SOCIAL WORK,
SOCIAL WELFARE, AND
AMERICAN SOCIETY

SOCIAL WORK,
SOCIAL WELFARE, AND
AMERICAN SOCIETY

second edition

Philip R. Popple · Leslie Leighninger
Auburn University *Louisiana State University*

ALLYN AND BACON

Boston • London • Toronto • Sydney • Tokyo • Singapore

Senior Editor: Karen Hanson
Editor in Chief, Social Sciences: Susan Badger
Series Editorial Assistant: Marnie Greenhut
Production Administrator: Susan McIntyre
Editorial-Production Service: Kathy Smith
Cover Administrator: Linda Dickinson
Composition Buyer: Linda Cox
Manufacturing Buyer: Megan Cochran

Photo credits continue on page 581, which constitutes a continuation of the copyright page.

Copyright © 1993, 1990 by Allyn & Bacon
A division of Simon & Schuster, Inc.
160 Gould Street
Needham Heights, MA 02194

Library of Congress Cataloging-in-Publication Data

Popple, Philip R.
    Social work, social welfare, and American society / Philip R.
Popple, Leslie Leighninger.—2nd ed.
        p.   cm.
    Includes bibliographical references and index.
    ISBN 0-205-14070-X
    1. Public welfare—United States.   2. Social service—United
States.   I. Leighninger, Leslie.   II. Title
HV91.P68   1993
361.973—dc20   92-26068
                                                    CIP

Printed in the United States of America

10 9 8 7 6 5 4 3   97 96 95 94

To Linda • *To Matt and Maggie*

Brief Contents

Contents

CHAPTER

three Social Work as a Profession   53

CHAPTER

nine   Child Welfare   **253**

CHAPTER

ten   Crime and Criminal Justice   **295**

CHAPTER

eleven   Mental Health and Developmental Disability   341

CHAPTER

twelve   Health Care   389

CHAPTER

thirteen   The Workplace   433

CHAPTER

fourteen   Housing and Homelessness   469

CHAPTER

fifteen Aging   **523**

CHAPTER
_____

Preface

Political events in the 1980s played a major part in the inspiration of the first edition of this book. Prior to Ronald Reagan's two terms in office, it was possible for most social workers to assume that many of the basic elements of a liberal welfare state were firmly entrenched in American society. True, the country had not yet achieved a nationalized health system, and programs like Aid to Families of Dependent Children did not seem to address adequately the problems of poor families. In addition, the 1970s had brought reductions in social welfare spending and criticisms of the programs and ideas developed during the New Deal and the 1960s' War on Poverty. Yet despite such setbacks, it remained possible for most social workers to anticipate continued progress toward the liberal goals of ensuring a minimum standard of living as well as adequate job opportunities, health care, and housing for all citizens. Government, especially the federal government, was to play the major role in achieving these goals.

Beginning in the 1980s, however, liberal ideas of progress toward a more complete social welfare system were severely shaken. Economic difficulties and growing federal budget deficits helped pave the way for a major reconsideration of the goals and shape of social welfare programs in our society. A revived conservative agenda emerged, forcefully articulated by Ronald Reagan. While Reagan was the most visible spokesperson for conservative ideas, such as scaling back the role of federal government in domestic social affairs and strengthening free enterprise in our society, he reflected the thoughts of large numbers of American citizens. Many of his ideas and programs were continued under the presidency of George Bush.

Most social workers, including the writers of social work textbooks, were slow to respond to the new social welfare era ushered in by the Reagan presidency. They failed at first to grasp that Reagan was acting not as a social renegade, but as a politician mirroring a wide growth of conservatism in the United States. This conservatism included resentment about the rise of "big government" and the expansion of the welfare state. Despite the political shift, many social work faculty continued to teach Introduction to Social Welfare courses with the liberal perspective and faith in continued progress as unexamined assumptions. Social welfare text writers failed to openly acknowledge their liberal approach or to examine that approach in light of a new political and social climate. Equally important, they neglected to describe and analyze the conservative critique and its alternate proposals.

Social work teachers, the authors included, gradually became aware that some students (majors as well as non-majors) did not share the liberal assumptions and were unconvinced by the standard liberal arguments. We found discussions of liberal and conservative approaches to problems creeping into our classes with increasing frequency. This led to another realization. While students had self-images of being liberal or conservative (or even radical), few had any real idea about what these labels meant. Not only were many unprepared to clearly articulate their points of view but also most were unable to either respond effectively to or appreciate the arguments of alternate political perspectives. Since we ourselves identify most clearly with a liberal approach, we were particularly concerned about our students' inability to evaluate and respond to the increasingly popular conservative critique of social welfare.

We thus felt the need to help students grasp the meaning of different political perspectives and understand social welfare developments in the light of those perspectives. Accordingly, we revised our outlines to begin the course with an analysis of the political context of social welfare. When we tried to find course material for this endeavor, we discovered that little was available. We realized that in order to achieve our goals, we would have to write the material ourselves. That realization was the beginning of this book.

This is not a book about American politics. It is a book about social welfare, but social welfare within a political context. It does not assume that the liberal perspective is the only relevant perspective in discussions of how we have chosen, continue to choose, and ought to choose the structure of our welfare programs and goals. It was written with the conviction that social work students and practitioners of the 1990s need to deal intelligently with all approaches to social welfare in order to be effective advocates for their clients.

PLAN OF THE BOOK

The book begins with a chapter outlining the concepts of *conservative, liberal,* and *radical.* Each concept is examined in terms of the following dimensions: attitude toward change, view of human nature, explanation of individual behavior, view of the social system, view of government and the economic system, and general value systems. In each of the remaining chapters, this material is integrated in analyses of the major concepts and areas of social welfare in terms of political perspectives.

Chapter 2 examines the concept of social welfare. It focuses on the important question: What is the function of social welfare in modern society? We argue that social welfare exists to manage issues of dependency and interdependency among and between individuals, communities, and social institutions. Our definition of dependency includes both a lack of concrete resources and a lack of skills, knowledge, and power necessary to cope with a particular set of circumstances. We also recognize that no one is truly independent in our society and that promotion of healthy interdependence can be an important goal of social welfare programs. The chapter concludes with an examination of conservative, liberal, and radical approaches to the management of dependency and interdependency.

Chapter 3 discusses the social work profession. It looks at the concept of professionalism and what the pursuit of professional status has meant for social work. The history of the profession is examined in light of that pursuit. The chapter also describes the effects of different political perspectives on social work's development. Then the important topic of values, ethics, and ethical dilemmas in social work practice is addressed. This is followed by a discussion of social work methods, a presentation of a model of social work practice, a description of the broad range of practice settings, and an identification and analysis of current professional issues. The chapter concludes by relating the three political perspectives outlined in Chapter 1 to contemporary social work.

Chapter 4 covers new ground for a social welfare text in its presentation of a comprehensive analysis of the interaction between religion, social work, and social welfare. Political changes in the 1980s have been accompanied by rising attention to the relationship between religion and public life. Increasing numbers of students seem to be drawn to social work out of religious impulses. This has been a topic of lively discussion among social work educators whenever they have gathered. The main source of concern has not been religion as a motive for social work per se, since as the historical discussion in the chapter explains, religious impulses have inspired social welfare efforts from their very beginnings. The current concern has been with the type of religious orientation of some students—a fundamentalist, often socially and politically conservative, and sometimes evangelical approach. Questions about the appropriateness of this particular religious orientation for social work practice have led to broader discussion of the general relationship between religion and social work. Chapter 4 looks at the issue in both its specific and its broader forms. In doing so, we have been careful not to preach and not to advocate our own motives and brand of religion. We try to affirm the appropriateness of social work as a career choice for people wishing to operationalize their faith. However, we attempt to sensitize students to the importance of a nonjudgmental attitude, the inappropriateness of evangelizing among clients, and the need to examine the various issues which a social worker with a strong religious orientation is likely to face.

Chapter 5 develops an understanding of issues of diversity and discrimination within the social welfare system. It discusses America's development as a country of many different racial and ethnic groups, and it describes the ways in which social welfare programs and policies have responded to these groups. The chapter analyzes the phenomena of discrimination and prejudice, as these relate to women, minorities of color, homosexual and lesbian individuals, and other frequently oppressed groups. As in the chapter on religion, this chapter encourages students to look at their own attitudes and biases in working with people.

Chapters 6, 7, and 8 deal with the topic of poverty. We chose to devote three chapters to this subject, as compared to one chapter for each of the other problems discussed, because of our belief that poverty is *the* central social welfare problem. Virtually every other social problem has poverty as one of its causative factors. Chapter 6 examines the complex topic of measuring and defining poverty. Chapter 7 describes the poverty population in the United States and presents a detailed discussion of major theories of the causes of poverty. Chapter 8 focuses on a historical presentation of the development of antipoverty programs in this country. All three chapters detail conservative, liberal, and radical perspectives on the definition and causes of poverty and the most effective ways of dealing with it.

The remainder of the book is devoted to a comprehensive discussion of a number of major areas in social welfare. These include child welfare, crime and delinquency, mental health and developmental disability, health care, and aging. The book also explores two crucial aspects of social welfare which have received far too little attention in preparing knowledgeable and effective social work practitioners. Chapter 13, on the workplace, analyzes work as a central factor in the welfare of individuals and thus as an important topic for all social workers, not just those who specialize in occupational assistance. Chapter 14, on housing and homelessness, not only discusses the causes and effects of the current crisis of rising numbers of homeless people but also places this discussion in the larger context of the relationship between housing, community life, and individual well-being. Each of these special topic chapters relates varying political perspectives to theory and practice in that particular area. In addition, each chapter details the role of social workers in that specific field. The book concludes with a chapter urging students to develop and articulate their own perspective on social welfare and social work practice.

The second edition has been updated and includes new or expanded material on such topics as chronic mental illness, proposals for national health insurance, the continued lack of success of anti-poverty policy, the incredible increase in the prison population, and new developments in child welfare, including court orders for massive system reform. The "Closer Look" boxes give more concentrated emphasis to case histories and examples. We believe that this revised edition should do an even better job of preparing students to understand social welfare issues in the real world.

ACKNOWLEDGMENTS

We would like to acknowledge the following people who have offered valuable guidance in writing the second edition of this book: Edward Allan Brawley, The Pennsylvania State University; Judith Brown, The College of New Rochelle; J. L. Chapis, Central Michigan University; Arnold Panitch, Boise State University; and Michael Lane Smith, Southwest Texas State University.

A number of students reviewed various drafts of this material and offered a "client's eye view." In addition, many colleagues read specific chapters and made useful suggestions: Gary Mathews, Marion Wijnberg, Danny Thompson, Linda Petersen, Linda Reeser, Dave Joslyn, Frederick MacDonald, Phil Brown, Peter Simbi, Bridgette Martin, Paul Hartrich, Paulette Hartrich, Toni Hartrich, Leslie Decker, and William R. Barnes. Unfortunately, Edith Pope and William Burian, who contributed thoughtful critiques, did not live to see the final result.

The production of this project was made smoother through the help of Ron DeVrou, Jane Ferguson, David Popple, Judy Moon, and Margaret Leighninger. We are appreciative of the enthusiasm shown by Bill Barke. Finally, we wish to acknowledge the cheerful support and impressive expertise of our two editors, Karen Hanson and Kathy Smith.

C · H · A · P · T · E · R

one

Competing Perspectives on Social Welfare

In Dallas, Texas, the manager of a twenty-four-hour convenience store called the police at about 11:00 one morning to report that there was a small child wandering around the store by himself. When the police arrived they found the little boy contentedly munching on a bag of potato chips and drinking a Coke. They asked him where he lived and where his parents were, and he pointed down the street to a number of large apartment complexes and said, "Mama's asleep." The officers took the child to the apartments and asked if anyone recognized him. The manager of the third complex knew the child. He told the officers, "This is Bobby Patrick. I think he turned three about two weeks ago. With his parents, I wouldn't be surprised if he never turns four. The father travels all the time for his job and returns home only long enough to scream at his wife and knock her around a little bit. The police have come out several times but Ms. Patrick won't press charges. She just stays in the apartment with the drapes drawn, watches soap operas on TV, and drinks. I don't think she ever wakes up before noon, and Bobby has learned not to disturb her. If he can't find anything to eat in the apartment, he goes outside to see if a neighbor will feed him. Lately he has started to wander off to the shopping center, which means he has to cross a very busy street." The manager looked at the officers, sighed, and said, "Something should be done about situations like this."

Five months into the fiscal year, the emergency welfare fund at First Church was out of money. Due to cuts in welfare programs the church had been deluged with requests for emergency assistance. The minister appealed to the congregation for more money explaining that people just couldn't live on the amount available from existing welfare programs. Everyone agreed that "Something should be done about situations like this."

In Detroit, a neighbor called the police one April to report that, for some time, she had seen no activity from the residence of the elderly lady next door, and she feared that something might be wrong. When the police entered the house they found the elderly lady's body. An investigation revealed that she had been dead for several months, having frozen to death after the power company shut off the electricity because she was behind on her payments. The lady had a son in town, but their relationship had not been good, and he was just as happy when he did not hear from her. Likewise, she had alienated her neighbors over the years, so no one visited her. The result was an impoverished elderly person who was completely at the mercy of her environment. When things began to go wrong, she had no personal or financial resources to correct them. The neighbor said, "Something should be done about situations like this."

In a small college town in the South, it was revealed one year that out of 246 girls in the junior high school, 6 were pregnant. Of the 6, 4 were in the seventh grade. The school board had a meeting, the PTA had a meeting, and the teachers' organization had a meeting. Everyone said, "Something should be done about situations like this."

Something should be done about situations like this. That is the subject of this book. How do we as a society deal with social issues that we collectively recognize as problems? While it is easy to find agreement on the general principle that we should do something, it is not so easy to agree on what should be done, who should do it, how much should be done, and how efforts should be financed. Because we believe that the central issue in social welfare is the perspective from which one addresses the topic, we begin this book with a look at these perspectives. In future chapters we will deal with individual social welfare problems in depth, paying constant attention to the importance of political perspectives in explaining and understanding each problem.

POLITICAL PERSPECTIVES AND SOCIAL WELFARE ISSUES

During the past year we have made it a practice to "eavesdrop" on conversations. The locations were parties, shopping malls, Sunday school classes, and similar settings. Our purpose was to learn what "people-on-the-street" were saying about social welfare issues. The following are paraphrases of typical statements we heard.

Regarding financial assistance for the poor:

An insurance agent. "I got lost last week and ended up driving around the housing projects. Have you ever seen those places? It's a shame; no, it's more than that, it's a crime, that people in this country have to live like that! If we can put a man on the moon, spend billions of dollars on arms, and give aid to third-world nations, you'd think we could provide a decent standard of living for our less fortunate citizens."

A small business owner. "Welfare is ruining this country. What made us a great nation is rugged individualism—the sure and certain knowledge that if we worked hard we would succeed, and that if we didn't we'd starve. But it's not like that anymore. If you succeed, the government takes away most of your profit in taxes and then pays it to the poor. If you don't want to work, all you have to do is go to the welfare office and they'll give you money. What we should do is cut out all welfare programs and then people will be forced to work."

Regarding child welfare:

A fourth grade teacher. "There's a boy in my class who comes to school at least half the time without breakfast. In the winter he is often without a coat and I don't think he gets a bath once a month. Last week he had a terrible black eye. He told the school nurse that he fell out of a tree, but we're both pretty sure his father hits him. Last fall I suggested to the father that he and the mother get counseling at the mental health center but he refused. After this last incident I called the child welfare office and made a report. I hope they take the parents to court and force them to get counseling. If that doesn't work, I hope they remove all the kids from that home."

A pediatrician. "I see abused and neglected children in my office quite often, but I rarely call the welfare department, even though legally I'm supposed to. People should not treat their children like that, but the government coming into people's homes and telling them how to rear their children is an even worse evil. In Sweden a parent can be jailed for just spanking his child. Once the government gets its foot in your door there will be no stopping it. I'm afraid that it may already be too late."

A college professor. "Look, we're bound to have child abuse in our society. The United States is a violent country. The domestic violence you see is just a mirroring of our arms race, our infatuation with guns, and our attempt to make the world safe for U.S. business by supporting military dictatorships which are pro-American. If we're really serious about helping kids, social work and psychology aren't the ways to do it. We need to change our oppressive and violent society."

Regarding juvenile delinquency:

A nurse. "Do you know that every day we are putting kids as young as twelve and thirteen in jail? They call it 'juvenile detention hall,' but let me tell you, I've seen it and it's jail! Often the things they lock these kids up for wouldn't even be a crime if they were adults. We need to hire more social workers to help these kids and their families. They need help, not jail. They have problems; they're not criminals."

An engineer. "My mother and father live in the same apartment that we lived in when I was growing up. Only now they are afraid to go out after dark and they have four locks on the door. Why? It's because the kids in the neighborhood spend their time terrorizing and mugging old people. If the courts would stop letting these kids off with a 'slap on the wrist,' that neighborhood would be safe again. If I had my way, everyone arrested and convicted would do time. Long time and hard time. I don't care if they're thirteen or thirty. If they're old enough to do the crime, they're old enough to do the time."

Regarding aging:

A plumber. "You know, it's really sad to see all the old people who just sit around in the park all day with nothing to do. I suppose the ones with money go to Florida, or to visit their kids or something, but most of them just sit around all day and stare at the ground. We need more things in this town for the elderly. We should build a senior citizens' center and hire a bunch of social workers to help people make the best of their 'golden years.' We also should build senior citizens' apartments so old people can continue to have their own homes, but help will be close at hand if it's needed."

A minister. "I think it's a shame that children no longer take responsibility for their parents. When I was growing up, when people became too old or ill to care for themselves, they would move in with their children. That's the way it should be—families looking out for their own. There is simply no need for the government to build senior citizens' centers, apartments, meals-on-wheels, and all that kind of stuff. People need to take responsibility for their own families."

These are just a few of many examples we could give illustrating clashing views on social welfare issues. Why are these views so different? Is one position right and the others wrong? One informed and the others ignorant? One progressive and the others old fashioned? The answer is "none of the above." Like the old fable about the blind men trying to describe the elephant, these people represent different political perspectives; stated another way, they represent different social attitudes.

Attitudes are our attraction to or revulsion from situations, objects, persons, groups, or any other identifiable aspects of our environment, including abstract ideas and social policies.[1] Attitudes are filters through which we screen our experiences and impose some sense upon them. Social attitudes express the psychological orientation of people to their social environment; they enable us to make sense of our incredibly complex world. As Kerlinger has said, "Whether directed toward social issues, ethnic groups, or abstract ideas, attitudes are efficient psychological mechanisms that strongly influence social behavior—they represent emotional, motivational, and cognitive reactions of people to the social 'objects' of the environment and their predisposition to act toward those social objects."[2]

Liberalism and conservatism are the two most common social attitudes that shape our beliefs and behaviors in the United States. Therefore they will receive most of our attention. Yet there is also a radical perspective. This is a minority view, described by one writer as a "small but frequently refreshing stream" of thought in American life.[3] A radical viewpoint has important implications for understanding the institution of social welfare, so we will include it in our discussion. Some people identify a fourth political perspective in the United States—the "Far Right." In most cases, this is an extreme version of the conservative position, so we will not discuss it separately.

We all have social attitudes, or political perspectives, which influence our behavior. In order to help you identify and analyze your own social attitudes, we will analyze the assumptions underlying the conservative, liberal, and radical points of view. We proceed with some caution here. Clearly delineating and defining labels such as these is a difficult task. Sibley has said of liberalism and conservatism that "neither is what might be called a tight political doctrine . . . each is more or less a tendency rather than a series of closely knit propositions."[4] The assignment of labels depends in part on an individual's perspective. In addition, the meaning behind the labels shifts over time. For example, the free market concept was originally associated with liberalism, but now it is a cornerstone of conservative doctrine. There can also be overlap between various perspectives, particularly between liberal and radical, and liberal and conservative world views. Thus, the following definitions should be viewed as approximations, or attempts to broadly sketch certain belief systems, rather than to definitively capture the "true meaning" behind each label.

Liberal, conservative, and radical ideologies can be differentiated in three areas: their attitudes toward change, their differences in philosophy, and their conceptions of the role of government in domestic affairs. Conservatives (derived from the verb "to conserve") tend to resist change. They believe that change usually results in more negative than positive consequences; thus, they wish to preserve things as they are. Conservatives strongly emphasize tradition. Liberals, on the other hand, are generally in favor of change; they believe that the world can be changed for the better. Liberals view history as progress, and they believe that continuing change will bring continuing progress. They usually view change as the reform, rather than the radical restructuring, of existing institutions. Radicals, on the other hand, are skeptical that moderate change can deal with what they view as pervasive inequities in society. Therefore, they stress the need for more fundamental alterations in the social system.

In the area of philosophy, conservatives emphasize, in addition to their general belief in tradition, the importance of religious freedom, private property, established

People with liberal and conservative world views often have strong, sometimes emotional, differences of opinion regarding many issues, including social welfare issues such as if abortion is an acceptable alternative for a problem pregnancy.

institutions and conventions, stability, and authority. Liberals in the United States present a wider philosophical spectrum. Initially, during the transition from the colonies to an autonomous United States, liberals spoke of an individual's right to life, liberty, and property, with the greatest stress being on property. As the United States became an industrialized nation, many liberals changed their focus from property rights to human rights and equality.[5] Today, although some "property rights liberals" still exist, most liberals emphasize the desirability of change, social reform, equality, and the rights of minorities and women. Radicals share these values. They also stress fair and equal distribution of power and wealth in society.

Conceptions about the role and authority of government in economic matters and domestic affairs provide further differentiations among conservatives, liberals, and radicals. According to conventional wisdom, conservatives favor "small government" and liberals promote large-scale government activity, particularly on the federal level. Yet the real picture is much more complex. In areas related to social welfare, such as health, mental health, and the maintenance of an adequate income, conservatives believe that the marketplace is a better tool than government programs for meeting these needs. Thus they see only a limited role for government in this arena, that of providing a basic "safety net," or minimal level of public aid to people who are dependent. However, they do not necessarily disapprove of additional government funding for health and welfare services, as long as these services are provided and controlled largely by private organizations.

Liberals have a different sense of the role of government. Although conservatives trust that the marketplace will provide equal opportunity for all to succeed, liberals feel government intervention and regulation is often necessary to control the excesses of capitalism, to safeguard human rights, and to provide equal chances for success. In addition, liberals see a positive role for government in providing various social welfare services to citizens.

Radicals generally view government as oppressive in capitalist societies. However, they differ in their ideas about the role of government after capitalism has been abolished. Some envision much less need for government in a non-capitalist society. Others suggest a strong role for government to play as the coordinator of the welfare state.

In the United States, the Republican party is considered to be relatively conservative and the Democratic party is considered to be relatively liberal. Although there are such things as conservative Democrats and liberal Republicans, the Democrats are generally to the left of the political spectrum and the Republicans are to the right. Kerlinger has noted that, "Although it has been said that there is no real difference between the policies and behaviors of Republicans and Democrats in the United States, there are actual and deep differences, especially in policies that affect the conduct of business and social welfare of people. Such differences spring, at least in part, from ideological concerns that are reflected in liberal and conservative attitudes."[6] At the same time, both liberals and conservatives reflect traditional American beliefs in property rights and in individualism, although the value they place on these beliefs differs.

There appear to be inherent contradictions in both liberal and conservative attitudes. Wolfinger, Shapiro, and Greenstein have noted that

[A] Republican favors big business and the free enterprise system; he is opposed to big government and welfare legislation. He feels strongly that individual freedom has to be

President Franklin D. Roosevelt, a liberal Democrat, was responsible for the Social Security Act, which created the framework for the social welfare system in the United States.

protected from government encroachments. Yet he may be a "law and order" advocate, singularly insensitive to the rights of the accused. In short, he may be strongly opposed to government limitations on the freedom of businessmen, but in favor of government limitations on the activities of alleged criminals.

In a similar fashion,

> [T]he liberal Democrat generally favors programs such as medicare and other such policies that lead to greater government involvement in the daily affairs of the people. On the one hand the liberal worries about F.B.I. or C.I.A. snooping, but on the other hand he may propose programs that give environmental and public health officials almost unlimited powers to dictate the terms and conditions under which individuals must earn their daily bread, use their own property, and engage in recreational pursuits.[7]

THE WORLD VIEW OF CONSERVATIVES, LIBERALS, AND RADICALS

Liberals and conservatives share a basic belief in maintaining our society as it is currently structured. Radicals have major reservations about the existing social arrangements. All three differ in important areas, including their views of human nature, individual behavior, the family, the social system, the government and the economic system, and basic values. These views have important implications for their positions on social welfare.

Views of Human Nature

Our views of human nature undergird and color our attitudes toward nearly everything else. The meaning and purpose of human life, what we ought to do, and what we can hope to achieve—all of these issues are fundamentally affected by our beliefs about the real or true nature of people. There are some basic differences between conservative and liberal views on this subject.

Conservatives tend to take a basically pessimistic view of human nature. People are perceived as being corrupt, self-centered, lazy, and incapable of true charity. They need to be encouraged to work. Conservative commentator Thomas Sowell says that those "who look everywhere for the mysterious causes of poverty, ignorance, crime, and war need look no further than their own mirrors. We are born into this world poor and ignorant, and with thoroughly selfish and barbaric impulses."[8] People need to be controlled because of their fundamentally negative nature, and they should be swiftly and sternly punished when they get out of line. This is the only way that they can live harmoniously with one another. Because of this view, conservatives have a basic distrust of democracy, doubting the ability of the masses to make decisions for the common good. They support democracy, however, because they believe it is much better than the available alternatives.

Liberals take a much more optimistic view of human nature. They accept the "blank slate" view of Locke that people are born with infinite possibilities for being shaped for the good, or the view of Rousseau or more recently Maslow, that people are born good and, if not corrupted, are naturally social, curious, and loving. People do not need to be controlled; they simply need to be protected from corrupting influences and given the freedom to follow their natural inclinations, which will lead to the good.

Like liberals, radicals believe people are basically good. Moreover, they believe people are inherently industrious and creative. Like conservatives, radicals regard hard work as a virtue. Unlike conservatives, who follow the Puritan assumption that people are naturally lazy and must be forced to work, radicals believe that if people have control over their working conditions they will take pleasure in working hard.

These different views of human nature have tremendous consequences for views of social welfare. If you regard people as being basically bad, you will design social welfare systems to control people. You will suspect that people will take advantage of the system whenever possible and thus will have the prevention of cheating as a major focus. You will view crime, drug dependency, child abuse, and similar problems as expressions of the basically negative nature of people and of the failure of external forces to control this nature. You will probably see punishment as the logical solution. On the other hand, if you regard people as being basically good, you will design social welfare systems to free people from problems that are preventing them from realizing their natural potential. You will be less concerned with control because people, if given the chance, will naturally do what is right.

Views of Individual Behavior

Our explanations of why people behave as they do are closely related to our views of human nature. The importance of heredity, the environment, and individual free will are all important components of our concept of individual behavior.

Conservatives generally view individuals as autonomous, that is, self-governing. Regardless of what a person's situation is or what problems he or she has had in the past, each person is presently responsible for his or her own behavior. People choose to do whatever they are doing, and they are responsible for whatever gains or losses result from these choices. The conservative theorist Irving Kristol, for example, asserts that individual behavior is a result of motivation, which he views as an innate (inborn) characteristic present in all people in varying degrees. People possess free will and thus can choose to engage in behaviors such as hard work that help them get ahead, or activities such as excessive leisure that contribute to failure.[9] Thus, poverty is often caused by individuals' lack of responsibility.

Although liberals and radicals do not completely deny free will and motivation, they put much more emphasis on the environment as the cause of individual behavior. An early expression of this view comes from Freud, who said that individuals are programmed by early experiences, primarily with their parents, and that an individual's behavior in later life results from this programming. More recent theorists, such as Erikson, Glaser, and Levinson, assert that the programming takes place throughout life, resulting in a series of developmental crises.[10] If people successfully resolve the crises, they will experience happiness and fulfillment, and if they do not, they will experience failure and discontent. Another view is based on the work of behavioral psychologists, notably Watson and Skinner.[11] According to this perspective, behavior is not the result of programming, but of the immediate consequences of behavior. If an individual perceives the consequences of a behavior as positive, the behavior will increase; behavior in which the consequences are perceived as negative will decrease.

Our explanations of human behavior have important implications for our approach to social welfare. If we assume that people are autonomous and guided completely by free will, poverty and other social welfare problems will be seen as a result of laziness, irresponsibility, or lack of self-control. Conservative scholar Thomas Sowell asserts that welfare recipients "are people who didn't bother to learn when they were in school, didn't bother to get work experience or job skills afterwards, and often don't bother to obey the law either. There are consequences to that kind of behavior. What the welfare state does is to force others to pay the consequences."[12] In other words, poor people would not be poor if they really wanted to be otherwise. Social welfare programs simply need to make sure that nothing interferes with people's efforts to better themselves and to solve their own problems.

If, on the other hand, we assume that people's behavior is strongly influenced by the environment, we will see changing the environment as the proper response to social welfare problems. Liberals, for example, support the Head Start Program, which attempts to solve the educational problems of poor children by means of early environmental enrichment. Head Start is an example of a reform in the present system. Radicals would push for even more fundamental changes in existing social institutions.

Views of the Family

Attitudes toward the family have an important, but often confusing, influence on social welfare policy. In this area more than others, it seems, theory and practice are farther apart for all groups. Conservatives and radicals have particular difficulty fitting ideals into the world in which they live.

Conservatives revere the "traditional" family and try to devise policies to preserve it. They see the family as a source of strength for individuals and as the primary unit of society. They oppose public funding of day-care centers, abortion, rights for homosexuals, sex education in schools, birth control counseling for minors, the Equal Rights Amendment, and other measures that might undermine parental authority or make family break-ups easier by giving too much independence to women and children.

In a recent symposium on the subject of the conservative agenda for the nineties, nearly every contributor addressed the need for a return to traditional family values and lifestyles as a key to the solution of social and economic problems. Adam Meyerson, for example, spoke of the need to "restore the family, the basic building block of a kinder and gentler America." Ken Tomlinson remarked that ". . . we've got to restore the role of the family in American life. Drug addiction, the emergence of a permanent underclass, virtually all the problems that plague urban America can be linked to the breakdown of the family structure. Policies that fail to address this problem are doomed from the start."[13]

The difficulty with this position is that the "traditional" model—father as sole wage-earner outside the home and mother as full-time homemaker and care-giver— was the majority situation for a relatively brief period of our history, and it is now obtainable by only a minority. A majority of women now work outside the home; many work because they have to. The argument against government intrusion in family life, which is used to resist sex education or birth-control counseling for minors, must be put aside when advocating the abolition of abortion. Divorce, long opposed by conservatives, has now been accepted by many of them. Thus, conservatives find themselves on a fairly small and uncomfortable base from which to defend the family.

Radicals regard the conservatives' traditional family perspective as oppressive and as a distortion of both male and female talents. It denies women a choice of careers and men an opportunity to participate in family life. However, radicals share with conservatives the recognition that strong families are essential to a healthy society. Accordingly, they favor ways of supporting "new" families—those consisting of two working parents, single parents, communal groups, or homosexual adoptive parents. Radicals, along with most liberals, favor equal rights and equal pay, day-care centers, maternity *and* paternity leaves, flex time and job sharing.

Yet radicals also have difficulty harmonizing theory and practice. Civil rights, antiwar, and other political groups supported by radicals often have been as oppressive to and patronizing of their women members as any conservative organization. In his own family, Karl Marx was a conventional, authoritarian father; the home lives of modern radicals do not always reflect the equal division of labor and power called for by their ideals.

Liberals may have the easiest time in this difficult area. They view the family as an evolving institution, and they can be more flexible and pragmatic in the ways in which they support it.

Views of the Social System

Is our social system fair? Do people really get rewards in proportion to their contributions to society? Do people have equal opportunities? How important is change in achieving the good society? Is conflict inevitable and, indeed, desirable? These are some of the questions that are related to our view of the social system.

Conservatives view society in a manner that is close to what sociologists call the *functional perspective*. The basic assumption of this perspective is that society is a system composed of interrelated and interdependent parts. Each part makes a contribution to the operation of the system, and thus the entire system is enabled to function. Each part fulfills a different function, but contributes to the overall well-being of society. In this way society is seen as analogous to a biological organism.

For our purposes, the most crucial aspect of the conservative perspective is the view that all parts of society, as they are, are beneficial to both society and the individuals within it. Society would not work as well without any of its existing arrangements, or with major changes in any of its arrangements. Thus, the average salary of physicians is over $100,000 per year and the average salary of preschool teachers is under $19,000 per year, because this is the arrangement that is most socially effective. Conservatives would argue that the large discrepancy in earnings is the result of the greater effort and ability necessary to become a physician, the greater work load and responsibility of a physician, and the greater importance to the general well-being of society of a physician's work. If the salary gap were narrowed, fewer highly qualified people would choose the rigors of becoming a physician, and society would suffer. Thus, social inequality is viewed as a device by which societies assure that the most important positions are filled by the most capable people.[14]

Liberals, like conservatives, tend to view society as an organismic system, but they have less faith that the system will regulate itself without intervention. They point out, for example, that nature is notoriously inefficient. The average tree sends out thousands of seedlings, but only a few will grow into mature trees. With the intervention of human horticulture, those seedlings can be replanted, watered, fertilized, protected from insects, and allowed to grow to maturity. The social system needs nurturing and regulating as well.

Liberals also see (and value) more diversity and friction in the social system than do conservatives. Different groups have different interests—things that are beneficial to them—and what is in the interest of one group may be to the disadvantage of another. These groups will struggle to promote their own interests, but will usually have to compromise with and accommodate to other groups in order to attain their goals. If there are enough interest groups and if none are powerful enough to dominate the others, the system will embody the "checks and balances" of the Constitution. Government provides the rules and limits that keep the contest fair and open. Liberal economists like John Kenneth Galbraith and political scientists like Robert Dahl describe the virtues of this pluralistic system.[15]

Radicals, who usually follow the analysis of Karl Marx, see the social system as a class hierarchy in which one class has predominant power and uses it to control the others. This is sometimes called the *conflict perspective*. To radicals, the interest-group politics that preoccupy liberals are only a sideshow. Behind the scenes, the important decisions are being made by an elite of wealthy and powerful people.[16]

Radicals believe that inequality is the result of the group with greater power using this power to perpetuate its position of advantage. Thus, the physician has seven times the income of the preschool teacher, not because physicians are seven times more valuable to the social system, but because they have wealth and power and use these resources to increase, or at least to maintain, their positions. The fact that the medical profession is predominantly male and early childhood education is predominately female is viewed as being very significant.

The conservative perspective views the social system as inherently fair. If some groups are poorer than others and have less power and lower status, it is because this situation is necessary for the well-being of society. Thus, change is viewed with a great deal of suspicion. What exists is useful and necessary. Rapid and major changes may benefit particular groups, but they will usually result in a net loss to society. Change is sometimes necessary, but it must be slow and incremental.

The liberal perspective views the social system as potentially fair, but frequently unfair. Some interest groups are more powerful than others and, if unchecked by government regulation, will use their power to take advantage of less powerful groups. Change takes place, sometimes rapidly and sometimes slowly, through the competition and compromise of interest groups.

Radicals believe that fairness is unattainable in the present system. It can only be achieved by restructuring existing social institutions to redistribute wealth and power.

It is not difficult to deduce the implication of these different perspectives for social welfare. Conservatives believe that everything in society has a function, and they are skeptical of proposals for change. If poverty were eliminated by, for example, the creation of millions of jobs and an increase in the minimum wage, conservatives would argue that:

1. The new jobs would compete with private business.
2. A tax increase would be necessary that would hurt the economy.
3. The increased minimum wage would force businesses to pay more, which would cause them either to go broke or to raise their prices.

The result would be a net loss to our economy. Thus, conservatives argue that our kind-hearted efforts to help the poor would only result in harm to society. Social welfare programs that help people adjust to society as it currently exists are supported by conservatives; programs that seek to change society are generally opposed.

Liberals do not view the existing society as the best possible world. They believe in changes that will reduce inequality and increase social justice. With regard to the previous example used, many liberals would assert that the wealthiest members of society are putting forth these arguments in a predictable effort to retain their power, resources, and positions. Liberals reject social welfare programs that simply help people to adjust to society as it is. They see these programs as means that the powerful use to keep the powerless "in their place," rather than as efforts to help them. Liberals view programs that change society more favorably than they do those that change individuals.

For radicals, the only way to avoid inequality is to completely change society. When power and wealth are distributed equitably and everyone is guaranteed the necessities of life, cooperation, rather than competition and conflict, will predominate. The struggle of oppressed groups to liberate themselves produces change in society. Some radicals believe that society can be restructured gradually and democratically; others see only revolutionary change as sufficient.

Views of the Government and the Economic System

Perhaps the area of the strongest and most emotional disagreement between liberal and conservative perspectives is the view of the proper role of government in the economy and in the lives of people. Conservatives embrace the old adage that "government governs best which governs least." They think that most government activities constitute grave threats to individual liberty and to the smooth functioning of the free market. Liberals believe that our social and economic systems contain imperfections that can only be corrected by governmental intervention, and therefore such intervention is justifiable and desirable.

Radicals see liberal tinkering with government as inadequate; they feel complete restructuring is necessary. What comes after the restructuring is less clear. Marx, who shared the Enlightenment belief in the basic goodness of people, assumed that once capitalism was swept away, basic human nature would assert itself and there would be little need for government. Little attention was paid to the transition from oppression to freedom. It is perhaps this assumption that left the door open to Soviet dictatorship after the Russian revolution.

The government is involved in the economy in two main areas, both of which have grown tremendously during this century, particularly during the past fifty years. The first area is taxation and government expenditure. Prior to 1913, there was no federal income tax and the spending by all levels of government (federal, state, and local) amounted to only $3 billion, less than one-twelfth of national income. Government spending in 1990 was $1,151.8 billion, nearly one-half of national income. One aspect of this area that is a special bone of contention between liberals and conservatives is the redistribution of income by the state. This refers to the government taking income from one group via taxes and giving it to another group in the form of cash grants (such as Social Security and public welfare) or some other form of benefit (such as food stamps and public housing). Prior to the onset of the Great Depression in 1929, the federal government spent almost nothing in this area. In 1990, the federal government spent $478 billion, over 40 percent of the total budget, on Medicare, Social Security, and income security programs.

The second area of government involvement in the economy includes laws, regulations, and executive orders governing economic affairs. For most of the nineteenth century there was virtually no governmental regulation of the economy. Samuelson has noted that:

> The result was a century of rapid material progress and an environment of freedom. There were also periodic business crises, wasteful exhaustion of irreplaceable natural resources, racial and sexual discrimination, extremes of poverty and wealth, corruption of government by interest groups, and at times supplanting of self-regulating competition by monopoly.[17]

Government regulation began to grow as a result of these problems. In 1887 the Interstate Commerce Commission was established; in 1890 the Sherman Antitrust Act was created; in 1913 the Federal Reserve System was established; and later the Federal Deposit Insurance Corporation, the Federal Power Commission, the Federal Communications Commission, the Pure Food and Drug Acts, the Securities and Exchange Commission, and a number of other commissions and laws were established and enacted. Of major importance were the Social Security Act of 1935, which made an "economic safety net" for all citizens a responsibility of the government, and the Employment Act of 1946, which established as a governmental responsibility the maintenance of "maximum employment, production and purchasing power."

With Adam Smith's *Wealth of Nations* as their bible and the University of Chicago's Milton Friedman as their leading contemporary spokesman, conservatives fear and resist this growth of governmental involvement in the economy.[18] They believe that for the economy to function efficiently, economic exchanges must be, to the greatest degree possible, unregulated. As stated by Friedman and Friedman:

> Adam Smith's key insight was that both parties to an exchange can benefit and that, *so long as cooperation is strictly voluntary,* no exchange will take place unless both parties do benefit. No external force, no coercion, no violation of freedom is necessary to produce cooperation among individuals all of whom can benefit. That is why as Adam Smith put it, an individual who "intends only his own gain" is "led by an invisible hand to promote an end which was not part of his intention. Nor is it always the worse for the society that it was no part of it. By pursuing his own interest he frequently promotes that of the society more effectually than when he really intends to promote it. I have never known much good done by those who affected to trade for the public good."[19]

In other words, a free-market economy is the best way to insure that the country prospers and individual needs are met.

Conservatives feel that government regulations substitute the "dead hand of bureaucracy" for the invisible hand of the free market. The result will be, they feel, that "sooner or later—and perhaps sooner than many of us expect—an even bigger government will destroy both the prosperity that we owe to the free market and the human freedom proclaimed so eloquently in the Declaration of Independence."[20] We should note again, however, that government involvement constitutes a conservative paradox; government intervention that benefits business, such as the periodic "bail-outs" of large corporations, is often viewed as necessary and desirable. The earliest examples of government involvement in the market were at the urging of conservative business people. In the early 1900s, for example, employers reacted to the spread of lawsuits against them from injured workers by pressing the government to establish worker's compensation laws.[21] Government intervention to support the free-market process is, therefore, legitimate. Intervention that subverts the market process is not.

The liberal perspective, based on the economic theories of John Maynard Keynes, is that the government must be involved in all areas of the economy in order to insure its optimal functioning.[22] Liberals believe that if the economy is left totally alone people with power will take unfair advantage of those with less power; people with more resources than they need will not necessarily share with those with less resources than they need; and, with totally free choice, people will not always make the right decisions (for example, a person may choose to buy heroin rather than food). They assert that certain goods, such as roads and national defense, must be provided by the government because they cannot be divided up and paid for as used by consumers. Liberals accept the capitalist system, but believe it needs regulation to avoid wild swings from prosperity to depression and back again. They contend that the government, through regulating the money supply (monetary policy) and expanding or decreasing government spending and taxation (fiscal policy), can stabilize the economy and prevent depressions.

Like conservatives and liberals, radicals have come to accept a "mixed" economy that contains both public and private elements. In terms of government involvement, they may prefer more public ownership of industry and services than do the other two groups, but they have seen in the experience of European socialist governments that public ownership does not guarantee either an equal distribution of power or a higher standard of living for workers. Some argue that ownership is irrelevant; what matters is who controls. American corporations are "owned" by stockholders, many of whom are elderly women, but they are controlled by a small group of mostly male managers.

Radicals would prefer an economic system where workers have control over the conditions of their work; where goods are produced for genuine need and not to satisfy whims created by advertising; where money is not the measure of worth; and where basic rights, such as medical care and housing, are not reduced to commodity status and sold in the marketplace to the highest bidder. Some radicals support the development of a welfare state where government organizes the provision of medical care, housing, and other social welfare benefits to all citizens.

The conservative economic perspective is profoundly suspicious of, but not entirely unsympathetic to, social welfare programs. Reid observes that "the 'new conservatives' do not deny that government has responsibility for society, they simply want that responsibility carried out in a particular way."[23] Harris has written that "it is a major failing of [conservatives] that more thought has not been given to the problem of public welfare and benevolence." He summarizes the basic principles of the conservative economic perspective on social welfare as:

1. The needy do not have a "right" to assistance, but those who are able have a moral duty to be benevolent "which, within certain limits, can be enforced by the state."

2. Social welfare programs should be designed to make use of the power of incentive. "It has been an assumption of capitalism since the time of Adam Smith that self-interest is a powerful motivating factor in human behavior. . . . In other words, we should use the natural motivating factors in human beings for moral ends."

3. "Finally, the advocate of the conservative welfare state will be suspicious of government programs to create jobs, remedy social ills, and care for the sick and the old. . . . The creation of new wealth and new jobs is the best way to alleviate poverty. Furthermore, governmental make-work programs can never be an adequate foundation for human dignity."[24]

Based on these principles, Harris argues that private retirement programs that invest contributions are preferable to government programs that immediately pay out contributions as benefits; a negative income tax would be preferable to the current welfare system; welfare benefits should be designed to increase incentive to work; and small, regional, private health programs such as health maintenance organizations (HMOs) are preferable to a large, centralized national health insurance program.

Many of today's conservatives find the voucher system a particularly appealing way to deal with poverty. Such a system works within the existing market economy. Vouchers are government certificates issued to people to use instead of money to pay for specific goods and services, such as housing and education. (Food stamps are a good example.) Government plays a role in financing the vouchers and in making them available to people with low incomes, but essentially the vouchers turn their recipients into "powerful consumers," able to exercise free choice in the open market. Rather than having the government provide public housing or education to the needy, vouchers enable low-income individuals to purchase such goods and services directly from private organizations or businesses.[25] President Bush recently proposed a voucher system as a means of providing health care to the poor while enabling the free market to work. The proposal failed to gain support due to cost containment concerns.

The liberal economic perspective generally prefers governmental welfare programs to private programs. One reason is that while private welfare programs may be preferable to government programs, as the conservatives argue, history has demonstrated that private charity is simply unable to deal with the massive problems of a modern industrial society. When the Great Depression began in 1929, the private relief organizations were overwhelmed within a few months. The government took over welfare programs not because it wanted to, but because it had to. A second argument is that welfare programs are good for the economy. The taxes that are taken from the wealthy come

TABLE 1–1	Comparison of conservative, liberal, and radical perspectives		
Attitudes Toward	Conservative	Liberal	Radical
Change	Change is generally not desirable; it is better to keep things as they are.	Change is generally good; it brings progress. Moderate change is best.	Change is a good thing, especially if it means a fundamental change in the system.
Human Nature	People are essentially selfish; they need to be controlled.	People are basically good; they need structures to reinforce good impulses.	People are basically good; they can be corrupted by institutions.
Individual Behavior	Individuals have free will; they are responsible for their own lives and problems.	Individuals are not entirely autonomous or self-governing; environment plays a part in the problems faced.	Individual behavior is strongly influenced by social and economic structures.
Family	The traditional family is the basic unit of society; it should not face government interference.	The family is changing; it needs social and government supports.	The traditional family is oppressive; the changing family needs government supports.
Society	Society is inherently fair, it functions well on its own, and it is a system of interrelated parts.	Society needs regulation to ensure fair competition between various interests.	Society contains inequalities, conflict between those with power and those without, and thus it needs change.
Roles of the Government and the Economic System	A free market economy is the best way to ensure prosperity and fulfillment of individual needs; the government role is to support, not regulate the market.	A free market economy needs regulation by government to ensure fairness; government programs are necessary to help meet basic human needs.	A market economy is exploitative and inherently unfair; alternatives include mixed public/private economy, and a socialist system.

from idle funds (such as bank accounts, real estate, and jewelry), which are not being spent and are therefore not contributing to national income. When they are given out in the form of welfare benefits, they are immediately spent and thus contribute to national income. Finally, liberals argue that governmental welfare programs have grown in response to increasing societal standards of health, nutrition, and security. Samuelson writes

> Society now rules that children shall not have rickets and bowed legs for life because of the bad luck or weakness of their parents. That poor people shall not die young because of insufficient money for operations and needed care. That the old shall be able to live out their years with some minimum of income.[26]

These increasing standards require programs beyond the capacity of private charity. They can only be met by the government.

A recent study examined the perceptions of governmental fairness by liberals and conservatives. It is interesting that both groups perceived government as basically unfair. The ways in which the groups perceived the unfairness were surprisingly predictable, however. The authors found that "liberals see government as favoring economic elites (including business, corporations, and the wealthy), while conservatives see government as favoring minorities such as black people and the poor."[27]

Value Systems

Underlying all of the differences among liberals, radicals, and conservatives that we have discussed are basically different, although occasionally overlapping, value systems. Values are based on what we find desirable; they are stated in terms of right or wrong, good or bad, beautiful or ugly, pleasant or unpleasant, and appropriate or inappropriate. The analysis of American value systems we draw upon here was developed by Alan Keith-Lucas in 1972.[28]

The value system that is the basis of conservative thinking in the United States is referred to by Keith-Lucas as the *capitalist-puritan value system*, or CP for short. He summarizes the basic assumptions of the CP value system as follows:

1. People are responsible for their own success or failure.
2. Human nature is basically evil, but can be overcome by an act of will.
3. A person's primary purpose is the acquisition of material prosperity, which is achieved through hard work.
4. The primary purpose of society is the maintenance of law and order so that this acquisition is possible.
5. The unsuccessful, or deviant, person is not deserving of help, although efforts should be made, up to a point, to rehabilitate or spur the person to greater efforts on his or her own behalf.
6. The primary incentives to change are to be found in economic or physical rewards and punishments.

The value system that is generally characteristic of liberals in America is referred to by Keith-Lucas as the *humanist-positivist-utopian value system*, or HPU for short. He summarizes the HPU value system as follows:

1. The primary purpose of society is to fulfill people's material and emotional needs.
2. If people's needs were fulfilled, then they would attain a state that is variously described, according to the vocabulary used by the specific HPU system, as that of goodness, maturity, adjustment, or productivity, in which most individual and social problems would be solved.
3. What hampers people from attaining this state are external circumstances, which are not generally under their individual control. In various HPU systems, this has been ascribed to lack of education, economic circumstance, childhood relationships, and social environment.
4. These circumstances are subject to manipulation by those who possess sufficient technical and scientific knowledge, and who use, in general, what is known as the "scientific method."
5. Consequently, individuals and society are ultimately perfectible.

Keith-Lucas identifies a third value system that he says is "behind, and yet parallel with these two systems." He calls this the *Judeo-Christian* tradition. Both liberals and conservatives accept parts of this value system, although they may interpret their meanings in very different ways. The basic assumptions of the Judeo-Christian tradition are summarized by Keith-Lucas as follows:

1. People are created beings; one of their major problems is the fact that they act as if they were not and try to be autonomous.
2. People are fallible, but at the same time capable of acts of great courage or unselfishness.
3. The difference between individuals in terms of good and bad is insignificant compared with the standard demanded by their creator, and, as a consequence, a person cannot judge others in such terms.
4. People's greatest good lies in terms of their relationship with others and with their creator.
5. People are capable of choice, in the "active and willing" sense, but may need help in making this choice.
6. Love is always the ultimate victor over force.

It is apparent that the conservative, capitalist-puritan value system will not lead to enthusiastic support of social welfare efforts. As Keith-Lucas has said, "If man is totally responsible for his own actions, if he can better his condition by an act of will, if he can be induced to change by punishment or reward, then helping becomes a simple matter of us arranging the appropriate rewards and punishments. There is no room for relationship, or concern for another, except in a highly condescending and judgmental way."[29] It is this value system that is behind work requirements for the receipt of welfare, even if the work is meaningless; prosecution and jailing of parents who neglect their children; jail as the solution to all crime regardless of the age or circumstance of the offender; and the general attitude of making the receipt of aid as unpleasant as possible to insure that "only those who really need it will be willing to apply."

The liberal, humanist-positivist-utopian value system is far more conducive to the support of social welfare efforts. Under this way of thinking people are not perceived as being totally responsible for their problems, so they are not totally responsible for the solutions. People are responsible for helping each other and, given enough time and resources, all problems are solvable. Therefore society can, and should, help inadequate parents to become good parents, provide poor people with the means necessary for a comfortable life, and help criminals become productive citizens.

It should be noted that Keith-Lucas does not think that the CP value system is all bad and the HPU is all good, as might easily be inferred from the brief description given earlier. In their extreme form both can have negative consequences that can be mitigated by the Judeo-Christian value system that undergirds them. The CP system can lead to a harsh and callous approach to social welfare needs that should be softened by the JC tenet that all people fall short of the standard expected of them, in addition to its emphasis on love as a virtue. The HPU system is criticized by Keith-Lucas as failing to recognize that, in the final analysis, it is the person in trouble who must bear the major responsibility for his or her own betterment.

THE AUTHORS' PERSPECTIVE

At one time it was contended that social scientists could be value free and, therefore, could write completely objective papers and texts. It is now generally agreed that this is not possible and that no matter how hard we try, our own social attitudes are bound to color our work. Therefore, we feel it is important that the reader know the authors' perspective before proceeding with this text.

The authors, both social workers, reflect the generally liberal bias of their profession. One author finds merit in many tenets of radicalism as well. Both vote Democratic, favor most welfare legislation, believe in social and racial equality for all men and women, and favor social action to further these ends. However, we recognize that there is also value in ideas to which many conservatives subscribe. We believe that individuals, where possible, should take primary responsibility for the solution of their own problems; we believe that there is fulfillment in meaningful work; we believe that the family, in both its traditional and newer forms, is a strong source of support for individuals; and we recognize that the economic consequences of welfare programs need to be carefully thought out before the programs are enacted.

It is not accidental that most social workers proceed from a liberal perspective. It is partly a matter of pragmatism, or in other words, what works. The conservative perspective leads to a very pessimistic view of both social welfare problems and the potential for their solution. If people are viewed as autonomous, if they are totally in control of their own fate and can change it by a simple act of will, if society is fair and change will most likely make it worse, if government is to be feared and governmental programs viewed as harmful to the economy, what is the use of trying to solve social welfare problems? Many conservatives agree with Thomas Sowell that there are no solutions, only trade-offs.[30] On the other hand, if we view people as being basically good and their problems as at least partially the result of factors they cannot control, and if we believe there are ways of structuring society that will make it more just and that government can be a force for good, then the opportunities for constructive social intervention are immense. Social attitudes are neither right nor wrong, they just are. However, as a matter of practicality the liberal perspective simply works better for those of us who are concerned with helping individuals and society solve problems.

The belief that the liberal perspective "works better" and is more hopeful has, unfortunately, led most authors in social work to ignore the conservative perspective. We believe that all competing ideas warrant careful consideration. In addition, in recent years our country has become increasingly conservative, and, in spite of President Bush's promise of a "kinder, gentler, America," the liberal renaissance that many of us keep hoping for does not appear to be close at hand. In fact, recent events such as the "victory" in the Gulf, the breakup of the Eastern Block, and now the apparent dissolution of the Soviet Union itself are being viewed by many as a complete vindication of the conservative perspective. Therefore, social welfare programs for the foreseeable future will have to be justified with an eye on the conservative point of view. It is crucial for social workers, and students of social work, to be conversant with conservative ideas, whether they accept these ideas or not.

E N D N O T E S

1. Daryl J. Bem, *Beliefs, Attitudes, and Human Affairs* (Belmont, CA: Brooks/Cole, 1973).
2. Fred N. Kerlinger, *Liberalism and Conservatism: The Nature and Structure of Social Attitudes* (Hillsdale, NJ: Lawrence Erlbaum Associates, 1984), 1.
3. Kenneth Dolbeare, *American Political Thought* (Monterey, CA: Duxbury Press, 1981), 7.
4. Mulford Q. Sibley, *Political Ideas and Ideologies: A History of Political Thought* (New York: Harper and Row, 1970), 513.
5. Dolbeare, *American Political Thought*, 9–10.
6. Kerlinger, *Liberalism and Conservatism*, 11.
7. Raymond W. Wolfinger, Martin Shapiro, and Fred I. Greenstein, *Dynamics of American Politics* (Englewood Cliffs, NJ: Prentice-Hall, 1976), 80.
8. Thomas Sowell, *Compassion versus Guilt and Other Essays* (New York: William Morrow and Company, 1987), 17.
9. Irving Kristol, *Two Cheers for Capitalism* (New York: Basic Books, 1978).
10. Erik Erikson, *Childhood and Society* (New York: Norton, 1963); Barney Glaser and Anselm Strauss, *Status Passage* (Chicago, IL: Aldine, 1971); Daniel Levinson, *The Seasons of a Man's Life* (New York: Alfred A. Knopf, 1978).
11. John B. Watson, *Psychology from the Standpoint of the Behaviorist* (Philadelphia, PA: J.P. Lippincott, 1919); B.F. Skinner, *The Behavior of Organisms* (New York: Appleton Century Crofts, 1938).
12. Sowell, *Compassion Versus Guilt*, 35–36.
13. Editors of *Policy Review*, "The Vision Thing: Conservatism for the Nineties," *Policy Review* 52 (Spring 1990): 4–37.
14. Kingsley Davis and Wilbert Moore, "Some Principles of Stratification," *American Sociological Review 10* (April 1945): 242–249.
15. John Kenneth Galbraith, *American Capitalism: The Concept of Countervailing Power* (Boston: Houghton Mifflin, 1952); Robert Dahl, *Who Governs?* (New Haven, CT: Yale University Press, 1961).
16. This analysis is advanced by sociologists like Robert and Helen Lynd, *Middletown in Transition* (New York: Harcourt Brace & Company, 1937); Floyd Hunter, *Community Power Structure* (Chapel Hill, NC: University of North Carolina Press, 1953); C. Wright Mills, *The Power Elite* (New York: Oxford University Press, 1956); and psychologists like G. William Domhoff, *Who Rules America?* (Englewood Cliffs, NJ: Prentice-Hall, 1967).
17. Paul A. Samuelson, *Economics,* 11th ed. (New York: McGraw-Hill, 1980), 142.
18. Adam Smith, *The Wealth of Nations,* 5th ed., Edwin Connan, ed. (London: Methuen & Co., 1930).
19. Milton Friedman and Rose Friedman, *Free to Choose: A Personal Statement* (New York: Harcourt, Brace and Jovanovich, 1980), 1–2.
20. Friedman and Friedman, *Free to Choose,* 1–2.
21. Edward Berkowitz and Kim McQuaid, *Creating the Welfare State* (New York: Praeger, 1980), 33–36.
22. John Maynard Keynes, "General Theory of Employment, Interest, and Money," in *Classics of Economics,* Charles W. Needy, ed. (Oak Park, IL: Moore Publishing Co., 1980), 324–338.
23. P. Nelson Reid, "Four Conservative Ideas," *Arete 8* (Summer 1983), 40.
24. Charles E. Harris, Jr., "Capitalism and Social Justice,"

The Intercollegiate Review 20 (Spring/Summer 1984): 35–49.

25. Stuart M. Butler and Anna Kondratas, *Out of the Poverty Trap* (New York: The Free Press, 1987), 77–79.

26. Samuelson, *Economics,* 147.

27. Henry B. Sirgo and Russell Eisenman, "Perceptions of Governmental Fairness by Liberals and Conservatives," *Psychological Reports* 67 (December 1990): 1331–1334.

28. From *Giving and Taking Help,* by Alan Keith-Lucas. © 1972 The University of North Carolina Press. Reprinted by permission. (pp. 138–142).

29. From *Giving and Taking Help,* by Alan Keith-Lucas. © 1972 The University of North Carolina Press. Reprinted by permission. (p. 142).

30. Sowell, *Compassion versus Guilt,* 21–24.

C · H · A · P · T · E · R

two

Social Welfare:
Basic Concepts

The four friends were having lunch together at the Rotary Club, and the conversation turned to the previous week's guest speaker, a United Way official who had spoken on the subject of social welfare. "He had some good things to say," said Ron, an energetic retired banker. "But, you know, I really resented his saying that Social Security and Medicare are social welfare benefits. They're insurance, not welfare, and after all the money deducted from my paychecks over the years for them I sure don't want anyone saying I'm on welfare." "Yeah," said William, the local Ford Dealer, "and what did he mean when he referred to the Family Guidance Clinic as a social welfare agency? My wife used to work there and they don't give away money or food, and most people who go there pay for counseling. One of my sales people went there for marriage counseling, and they charged her forty-five dollars an hour." "I'll tell you what social welfare is," said Hank, a retired Marine Lieutenant Colonel. "Welfare is freebies given to people who are too lazy to work and to people who have so many illegitimate kids that they can't afford to work." "Garbage!" said Hal, the youngest member of the group, whose generally disagreeable nature was widely suspected to be caused by his having taken too many drugs during the sixties. "I'll tell you what welfare is. Welfare is government handouts to people who are already rich, like the Chrysler Corporation or big farmers."

The preceding discussion illustrates various popular conceptions about what is meant by the term *social welfare*. The first is the belief that social welfare involves a stigma, or in other words, it is shameful and involves only low-status people. Thus, Hank believes that social welfare involves only the able-bodied unemployed and mothers of illegitimate children (two very low-status groups), and Ron was offended by the reference to benefits he receives as being social welfare because, as a retired banker, he is not a low-status person. The second conception is that social welfare only involves the receipt of material goods (such as money or food) or perhaps counseling to help people obtain these goods on their own. Thus, William took issue with the speaker's characterization of a family guidance agency as providing a social welfare service. The third conception is that social welfare is anything given away (generally by the government) for free or below market value. Thus, Ron does not feel his social security benefits are social welfare because he has paid for them. William does not view a family guidance clinic as a social welfare agency because many clients pay for the service they receive, and Hal argues that rich people are the major recipients of social welfare benefits.

The main idea with which we begin this chapter is that social welfare is a very difficult concept to define. It is difficult, confusing, and debated not only among lay people like our group of Rotarians, but also among social welfare professionals. As Joseph W. Heffernan, a leading scholar of social welfare policy, says, "We could search in vain . . . for a . . . central element in the study of social welfare. . . . While politics and economics are fuzzy at their boundaries, social welfare is fuzzy at its core."[1] We believe this fuzziness in our understanding of the concept of social welfare is the result of two major factors. The first is that social welfare *does* carry a stigma. Therefore, people do not want to include in their definition of social welfare benefits and services that they or people they care about receive. The second problem is that most definitions are descriptive. They try to capture what social welfare "looks like," that is, types of agencies, methods of finance, and types and numbers of people served. These defi-

The popular stereotype of social welfare programs is that the beneficiaries are poor people, generally members of minority groups.

nitions generally ignore the *function* of social welfare, in other words why we provide the services described. In our attempt to define the concept of social welfare, we will begin with a discussion of stigma and then present a brief review of descriptive definitions. We will then move to what we consider to be the critical element in the concept of social welfare—its function in society. We will then present a categorization of major social welfare services, and finally we will discuss perspectives on the function of, and motivation for, social welfare.

STIGMA AND SOCIAL WELFARE

The term *stigma* as used by sociologists refers to an aspect of a person's life that ruins his or her identity. Because of some characteristic that others consider to be a disgrace, the individual is disqualified from full social acceptance.[2] There is no doubt that in American society there is considerable stigma attached to the receipt of social welfare services. The British sociologist Paul Spicker asserts that "a stigma marks the recipient of welfare, damages his reputation, and undermines his dignity."[3] Some sociologists have argued that stigma is such an important concept that it is the central issue in the study of social welfare.[4] Beck argues that the only meaningful way to define social welfare is as a moral category in which the recipients are stigmatized because they are believed to lead lives that are "morally suspect and reputationally degraded."[5]

Why is social welfare a moral category and why are recipients stigmatized in our society? The first thing to note is that most people who have written about this subject tend to view social welfare as synonymous with poverty and the receipt of financial or material assistance, as was noted at the beginning of the chapter. Matza asserts that poverty itself is considered disreputable, but to be poor and to receive financial assistance is even more disreputable.[6] Sociologists relate this to two factors—the value placed on work in our society and the norm of reciprocity. Spicker argues that the amount of stigma attached to welfare benefits is directly related to how closely the benefits can be related to contributions from work. "Contribution is measured largely by work status. Pensioners are respectable; they have paid their dues by working most of their lives. Student [aid recipients] are accepted, perhaps with some reservations, because they are going to contribute in the future."[7] Recipients of Aid to Families with Dependent Children (AFDC) are viewed as unacceptable because the benefit is generally not tied to work.

A related but more general explanation of the stigma attached to social welfare benefits involves the norm of reciprocity. This means that it is considered in our society to be a general obligation to make some return for the things received. Exchange, the anthropologist Claude Levi-Strauss writes, "provides the means of binding men together."[8] Because the recipient of welfare benefits is seen as unable to offer anything in return for those benefits, he or she violates this norm and is stigmatized as a result.

These explanations may be adequate to explain why there is a stigma attached to the receipt of financial and material assistance, but what of other types of social welfare services? As will be discussed later in this chapter, there are a number of social welfare services that do not involve material assistance, such as child welfare services, child guidance, marriage and family counseling, drug and alcohol services, employee assistance programs, and many others. Do these services also involve a stigma? The authors argue that they do, although not to as great an extent as material assistance services. The explanation for the stigma attached to these services is related to what Wilensky and Lebeaux identify as one of the primary components of American culture, the concept of individualism.[9]

Wilensky and Lebeaux argue that of central importance to American society, which they characterize as the "culture of capitalism," is its great emphasis on the rational, acquisitive, self-interested individual. They explain individualism as two sets of beliefs, one set about what *should be* and another set of beliefs about what *is*. "Large and

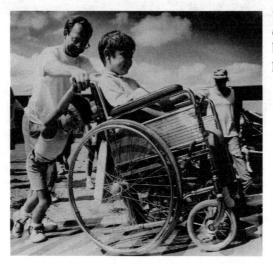

In reality the majority of recipients of social welfare benefits are non-poor white people.

influential segments of the American people (not just businessmen) believe strongly that:

1. The individual should strive to be successful in competition with others, under the rules of the game.
2. These rules involve 'fair play': (a) everyone should start with equal opportunity; (b) no one should take unfair advantage through force, fraud, 'pull.'
3. The test of reward should be ability (especially ability to contribute to the productive and other purposes of the enterprise). There should be unequal reward for unequal talents and unequal contributions.

Americans also believe strongly that:

1. Those who work hard and have the ability will be rewarded with success. (Success is a tangible package which mainly includes income and wealth, possessions, occupational prestige, and power—along with the style of life those permit.)
2. Success is the reward also of virtue; virtue will bring success. Failure (if it is not a temporary way-station to success) is sin and reveals lack of virtue.
3. When the lazy, incompetent, and unvirtuous attain success it is purely a matter of luck; it could happen to anybody. Besides, it does not happen too often."[10]

The upshot of the idea of individualism is that success and failure are directly attributable to the individual. He or she gets all the credit and also all the blame. Individualism has strong moral overtones. Those who achieve at high levels are, by definition, virtuous, and those who do not are at least incompetent, and perhaps even lazy and immoral. Although Wilensky and Lebeaux are speaking mainly of economic success, the idea is generalizable to noneconomic areas of life as well. Individuals are considered to be totally responsible for the success or failure of their children, their career, their marriage, and their mental health. When something goes wrong with one of these, such as when a couple's marriage begins to crumble, society and the individuals affected tend to feel it is a personal failure and perhaps an indication of some moral defect. Social workers in family guidance settings often hear statements like the following:

Ever since Bill and I separated I feel like such a failure. I need to look for a better job, but every time I hear about an opening I'm overwhelmed by the feeling that no one would want to hire a woman who can't even keep a marriage together. I guess I'm just not worth very much.

The fact that stigma is attached to social welfare complicates any discussion of the concept. People do not want to be associated with a stigmatized entity and therefore tend to define benefits and programs with which they are personally involved as outside the boundaries of social welfare. Therefore, Grandma's Supplemental Security Income grant is not social welfare; it is a "pension"; Uncle Ed's vocational rehabilitation program is not social welfare, it is "career guidance"; cousin Bob's family, who are receiving help with family problems that affect Bob's school performance, are not receiving social welfare services from the school social worker, but are being helped by a "visiting teacher." This is the main reason that descriptive definitions of social welfare rarely are satisfactory. In the following section we will discuss two descriptive definitions and the problems with each one.

DESCRIPTIVE DEFINITIONS OF SOCIAL WELFARE

Numerous authors have attempted to develop clear and adequate descriptive definitions of social welfare. All have fallen short of their goal because of the problem of arriving at a definition of *social welfare* that is exclusive (fitting no other activity) and inclusive (encompassing every social welfare activity). As Macarov notes

> Definitional problems arise both because social welfare actually overlaps with the activities of many other institutions and because the activities of social welfare itself are so varied.[11]

The descriptive definitions that have been developed fall into two categories.

1. Social welfare defined as economic transfers outside the market system.
2. Social welfare defined as benefits and services to help people meet basic needs. Some restrict the definition to economic needs, and some include other areas of well-being such as physical and mental health.

Social Welfare as Nonmarket Economic Transfers

In a market economy such as the United States, the primary mode of economic life is that when one person desires a good or a service, he or she pays for it at market value—the amount it is worth. An obvious feature of social welfare services is that many do not operate this way. People receiving Medicare get medical services for free, food stamp recipients do not pay cash for their groceries, and couples going to a United Way Family Guidance agency frequently pay much less than full cost for the services they receive. Some analysts have seized on this aspect of social welfare and use it as a basis of their definition. For example, Burns says

> To an economist the most significant fact about social welfare as an institution is that it is a set of organizational arrangements which results in the production and distribution to consumers of economic output by methods, or on the basis of principles, which differs from those of the free economic market or prevailing under the family system.[12]

In a similar manner, Gilbert and Specht speak of social welfare as "a benefit-allocation mechanism functioning outside the economic marketplace."[13]

This method of describing social welfare has two distinct advantages. The first is that it is conceptually clear and unambiguous. It is very easy to separate social welfare services from other services. If someone pays full price for something, such as a shopping cart full of groceries, they are not involved with the social welfare system. If someone pays less than full value and buys his groceries with food stamps, that person is receiving social welfare.

The second advantage of this means of defining social welfare, one much touted by social workers who are often political liberals, is that it includes many services to nonpoor, nonstigmatized people, and thus it is viewed as reducing the stigma of welfare. Walz and Askerooth use this definition in an entertaining little book titled *The Upside Down Welfare State* in which they say, "Somebody is getting something for nothing, but as usual, it's not the folks who had nothing in the beginning."[14] On the same theme, Bell says

A C L O S E R L O O K

A Rugged Individualist

A veteran returning from Korea went to college on the GI Bill; bought his house with an FHA loan; saw his kids born in a VA hospital; started a business with an SBA loan; got electricity from TVA and, then, water from a project funded by the EPA. His kids participated in the school-lunch program and made it through college courtesy of government-guaranteed student loans. His parents retired to a farm on their social security, getting electricity from the REA and the soil tested by the USDA. When the father became ill, his life was saved with a drug developed through NIH; the family was saved from financial ruin by Medicare. Our veteran drove to work on the interstate; moored his boat in a channel dredged by Army engineers; and when floods hit, took Amtrak to Washington to apply for disaster relief. He also spent some of his time there enjoying the exhibits in the Smithsonian museums.

Then one day he wrote his congressman an angry letter complaining about paying taxes for all those programs created for ungrateful people. In effect, he said, the government should get off his back.

Source: Senator Ernest F. Hollings, as quoted in Jonathan Yates, " 'Reality' on Capitol Hill," *Newsweek*, (November 28, 1988), 12.

Perhaps the most frequent misconception about social welfare is that it serves only the poor. Nothing could be further from the truth. Around the world, as nations grow in complexity, people have recognized that collective efforts are necessary to satisfy social needs and to resolve social problems. . . . When provisions spread benefits over all income classes, they are known as *universal* programs. When they are designed solely for the poor they are called *selective* programs. . . . By the late 1970s, less than one-fifth of public social welfare expenditures in the U.S. were for selective measures. . . . The other four-fifths was spent on universal programs . . .[15]

This means of defining social welfare is extremely appealing because it emphasizes that the stigmatization of welfare recipients as people who get "something for nothing" is irrational because *many* people get "something for nothing" and, in fact, the nonpoor get much more than the poor. However, conceptually this approach is of limited value. There are many social welfare programs that do not involve economic transfers or, if they do, the transfers are within the market system. For example, the recipients of services at a mental health clinic do not obtain anything of direct economic value, and furthermore, they often pay market value for the services they receive. Residents in a retirement home are generally considered to be recipients of social welfare services, but not only do many pay the full cost of their care but also a number of homes are run as for-profit businesses. Hence, this definition is not inclusive because it does not cover all social welfare services. The second problem is that this definition is not exclusive; it includes many things that most people would not define as social welfare. Most people do not consider agricultural subsidies, loans to Chrysler Corporation, and FHA home loans to be social welfare programs. The second major class of definitions, to which we now turn, addresses this problem.

Social Welfare as Services to Meet Basic Needs

The philosopher Nicholas Rescher points out that the word *welfare* as currently used is derived from the original root meaning of "having a good trip or journey," thus conveying the idea of traveling smoothly on the road of life. However, Rescher argues, upon reflection it becomes clear that welfare does not relate to all aspects of a smooth journey, but only to the basic requisites of a person's well-being in general, and it deals most prominently with health and economic adequacy. "This characterization—with its explicit reference to the basic—makes transparently clear one critical negative feature of welfare in its relationship to human well-being in general, namely, that welfare is a matter of 'well-being' not in its global totality but in its 'basic requisites,' its indispensable foundations."[16]

This approach to social welfare, which defines it as services designed to bring people's well-being up to some minimum level, is very popular. Coll, writing in the *Encyclopedia of Social Work,* the standard reference source in the field, gives the following definition.

> Social welfare is an organized effort to insure a basic standard of decency in relation to the physical and material well-being of the citizenry.[17]

In his 1955 text on social welfare, Walter Friedlander gave the following definition.

> *Social Welfare* is the organized system of social services and institutions, designed to aid individuals and groups to attain satisfying standards of life and health. It aims at personal and social relationships which permit individuals the development of their full capacities and the promotion of their well-being in harmony with the needs of the community.[18]

Martin and Zald say

> Our definition of social welfare is relatively exclusive: Social welfare attempts to enable people in need to attain a minimum level of social and personal functioning.[19]

Finally, Wickenden defines social welfare as

> including those laws, programs, benefits, and services which assure or strengthen provisions for meeting social needs recognized as basic to the well-being of the population and the better functioning of the social order.[20]

Rescher notes that social welfare is broader than physical and material welfare. It also deals with people's relations with each other and their personal and close-range interactions (family contacts, professional interactions, friendships, and other human relationships) which are key aspects of well-being. Therefore, this means of defining social welfare includes services such as recreation, socialization, and counseling. "Yet," Rescher cautions, "it is important to recognize that despite its diversified and multi-faceted character, the issue of a man's welfare has a certain *minimality* about it. Welfare—in all its dimensions—deals only with the basic essentials."[21]

The authors agree that this definition—social welfare as laws, services, and programs designed to bring people's level of well-being up to some minimum—offers a fairly adequate description. By and large it meets the tests of being inclusive and exclusive. However, it offers no explanation of what we consider to be the most interesting part of the definition of social welfare, namely, what is the function of social welfare in society? We now turn to this question.

Our preliminary functional definition of social welfare is as follows.

> For society to survive, individuals must function as interdependent units, each carrying out the full range of his or her roles and responsibilities. A society cannot survive if it contains too many individuals who cannot function in an interdependent manner (i.e., who are dependent). On the other hand, the social system cannot endure if it contains too many dysfunctional culture patterns and inefficient structures that inhibit people's ability to function in an interdependent manner.
>
> Up until the late nineteenth century, the basic institutions of family, economy, religion, and politics were able to handle the problem of dependency. It should be noted that when we say that these institutions handled the problem of dependency we do not mean to imply that they handled it well. People were poor, sick, mentally ill, and starving to death. Dependent people were relatively few in number, and were spread out, and the basic institutions were able to do enough so that they did not constitute a threat to the stability of society. As society evolved from rural agricultural to urban industrial, these institutions lost the ability to handle dependency. When society recognized dependency as a threatening state of affairs, social welfare as an institution began to emerge to handle dependence and to facilitate interdependence.

At this point it is likely that this definition does not mean much to you because it contains a number of terms with which you are probably not familiar, such as *role* and *institution,* which are two concepts sociologists use to explain *social structure,* or how society works. The terms *dependence* and *interdependence* may also be unfamiliar. These are explained next.

Social Structure

When sociologists speak of social structure, they are referring to how individuals achieve identity (status and role) and fit into groups and organizations, and how these in turn fit into institutions, communities, and finally society. In order to understand our functional definition of social welfare, it is necessary to understand some basic concepts of social structure, including status, role, and institution.

Status and Role A *status* is simply a socially defined position in a group or society. Statuses include things like being black, male, a social worker, father, or student. The most familiar statuses are related to gender, marital status, age, education, ethnic background, religion, and occupation. Obviously, any one person will occupy a large number of statuses, and many will change and evolve throughout a person's life span.

Each status, or set of statuses, has connected with it a *role,* which is a set of expectations and behaviors. Most statuses have a number of roles associated with them, and the term for all the roles associated with a particular status is a *role set.* Roles associated with the status of parent, for example, generally include breadwinner, disciplinarian, household maintenance and repairperson, and family business representative. The role set for a social worker teaching in a university includes teaching classes, arranging for field placements, advising students, doing research, participating on university committees, and volunteering in community social agencies, among other things.

People do not always fulfill roles in ways that meet with everyone's approval. The *role expectation* is the generally accepted way a role should be played, and *role performance* is the way a person actually plays a role. Role expectation of the status of mother generally includes being married and financially supporting the children in some way. When a woman gives birth out of wedlock and supports the child through a public welfare grant, we perceive a gap between role expectation and role performance.

Our description of the concept of role is highly simplified. There is a large area of sociology called *role theory* that studies roles in society. Sociologists in this area are interested in the roles that make up groups and organizations; how people assume roles and learn the roles associated with various statuses; and special problems such as role strain, role conflict, and roles and self-identity, as well as numerous other questions. For our purposes, however, it is sufficient to understand that a basic component of social structure (how society works) is the concept of status and role. People occupying various statuses have to appropriately carry out the roles associated with those statuses in order for society to function smoothly. For example, the status of parent has associated with it roles of providing financial support for children, providing nurturance and supervision, and providing appropriate discipline. If parents are unable to fulfill any of these roles, for example they do not support their children, it creates a problem for society. We will return to this later. Now we need to deal with another component of social structure related to our functional definition of social welfare, social institutions.

Social Institutions   Sociologists and anthropologists have developed a list (actually several similar lists) of essential functions that must be performed if a society is to survive. To illustrate these functions, we ask you to imagine that you are a member of a group of the last two hundred surviving people on earth. Everyone else in the world has died of some strange disease, and you and your companions survived because you were on a cruise ship far out to sea. You have landed on a tropical island and, upon taking inventory, you discover you have all the basic resources necessary for survival (such as tools, books, and seeds) and all the basic skills needed (doctors, dentists, engineers, teachers, and farmers). The only thing you do not have is a society. You have no rules, laws, family structure (you are all single), or anything. Think about this—what functions will have to be accomplished in order for your group of two hundred individuals to remake and continue society? Your answer will probably, in some forms, include the following:

- **Production-Distribution-Consumption.** How will you produce the many things needed for your group to survive? Will people grow their own food, or will certain people be given the status of farmer and its associated roles? If the tasks are divided up (sociologists call this "division of labor") with some people being farmers, some builders, and so on, how will the fruits of their labor be divided up? Will the physicians be entitled to a larger share of what your society produces than the farmers, for example?
- **Population and Socialization.** What arrangements will be made for having children? And, once the children arrive, some provisions must be made to induct them into the knowledge systems, social values, roles, and behavior patterns of the group.

- **Social Integration.** Processes will have to be established by which individuals will come to value their membership in your society and to feel a responsibility for abiding by its rules. These processes are aimed at developing a level of solidarity and morale necessary for the ongoing life of the group.
- **Mutual Support.** It will be necessary for members of your group to feel some obligation to help each other out. Mutual support is necessary among members of any social group if individuals within the group are to grow, develop, and function comfortably and effectively as human beings.
- **Social Control and Social Order.** Arrangements will need to be made by which your society attempts to assure that its members behave in conformity with its generally accepted norms of social behavior.
- **Social Change.** Finally, if your group, like any group, is to survive it must develop means to provide for orderly, lawful change in the ways in which the institutions of your society function and interrelate.

All societies, whether simple as in the preceding example or highly differentiated and complex like the United States, must perform the functions listed earlier. How is this done? Sociologists explain that societies organize life into enduring patterns of statuses and roles that ensure that these functions are carried out. These patterns are called *social institutions*. Sociologist David Popenoe says that "institution" is one of "the most abstract concepts sociologists use." He goes on to define an *institution* as "a stable cluster of social structures that is organized to meet the basic needs of societies."[22] Lenski and Lenski say that "a social institution is essentially a system of social relationships and cultural elements that has developed in a society in response to some set of basic and persistent needs. These cultural elements are such things as rules, laws, customs, role definitions, and values that serve to regulate people's behavior and organize their activities in certain basic areas of life."[23] The basic needs of society referred to by these sociologists are, of course, the list of functions given earlier.

What are these vague and abstract things called social institutions? You may be surprised to learn that they are really very familiar and everyday things. There is one basic social institution present in every society, no matter how simple—the family. There are three other institutions in all but the most primitive societies: government, the economy, and religion. As societies modernize, two other institutions develop. Education is one, and it is accepted by nearly all social theorists as a basic social institution in modern societies. Finally, many people, including the authors, now consider social welfare to be a basic institution in modern societies. Let's look at each of these institutions in more detail, with special emphasis on the social welfare institution.

Family and Kinship   The family is the most basic institution, and in simple societies it fulfills all necessary functions. In modern societies the family's main functions are population and socialization, and mutual support; its secondary functions include social integration and social order—social control. One of the decisions you will need to make in your island society is what kind of family you want to have. Will you want to establish the institution as it presently exists in the United States, with a nuclear family where the husband and wife are almost entirely responsible for each other's emotional needs and for the care and upbringing of their children, or will you want to establish something else, perhaps like an Israeli kibbutz where there is more shared responsibility for child rearing?

Government and Politics   Two of the earliest questions you will deal with in your island society are how decisions are going to be made and how the power to enforce these decisions is going to be exercised. These are the central questions of the political institution. The primary functions of the political institution are social control/social order and social change. Secondary functions are mutual support, social integration, and production-distribution-consumption.

Economics   A central principle in the study of economics is that of scarcity. That is, there are never enough goods and services available to satisfy 100 percent of everyone's needs and desires. Therefore, the economic institution develops to regulate the production, distribution, and consumption of goods and services. As Compton says, "a society must organize a system to assure the production of enough goods and services for its own survival and must arrange for the distribution of the fruits of its production so that more production can take place."[24] In our island example you must decide if each person will be expected to produce as much as he or she is capable of and will be entitled to receive an equal share of the total production (basically a socialist system) or if each person will sell as much as he or she can produce for as much as possible (basically a capitalist system). If you choose the latter, you will then need to decide how to deal with people who, because of illness, injury, old age, or whatever, produce less than they need to survive.

Religion   The religious institution seeks to answer our questions about the meaning and purposes of life. The major functions of religious institutions are social integration and mutual support. Secondary but still very important functions are socialization, social control/social order, and social change.

Education   The primary function of the educational institution is one part of socialization, that of passing along formal knowledge systems. Until the nineteenth century this function was generally carried out by the family, with some help from the church. However, as knowledge rapidly expanded and there was a corresponding increase in the amount individuals had to master to function adequately in society, the ability of the family to serve this function deteriorated. At the beginning of the nineteenth century the family was held responsible for passing along knowledge; by the end of the century this function was assigned to the schools—it had become institutionalized. As the twentieth century has progressed we have seen an ever-increasing number of functions assigned (often with considerable controversy) to the educational institution. In addition to traditional education, schools are often asked to pass along values, career counseling, vocational training, sex education, and general life skills training. Schools not only are expected to provide sex education, but also we are now seeing pressure to provide medical family planning services. Many people, mainly but not exclusively conservatives, think this is a bad trend and that the schools are serving functions that are the proper territory of the family and religion.

Dependence, Interdependence, and the Social Welfare Institution

You may already have observed that statuses and roles nearly always come in groups. The status and role of physician assumes that of patients, teacher assumes students, husband assumes wife, and parent assumes child. You may also have observed that roles occur within (and in fact they are one of the defining characteristics of) social institutions. The statuses and roles of parent and children occur within the institution of the family; citizen, voter, and taxpayer occur within government. Therefore, although we often speak of people as being independent, no one really is. It is common to hear statements such as, "My grandfather is 86 years old, but he is still completely independent." In actuality, unless he is a hermit, he is not independent. He depends on his wife, his children and grandchildren, dentist, neighbors, police, and grocer—the list goes on and on. These people, in turn, depend on him. The proper term is *interdependent*, which, according to Atherton, means "carrying one's own load in a social situation in which other actors do the same."[25] In other words, an interdependent person adequately performs all the roles connected with a given status and his or her role partners do the same.

Adequate societal functioning has two levels. One is that of individual role performance. For example, for society to function well, parents must fully discharge their roles. If they do not feed and supervise their children and the kids wander the streets searching for food or begging, we have a social problem. The other level is that social institutions must function well enough so people are able to perform their individual roles. One role of parents is to financially support their children. However, if the economic institution does not function well enough for everyone to be employed (and it in fact does not), many people are not going to be able to fulfill this role. Another role of parents is to supervise, or arrange for the supervision of, their young children. If the economic and governmental institutions do not provide affordable, accessible day care for everyone who needs it (and in fact they do not), many people are not going to be able to fulfill this role. Individuals are interdependent with institutions as well as with each other for role performance.

When people are unable to perform their roles in an interdependent manner, whether the problem is on the individual or the institutional level, we speak of them as being *dependent*. To quote Atherton again,

> Dependent is intended to connote a state of being in which one is not able to participate as a social being in rewarding ways and, thus, is the proper opposite for interdependent. . . . The point is that, in all human societies and in all human actors, situations come about in which people are unable to perform their roles in ways that satisfy both themselves and the society. Quite obviously, dependency is only one of a whole series of problematical conditions which societies and actors face. It is, however, a very basic problem to the continued existence of the social system and the individual actor.

> Since dependency, deviant behavior, and social dysfunction constitute threats to society, such conditions must be kept in bounds if society is to survive. Some way must exist either to repair or to change the social system so that it is as organized as well as it can be to fulfill the needs and requirements of its actors. There must also be some way of focusing on the problematical aspects of actors' behavior and life situations, assuring the actor satisfying role performance within the limits of social norms and offering corrective experiences for harmful forms of deviance and dependency.[26]

For people living in extended families, as was once common, dependency is less of a problem than for those living in nuclear families. Now that most people live in nuclear families, often hundreds of miles from their nearest relatives, social welfare programs are necessary to help with problems formerly dealt with by the family.

Social welfare is the institution in modern industrial society that functions to promote interdependence and to deal with the problem of dependence. Prior to industrialization this function was performed by the other basic social institutions, mainly by the family and religion. If a person was sick, elderly, out of work, or whatever, that person was generally cared for by his or her family (often extended) or was aided by the church. As industrialization progressed, two things happened which impaired the ability of these institutions to deal with dependency. The first is that the combination of urbanization, industrialization, immigration, and mobility caused some deterioration in these institutions. Fewer and fewer people lived close to their extended family, had life-long ties to one church, or lived in an area with a strong sense of community and neighborly obligation. People came to be pretty much on their own. A large number of people who were sick, elderly, or out of work found themselves with no one to help them. The second factor is that along with industrialization, urbanization, and immigration came a massive increase in the risk of becoming dependent. A family living in the country in a house they built and owned themselves, with land for a garden, a few animals, and opportunities to hunt, fish, and gather, could weather a temporary period of misfortune. A family living in a city, working in a factory, buying food at a grocery store, and living in a tenement where rent was due weekly was only one paycheck away from destitution.

Radical theorists argue that the changes brought about by rapid industrialization were not accidental. They see a deliberate attempt on the part of employers and other members of the power structure to reorganize working-class life in order to ensure the survival of capitalism in the United States. As Ehrenreich notes "the reorganization of the working class involved the fragmentation of the labor process at the workplace and the radical isolation of worklife from home life and of workplace from home. In the process, indigenous networks of support and mutual aid were disrupted, and central aspects of working-class and immigrant cultures were destroyed and replaced by 'mass culture,' as defined by the individual, privatized consumption of commodities."[27] This meant not only an increase in levels of dependency, but also a weakened working class that was unable to promote changes in the system necessary to ensure against unemployment, industrial accidents, and other factors leading to dependency.

In a process similar to what occurred with education, social welfare began to emerge as an institution when it became apparent that the family and the church were unable to deal with the problem of dependency. When the number of people needing food, shelter, and financial assistance because of unemployment became too great for churches to deal with, first private and then public welfare programs developed; when the number of orphans became so great as to be seen as a threat to social order, child welfare services evolved; and when more and more elderly were left with no family to care for them, services for the aged developed. The list could go on and on; specific details of the emergence of various welfare services are provided in later chapters.

Private Troubles and Public Issues The social theorist C. Wright Mills spoke of the distinction between "the personal troubles of milieu" and "the public issues of social structure," or, more simply, private troubles and public issues. According to Mills, "*Troubles* occur within the character of the individual and within the range of his immediate relations with others; they have to do with his self and with those limited areas of social life of which he is directly and personally aware . . . . A trouble is a private matter; values cherished by an individual are felt by him to be threatened." Issues, on the other hand, "have to do with matters that transcend these local environments of the individual and the range of his inner life. They have to do with the organization of many such milieu into the institutions of an historical society as a whole, with the ways in which various milieu overlap and interpenetrate to form the larger structure of social and historical life. An issue is a public matter: some value cherished by publics is felt to be threatened." The point Mills was making is that public issues, such as structural problems with the economy, are generally experienced as private troubles; an example is individuals who are unable to pay their bills because they are unemployed. We have to be able to look beyond the private trouble to the public issue to find solutions.[28]

Mills's discussion of private troubles and public issues leads to the observation that because dependency has two sources, individual role failures and institutional failures, social welfare services have two targets. One target, private troubles, is at the level of individual role performance and involves what is generally known as *social treatment* or *casework*. At this level, a social worker attempts to help a client find and deal with the cause of his or her dependency. If the problem is financial, the social worker and client might attempt to identify and correct problems the client has in getting and keeping a job. The other target of social welfare services is on the level of public issues, the institutions that are supposed to support individual role performance. If the client in the preceding example is living in a community with a 25 percent unemployment rate, this is a public issue and the client's problem is probably institutional. In this case the social worker, in conjunction with others, will attempt to address the institutional malfunctioning, perhaps by developing a plan to attract industry to the community. In social work this approach of addressing both levels of dependency at once, the private trouble in the context of the public issue, is known as working with *person-in-situation*.

Institutional and Residual Conceptions of Social Welfare   In this chapter we have identified social welfare as the sixth major social institution, which emerged in the nineteenth and twentieth centuries to deal with the problem of dependency when the other major institutions, mainly family and the church, were no longer able to deal with this problem. At this point we need to note that although most social workers and social scientists accept this conception of social welfare, it is not shared by everyone in our society.

Writing in the late 1950s, Wilensky and Lebeaux identified in American society two opposing conceptions of social welfare which they labeled *institutional* and *residual*. The description of social welfare in the preceding section represents a straight institutional view which Wilensky and Lebeaux say

> implies no stigma, no emergency, no "abnormalcy" [on the part of those receiving services]: Social welfare becomes accepted as a proper, legitimate function of modern industrial society in helping individuals achieve self-fulfillment. The complexity of modern life is recognized. The inability of the individual to provide for himself, or to meet all his needs in family and work settings, is considered a "normal" condition; and the helping agencies achieve "regular" institutional status.[29]

In other words, the *institutional conception* recognizes that life in modern society is so complex that nearly everyone will need help achieving and maintaining interdependence and that the level of this help needs to be greater than the forms the basic institutions can provide. Families cannot provide 100 percent of the care needed by their children; the economy cannot provide 100 percent employment for the whole population at all times; and families and churches cannot care for all the elderly now that people are living many years past retirement and an ever-increasing proportion of the population is elderly. Social welfare is viewed as a first line, permanent social institution.

Wilensky and Lebeaux call the other view of social welfare present in American society the *residual conception.* This is

> based on the premise that there are two "natural" channels [institutions] through which an individual's needs are properly met: the family and the market economy. These are the preferred structures of supply. However, sometimes these institutions do not function adequately: family life is disrupted, depressions occur. Or sometimes the individual cannot make use of the normal channels because of old age or illness. In such cases, according to this idea, a third mechanism of need fulfillment is brought into play—the social welfare structure. This is conceived as a residual agency, attending primarily to emergency func-

tions, and is expected to withdraw when the regular social structure—the family and the economic system—is again working properly. Because of its residual, temporary, substitute characteristic, social welfare thus conceived often carries the stigma of "dole" or "charity."[30]

In this conception social welfare is not an institution, but an emergency back-up system. If the other institutions of society could be made to perform properly—the family to take responsibility for its elderly members, the church to care for the less fortunate, and the economy to provide enough jobs for everyone—social welfare would not be necessary.

Throughout this century, until the last ten or fifteen years, we have seen a steady movement away from a residual approach toward an institutional approach to social welfare. Unemployment insurance recognizes that everyone is at risk of periods of unemployment and a provision must be made to help people deal with this "normal" problem of modern industrial life; Old Age, Survivors, and Disability Insurance (Social Security) recognizes three major hazards of living in an urban society and depending on a paycheck and these are, once again, viewed as "normal"; and Medicare recognizes that the cost of medical care for the elderly is likely to be beyond the reach of all but the very wealthy. In other words, "normal" people will need help. In recent years we have seen a reversal of this trend. The social philosophy of recent Republican administrations has been that the family should care for children (that is, mothers should stay home) and thus they have opposed increased provision of day care; that work should be required of welfare recipients because the solution to financial dependency resides in the economic institution (that is, welfare mothers should not stay home, even though there is no day care); and that social welfare is really the proper role of the church. This is a traditional conservative approach emphasizing individual responsibility, minimum government, tradition, and fiscal restraint. The authors believe that this is a temporary phenomenon. Society continues to become larger, more technological, more urbanized, and more fragmented, and these developments continue to erode the ability of the basic institutions to deal with dependency in society.

Is the United States a Welfare State?   A term often used in the press and in political dialogue to refer to a society that has thoroughly accepted the institutional conception of social welfare is *a welfare state*. From the passage of the Social Security Act in 1935 until the early 1970s, a period Blau refers to as "the ideological consensus," liberals and conservatives alike generally accepted that the United States either was, or was well on its way to becoming, a European-style welfare state.[31] Since this time there has been a spirited debate on whether or not we are a welfare state, and if it is even desirable to be one.

Atherton has pointed out that it is important to recognize that there are at least two views of the welfare state. The first, which he refers to as the *programmatic welfare state,* is "a capitalist state that devotes a portion of its gross national product, through taxation, to the solution of certain social problems without changing the basic nature of the economy." The programmatic welfare state is closely tied to the labor market; its intended beneficiaries are workers who are experiencing temporary problems. Atherton calls the other view the *redistributive welfare state.* According to this perspective the primary aim of the welfare state is the redistribution of wealth and resources.[32] The popular press sometimes refers to this as *welfare socialism*.[33]

Atherton argues that if you are referring to the programmatic view of the welfare state, the United States certainly is one, and even conservatives will not forcefully argue against this as a desirable social goal. However, if you are referring to a redistributive welfare state, there is little evidence that much support for this exists in the United States.[34] Putting this together with Wilensky and Lebeaux's work on conceptions of social welfare, it is probably accurate to say that the United States is a residual welfare state. There is strong support for the belief that the government should provide a "safety net" of services and benefits for all citizens, and that no one should have to go without food, clothing, and medical care, but that our economic system is basically sound and that the institutions of family, economy, and religion, with a little help from government, should be able to meet the needs of all citizens.

A CLASSIFICATION OF SOCIAL WELFARE SERVICES

For two chapters we have been discussing social welfare based on the presumption that the reader has a pretty good idea about what social welfare services are. This is probably an accurate presumption because nearly everyone is familiar with at least the major service categories, such as financial assistance and child welfare. However, social welfare covers a wide spectrum of services, and few people are familiar with the whole picture. We will now present a fairly complete, although perhaps not exhaustive, description of the social welfare system.

There are a number of ways to classify social welfare services. Compton identifies four major schemes; the first is classification by the type of client served.[35] Under this scheme fourteen types of programs are listed serving the aged, dependent children, neglected and abused children, delinquent offenders, the unemployed, the emotionally disturbed, the physically handicapped, the mentally retarded, the mentally ill, veterans, railroad workers, the disabled, and various special interest groups. These groups can be combined to form fewer groups, or further subdivided to form more groups. They are not mutually exclusive; one client can be classified under several categories. The second method of classification is by source of funding. Using this method we get two large groups of services: those that are financed by public (tax) monies and those that are private or voluntary. The third classification method is by level of administration. This method only classifies public programs, and it divides them into federally administered programs, federal-state programs, and state, state-local, and local programs. The final method, which is widely disseminated in the work of Kamerman and Kahn, is classification by nature of service. They list six categories: income maintenance, health care, housing, education, employment, and personal social services.[36]

The preceding classification methods are all useful and valid ways of describing the social welfare system. However, we are going to use a different method. In keeping with our functional definition of social welfare we are going to classify services according to broad societal function. To do this we first need to expand on our definition of *dependency*. You will recall that dependency connotes a state of being where a person, because of either individual or institutional dysfunction, is unable to adequately carry out essential social roles. For the purpose of our definition we will divide dependency into three broad types. The first type of dependency is *economic dependency*, where the fundamental problem is a lack of sufficient resources to meet basic needs. If enough resources are made available, the person will resume his or her position as an inter-dependent member of society. An example of this type of service is food stamps which are given to people who lack sufficient resources to adequately feed themselves and their families. The second type of dependency is *role dependency as defined by self*, where the person defines himself or herself as needing help fulfilling some social role. Examples of this are parent effectiveness training classes offered by a family service agency for people who feel they are having difficulty fulfilling their parental roles and job counseling services offered by a YWCA for women who want to enter or re-enter the work force but are having difficulty with the role change. The third type of dependency is *role dependency as defined by others*, where the person is defined *by others* as needing help fulfilling some essential social role. Examples of this are child welfare services that protect children from harm by helping parents fulfill their roles and probation services that offer supervision and counseling instead of prison to people convicted of crimes. In this third type of service the clients are referred to as "invol-untary" because, at least initially, they do not want to receive help. The following is a description of the major social welfare services in each of the three categories.

I. Services for People Who Are Economically Dependent
    A. Cash Support Programs. These are programs that seek to mitigate or to alleviate economic dependence by the direct provision of money.
        1. Old Age, Survivors, and Disability Insurance (OASDI). This is the program that is generally called "Social Security." It is an insurance type program where in order to receive benefits you must have paid into the program. As the name implies, this program provides a cash income to retired or permanently disabled workers that is related to the worker's age and income at the time benefits commence. Dependents and survivors can receive set proportions of this benefit, subject to a family maximum. Coverage under this program is vast and ex-tensive—93 percent of the work force is covered, and of those who reach age 65, 19 out of 20 are eligible for some benefits.[37]
        2. Public Assistance Programs. These programs assist people who are needy (eco-nomically dependent), but who are not eligible for OASDI, or whose OASDI benefits are below a minimum level. These are not insurance programs because recipients of benefits have not directly paid into the system. (However, it can be argued that everyone who has ever worked has paid into public assistance because it is funded by tax revenues.) When people speak of "welfare," they are usually referring to public assistance. Major categories of public assistance are:
            a. Aid to Families with Dependent Children (AFDC). This is the costliest and most controversial public assistance program. There are currently 10.9 mil-lion recipients, living in 3.7 million families with 7.3 million children, or nearly one child in every nine. Benefit levels are very low, and range from an average of $101.43 per month in Puerto Rico to $598.59 per month in Alaska. In the contiguous forty-eight states benefit levels range from $113.83 in Alabama to $589.74 in California. The main beneficiaries of AFDC pay-ments are children in fatherless families where the mother is either unem-ployed or employed with an income greatly below the poverty level.
            b. Supplemental Security Income (SSI). This really includes three programs: SSI for the aged, SSI for the blind, and SSI for the disabled. It provides benefits for people in these three groups who are without adequate support. Benefits are considerably more generous than AFDC because of the fact that

these groups are less stigmatized. The federal benefit rate is currently $386.00 per month for an individual with no other income, and $579.00 for a couple. Many states with a high cost of living further supplement this amount.

  c. General Assistance. AFDC and SSI are largely federally financed. For the needy who do not qualify for these programs, most states provide some benefits through a general assistance program. Some states provide cash assistance for a limited period of time; others limit the benefits to health care or burial expenses. Benefits under this program are generally very meager.

  d. Veteran's Compensation and Pensions. Veterans as a group have received preferential treatment in the United States since the Revolutionary War. Compensation is paid to veterans (or their dependents) for an injury, disability, or death incurred while in the armed forces. Pensions are paid to war veterans (or their dependents) whose annual income is below a specified level and who are permanently and totally disabled.

  e. Unemployment Insurance. This is an insurance program to protect workers against need during temporary periods of unemployment. Benefits are related to past earnings and work experience and are not based on level of need. Therefore, the poor are often excluded or receive meager benefits.

  f. Worker's Compensation. This program is administered by private insurance companies under state regulation. It is designed to protect workers and their families from financial need during periods when wages are interrupted because of work-related injuries. It provides cash benefits, medical care, and rehabilitation services for injured workers. The program also compensates workers' survivors in the event of fatal injuries.

  g. Private Pensions. A growing proportion of the elderly are protected from economic dependency by private pensions that generally supplement their OASDI benefits. There are no accurate statistics available, but it is estimated that more than half of all private sector employees and three-fourths of government employees are protected by pension plans.[38]

B. In-kind Programs. These programs seek to mitigate or alleviate economic dependency by the direct provision of various goods and services to needy people as supplements to, or instead of, cash benefits.

  1. Medical Services

  a. Medicaid and Medicare. These programs were added to the Social Security Act in 1965. Medicare covers most hospital and medical costs for people age 65 or older, as well as for disabled Social Security recipients. Medicaid, funded by the states, provides health care coverage to persons receiving federally supported public assistance in all states except Arizona. Thirty-four states extend this coverage to persons not actually receiving public assistance but whose incomes are low enough to qualify them as "medically needy."

  b. Community, Maternal, and Child Health. With funding primarily from federal block grants, states provide a number of services to supplement Medicare and Medicaid. Among these are community health centers, programs to reduce infant mortality, rehabilitative services for blind and disabled children, and prenatal health services.

  c. Veterans Health Services. The Veterans Administration health care system provides free medical services to low-income veterans regardless of whether their problems are connected to their term of service. The system is currently composed of 172 hospitals, 119 nursing homes, 26 domiciliaries, and 233 outpatient clinics.[39]

d. Native American Health Services. Because of poverty and geographic isolation, Native Americans fare very poorly on almost any measure of health. To deal with this, the Indian Health Service has been established within the U.S. Department of Health and Human Services. This service directly operates 43 hospitals, 66 health centers, and 65 smaller health stations and satellite clinics. In addition, the Service contracts with tribes for the operation of an additional 7 hospitals and more than 300 outpatient clinics.

2. Shelter

a. Public Housing. This is a federally sponsored program that provides apartments for families whose incomes are less than 80 percent of the median income in their area; however, in most areas eligibility is restricted to those below the 50 percent median income. The apartments are rented at well below market value, with the rent being proportionate to the tenant's income. There are currently 1.4 million public housing apartments.

b. Subsidized Housing. In this program the federal government does not provide an actual apartment, but subsidizes the rent for a privately owned house or apartment. The largest rent supplement program was established by Section 8 of the Housing and Community Development Act of 1974. Section 8 has overtaken public housing as the largest federal housing assistance program and currently serves approximately 2.3 million families.

c. Energy Assistance. Because of the drastic increase in fuel costs in recent years, fuel and weatherization assistance programs have become a part of the social welfare system. The Low-Income Home Energy Assistance Program (LIHEAP) was begun in 1978 by the Department of Health and Human Services. The program distributes block grants to states to use to cover residential heating and cooling costs for the poor and very poor. In addition to public programs, a number of private programs have begun, often as a cooperative effort between utility companies and social agencies like the Red Cross.

3. Nutrition

a. Food Stamps. This is by far the largest nutrition program providing $12.7 billion in benefits to a monthly average of over 18 million people. The benefits are in the form of coupons that can be used just like money to purchase any food for human consumption. All recipients of public assistance are eligible for food stamps, as well as households not eligible for public assistance which have incomes at or below the poverty level. Currently the maximum monthly food stamp allotment for a family of four is $300.00.

b. Child Nutrition. In addition to food stamps, there are several nutrition programs focused on children. A number of programs now provide breakfast, lunch, and milk to over 30 million children in private and public schools and day care centers at a federal cost of $4.5 billion. The largest of these programs is the school lunch program which provides subsidized lunches to about 24 million children, about half of the entire child population.

II. Services for People Who Are Dependent Because They Are Unable to Fulfill Roles, as Defined by Themselves

A. Mental Health Services. There are a wide variety of services, both public and private, provided for people suffering from mental health problems. Public services are provided in most areas by community mental health centers. These centers offer individual and group counseling and drug and alcohol treatment, as well as other services. They are staffed by psychiatrists, psychologists, social workers, nurses, and other specialists. These services are also available in the private sector through

United Way and church affiliated agencies, as well as from providers in private practice.

B. Family and Relationship Counseling. Family counseling is available in most larger communities either through the community mental health center or from a private family service agency. These agencies are generally sponsored by the United Way or by one of the major religious denominations. The Catholic, Jewish, and Lutheran religions all have extensive networks of family service agencies. The counselors in these agencies are mostly master's level social workers.

C. Employment Services. There are a number of services provided for people having problems with employment-related roles. The largest provider is the Federal-State Employment Service, with over 1,700 offices throughout the country. This is primarily a placement service with about 20 million individuals applying for services annually. The federally sponsored vocational rehabilitation programs provide job training and medical, educational, and other services to the physically and mentally handicapped in order to help them become employable.

D. Recreation and Socialization Services. There are a wide variety of services available which provide recreation and socialization for children and youth. There are a number of government recreation services (such as swimming pools and soccer leagues), but those that combine recreation with socialization are generally private. Notable among these are Young Men's and Young Women's Christian Associations (YMCA and YWCA), Jewish Community Centers Association (JCCA), Boy Scouts and Girl Scouts, and Boys and Girls Clubs. In recent years an increasing number of such services have been made available to the elderly through senior citizens' centers.

E. Advocacy, Liaison, and Access. With the growing complexity of the social service system, mechanisms have been developed to help people find the services they need and to make sure they are provided the services to which they are entitled. Examples are the information and referral services provided by most United Way organizations and ombudsman services provided by some government agencies.

III. Services for People Who Are Dependent Because They Are Unable to Fulfill Roles, as Defined by Others

A. Probation and Parole. Often a person convicted of a crime will be placed on probation rather than actually being sent to prison. People released from prison are generally not released unconditionally but are placed on parole, which means they are released before their sentence is completed on the condition that they submit to supervision and a stringent set of rules. Parolees are defined by society as needing help in fulfilling all the roles of citizenship and they are required to accept this help as a condition for being out of jail.

B. Child Protective Services. Parents having difficulty adequately caring for their children may be required by court action, or threat of court action, to accept help in better fulfilling their roles as parents. Common reasons for intervention are abuse, neglect, and exploitation. In severe cases it may be determined that the parents will never be able to adequately fulfill their roles and the children will be permanently removed.

C. Adult Protective Services. Elderly and disabled people who are heavily dependent on others for care face some of the same problems of abuse, neglect, and exploitation as children. Our society has only recently begun to recognize this problem and to provide services to protect this vulnerable group.

D. Mandatory Employment and Training Programs. The previously discussed services for the economically dependent could also be described as helping people who are having difficulty with various roles associated with being a breadwinner. Assistance is given to many of these people on the condition that they accept help in becoming able to fulfill these roles. The largest such program is the Work Incentive Program (WIN). Welfare recipients with no children under the age of six are required to register with WIN for job placement and/or training. Currently over one million people a year register with WIN and about one-fifth of them obtain employment.

E. Involuntary Mental Health Services. Mental health services were classified under section II as services for people who define themselves as being unable to fulfill roles. We need to note that there are also mental health services for people who are defined by others as being unable to fulfill their roles. The most obvious situation is a person who is involuntarily committed to a mental hospital. Community mental health centers also provide out-patient services to people who have been ordered by a court to receive services for problems such as alcoholism, drug addiction, a violent temper, and various compulsions such as stealing. (In a case one of the authors is familiar with, a man was ordered into treatment because of a compulsion to stomp on women's feet.) Generally these people are given the choice of going into treatment or going to jail.

PERSPECTIVES ON SOCIAL WELFARE

In this chapter we have developed the definition of social welfare as the institution that serves the function of managing the problem of dependency in society. We have said that liberals agree that social welfare has become a major social institution, and conservatives argue that it is (or should be) a residual function of other institutions. Two targets for social welfare intervention have been identified: individual role performance and the functioning of social institutions. We noted that conservatives think that the individual should be almost exclusively the target of services, but liberals are much more willing to support strategies for institutional change. We now turn to another major difference among conservative, liberal, and radical perspectives on social welfare. That is, what are the major motivations behind social welfare activities, and what are the major goals?

The Conservative Perspective

Basically, conservatives view the purpose of social welfare as the maintenance of the status quo. Social welfare is perceived as fulfilling an integrative social function; it sustains morale and cohesiveness in society and thereby contributes to efficiency, stability, and order.[40] As Room observes, conservatives believe that social welfare should "reinforce and uphold the capitalist market system and that would therefore not hinder but multiply the benefits of a market civilization."[41] Conservatives believe that dependency should be addressed on a case-by-case basis and that economic growth will, without redistribution of income, eliminate poverty and thus the need for most social welfare services. There are two central ideas behind the conservative definition of social welfare: *noblesse oblige* and enlightened self-interest.

Noblesse Oblige   This term is French for "nobility obligates." It refers to the obligation of honorable, generous, and responsible behavior associated with high rank or birth.

The idea is that those who are fortunate, originally because of birth, but now also because of achievement, have a moral obligation to assist those who are less fortunate. Thus, the motivation to help the dependent in society stems not from any *right* of these people to demand help, but rather from a moral *obligation* of the more fortunate to provide it. This approach is paternalistic, it views welfare as charity to the unfortunate, and it leads to clear distinctions between givers and receivers and worthy and unworthy poor.

Enlightened Self-Interest   Conservatives believe that in order for the status quo to be maintained, dependency must be managed in a humanitarian way that prevents it from disrupting society while hopefully not costing too much. As Rescher remarks, "Under current conditions in technologically advanced societies, we are brought back with a vengeance to the doctrine of the Stoics of antiquity that due care for this interest of others with whom one coexists in a social context is, in the final analysis, a matter not just of altruism but of enlightened self-interest."[42] In other words, conservatives realize that helping others is simply a cost of living in modern society and that it is in their own self-interest.

The Liberal Perspective

The liberal position on social welfare is known in Europe as *social democracy or citizenship*[43] and in the United States as the *mass society thesis.*[44] This position views social welfare as more humanitarian and less utilitarian than the conservative position. Social welfare programs are viewed as basically humanitarian responses by the state to social problems *endemic* to industrialized society. The central feature of the liberal perspective on social welfare is a conception of individual rights.

The liberal position views the history of western society as characterized by an ever-expanding conception of individual rights. First, people were accorded civil rights, such as the right to vote, the right to move freely about the country, and the right to accumulate wealth. More recently society has evolved, according to this perspective, to a point where people are accorded social rights. The concept of social rights means that people are guaranteed, by virtue of being citizens, a certain, generally minimum, standard of living as well as other life-sustaining, life-enhancing services. Schram and Turbett explain that under the liberal definition, "all persons are seen by the state as having legitimate entitlements as citizens. The movement toward a 'mass society' constitutes an expansion in the concept of citizenship beyond basic political rights to include social and economic rights. In a 'mass society,' poor people as citizens are vested with the right to receive government assistance when their basic social and economic rights cannot legitimately be fulfilled through private means."[45] Under the conservative approach, people who are dependent are assisted by those who are able because helping is considered a *moral obligation*. Under the liberal approach, people are assisted because they have a *right* to assistance.

Conservatives agree with liberals that there has been a tremendous expansion of individual rights, but unlike liberals, they believe that it has gone too far. Donahue argues

A CLOSER LOOK

Altruism Among Conservatives Avoids Ruin

Conditions have changed, but attitudes haven't very much, in the century since Charles Dickens was writing novels about the impact of the Industrial Age upon Victorian England.

In the novel "Hard Times," depicting the situation of the factory worker in his day, Dickens penned the ironic paragraph which, *mutatis mutandis,* is as true in 1986 as it was a hundred years ago:

"Factory owners insist that they will be 'ruined' if they are obliged to do anything at all. They were ruined when they were required to send laboring children to school; they were ruined when inspectors were appointed to look into their works; they were ruined when such inspectors considered it doubtful whether they were justified in chopping up people with their machinery; they were utterly ruined when it was hinted that perhaps they need not always make quite so much smoke."

But the children were taken out of the mines and sent to school, and the factory owners were not ruined; the inspectors enforced safety rules, and they were not ruined; the smoke was gradually cleared up, and they were not ruined.

In fact, decade after decade, they did better and better, got richer and richer, despite these fearsomely resisted reforms.

What is the moral here? The moral here, I think, is that many people do not recognize their own true self-interest, and fight against the very things that would benefit them in the long run.

Intelligent conservatives—a group that America is not too crowded with—have always recognized that making concessions to the less fortunate is the best way of retaining one's privileges, and that cold exploitation is the surest way to lose such privileges sooner or later.

It was a conservative in Germany, Bismarck, who instituted the first form of social security for workers there; it was a conservative in England, Disraeli, who formed a political partnership with the working classes, and insisted that they be treated with more fairness.

Students of modern history agree that the Russian Revolution could have been averted had the Czar and the royal court been willing to make concessions to the oppressed workers and peasants, and mitigated their tyranny. Revolution is always preceded by oppression.

Sometimes I think we have the dumbest conservative class in the world. By opposing virtually every reform that seeks to ameliorate the condition of the poor, it sows the seeds of rebellion and discontent, and provides ammunition for "subversive" forces. What "ruins" factory owners is mistreatment, indifference and high-handedness; what will save them is giving a little in order to retain a lot.

Source: Sydney Harris, "Altruism Among Conservatives Avoids Ruin," *Columbus Enquirer,* April 7, 1989. Reprinted with permission.

Rights mania began once liberty was seen as rights alone and freedom from responsibility became respectable. The behavior of government had a lot to do with both. The creation of new rights for the individual, many of them long overdue, had the unanticipated effect of raising the expectations for yet more rights, rights without a grounding in justice and the common good. This occurred at the same time government was redistributing responsibilities from the individual to institutions. It was the interaction between the two—more individual rights and less individual responsibilities—that proved to be decisive.[46]

The Radical Perspective

Radicals view social welfare as a deliberate effort by the power elite in society to control the masses and to prevent any meaningful social change. By "meaningful social change" they mean radical change in the distribution of resources and power. Room, for example, says that

> [Radicals] deny that attempts at non-revolutionary reform are other than misconceived or that the social policies developed over the past century introduce fundamental changes in the dominant mode of social integration. On the contrary, welfare state institutions have served as relatively successful agencies for the perpetuation of a "false consciousness" among members of the working class. Through its social policies, the state is able to mitigate the most glaring deprivations wrought by the capitalist system and to pretend to a concern with social welfare.[47]

An extremely influential book promoting a radical perspective on social welfare, *Regulating the Poor: The Functions of Public Welfare* by Frances Fox Piven and Richard A. Cloward, was published in 1971 and its contents are still being debated. Piven and Cloward argue, and support their argument with historical data, that the social welfare system is a servant of the economic system and that its chief function is to regulate labor. The system regulates labor in two ways. "First, when mass unemployment leads to outbreaks of turmoil, relief programs are ordinarily initiated or expanded to absorb and control enough of the unemployed to restore order; thus, as turbulence subsides, the relief system contracts, expelling those who are needed to populate the labor market." In addition, the welfare system serves as a motivator for the labor force because the treatment of the dependent "is so degrading and punitive as to instill in the laboring masses a fear of the fate that awaits them should they relax into beggary and pauperism. To demean and punish those who do not work is to exalt by contrast even the meanest labor at the meanest wage."[48]

Summary

All three perspectives would agree with our functional definition of social welfare as being concerned with managing the problem of dependency in society. They strongly disagree on whether this function is residual or institutional; whether the major target for services is the individual with role difficulties or social institutions failing to support role performance; and whether the function of social welfare, as currently carried out, is good or bad.

Conservatives believe that:

1. Social welfare should be a residual social function. The family, church, and economy should be the front line of defense against dependency, and social welfare should only be a temporary function that comes into play when these institutions are overwhelmed.

2. Society as it is presently structured is functional and therefore dependency is a result of individual role failure. Thus, the proper target of social welfare services is the individual.

3. The motivation for social welfare is twofold. First, dependent individuals are non-productive and therefore costly for society, so it is in society's interest to help them. Second, charity is a moral virtue and thus we are all obligated to help the less fortunate.

Liberals believe that:

1. Social welfare has become, or is fast becoming, a first line social institution. Society, they argue, has become so fragmented and so complex, and the traditional institutions have deteriorated to such a point that very few individuals can function in a totally interdependent manner without some help. Employment services, family counseling, mental health, and day care are all necessary supports for life in modern society.

2. Individual problems in role performance are a result of an interaction between individual and institutional causes. Thus, social welfare has two targets—individual change through counseling, therapy, education, and training and social change through environmental manipulation, social planning, and political action. This is the traditional position of the social work profession, and it is referred to as viewing problems from the perspective of person-in-situation.

3. The motivation for social welfare is seen as primarily humanitarian. People help each other out of a true caring for one another and out of the gradually evolving recognition that everyone has a right to a share of society's resources.

Radicals believe that:

1. Social welfare has become institutional, but it is an institution set up, controlled by, and serving the interests of the elite in society.

2. Problems of dependency are almost entirely the result of repressive social institutions. The goal of the social welfare institution *is* to keep the masses in line by promoting the idea that individuals are to blame for their own problems and by helping people adjust to a repressive society. The goal of social welfare *should be* to promote radical social change that results in a more humane, equalitarian social order.

3. The motivation for social welfare is social control. Social welfare institutions keep the masses in their place and head off any really meaningful social change.

CONCLUSION

Most likely, after reading this chapter you are a little confused. This is typical and is not something to be concerned about. Social welfare is an extremely confusing concept. When you take a geology course you learn exact properties of various types of rocks. All rocks of any one type share the same properties, and all geologists agree on what they are. Those of us who study social welfare are not so fortunate. Two concepts we have been discussing make social welfare extremely difficult to understand. The first is ideology. Social welfare is an extremely ideological thing. Liberals, conservatives, radicals, and people with perspectives in between will define and discuss social welfare on

entirely different terms. The second concept is stigma. Because social welfare tends to be highly stigmatized in our society, people tend to define social welfare as not including services they themselves, or the people they care for, are involved in.

One thing, however, is very clear. The social welfare institution has grown steadily for over four centuries, and the growth this century, especially since World War II, has been explosive. In 1900, government expenditure for social welfare was virtually nothing; in 1929 state and federal expenditures were a little less than $4 billion; by 1950 this had grown sixfold to nearly $24 billion; and by 1988 federal, state, and local governments spent more than $885 billion on social welfare programs. Cash assistance to the poor was about $2.5 billion in 1950; it amounted to $120 billion in 1988.[49] The total cost of social welfare expenditures in the United States, public and private, was 13.5 percent of the Gross National Product in 1968; it had risen to 30.8 percent by 1988.[50]

During recent years, very conservative federal administrations, supported by a public reacting to the tremendous increase in expenditures, have succeeded in slowing the growth of many social welfare programs and have actually reduced the size of some others. However, most agree that this is a temporary phenomenon and that over the long haul the growth will continue, probably at a slower rate than during the sixties and seventies. The administrations have not succeeded in reversing any of the social forces that have created the need for social welfare services. We continue to see an increase in births out-of-wedlock, divorces, desertion, illiter-

acy, unemployment, school dropouts, and drug abuse. The unemployment rate remains unacceptably high, and the underemployment rate even higher. New problems are being recognized that call for social welfare services, including eating disorders, agoraphobia, spouse abuse, and new sexually transmitted diseases, to name a few recent ones. In addition, our society continues to become more complex and in many ways less secure. Unions do not provide the security they once did; an increasing proportion of new jobs are "high tech," but low in pay and in job security; and vocational experts predict that soon it will be common for a person to have to train for and enter completely new careers two or three times during his or her working life. All of these factors create or reflect individual and societal stresses and tensions that will require new responses, and many of them will involve the expansion of the social welfare institution.

E N D N O T E S

1. Joseph W. Heffernan, *Introduction to Social Welfare Policy: Power, Scarcity and Common Human Needs* (Itasca, IL: F.E. Peacock, 1979), 8.
2. Erving Goffman, *Stigma: Notes on the Management of Spoiled Identity* (Englewood Cliffs, NJ: Prentice-Hall, 1963), preface and 1.
3. Paul Spicker, *Stigma and Social Welfare* (New York: St. Martin's Press, 1984), 175.
4. Robert Pinker, *Social Theory and Social Policy* (London: Heinemann, 1971), 139.
5. Bernard Beck, "The Military as a Welfare Institution" in *Public Opinion and the Military Establishment,* Charles C. Moshos, Jr., ed. (Beverly Hills, CA: Sage Publications, 1971), 172.
6. David Matza, "Poverty and Disrepute" in *Contemporary Social Problems,* 3rd ed., Robert K. Merton and Robert Nisbet, eds. (New York: Harcourt, Brace and Jovanovich, 1971), 601–616.
7. Spicker, *Stigma and Social Welfare,* 96.
8. Claude Levi-Strauss, *The Elementary Structures of Kinship* (Andover, Great Britain: Eyre and Spottiswoode, 1949), 480.
9. Taken from *Industrial Society and Social Welfare,* en-larged paperback edition by Harold L. Wilensky and Charles N. Lebeaux. © The Russell Sage Foundation, 1958. Used with the permission of the Russell Sage Foundation. (pp. 34–35).
10. Taken from *Industrial Society and Social Welfare,* enlarged paperback edition by Harold L. Wilensky and Charles N. Lebeaux. © The Russell Sage Foundation, 1958. Used with the permission of the Russell Sage Foundation. (pp. 34–35).
11. David Macarov, *The Design of Social Welfare* (New York: Holt, Rinehart and Winston, 1978), 22–23.
12. Eveline M. Burns, "Some Economic Aspects of Welfare as an Institution" in *Social Science and Social Welfare,* John M. Romanyshan, ed. (New York: Council on Social Work Education, 1974), 89.
13. Neil Gilbert and Harry Specht, *Dimensions of Social Welfare Policy,* 2nd ed. (Englewood Cliffs, NJ: Prentice-Hall, 1986), 34.
14. Thomas H. Walz and Gary Askerooth, *The Upside Down Welfare State* (Minneapolis, MN: Elwood Printing, 1973), 2.
15. Winifred Bell, *Contemporary Social Welfare,* 2nd ed. (New York: Macmillan, 1987), 3.

16. Nicholas Rescher, *Welfare—The Social Issues in Philosophical Perspective* (Pittsburgh, PA: The University of Pittsburgh Press, 1972), 4–5.

17. Blanche D. Coll, "Social Welfare: History" in *Encyclopedia of Social Work,* 17th ed., John B. Turner et al., eds. (Washington, D.C.: National Association of Social Workers, 1977), 1503–1512.

18. Walter A. Friedlander, *Introduction to Social Welfare* (New York: Prentice-Hall, 1955), 4.

19. George T. Martin, Jr., and Mayer N. Zald, eds. *Social Welfare in Society* (New York: Columbia University Press, 1981), 4.

20. Elizabeth Wickenden, *Social Welfare in a Changing World* (Washington, D.C.: Department of Health, Education and Welfare, 1965), vii.

21. Rescher, *Welfare,* 8.

22. David Popenoe, *Sociology,* 4th ed. (Englewood Cliffs, NJ: Prentice-Hall, 1980), 85.

23. Gerhard Lenski and Jean Lenski, *Human Societies—An Introduction to Macro-sociology,* 3rd ed. (New York: McGraw-Hill, 1978), 74.

24. Beulah R. Compton, *Introduction to Social Welfare and Social Work: Structure, Function, and Process* (Homewood, IL: Dorsey, 1980), 41.

25. Charles Atherton, "The Social Assignment of Social Work," *Social Service Review* 43 (May 1969): 421–429. Used with permission.

26. Atherton, "The Social Assignment of Social Work," 423. Used with permission.

27. John H. Ehrenreich, *The Altruistic Imagination: A History of Social Work and Social Policy in the United States* (Ithaca, NY: Cornell University Press, 1985), 30–33.

28. C. Wright Mills, *The Sociological Imagination* (New York: Oxford University Press, 1959), 8–10.

29. Taken from *Industrial Society and Social Welfare,* enlarged paperback edition by Harold L. Wilensky and Charles N. Lebeaux. © The Russell Sage Foundation, 1958. Used with the permission of the Russell Sage Foundation. (p. 140).

30. Taken from *Industrial Society and Social Welfare,* enlarged paperback edition by Harold L. Wilensky and Charles N. Lebeaux. © The Russell Sage Foundation, 1958. Used with the permission of the Russell Sage Foundation. (p. 139).

31. Joel Blau, "Theories of the Welfare State," *Social Service Review* 63 (March 1989): 22–29.

32. Charles R. Atherton, "The Welfare State: Still on Solid Ground," *Social Service Review* 63 (June 1989): 169.

33. See, for example, David Moller, "The Nation That Tried to Buy Happiness," *Readers Digest* (September 1991): 100–104.

34. Atherton, "The Welfare State," 177–178.

35. Compton, *Introduction to Social Welfare and Social Work,* 60.

36. Sheila Kamerman and Alfred J. Kahn, *Social Services in the United States* (Philadelphia, PA: Temple University Press, 1976), 4.

37. Sar A. Levitan, *Programs in the Aid of the Poor,* 6th ed. (Baltimore, MD: The Johns Hopkins University Press, 1990), 41.

38. Levitan, *Programs in the Aid of the Poor,* 50.

39. Levitan, *Programs in the Aid of the Poor,* 68.

40. Gilbert and Specht, *Dimensions of Social Welfare Policy,* 10.

41. Graham Room, *The Sociology of Welfare—Social Policy, Stratification and Political Order* (New York: St. Martin's Press, 1979), 51.

42. Rescher, *Welfare,* 35.

43. Richard M. Titmuss, *Essays on the Welfare State* (London: Allen and Unwin, 1963); T.H. Marshall, *Class, Citizenship and Social Development* (Garden City, NY: Doubleday, 1964).

44. Kirsten A. Gronbjerg, *Mass Society and the Extension of Welfare, 1960–1970* (Chicago: University of Chicago Press, 1977).

45. Sanford F. Schram and Patrick Turbett, "The Welfare Explosion: Mass Society versus Social Control," *Social Service Review* 57 (December 1983): 616.

46. William A. Donahue, "The Social Consequences of the Rights Revolution," *The Intercollegiate Review* 22 (Spring 1987): 41–46.

47. Room, *The Sociology of Welfare,* 46.

48. Frances Fox Piven and Richard A. Cloward, *Regulating the Poor: The Functions of Public Welfare* (New York: Vintage Books, 1971), 3–4.

49. Ann Kallman Bixby, "Overview of Public Social Welfare Expenditures, Fiscal Year 1988," *Social Security Bulletin* 53 (December 1990), 28.

50. Wilmer L. Kerns and Milton P. Glanz, "Private Social Welfare Expenditures, 1972–1988," *Social Security Bulletin* 54 (February 1991), 3.

C · H · A · P · T · E · R
three

Social Work as
a Profession

W hat happens when you tell family friends, your spouse, or Great-Aunt Ella that you would like to major in social work? A gasp, then, "Oh, but you know you won't make any money," or "Do you *really* want to work with poor people?" or "You'll never get a job—unless maybe you go on for your Master's degree." Then there is a moment's reflection, and, "But on the other hand, since you're so patient and self-denying, maybe it is the right career for you after all . . ." Such responses give you a good idea of the confused, often negative image of social work in our society. It is an image reflecting a number of factors, including ambivalence about the degree of responsibility society should take in dealing with dependence, negative feelings about the "typical" clients of social workers, and questions about the status of a "woman's profession" in our society. Consider, for example, the most popular TV shows involving working people and professions. Rarely is a series based on the job of a social worker. Instead we are caught up in the glamour and excitement of police detectives, lawyers, doctors, and even bartenders at work. Sometimes these actors are portrayed performing tasks which are really those of a social worker. When social workers do appear directly on these or other shows, they are often depicted as grim public welfare workers who are determined to remove a child from a home; well-meaning but naive young women; or bureaucrats wedded to their paper work.

This chapter will explore the reality behind such images. It will examine some of the reasons for society's stereotypes and ambivalence about social work. An introduction to the broad outlines of social work's history in the United States will help you understand both the bases for stereotypes as well as the sources of social work's strengths. An analysis of varying political perspectives on social work's functions will offer you further insight into the conflicting expectations of the field. In addition, the chapter provides an overview of social work's current practice settings and methods, values and value conflicts, professional issues, education and knowledge base, and relation to the broader field of social welfare. The intent of this chapter is to increase your understanding of the current shape and scope of social work, its traditions, and its mixed reception by the public.

SOCIAL WORK AND PROFESSIONALISM

One frequent confusion about social work emerges in the question "Is social work a 'real' profession?" In order to attempt an answer, we should recognize that there are several models for describing what "profession" and the act of becoming a profession mean. One model looks to the traditional professions—medicine, the clergy, and law—and sees these as possessing a specific group of attributes.[1] Although lists of attributes differ somewhat from theorist to theorist, most include: (1) possession of a unique skill valued by society; (2) expectation of lengthy, specialized training for practitioners; (3) possession of systematic theory upon which such training is based; (4) existence of a code of ethics to guide practice; and (5) organization of members of the profession into associations that protect their interests. Occupational groups claiming professional status can be measured against these specific attributes. If they possess them, they have earned the label of profession.

A number of observers of occupations are critical of this way of thinking about professionalism.[2] They argue that the attributes model is a static approach. A more realistic perspective would be to concentrate on the process groups go through in trying to establish a cohesive professional identity (and to worry less about finding a universal definition of that identity). What is most interesting and important about professions, according to proponents of the process model, are the ways in which they try to build internal unity, to win public acceptance of their functions, and to compete with other groups to establish their exclusive expertise and right to practice in a particular area. For example, physicians and midwives can be viewed as two groups vying for control over delivering babies in our society. The winner of the conflict will be labeled the professional group in that area of practice. In the United States, physicians, the stronger group, have so far won out; they have been able to establish themselves as the major profession handling childbirth. As you can see, this way of thinking about professions often stresses power—for example, the ability of one group to "control the market" for a particular social function, or the authority gained by an occupation which convinces the public that its definitions of social or health problems and its solutions to them are the correct ones. The process model stresses conflict and diversity, not only among occupations, but also among segments within them. These internal segments struggle over defining the profession's goals and functions and deciding just who will be a member. The conflict within social work about whether or not professionals can be trained at the baccalaureate level is an example of such a debate. As you will see in our discussion of social work history, we view the process model as a fruitful way of understanding social work's development and search for professional identity.[3]

So far, this discussion has not answered the question "Is social work a profession?" Those who study professions have given a variety of responses. A widely read article by sociologist Ernest Greenwood uses the attributes approach to defining professionalism. Measuring social work against a list of professional characteristics, Greenwood asserts that the field has "passed the test" and that it is a true profession. Others are less sure. Using Greenwood's own list of professional attributes, Toren defines social work as a "semi-profession" because not all of its attributes are fully developed. She argues that social work's theory base, for example, is not yet well articulated. In a similar vein, Gilbert, Miller, and Specht define social work as a "developing profession," which has at this point a fairly low degree of professional authority and community sanction. (Requirements for social work licensing, for example, are far less stringent than those for the practice of medicine.)[4] Using the process model of professionalism presented earlier, one might argue that social work is not yet powerful enough to lay claim to an exclusive area of practice. Social work shares some of its methods and goals with members of other occupational groups, including counselors, public health nurses, and psychologists, and so faces a challenge in trying to establish its own autonomy and legitimacy as a profession.

Rather than prolonging the debate about social work's professional status, we would prefer to examine some different issues. These include: (1) the effects the process of seeking a professional identity has had on the development of social work and (2) the social functions social work might stress in its attempt to define its particular role in society.

The first issue will be examined in some detail in the section on social work history. The second issue involves a different way of looking at the concept of profession. One might say that the professions exist to deal with particular problems faced by society.

The occupational group which seems most effective in handling a specific problem is "assigned" this social function by society. In other words, this is the problem that officials and the public expect it to handle. That problem then becomes the occupation's professional domain. Does social work possess such a professional domain? We suggest that the field does indeed have a legitimate social assignment or professional task: that of managing dependency and promoting productive interdependence in our society. As we discussed in Chapter 2, dependency can be defined as the inability to adequately fulfill one's social roles. This inability can stem from a lack of resources, skills, knowledge, or power. Institutional failings contribute to inadequate role functioning. Therefore, social work deals with dependency both by changing the behavior and life situations of individuals and by changing dysfunctional elements in society itself.[5]

This discussion of social work and the concept of profession should help you gain perspective on the goals, functions, and identity-seeking activities of the field. Yet it may seem less helpful in terms of your developing a personal sense of professional identity. In other words, the discussion has focused on the meaning of "profession" for an occupational group, rather than on the significance of being a "professional" to an individual. When we discuss the latter with our classes, we find that while students may be critical of professions and the way some professionals behave, they tend to have a strong personal sense of what it means to act in a professional manner. They speak of having a commitment to clients, being honest and reliable, and becoming as knowledgeable and skilled as possible in regard to dealing with social problems. We would urge you to think about professionalism on this level as well, and to draw upon your experience and education to develop your own definition of "being professional."

SOCIAL WORK'S HISTORICAL DEVELOPMENT

A description of social work's history illustrates how a search for professional identity has shaped social work's growth. It also sheds light on current stereotypes and the conflicting expectations of the field. In keeping with the major focus of this book, the following history is in part a political history of social work. That is, it discusses how three ideological perspectives—conservative, liberal, and radical—have been used by social workers and others to define the desired goals and practice of the profession.

A conservative approach to social work's task reflects two major tenets of conservative ideology: a belief in individual and family responsibility and a preference for private rather than public action. Individual factors are viewed as the dominant force in social problems. Individual strengths and weaknesses are seen as being rooted in family and community structures and traditions. Social work's major function, in this view, is that of helping individuals and families resolve their own difficulties. This sometimes involves dealing with environmental conditions, but most often stresses personal adjustment or change. Often, some personal "defect," such as inadequate education or a lack of willingness to work, needs to be attended to. In the conservative view, the job of social work should be carried out under private auspices wherever possible. A minimum "safety net" of government services may be necessary to support the elderly and the "truly needy." But beyond this, governmental involvement in social welfare only furthers individual or family dependency.

The liberal perspective does not deny individual autonomy and responsibility. Yet it emphasizes the ways in which existing economic and social institutions contribute to problems and inequities in our society. Social workers should therefore attend to both individual and institutional change. A legitimate role for the profession is the promotion of governmental involvement in the social welfare system. Government policies can safeguard against the hazards of modern industrial life both through regulation (such as laws forbidding child labor) and through the provision of social welfare benefits to ensure that all citizens have adequate food, shelter, and health care. Social workers can play the role of advocates in the system, ensuring that existing public welfare programs do their jobs effectively. Private agencies are seen as supplementing the work of government programs. Thus, liberals often envision social services as being carried out through a partnership of public and private services.[6]

A radical approach to social work stresses the need for a broad restructuring of existing political, social, and economic institutions. Such restructuring is necessary in order to redistribute income in our society, increase democratic control over economic and other institutions, and provide comprehensive social welfare benefits for all. Radicals, both within and outside the field, criticize social workers for seeking to adjust individuals to society and for pursuing only minimal social change. Some see the profession's major function as helping to manage the workforce so as to produce a docile labor supply for the capitalist system. Others portray social workers more generally as pawns in a social welfare industry whose main aim is to control the poor and powerless and to keep them from causing trouble. One book on welfare, by Betty Reid Mandell, even uses this idea in its title: *Welfare in America, Controlling the "Dangerous Classes."*[7]

Radicals are often critical of social work's pursuit of professionalism. They argue, as Malcolm Payne notes, that "professionalisation of social work leads to social workers being rewarded by society with status, income and other advantages of the profession, thus promoting their acceptance of the status quo and rejection of critical analyses of the problems they are dealing with." Radical thinkers urge social workers to reject this stance and to join clients in working for meaningful change in the system.[8]

Proponents of all three perspectives can be found throughout social work's history. Various social work programs and approaches to practice can be categorized as conservative, liberal, or radical, or even as combining elements of several perspectives. These categories thus become broad lenses through which to view social work's development.

These broad ideological outlines do not present the entire picture, however. Social work's history is also the story of internal professional conflicts and debate. These issues often relate to various political perspectives, but they also have a life of their own. Chief among social work's internal conflicts are the following: (1) Should social workers put major stress on building a profession or on delivering a service? (2) How should social work relate to a national system of public welfare? and (3) What is the appropriate role of a profession in political activity and social change?[9]

The following history looks at both the internal struggles and the effects of larger ideological perspectives in shaping social work. This discussion focuses specifically on the development of the profession. A fuller history of the United States' social welfare system will be presented in Chapter 8.

State Charitable Institutions

Although one could trace the antecedents of social work in the United States back to early Judeo-Christian practices of almsgiving to the poor, the more relevant place to begin is the rise of state charitable institutions in the mid–1800s. Prior to such institutions, communities in the United States dealt with the dependent poor by "auctioning out" their care to the lowest bidder, or, more commonly, by distributing public outdoor relief—small amounts of money or goods provided directly to the poor by local governments. Another alternative was the dreaded poorhouse, where orphans, the elderly, the unemployed, and those with physical or mental handicaps were crowded together in often unpleasant surroundings. The state institutions, in their inception, represented a progressive experiment in a more scientific, state-supported response to the needs of dependent groups. Social reformers like Dorothea Dix led the way by campaigning for special state institutions for the mentally ill. Shocked at the conditions in which many people with mental problems were forced to live, such as unheated jail cells or dismal attics, Dix successfully lobbied state legislatures to create mental hospitals which could provide more humane treatment. Similar movements grew up around the needs of delinquents, poor children, the developmentally disabled, and those with physical handicaps. At the same time the earlier system of poorhouses expanded. The result was what one historian has called "the discovery of the asylum"— the creation of large, specialized, often state-financed institutions which attempted to deal more adequately with dependent populations.[10]

By the late 1800s, although public outdoor relief remained in use, these large institutions dominated the care and treatment of dependent people. Eighteen state governments had set up boards of charities to monitor and coordinate the growing system of poorhouses, mental asylums, state schools for the blind, and reformatories. The growth and regulation of these institutions led to increased occupational identity among administrators and a cohesiveness among the philanthropists appointed to state boards. Annual conferences, such as the National Conference of Charities and Correction, drew these people together to discuss common problems, staff training procedures, and other administrative issues. Their growing professional identity was one contribution to the development of social work.[11]

By the end of the 1800s, however, state institutions had greatly deteriorated. Their initial aim—to offer rational, humane care to various groups of dependent people— had been subverted by high numbers, high costs, and a recurring tendency on the part of public officials and others to use such institutions to isolate certain groups from society and to maintain social control. Although they persisted well into the twentieth century, it became increasingly clear that large, overcrowded asylums and reformatories could not solve the problems of dependency.

The Charity Organization Society

As the state institutions began their decline, two new social welfare movements held forth promise for dealing with dependency. Each was to have significant impact on the creation of social work as a profession. The first, the Charity Organization Society (COS), was initially established in England and was transplanted to the United States in 1877. The COS stressed individual factors in the development of poverty. The second movement, the rise of the social settlement, also had its roots in England and began its growth in the United States in the 1880s. The settlement house movement proposed a different approach to dependency and focused on the environmental and social aspects of human problems.

The charity organization movement developed in part as a reaction to the proliferation of small private charities in the United States and England during the nineteenth century. Some of these organizations, notably the New York Association for Improving the Condition of the Poor, used systematic home visiting by volunteers to ensure that the "moral deficits" of poor families would be attended to as well as their economic needs. Yet by the 1870s the private charity scene consisted mostly of perfunctory almsgiving with little organized investigation of the recipients. There was also a lack of coordination among the various charitable groups. In both England and the United States, charity reformers began to call for a more systematic, "scientific" approach. In the United States particularly, the ill effects of industrialization—overcrowded cities; an exploited, low-paid working class; periodic depressions; and structural unemployment—led to great increases in the numbers of people asking for relief. These same social phenomena fanned the fears of middle- and upper-class people that the lower classes would revolt. At the same time, faith in progress and in the visible signs of prosperity around them allowed most Americans to view poverty as individual deviation, rather than as the fault of economic and social institutions.

This mixture of concerns—awareness of increasing demands for relief made on a poorly organized system, fear of militancy among the poor and working classes, and a belief in individual responsibility for dependency—led to the rise of the COS in the United States. The main premise of the movement held that private, carefully orchestrated relief efforts offered the greatest promise for the eradication of poverty. Charity organization societies proposed to coordinate the work of all private charities in a given locality in order to prevent recipients from receiving aid from several sources. Each family's application was to be thoroughly investigated. Then, in a revival of the earlier system of home visiting, volunteer "friendly visitors" were assigned to needy families. Visitors were urged to be friendly but firm; their primary functions were to correct the character flaws of the poor and to inspire them to strive for independence and the moral life.[12]

The goals and values of the movement reflected a conservative interpretation of the causes of poverty. As espoused by leaders like Josephine Shaw Lowell, a reformer from a well-to-do Boston family, this interpretation viewed individual dependency as one of the greatest evils of modern industrial life. The poor were in need largely because of their own shortcomings, including drunkenness and idleness; haphazard charity furthered their dependency. Government-sponsored outdoor relief was an even greater obstacle to rehabilitation. Only patient, skilled visiting by dedicated volunteers could guide families to economic independence. In Lowell's words, well-to-do visitors, generally women, brought not *alms,* but "kind action" and served as good moral examples for the poor.[13] Direct cash help was to be avoided if at all possible. Loans and assistance in finding jobs were the preferred type of aid to "deserving" families.

Charity organization societies spread rapidly among American cities in the late 1800s. However, the initial goals of COS leaders were difficult to sustain. Individual approaches to the problems of poverty failed to stem its growth. The continuing demand for relief led many charitable societies to rely on direct cash payments to the poor. In

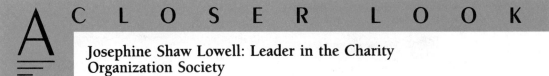

Josephine Shaw Lowell: Leader in the Charity Organization Society

Josephine Shaw Lowell was born into a wealthy Bostonian family in 1843. Her parents had strong social reform commitments, and from her family and its circle of friends, Lowell inherited a belief in the importance of public service. Her life was greatly affected by the Civil War. Her parents were abolitionists and she herself joined a women's relief organization which provided aid to Union soldiers. In 1864, Lowell's husband of one year was wounded in combat; when he died, she was pregnant with their only child. This loss seemed to spur Lowell to even greater involvement in social reform. She became a major figure in the organized charity movement of the late nineteenth century. In 1872, as chair of a committee of the New York State Charities Aid Association, she conducted a statewide investigation of pauperism. Impressed by this study, the governor appointed her the first woman Commissioner of the State Board of Charities, a position she held for thirteen years. This board dealt with both public and private charitable organizations. However, Lowell was particularly drawn to the field of private charity. She helped organize the New York Charity Organization Society in 1882 and guided its activities over the next two decades.

Lowell dressed in black and seemed to be the symbol of a self-sacrificing reformer, but she was also tough, sharp, and pragmatic. She held strong views about the causes of poverty and the appropriate remedies for it. Many of these are expressed in her book *Private Charity and Public Relief* (1884).

While she is sometimes portrayed as exhibiting a moralistic and punitive attitude toward the poor, Lowell displayed a mixture of values and beliefs about dependency. On the one hand, she saw idleness as a major defect of the poor and she believed that government aid to paupers made matters worse by decreasing the incentive to work. Only private charity, through its program of friendly visiting, could elevate the moral nature of the poor. Lowell also had little sympathy for "drunkards" and felt that aid to their families would simply encourage such men to count on charity to feed their wives and children. Similarly, she had little use for vagrant women and mothers of illegitimate children, and she recommended that they be committed to long terms in reformatories.

On the other hand, Lowell believed that certain people, such as orphans, widows, and the sick, were poor through no fault of their own. In these cases, she regarded public responses, such as institutions or widows' pensions, as appropriate forms of relief. She viewed low wages as one cause of poverty, and she fought to improve job conditions for working women. As part of this fight, she supported labor unions. In these situations, Lowell appreciated the importance of environmental factors in poverty. Yet she tended to apply these insights and responses only to the situation of the "deserving" poor (those showing a desire to work, for example). In essence, then, she believed that personal character was the most significant element determining one's position in life.

Sources: Barbara R. Beatty, "Josephine Shaw Lowell, in Walter I. Trattner, ed., *Biographical Dictionary of Social Welfare in America* (Westport, CT: Greenwood Press, 1986), 511–515; Michael Katz, *In the Shadow of the Poorhouse* (New York: Basic Books, 1986), 68–72.

addition, there was an insufficient pool of volunteers to maintain effective friendly visiting. For this reason, and because of a growing sense of the need for a permanent, trained staff, charities turned increasingly to the use of paid staff, called "agents," to investigate applications and to visit the poor.

These agents were a major forerunner of professional social workers. Like the volunteers before them, they were chiefly women, and they were usually Protestant, white, and middle class. This job offered an outlet for college-educated women at a time when nurturance of a family took center stage and career possibilities for women were few and far between. Charity work was a reasonably acceptable endeavor for women as it made use of traditional feminine characteristics, such as caring for others.

Gradually, agencies began to train their visitors. They offered informal lectures and short courses on working with poor families. The realization that friendly visiting demanded specific skills which could be generalized and taught was particularly well articulated by Mary Richmond, head of first the Baltimore and then the Philadelphia COS. Richmond had risen from the position of clerk to administrator, an unusual role for a woman at a time when most charity societies were headed by men. A dynamic administrator and a fervent believer in charity organization, Richmond worked hard to define and to publicize the particular tasks performed by charity workers, especially the job of careful investigation into the causes of a family's dependency. In a famous speech at the National Conference of Charities and Corrections in 1897, she called for the creation of training schools in charitable work.[14] The following year, the New York Charity Organization Society responded by founding the New York Summer School of Applied Philanthropy. This series of courses for charity workers soon expanded to become the first school of social work in the United States (now Columbia University School of Social Work). And of course, formal training called for textbooks; Richmond wrote the first one, *Social Diagnosis,* in 1917.

The Social Settlement

While the charity movement was beginning to become professionalized, another approach to poverty was taking shape. The social settlement, again an idea imported from England, added a different dimension to the development of social work. Unlike the charity movement with its stress on individual defects, social settlements focused on environmental factors in poverty.

During the 1880s and 1890s, a number of American reformers visited Toynbee Hall in a slum area of London; this was a large house which served as a sort of live-in laboratory for the study of poverty by young university students. Toynbee Hall brought students in close contact with the poor and encouraged efforts at social reform. One of the American visitors who found the idea appealing was Jane Addams. Together with her friend Ellen Gates Starr, Addams founded Hull House in a poor immigrant neighborhood in Chicago in 1889. Although it was not the first American settlement, Hull House came to exemplify the particular brand of research, service, and reform which was to characterize much of the American settlement movement.

Jane Addams grew up in a comfortable home in a small town in Illinois. Like a growing number of young, well-to-do women of her generation, she received a college education. Yet, like her peers, she faced constraints on the uses to which this education could be put. Hull House offered a way to put her education and commitment to service into action. When she and Starr first moved into the settlement, they had vague notions of being "good neighbors" to the poor around them and studying the conditions in which they lived. As they observed the structural elements of poverty, however, the two began to create a specific agenda of services and reform. Exploitation of immigrants

A CLOSER LOOK

Mary Richmond: Pioneer in Social Casework

Unlike many early charity organization and settlement leaders, Mary Richmond did not come from a well-to-do family. She was born in 1861, the daughter of a carriage blacksmith. Her mother died when Richmond was three, and she was brought up by a widowed grandmother and two maiden aunts. Her grandmother operated a boarding house in a lower-middle-class neighborhood in Baltimore. Richmond graduated from a highly academic girls' high school, but did not go on to college. Instead, she held a series of clerical and bookkeeping jobs. In 1889 she became assistant treasurer of the Baltimore Charity Organization Society, thus beginning her career in social work.

Growing up in a household where discussions

of women's rights, race relations, education, and political reform were commonplace, Richmond inherited a concern for the weak and the oppressed. This was strengthened by involvement in church activities and volunteer work with working-women's clubs. In addition, prominent women reformers in Baltimore served as mentors and friends. The support of one of these women helped Richmond to secure the position of director of the Baltimore COS in 1891; this post had formerly been held by men with graduate training. Richmond soon rose to prominence in the charity movement. As an administrator, author, and promoter of research and training, Richmond was instrumental in establishing "scientific" casework as the foundation of social work practice.

Sources: Muriel W. Pumphrey, "Mary Ellen Richmond," in Walter I. Trattner, ed., *Biographical Dictionary of Social Welfare in America* (Westport, CT: Greenwood Press, 1986), 622–625; Peggy Pittman-Munke, "Sisterhood is Powerful: The Role of Women and Women's Clubs in the Early Career of Mary Richmond," Social Welfare History Symposium, Council on Social Work Education Meetings, March, 1986.

from southern and eastern Europe, poor employment conditions and inadequate wages, lack of educational opportunities, substandard housing, and inefficient city government were the factors that contributed greatly to the poverty of the area and called for specific responses. Hull House soon offered a day nursery for children, a club for working girls, lectures and cultural programs, and meeting space for neighborhood political groups. Along with a remarkable group of reformers who came to live at the settlement, Addams supported labor union activity, lobbied city officials for sanitary and housing reforms, and established the Immigrants' Protective League to fight discrimination in employment and other exploitation of newcomers. In addition, Hull House members carried on an active program of research. Residents surveyed conditions in tenements and work places. They publicized their results widely, with an eye to creating an atmosphere conducive to governmental and legislative reform.[15]

As with the Charity Organization Movement, the settlement experiment spread to cities across the country. While approaches varied and some settlement workers spoke disapprovingly of the "city wilderness" around them, most employed a liberal interpretation of the causes of poverty.[16] Living alongside the poor, they saw firsthand the role of environmental factors in dependence. They did not subscribe to the belief that poverty was a matter of individual defect; they felt it stemmed largely from social and economic conditions, which they worked to change. While settlements were supported by private donations, they often looked to government as the source of reforms, both on a local level (such as city sanitation regulations) and on a national scale (as in child labor laws). In their attempts to empower the poor through support of the labor movement and democratization of political institutions, settlements like Hull House verged on a radical view of the need for fundamental social change.[17]

Those who worked in the settlements resembled the charity workers in many respects. Residents were generally middle- to upper-class, white, and Protestant (although settlements were also founded by black and Jewish groups). Interestingly, however, the fields differed in terms of the roles played by women and men. Male administrators dominated the leadership of the COS, with women making up the vast majority of the societies' friendly visitors. The settlement movement, on the other hand, included a fair proportion of men (about a third) among its "front line" workers. Women took on a more visible leadership role, constituting about two-thirds of all settlement directors.[18] A powerful network of women social reformers emerged from the Hull House setting, including Julia Lathrop and Grace Abbott, prominent figures in the U.S. Children's Bureau; Florence Kelley, labor and consumer advocate; Alice Hamilton, physician and social activist; and Edith Abbott and Sophonisba Breckinridge, social researchers and key leaders in the development of social work education.

In contrast to many charity workers, settlement residents were wedded to a cause rather than to a set of skills. While less conscious of building an occupation, they developed a sense of shared purpose and cooperated with each other in campaigns for women's suffrage, protective legislation for working women and children, and municipal reform. Because they often worked with groups, they contributed to the development of group work as a social work method.

At first charity workers and settlement residents regarded each other with suspicion. As one friendly visitor put it, the settlement house worker was like "a man who found a drunkard lying in the gutter and said to him, 'I can't help you, my friend, but I will sit down in the gutter beside you.' "[19] Gradually, however, both types of workers began to mingle in settings such as the annual meetings of the National Conference of Charities and Correction. Broadened since the days of state institutions, this group now served as a national forum for ideas about social welfare and social reform. Rapprochement between settlement and charity folk was made more possible by a shift in philosophy on the part of charity organization leaders in the early 1900s. Key figures like Mary Richmond and Edward Devine began to recognize that work with individual poor people needed to be coupled with broader social change. A growing awareness of the importance of the economic and social causes of poverty allowed charity workers to develop a greater sense of common cause with their settlement colleagues.

Growth of a Profession

The notion of a distinct occupation—social work—was beginning to take shape. Settlement and charity work were soon joined by two new specialties, social work in medical settings and school settings. In 1915, organizers of the National Conference

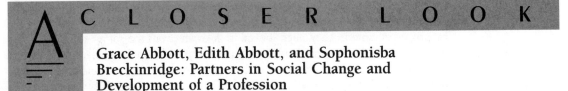

Grace Abbott, Edith Abbott, and Sophonisba Breckinridge: Partners in Social Change and Development of a Profession

The Abbott sisters and their colleague, Sophonisba Breckinridge, represent a formidable trio in the development of public welfare and professional social work in the United States. Grace Abbott is perhaps the best known of the three, because of her position as head of the U.S. Children's Bureau from 1921 to 1933. Yet as educators, researchers, and active members of social work and social welfare organizations, Edith Abbott and Sophonisba Breckinridge also made a major impact on the profession and its practice.

The three had excellent backgrounds for their work. Breckinridge came from a distinguished Kentucky family which had a long history of political and philanthropic service. Her father was a lawyer and member of the U.S. House of Representatives. Several women relatives had been involved in charitable work. Breckinridge herself studied law and became the first woman to pass the Kentucky bar exam. Failing to be accepted as a "woman lawyer," however, she completed a doctorate in political science at the University of Chicago in 1901 and remained there to teach. She met the Abbott sisters as students in her series of lectures on social welfare.

Grace and Edith Abbott came from a small town in Nebraska. Their lawyer father held a state political office; their mother had been a school principal. Both parents imbued their children with a strong commitment to education, women's rights, and progressive ideas. Edith Abbott studied at the London School of Economics and received a Ph.D in economics at the University of Chicago in 1905. Her sister, more an activist than a scholar, received a master's degree in political science several years later.

All three women had important connections to Jane Addams's Hull House. The Abbott sisters lived there during their early years in Chicago; Breckinridge joined them every summer. The settlement and its immigrant neighborhood served as the setting for Breckinridge and Edith Abbott's research on housing conditions of the poor, the employment situation of working women, juvenile delinquency, and child labor. Grace Abbott, with her more activist bent, became head of the Immigrants' Protective League, an organization established by Addams and others as an advocacy group for newcomers to the United States. This division of labor was typical of their activities in later years. Grace Abbott went to Washington to administer the Children's Bureau; there she played an active role in developing policy and creating programs serving women and young children. Edith Abbott and Breckinridge chose to make their contribution to society as educators, scholars, and analysts of public policy. The two helped establish the School of Social Service Administration at the University of Chicago, a social work school with a primary focus on public welfare. Both were active in social work organizations and used them as forums for several major concerns: the development of a fair and comprehensive government-sponsored welfare system, the promotion of public welfare as a legitimate concern of social work, and the creation of a social work profession based on scientific knowledge gained in graduate education. The three women's major legacy was thus a wedding of professionalism with a concern for social reform.

Sources: Lela B. Costin, *Two Sisters for Social Justice* (Chicago, IL: University of Illinois Press, 1983); Judith Sealander, "Sophonisba Breckinridge," in Walter I. Trattner, ed., *Biographical Dictionary of Social Welfare* (Westport, CT: Greenwood Press, 1986), 126–129.

of Charities and Correction invited Abraham Flexner, who was an educator nationally known for his expertise in evaluating professional standards, to discuss "Is Social Work a Profession?" In a frequently quoted reply, Flexner answered *no*. He described social workers as mediators between clients and other professionals, such as lawyers and doctors, rather than as practitioners with their own specific competency and set of skills. Social workers appear to have taken Flexner's words as a challenge. As they pursued professional standing, they heeded the observations of Flexner and others that professions need systematic technique and specialized education based on scientific knowledge. This seemed to many of them to justify further development of individualized charity work, or, as it was coming to be called, *social casework,* and a turn away from social reform. The climate of the country in the years following World War I supported such a shift. The public was becoming suspicious of social activists, including some social workers, who seemed to promote radical change. The United States was moving away from interest in broad social reform and toward a concern with rationality and scientific expertise in government and industry. The move to build a scientific and professional social work, which came particularly from caseworkers out of the charity tradition, fit nicely with this new approach.[20]

The 1920s witnessed an expansion in the kinds of settings in which social work was carried out, as well as the growth of professional and educational organizations. Many social workers practiced in private family welfare agencies, as most charity organization societies were now called. Others worked in schools, hospitals, and children's aid societies. A new method, social work with groups, was developing within settlement houses and the YMCA/YWCA. Social workers also staffed the Home Service Program set up by the American National Red Cross soon after World War I. This program marked the beginnings of rural social work, providing casework services to the families of servicemen and disaster victims in small towns and rural areas, as well as in larger communities. Child guidance clinics and other mental health facilities offered a prestigious new area for practice. These settings, which were the products of a mental hygiene movement that stressed treatment and prevention rather than custodial care, spurred social workers' interest in the use of psychological theory in their practice. One school of social work, founded by Smith College in 1918, chose to focus specifically on the new area of psychiatric social work. Settlement work and legislative reform activity continued as well, although these had lost strength since the early 1900s.[21]

The 1920s saw the establishment of the private social agency as the prototypical setting for social work practice. While social workers were also employed in public welfare establishments, hospitals, and clinics, the social agency set the tone for much of professional development. As Roy Lubove has noted, the fact that the private agencies of the 1920s focused increasingly on administrative hierarchy, order, rational procedures, and the use of specialized skills made these agencies a compatible home for an occupation moving from volunteerism to a "scientific" professionalism.[22]

There has been a tendency among historians to think in terms of a strict division between private agencies and the various levels of government that was bridged beginning in the 1960s, and particularly in the 1980s and 1990s. Yet government support for non-profit social service organizations has long been extensive. In the late 1800s, many large cities paid private institutions to care for the dependent. A study of private organizations for orphans and elderly people in New York State, for example, showed

A CLOSER LOOK

Edward T. Devine: From Charity Work to Social Reform

Born in 1867, Edward Devine was raised on a farm in Iowa. He first worked as a teacher in several small Iowa communities. After receiving a Ph.D. in economics from the University of Pennsylvania, he became a university lecturer in Philadelphia. The suffering he witnessed in that city during the Depression of 1893 led him toward a more direct involvement in human service. At the age of twenty-nine, he became head of the New York Charity Organization Society, the largest COS in the country. Shortly after taking on the position, Devine launched a journal on charity work, first called *Charities,* and later the *Survey.* Devine edited the journal for over ten years, during which time its content changed from an emphasis on the techniques of charity work to coverage of a variety of social problems.

A vigorous, imaginative, and hard-working in-

dividual, Devine not only ran the journal and the COS but also helped to launch the New York School of Philanthropy (the first school of social work in the United States). He served both as instructor and as the School's director for a number of years. Gradually Devine broadened his concerns from direct charity for individuals to an interest in more fundamental social reform. By the early 1900s, he was convinced that social work must move beyond relief to address the larger social problems causing dependency. Accordingly, he played an important role in campaigns for child labor laws and tenement house improvements. Toward the end of his career in the 1930s, Devine became involved in the new federal relief programs initiated by Franklin Roosevelt. His work thus spanned the prewar Progressive movement and New Deal reforms.

Sources: Clarke A. Chambers, *Paul Kellogg and the Survey* (Minneapolis, MN: University of Minnesota Press, 1971), 6–8, 27; William W. Bremer, "Edward Thomas Devine," in Walter I. Trattner, ed., *Biographical Dictionary of Social Welfare* (Westport, CT: Greenwood Press, 1986), 228–231.

that twice as much of their support came from public as from private sources. In Chicago, many private children's institutions received public subsidies. A national survey in 1901 concluded that in almost all of the states, some financial aid was given to private charities by the state, counties, or cities. Private agency social workers of the 1990s will find this a familiar theme, as they note the importance in their own organizations' budgets of government grants and contracts with public agencies.[23]

Diversity and Unification

Although the field of social work was predominantly white and Protestant, the profession also included Catholic, Jewish, and African American practitioners. Jewish and Catholic groups often formed their own agencies and professional schools. African Americans had little choice but to follow a similar path. Several prominent African American social workers were influential in the National Conference of Social Work and similar forums, yet by and large the African American social work community found it difficult to win acceptance in the field. Because of segregation laws and customs, African Americans were often unable to enroll in white graduate schools or to intern and practice in white agencies. Atlanta University School of Social Work and the National Urban League were two institutions that were created by African Americans partly in response to this exclusion from mainstream social work. In addition to professional development, there was a strong tradition of self-help in many African American communities, with members of African American women's clubs and churches being particularly involved in social welfare activities.[24]

As social work diversified and expanded, it also created unifying mechanisms. The growing number of schools of social work joined together in the American Association of Schools of Social Work in 1919. These schools varied in their structure; some were undergraduate programs, some were graduate programs, some were affiliated with universities, and others were freestanding schools closely tied to social work agencies. However, by the 1920s, a movement was growing to standardize schools and to promote a master's degree as the only qualifying degree for professional practice. While some social work educators and practitioners argued for a broader, more flexible approach to training, others successfully convinced Association members that the symbol of professionalism in the United States was a graduate degree. By the mid–1930s, member schools had to offer at least one year of graduate training and to follow prescribed guidelines on course content.[25]

Similar standardization and emphasis on professionalism was beginning to be seen in the practice organizations. By the 1920s, a number of specialist organizations existed—one for school social workers, another for hospital social workers, and so on. In addition to these organizations, the American Association of Social Workers developed; this was a broader group which offered membership to caseworkers across fields. The Association tended to exclude settlement and group workers, however, as they often lacked the formal specialized training required for membership. In the late 1920s, a move within the AASW to legislate even stiffer membership requirements caused much controversy. At stake was the concept of how broad a profession social work should be. Should it, as some members argued, include a diverse group of people with different levels of professional training, or should it, as others contended, concentrate on developing itself as a select professional group with high educational standards? The latter group won out, convincing the membership that selective professionalism was a good thing. From the early 1930s until the end of the 1960s, the major social work professional association mandated graduate training as a requirement for membership.[26]

Social work at the end of the 1920s had become rather complacent. Professional development was proceeding, and services concentrating on an individual approach to people's problems were expanding. In a famous series of meetings, the Milford Conference, caseworkers produced a report which affirmed that a core of casework skills existed, uniting the various fields of practice. These changes were summed up in a famous speech by Porter Lee, the Director of the New York School of Social Work. As Lee explained, social work had changed from a "cause" to a "function," from social reform to the organized provision of casework and other help to individuals with problems.[27]

A CLOSER LOOK

George Haynes

George Haynes was the first executive director of the National Urban League, which he helped to found in 1910. He was born in a small Arkansas community in 1880, where his mother worked as a domestic servant and his father was an occasional laborer. Haynes's mother instilled in her children strong religious and moral ideals and a belief in the importance of education. A visit to the Chicago World's Fair brought exposure to philosophical and political ferment within urban black communities and helped Haynes develop his view that the problems of blacks in America would not be solved by emigration to Africa, but rather through interracial cooperation to create equity and justice in the United States. Improved education for African Americans would help in achieving such equity.

Haynes attended Agricultural and Mechanical College in Alabama for one year, and then he transferred to Fisk University, where he completed his degree in 1903. Building on an excellent academic record, he received a master's degree from Yale. In his first job as Secretary of the Colored Men's Department of the International YMCA, Haynes traveled through the South working with African American college students and encouraging high academic standards. Continuing his interest in bettering conditions for blacks, Haynes attended the New York School of Philanthropy and became its first black graduate in 1910. He completed a Ph.D in economics at Columbia University two years later. While pursuing these degrees, the energetic Haynes maintained his involvement in the community. He worked with several organizations aimed at dealing with the problems of the large numbers of African Americans moving into New York City in the early 1900s. With Haynes's help, the activities of these groups led to the formation of the National Urban League. The new organization had a social work orientation and a commitment to interracial efforts to help African Americans achieve better employment and living conditions in urban areas. In a creative effort to provide training for black social workers who could then staff the League, Haynes assumed a teaching position at Fisk University. In consultation with his New York School mentor Edward Devine, Haynes set up a program in which Fisk social science students engaged in field work at the League offices. At a time when little social work training was available to minorities of color, Haynes's efforts were an important impetus to the entry of African Americans into the profession.

Sources: Rayford Logan and Michael Winston, *Dictionary of American Negro Biography* (New York: W.W. Norton, 1982), 297–301; Guichard Parris and Lester Books, *Blacks in the City: A History of the National Urban League* (Boston, MA: Little, Brown & Co., 1971), 23–28.

The Depression and the Development of Federal Social Welfare Programs

The Stock Market Crash of 1929 brought a severe jolt to social work practice. As the Depression spread, social workers were often the first to view its effects. In family welfare agencies, settlements, and elsewhere, they encountered increasing numbers of the unemployed. Their case loads included not just the traditional poor—the elderly, minorities, and those with handicaps—but also growing numbers of working- and middle-class families. Slowly, as they looked at clients often much like themselves, social workers began to shift their ideological perspective from a focus on individual defect back to an appreciation of the social and economic factors causing dependency. As they did so, they embraced the liberal view that government should help to ensure an adequate standard of living for all citizens.

Social workers joined other groups in demanding a federal response to the problems of unemployment. They testified in congressional committee hearings on relief and helped to draft welfare legislation. Most supported President Franklin Roosevelt's creation of federally funded relief and the subsequent development of unemployment insurance and a Social Security system which dealt with financial needs of the elderly, dependent children, and individuals with physical handicaps. It was no coincidence that Roosevelt's emergency relief program was headed by social worker Harry Hopkins and that the public assistance part of the Social Security program was directed by another member of the profession, Jane Hoey.[28]

This was the first time that the federal government had entered the realm of social welfare on a major scale. The Freedmen's Bureau, set up after the Civil War to offer aid to freed slaves, and the Children's Bureau, established by social workers in 1912, were significant, though limited early endeavors. A system of veterans' pensions and services, beginning as early as 1818 with the Revolutionary War Pension Act, provided a broader precedent for federal involvement.[29] Now, during the Depression, state and local public relief departments, dispensing a combination of local and federal funds, expanded at a rapid rate and provided countless jobs for social workers. As new, young workers, often without professional training, swelled social work's ranks, they helped found a movement with a more radical perspective on social welfare problems. The Rank and File movement was a loose coalition of social work unions and other activist groups which grew up in the Depression era. Many of the unions were formed by the new public welfare workers in an attempt to deal with demanding working conditions: huge case loads, crowded work places, little job security, and salary cutbacks. While the unions stressed improvements in job conditions, they also joined groups of established social work professionals in calling for far-reaching changes in American economic and political life. Believing that only radical changes could eradicate poverty, many Rank and File members called for such measures as a planned national economy and redistribution of income. They stressed working through America's organized labor movement in their attempt to create a better society. Although it represented a minority faction within social work, the Rank and File movement provided a useful challenge to more traditional social work professional organizations and attracted prominent social workers to its cause. Harry Lurie, a well-respected Jewish charities executive, was one example; Bertha Reynolds, Associate Dean of the Smith College School of Social Work, was another. A leading psychiatric social worker, Reynolds sought to reconcile the ideas of Marx and Freud in a holistic view of human problems.[30]

The Rank and File movement and social work's involvement in New Deal reforms brought a new political activism to the field. Yet social workers debated the degree to which political action conflicted with professional development. While some argued that politics and union activity were compatible with professionalism, particularly in a field concerned with bettering social conditions, others embraced a more traditional view of professions as objective, nonpolitical bodies. This debate remains an ongoing dilemma in social work.[31] In the Depression Era, mainstream social work chose to resolve the dilemma by endorsing the role of the expert witness and the consultant to the policy makers, rather than that of the more direct political activist.

A growing national backlash against New Deal reforms, along with the escalation of war in Europe and Asia, contributed not only to the demise of the Rank and File movement in the early 1940s, but also to social work's renewed interest in the individual treatment aspects of the field. At the same time, social workers felt that government welfare programs were well on their way to solving the most pressing problems of poverty. Relief giving was now almost entirely the responsibility of public, rather than private agencies. This meant that social workers could concern themselves with the more personal aspects of family and individual difficulties. They could deal with these issues in private family and children's agencies and expand their services to a middle-class clientele. The psychology of Sigmund Freud took on a tremendous appeal, and social work educators incorporated his theories in their teaching. Practitioners were even urged to undergo psychoanalysis to improve their therapeutic skills.

The commitment to an involvement in public welfare and the social policy arena did not completely disappear, however. While many schools of social work trained students primarily for casework practice in a private agency, the School of Social Service Administration at the University of Chicago, under the guidance of Edith Abbott and Sophonisba Breckinridge, carried on a tradition of educating students for leadership positions in public welfare. Jane Hoey in the Social Security Administration worked tirelessly to raise professional standards among workers in the federal public assistance programs. This was a difficult job, partly because many local communities, especially in rural areas, lacked trained social workers. These communities did not always welcome what they viewed as the intrusion of the outside expert. State and federal politicians, who wanted to grant favors by employing local residents, sometimes railed against those "damned social workers [who] are going to . . . tell our people whom they shall hire."[32]

During this time, a number of undergraduate social work programs were established in state universities and land grant colleges, with the primary goal of preparing personnel for the expanding public welfare arena. These programs, often growing out of sociology departments, formed their own organization, the National Association of Schools of Social Service Administration, in 1942. The organization grew to number

During the Depression years of the 1930s, drought and farm foreclosures forced many families to abandon their farms and move West in search of work.

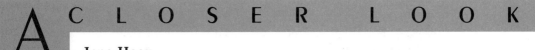

Jane Hoey

As head of the federal Bureau of Public Assistance from 1936 to 1954, Jane Hoey sought to build a professional public welfare service in the United States. The Bureau was a part of the new Social Security program developed by Franklin Delano Roosevelt during the Depression years. Hoey came to the position as a trained social worker. The youngest of nine children in an Irish immigrant family, she had attended college with the financial help of her brothers and sisters. After earning a master's degree in political science and a diploma from the New York School of Philanthropy in 1916, Hoey worked in a variety of health and public welfare jobs in New York City. She was a good friend of Harry Hopkins, the social worker who would later head Roosevelt's federal emergency relief operation. Hoey was Hopkins's assistant when he was Secretary of the New York Board of Child Welfare. Hoey's brother served two terms in the state legislature, and through him she met Roosevelt and New York's governor, Al Smith. Smith appointed her as the first woman member of the State Crime Commission.

Hoey brought to her position in the Roosevelt administration a sound knowledge of state and local government and a commitment to social work in the public arena. The new Bureau was in charge of developing the congressionally mandated programs of federal aid for the poor elderly, the blind, and dependent children. Hoey began with a staff of three; all were filled with excitement and enthusiasm for the new ideas being generated in New Deal Washington. Her task was to guide states in developing their own systems for administering these jointly funded programs. She promoted the use of professionally trained social workers on both the state and federal levels, against the objection that any educated person of good will could be a social worker. She fought vigorously against the attempts of several states to discriminate against African Americans, Native Americans, and Mexicans in providing welfare grants. One state official angrily complained to the head of the Social Security Board, "That red-headed devil of yours is in my office. She's telling me certain things that I need to do. Do I have to?" "Yes, sir," was the unwelcome reply. Hoey was not always successful in her attempts to improve public welfare, however. Lack of state funds and trained personnel, as well as a continued aversion to the idea of government welfare programs on the part of many Americans, prevented the United States from developing the type of comprehensive social welfare system that was common in Europe. However, Hoey left her mark by bringing professionalism to most state welfare departments.

Sources: *The Reminiscences of Jane Hoey,* Social Security Project, 1965, Oral History Research Office Collection of Columbia University, The Trustees of Columbia in the City of New York; Blanche D. Coll, "Jane Marguereta Hoey," in Barbara Sicherman and Carol Hurd Green, eds., *Notable American Women: The Modern Period* (Cambridge, MA: Belknap Press, 1980), 341–343.

over thirty members, with a nucleus of Southern and Southwestern institutions, but including schools from all over the United States. The group argued that social work's stress on graduate education as the only way into the profession was both elitist and impractical in a time of growing staffing needs. By and large, however, the field of social work resisted wide-scale involvement in the developing public welfare system, perhaps because it seemed less glamorous and less professional than psychologically oriented casework in a private agency. Undergraduate social work programs were among the major victims in the debate between a public service commitment and the maintenance of high professional standards. By not allowing undergraduate programs to become members, the American Association of Schools of Social Work successfully blocked their attempt to offer accredited social work professional training on the undergraduate level. Although this would have been a practical way to staff public welfare programs, the Association continued to argue that social work needed graduate training to build its public image.[33]

Continued Professional Growth

New, broader social work organizations emerged in the 1950s. These embraced a number of factions of social work, although they maintained a stress on graduate education as the symbol of professional status. The National Association of Social Workers (NASW), formed in 1955, brought together all the existing specialist organizations, including psychiatric social workers, medical social workers, group workers, and practitioners in the emerging fields of community organization and social work research. In 1952, the Council on Social Work Education (CSWE) encompassed graduate schools and undergraduate programs, although the latter were restricted to a pre-professional curriculum.

By the 1950s, social work had matured and solidified. The NASW adopted a Code of Ethics for practice and began to explore the possibility of state licensing for social workers. Schools of social work experimented with a "generic" curriculum that exposed students to a variety of practice methods and stressed the similarities among them. The idea was that whether social workers dealt with groups, communities, or individuals, they used certain common skills that should be taught to all students. The field was no longer strictly a woman's profession; during the preceding several decades, men had been entering its ranks. Ironically, they tended to replace women in leadership roles in the professional organizations and schools.[34]

Once again, however, national events placed new demands upon the field. The 1960s were a time of great social change. The Civil Rights movement, spearheaded by leaders like Martin Luther King, Jr., forced Americans to recognize the extent of prejudice and discrimination in a supposedly open society. A renewed concern about poverty emerged at the same time. One factor in this rediscovery of the poor was the publication of Michael Harrington's *The Other America,* which called attention to pockets of poverty in the midst of plenty, and was influential in the thinking of President John F. Kennedy and other national leaders. This revived interest in poverty led to a variety of new social welfare initiatives, such as Head Start and community-based antipoverty programs.

In the ferment of the 1960s, social work was challenged to respond effectively to the needs of African Americans, Hispanic Americans, and other minorities and to facilitate the entry of minorities into the profession. In addition, the renewed focus on poverty revived a call for political activism. Critics within and outside the field denounced social work's stress on individual treatment and a narrow, "objective" professionalism. Some social workers became community workers in President Lyndon Johnson's War on Poverty programs. Others, remaining in the casework field, began to include a stress on advocacy for clients' rights within the various social welfare systems. The traditional emphasis on individual change was again augmented by attention to social and economic problems.

Other shifts took place in social work education and practice. The expansion of social services brought renewed interest in undergraduate social work training. Baccalaureate-level workers were needed to fill the increasing demand for personnel, and this time the undergraduate movement achieved legitimacy within the field. The federal government began to provide funding for undergraduate as well as graduate education. In the early 1970s, both the NASW and the CSWE accepted the BSW as an entry-level professional degree in social work. In addition to federal funding for public social services, support for social work training and activities in the field of mental health was provided by the National Institute of Mental Health. As it developed a new approach called "community mental health," NIMH gave substantial assistance to social work and other disciplines, including generous fellowships for MSW students.

Since the 1970s, social work has broadened its membership base to include baccalaureate-level workers and a more diverse group of practitioners. Currently, minorities of color make up about 12 percent of the field. They constitute about 17 percent of the students enrolled in graduate schools of social work and 24 percent of those enrolled in undergraduate social work programs. There is an Association of Black Social Workers, and African American, Hispanic American, Native American, and Asian American social workers are represented on committees in NASW and CSWE. Approximately one-third of all social workers are men. This percentage may soon decrease, however. Today, men represent 18 percent of all students enrolled in MSW programs and about 15 percent of those in BSW programs.[35]

The social work practice base maintains a healthy diversity. While social workers have recently been less involved in political activity, they have been active as lobbyists, chiefly within the NASW, and as advocates for client rights in areas such as developmental disability and domestic violence. Schools of social work offer training in administration, planning, and policy analysis. However, clinical social work remains the preferred area of practice for many, and an increasing number of social workers have been attracted to the private practice arena.

A politically conservative national climate, as well as continued cutbacks and underfunding of public social welfare programs, has bolstered both an emphasis on individual problems rather than on systems reform and a stress on private agency, and even entreprenurial practice. Less investment in social services of all kinds has led to decreased financial aid for social work students, particularly from federal sources.

The public continues to be ambivalent in its expectations of social workers—should they be change agents, or skilled providers of services to families and individuals? The profession itself struggles with perceived conflicts between public service and profession building, and political involvement and professional objectivity. As social work matures, it may find ways to reconcile these competing goals within a broader conception of professional practice.

SOCIAL WORK VALUES, ETHICS, AND ETHICAL DILEMMAS

As a diverse profession, social work finds unity both in its values and in its historically developed perspective on dealing with social problems. First, social work has a tradition

Important Dates in Social Work History

1843	Dorothea Dix begins her campaign for state sponsorship of special institutions for the mentally ill.
	Establishment of New York Association for Improving the Condition of the Poor.
1874	Formation of National Conference of Charities and Correction.
1877	Foundation of first American Charity Organization Society in Buffalo, New York.
1889	Jane Addams and Ellen Gates Starr found Hull House.
1904	Establishment of first training school for social work, the New York School of Philanthropy (now the Columbia University School of Social Work).
1908	Establishment of Chicago School of Civics and Philanthropy (now the School of Social Service Administration at the University of Chicago).
1912	Formation of U.S. Children's Bureau.
1915	Abraham Flexner invited to National Conference of Charities and Correction to discuss "Is Social Work a Profession?"
1917	Mary Richmond publishes first social work textbook, *Social Diagnosis*.
1919	Organization of American Association of Schools of Social Work.
1920	Establishment of Atlanta School of Social Work to train African American social workers.
1921	Formation of American Association of Social Workers (professional organization preceding National Association of Social Workers).
1933	Franklin Roosevelt initiates Federal Emergency Relief Administration under Harry Hopkins.
1935	Passage of Social Security Act.
	First national conference of Rank and File Movement in Social Work (collection of social work unions).
1942	Rise of undergraduate social work education movement with formation of National Association of Schools of Social Administration.
1952	Establishment of single social work educational association, the Council on Social Work Education.
1955	Formation of National Association of Social Workers.
1964	Passage of Economic Opportunity Act, heralding War on Poverty.
1970	NASW grants full membership to baccalaureate social workers graduating from CSWE-approved undergraduate programs.

of valuing people—of appreciating and understanding individual strengths, needs, and rights. Second, although the profession's history of swings between an individual and an environmental focus may suggest a dichotomy between these emphases, it can be interpreted in another way. That is, social work can be viewed as having developed a unique dual perspective—an awareness of the interplay between individual behavior and larger social, economic, and political structures. Social work practice can in fact be rather schizophrenic, as workers try to deal both with individual and family issues and with the impact of the larger environment. But it is this dual perspective which, when adhered to, offers social work its greatest strength.

Many of social work's values are embedded in the NASW Code of Ethics. The Code affirms the profession's primary responsibility to clients. It also calls on social workers "to foster maximum self-determination" among the people they serve. This means respecting individuals' rights to make their own decisions. Another important client right is that of confidentiality of records and information given during interviews. In addition to these obligations to clients, social workers face other responsibilities. The Code calls for adherence to commitments made to employing organizations. Social workers must uphold the ethics and mission of the profession, make social services available to the general public, and promote the overall welfare of society.

Fulfilling responsibilities to so many groups is a tall order, and in fact it is at times an impossible task. Although the Code is useful as a general set of guidelines, it contains built-in conflicts, which are partially related to social work's pull between individual and society. For example, suppose you are a social worker employed by a community center. The center is in a poor neighborhood, and many of the residents are trying to improve their surroundings by fixing up buildings, planting flowers, and asking the city for better garbage collection and street lights. One community resident, a seemingly eccentric man, persists in filling his yard with carefully hoarded trash. If residents complain to you, what do you do? How do you, as the community worker, choose between the principle of client self-determination and the concept of promoting the general welfare of the neighborhood?

Similarly, an agency policy may lack the flexibility to deal with a particularly needy client. In that case, how does one reconcile commitment to agency regulations with a responsibility to client needs? Even if the worker were able to keep the commitment to clients as his or her priority, there are no easy answers to questions such as "who is the primary client?" An early childhood interventionist may witness a certain amount of benign neglect of a young child on the part of a confused and dependent teenage mother; yet the mother is genuinely trying to increase her independence by studying for her high school equivalency certificate. Whose needs should the social worker attend to, mother or child? What if these needs conflict?

Some of the thorniest ethical dilemmas for social workers arise from attempts to carry out the concept of client self-determination. Philosopher Raymond Plant has noted the difficulties this concept poses for a profession so committed to caring for people and to developing effective responses to problems of dependency.[36] After all, social workers believe they have developed a certain expertise in diagnosing individual and environmental problems and in working toward solutions. Sometimes it seems much more effective and humane to guide clients to these solutions, rather than to leave them "floundering" by themselves. And yet, when a social worker counters an elderly woman's decision to live on the city streets rather than to accept the regimentation of a downtown mission, on the grounds that the woman is "too confused to know what's best for her," the social worker denies the woman's right to self-determination. Respect for individual autonomy can clash not only with the social worker's

A CLOSER LOOK

Summary of NASW Code of Ethics

Summary of Major Principles

I. The Social Worker's Conduct and Comportment as a Social Worker

  A. **Propriety.** The social worker should maintain high standards of personal conduct in the capacity or identity as social worker.

  B. **Competence and Professional Development.** The social worker should strive to become and remain proficient in professional practice and the performance of professional functions.

  C. **Service.** The social worker should regard as primary the service obligation of the social work profession.

  D. **Integrity.** The social worker should act in accordance with the highest standards of professional integrity.

  E. **Scholarship and Research.** The social worker engaged in study and research should be guided by the conventions of scholarly inquiry.

II. The Social Worker's Ethical Responsibility to Clients

  F. **Primacy of Clients' Interests.** The social worker's primary responsibility is to clients.

  G. **Rights and Prerogatives of Clients.** The social worker should make every effort to foster maximum self-determination on the part of clients.

  H. **Confidentiality and Privacy.** The social worker should respect the privacy of clients and hold in confidence all information obtained in the course of professional service.

  I. **Fees.** When setting fees, the social worker should ensure that they are fair, reasonable, considerate, and commensurate with the service performed and with due regard for the clients' ability to pay.

III. The Social Worker's Ethical Responsibility to Colleagues

  J. **Respect, Fairness, and Courtesy.** The social worker should treat colleagues with respect, courtesy, fairness, and good faith.

  K. **Dealing with Colleagues' Clients.** The social worker has the responsibility to relate to the clients of colleagues with full professional consideration.

IV. The Social Worker's Ethical Responsibility to Employers and Employing Organizations

  L. **Commitments to Employing Organizations.** The social worker should adhere to commitments made to the employing organizations.

V. The Social Worker's Ethical Responsibility to the Social Work Profession

  M. **Maintaining the Integrity of the Profession.** The social worker should uphold and advance the values, ethics, knowledge, and mission of the profession.

  N. **Community Service.** The social worker should assist the profession in making social services available to the general public.

  O. **Development of Knowledge.** The social worker should take responsibility for identifying, developing, and fully utilizing knowledge for professional practice.

VI. The Social Worker's Ethical Responsibility to Society

  P. **Promoting the General Welfare.** The social worker should promote the general welfare of society.

Source: Copyright 1990, National Association of Social Workers, Inc., *NASW Code of Ethics.*

sense of expertise, but also with his or her desire to protect clients. The worker may be concerned, as well, with the consequences of a client's decision for others. How does the social worker with a commitment to alleviating suffering respond to the woman with an abusive husband who elects to return home after hospitalization for the beatings? And should the worker attempt to remove the children from what seems to be a destructive home environment?

A particularly complex situation involving parental rights, client self-determination, and social sanctions against child abuse was described in the *New York Times* on September 15, 1991. Under the dramatic headline "Teen-ager Found Chained in Bronx," the story unfolds of a fifteen-year-old girl whose parents chained her to an iron pipe in their apartment in order "to protect her from drugs and other dangers in the community." One's immediate impulse is to react with horror at such treatment. Yet according to testimony by the parents and other relatives, this drastic step was taken out of desperation: The teenager had a history of drug addiction and frequent long disappearances from home, after which she would return emaciated and in poor health. Although the girl reportedly told police that she had been chained up for a year, she later explained to a reporter that the time period was only several months and that she had been able to move around the apartment, watch television, play Nintendo games, and visit with her relatives. Her parents, she said, "were afraid I would go back to the old ways. I'm glad they chained me." The girl's mother told the same reporter that she had sought help for her daughter from various social agencies since the girl was twelve years old. "Nobody ever helped."[37] What is the appropriate role of a social worker in such a case? Should an investigation of child abuse be pursued? (In this situation, for example, the police intervened after an anonymous tip from a state agency.) Should the social worker discuss with the parents and daughter issues of individual freedom versus the need to control the girl's behavior? Can it be assumed that the parents' method of control was wrong?

There are no easy ways out of these dilemmas. In some cases, agency guidelines exist. A number of state departments of social services, for example, have developed policies regarding the rights of individuals referred to Adult Protective Services. An adult who refuses needed medical help, for example, and who understands the consequences of that decision, cannot be forced to accept medical treatment. Many cases lack formal guidelines, however. For this reason, the examination of social ethics, or the values and ethics guiding social policy, has become a growing focus in social work.

As a general approach, social workers faced with ethical conflicts can try to face such conflicts honestly and to think as carefully as possible about the implications of potential decisions and actions for the clients, the agency, and the community. They can explore their own value systems, including religious beliefs, and assess the impact of these values on their decisions. In addition, social workers can now avail themselves of recent publications by those studying social and professional ethics. Ethical decision-making models have begun to appear in the social work literature and to be discussed in social work classes and practitioner workshops. One model, developed by Joseph, includes the following steps:

1. Identify the ethical dilemma as precisely as possible;
2. Gather information on both sides of the issue;
3. Identify the central values in the situation and prioritize them;

4. Formulate alternatives for action and present the reasons justifying each option and the possible consequences of each;

5. Choose an ethical position after reviewing the data, examining the values, and analyzing all the options. Strive for a position that protects both parties if possible.

Although no model can provide easy answers to ethical dilemmas, using a model like the preceding one can at least increase the ability of both the social worker and the client to deal with difficult situations.[38]

SOCIAL WORK METHODS

Social work methods, or interventions, are the specific ways in which practitioners work with clients and communities. These interventions are influenced by the profession's value system and particularly by its historically developed dual commitment to individual and environment. As we noted in Chapter 2, one succinct definition of social work describes it as work with a person-in-situation, that is, as an effort to help individuals interact effectively with their environments.[39] This dual perspective has given rise to a broad range of social work methods, which include interventions with individuals, families, groups, organizations, and communities.

Describing and categorizing methods has not been an easy task for social work. At first, practitioners saw the field as consisting of casework and group work. The term *casework* was used to encompass a variety of interactions with individuals and families, including helping people get financial resources, providing counseling about personal and family problems, and serving as a link between clients and community services such as health care and educational programs. Group work, with its roots in the social settlement and recreation work, meant providing recreational and socializing experiences to groups of clients. By the 1930s, community organization was accepted as a third method; it generally meant community planning activities such as those carried out by the Community Chest, which helps coordinate and raise funds for private social agencies. In the 1950s, administration and social work research were added to the list. More recently, schools of social work have collapsed this array of methods into two categories, or tracks, often labeled "social treatment of individuals, families, and groups" and "planning, administration, and community organization." Planning and community organization are now listed separately because the latter has come to mean work with neighborhood groups and individual residents to strengthen communities and to help the people within them achieve greater power over their lives.

Conceptualizing social work methods as a division among casework, group work, and community organization, or between the two tracks mentioned earlier, creates some problems. First, it encourages the idea that practitioners must choose a single area in which to work. Second, it can lead to the assumption that all social change activity belongs on the community organizing and social planning side of the dividing line and that the social treatment/casework side is concerned only with adjusting clients to the status quo. Finally, this rather arbitrary separation fails to take into account skills and roles that cut across the categories.

One way to deal with these problems is to add to the picture an understanding of the various roles social workers play. These include behavior changer, advocate for client rights, consultant, mediator, and evaluator. Most of these roles apply to the whole range of methods described previously. For example, advocacy for the right of an individual with a developmental disability to receive a public education can be a part of the job of the social treatment person, the group worker, or the community organizer. The interchangeability of such a role indicates that certain commonalities exist among the various methods and that social change activity is not limited to one side of the dichotomy.

Social work methods and roles have evolved over the years. Group work, for example, now includes group therapy, self-help groups, and problem-specific groups, such as those focusing on adult children of alcoholics. Social treatment of individuals and families draws on a wide variety of therapeutic approaches, including behavior modification, short-term counseling models, and cognitive therapy. An increasingly important social work role within social treatment is that of case manager, which is a variation of the broker role described in the box on page 80. Case managers coordinate and monitor the delivery of services to individual clients. To illustrate, a case manager for an elderly client would assess that individual's needs—such as health care in the home, meals-on-wheels, and outlets for socialization with others—and would arrange with different social and health organizations to meet these needs. The case manager would not end the relationship with the client at this point, but would remain involved in order to make sure that services were provided in a helpful and effective way.[40] Finally, social workers in the area of planning and administration use a range of skills, including budgeting, evaluation of social agency programs, and personnel administration.

A MODEL OF SOCIAL WORK PRACTICE

Social work methods are a part of the larger phenomenon of social work practice. This larger picture includes additional elements: fields of practice, social problems, and the different sizes and types of social groupings with which practitioners are concerned. Fields of practice are the broad areas in which social work takes place, including the medical, juvenile justice, and mental health systems. A social problem is anything that either the majority of people in society or the people in power decide needs special attention. Social problems include mental illness, substance abuse, and poverty. Finally, the social groupings that social workers relate to range from individuals to whole communities.

A social worker might choose, for example, to practice in school social work. In this job, the worker would be concerned with a variety of social problems, such as juvenile delinquency, substance abuse, and racial discrimination. He or she might work with individual students, families, and groups of staff, including teachers. Finally, the school social worker would engage in whatever methods were appropriate to the particular situation, including individual counseling, group work, and social planning.

Nancy K. Carroll has developed a three-dimensional model to illustrate the interaction of these variables in social work practice. We have adapted the model here by

A CLOSER LOOK

Social Work Roles

Outreach Worker—identifies individuals, groups, or communities that are experiencing difficulty (in crises) or that are in danger of becoming vulnerable (at risk). A further objective is to detect and identify conditions in the environment that are contributing to the problems.

Broker—steers people toward existing services that may be useful to them. A goal is to enable people to use the system and to negotiate its pathways.

Mediator—intervenes between two individuals, an individual and a group, or two groups to assist people in resolving differences and working productively together.

Advocate—fights for the rights and dignity of people in need of help. This includes fighting for services on behalf of a single person, group, or community (case advocacy) and fighting for changes in laws or practices on behalf of a whole class of persons or segment of society (class advocacy).

Evaluator—gathers information; assesses individual, group, or community problems; and helps make decisions for action.

Mobilizer—assembles, energizes, and organizes existing groups or new groups to deal with prob-

lems. Mobilization can also be carried out on the individual level.

Teacher—conveys information and knowledge and helps people develop skills.

Behavior Changer—works to bring about changes in behavioral patterns, habits, and perceptions of individuals or groups.

Consultant—works with other workers or agencies to help them increase their skills and solve clients' problems.

Community Planner—assists neighborhood planning groups, agencies, community agents, or governments in the development of community programs.

Data Manager—collects, classifies, and analyzes data generated within the social welfare environment.

Administrator—manages an agency, an institution, or a program or service unit.

Care Giver—provides concrete, ongoing care (physical, custodial, financial), in either an institutional or a community setting.

Sources: Adapted with permission of the Southern Regional Education Board from Harold L. Mc-Pheeters and Robert M. Ryan, *A Core of Competence for Baccalaureate Social Welfare* (Atlanta, GA: Southern Regional Education Board, 1971), 18–20.

Also from Betty J. Piccard, *Introduction to Social Work,* 4th ed. (Chicago, IL: Dorsey Press, 1988), 27–28. Reprinted by permission of Brooks/Cole Publishing Company, Pacific Grove, California 93950.

adding the element of fields of practice. We find it a useful way to envision the many facets of social work.[41] (See Figure 3–1.)

The various dimensions of practice offer a number of opportunities for specializations in social work. One could opt to be a medical social worker, a community organizer, or a psychiatric social worker with a particular expertise in treating substance abuse. While some social workers view specialization as an effective and indeed necessary division of labor within an unusually broad field, others argue that practitioners should be generalists who are familiar with a variety of methods, settings, and social

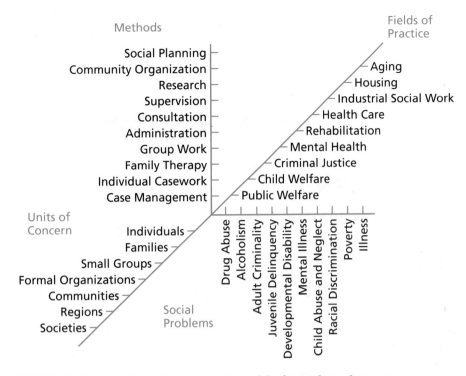

Methods

Fields of Practice

Social Planning
Community Organization
Research
Supervision
Consultation
Administration
Group Work
Family Therapy
Individual Casework
Case Management

Aging
Housing
Industrial Social Work
Health Care
Rehabilitation
Mental Health
Criminal Justice
Child Welfare
Public Welfare

Units of Concern

Individuals
Families
Small Groups
Formal Organizations
Communities
Regions
Societies

Social Problems

Drug Abuse
Alcoholism
Adult Criminality
Juvenile Delinquency
Developmental Disability
Mental Illness
Child Abuse and Neglect
Racial Discrimination
Poverty
Illness

FIGURE 3–1   A Four-Dimensional Model of Social Work Practice

problems. The advantage of the specialist approach lies in the depth of expertise a worker can offer in a particular area. The merit of a generalist stance is its flexibility. The worker can view the client situation in a holistic manner, and can either use a variety of methods or refer clients to other resources for these different approaches. The specialist-generalist debate has a long history in social work.[42] The debate raises several important issues: how clients can best be served, how specialization can be reconciled with a need for coherence within the profession, and how social work can best gain public recognition for its expertise—through developing specializations or promoting an integrated set of skills? The tension between specialization and generalist practice may never be completely resolved, and the profession may continue to combine both approaches. One way this has been formalized since the mid–1970s is the Council on Social Work Education's designation of baccalaureate training as education for generalist practice and MSW programs as the arena for specialization. However, even this tidy division can break down as graduates pursue subsequent careers.

PRACTICE SETTINGS

Beyond the diversity of methods, fields of practice, and social problems, social workers face additional variety in the broad range of settings in which their work is carried out. Social workers practice in nursing homes, hospitals, county social service departments, mental health clinics, family and children's services agencies, centers for independent living for clients with handicaps, homes for delinquent youth, crisis phone line programs, private counseling practice, schools, community centers, social research and planning organizations—and the list goes on. Indeed, one of the advantages of social work is the choices it offers in places to practice.

As one surveys this vast array of settings, it is helpful to keep a few general categories in mind. First, social work is generally divided between practice in host institutions and practice in more specifically social-work-oriented agencies. Host organizations include public schools, hospitals, and nursing homes—places where the dominant goal of the organization is not social service, but education, health maintenance, or the like. Social workers, who usually make up a small proportion of the organization's staff, work with teachers, nurses, and others to help bring about organizational goals. Social workers in these organizations provide a specific skill, such as counseling or intervention with families, that the organization feels it needs. Beyond this, they play a unique mediator role, interpreting organizational aims and restrictions to clients and conveying client needs to the organization. Thus, a hospital social worker may explain the importance of the physician's prescribed medication program to a patient and at the same time convey to the nursing staff that the patient's "troublesome behavior" regarding medication stems from a fear of dependence on drugs.

An alternate kind of setting is the one that is staffed primarily by social workers and that pursues social work goals. Family and children's services agencies, which provide individual counseling, family therapy, referral services, and parent education, are a good example. The children's services sections of county social services departments are another example. One advantage of these settings is the sense of professional cohesion and common identity they can offer. (See Figures 3–2 and 3–3.) Finally, there exists a middle ground between the host institution and the social work setting. A number of human services organizations, such as out-patient mental health centers and educational programs for teenage parents, utilize staff from a variety of disciplines, with no one group predominating. In those settings, professionals can work together in complementary ways to provide a broad set of services for clients.

Another traditional distinction between social work settings has been the division between public and private sponsorship. The growth of the public social services increased dramatically during and after the Depression. Federal involvement in mental health and veterans' programs has also expanded. And, of course, state and local governments continue to play an important role in providing health and human services. Alongside these exists the longstanding network of privately funded social agencies, including those sponsored by religious denominations. However, the distinction between public and private institutions obscures the great degree of interdependence between the two. Today, many public agencies contract out their services to private organizations; for example, a county social services department may delegate its adoptions work to a family and children's services agency. In addition, a number of private organizations receive state or federal funding for particular facets of their programs. A comparatively small but growing area for social work practice is the private for-profit organization, such as a for-profit nursing home or medical facility. A survey of NASW members indicated that 15 percent worked in such settings in 1987, compared to 3 percent in 1972 and 12 percent in 1982.[43]

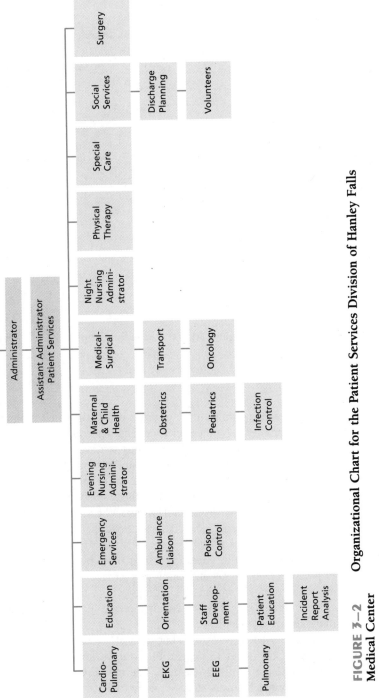

FIGURE 3–2   Organizational Chart for the Patient Services Division of Hanley Falls Medical Center

Note: The social work staff are located in the Social Services Department.

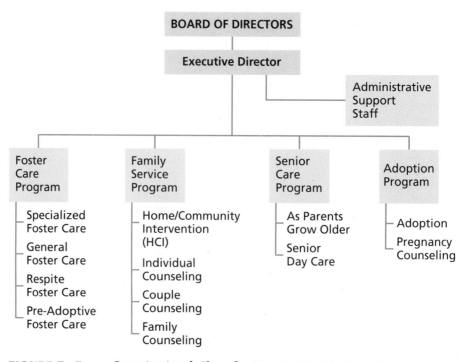

FIGURE 3–3   Organizational Chart for Utopian Family Organization, Inc.

Source: Courtesy of Danny Thompson and John Flynn, School of Social Work, Western Michigan University.

Finally, practice settings differ in terms of whether their programs are mandatory or voluntary for clients. While social work students are sometimes led to believe that all services are freely chosen by clients, many settings are required by law to constrain clients and to mandate their involvement in particular programs. These are the "involuntary services" referred to in Chapter 2 for people whose dependency stems from an inability to fulfill roles as defined by others. Obvious examples are juvenile homes and other parts of the penal system. However, clients are also involuntarily committed to mental institutions, ordered by courts to attend therapy sessions in marital counseling programs, and required to work with social workers in cases of child abuse. Even "voluntary" clients may be attending a substance abuse treatment group, for example, under pressure from family and employers. Greater attention to this voluntary-involuntary continuum within practice settings would help social workers grapple with issues surrounding authority, as well as increase their skills at intervening effectively with involuntary clients.

No matter what the setting, almost all of social work is practiced in a complex organization. Only about 15 percent of social workers engage in private practice, and not all of these are involved full-time. The importance of the organizational context for practice cannot be overstated. While not all settings are as highly bureaucratic as a Veteran's Administration hospital or a large county department of social services, most agencies (even small ones) contain some bureaucratic features. These include specialization of tasks, a hierarchy of authority, formal rules and guidelines, and documentation of activities and procedures—the famous "paperwork." Some practitioners view organizational rules and structure as obstructions to practice, and in fact, the desire to escape such perceived constraints has been one motivation for entering private practice. Others concentrate on realizing the organization's potential for providing equitable and effective services to clients and on developing their own ability to shape organizational goals.[44]

SALARIES AND JOB OPPORTUNITIES

Detailed, current, and comprehensive data on social work jobs and salaries is often hard to find. Much of the available data has been gathered by NASW, but this information needs to be viewed with some caution, since not all professionally trained social workers belong to the organization. United States Census Bureau information is even more problematic, because of the broad definition of "social worker" employed by the Bureau and the inclusion in the figures of a number of people without professional training. Data on undergraduate social work careers is particularly sketchy, because many BSW practitioners are not members of NASW and because government surveys do not differentiate between workers with BA degrees in other fields and those with BSWs.

However, a general picture of social work jobs and salaries can be gathered from recent studies. A 1986 NASW survey of members found a mean salary of $27,700 for those with an MSW, and $22,900 for BSWs. In 1988, according to the U.S. Department of Labor, full-time social workers, including those with graduate as well as undergraduate degrees, had median earnings of $22,000. The salary range was about $16,000 to $30,000 for BSWs, and $17,000 to $45,000 for MSWs.[45]

The number of job openings in social work varies from area to area. An undergraduate program in one state might report that 80 to 90 percent of its graduates have found social work positions. A program in another state might place only 60 percent (although most of the rest will be found working in non-social-work jobs or attending graduate school). MSW programs generally report high rates of employment for their graduates.

According to the 1986 NASW survey, the field of mental health employs the largest number of social workers, and in fact, social workers represent the largest single group of mental health professionals. Only about one percent of social workers surveyed were employed in public assistance positions. The majority of MSW workers worked in private, non-profit social service agencies, such as a Family and Children's Service. A recent study of BSW practitioners found that they were "overwhelmingly engaged in direct practice with diverse client populations and with a wide variety of problem situations." The primary areas in which BSWs work are children and youth, services to the aged, family service, health care, and mental health.[46]

As we noted at the beginning of this chapter, you will encounter a certain amount of skepticism regarding the ability of BSW graduates to find a "real" social work position. However, while a few areas in the field, such as school social work and intensive individual counseling, are normally closed to BSWs, most other types of social work have opportunities and challenges for practitioners at both the baccalaureate and masters levels.

SOCIAL WORK EDUCATION AND KNOWLEDGE FOR PRACTICE

Social work's breadth and diversity present a particular challenge to professional education. How can practitioners be trained in all the diverse aspects of the field? How can they develop an effective grounding in the dual perspective of individual behavior and environmental influence? A part of the solution is to use knowledge from many disciplines in educating social workers. Sociology, anthropology, psychology, political science, and economics are among the fields from which social work draws. This is why many social work undergraduate programs require students to take courses in the social sciences. Yet this use of knowledge from other areas can be problematic. A familiar complaint of social work students is "That sociology [or psychology or economics] course has too much theory in it and it doesn't have anything to do with social work!" Application of theoretical material to practice is a difficult task, especially if the material has been developed by another discipline. In addition, profession building seems to some social workers to call for an independent knowledge base. This might imply less use of other disciplines.

The desire for autonomy, in addition to conflicting goals of different fields, has led to tensions between social work and other disciplines, especially sociology.[47] Over the years, social work has struggled to deal with these dilemmas through the adaptation of knowledge borrowed from other fields as well as the development of its own body of theory and research. The discovery of unifying intellectual frameworks, such as social systems theory, has helped social work to bring some coherence to this diversity of facts and theories.

Social work research has been emphasized particularly in the field's doctoral programs, which have expanded greatly since the 1950s. Fifty-one schools now offer doctoral degrees in social work. These schools prepare students primarily for positions as teachers and researchers, although a few programs specialize in advanced clinical work. The BSW and MSW degrees equip individuals for beginning and advanced level professional practice. A final piece of the social work educational continuum is the two-year college degree in social work or human services, which prepares students for work as social work aides or technicians in mental health, social services, or similar settings.

CURRENT PROFESSIONAL ISSUES

The several levels of social work education are often seen as relating to a continuum of practice. Defining the steps in this continuum has been a difficult task for social work, yet it seems a necessary response to the need to staff a large number and variety of social work positions. Although over the years many professional leaders have stressed that social work jobs should be filled by those trained on the master's level, MSW programs have never produced enough graduates to meet staffing requirements.

Social work has faced a peculiar situation in which many of those bearing the occupational title are in fact college graduates with no specific social work training. Attempts to rectify this situation by providing professional training on the undergraduate level have led to confusion about the differences between MSW and BSW practitioners. Building an educational and practice continuum is one way to clarify the abilities and skills levels of practitioners with different backgrounds. The National Association of Social Workers has developed such a continuum, which attempts to differentiate between tasks carried out by master's level practitioners and those engaged in by baccalaureate social workers. Although this is an important step in clarifying practice, guidelines such as these are necessarily general and abstract. Moreover, they may not always represent the actualities of practice. BSW social workers, for example, have been found to engage in more administrative and supervisory activity than the classification of their responsibilities would suggest.[48]

The movement to license social work represents another effort to organize and control practice. In part, it reflects the professional tendency toward gate-keeping, or restricting entry to a field. Social workers with a more democratic view of professionalism criticize the gate-keeping aspect of the licensing movement, but others argue that licensing signifies public sanction for the profession and offers protection to clients. As of January, 1990, forty-seven states had developed some form of legal regulation of social work. The type of regulation varies from state to state and includes both certification (in which the use of the title "social worker" is limited to those with special knowledge and skills) and actual licensure (in which the state spells out specific requirements and limits the actual practice of social work to those meeting the requirements).[49]

Pursuing a parallel, nongovernmental approach to controlling practice, NASW has established a voluntary certification program, the Academy of Certified Social Workers. NASW members may belong to the Academy and put the letters ACSW after their names if they possess the master's degree, have two years of post-MSW experience, and have satisfactorily passed a qualifying exam. The program for MSW social workers has existed for a number of years. Recently, an Academy of Certified Baccalaureate Social Workers was created, which uses two years of post-BSW work as the experience requirement and also includes an exam. In addition, in response to lobbying by clinical social workers for licensing or other forms of recognition for their functions, NASW has developed a Qualified Clinical Social Worker credential which offers yet another set of letters: QCSW. While this array of credentials and letters may be a bit bewildering, our discussion underscores both social work's concern to increase its professional standing and the existence of a variety of interest groups within the field.[50]

SOCIAL WORK IN THE LARGER FIELD OF SOCIAL WELFARE

Social work's interest in continuum and licensing issues reflects the profession's need to define itself and its role within a larger social welfare system. A number of occupations have some relationship to this system, and each struggles to maintain a professional identity and control over a particular domain or realm of practice. These tendencies toward competition are countered by the desire to help clients, which often means cooperation with members of other disciplines. Thus, social workers are challenged to develop positive working relations with nurses, psychologists, planners, and others. Much of current practice is multidisciplinary and ranges from interdisciplinary treatment teams in mental health facilities to ongoing consultation between teachers and social workers in school settings. Social workers bring unique skills and perspectives to these joint endeavors: an expertise in helping clients utilize a broad network of social welfare services, an appreciation of the individual's right to self-determination, and most significantly, an ability to focus on both individual and social change in dealing with issues of dependency.

PERSPECTIVES ON PRACTICE

Present-day social work continues to encompass several ideological perspectives on practice. The conservative approach, bolstered in the 1980s by the philosophies of the Reagan administration and reinforced in the 1990s under President Bush, holds that individuals, families, and communities, rather than the federal government, should take the major responsibility for dealing with social problems. These problems, including poverty, out-of-wedlock births, and substance abuse, are defined primarily in individual terms. That is, poverty stems from a person's unwillingness to work, and hunger arises from a lack of knowledge of community programs which provide food. While few social workers adopt this position in its entirety, a number have embraced another tenet of recent conservatism: a focus on the private marketplace as the provider of social services. Thus, social workers can currently be found working in private, for-profit nursing homes, drug treatment centers, and similar organizations, or conducting their own private counseling practice.

Social workers who see themselves as liberals generally argue against both the individualization of social problems and the growth of a "privatized" social welfare system. They view individual problems as being related both to personal factors and to larger structural difficulties in our country. Such structural problems include wide-

An increasingly common sight in America, homelessness is one of the many problems social workers must deal with. How they deal with it depends in part on their political perspective.

spread unemployment and the lack of opportunities for women and minorities to advance into meaningful roles in society (hence, the often dead-end position of the minority teenage mother who sees few options in life other than childbearing). While liberal social workers support individual and local community involvement in problem solving, they tend to stress the necessity for broader governmental intervention, particularly on the federal level. They deplore the breakup of the federally supported system of social welfare benefits and guidelines that was begun during the Reagan presidency.

Finally, radicals within social work continue to push for greater client involvement in the planning and provision of services, more attention to the social control function of social welfare, and fundamental changes in social and economic structures. For example, radical social workers working with the homeless might argue that homeless families should be given a chance to develop and run cooperative low-income housing units. Such social workers would be publicly critical of what they would term city merchants' efforts at social control, such as "sweeping the homeless off of downtown streets" and relegating them to large shelters. Finally, radical practitioners would draw connections between homelessness and the market economy's stress on the development of profitable luxury housing rather than on the provision of decent accommodations for people with modest incomes.

CONCLUSION

Social work, like other professions, contains conflict and diversity (although social work is probably broader and more diverse than most). One internal debate centers on whether dependency is caused by individual or broad social factors. Out of this debate has arisen a dual focus on individual and social change, and on the personal and the environmental factors in social problems. The liberal and radical perspectives express this duality most clearly. Even at the conservative end of the continuum, however, social workers acknowledge some degree of external influence on individual difficulties.

This consciousness of an interrelatedness between what C. Wright Mills terms "private troubles" and "public issues" is one of social work's greatest strengths. In fact, this sense of the tie between individual and environment constitutes the profession's major contribution to the social welfare arena.[51]

ENDNOTES

1. Ernest Greenwood, "Attributes of a Profession," *Social Work* 2 (July 1957): 45–55; William J. Goode, "The Theoretical Limits of Professionalization," in *The Semi-Professions and Their Organization,* Amitai Etzioni, ed. (New York: Free Press, 1969), 266–313; Wilbert E. Moore, *The Professions: Roles and Rules* (New York: Russell Sage, 1970).
2. Harold Wilensky, "The Professionalization of Everyone?" *American Journal of Sociology* 70 (September 1964): 137–158; Jeffrey Berlant, *Professions and Monopoly* (Berkeley, CA: University of California Press, 1975); Eliot Freidson, *The Professions and Their Prospects* (Beverly Hills, CA: Sage, 1973); Rue Bucher and Anselm Strauss, "Professions in Process," *American Journal of Sociology* 66 (January 1961): 325–334.
3. Leslie Leighninger, *Social Work: Search for Identity* (Westport, CT: Greenwood Press, 1987) is a history

of social work based on the process model of professionalism. See also Gary Lowe, "Social Work's Professional Mistake: Confusing Status for Control and Losing Both," *Journal of Sociology and Social Welfare 14* (June 1987): 187–206.

4. Greenwood, "Attributes of a Profession," 54; Nina Toren, *Social Work: The Case of a Semi-Profession* (Beverly Hills, CA: Sage, 1972), 37–42; Neil Gilbert, Henry Miller, and Harry Specht, *An Introduction to Social Work Practice* (Englewood Cliffs, NJ: Prentice-Hall, 1980), 14–16.

5. The use of professional domain as a more satisfactory model for understanding professionalism than the process or trait models is further detailed in Philip Popple, "The Social Work Profession: A Reconceptualization," *Social Service Review 59* (December 1985): 560–574.

6. James Leiby, *A History of Social Welfare and Social Work in the United States* (New York: Columbia University Press, 1978), 340–358; Willard C. Richan and Allan R. Mendelsohn, *Social Work: The Unloved Profession* (New York: New Viewpoints, 1973), 126–162.

7. Peter Leonard, "Towards a Paradigm for Radical Practice," in Ron Bailey and Mike Brake, eds., *Radical Social Work* (New York: Pantheon Books, 1975), 46–61; Jeffrey Galper, *Social Work Practice: A Radical Perspective* (Englewood Cliffs, NJ: Prentice-Hall, 1980), 3–15, 68–88; Ann Withorn, *Serving the People: Social Services and Social Change* (New York: Columbia University Press, 1984), 121–158; Michael B. Katz, *In the Shadow of the Poorhouse* (New York: Basic Books, 1986), 164–167; Mimi Abramovitz, *Regulating the Lives of Women* (Boston: South End Press, 1988); Betty Reid Mandell, ed., *Welfare in America* (Englewood Cliffs, NJ: Prentice-Hall, 1975).

8. Malcolm Payne, *Modern Social Work Theory: A Critical Introduction* (Chicago: Lyceum Books, 1991), 201–217.

9. For a more complete discussion of these debates as they affected social work between 1930 and 1960, see Leighninger, *Social Work: Search for Identity.*

10. David Rothman, *The Discovery of the Asylum: Social Order and Disorder in the New Republic* (Boston: Little, Brown, 1971).

11. Leiby, *A History of Social Welfare and Social Work in the United States,* 344; Katz, *In the Shadow of the Poorhouse,* 27–28.

12. Blanche D. Coll, *Perspectives in Public Welfare* (Washington, D.C.: U.S. Department of Health, Education, and Welfare, 1969), 40–62; Roy Lubove, *The Professional Altruist* (New York: Atheneum, 1969), 22–54; Katz, *In the Shadow of the Poorhouse,* 66–84.

13. Katz, *In the Shadow of the Poorhouse,* 71.

14. "The Need for a Training School in Applied Philanthropy," National Conference of Charities and Correction, *Proceedings* (1897), 181–188.

15. An excellent discussion of Addams and the settlement movement can be found in Allen F. Davis, *American Heroine: The Life and Legend of Jane Addams* (New York: Oxford University Press, 1973).

16. William I. Cole, "Introduction," in *The City Wilderness,* Robert A. Woods, ed. (Boston: Houghton Mifflin, 1898), 1–9; Barbara Solomon, *Ancestors and Immigrants* (New York: John Wiley, 1956), 14–143; Allen F. Davis, *Spearheads for Reform: The Social Settlements and the Progressive Movement, 1890–1914* (New York: Oxford University Press, 1967), 3–25.

17. Christopher Lasch, *The New Radicalism in America* (New York: Alfred A. Knopf, 1965), xiv–xv, 141–180.

18. Clarke Chambers, "Women in the Creation of the Profession of Social Work," *Social Service Review 60* (March 1986): 8–12.

19. Walter Trattner, *From Poor Law to Welfare State,* 4th ed. (New York: The Free Press, 1989), 154.

20. Abraham Flexner, "Is Social Work a Profession?" National Conference of Charities and Correction, *Proceedings* (1915), 576–590; Lubove, *The Professional Altruist,* 118–156.

21. Leighninger, *Social Work: Search for Identity,* 7–26.

22. Lubove, *The Professional Altruist,* 157–167.

23. Lester A. Salamon, "Of Market Failure, Voluntary Failure, and Third-Party Government: Toward a Theory of Government-Nonprofit Relations in the Modern Welfare State," *Shifting the Debate: Public/Private Sector Relations in the Modern Welfare State,* Susan A. Ostrander and Stuart Langton, eds. (New Brunswick, NJ: Transaction Books, 1987), 31–32; Katz, *In the Shadow of the Poorhouse,* 42–46.

24. Leighninger, *Social Work: Search for Identity,* 10–11; Wilma Peebles Wilkins, "Black Women and American Social Welfare: The Life of Fredericka Douglass Sprague Perry," *Affilia 4* (Spring 1989), 33–44; Anne Firor Scott, "Most Invisible of All: Black Women's Voluntary Associations," *The Journal of Southern History 56* (February 1990), 3, 22.

25. Leighninger, *Social Work: Search for Identity,* 15–16; David M. Austin, *A History of Social Work Education* (Austin, TX: School of Social Work, University of Texas at Austin, Social Work Education Monograph Series, 1986), 1–9; Gary Lowe, "The Graduate-Only

Debate in Social Work Education, 1937–1959, and Its Consequences for the Profession," *Journal of Social Work Education 21* (Fall 1985): 52–62.

26. Leighninger, *Social Work: Search for Identity,* 27–36.

27. Porter Lee, "Social Work as Cause and Function," National Conference of Social Work, *Proceedings* (1929), 3–20.

28. William Bremer, *Depression Winters: New York Social Workers and the New Deal* (Philadelphia, PA: Temple University Press, 1984), 63–75, 88–113; Leighninger, *Social Work: Search for Identity,* 52–68.

29. Trattner, *From Poor Law to Welfare State,* 59, 78–79, 195–197.

30. Bertha Reynolds, *An Uncharted Journey* (New York: Citadel Press, 1963), 135–187. Jacob Fisher's book, *The Response of Social Work to the Depression* (Cambridge, MA: Schenkman, 1980) is a detailed description of the movement by one of its leaders.

31. Marian Mahaffey, "Political Action in Social Work," in *Encyclopedia of Social Work,* 18th ed., Vol. II (New York: NASW, 1987), 283–293; Karen S. Haynes and James S. Mickelson, *Affecting Change,* 2nd ed. (New York: Longman, 1991).

32. Quoted in George Martin, *Madame Secretary: Frances Perkins* (Boston: Houghton Mifflin, 1976), 354–355.

33. Leighninger, *Social Work: Search for Identity,* 86, 92–94, 125–143.

34. Chambers, "Women in the Creation of the Profession of Social Work," 1–4, 22–24.

35. Elaine C. Spaulding, *Statistics on Social Work Education in the United States: 1990* (Alexandria, VA: Council on Social Work Education, 1991), 23, 27–28.

36. Raymond Plant, *Social and Moral Theory in Casework* (London: Routledge and Kegan Paul, 1970), 6–34.

37. Seth Faison, Jr., "Teen-ager Found Chained in Bronx," *New York Times* (September 15, 1991), 184.

38. M. Vincentia Joseph, *Developing and Teaching Models of Ethical Decision Making* (School of Social Work, Loyola University of Chicago, 1988); see also Frederic G. Reamer, *Ethical Dilemmas in Social Service* (New York: Columbia University Press, 1982), 24–25.

39. Florence Hollis, *Casework: A Psychosocial Therapy,* 2nd ed. (New York: Random House, 1972), 10.

40. Karen Orloff Kaplan, "Recent Trends in Case Management," *Encyclopedia of Social Work, 18th Edition, 1990 Supplement* (Silver Spring, MD: NASW Press, 1990), 60–77.

41. Nancy K. Carroll, "Three-Dimensional Model of Social Work Practice," *Social Work 22* (September 1977): 428–432.

42. Leslie Leighninger, "The Generalist-Specialist Debate in Social Work, *Social Service Review 54* (March 1980): 267–273; Paul Stuart, "School Social Work as a Professional Segment: Continuity in Transitional Times," *Social Work in Education 8* (Spring 1986): 141–143.

43. Leon F. Williams and June G. Hopps, "The Social Work Labor Force: Current Perspectives and Future Trends," *Encyclopedia of Social Work, 18th Edition, 1990 Supplement* (Silver Spring, MD: NASW Press, 1990), 290.

44. Phil Brown, "Social Workers in Private Practice: What Are They Really Doing?" *Clinical Social Work Journal 18* (Winter 1990): 407–421; Robert Pruger, "The Good Bureaucrat," *Social Work 18* (July 1973): 26–32; Rino J. Patti and Herman Resnick, "Changing the Agency from Within," *Social Work 17* (July 1972): 48–57; Edward J. Pawlak, "Organizational Tinkering," *Social Work 21* (September 1976): 376–380.

45. Williams and Hopps, "The Social Work Labor Force," 292–296; "Social Workers," *Occupational Outlook Handbook: 1990–91 Edition* (U.S. Department of Labor, Bureau of Labor Statistics, Bulletin, April 1990), 118.

46. Mary Ann Suppes and Carolyn Cressy Wells, *The Social Work Experience: An Introduction to the Profession* (New York: McGraw-Hill, 1991), 393–394.

47. Leighninger, *Social Work: Search for Identity,* 151–170.

48. Natalie Edelman-Bastian and Leslie Leighninger, "The Value and Marketability of Undergraduate Social Work Education: Alumni Perspectives," *Journal of Applied Social Sciences 7* (Spring/Summer 1983): 152–154; Michael S. Kolevson and Marilyn A. Biggerstaff, "Functional Differentiation of Job Demands: Dilemmas Confronting the Continuum in Social Work Education," *Journal of Education for Social Work 19* (Spring 1983): 26–34.

49. David A. Hardcastle, "Legal Regulation of Social Work," *Encyclopedia of Social Work, 18th Edition, 1990 Supplement* (Silver Spring, MD: NASW Press, 1990), 203–217.

50. Mark G. Battle, "National Association of Social Workers," *Encyclopedia of Social Work, 18th Edition, 1990 Supplement* (Silver Spring, MD: NASW Press, 1990), 231–233; Ann Farwell, "The History and Metamorphosis of the National Registry of Health Care Providers in Clinical Social Work," *Clinical Social Work Journal 16* (Winter 1988): 430–439.

51. C. Wright Mills, *The Sociological Imagination* (New York: Oxford University Press, 1959), 8–11.

C·H·A·P·T·E·R
four

Religion and
Social Work

An interesting and little researched question is "Why do people choose social work as a career?" Although, as discussed in the last chapter, the career prospects are nowhere near as bleak as popularly believed, there is little doubt that few people choose social work for the money. People whose main career objective is to make a lot of money generally choose business, law, or perhaps engineering. Social work, we presume, is chosen for other reasons.

Historically, one of the major reasons for choosing social work as a career has been personal religious belief. There is speculation among social work educators, although it is not yet supported by formal data, that the number of students choosing to major in social work because of religious commitment is increasing. At the school of one of the authors an essay is required of students entering the social work program; in the essay students are asked to explain their reasons for choosing social work as a major. From a steadily increasing number of students we are receiving statements like the following:

> I believe my main qualification as a social work candidate has been my life because I've been where a lot of people needing services are today, and with God's grace and a lot of help, I hope to become what I dreamed of being . . . a social worker.

Another student wrote

> As I sit back and look over the last few years, I can honestly say there is only one major reason why I am in social work. I have been called into the field because of my love for people and their needs, along with my whole hearted desire to serve God.

The fact that a person chooses social work out of a desire to live his or her faith is commendable and in most cases desirable. However, the relationship between social work and religion is not without problems. Although social work grew out of organized religion, during the course of this century it has become increasingly secularized. People with strong religious values sometimes find it difficult to subscribe to certain social work values. For example, one of the students cited earlier also said in her essay "One issue that I have difficulty in is being accepting of all people, especially homosexuals. I believe this lifestyle is against the will of God and therefore have difficulty condoning it." As a professional social worker, this person will be expected to work with all kinds of people, homosexuals included, and to do so in a nonjudgmental and accepting manner, although there is no requirement that she personally approve of the lifestyle. The potential conflict between the values currently dominant in the social work profession and the religious values of a number of individual social workers can be problematical for both the individual social workers and the profession. The individual worker in a secular agency is often worried that he or she will be required to compromise his or her own values, and the agency is concerned that religiously oriented workers will use their position within the agency to attempt to convert clients to their belief system.

In this chapter we discuss the relationship between social work and religion, as well as some of the problems inherent in this relationship. We will conclude that these problems are by no means unsolvable. The student cited earlier was well on the way to solving her own problem in this area. She concluded her essay with the following statement:

> This area I am still working on. Besides acceptance being important to social work, it is even more important as a Christian to love *everyone*: even those different than myself. I John 4:20 is why I see such a need to love *all* people, "If anyone says, 'I love God' yet hates his brother, he is a liar. For anyone who does not love his brother whom he has seen, cannot love God, whom he has not seen."

THE RELIGIOUS ROOTS OF SOCIAL WELFARE

One of the leading scholars in the area of social work and religion, Alan Keith-Lucas, points out that the desire to help someone is not, as far as we know, instinctive.[1] The very desire to help others and, therefore, the beginning of social welfare, seems to have developed as a part of religion. Almost all religions have obligated their followers to engage in acts of charity, sometimes only to members of their sect and sometimes to anyone in need.[2] All major religions have to some extent stressed responsibility for one's fellows, kindness or justice to the needy, and self-fulfillment through service.

Early Egyptian Roots

Egyptian civilization is the oldest culture to have left a substantial written record. It is therefore used here to illustrate the early development of religious injunctions regarding social welfare. Morris points out that a similar evolution was taking place in Assyrian, Mesopotamian, and Chinese societies.[3] The early Egyptian holy book, called the "Book of the Dead," was a group of writings collected around 3500 B.C. In the book is a list of seven acts of mercy, including relief of hunger, thirst, nakedness, prisoners, help for the stranger, and care for the sick and the dead.[4] The book also contains an early version of what we now call the Golden Rule, "Do to the doer in order to cause him to do [for thee]."[5] The "Book of the Dead" contains mainly negative injunctions; that is, it focuses more on not doing harm than on actively doing good. It suggests behaviors that should be avoided because doing so will assure a good life after death. Writings buried with the dead for the apparent purpose of providing evidence that the person had lived a correct life contain statements such as "I have not done violence to a poor man"; "I have not made anyone sick or weak"; and "I have not taken milk from the mouths of children." There is also some evidence of positive injunctions such as "I gave bread to the hungry, clothed the naked, I ferried him who had no boat."[6]

Jewish Roots

In Jewish thought there is no concept of salvation or damnation, so thoughts of a good afterlife did not provide any motive for charitable behavior. However, it was believed that once a year there should be a Day of Atonement in which people would be afflicted with earthly torments—flood, fire, plague, death, and the like—in punishment for their misdeeds. Repentence, prayer, and charity were ways a person could avoid the evil decree. Thus, while charitable behavior was not believed to assure a good afterlife as the Egyptians thought, it could at least help one escape some earthly torments.

Probably the most significant advance of Jewish charitable thought over Egyptian thought was the assertion that individuals have a positive obligation to perform acts of helping and doing good for others. For example:

> If there is among you a poor man, one of your brethren, in any of your towns within your land which the Lord your God gives you, you shall not harden your heart or shut your hand against your poor brother, but you shall open your hand to him, and lend him sufficient for his need, whatever it may be. Take heed lest there be a base thought in your heart, and you say, "The seventh year, the year of release is near," and your eye be hostile to your poor brother, and you give him nothing, and he cry to the Lord against you, and it be sin in you. You shall give to him freely, and your heart shall not be grudging when you give to him because for this the Lord your God will bless you in all your work and in all that you undertake. [Deuteronomy 15:7–10]

The Egyptian concept of charity mainly means the avoidance of doing harm to others. The Jewish concept added the obligation to do positive acts of good.

Interestingly, the Hebrew word *Tsedakah,* which has generally been translated as *charity,* actually could more accurately be translated as *justice*.[7] From this can be inferred that not only did people have an obligation to help those in need but also the needy had a right to help. Charitable acts were to be done simply because they were the right thing to do and the giver should expect no repayment from the recipient. The Jewish philosopher Maimonides outlined eight degrees of charity, from lowest to highest.

> Give, but with reluctance and regret. This is the gift of the hand but not of the heart.
>
> The second is to give cheerfully, but not proportionately to the distress of the sufferer.
>
> The third is to give cheerfully and proportionately, but not until we are solicited.
>
> The fourth is to give cheerfully and proportionately, and even unsolicited; but to put it in the poor man's hand, thereby exciting in him the painful emotion of shame.
>
> The fifth is to give charity in such a way that the distressed may receive the bounty and know their benefactor, without being known to him.
>
> The sixth, which rises still higher, is to know the objects of our bounty, but remain unknown to them.
>
> The seventh is still more meritorious, namely, to bestow charity in such a way that the benefactor may not know the relieved persons, nor they the name of their benefactor.
>
> Lastly, the eighth and most meritorious of all, is to anticipate charity by preventing poverty; i.e., to assist a reduced person so that he may earn an honest livelihood and not be forced to the dreadful alternative of holding up his hand for charity.[8]

From these factors, along with the Ten Commandments, prophetic exhortations, the Proverbs, and general moral teachings, the Jews developed a number of social welfare practices. Among them were hospitable reception of strangers; education of orphans; redemption of lawbreakers; endowment of marriages; visitation of the ill and infirm; burial of the dead; consolation of the bereaved; and care of widows, slaves, divorcees, and the aged.

Christian Roots

To the moral teachings and concept of justice from the Old Testament, the early Christians added an emphasis on love and compassion. The "theological virtues" were set forth as faith, hope, and charity, the greatest of these being charity.[9] The basis of the Christian approach to social welfare is generally considered to be in Jesus' depiction of the welcome to the righteous as blessed inheritors of the Kingdom.

> "For I was hungry and you gave me food, I was thirsty and you gave me drink, I was a stranger and you welcomed me, I was naked and you clothed me, I was sick and you visited me, I was in prison and you came to me." Then the righteous will answer him, "Lord, when did we see thee hungry and feed thee, or thirsty and give thee drink? And when did we see thee a stranger and welcome thee, or naked and clothe thee? And when did we see thee sick or in prison and visit thee?" And the King will answer them, "Truly, I say to you, as you did it to one of the least of these my brethren, you did it to me." [Matthew 25:35–40]

In Christian doctrine Jesus is seen as the revelation of God and as the model which believers are to follow and emulate. The teachings of Jesus centered around the law of obedient love, which takes its cue from the nature of God rather than from the worthiness of any other object. Miller contends that the Good Samaritan parable, which emphasizes this love response, has probably done more to encourage humanitarian social welfare than any other single influence in all of history.[10]

A somewhat different, although not conflicting rationale for charity is found in the writings of St. Paul. As discussed by Douglas

> St. Paul, in his famous description of the virtue of charity, implies an almost total merging of the interests of the individual with those of the collectivity of which he or she is a member. In the Church of Corinth, he was faced with the fairly typical problem of a collectivity riven by doubts, jealousies, and schisms. His principal response was to elaborate the analogy between a collectivity, the church, and a human body. "A man's body is all one although it has a number of different organs and all this multitude of organs goes to make up one body, . . . The eye cannot say to the hand, I have no need of thee." [I Corinthians 12:15–21] The diversity is to be prized. After all, "if the whole were one single organ, what would become of the body?" Charity is the unifying force: "God has established a harmony in the body—all the different parts of it were to make each other's welfare their common care." [Ephesians 4:16]. He follows the analogy immediately with the famous description and praise of charity of Chapter Thirteen. The same point, also in relation to the analogy of the body, is made more succinctly in the Letter to the Ephesians: "Thus each limb receiving the active power it needs; it [the body] achieves its natural growth building itself up through charity." [Ephesians 4:16][11]

Thus, charity was not only viewed as a theological virtue but also as a practical necessity to maintain the organic unity of the church and community.

The early Christian church, and the generations which followed, took seriously the command of Jesus to carry out the expression of love which occurs so frequently in the New Testament. Since its earliest days the church has engaged in at least twelve areas of social ministry: care of widows, orphans, sick, poor, disabled, prisoners, captives, slaves, victims of calamity; burial of the poor; provision of employment services, and meals for the needy.[12] Because the roots of the Christian church are in Judaism, the lists of charitable activities of the two groups are very similar.

THE RELIGIOUS ROOTS OF ORGANIZED SOCIAL WORK

Because the philosophical basis for social welfare was largely based on religious teachings, it is not surprising that the earliest forms of organized social work also had their roots in the church. Even before the rise of modern European states, the church was providing social services of a primitive sort. The early church provided alms to the poor, shelter for the homeless, and care and comfort for the sick; monasteries often served as all-purpose social service agencies acting as hospitals, homes for the aged, orphanages, and travelers' aid stations. However, as discussed in Chapter 2, it was not until the onset of industrialization and urbanization, when the informal helping systems of the church and family began to break down, that organized social welfare services began to emerge. The natural first step was for the church to begin to formalize what it had previously done on an informal basis.

As we noted in Chapter 3, the profession of social work is generally considered to have emerged from three general movements. These are: the Charity Organization Society movement, the settlement house movement, and a third, less clearly defined movement, the development of institutions to deal with a whole range of social problems. All of these had their period of most rapid growth during the nineteenth century, and all grew out of the church.

Churches and the Charity Organization Society Movement

We have already described the impact of the Charity Organization Society movement (COS) on the development of social work as a profession. Now we will consider its religious roots. The earliest development of the COS has been traced to Thomas Chalmers, a minister of the Church of Scotland. Chalmers was called to Glasgow in 1814 to be the minister of one of its most important churches. Appalled by the poverty he witnessed in the parish of St. John's, and detesting the Poor Law, he set out to do something about it. What he did was to divide the parish into twenty-five units and

The provision of social services is one of the main ways in which churches express their concern for worldly problems.

to assign the direction of each unit to a deacon of his church. Each unit was composed of approximately fifty families who had requested aid from the church. The deacon in charge was to get to know each of the families, thoroughly investigate their situation, and help them solve the problems that had led to their state of dependency.[13] Chalmers is credited with conceiving the individualized approach and the person-centered philosophy which have become the central tenets of social work practice.

In 1819, five years after Chalmers began his work in Glasgow, a Unitarian clergyman, Joseph Tuckerman, was beginning similar work in Boston. Until failing health caused his retirement in 1833, Tuckerman pursued many projects in his efforts to better the condition of the poor. "Housing, wages, education, delinquency, and relief all occupied his attention. From his 'Poor's Purse,' derived from contributions from wealthy supporters of his ministry, he gave charitable assistance to the needy . . ."[14] In 1834, one year after his official retirement, Tuckerman began an association of over twenty benevolent societies operating in Boston for the purpose of cooperation and coordination of services to the poor.

The Charity Organization Society movement, widely recognized as the parent of organized social work, began in England in 1869 and in the United States in 1877, building upon the work of Chalmers and Tuckerman. In the United States a cleric was once again credited with the development of the COS, this time an Episcopalian, the Reverend S. Humphries Gurteen of Buffalo, New York. Gurteen was alarmed by what he perceived as the chaotic and indiscriminant approach to poor relief in Buffalo. He traveled to London and observed the work of the Charity Organization Society there; then he returned to the United States to implement a similar system. His basic goal was to set up a rational, objective system of poor relief, emphasizing the investigation of each individual case and the coordination of the activities of all charitable agencies to avoid duplication of services. In 1882 Gurteen stated the basic philosophy of the Charity Organization Societies:

> If left to themselves . . . [the poor] will inevitably sink lower and lower, till perchance they end their course in suicide or felony. If . . . our charity is not tempered by judgment, they will inevitably learn to be *dependent* . . . To avoid these two extremes, both of which are fatal, is the grand object of the Charity Organization Society. It views man as God has made him, with capabilities of manliness and self-respect and holy ambition. . . . Its axiom, accordingly, is, "HELP THE POOR TO HELP THEMSELVES."[15]

Unlike the work of Chalmers and Tuckerman, the COS movement was an immediate success. Within twenty years virtually every city of any size in the country had a Charity Organization Society, or an Associated Charities as they were sometimes called. Interestingly, although begun by a minister and often directed and staffed by clergy, the charity organization societies always viewed themselves as secular and put their faith in science and professionalism, rather than in religion as the solution to social problems.

Churches and the Settlement House Movement

The settlement house movement began in Victorian England as part of a broad attempt to preserve human and spiritual values in an age of urbanization and industrialization. The first settlement was Toynbee Hall, founded in 1884 by Canon Samuel A. Barnett. Barnett's idea was to have university men move into the worst area of London and get to know the people living there. He felt that university men were cut off from the real work of the world, and that they were restless and needed to do something useful. On the other hand, he felt that working men were cut off from culture and civilization. Toynbee Hall was strongly Protestant in nature, and Barnett hoped that it would result in a spiritual reawakening in both the laborer and the university man.

Although it was founded in England by a clergyman and was strongly religious in nature, the settlement movement was imported to the United States by laypeople who had little interest in its religious aspects. Stanton Coit, a young American who had just finished a Ph.D. at the University of Berlin, visited Toynbee Hall in 1886, was greatly impressed with the concept, and returned to New York to found the Neighborhood Guild, the first settlement in the United States. Jane Addams visited Toynbee Hall in 1888 and returned to Chicago to found Hull House, the most famous settlement in the world. Neighborhood Guild and Hull House, like many settlements in the United States, were secular from the very beginning, and their focus was social change rather than spiritual goals.

Although historians have generally characterized settlements as largely secular in nature, it has always been recognized that a number grew from religious roots. Probably the best known is Chicago Commons, founded by the Reverend Graham Taylor, who was the first professor of "Christian Sociology" at Chicago Theological Seminary. He founded the settlement in 1894, partially as a social laboratory for his students. Although Taylor's work is almost always characterized in the most positive possible light, the religious roots of the settlements are not always regarded so kindly. Mohl and Betten, for example, have written

> [M]ost settlements were religious missions that reflected, acted upon, and transmitted the values and attitudes of the larger society; beyond their proselytizing activities, they adopted a derogatory view of ethnic traditions and assumed that their proper role was that of Americanizing the immigrant with all possible speed.[16]

The Church and the Institutional Roots of Social Work

Probably the most popular way of dealing with dependency during the early years of social welfare was the establishment of institutions, such as orphanages, poorhouses, and asylums, to deal with the problem. The church had a leading role in establishing this approach to social problems and, ironically, it had a leading role in seeking alternatives once the shortcomings of institutions became known.

Residential institutions for children and the aged in America were initially established by Catholic orders; the first was an orphanage opened by the Ursuline Sisters in New Orleans in 1727. "These early Catholic institutions were American transplants from established institutional networks maintained by Catholic sisterhoods in Europe. The European sisterhoods continued to be a source of the development of specialized residential institutions in this country, including such innovations as institutions providing protective care for girls."[17]

A number of institutions were established by Lutherans, a group not often associated with early developments in social welfare. The person associated with the beginning of these activities was a German pastor, Johann Hinrich Wichern. Wichern worked in Hamburg's poorest area and became concerned about the great problems he was seeing that were related to industrialization and immigration. His first project was the opening of a home for delinquent boys, *Das Rauhe Haus* (the rescue home). Within a short time, people trained by Wichern had established "rescue homes" for alcoholics, the poor, seamen, and inner city dwellers. Wichern's work, which came to be known as the "inner mission" of the church, was carried over into American Lutheranism by William Alfred Passavant. Passavant was called to Pittsburgh as a pastor in 1844. Shortly after coming to Pittsburgh, he visited Europe and observed the work of Wichern's followers. He returned to the United States and established a large number of orphanages, hospitals, homes for the aged, and other "rescue home" type services.[18]

It was not long before the shortcomings of institutions, especially those for children, were recognized. These institutions tended to be overcrowded, understaffed, impersonal, and generally ineffective in meeting the developmental needs of the residents. Thus, people began to look for alternatives almost as soon as the institutions were built. One of the earliest and best known alternatives came from a churchman, the Reverend Charles Loring Brace, who established the Children's Aid Society in New York City in 1853. Brace's main idea was to remove orphan children from the streets of the city and, instead of sending them to an institution, to send them to the midwest where they could be cared for by families. As will be discussed in greater detail in Chapter 9, Brace's program was subjected to harsh criticism both from his contemporaries and from historians. However, he should at least be credited with an idea that led to some real advances in child welfare.

As the preceding brief review indicates, the interest of social workers in religion, and the interest of religious people in social work, is hardly a new one. F. Ernest Johnson has gone so far as to say that the church is the "mother of social work."[19] Reid argues that virtually all social work in the voluntary sector originated from religion. He states that voluntary social services either currently operate under religious auspices (sectarian services), or else they began under religious auspices and over time have become secularized. It is to this secularization of social work that we now turn.

The Secularization of Social Work

Although religion has provided the philosophical basis of most social welfare activities, and most modern social work agencies can trace their origins to religion, social work has always had a strong secular leaning. There is no evidence that S. Humphries Gurteen or Charles Loring Brace ever intended for their agencies to be anything but secular. Graham Taylor envisioned his "Christian sociology" as more firmly rooted in science than theology. Social work has evolved so far from its religious roots that Spencer observed in 1961 that ". . . social work literature [is] almost totally lacking in any treatment of the subject of man's spiritual needs and practices and their interrelatedness with his other needs and adjustment."[20] Marty observed in 1980 "Secularization has many meanings, but at least it includes [among social workers] the notion that religion in both ideological and institutional senses has little part in informing the world of social work. . . . most of the time the literature of the profession genially and serenely ignores religion."[21]

Why did social work, with its clear and strong religious roots, become so secular so quickly? There appear to be a number of factors that worked simultaneously over the past century to accomplish this end. The most important factors are the general secularization of society, the growth of government within the field of social welfare, and (more speculatively) the development of the New Left and student movement of the 1960s and early 1970s.

The Secularization of Society   When we discuss the secularization of social work, it has to be viewed in the context of a more general secularization of society. Scholars working in the area of the sociology of religion identify two general understandings of this phenomenon. The first is the assertion that beginning in the nineteenth century and continuing until the present time

> there has been a displacement of religious interpretations of reality and religious orientations toward life by an orientation that seeks explanations for and justifications of human behavior and other phenomena in scientific and rational terms. One has undergone a secularization process if, for example, instead of asserting that marriages are made in heaven and for eternity, he or she says that marriages are made by human beings, in time, on the basis of propinquity, and in response to biological and psychological needs.[22]

Because of the trend of secularization, people see fewer things as being explained in terms of "God's will," and they seek scientific, rational explanations for more of life's events.

The secularization process can be clearly seen in the history of social work. In the early years the causes of many types of dependency were believed to be related to moral factors. The Charity Organization Societies, for example, felt that poverty was a result of a lack of abstinence, diligence, and thrift among the poor—all are moral factors. After thousands of contacts with families of "exemplary piety" and diligence who were overwhelmed by circumstances beyond their control—abominable housing, illness, low wages, and unemployment—the COS people were forced to conclude that in many, and perhaps most, cases of dependency, morals had little to do with the problem. The failure of the moral explanation of problems made the problems, and hence social work, less religious and more secular. Charity Organization Society workers, as well as other social workers, quickly began to search for scientific explanations to replace the moral explanations of problems.

The second general understanding of secularization is that "it is a process of increasing differentiation between the religious and the secular (nonreligious) spheres of life—a process, moreover, coinciding with and perhaps in part resulting from increasing specialization within society as it grows and becomes more urbanized and industrialized."[23] This relates to the process of professionalization discussed in Chapter 3. During this century the ministry, like many other professions, has come to be considered a specialized profession. The specialty of ministers is now considered to be limited to worship and spiritual matters. Ministers who wish to engage in counseling, for example, are no longer considered to be qualified for this role simply by virtue of being ordained. They are expected to have training beyond the seminary level in either pastoral counseling or social work. At one time a person wanting to enter social work could do so by attending seminary. This is no longer true. If a person wants to enter social work, he or she must attend a specialized social work school or program, which is generally located in a secular college or university.

The Growth of Government Services   When social work first began during the nineteenth century, virtually all services were privately funded, and the source of the great majority of funds was religious groups. Thus, most of social work occurred under religious auspices. During the twentieth century, government has rapidly assumed responsibility for more and more social services. The biggest development in this process was the Social Security Act of 1935, which firmly established the federal government as the major source of social welfare funding. Currently over 90 percent of social welfare funding in the United States comes from governmental sources. With the longstanding tradition of separation of church and state in the United States, the fact that most social workers work for government-funded programs virtually mandates the secularization of social work.

The New Left and the Student Movement of the 1960s and 1970s   The final reason for the secularization of social work is, admittedly, more speculative on the part of the authors, but we think it is valid. Although social work was considered to be a secular profession, for most of the twentieth century a large number of people who entered social work continued to do so out of religious motives. During the 1960s and 1970s the social work profession grew at a tremendous rate; it more than doubled in size. Among the reasons for this rapid growth was the fact that many young people of that generation viewed it as a "relevant" profession. That is, they saw it as related to the liberal, social-change-oriented ethos that was characteristic of college-age people at that time. Thus, a large, perhaps dominant, proportion of the huge cohort of new social workers was entering the profession out of political rather than religious motives. The authors speculate that this cohort fundamentally changed the nature of the social work profession. Among these changes was the completion of the process of secularization that had been evolving for most of the profession's history.

THE REVERSAL OF SECULARIZATION?

While it is a difficult speculation to prove, there are indicators that the trend toward secularization in society in general, and in social welfare and social work in particular, is slowing and perhaps even reversing. In society in general, the clearest indicator seems to be the large amount of growth that conservative churches have been experiencing.[24] Another indicator is illustrated in Figure 4–1, which graphs responses over time to an item on the Gallup Poll. The item asked respondents to indicate whether they thought religion was increasing or losing its influence in American life. The graph illustrates that from 1957 to 1970, a steadily increasing percentage of respondents believed that religion was declining in influence and a steadily decreasing percentage felt that its influence was increasing. Then a remarkable thing happens. Beginning in 1970 and continuing until 1976 the trend reverses, with more people each year thinking that the influence of religion is increasing and fewer thinking it is decreasing.[25] In 1976 the pattern stabilizes with small changes probably due to temporary factors, such as the rash of church scandals that occurred in 1988, or random statistical variation.

In social welfare in general, the reversal of secularization has been forced by the trend in government in recent years, beginning with the first Reagan administration

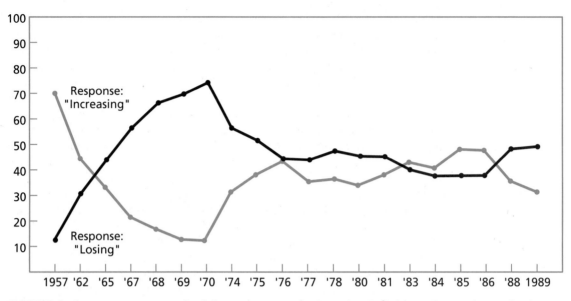

FIGURE 4–1   **Proportion of Adult Americans Who Perceive Religion as Increasing or Losing Its Influence in American Life**

Source: Adapted from Ronald L. Johnstone, *Religion in Society: A Sociology of Religion,* 2nd ed. © 1983, p. 260. Reprinted by permission of Prentice Hall, Inc., Englewood Cliffs, New Jersey. Based on data reported in Princeton Religious Research Center, *Emerging Trends,* 11 (April 1989), 1.

and continuing under George Bush, to abdicate responsibility for social welfare. The argument that social welfare is "the historic mission of the churches" has been used as the justification for cutting government programs. Since early in the Reagan administration, the stance of government has been that it should do less and the churches should do more because social welfare is really the proper role of the church rather than government.[26] Unfortunately, although churches are aware of the challenge, it is plain that they are not up to it. A survey by the Council on Foundations reported that churches felt "inundated since the federal budget cuts, in 1983 receiving the largest volume of requests for aid in their history. Several warned that no methods could come close to replacing government funds and that religious organizations would never be able to take over the role of government in meeting human needs."[27]

In the social work profession there is also evidence of a reversal of the trend toward secularization. One indicator is the establishment and growth of a professional organization specifically devoted to the interests of Christians in social work, the North American Association of Christians in Social Work. This organization currently has about 1,000 members, holds a well-attended annual convention, and publishes a journal, *Social Work and Christianity.* There is also a journal devoted to the interests of Catholics in social work, *Social Thought,* and one devoted to the interests of Jews, the *Journal of Jewish Communal Service.* Another indicator of the renewed interest of social workers in religion is the topics chosen for journal articles and doctoral dissertations. In the 1960s and early 1970s one rarely encountered an article or dissertation dealing with a topic related to religion. In recent years this too has changed, and we find, often in main-line journals, articles dealing with moral philosophy, research and religion, the funding of church-related agencies, and the relation of secular and sectarian social services, as well as many others.[28] Social work educators have begun to demonstrate a renewed interest in the subject of religion, with articles being published discussing religion in social work education, religion as a component of both micro and macro practice courses, and spirituality as an important component in human behavior courses.[29] We are also witnessing doctoral degrees being granted by major graduate schools of social work for dissertations on topics such as the development of social responsibility among Lutherans, evangelical Christianity and social work, a Christian interpretation of humanity for social work, a conceptualization of spirituality for social work, and the relationship of social work to religion and the church.[30] Another indicator has been the development of social work education programs with a religious focus. On the undergraduate level, programs in "bible social work" have been developed and accredited by the Council on Social Work Education at schools such as Eastern College and the Philadelphia College of the Bible. On the graduate level, schools of social work and seminaries are cooperating in offering joint degree programs. The University of Texas at Arlington and Southwestern Baptist Theological Seminary have such a program that enables a student to earn both a Master of Social Work degree and a Master of Religious Education degree at the same time. At least one seminary, Southern Baptist Theological Seminary in Louisville, Kentucky, has developed its own accredited MSW program.

It would be a mistake to interpret these developments as an indication that social welfare and social work will return to being primarily religious endeavors. If for no reason other than their immense size, social welfare and social work will continue to be largely secular enterprises. However, there is a natural alliance between the church and social work/social welfare. These recent trends seem to indicate that after some years of neglect, the importance of this alliance is once again being recognized, and it will probably continue to develop in a productive manner. In the next section, we turn to a brief examination of services provided by agencies with a connection to organized religion, generally known as *sectarian agencies*.

CURRENT SECTARIAN SERVICES

If you look in the yellow pages under the heading "social services" in any large city, the enduring religious connection of social welfare is clearly illustrated. Take, for example, Atlanta, Georgia. Out of 213 agencies listed, 46 have names that clearly indicate some formal religious ties. Listed are B'Nai B'Rith Youth Organization, Catholic Social Services, Jewish Family and Children's Bureau, Lutheran Immigration and Refugee Service, United Methodist Children's Home, Salvation Army, St. Vincent De Paul Society, and 39 others.

It is not possible to give accurate figures on the number of sectarian agencies in the United States. As Reid has noted, "Data on numbers and types of sectarian organizations are, at best, fragmentary, and at worst, misleading. One must rely on information furnished by the groups themselves. Lack of complete and current data, uncertainties about what constitutes a sectarian organization, and variations among groups in classifying agencies limit the usefulness of this information . . ."[31] The best

TABLE 4—1   Populations funded or served by different religious groups

	Anyone In Need		Adults Over 65		Adults 21–65		Children and Youth		Low Income	
	No.	%	No.	%	No.	%	No.	%	No.	%
Protestant (Baptist, Episcopal, Lutheran, Methodist, Presbyterian, Other)	239	49	21	162	68	159	67	170	71	158	66
Catholic	156	15	10	101	65	119	76	129	83	130	83
Jewish	38	6	16	26	68	27	71	27	71	22	58
Inter-religious Groups	23	5	22	10	43	11	48	11	48	14	61
Non-denominational Groups	29	4	14	16	55	18	62	20	69	18	62
Total[2]	485	79	16	315	65	334	69	357	74	342	71

[1]Unmarried parent; the terminally ill; rural farm households; the gay and lesbian community; seasonal farmworkers.
[2]Percentages do not total 100 because categories are not mutually exclusive and most respondents funded more than one.
Source: Adapted from Council on Foundations, *The Philanthropy of Organized Religion* (Washington, DC: The Council on Foundations, 1985), p. 18.

figures currently available on the number of sectarian agencies comes from a 1982 survey conducted by Netting, who surveyed the national headquarters of religious groups in the United States to obtain the number of social service agencies affiliated with each group. Approximately 14,000 agencies were reported to be affiliated with national religious groups. Netting explains that this is an underestimate of the total number of sectarian agencies because it does not include those that are not affiliated with a national body.[32]

We should also note that sectarian agencies have differing degrees of relatedness to the religious group with which they are affiliated. Reid posits a sectarian-secular continuum,[33] varying on criteria such as degree of control exercised by the parent religious body, the amount of financial support derived from sectarian sources, the proportion of board members who are of the faith, the extent to which decisions of the board and administration are guided by religious considerations, the amount of religious content in agency programs, and the religious identification of the agency's clientele. At the sectarian end of the continuum might be a Catholic adoption program that is funded entirely by Catholic sources, has a board consisting of only church members, provides services mainly to pregnant, unmarried, church-related women, and will only place children in Catholic homes. At the secular end of the continuum might be a Methodist community center that began as a settlement house with strong church ties, but over the years has evolved to the point where the board is only nominally Methodist, the staff is hired on the basis of professional credentials with no

| Respondents | | | | | | | | | | | | | |
| Handicapped | | Homeless and Runaways | | Prisoners and Ex-Offenders | | Refugees and Immigrants | | Women | | Veterans | | Other[1] | |
No.	%	No.	%	No.	%	No.	%	No.	%	No.	%	No.	%
92	38	59	25	77	32	126	53	98	41	7	3	7	3
72	46	61	39	44	28	87	56	83	53	6	4	6	4
22	58	9	24	4	11	21	55	13	34	6	16	1	0
9	39	5	22	10	43	12	52	9	39	1	4	2	9
15	52	8	28	3	10	12	41	12	41	0	0	3	10
210	43	142	29	138	28	258	53	215	44	20	4	18	4

consideration of church affiliation, funding comes mainly from the United Way and government sources with only a very small percentage coming from the Methodist church, and the clients reflect the changing character of the neighborhood in which the center is located, which is currently not very Methodist.

For the reasons discussed earlier, the data on the services of major religions is sketchy and fragmentary, at best. One useful source is a survey conducted in 1984 by the Council on Foundations. The Council surveyed 2,700 national and regional religious organizations. Most of the data contained in this section is from this survey.[34]

The data on populations funded or served by the various religious traditions are summarized in Table 4–1. As can be seen, differences between the groups served by the various traditions are not great. Note that all traditions concentrate on children and youth and all give less emphasis to veterans. The data is broken down for Protestant groups in Table 4–2 on pages 108–109. The "Other" category is composed of smaller groups such as Seventh Day Adventists and the Salvation Army.

The Council was surprised at the amount of services provided by religious groups. The authors concluded, "The results demonstrate not only that religious groups are a significant philanthropic force, but they may in fact have spent as many dollars to meet human and social needs as corporations and foundations."[35] Using responses to the survey supplemented by supporting data, such as annual reports, handbooks, directories, yearbooks, and previous studies, the authors concluded that the national religious bodies surveyed spent more than $1.03 billion on charitable activities in 1984.

TABLE 4—2   **Populations funded or served by different Protestant groups**

		Anyone In Need		Adults Over 65		Adults 21–65		Children and Youth		Number of Low Income	
		No.	%	No.	%	No.	%	No.	%	No.	%
Baptist	31	14	45	20	65	19	61	21	68	15	48
Episcopal	37	3	8	29	78	26	70	28	76	28	76
Lutheran	37	9	24	26	70	26	70	27	73	23	62
Methodist	20	4	20	11	55	14	70	15	75	12	60
Presbyterian	53	4	8	42	79	40	75	42	79	46	87
Other Traditions	61	15	25	34	58	37	56	37	61	34	56
Total	239	49	21	162	68	159	67	170	71	158	66

[1]Unmarried parents; the terminally ill; rural farm households; the gay and lesbian community; seasonal farmworkers.
Source: Adapted from Council on Foundations, *The Philanthropy of Organized Religion* (Washington, DC: The Council on Foundations, 1985), p. 18.

The authors estimated that when funds from government, United Way, and local congregations were totaled, the budgets of religiously affiliated agencies might be as high as $8.5 billion.

The Council's survey found that religious organizations are funding virtually every type of service. The ten most frequently provided services are listed in Table 4–3 on page 110. Two significant facts can be inferred from Table 4–3. The first is that religious groups give greatest emphasis to "hard" services, such as providing food, shelter, and recreation. The second is that almost as many groups are working for justice, advocacy, and human rights as are offering direct aid to the hungry and homeless. A very interesting finding is that while social change activities were given more emphasis by traditional liberal groups, such as the United Methodist Church, a significant number of traditionally conservative groups, including those identifying themselves as evangelical, were also involved in activities designed to produce social change.[36] Although the researchers found this surprising, it should not be startling to those familiar with the history of religion and social welfare. This topic will be dealt with in more detail in the following section.

SOCIAL WORK AND RELIGION—UNEASY BEDFELLOWS

The discussion so far has demonstrated that there is a definite and complex relationship between social work and religion. In addition, the relationship, which weakened for many years, is showing signs of intensifying. The reader is justified at this point in

Respondents

Handicapped		Homeless and Runaways		Prisoners and Ex-Offenders		Refugees and Immigrants		Women		Veterans		Other[1]	
No.	%	No.	%	No.	%	No.	%	No.	%	No.	%	No.	%
9	29	2	6	5	16	14	45	6	19	0	0	2	6
16	43	14	38	18	49	25	68	15	41	2	5	1	3
20	54	12	32	12	32	20	54	15	41	4	11	1	3
5	25	3	15	3	15	5	25	5	25	0	0	0	0
22	42	14	26	14	26	32	60	33	62	1	2	0	0
20	33	14	23	16	26	30	49	24	39	0	0	3	5
92	38	59	25	77	32	126	53	98	41	7	3	7	3

asking "So what's the big deal? For this you spend a whole chapter?" The "big deal" is that the relationship between social work and religion is by no means problem-free, as the following situation illustrates.

> In an earlier time Penny might have become a nun. She had been reared in a conservative and devout Catholic family and had grown up with the idea that her role in life was to serve the Church and her fellow human beings. When she took a social work class during her freshman year, she felt she had found her calling. She did her senior field placement at Catholic Social Services and hoped to be offered a job upon graduation. However, no positions were available at CSS and so she went to work for the local public health clinic as a social worker. She loved her job and felt she was doing what she was meant to do. That is, until this morning.

> Penny stared numbly at the doctor's referral before her. The doctor had written: "I am referring for counseling Monica Freeman, white female, age thirteen years five months. Patient is pregnant, still in the first trimester. Please explore options with patient and her parents. Medically, the obvious choice is abortion. This child is not mature enough physically or emotionally to go through a pregnancy and birth."

> Penny went to her supervisor for help. Her supervisor said "Well, Penny. You're aware that this clinic subscribes to the NASW Code of Ethics, which among other things states 'The social worker should provide clients with accurate and complete information regarding the extent and nature of the services available to them' and 'The social worker should make every effort to foster maximum self-determination on the part of clients.' This means that you don't need to actually advocate for an abortion as the physician apparently wants you to, but it does mean that you need to make the family aware that it is an option, and do all you can to help them reach their own decision, not yours."

TABLE 4-3	Most frequently mentioned activities, all religious groups	
Activity		**Percent of Respondents**
1. Food, nutrition		56%
2. Refugee aid, resettlement		49
3. Day care, camps, recreation for youth		47
4. Issue education, advocacy		47
5. Justice, human rights for particular groups		47
6. Emergency assistance, disaster relief		46
7. Clothing		43
8. Temporary shelter		41
9. Schools (pre-school through high school)		41
10. Adult education, tutoring		40

Source: Council on Foundations, *The Philanthropy of Organized Religion* (Washington, D.C.: The Council on Foundations, 1985), 21.

Penny replied, "I understand that, but you must realize that my religion teaches that abortion is murder, regardless of the fact that it is legal. I could no more help those people obtain an abortion than I could help them go upstairs to the nursery and murder one of the babies." The supervisor ended the discussion saying "OK Penny. I'll assign this case to one of the other social workers. However, working in a public clinic you'll run into situations like this fairly often, and I'll not always be able to get you off the hook. You need to resolve this within yourself, and if you can't, you'll need to look for work in a setting where you won't face this dilemma."

In this section, we will be discussing the major areas where there is the potential for conflict between social work and religion. To be more precise, we will be talking about the relationship between social work and Christianity. The other major religion in America, Judaism, has always had a more comfortable relationship with social work than has Christianity. There are two reasons for this. The first is "As far as Judaism is concerned, there [is] little competition between religious and secular understandings of social work." Also, "from the first, American Jewish social service was relatively independent of the synagogue, while Christian effort grew from the churches."[37] The second reason is that Jews have no equivalent of the Great Commission. Thus, they are under no obligation to seek converts to their faith. In this section, we will consider several broad issues—the first is whether the church has any business being involved in social welfare in the first place. Next, we will consider the problems resulting from conservative religion and the social change mission of social work. We will conclude with a discussion of the general question of the fit between religious values and social work values.

Should the Church Be Involved in Social Work and Social Welfare?

There are those both in the church and in the social work profession who do not feel that the church should be involved in social welfare. From the perspective of the church, this is an issue that assumed more importance in the past than it does now. The major argument is that the church should be concerned with saving souls, not with redeeming society. The colorful nineteenth century evangelist Billy Sunday is quoted by Marty as having said, "the road to the kingdom of God is not by the bathtub or the gymnasium [two common services provided by social welfare agencies of the time], nor the university, but by the blood red hand of the cross of Christ." Sunday criticized Christian social welfare agencies of the time, such as the YMCA, because "they have taken up sociology and settlement work but are not winning souls to Christ." He was overheard by a reporter as saying, "We've had enough of this godless social service nonsense. I'll go with you in eugenics, in social service, oyster soup, and institutional churches, but when you leave Jesus Christ out of it, good night."[38] Very few people in the church are concerned with this today, but it does still, on occasion, pop up. For example, an essay in *Evangelical Missions Quarterly* suggested that social service directed toward community development "probably is the greatest foe of Christianity." Douglas Johnson, a British author, wrote in 1979 that, ". . . we can see nothing in scripture or in history to lead us to believe that social work or any other foundation lasts to eternity, or is to the glory of God."[39] Loewenberg observes that, "Some ministers view social workers as competitors. They are especially concerned that nonreligious social workers provide help that they believe to be incompatible with the teachings of their church."[40]

There are few people on the social work side of the relationship who feel that, as a general principle, social work and religion are not compatible. The only general concern is that a number of persons, probably a majority of the profession, feel that the mission of social work is to become an empirically based, scientific profession, and they fear that religion, which they often associate with dogma, will retard this development. Imre observes

> The tendency to equate dogmatism with religion . . . can be seen to be rooted in the history of science. The development of logical positivism is intertwined with this history. Academic social work, where much of the current literature originates, is still very much committed to the positivistic definition of science. [The social work profession has] hidden assumptions, such as that all religion is dogmatic and ideological [that] continue to operate, even while recognition is given to the roots of [social work] values in religious and moral tradition.[41]

Conservative Religion and Social Change

Many within social work are uncomfortable with what we discussed earlier as the reversal of secularization. This discomfort is a result not of disapproval of religion, but of disapproval of a particular kind of religion. Social workers are generally very comfortable with main-line liberal Protestant, Catholic, and Jewish faith. However, many people now entering social work out of religious motivation are coming from somewhere else. They are generally perceived as being "conservative," "fundamentalist," or "evangelical." Mike Elliott, a social worker on the staff of a Baptist church in Kentucky, relates the following:

> [C]hurch related social workers are often considered "unclean" by secular social workers. It seems as if I was regarded as an evangelist who had the ulterior motive of conversion in mind for my clients. I was pegged a social work evangelist who, with or without hair spray or wing-tipped shoes, only used social work to rack up conversions.[42]

However, the concern of secular social workers goes deeper than a fear that social workers with conservative religious orientations will use their profession to evangelize. The major concern is that conservative religion goes hand-in-hand with conservative politics and will tend to blunt, or even thwart, the social change mission of social work.

Social workers are not the only people with the fear that conservative religion will hamper efforts at achieving a just society. Magnuson relates

> When Ernest Fremont Tittle, the noted liberal preacher, wrote more than three decades ago that "Evangelical religion" could never hope to produce a humane social order, he gave voice to what has been the opinion of many throughout the present century. Tittle thought that evangelicals had since the reformation era habitually sanctioned the social order and refused "to cry out against social injustice," thus clearly demonstrating the social impotence of a gospel of individual salvation.[43]

Is this the case? Is conservative Christianity incompatible with the social change aspect of social work? The answer, found mainly in the writings of Christian social workers, is interesting. It is that yes, this is often the case, but no, it should not and need not be.

The criticism of conservative Christianity as being opposed to social change has some justification and Christian social workers are the first to admit this. Keith-Lucas says that the Christian is "looked on with suspicion by social work educators, and most rightly, too." The reason for this suspicion is "the noninvolvement in human problems that can all too easily accompany a religion that has metaphysical or other worldly interests."[44] Speaking of the renewed interest in social change that emerged in social work in the 1960s, Kuhlmann observes, "Christians, particularly those holding an evangelical viewpoint, have tended to resist these trends, both in social work as well as in the larger society."[45] Speaking specifically of social work's interest in equity for the sexes, Faver and Hunter report that some students "have reacted with indifference or hostility to curriculum content on women's issues. And, alarmingly, some of those most strongly opposed to this material openly assert incompatibility of the material with their Christian beliefs. . . . They counter the notions of freedom and equality by maintaining that the Bible teaches women to be subordinate to men, and to confine their activity primarily to homemaking, childrearing, and volunteer work."[46]

Why have conservative Christians tended to resist social change? Eckardt traces the problem to the development of "higher criticism" of the Bible which developed in Europe during the first half of the nineteenth century, and to the growth of the ideologies of communism and socialism during the late nineteenth and twentieth centuries. Basically, higher criticism refers to the intellectual analysis of the scriptures, which includes interpreting them in relation to the social and historical context in which they were

Leaders of the religious right such as Pat Robertson are conservative to the point of being reactionary and are generally viewed as opponents of social welfare services provided by the public sector.

written, as well as the motivations of the author. The bottom line is that the scriptures are viewed as being written by humans, although they are God-inspired, and therefore, they are fallible. The hallmark of conservative, or evangelical, Christians is their belief that the scriptures represent the actual word of God and are thus infallible, and therefore, they are not open to interpretation by mere humans. A popular bumper sticker reflecting this attitude reads: "God said it; I believe it; That settles it!" As a result of higher criticism, fundamentalist Christians became preoccupied with defending their faith, and this has tended to cause them to withdraw from worldly concerns such as social justice and equality. The great theological debates among conservative Christians during the late nineteenth and early twentieth centuries centered around the "fundamentals" of faith rather than on any social issues. These issues became the territory of the liberal sects, which made them even less attractive to the fundamentalists, who rejected "anything associated with liberal theology [because they] feared that if part of it was bad all the rest would soon be contaminated."[47]

The second reason for the rejection of social change by conservative Christians is the development of the ideologies of communism and socialism. These ideologies, particularly communism, are often militant in their rejection of religion in general and Christianity in particular. This led to "an alignment of evangelical Christianity with conservative politics and economics. There developed an unquestioned acceptance of capitalism as the Christian's economy and of democracy as God's political preference."[48] This acceptance of the political status quo as being ordained by God has resulted in evangelical Christians viewing any effort to change the social system as being, by definition, against the will of God.

A number of recent writers have pointed out that the identification of conservative Christians with a reactionary position on social change is strange because, historically, evangelicals have been heavily involved in social change, with their activities often exceeding those of their liberal counterparts. Magnuson did an in-depth study of evangelical social work from 1865 to 1920. He found that although liberals talked about social change and conservative Christians tended to avoid such rhetoric, when actual behaviors were studied it was the evangelicals who had the greater record of social change activities. He observes

> No matter how troublesome the persons they helped—former prisoners, prostitutes, unwed mothers, vagrants, or the unemployed—revivalists accepted them with openness and warmth. Placing the blame largely on environmental pressures, rescue workers argued that given a proper chance even the most difficult persons would perform creditably. Frederick Booth-Tucker, commander of the Salvation Army in the United States from 1896 to 1903, estimated that 90 per cent or more of the unemployed would gladly work if they had the opportunity. That kind of optimistic acceptance generally characterized these organizations.[49]

Magnuson contrasts this attitude with that of many liberal religious reformers, such as Washington Gladden, whose attitude was often somewhat harsh, advocating that applicants for assistance should be treated with "prison-like restraint."[50]

The attitude of Christian social workers writing today is clearly that the identification of conservative Christianity with conservative politics, although often a fact, has been a sort of historical accident and is really based on a misinterpretation of faith. Keith-Lucas says, ". . . these are not actually beliefs in the Judeo-Christian or biblical tradition. They are perversions of these beliefs in the capitalist-puritan set of assumptions."[51] Kuhlmann says, ". . . such a view [that social action is not good], although it is quite prevalent in the contemporary evangelical community, and also reflects much that is consistent with Biblical Christianity, is not fully Christian, in the sense that it does not reflect the whole of Biblical truth on the subject."[52] Moberg asserts that concern among Christians for individual salvation at the expense of social change ". . . leaves out significant aspects of the teaching of the Bible. It easily results in loving only 'our own brethren,' avoiding needy neighbors in our own community and other parts of the world . . . and it reflects paying greater attention to cultural values than to biblical norms."[53]

In an interesting article, theologian Richard F. Lovelace argues that revival movements have historically begun with concentration on individual salvation and have then moved into a period of emphasis on social change. He argues that America is in the early stages of a great religious awakening and predicts that it will eventually move into an era of social change based on this awakening.[54] There are signs that this may be already happening. In 1973 on Thanksgiving weekend a meeting took place among evangelical leaders during which they wrote "A Declaration of Evangelical Social Concern."[55] The survey of philanthropic activities by organized religion conducted by the Council on Foundations found that groups who identified themselves as conservative were funding social justice activities "just like [their] non-conservative brethren."[56]

To sum up this section, we will refer to Ralph Eckardt, a well-known figure among Christian social workers. Eckardt makes two general points regarding Christianity and social action. The first is that political involvement is a legitimate activity for Christian social workers. The second is that conservative Christianity is not synonymous with conservative politics. Eckardt says

> I am a patriotic American and support the democratic way of life, but it is not God breathed. I also assert my allegiance to Jesus Christ. The two are very important to me but they are not synonymous. In this regard my allegiance to Jesus Christ stands above

any other and I must serve Him primarily and I assert my obligation to criticize this or any government, when what it does is not in consonance with the revealed will of God.[57]

In a similar vein, the British social worker Robert Holman says

> So I argue that Christians in general and Christian social workers in particular should have a collective voice to address society. Its support for the poor might seem to lean towards the left, its views on the sanctity of life and marriage towards the right. It belongs to no political party. It should be an attempt to show that a distinct Christian opinion can be expressed about those social issues which confront social workers every day of the week.[58]

Social Work Values and Christian Values—Conflict or Consensus?

There is little doubt that there is perceived conflict between the secular, humanistic values of the social work profession and the religious values of many practitioners. Eckardt describes

> the preconceived notion on behalf of many in the profession that social work and religion do not mix. More specifically, this attitude suggests that if a person is a committed evangelical Christian his values are so different from those of the social work profession as to render him an unacceptable, or at least second rate, practitioner in the field. Most professionals would deny this discrimination and bias; but as an evangelical I have felt it when I have applied for positions in the profession, sought further education, or attended gatherings of professionals discussing professional issues.[59]

In a study of social work in church-related agencies, Netting found that church representatives feared that "spiritual values will be sacrificed on the altar of professional know-how," and social workers felt that religion interfered with maintaining a nonjudgmental attitude.[60]

This conflict of values has grown out of the process of secularization of the profession. Siporin, in an article that is sharply critical of the profession, asserts that social work was once based on a normative philosophy. That is, social work was seen as being a moral agent of society, charged with enforcing social, religiously based norms. As such, social workers actively sought to prevent in their clients behavior that was generally considered by society to be undesirable or immoral, such as divorce, premarital sex, homosexuality, and the use of alcohol or drugs. Siporin asserts that, "In recent years, however, this social work value system and its moral vision have been fragmented and weakened. Many social workers now believe that people should be free to choose their own life-styles, values, and moral norms." He calls this the *libertarian philosophy* and observes that it rejects the labeling of behaviors such as those listed earlier as deviant, and that it instead labels them as "variant" or "normal." "It is further argued that the social work profession should advocate and support the social redefinition of such conduct as 'normal,' and should actively support or approve these behavior patterns as rightful, viable options for people in our society." Siporin believes that this trend has been harmful to the profession and that it has led to the perception by much of the public of social work as an immoral, or at least amoral, profession.

He thinks that, "Social work as a profession needs to regain its moral vision and idealism and even the moral passion that the old-time social workers had. Social work also needs to be able to present itself again as a representative moral agent of society. . . ."[61]

Keith-Lucas takes a much less extreme view than Siporin, with regard to both social work's current moral state and what its position should be. Rather than viewing social work as having abandoned a normative position and adopted a libertarian position, Keith-Lucas believes that social work has simply abandoned the concept of sin, and with good reason. The concept of sin has often been used to justify harshness toward people with problems, and it has been interpreted legalistically and simplistically. This often led to punitive attitudes toward clients, which Keith-Lucas believes are both "bad social work and questionable Christianity."[62] Keith-Lucas also believes that Christian values have sometimes been perverted by our society and "To the extent that Christian doctrine has been identified with capitalism, to the extent that it assures, even implicitly that worldly success and grace have anything to do with each other, to the extent that there is any room in it for judgmentalism, or distinction between people on the basis of their supposed goodness or badness, to the extent that it rejects the sinner rather than his sin, the church . . . deserves all that the humanists have said about it."[63]

Whatever the reasons, it is clear that there is the potential for conflict between the values of the social work profession and those of religion, particularly conservative Christianity. The basis for the conflict lies in the values considered almost sacred by social work, and referred to earlier in the case of Penny, of the client's right to self-determination, the worker's obligation to provide information on all options, and the worker's need to maintain a nonjudgmental attitude. In practice terms this means that a social worker, at least when working in a secular agency, is obligated to consider all legal options for clients. These options sometimes involve practices which certain religions consider to be sinful. Common examples are homosexuality, abortion, premarital sex, and contraceptives and sexual information for teenagers, as well as many others.*

Problems stemming from the relationship of social work and religion have two sides; they present difficulties for both the agency and the individual social worker. From the standpoint of the agency, religion presents several problems. The first has to do with a problem noted by Keith-Lucas, that social workers with strong religious beliefs tend to be less concerned than social workers in general about the material needs of clients "and more concerned that their clients should behave in a generally acceptable way."[64] The policy of most social work agencies is that the client's material needs should be taken care of before the social worker deals with behavioral change. The second problem has to do with agency administrators' concern that agency policies regarding client self-determination and worker nonjudgmentalism be followed. They

---

*We should note that the problem of helping clients find solutions which are at variance with the personal values of the social worker is by no means confined to social workers with strong religious convictions. For example, many social workers with strong feminist convictions find themselves in the position of helping women strengthen traditional marriages where the husband is the "boss" and the wife is the "helpmate." The social worker may find this type of relationship personally distasteful, but if it is the kind of marriage the client desires, the social worker has no right to impose his or her own values of equalitarian relationships on the client.

are generally concerned, and rightly so, that social workers with strong religious beliefs will have difficulty following these policies. The third problem for agencies has to do with witnessing. It is not uncommon for social workers with strong Christian beliefs to feel that the root of many clients' problems is that they are out of alignment with God, and that finding and accepting Jesus Christ is the only solution to their problems. Be that as it may, in secular agencies the practice of witnessing is almost always against policy. MacDonald, a graduate student at the University of Chicago, recalls that at the end of his first week of field placement, "the executive director and another staff member confronted me with the policy of not overtly expressing my personal faith in the agency (they knew of my strong Christian background). I began to realize that the agency desired to approach only the physical and emotional/mental needs of an individual, not the spiritual. I knew that as a Christian I could not agree with this kind of incomplete therapy."[65] Whether a social worker agrees with a nonspiritual approach to client problems is not a concern of the agency; however, assuring that workers follow policy and refrain from using their positions to witness to clients is very much a concern.

From the standpoint of the social worker with strong religious beliefs, the issue is one of balancing the sometimes conflicting values of profession and religion without unacceptably compromising either. Social workers writing in this area have developed guidelines which are of help. The following list is based on writings of Sherwood and Keith-Lucas[66]

1. Integrating faith and practice involves difficult judgments and *compromise,* since every choice will advance certain values at the expense of other values.

2. Religion will provide a fundamental value base from which to practice but will not give prescriptive, mechanical guidance.

3. It is possible to work with clients whose values and goals are at variance with your own. Sherwood recalls "In doing marriage counseling in a secular setting this author often found clients choosing goals counter to his own. One consequence was that he often found himself doing divorce counseling. It was neither his right nor in his power to prevent such a choice on the part of his clients. And once the choice was made, he believes he served them better by helping to minimize the damage of the divorce . . ." (p. 49)

4. It is acceptable to express one's own values, when appropriate, as long as they are clearly labeled and with emphasis on the client's right and responsibility for his or her own choices and their consequences.

5. The agency setting and the social worker's position should never be used in a manipulative or coercive way even when it is perceived to be for the client's own good. This means, among other things, that a social agency, particularly a secular one, is not an appropriate setting for witnessing.

6. When working in a social agency, the social worker has an obligation to carry out the policy of the agency. A social worker in a public health clinic must discuss abortion as an alternative to a problem pregnancy, must discuss the use of condoms with homosexuals and unmarried clients as a means of AIDS prevention, must furnish birth control information to teenagers, and must discuss with drug addicts ways to get clean needles. About this Keith-Lucas says "One has no right to ignore policies or give them subtly some other meaning than that which the agency intends. Clients have a right to rely on an agency's consistency and Government or a Board of Trustees that its money be spent as it directs."[67]

A CLOSER LOOK

Guidelines from North American Association of Christians in Social Work

As a member of NACSW I practice, learn and teach social work within the following philosophical frame:

1. Human beings are of infinite worth, irrespective of gender, race, age or behavior.

2. At the same time human beings, including myself, are fallible, limited creatures. They are not capable, and never will be, of solving all their problems or of creating the perfect society. Nevertheless they are sometimes capable, with appropriate help, of transcending their nature in acts of courage and compassion.

3. As a fallible being myself I have no right to pass moral judgments on others, to assume authority over them except as mandated by law, or to imagine that I know everything about them.

4. Human beings have been endowed with the faculty of choice, which must not be denied them except by due process of law, or where their actions or threatened actions are demonstrably gravely harmful to others or self-destructive, or where they voluntarily surrender this right for a prescribed purpose.

5. They are, however, responsible for the consequences of their choices, and may need help in perceiving what these are likely to be.

6. No person is beyond help, although at this time we may not have the knowledge or skill to help.

7. All programs and policies that depreciate people, treat them as objects rather than as subjects, seek to impose on them behavior not mandated by law, manipulate them without their knowledge and consent or deny them choices permitted others in our society, are to be avoided or resisted.

8. Our society is far from perfect, and it is not my business to act as its representative, but rather to help people determine their relationship to it.

9. Love, understanding and compassion are the source of wellbeing and acceptable behavior, rather than the reward for them.

10. While force is sometimes the quickest way of obtaining an immediate result, in the long run it is self-defeating. Compassion, understanding and concern are the eventual victors.

11. The social sciences provide much useful knowledge for practice, but cannot explain all phenomena and their pronouncements need constantly to be evaluated in terms of the values they subsume.

12. There are outcomes to human helping that cannot be measured statistically as well as those which can.

13. All human institutions, ideals and commitments are liable to subtle perversion of their values, unless these are constantly examined. The new is not necessarily the best, nor does new knowledge always invalidate the old.

14. Professional education and training in self-discipline are indispensable to good social work.

15. As a Christian committed to the dissemination of what I believe to be the truth, my task as a social worker is not so much to convince others of this truth, as to provide them with the experience of being loved, forgiven and cared for so that the Good News I believe in may be a credible option for them.

Source: Alan Keith-Lucas, *So You Want to be a Social Worker: A Primer for the Christian Student* (St. Davids, PA: North American Association of Christians in Social Work, 1985): 34–35. Used with permission.

What if a social worker is asked to do something which he or she cannot in good conscience do? Keith-Lucas says the worker has two choices. One is to resign and the other is to openly refuse to carry out the policy, in which case the worker will probably be fired.

Incidentally, these guidelines can be turned around. Many religiously affiliated agencies employ social workers who are themselves not very religious. It is entirely possible for a social worker who believes in abortion as a viable alternative to pregnancy to be employed by a Catholic agency which has a strict policy against offering abortion to clients as an option.* The worker in such a setting is also under an obligation to follow agency policy and to not discuss abortion.

The North American Association of Christians in Social Work has developed a very useful set of guidelines for Christians in social work. These are presented in the box on page 118.

CONCLUSION

Religion and social work have a long and heavily intertwined history. They are natural allies and collaborators, both being concerned with the well-being of people, justice, and problems of the oppressed, as well as many other mutual interests. As social work has become more secularized and more tolerant of atypical behavior, and as conservative religion has become a more powerful force in society, the potential for problems between these old allies has increased.

How great have these problems actually proven to be? Because it has only been in the past few years that many people have even perceived the potential for conflict, we really do not have much data on which to base a hard and firm conclusion. However, the data which are beginning to come in indicate that the relationship between religion and social work is not presenting as great a problem as feared. A study by Eckardt which compared the practice of graduates of the Social Work Program at Temple University, who identified themselves as secular in orientation, with graduates of the Social Work Program at the Philadelphia College of the Bible, who identified themselves as evangelical Christians, concluded

> The overwhelming difference in religious beliefs was matched by an equally overwhelming similarity in practice. There was not always a positive affirmation of the values of the profession through the practice decisions, but the nature of the responses was similar. A generalization which can be made from this study is that although the groups tested were diverse in religious beliefs, they were similar in professional practice.[68]

A similar finding was reported by Epstein and Buckner, who surveyed practicing social workers in Georgia, in the heart of the "Bible Belt." Of the 214 social workers surveyed, only 4.4 percent identified themselves as fundamentalist Christians, but 35.5 percent identified their religion as "Central to my life and philosophy." Epstein and Buckner found "that those social work professionals participating in the study have not experienced significant conflicts or pressures related to Fundamentalism or to differences in religious beliefs."[69]

---

*It is perfectly ethical for an agency to have such a policy as long as clients know ahead of time that this is the policy. It is not ethical for an agency to call itself something like "Pregnancy Counseling Center" and imply that it offers all options when, in fact, it is a pro-life front which will go to almost any length to prevent a client from obtaining an abortion.

1. Alan Keith-Lucas, *Giving and Taking Help* (Chapel Hill, NC: University of North Carolina Press, 1972), 200.

2. David Macarov, *The Design of Social Welfare* (New York: Holt, Rinehart, and Winston, 1978), 76.

3. Robert Morris, *Rethinking Social Welfare: Why Care for the Stranger?* (New York: Longman, 1986), 66.

4. Bob Brackney and Derrel Watkins, "An Analysis of Christian Values and Social Work Practice," *Social Work and Christianity* 10 (Spring 1983): 6.

5. Morris, *Rethinking Social Welfare,* 66.

6. Morris, *Rethinking Social Welfare,* 67.

7. Morris, *Rethinking Social Welfare,* 72.

8. Macarov, *The Design of Social Welfare,* 78–79.

9. Macarov, *The Design of Social Welfare,* 79.

10. Cited in Brackney and Watkins, "An Analysis of Christian Values and Social Work Practice," 7.

11. James Douglas, *Why Charity?* (Beverly Hills, CA: Sage Publications, 1983), 78.

12. Brackney and Watkins, "An Analysis of Christian Values and Social Work Practice," 7.

13. Arthur E. Fink, Everett E. Wilson, and Merrill B. Conover. *The Field of Social Work,* 4th ed. (New York: Holt, Rinehart and Winston, 1964), 29–30.

14. Robert H. Bremner, *From the Depths: The Discovery of Poverty in the United States* (New York: New York University Press, 1956), 33.

15. S. Humphries Gurteen, *A Handbook of Charity Organization* (Buffalo, NY: author, 1882), 129.

16. Raymond Mohl and Neil Betten, "Paternalism and Pluralism: Immigrants and Social Welfare in Gary, Indiana, 1906–1940," *American Studies* 15 (Spring 1974): 6.

17. William J. Reid, "Sectarian Agencies," in John Turner, ed., *Encyclopedia of Social Work* 17 (New York: National Association of Social Workers, 1977), 1245.

18. Robert R. Hildebrandt, "The History of Developing Responsibility Among Lutherans Through Co-operative Efforts of the Church Bodies and the Place of Social Welfare in the Mission of the Lutheran Church Today" (DSW Dissertation, Tulane University, 1978), 32–35.

19. F. Ernest Johnson, "Protestant Social Work," in *Social Work Yearbook* 6, Russell H. Kurtz, ed. (New York: Russell Sage Foundation, 1941), 404.

20. Sue Spencer, "What Place Has Religion in Social Work Education?" *Social Service Review* 35 (April 1961): 161.

21. Martin E. Marty, "Social Service: Godly and Godless," *Social Service Review* 54 (December 1980): 465.

22. Ronald R. Johnstone, *Religion in Society: A Sociology of Religion,* 2nd ed. (Englewood Cliffs, NJ: Prentice-Hall, 1983), 270.

23. Johnstone, *Religion in Society,* 271.

24. Dean M. Kelley, "Comment: Why Conservative Churches are Still Growing," *Journal for the Scientific Study of Religion* 17 (June 1978): 21–38.

25. Johnstone, *Religion in Society,* 260.

26. F. Ellen Netting, "The Religiously Affiliated Agency: Implications For Social Work Administration," *Social Work and Christianity* 13 (Fall 1986): 50.

27. Council on Foundations, *The Philanthropy of Organized Religion* (Washington, D.C.: Council on Foundations, 1985), 63.

28. Max Siporin, "Moral Philosophy in Social Work Today," *Social Service Review* 56 (December 1982): 516–538; Catherine A. Faver, "Religion, Research, and Social Work," *Social Thought* (Summer 1986): 20–29; F. Ellen Netting, "Secular and Religious Funding of Church-related Agencies," *Social Service Review* 56 (December 1982): 586–604; Marty, "Social Service: Godly and Godless," 463–481.

29. Larry P. A. Ortiz, "Religious Issues: The Missing Link in Social Work Education," Paper presented at the 37th Annual Program Meeting of the Council on Social Work Education, New Orleans, LA, March 14–17, 1991; Edward R. Canda, "Religious Content in Social Work Education: A Comparative Approach," *Journal of Social Work Education* 25 (Winter 1989): 36–45; F. Ellen Netting, Jane M. Thibault, and James W. Ellor, "Integrating Content on Organized Religion into Macropractice Courses," *Journal of Social Work Education* 26 (Winter 1990): 15–24; M. Vincentia Joseph, "Religion and Social Work Practice," *Social Casework* 69 (September 1988): 443–452; James R. Dudley and Chava Helfgott, "Exploring a Place for Spirituality in the Social Work Curriculum," *Journal of Social Work Education* 26 (Fall 1990): 287–294.

30. Robert R. Hildebrandt, "The History of Developing Social Responsibility Among Lutherans Through Cooperative Efforts of the Church Bodies and the Place of Social Welfare in the Mission of the Lutheran Church Today"; Ralph William Eckardt, "Evangelical Christianity and Social Work: A Study of the Beliefs and Practices of Graduates of the Social Work Majors

at Philadelphia College of the Bible and Temple University" (DSW dissertation, The University of Pennsylvania, 1974); Edward G. Kuhlman, "A Christian Interpretation of Humanity for Social Work" (DSW Dissertation, The University of Pennsylvania, 1982); Edward R. Canda, "A Conceptualization of Spirituality for Social Work: Its Issues and Implications," (Ph.D. Dissertation, The Ohio State University, 1986); Barbara Jean Manthey, "Social Work, Religion, and the Church: Policy Implications," (Ph.D. Dissertation, The University of Texas at Austin, 1989).

31. Reid, "Sectarian Agencies," 1247.

32. Netting, "The Religiously Affiliated Agency: Implications for Social Work Administration," 55.

33. Reid, "Sectarian Agencies," 1251.

34. Council on Foundations, *The Philanthropy of Organized Religion.*

35. Council on Foundations, *The Philanthropy of Organized Religion,* xiv.

36. Council on Foundations, *The Philanthropy of Organized Religion,* 21–22.

37. Marty, "Social Service: Godly and Godless," 467–468.

38. Marty, "Social Service: Godly and Godless," 463–481.

39. Douglas Johnson, *Contending for the Faith* (Oxford, England: Inter-Varsity Press, 1979), quoted in Robert Holman "The Christian Social Worker: A British View," *Social Work and Christianity 11* (Spring 1984), 52.

40. Frank M. Loewenberg, *Religion and Social Work Practice in Contemporary American Society* (New York: Columbia University Press, 1988), 12.

41. Roberta Wells Imre, *Knowing and Caring* (Lanham, MD: University Press of America, 1982), 57.

42. Michael Elliot, "The Church Related Social Worker," *Social Work and Christianity 11* (Fall 1984): 41.

43. Norris Magnuson, *Salvation in the Slums: Evangelical Social Work, 1865–1920* (Metuchen, NJ: Scarecrow Press, 1977), ix.

44. Alan Keith-Lucas, "Christianity and the Church in Today's Social Scene," *The Paraclete 1* (Spring 1974): 4–5.

45. Edward G. Kuhlmann, "A Christian View of Man for Social Action," *The Paraclete 1* (Spring 1974): 4–5.

46. Catherine A. Faver and Mary "Ski" Hunter, "Feminism, Christianity, and Social Work Education," *Social Work and Christianity 9* (Spring–Fall 1981): p. 57.

47. Eckardt, "Evangelical Christianity and Social Work," 54–57.

48. Eckardt, "Evangelical Christianity and Social Work," 55–56.

49. Magnuson, *Salvation in the Slums,* xii–xiv.

50. Magnuson, *Salvation in the Slums,* xii.

51. From *Giving and Taking Help* by Alan Keith-Lucas. © 1972 The University of North Carolina Press. Reprinted by permission. (pp. 201–202).

52. Kuhlmann, "A Christian View of Man for Social Action," 23.

53. David O. Moberg, "The Christian and Social Change," *The Paraclete 4* (Summer 1977): 17.

54. Richard F. Lovelace, "Completing An Awakening," *The Christian Century* (March 18, 1981): 296–300.

55. John D. Bower, "Social Action: A Christian Mandate," *The Paraclete 2* (Summer 1975): 40–50.

56. Council on Foundations, *The Philanthropy of Organized Religion,* 22.

57. Ralph W. Eckardt, "Christianity and Government: A Plea for Sane Social Action," *The Paraclete 1* (Spring 1974): 45.

58. Holman, "The Christian Social Worker: A British View," 59.

59. Eckardt, "Evangelical Christianity and Social Work," iv.

60. F. Ellen Netting, "Social Work and Religious Values in Church Related Social Agencies," *Social Work and Christianity 9* (Spring–Fall, 1982): 10–11.

61. Siporin, "Moral Philosophy in Social Work Today," 519–520.

62. Alan Keith-Lucas, *So You Want to be a Social Worker: A Primer for the Christian Student* (St. Davids, PA: North American Association of Christians in Social Work, 1985), 20–22.

63. From *Giving and Taking Help* by Alan Keith-Lucas. ©1972 The University of North Carolina Press. Reprinted by permission. (p. 201).

64. Keith-Lucas, *So You Want to be a Social Worker,* 30.

65. Mark MacDonald, "The Christian Social Worker in a Secular Drop-In Center Setting," *Social Work and Christianity 10* (Spring 1983): 68–69.

66. David A. Sherwood, "Add to Your Faith Virtue: The Integration of Christian Values and Social Work Practice," *Social Work and Christianity 8* (Spring–Fall 1981): 41–54; Keith-Lucas, *So You Want To Be A Social Worker: A Primer for the Christian Student,* 31–33. Used with permission.

67. Keith-Lucas, *So You Want to be a Social Worker,* 32.

68. Eckardt, "Evangelical Christianity and Social Work," 32.

69. Howard Epstein and Ed Buckner, "Social Work and Fundamental Religious and Political Values," (Unpublished paper, Social Work Department, Georgia State University, Atlanta, GA, 1987), 9.

C · H · A · P · T · E · R
five

Responses to
Human Diversity

W ell, I don't think it's fair," one college student says to another. "I applied to the Social Work Major this semester but I didn't get in. My grade point average is 2.7 and I spent the whole summer volunteering—I should have been fine. But what makes me *really* mad is that Towanda Moore got accepted even when I didn't. I bet her grades aren't as good as mine. They must have let her in because she's black."

A social worker from a rehabilitation center is addressing an introductory social work class. Describing a recent client, he tells them "I just *knew* he was gay—because of the way he dressed and talked. You know—you can tell." A nervous giggle arises among the students in the class. Not sharing in the laughter are two students. Kate, a lesbian, and Tom, a gay man, both wonder to themselves: "Do they know about me? What would they think if they found out?"

Maryann Rogers works in the Child Welfare Division of the welfare department of a western state. "I'm concerned about Ruth Redthunder," she tells her supervisor. "I know the decision has been made to remove her from her home and put her in a boarding school. But her family's pretty upset. Do you really think it's right that we keep taking these Native American kids from their homes and sending them off to boarding schools run by white teachers and administrators?" Her supervisor replies: "Look, I know it's become a hot issue to talk about bringing people up in their own culture, so they know their own roots. But when you look at the poverty and neglect most of these kids face, you know the best thing for them is to get them out of it—and 'white' boarding schools are one way out."

Hector Diaz lives in a small Texas community in the lower Rio Grande Valley. Located on the Mexican border, the area is now the poorest region in the United States. Diaz has no trouble believing this is so. His family of two adults and eight children lives in a three-room shack with no heat or sewage system. A contaminated water supply causes health problems for the Diaz family and their neighbors. Poverty and poor living conditions lead to a high rate of chronic disease. Mr. Diaz's youngest child, for example, has diabetes and faces blindness. Over half of the inhabitants of the community, almost all first-generation Mexican Americans, are unemployed. Drawn to the United States in search of a decent living, Mr. Diaz and others bought small plots of land from wealthy developers. These developers provide little in the way of sanitation or other services. Local and state governments have generally ignored the Rio Grande Valley, tending to see it as just another part of Mexico, rather than as an American community.[1]

The director of the field internship program in a School of Social Work is discussing a problem with her advisory committee. "Frankly, I don't know how to handle this," she exclaims. "I still can't get placements for our two visually impaired students. The agencies I've approached are either subtle or direct—but the basic answer is 'a blind student wouldn't be able to function here.' It doesn't help for me to point out that there are at least two blind social workers who work in this town." "How can they do that?" a committee member interjects. "Don't they realize they're admitting they wouldn't hire a visually impaired worker—and isn't that against the law?"

The staff meeting at the Union County Family and Children's Services Center is just breaking up. The members of the Policies Subcommittee are being congratulated by other members of the staff. They have just received approval of a proposed policy on sexual harassment. The policy covers any employee who complains of sexual harassment on the job, and spells out an investigation process and appropriate penalties for harassers. "I can't believe it," one female staff member sighs. "It takes something like Senate Hearings on charges of sexual harassment by a Supreme Court nominee to raise consciousness enough to finally get this policy passed. Did the staff think that human service agencies are immune from these problems?"

The United States is a country of diversity. Its population is composed of members of a variety of races and ethnic groups, some recently arrived and others long-time residents. And, like any other country, the United States contains other groups that are often singled out and labeled as "special": the aged, those with physical or mental handicaps, gays and lesbians, and even that group which makes up half the population—women. Such diversity can bring great strength to a society, providing a wide variety of values, talents, and points of view. Yet all too often, difference has been accompanied by prejudice and discrimination, and has been used to justify oppression. Currently, our country is witnessing a heightened awareness of issues related to race and gender, as evidenced in debates about quotas, affirmative action, "politically correct" speech, and the place of multiculturalism in American society.

National, regional, and community patterns of acceptance of difference, or of prejudicial treatment, are reflected in our social welfare policies and services. In addition, the variables of ethnicity, race, gender, sexual orientation, age, and physical and mental capabilities often have profound impact on people's lives. These variables can determine income level, job and educational opportunities, access to housing and health care, and participation in various political and social institutions. Finally, the existence of diversity raises questions about the type of society we want to foster. Should that society be pluralistic, allowing a certain autonomy for a variety of groups and cultures? Should it go farther and support separatism—where groups that wish to can maintain their own very separate and distinct lifestyles? Or should it instead strive for a more homogenized whole—perhaps even endeavoring to fit all people into a white, Anglo-Saxon model?

All three areas related to diversity: social policy, individual development, and the relationship between groups and the larger community, are of vital importance to social workers. This chapter looks at the impact and meaning of "difference" for individuals, groups, and society, and explores the ways in which the social welfare system has responded to diversity. Its ultimate aim is to encourage you to think about how these issues affect your own life and the ways in which you judge and interact with others.

DEFINITION OF THE PROBLEM

There is no single problem related to human diversity. Rather, there are a variety of issues and consequences, some negative and some positive, related to belonging to a group that is seen as somehow different from the "majority." (We will discuss the concepts of majority and minority in the next section of this chapter.) While it is important to appreciate the strengths of being part of such a group, it is the negative aspects which often draw our attention and mobilize us to seek change. Racism, for example, remains a prominent feature of our society. Despite the gains of the Civil Rights movement of the 1950s and 1960s and the various social policies and programs aimed at eradicating discrimination and its effects, for many, being African American still means being disadvantaged. This disadvantage extends to other minorities of color, including Hispanic Americans, Asian Americans, and Native Americans. As Figure 5–1 shows, African Americans and Hispanic Americans are far more likely than whites to live below the poverty line. African American children have a four in nine chance of being poor and Hispanic American children have a three in eight likelihood of poverty, while the figure for white children is only one in seven.[2] The poverty section of this book will give further evidence of the impact of minority status on income and employment rates.

Upcoming chapters will also describe the effects of race and minority status on health, housing, and other areas of social welfare. To summarize some of those effects

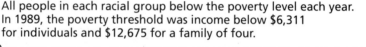

All people in each racial group below the poverty level each year. In 1989, the poverty threshold was income below $6,311 for individuals and $12,675 for a family of four.

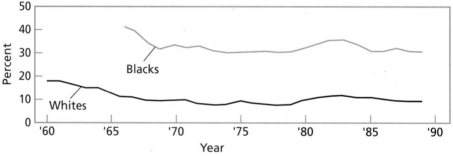

Percent of each group living below poverty level in 1989.

FIGURE 5–1   **Below the Poverty Level . . .**

Source: New York Times (January 21, 1991), 15. Copyright © 1990/91 by The New York Times Company. Reprinted by permission.

    Chapter Five • *Responses to Human Diversity*

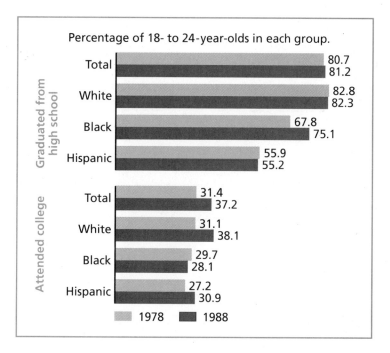

Percentage of 18- to 24-year-olds in each group.

Graduated from high school

Total	80.7	81.2
White	82.8	82.3
Black	67.8	75.1
Hispanic	55.9	55.2

Attended college

Total	31.4	37.2
White	31.1	38.1
Black	29.7	28.1
Hispanic	27.2	30.9

1978   1988

FIGURE 5–2   Disparities in Education

Source: New York Times Education Life (Supplement), April 8, 1990. Copyright © 1990/91 by The New York Times Company. Reprinted by permission.

here: minorities of color face disparities in disease rates and access to adequate health care. African Americans have twice the rate of high blood pressure as whites and as much as seven times the rate of severe hypertension. African Americans are over three times as likely to die of AIDS as whites; Hispanic Americans are about twice as likely.[3] Hispanic Americans typically have low rates of utilization of government health services, because of such factors as lack of knowledge about these services, a sense of pride, lack of bilingual workers, and the inadequacy of health services in many Hispanic American communities. Housing is a major arena for discrimination, with housing segregation rates remaining high in many American cities. In addition, Native Americans, Hispanic Americans, and African Americans are often consigned to separate small, poor, rural communities (such as the one in which the Diaz family lives). The education system also shows the effects of discrimination. The use of busing to desegregate public schools has only partially eradicated widespread segregation based on residential patterns. Rates of college enrollment vary by group membership. Hispanic Americans, for example, continue to lag behind whites and other minority groups in the percentage graduating from high school.[4] (See Figure 5–2.)

Being a minority of color has ramifications in the crucial areas of income, health, housing, and education. New waves of immigration can add to the problem by increasing existing inequities. The latest influx of immigrants has also rekindled debate over the country's ability to absorb large numbers of newcomers. About ten million immigrants entered the United States in the 1980s, even more than the huge influx

TABLE 5–1	Legal immigrants in the United States		
	Immigrants Admitted (in millions)	Number of New Immigrants Admitted per 100 Native Births	Percent of U.S. Population that Is Foreign Born
1901–1910	8.8	N/A	14.2%
1911–1920	5.7	19.9	13.6
1921–1930	4.1	14.4	12.1
1931–1940	0.5	2.2	10.1
1941–1950	1.0	3.3	8.2
1951–1960	2.5	6.2	6.0
1961–1970	3.3	8.5	5.0
1971–1980	4.5	13.5	5.5
1981–1987	4.1	15.8	6.0

Source: New York Times (April 15, 1990), Section E, 4. Copyright © 1990/91 by The New York Times Company. Reprinted by permission.

of immigrants from Southern and Eastern Europe at the turn of the century. (See Table 5–1.) Over three million people came into this country illegally in the last decade.[5]

As Figure 5–3 indicates, most of the new arrivals are of Asian and Hispanic descent. About a quarter of them are undocumented immigrants. They bring an energizing diversity of cultures and ethnic backgrounds to American society. Yet some people argue that new immigrants strain existing housing, education, and health facilities, as well as the job market, particularly in areas where they settle in large numbers. Public backlash against the surge of newcomers has fueled efforts to reaffirm English as the official language of the United States. By 1989, seventeen states had passed legislation formally adopting English as our official language. Interestingly, although anti-immigrant feeling is often fueled by fears that newcomers take jobs away from native-born workers, research suggests that recent arrivals have had little impact on either the earnings or employment prospects of American workers.[6]

Inequities and discrimination also continue for women, the elderly, those with handicaps, and people with a different sexual orientation. Statistics on economic inequities are all too familiar: women earn only 70 percent of men's salaries; female-headed families represent the largest group of poor Americans; the elderly, while their collective situation has improved, still constitute 11 percent of the poor; and Social Security benefits for people with physical and mental handicaps remain at low levels. But beyond the statistics lie issues of prejudice and unequal access to opportunities and services in our society. The AIDS epidemic, for example, has fanned existing negative attitudes toward homosexuals, strengthening attempts to bar gay men and lesbians from teaching jobs and to repeal local government ordinances assuring their free access to housing, employment, and public services. While legislation exists to protect employment rights and access to public buildings for people with physical handicaps, such legislation is not always enforced. Our illustration of social workers who are blind being denied field placements or jobs is just one example of society's continued failure to see the person behind the handicap. Even though laws exist to prohibit such discrimination, legal action may prove too costly or too risky for an individual to pursue.

In sum, diversity can bring discrimination and exploitation. We have even invented terms to capture this phenomenon: sexism, racism, ageism, and homophobia (the fear of homosexuals and homosexual lifestyles). On the other hand, diversity has great advantages, both for the nation as a whole and for members of groups viewed as "different." The social and kinship ties within ethnic communities, the cultural traditions of Hispanic American and African American families, the coping skills of the "physically challenged" (a new term for handicapped) and the working mother, the wisdom of the older person—all can enrich individual and communal life. An understanding of both the positive and negative impacts of diversity is a vital part of social work practice.

DEFINITION OF TERMS

A number of terms emerge in discussions of diversity and difference, particularly in the United States. *Minority group* and *majority* are common labels, for example. Their use suggests that exploitation or discrimination focuses on a group smaller in number than the exploiters. Further, minority often implies nonwhite. Lately, the term *minority* has been expanded. Women constitute more than half of the United States population, yet they are often considered a minority group. Black South Africans, while they are numerically the majority in their country, are seen as a minority group in terms of their subjugation in a white-controlled society. More useful terms for analyzing ex-

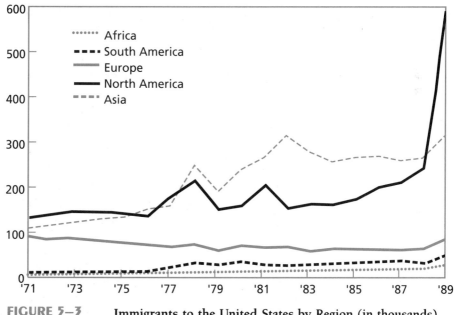

FIGURE 5–3   **Immigrants to the United States by Region (in thousands)**

Source: New York Times (October 14, 1990), Section E, 4. Copyright © 1990/91 by The New York Times Company. Reprinted by permission.

ploitation and discrimination might be *dominant* and *subordinate* groups. A subordinate group is one that is singled out for differential or unequal treatment by a dominant group that has higher rights and privileges.[7]

The concepts of *race* and *ethnic group* are also used in varying and sometimes overlapping ways. Traditionally, the word *race* has meant "a distinct category of human beings with physical characteristics transmitted by descent."[8] In other words, people throughout the ages have found it reasonable to divide each other into groups based on obvious external criteria, such as skin color or eye shape, even though over time, these characteristics have blurred because of intermarriage. The concept of race also carries social connotations which are particularly attached to differences in skin color. That is, from the early days of European colonization, dominant white groups have viewed color as a symbol of status and cultural difference. They have defined dark-skinned people as backward or less evolved. This outlook underlies *racism,* or the idea that physical differences between groups of people signify meaningful differences in intelligence and ability. The racist belief that one group is inherently inferior and another is inherently superior allows one group to justify its oppression of another.[9]

The term *ethnic group* is an even broader concept than race. Ethnic groups can be defined as those "whose members share a unique social and cultural heritage passed on from one generation to the next." Such groups often have distinctive patterns of language, family life, religion, and other customs.[10] Race and nationality might be subsumed under the term *ethnic group,* and a number of present writers use *ethnicity* to talk not only of Jews and Polish Americans but also of African Americans. This book, however, limits the term to groups distinguished primarily by cultural or nationality characteristics, rather than by race.

Ethnic and racial relations are all too often marred by prejudice and discrimination. The term *prejudice* applies to attitudes, and the term *discrimination* applies to behaviors. To be prejudiced is to have unfavorable feelings about a group and its individual members; these feelings are based on stereotypes rather than on comprehensive knowledge. Discrimination is differential (usually negative) treatment of individuals from certain groups or social categories. To say Jews are only interested in making money is prejudice; to prohibit Jews from living in certain suburban neighborhoods is discrimination.

Racism, sexism, ageism, and similar phenomena are forms of prejudice. It is important to note that these attitudes take both an individual and an institutional form. As an example of individual racism, a college professor might routinely ignore the comments and questions of minority students, even though university regulations prohibit such differential treatment. *Institutional racism,* on the other hand, refers to beliefs and actions of large numbers of people which are supported by organizational or community norms. Institutional racism means that a belief in white supremacy has become deeply ingrained in the dominant culture. That belief is reflected in customs and laws, and it leads to discriminatory patterns that many take for granted. These patterns are so deeply and subtly ingrained that it is possible to act in a racist way without being consciously aware of it. At a high school dance, for example, the security staff may turn away African American students who say they have forgotten their tickets, while letting in white students with a similar story. To the extent that members of the white student body ignore this discriminatory action, they are a part of a racist response.

The presence of diverse racial, ethnic, and other distinct groups in society gives rise to various notions about the proper relationship between individual groups and "the whole." Such notions emerge particularly in discussions of immigration, although they have relevance also to the situation of long-time residents (African Americans and Native Americans) and of those belonging to categories such as the aged or people with handicaps. A traditional version of "ideal group relations" in the United States is the idea of a melting pot, in which the cultures of all groups are "melted down" to produce a new, distinctly American culture. In real life, this early twentieth century idea of a "blended American" proved unrealistic. Newcomers were unwilling to give up all of their traditions and customs, and perhaps more significantly, the dominant society had a stake in maintaining its own distinct identity.

A more common and attainable goal for intergroup relations has been that of *assimilation,* in which new and subordinate groups are expected to adapt to American ways and to pattern themselves on a white, Protestant, Anglo-Saxon model. Theorist Milton Gordon has divided the concept of assimilation into a variety of categories. *Structural assimilation,* for example, means the penetration of the new group into "the cliques and associations of the core society at the primary-group level," that is, at the level of family, club, and social relations. Acceptability of intermarriage between dominant and subordinate groups, or of minority membership in the local country club are the signs of structural assimilation. *Cultural assimilation* occurs when the group changes its cultural patterns and beliefs as well as its behaviors to match those of the core society. For example, cultural assimilation was at work when European immigrants of the early 1900s adopted the American preoccupation with material success. Gordon and others note that assimilation of ethnic groups in America has most frequently been of the cultural rather than the structural type.[11] The lack of structural assimilation may stem from ethnic or racial group reluctance to interact with the dominant group on the level of family and social networks, or, more likely, it indicates "mainstream" society's intention of keeping them out.

A final image of intergroup relations is that of *cultural pluralism.* This occurs when people of different cultures retain their own unique individual character and traits, but at the same time interact with other groups, taking on additional traits, such as a common language. In the United States these common traits have tended to supplant individual group practices and attitudes, so full-scale cultural pluralism cannot be said to exist. However, social scientists like Andrew Greeley, Nathan Glazer, and others have documented various types of ethnic group persistence in our country. Looking at the continuing presence of ethnic ties among third and fourth generation European immigrants (seen, for example, in tight-knit Italian or Polish communities), Greeley and Glazer conclude that ethnicity is still alive and well in America.[12] Furthermore, the prospect of a pluralistic society which draws on the unique contributions of a variety of groups remains an attractive ideal for many, including the authors of this text.

Different possibilities for intergroup relations, then, include: (1) assimilation (taking on the characteristics of the dominant group); (2) blending ("melting" together to create a new type of dominant group); and (3) pluralism (maintaining a degree of group distinctiveness). As we will see in succeeding sections of this chapter, the element of power plays a role in all of these alternatives. In addition, these models have been more available to some groups than to others. In some cases, two final models of intergroup relations have relevance: colonialism and separatism. *Colonialism,* or control by a nation or a dominant group over a dependent territory, can be used to describe the relations between Americans of European descent and Native Americans, or even perhaps the subjugation of regions such as Appalachia. The notion of colonialism is sometimes extended to describe the continued oppression of African Americans, whose ancestors were brought into this country as slaves.[13] Another concept, *separatism,* characterizes situations in which groups attempt to divorce themselves as much as possible from mainstream society, as in the case of Amish communities.

DYNAMICS OF INTERGROUP RELATIONS

What lies behind the prejudice and discrimination which are often part of relationships between different groups? Social and behavioral scientists have come up with a variety of theories to explain negative feelings and actions toward groups and individuals perceived as *different.* One set of theories focuses on internal personality traits. Prejudice might spring from inner frustrations and aggressive urges, which are converted into hatred or suspicion of a convenient scapegoat. Sexual feelings may also play a part. Homophobia, fears of sexual aggression by African American men toward white women, beliefs that Jewish (or Italian, or Mexican) women are sexually promiscuous—all seem to express an uncomfortableness with sexuality and a fascination with the "forbidden fruit" represented by other groups with whom close interaction is forbidden. Still another psychological interpretation has been offered by social psychologist T.W. Adorno. Adorno's work on the concept of an authoritarian personality holds that some people are more likely than others to be prejudiced. These individuals have the following traits: they glorify power, they tend to view people as good or bad, they repress their sexual feelings, they are concerned about status and toughness, and they generally "blame others rather than themselves for misdeeds and troubles." Subsequent studies of Adorno's theories, however, find that prejudice is not confined to the authoritarian personality.[14] While prejudice cannot be explained solely by psychological traits, these traits no doubt play a part in the larger picture of bias against others.

Prejudice may often relate to social and economic factors. In a situation of scarce resources, groups compete for jobs, educational opportunities, and other necessities of life. The chapter on housing, for example, gives abundant evidence of how competition over affordable living space can lead to discriminatory housing policies and even race riots. A major part of prejudice against immigrants to the United States has no doubt been the fears of working-class people that the newcomers would take their jobs.

In addition to economic competition, a more subtle social competition may take place. That is, one group defends its status in society by looking down on another. Sometimes, groups who already feel discriminated against may try to characterize other groups as being even lower in the social "pecking order." For example, African Americans may at times express prejudice against those of Puerto Rican descent. Also, a group might seek to maintain solidarity and to define its values by contrasting itself to "outsiders." This may explain some of the bias shown by white Anglo-Saxon Americans against people of divergent backgrounds (or the existence for most of our history of men's groups which prohibit membership by women).

Many observers argue that the element of power is the most important component of prejudice and discrimination. This power may be used to maintain a particular social status. In other words, certain elements in the United States have assumed positions of social superiority, and they have attempted to keep these positions by setting up psychological and physical barriers against other groups. White Americans, for example, have bolstered their status through beliefs about the inferiority of African Americans and other people of color. They have constructed discriminatory policies leading to segregated education, housing covenants, and lack of access to the ballot box. Those upholding such policies are not necessarily bigots in the blatant sense. Their aim is to maintain the advantages of the status quo.[15]

The power element is sometimes displayed through a more direct exploitation of subordinate groups. Labeling such groups as inferior helps to justify their oppression. As one form of such oppression, American employers have frequently sought a cheap labor force, such as African slaves in the early years of this country, Chinese railroad workers in the mid–1800s, unskilled immigrants from Europe at the turn of the century, or Mexican farm workers in the present day. Discriminatory practices have helped to control this labor force. For example, if access to better paying jobs is denied to them, members of subordinate groups have no choice but to remain in menial labor. Feminist scholars point out that white males have similarly exploited women in America. In *Regulating the Lives of Women,* Abramovitz describes male domination of women both at work and at home. Discrimination has channeled women into low-paying jobs, thus sustaining the market supply of low-cost labor. Stereotypes about women's inferior

Back-breaking field work is typical of the exploitation of cheap labor which has continued to occur since the abolition of slavery.

intelligence and lack of drive have also helped keep women "in their place" at home, where they do unpaid work to support the family.[16]

These examples lend credence to the idea that the roots of racial, ethnic, and gender inequities, as well as prejudices, are grounded in the U.S. economic system, which encourages competition. In addition, race, ethnicity, and gender help dictate the economic class to which one will belong. Recently, African American scholar William Julius Wilson has taken this argument in a different direction, contending that in the present day, class differences are more important than race in explaining the plight of African Americans in U.S. society. In *The Declining Significance of Race* and *The Truly Disadvantaged*, Wilson writes that racism is not the major cause of current problems in the inner city ghetto. Instead, the exodus of "more stable working- and middle-class" African Americans from the ghetto has left behind an underclass, a grouping of families and individuals who remain outside the occupational mainstream.

> Included in this group are individuals who lack training and skills and either experience long-term unemployment or are not members of the labor force, individuals who are engaged in street crime . . . , and families that experience long-term spells of poverty and/or welfare dependency.[17]

African American dependency, Wilson contends, stems more from factors like the lack of skills among the men and the growth of female-headed families, than it does from racial discrimination. If discrimination were still widespread, he asks, how does one explain the recent economic rise of the African American middle class?

Critics of Wilson's arguments have pointed out that even the more privileged African American middle class is not as well off or as well treated as the white middle class. Racism has affected the lives of even these "successful" African Americans. In addition, Wilson has been taken to task for failing to acknowledge that poverty in female-headed families occurs largely because discrimination based on race and sex keeps women's salaries low. Finally, as sociologist Charles Willie notes, discrimination and segregation created the African American urban ghetto. This residential segregation leads to lessened economic opportunities, since businesses and industrial plants tend not to locate in or near these areas.[14] Thus despite Wilson's thesis, many scholars continue to stress the importance of discrimination in shaping the lives of those in subordinate groups.

PERSPECTIVES

The Conservative Perspective

Conservatives, liberals, and radicals take different ideological positions on how best to deal with the discrimination and disadvantages faced by subordinate groups. Consistent with their approach to other social problems, conservatives warn against relying on government regulation to deal with discriminatory practices, and they are particularly critical of affirmative action policies. Sometimes, conservatives question whether significant discrimination even exists in the United States today. Those who take this position argue that individual defects—in the form of lack of skills, motivation for work, or commitment to independence—are the real factors behind the problems of groups like African Americans, Native Americans, and Hispanic Americans. Similarly, the low salaries of women are attributed to such factors as their having less education and a tendency to leave work "to have children."

Both those conservatives who question the existence of discrimination and those who accept its presence agree that the major solution to the problems of minority or subordinate groups is extension of opportunity. Given opportunities in employment, education, and housing, individuals will be able to overcome their minority group status. The chance to change is to be offered through freedom of choice in the marketplace, rather than through government regulation. For example, provision of vouchers to poor African Americans and Hispanic Americans to use for housing and education will allow them to move into "better" neighborhoods and to equip their children with the type of schooling necessary for occupational success.

The Liberal Perspective

Liberals generally relate the problems of subordinate groups to social-structural causes rather than to individual causes. They see discrimination as an important factor in the difficulties faced by women, African Americans, and others. Some liberals believe in the modified version of the "individual defect" argument, stressing inadequate education, poor health, and lack of role models who could point the way to success. Yet this view differs from the conservative interpretation of defect because it emphasizes that these individual problems are caused by larger socioeconomic forces.

Liberals stress the necessity of government intervention to counteract discrimination in our society. They question the ability of the market to enforce equality in jobs and living arrangements. They back legislation and regulation to guarantee equal employment, education, and housing opportunities. In the case of persons with physical disabilities, for example, liberals would support laws that mandate accessibility in both public and private buildings. Conservatives would prefer that such accessibility be provided on a voluntary basis, particularly in buildings within the private sector.

In addition to their emphasis on regulation, liberals look to government to provide welfare benefits and compensatory programs to deal with those problems caused in part by discrimination: poverty, unemployment, and the lack of adequate education and skills. The War on Poverty in the 1960s constituted one such attempt to "break the cycle of poverty," particularly minority group poverty, by increasing welfare benefits and services and committing large amounts of public monies to job training programs and early childhood education.

The Radical Perspective

Radicals agree with liberals that social-structural factors are the basis for difficulties faced by African Americans, Hispanic Americans, and women. However, the radical viewpoint places major emphasis on the role of power in dominant/subordinate group relations. Many radicals argue, for example, that a capitalist society creates oppressed groups in order to ensure a supply of cheap labor. Radical feminists contend that men have historically discriminated against women in order to control their work. Radicals also point out that those in power may encourage competition between subordinate groups in order to maintain their own control. If Hispanic Americans and African

Americans feel they must compete over what they are told are scarce resources, they will be less likely to join together to question the existing system. By exploiting white fears that their taxes were being used to subsidize an African American underclass, conservative politicians diverted attention from the massive transfer of wealth to the upper class during the Reagan era. In general, the radical perspective depicts prejudice as a mask for privilege, or a way in which dominant groups can maintain their own status and power.[19]

To combat discrimination, radicals support the same sorts of government regulation that liberals stress. But they also point to the importance of equalizing income and wealth so that oppressed people can gain more power in the system. In order to overcome powerlessness among subordinate groups, radicals seek ways to increase people's control over resources and over the major decisions that will affect their lives. Strategies of empowerment include raising consciousness (that is, helping people see that they are oppressed), teaching people how to analyze the existing power structure, and fostering the use of groups—advocacy groups, unions, and protest groups—to counter that power structure.[20] Finally, radicals look to the restructuring of social institutions to eradicate discrimination and oppression.

HISTORY OF INTERGROUP RELATIONS IN THE UNITED STATES

A comprehensive history of intergroup relations in the United States is too large a task for the present book. In this section, we will instead take a brief look at society's treatment of European ethnic groups, African Americans, and women, with a primary stress on these groups' relationships with the social welfare system.

Social Workers, Social Welfare Institutions, and the "New Immigration"

At the end of the nineteenth century and the beginning of the twentieth century, the United States witnessed the greatest influx of European immigration in its history. In fact, nearly 40 percent of today's Americans can trace their roots to a relative who immigrated during this period. Between 1901 and 1910, 8.7 million people, largely from Southern and Eastern Europe, landed on American shores. These were called the "new immigrants" because they appeared fundamentally different from those groups—the British, Germans, French, Scandinavians, and other Northern Europeans—that had come before. Only the Irish, largely poor folk escaping poverty and famine, had some characteristics in common with the newer arrivals. Often uprooted peasants, at least half of the new immigrants were classified as unskilled laborers. One-third were illiterate. Many of them had little or no experience in the process of representative government. Most joined friends and families in the slum neighborhood of large cities. This influx strained the facilities of existing health and welfare services and posed a potential job-market threat to native-born workers (even though their coming had in part been fostered by industrialists in search of cheap labor).[21]

In addition, the newcomers looked different. Often they wore "peasant clothes," such as the *babushka,* or Russian woman's head scarf. Some, like many Italians, had dark complexions. They ate unusual foods and spoke a variety of languages: Yiddish,

Russian, Polish, Greek, and many more. Unlike the Protestant Anglo-Saxon mainstream, they attended Catholic and Greek Orthodox churches and Jewish synagogues.

Because of these differences, and because of their potential as competitors for jobs, the new immigrants encountered fear and prejudice on the part of many Americans. Large numbers of the public felt that the newcomers represented an inferior stock, lacking the intelligence and physical attributes of northern Europeans. Discrimination in jobs, education, and housing soon developed. In addition, businesses exploited this cheap and powerless labor force, paying low wages, demanding long hours, and failing to provide safe and healthy working conditions.

Social welfare institutions—in particular, the social settlement—developed a variety of responses to the new immigrants. The newcomers were, after all, the major "clients" of most settlement houses. Jewish neighborhoods in New York, Polish enclaves in Cleveland, and Italian communities in Boston each had their own neighborhood settlements. In some cases, settlement workers' philosophies and actions regarding the immigrant community mirrored reactions in the larger public. In others, settlements led the way in thinking about the possibilities of a pluralistic society.

One segment of the settlement movement, located primarily in Boston, stressed assimilation as the appropriate path for immigrants to take. This emphasis stemmed from a belief in the importance of social harmony in American communities, and in some cases from negative stereotypes about the newcomers. A particularly blatant example of prejudice against immigrant groups appears in the 1911 Annual Report of Boston's Peabody House.

> This district is virtually transplanted from another order of civilization. Our foreign neighbors bring with them habits which cannot be followed in this country without danger to our own standards . . . the constituents of our district [must] sink individuality in common neighborhood purposes.[22]

Sinking individuality in common purposes often meant assimilation into a "coherent and distinctively American nationality." For most Boston settlement workers, "American" meant "Anglo-Saxon." Fearful of the lowering of Anglo-Saxon standards, and concerned to build close-knit, harmonious communities, these workers strove to Americanize their foreign neighbors.[23] They promoted English and "good citizenship" classes and stressed such behaviors as responsible voting, obedience to the law, hard work, and thrift.

Other settlement workers followed a different tack. In cities like New York, Cleveland, and particularly Chicago, a philosophy of cultural pluralism characterized many settlements' work with immigrants. Jane Addams was a particularly articulate champion of the pluralist ideal. Unlike those who looked to a past Anglo-Saxon harmony in America, Addams applauded newness and change. Society's new unity would be based on synthesis rather than standardization. Addams envisioned a cosmopolitanism which allowed for the appreciation of cultural differences along with the recognition of commonalties among all human beings.[24]

As director of Hull House in Chicago, Addams stressed the strengths and "immigrant gifts" of her Greek and Bohemian neighbors. "One thing seemed clear in regard to . . . immigrants," she noted, and that was "to preserve and keep whatever of value their past life contained."[25] To this end, Hull House developed a Labor Museum, where people exhibited the tools and processes used in their countries of origin. The settlement sponsored foreign language plays and provided a meeting place for nationality groups. Through such activities, Hull House strove to publicize the immigrants' contributions to the larger community and to encourage immigrant children to respect their parents' culture. Above all, Addams hoped "to have made a genuine effort to find the basic experience upon which a cosmopolitan community may unite."[26]

Hull House also pioneered in another response to the immigrant situation—immigrant protection work, or what we might now describe as advocacy for the newcomers' rights. This activity led to new governmental structures designed to deal with immigrants' problems. Recognizing the varieties of exploitation and fraud perpetrated upon immigrants by employment agencies, banks serving the newcomers, and employers, Hull House resident Grace Abbott helped found the League for Protection of Immigrants. The League acted as an advocacy group for a number of years; it helped bring about state legislation protecting immigrants from fraudulent practices by employment agencies and it was instrumental in the creation of an Illinois Immigration Commission. In promoting government regulation to counteract discrimination and exploitation of European immigrants, the League's work reflected a liberal approach to the problems of subordinate groups.[27]

The influx of southern and eastern Europeans was ended abruptly by immigration restriction legislation in 1924. Fears of job competition, uneasiness about "foreign radicalism" after the Russian Revolution and World War I, and outright prejudice against the newcomers helped create an atmosphere conducive to exclusion. Rejecting notions of cultural pluralism and skeptical of the ability of immigrants to assimilate, many Americans saw restriction as the only reasonable solution to the "immigrant problem."

Social Workers, Social Welfare Institutions, and African Americans

Settlement house work with the new immigrants constituted an early arena for testing out the relationship between subordinate groups and social welfare programs and goals. Social workers were slower to identify African Americans as a specific client group, in part because a large proportion lived in Southern rural areas, where few social work organizations existed. Also, inattention to the problems faced by African Americans reflected either overt prejudice or an unthinking involvement in institutional racism on the part of a number of social workers and social reformers.

African Americans came to the United States under circumstances different from other immigrant groups. Brought over by force, they began their experience as an enslaved and colonized people. Prejudices used to justify such oppression persisted even after the Civil War ended the institution of slavery. Biases against African Americans were kept alive partly by white laborers fearing competition from freed slaves in the Southern job market and partly by a white Southern elite wishing to retain the traditional system of agricultural production and to keep African Americans in subordinate positions.[28]

Prejudice against African Americans and the desire to keep them in their place played a role in the difficulties faced by the Freedmen's Bureau, a social welfare program established by the national government in 1865 to foster the economic rehabilitation of freed slaves. The first federal social welfare program other than veterans' benefits

The U.S. Supreme Court ruled in 1948 that the University of Oklahoma admit G. W. McLauren, but the University made him sit outside the classroom.

in the United States, the Bureau promoted education for African Americans and public relief for both freedmen and displaced whites. It also proposed to furnish land and tools to former slaves. While accomplishing a good deal in the area of education, the Bureau was unable to fulfill its economic objectives. Inadequate funds, lack of support by President Andrew Johnson, and opposition from the Southern gentry contributed to the abolishment of the Freedmen's Bureau in 1872.[29] Soon after, in the 1880s, Southern states and cities began enacting statutes (the infamous Jim Crow laws) to legalize segregation and to deny African Americans access to good jobs, public services, and equal education.

In increasing numbers after the turn of the century, African Americans moved to Northern cities in search of jobs and greater equality. More often than not, they encountered the same racism and discriminatory practices they had left behind. The growth of segregated communities in the North gave rise to new issues in intergroup relations. Were African Americans simply another group, like the Italian or the Polish immigrants, in a pluralistic society? Or did they "constitute a people apart?" These questions were particularly relevant for settlement workers. Reactions of Chicago settlement personnel, as examined by historian Steven Diner, indicate a range of responses probably typical of settlement and charity workers across the country.[30]

Chicago settlement workers, Diner reports, developed different perspectives regarding African Americans. One response, perhaps that of the majority, was to recognize their poverty and difficult living situations, but at the same time to believe that these difficulties were best overcome by hard work and initiative. African Americans did not face any greater hardships than the immigrants, although they were probably so "inherently different" from whites that they would never really assimilate into American society.[31]

A smaller group of settlement leaders, including Jane Addams, argued that African Americans faced distinctive difficulties which caused their situation to be even worse than that of the immigrants. In particular, they encountered greater economic and political discrimination, and almost total residential segregation. In attempts to help them deal with these problems, Addams and other settlement leaders helped found the NAACP and the Chicago Urban League. They researched the specific problems of African American residents of Chicago, and they publicized their findings to the larger community.[32]

Yet despite greater understanding of the problems faced by African Americans, these leaders joined the rest of the Chicago settlement movement in maintaining the color line. None of the white settlements worked directly with residents of the ghetto. Perhaps because it seemed to them the only possibility in the context of the times, Addams and her colleagues did not push for integration. Instead, they promoted exclusive settlements founded and run by African Americans. These centers were poorly funded and often lasted only a few years.[33]

Social service agencies in Chicago (and no doubt in other Northern cities) followed similar patterns of separation. In addition, most lacked the special concern for African Americans expressed by reformers like Addams. Public agencies were required by state law to serve both races, but wherever possible they kept the two groups separate. For example, clinics and other facilities were located in areas where African Americans and whites were unlikely to mingle. Private welfare agencies could, and did discriminate. Some refused to serve African Americans at all. Others offered separate services at different times or in different offices. Goodwill Industries, for example, would help all people with handicaps except disabled African Americans. The United Charities, a relief organization, maintained separate branches in the ghetto.[34]

In response to the needs of their communities and the failure of the larger society to meet those needs, African Americans developed their own network of charitable organizations. African American churches were the major source of social welfare activity after the Reconstruction era. By the turn of the century, they were joined by African American women's clubs, whose membership was made up largely of educated middle-class African American women. These clubs were similar to the philanthropic white women's groups from which African Americans were barred. They supported a host of social welfare organizations, particularly in urban areas, which included children's nurseries, homes for young working women, settlements, and homes for the aged. However, these institutions lacked the financial resources available to most white charitable endeavors. In the city of Chicago, for example, only the Urban League, which concentrated on employment services and became the city's dominant African American social welfare organization after World War I, was able to obtain substantial support from white philanthropists.[35]

Discrimination and lack of financial support continued to characterize the treatment of African Americans in the social service system during and after the 1930s. While some moves were made toward integration and improvement of services, elements of racism found their way into the new federal public welfare programs developed during the New Deal. The state of Mississippi, for example, instructed its county relief offices to put a 10 percent quota on the number of African American citizens receiving assistance, even where they were in the majority. (In a similar vein, Texas excluded Mexican American applicants from its programs, and Nevada had no Aid to Families with Dependent Children program for twenty years, to avoid giving benefits to Native American families.)[36] On the other hand, New Deal social welfare programs, with their greater resources and introduction of some national standards, provided improved levels of benefits and services for large numbers of African Americans.

The relationship between the social welfare system and African Americans remains a highly complex one. It has been characterized both by institutional racism and discrimination and by provision of appropriate aid. To the extent that it has been effective, the system owes a good degree of credit to the efforts of African American churches, women's clubs, and social welfare workers. African American scholars and social work educators like E. Franklin Frazier, George E. Haynes of Fisk University, and Forrester B. Washington, Director of the Atlanta School of Social Work, contributed by helping to train social work practitioners. Together, these individuals and organizations struggled to provide benefits to the African American population and to publicize inadequate and unequal treatment in the American social welfare institution.

Social Workers, Social Welfare Institutions, and Women

One unique aspect of the relationship of women and social welfare is the fact that women represent both the majority of clients and the majority of workers in the system. Women, for example, constitute a large percentage of Social Security recipients and mental health clients. The biggest program within the federal public welfare system, Aid to Families with Dependent Children, serves primarily women and their children. The social welfare system, built on the need to deal with dependency, has traditionally included widows, deserted wives, and young, unmarried women (potential "wayward girls") among its concerns.

How well has the system served women? What have been its major goals in dealing with a female clientele? To a certain degree, one can argue that these goals have been humanitarian and supportive ones. This seems most characteristic of the programs developed and advocated to a large part by women themselves. For example, women's organizations and female settlement and charity leaders played an important role in the creation of a system of state pensions for destitute mothers between 1910 and 1920. These pensions marked a move away from temporary charity and toward a more lasting form of assistance for female-headed families. They constituted a precedent for the Aid to Dependent Children program established in 1935.[37]

Similarly, a powerful lobby of feminist groups and individual women leaders, many of them connected with Hull House and the U.S. Children's Bureau, was instrumental in the passage of the Sheppard-Towner Act in 1921. This act provided federal matching grants to states for maternal and child health services. The American Medical Association, anti-women's suffrage groups, and self-styled patriotic organizations attacked the program for its "encroachment" into the medical domain, its involvement of the federal government in social welfare activities, and its undermining of men's capacity to care for their families. This opposition helped bring about the program's demise in 1929. Yet the Sheppard-Towner Act was significant in establishing official attention to the needs of women and children, and it led the way for subsequent government programs protecting infant and maternal health.[38]

Women also set up private organizations and agencies which provided social welfare services specifically for women. These included the YWCA, boarding houses for single working women, mother's clubs in settlement houses, and county cooperative extension services.

Of course, it would be a mistake to assume that programs and services developed or administered by women were automatically free of bias, nonjudgmental, and helpful to their clients. Well-to-do women charity workers, for example, generally felt little compunction about applying their moralistic standards to the lives of poor women. Even mothers' pensions laws often restricted benefits to those women deemed "fit and deserving." By the same token, services developed and supported by men could be appropriate and sympathetic to the needs of women.

On the other hand, some scholars argue that the social welfare institution has been used by the male patriarchy, or authority system, as a means of controlling the lives and labor of women. In an analysis of social welfare policy in relation to women, Abramovitz contends that historically, welfare programs have supported certain roles for women and discouraged others. The system has tended to reward women whose lives combined the traditional roles of wife, mother, and homemaker. It has often penalized those, like working wives or unmarried women, who either by choice or by necessity followed a different path. In addition to reinforcing a certain view of women's roles, the welfare system has "helped to meet the economy's need for women's unpaid labor in the home."[39]

As evidence of the system's aim of regulating women's lives, Abramovitz and others point to the practices of the Charity Organization Societies (COSs) in the late nineteenth century and early twentieth century. The COS workers were urged to "dissuade restless wives from seeking outside employment" and to deny aid to immoral, vagrant, or degraded women. The majority of clients accepted for assistance were "deserving" married couples or widows.[40] A goal of controlling women can be seen in public welfare policies as early as the 1820s. It was not unusual, for example, for local public relief authorities to remove children from poor families and to place them in almshouses or children's institutions. The grounds for doing so were that such families offered harmful home conditions and that many poor mothers were unfit to raise their children.[41]

In addition, critics argue, welfare policies have been used to maintain a low-paid female labor force for work outside the home. While AFDC was begun as a program to allow poor women to stay home with their children, since the late 1950s either subtle or overt pressure has been put on "welfare mothers" to "get off the welfare rolls" and seek employment. President Nixon's WIN program and the welfare/workfare re-forms of the late 1980s are two such attempts to put women on AFDC to work. Because many women in this situation either lack the proper skills or are denied access to decently paying jobs, they are forced to join a convenient pool of low-wage labor. A particularly blatant example of this manipulation of women's labor in the past was the refusal of many states to grant assistance to black women "if their eligibility for AFDC conflicted with local labor market demands."[42]

This analysis of women and the welfare state suggests a type of colonization of a subordinate group by a dominant group. Similar concepts have been applied to dis-cussions of women as professionals working in the social welfare system, although there the picture seems more diverse. Some have argued that women were channeled into social work jobs by men who saw this occupation as appropriate to women's nurturing and "emotional" natures. At the same time, men maintained control over the powerful supervisory positions in the field. It is true that women filled most of the front line jobs in charity work, as well as many of the jobs in the settlements in the late 1800s and early 1900s. Yet at the same time, women assumed leadership roles in these fields. This was particularly true in the settlement movement, which boasted such prominent figures as Jane Addams, Grace Abbott, Lillian Wald of New York's Henry Street Settlement, and many others. In 1910, women constituted about two-thirds of all settlement directors.[43] Charity work was more likely to be under the direction of a man, although the movement produced important figures like Josephine Shaw Lowell and Mary Richmond, who occupied a number of leadership positions in the field. In social work education, up through the 1930s and 1940s, women shared leadership roles with men. Most of the early developers of methodologies in social work—casework, group work, and Freudian and other therapies—were women.

A number of these early leaders saw in social work the chance to build a new career for women. Edith Abbott and Sophonisba Breckinridge were instrumental in founding and developing the social work graduate school at the University of Chicago. Although they had degrees in other fields—Abbott in economics and Breckinridge in law—they faced discrimination in these disciplines. In their development of graduate education for social work, they consciously molded a new occupation for women.[44]

Although women held prominent leadership positions in social work's earlier years and the number of women administrators increased when men left for war in the 1940s, by the 1950s men were increasingly taking over administrative roles in social welfare organizations. Between 1957 and 1976, for example, the percentage of women heading member agencies of the Family Service Association of America fell from 60 to 20 percent.[45] (See also Table 5–2.) Men had also come to predominate in the social work education hierarchy. Whereas two out of three women were deans of schools of social work in 1925, the ratio had dropped to only one out of three by 1990. While more men were entering the field at lower levels, women continued to constitute the majority of workers.

Varied explanations have been put for these changes. Some feminist scholars argue that the increase in male leadership is evidence of the ability of the male patriarchy to continue to control the lives of women. Additional factors have been cited by historian Clarke Chambers in a study of the rise of male leadership in social work from the 1950s through the 1980s. Chambers suggests that women's new freedom to combine both career and marriage may have, paradoxically, undercut their chances to rise within

TABLE 5–2 **Percentage of women and men in social welfare administration, 1950–1984***

	1950	1960	1977	1984
Female administrators as percentage of all female social welfare workers	16	15	29	13
Male administrators as percentage of all male social welfare workers	33	29	43	30

*Statistics are not directly comparable across years because of different data bases. All percentages are rounded.

Source: Paula Dressel, "Patriarchy and Social Welfare Work." © 1987 by the Society for the Study of Social Problems. Reprinted from *Social Problems,* Vol. 34, No. 3, June 1987, 298.

History of Intergroup Relations in the United States

the profession. Unlike the earlier unmarried leaders, women who now took some time out for family involvement, or who worked part time, found themselves unable to stay on the "promotion track" in a university or agency. In addition, the expansion of welfare bureaucracies following the New Deal opened up career positions in public adminis-tration that tended to favor men.[46] Also, women social work leaders actively recruited men into the profession after World War II, partly in an attempt to increase the field's prestige. On a similar ironic note, the expansion of women's job opportunities has drawn a number of bright and ambitious women away from the more traditional "women's fields" and into the challenging areas of the sciences, medicine, engineering, and law.

Increasingly, a number of women social workers (as well as men) have become conscious of what they see as the power imbalance within the profession as well as the need to address the needs of women clients more appropriately. Groups fostering attention to women's concerns have emerged within the National Association of Social Workers and the Council on Social Work Education. A growing scholarship addresses women's issues within the social welfare system. These developments have taken place within the context of a national women's movement, which began in the 1960s and which in many ways represents the attempts of a subordinate group to gain greater control over its position in society.

CURRENT ISSUES REGARDING SOCIAL WELFARE AND HUMAN DIVERSITY

Many groups in today's society—women, African Americans, ethnic groups, people with handicaps, and homosexuals—have their own specific concerns and needs. Rather than focus specifically on each group, however, we find it more useful to analyze several broad policy debates concerning how best to deal with patterns of discrimination and inequality emerging in a diverse society.

One response to inequities in education and employment has been the development of affirmative action policies. These represent both an attempt to compensate for past discrimination and an effort to eliminate barriers to the participation of all groups in educational, occupational, and other opportunities. Most affirmative action programs and policies stem from the 1964 Civil Rights Act, which declared that it was illegal for any employer or labor union with twenty-five or more persons "to discriminate against any individual . . . because of race, color, religion, sex, or national origin." The act also ordered the Attorney General to undertake civil actions to support de-segregation of public schools, a process begun after the Supreme Court's ruling against segregated schools in the 1954 *Brown* v. *Board of Education* case.[47]

Discrimination continued despite these prohibitions. Policy makers soon concluded that more specific direction was needed. By the 1970s, federal regulations and court decisions began specifying that employers and educational institutions had to take "affirmative actions" to end discrimination and to ensure equal opportunity in education and employment "without regard to race, color, religion, sex, or national origin." Organizations were to do this by working under guidelines and setting specific goals and timetables. For example, the Office of Federal Contract Compliance began requiring that firms send in plans which included data on current employees as well as on the background of job applicants and reasons for rejection. They could then ask such questions as, "Why did you hire the one white man out of a pool of women and African American men?" Similarly, a court might rule that a school system have a certain proportion of members of each race in each school.[48] Recently, such guidelines and protections have been extended to older Americans and to people with handicaps, although generally not to gay men and lesbians.

Although affirmative action policies and programs have improved opportunities for many Americans, they have also received a good deal of criticism. A part of this stems from the use of formal and informal quotas in some affirmative action systems. Another basis for criticism is an unwillingness on the part of some to "accept the guilt of the fathers" and to see affirmative action as a just compensation for those groups which have been discriminated against in the past. Critics also argue that affirmative action programs, especially those allowing lower merit test scores for minorities, lead to a lowering of standards and the hiring of "unqualified persons." (Defenders of affirmative action counter that standard-test-type measures of merit may be biased against nonwhites and women and that test scores do not correlate well with actual job performance.) Finally, the claim has been made that affirmative action can lead to "reverse discrimination" against majority groups. Such criticisms found expression in the well-known Bakke case (U.S. Supreme Court, 1978), in which a white man in California successfully gained entry to medical school after having been denied admission because of a quota system which saved spaces for minorities.[49]

In the 1990s, a stagnant economy and ongoing concern about interventions by "big government" have created a fertile ground for continued attacks on affirmative action. For over a year, President Bush delayed passage of the 1991 Civil Rights Act, which makes it easier to sue over job discrimination, by referring to it as a "quota bill." Bush argued the bill would force employers to choose between quotas and costly litigation.[50]

At times, critiques of affirmative action have been used to appeal to racist tendencies, as in the recent political campaigns of David Duke, a public figure with a White Supremacist background. In an uncertain job market, the concern that "other people"—including minorities and immigrants—are "taking our jobs" can reinforce such tendencies.

Despite this opposition, many liberals and members of subordinate groups continue to argue that affirmative action policies of some type will be necessary to combat persistent discrimination and inequality in American society. These policies need not take the form of formal quotas, but can stress such measures as active recruitment of minorities and women by employers, and in cases of applicants with comparable qualifications, giving preference to these groups in hiring.

Another controversial discussion in the United States has reemerged around the issue of how best to encompass diverse racial and ethnic groups in one society. This discussion is occurring in part because of the growth of minority populations, particularly in certain segments of society and certain geographical regions. In 1960, for example, 94 percent of all college students were white. Now, at least 20 percent of college students are nonwhite or Hispanic Americans. In the state of California, the white non-Hispanic American population will soon be a minority group. Such demographic changes, along with the continued growth of organized movements among women and minorities of color, have led to a stress on *multiculturalism,* a concept which calls for focusing as much attention on the history, culture, and interests of minority groups as on that of the dominant white Anglo-Saxon (male) population. The multicultural approach most frequently manifests itself in education. For example, books by women, African Americans, Native Americans, and others are now included in many college literature courses. Elementary school history texts have been rewritten to reflect the stories of the myriad groups which make up the United States. Now, as in the time of the New Immigration at the turn of the century, some people criticize the multicultural focus, arguing that it threatens to undermine the common goals and ideals vital to the maintenance of a national identity. Others maintain that attention to difference is a necessity in a diverse society, but that it can be carried out in a way that still recognizes basic commonalities.[51]

A third debate related to the needs and preferences of specific groups revolves around issues of separatism versus integration. Although the "separate but equal" principle in education was long ago discarded by the Supreme Court, separatism is still practiced, and debated, in other realms. In the area of housing, for example, questions have been posed about whether it is more desirable for the elderly to live in separate housing complexes or to be in age-integrated housing and communities. Similarly, one might ask whether Native Americans should remain on reservations, where their unique culture can best be preserved. Finally, even in public education a major debate has developed over whether states in the South should preserve and enhance their historically black colleges and universities.

Gay men, and more recently, lesbian women, tend also to see themselves as representing separate communities of interest. At an earlier point in history, homosexuals were often integrated into society and not viewed as "different" people. But since the 1700s, homosexuality has been considered illegal in most European countries, with the Scandinavian countries and the Netherlands as notable exceptions. In reaction, a male homosexual underground had become well established in Europe and the United States by the nineteenth century. Because women were tied to the private world of the home until relatively recently, the practice of lesbianism remained hidden for a longer period. Following the development of social networks, political movements promoting gay and lesbian rights emerged first in Europe and then spread to the United States in the 1900s. Many lesbians and gay men have seen creation of these separate social groups and advocacy organizations as crucial to their emotional and physical survival in an insensitive, frequently hostile world.[52]

In the social welfare arena, issues of separate treatment arise in discussions of special agencies for special groups, mainstreaming, and the matching of workers and clients. A number of those concerned about women's issues, for example, have argued the need for alternative social services for women. Thus, we have witnessed the emergence of women's health clinics, counseling centers, programs for female victims of sexual abuse, and the like. While less prevalent today, African Americans and European ethnic groups have a history of group-specific services, such as the black settlement or the Jewish charitable organization. (At the present time, religiously affiliated organizations tend to serve clients of all denominations.) The presence of new immigrant groups, including people from Southeast Asia and Central America, has led to the

Marches like these attest to a growing activism within the gay and
lesbian population.

development of agencies attending specifically to their needs, including the use of
workers who speak the appropriate language.

The alternative to separate services and treatment is integration of diverse groups
into a common social welfare system. Mainstreaming of the handicapped, a policy
applied most often to the education arena, has relevance for social welfare programs
as well. During the 1970s, state and federal legislation developed which guaranteed
the right of handicapped youngsters to receive a public education. Wherever possible,
such education is to take place in regular classrooms in the public schools. This notion
of mainstreaming has most recently been expanded to job training and job placement.
"Supported employment" programs place those with physical, mental, or emotional
handicaps in normal job situations rather than in the traditional, separate sheltered
workshop.

Another version of the debate between separatism and integration emerges in
discussions of client-worker matching. Such matching entails the selection of a social
service worker who has the same background as the client. For example, one might
argue that only a counselor who is herself lesbian can understand the specific issues
faced by a lesbian client. Some women feel most comfortable with a woman gynecol-
ogist. An African American teenager might identify best with an African American
guidance counselor.

The idea of matching plays an important role in policies regarding adoption and
foster care placement. There the issue centers on the importance of placing children
in settings which duplicate their own racial, religious, or ethnic backgrounds. The
National Association of Black Social Workers, for example, has successfully argued that

African American children should be placed in African American families in order to maintain an awareness of their cultural heritage. Many states have policies requiring that adoption workers, when seeking permanent placements, choose African American homes for African American youngsters. This has sometimes led to cases where an African American child placed in a white foster home was not available for adoption by those foster parents. Critics of the system argue that the offer of a loving home outweighs the need to match the child's own background. On the other hand, many minority group members counter that the maintenance of ethnic or racial identity is an important goal for all children. They also question whether someone from a different, particularly nonminority group background can really empathize with the personal experience of discrimination and prejudice and teach children how to deal with these issues. One way to provide minority homes for minority children, they suggest, is to actively recruit adoptive parents from these backgrounds.

Native Americans living on reservations have had particular concerns about matching children in foster and institutional care and adoptive homes. For many years, they have witnessed an excessive rate of placement of Native American children in white institutions or homes. The problem stems in part from the tendency of state welfare departments to see Native American families as unfit and to ignore the usefulness of extended families in caring for children. A long period of opposition to these practices by Native American groups and civil liberties advocates led to passage of The Indian Child Welfare Act of 1978. This legislation establishes minimum federal standards for the removal of Native American children from their families and states that placement of such children should reflect the unique values of Native American culture.[53]

Questions relating to separate services, mainstreaming, and matching are thorny ones for social workers. On the one hand, separatism can mean much closer and empathetic attention to client needs and to the experience of subordinate group membership. The women's counseling center might provide babysitting services to clients during their appointments and a more sensitive understanding of women's issues, such as the conflict between job and home, or the difficulties in leaving an abusive marital situation. The school social worker who is himself Chinese might best understand the conflict of a first generation Chinese high school student who feels the pull between a family structure that stresses obedience to authority and a school setting that encourages assertive behavior.

On the other hand, matching may not always be helpful or appropriate. An African American middle-class social worker in the Department of Social Services might unfairly expect greater self-initiative from her African American clients than her white ones.[54] And a homosexual man would not necessarily choose a gay therapist if the areas he wanted to deal with were phobic behaviors or substance abuse. In such situations, the therapist's ability to deal with those areas might well be his primary criterion, rather than an intimate understanding of what it means to be gay.

Perhaps the best approach to these issues is to ensure choice within social welfare settings. Clients could then decide for themselves whether in some situations they would be more comfortable with a worker of their own particular background, and if they would prefer services delivered within special settings. On the other hand, they should always be assured fair and sensitive treatment within "mainstream" agencies and programs.

SOCIAL WORK ROLES RELATED TO DIVERSITY

Social workers have a long history of dealing with diversity. Their concerns with the needs and problems of specific groups can be traced through the social work literature and through changing curricula in social work educational programs. The charity worker or settlement worker in the early 1900s heard conference papers or read articles on the plight of the new immigrants. Social workers of the 1930s and 1940s were exposed to discussions of "Cultural Factors and Family Case Work" or "The Case Worker's Need for Orientation to the Culture of the Client." The 1940s also brought national attention to race relations. Social workers joined social scientists and others in their concern for the problems of African Americans in a country which had just fought "to make the world safe for democracy." The development of the civil rights and women's movements in the 1960s and 1970s furthered pressure on the social work curriculum to provide meaningful material on the concerns and lifestyles of subordinate groups.[55]

All this is not to say that the social work profession has a perfect record of attention to issues of discrimination and diversity. And, as you read in the vignette at the beginning of this chapter, individual social workers are not immune from prejudices such as homophobia. All too often, curriculum or practice changes have been a belated response to outside pressure (or to internal pressure from diverse groups within the profession). Yet at the same time, social work's traditions of valuing client self-determination, stressing the importance of environmental factors in people's lives, and working with a broad range of populations in our society should make the profession particularly sensitive to the problems and strengths of subordinate groups.

How might this sensitivity be translated into social work practice? First, as one hears in numerous social work courses, it is important "to recognize one's own biases and assumptions about others." Yet even for well-intentioned students (and practitioners), such advice is easier to give than to carry out. For example, a group of social work students in a field work seminar was asked to go around the room and provide social/psychological information on one of their clients. Each student spoke in turn. Each provided all conceivable kinds of information except for his or her client's race—even when this fact might have been particularly pertinent in understanding that individual's life situation. When asked about this omission by the instructor, class members responded that it would be "impolite" to speak openly of someone's racial background. This answer suggests that we are often uncomfortable about openly acknowledging race, ethnicity, and subordinate group membership as significant factors in people's lives. Then too, it is difficult to perceive the subtle power of institutional racism, sexism, and other forms of discrimination over our own beliefs and behaviors.

There is no easy answer to this problem. One starting point is the simple determination to try to be sensitive to issues of discrimination and difference. This sensitivity can be enhanced through learning a foreign language; traveling to other countries; reading feminist novels and books about members of various ethnic or racial groups; living in racially integrated neighborhoods; learning about gay and lesbian issues; visiting agencies with a large proportion of minority, elderly, or handicapped clients; and most of all, working with people of different backgrounds on common projects.

The next step is to translate an awareness of the needs and strengths of people of diverse groups into practice, both in building relationships with individual clients and families and in developing agency services. On the individual level, this means such things as understanding the importance of extended family support for an African American teenage mother, appreciating the devastating effects of unemployment on the self-image of a Hispanic American father, and acknowledging the frustration of a woman trapped in the "pink collar ghetto" of a low-paying office clerk job. On the agency level, awareness means thinking about whether agency services are appropriate to the needs of specific client groups, and developing policies to combat discriminatory practices. On a broader level, it means helping to develop legislation against discrimination on the local, state, and national levels. It also means confronting prejudices and stereotypes where they occur. In our vignette on homophobia, for example, the teacher might discuss the implications of the speaker's remarks with the class, and might also talk with the speaker about the unfavorable impression these sorts of comments creates. Finally, sensitivity to issues of diversity should include an understanding of power differentials between dominant and subordinate groups in our society. This can lead to a goal of empowering clients on individual, group, and community levels and assisting them in their attempts to bring about structural change.

In addition, attention to diversity really ought to include a sense of the type of society in which we would like to live. Is greater homogeneity a desirable goal? Is cultural pluralism our ideal? What is the proper balance between common beliefs and values and the maintenance of separate customs and traditions? These are important questions for social workers, as well as for all citizens. One version of an answer is contained in the following article written for a high school newspaper:

"The World is a Box of Crayons"
by Rachel Morris

10:06 a.m. The buzz of an artificially lit classroom swarms around its third hour occupants. Slouched in my chair at the back of the room, I try to ignore the sweat running into the collar of my t-shirt, the incessant tapping of my foot. I chew anxiously on my pen top, and the words on the paper before me swim around in a mocking blur.

No, I'm not struggling over a physics test, or an essay question in College English. This is simply a survey on student-teacher relationships given to the whole school and I haven't made it past the first section.

Name _____. Okay, got that one. Age _____. Grade _____. Sex _____.
Yeah, these are easy. Race _____. What? RACE. 1. White. 2. Black. 3. Oriental. 4. Hispanic. 5. American Indian. This is where my panic begins. I read my choices again, and my brow furrows. Basically, the problem is this: I'm racially mixed, and there is no option for me.

Now, this is not the first time this has happened. All my life, I've had to decide what race I am, which half of me to deny. I remember asking my sister one day in third grade which one I was. "We're mixed, Rach," she told me. Mixed. And for every survey, every technical form I received in every grade after, I looked for that word. The closest I ever found was "other." That always kind of amused me, but I tried it. Other: mixed. But my teachers came to me. "Mixed what, honey?" And they looked at me. "You're black. Next time, just put black, okay?" And I would go home to my mother, my single, cream-colored mother, who wanted nothing but to raise us well. Even as an intelligent 8-year-old, I was a bit confused.

My next practice, starting about seventh grade, was to circle both white and black. It made the most sense, really, but even here in high school I got trouble. Again, the tender pressure: "Hon, you can't be *both*." So I ended up selecting "Caucasian" for the day. Recently, I went to my counselor and had that changed. See, I'm a junior, and considering colleges, and I know that as a "minority student" I'll be eligible for certain scholarships. Also, it will give me an edge at schools that are looking for a diverse student body. So I figure I'll be black for the next 5 years or so, and then go back to being myself.

But can I really go back? Can I really be comfortable with who I am if society ignores that people like me exist? Well, I can—but you must realize that I'm lucky. I grew up in Hyde Park (in Chicago), one of the most liberal integrated neighborhoods in America. My 14 years there taught me that I could exist as a mixed person, with both black and white friends. That I could be proud of my brown skin, even have fun with it. It's always great to see the look on people's faces when my mom and sister and I go out, especially with my white stepfather.

But for some kids, there is no joke. Only confusion, and the total lack of a sense of identity. These children are pressured to choose a group of friends, and in effect to choose a parent, a race, a way of life, a heritage—and to completely deny the other. But do black people really want a friend who's only half black, and vice-versa?

That was the problem facing the first mixed kids—the children born of slaves and their owners. It should not exist now. In this age, the so-called "modern civilization" we're supposed to have reached, being racially mixed shouldn't be a dilemma, it should be considered a blessing. We are graced with the best of both worlds, exposure to two entirely different walks of life. In fact, our parents should be congratulated for creating a higher, enlightened race with such a large sphere of influences and possibilities. Instead, they have been scolded. God forbid we should pollute one race by adding another to it.

The world is a box of crayons. Though they're all different colors, they're all made of the same thing. And even though yellow and blue are combined to make green, once the wax has set, it's a green crayon, and that's all. It's never asked to make a choice between blue and yellow. One of the things my sister and I did together is draw pictures of the family, coloring them from our big box of Crayolas. And I always thought it was neat that a drawing of four people could use up three crayons—peach, light brown, and dark brown, when the other kids only got to use one.[56]

ENDNOTES

1. "In Texas, a Grim New Appalachia," *Newsweek* (June 8, 1987): 27.
2. *Children, 1990* (Washington, D.C.: Children's Defense Fund, 1990), 28.
3. Warren E. Leary, "Black Hypertension May Reflect Other Ills," *New York Times* (22 October, 1991), B6; *Health, United States, 1990,* DHHS Pub. No. (PHS) 91-1232, Public Health Service (Washington, D.C.: U.S. Government Printing Office, 1991), 15.
4. U.S. Bureau of the Census, *Statistical Abstract of the United States: 1990* (Washington, D.C.: 110th Edition, 1990), 132–135.
5. Sharon Begley, "America's Changing Face," *Newsweek* (September 10, 1990): 47.
6. Lisa Belkin, "Wave of Poor Immigrant Children is Straining Schools and Housing," *New York Times* (29 January, 1989), 1, 16; Peter Passell, "So Much for Assumptions about Immigrants and Jobs," *New York Times* (15 April, 1990), E4.
7. Joe R. Feagin, *Racial and Ethnic Relations,* 2nd ed.

(Englewood Cliffs, NJ: Prentice-Hall, 1984), 10; Peter I. Rose, *They and We: Racial and Ethnic Relations in the United States,* 3rd ed. (New York: Random House, 1981), 8–9.

8. Feagin, *Racial and Ethnic Relations,* 5.

9. R.A. Schermerhorn, *Comparative Ethnic Relations* (New York: Random House, 1970), 73–74, 102–103.

10. Rose, *They and We,* 7.

11. Milton M. Gordon, *Human Nature, Class, and Ethnicity* (New York: Oxford University Press, 1978), 166–180.

12. Gerard A. Postiglione, *Ethnicity and American Social Theory* (Lanham, MD: Universal Press of America, 1983), 18–21, 125–148; Leonard Dinnerstein, Roger L. Nichols, and David M. Reimers, *Natives and Strangers: Blacks, Indians, and Immigrants in America,* 2nd ed. (New York: Oxford University Press, 1990), 285–292, 328–332.

13. Denise Giardina, "America's Exploited Colony of West Virginia," *Manchester Guardian Weekly* (15 September, 1985), 17; Hermon George, *American Race Relations Theory: A Review of Four Models* (Lanham, MD: University Press of America, 1984), 85–120.

14. Rose, *They and We,* 105–106.

15. Rose, *They and We,* 115–138; Feagin, *Racial and Ethnic Relations,* 15.

16. Mimi Abramovitz, *Regulating the Lives of Women: Social Welfare Policy from Colonial Times to the Present,* (Boston: South End Press, 1988).

17. William Julius Wilson, *The Truly Disadvantaged* (Chicago: The University of Chicago Press, 1987), 8.

18. Andrew Billingsley, "The Sociology of Knowledge of William J. Wilson: Placing *The Truly Disadvantaged* in Its Sociohistorical Context," *Journal of Sociology and Social Welfare 16* (December 1989): 7–41; Charles Vert Willie, *The Caste and Class Controversy* (Bayside, NY: General Hall, Inc., 1979), 145–158; Maxine Baca Zinn, "Family, Race and Poverty in the Eighties," *Signs: Journal of Women in Culture and Society 14* (Summer 1989): 856–873.

19. Paula Dressel, "Patriarchy and Social Welfare Work," *Social Problems 34* (June 1987): 294–309; Jim Fain, "GOP Wielding Racist Wedge," *Kalamazoo Gazette* (25 April, 1991), 9.

20. Barbara Bryant Solomon, *Black Empowerment: Social Work in Oppressed Communities* (New York: Columbia University Press, 1976); Ann Bookman and Sandra Morgen, eds., *Women and the Politics of Empowerment* (Philadelphia: Temple University Press, 1988).

21. Begley, "America's Changing Face," 49; Leslie Leighninger, "Social Workers, Immigrants, and Historians: A Re-examination," *Journal of Sociology and Social Welfare 2* (Spring 1975): 327.

22. Elizabeth Peabody House, *Fifteenth Annual Report* (Boston, 1911), 10–13.

23. Leighninger, "Social Workers, Immigrants, and Historians," 331–334.

24. Jane Addams, *Newer Ideals of Peace* (New York: Macmillan, 1911).

25. Addams, *Newer Ideals,* 69–75.

26. Addams, *Newer Ideals,* 204.

27. Leighninger, "Social Workers, Immigrants, and Historians," 337–338.

28. Charles Marden and Gladys Meyer, *Minorities in American Society,* 4th ed. (New York: D. Van Nostrand Company, 1973), 162; Feagin, *Racial and Ethnic Relations,* 227.

29. Marden and Meyer, *Minorities in American Society,* 162–165; Eric Foner, *Reconstruction: America's Unfinished Revolution* (New York: Harper and Row, 1988), 68–69, 144, 159–161, 170.

30. Steven J. Diner, "Chicago Social Workers and Blacks in the Progressive Era," *Social Service Review 44* (December 1970): 393–410.

31. Diner, "Chicago Social Workers and Blacks in the Progressive Era," 400–401; Thomas Lee Philpott, *The Slum and the Ghetto: Neighborhood Deterioration and Middle-Class Reform, Chicago 1880–1930* (New York: Oxford University Press, 1978), 295–299.

32. Diner, "Chicago Social Workers and Blacks in the Progressive Era," 396–408.

33. Philpott, *The Slum and the Ghetto,* 301, 314–342.

34. Philpott, *The Slum and the Ghetto,* 301–308; Philip Johnson, "Black Charity in Progressive Era Chicago," *Social Service Review 52* (September 1978): 400–415.

35. Johnson, "Black Charity in Progressive Chicago"; Anne Firor Scott, "Most Invisible of All: Black Women's Voluntary Associations," *The Journal of Southern History 56* (February 1990): 4–22; Gerda Lerner, "Community Work of Black Club Women," *The Journal of Negro History 59* (April 1974): 158–167; Philpott, *The Slum and the Ghetto,* 320–342.

36. Leslie Leighninger, *Social Work: Search for Identity* (Westport, CT: Greenwood Press, 1987), 90–91.

37. Michael B. Katz, *In the Shadow of the Poorhouse: A Social History of Welfare in America* (New York: Basic Books, 1986), 128–129.

38. Lela Costin, *Two Sisters for Social Justice: A Biography of Grace and Edith Abbott* (Urbana, IL: University of Illinois Press, 1983), 132–150.

39. Abramovitz, *Regulating the Lives of Women,* 4; Paula Dressel, "Patriarchy and Social Welfare Work," 294–309.
40. Abramovitz, *Regulating the Lives of Women,* 152–154.
41. Ruth Sidel, *Women and Children Last* (New York: Penguin Books, 1986), 80–81.
42. Abramovitz, *Regulating the Lives of Women,* 333.
43. Dressel, "Patriarchy and Social Welfare Work," 294–295; Clarke Chambers, "Women in the Creation of the Profession of Social Work," *Social Service Review* 60 (March 1986): 12.
44. Leighninger, *Social Work: Search for Identity,* 10–11; Costin, *Two Sisters for Social Justice,* 21–25, 44.
45. Dressel, "Patriarchy and Social Welfare Work," 298.
46. Chambers, "Women in the Creation of the Profession of Social Work," 22–24.
47. Elizabeth D. Huttman, *Introduction to Social Policy* (New York: McGraw Hill, 1981), 124, 322–323.
48. Huttman, *Introduction to Social Policy,* 321–346.
49. Joe R. Feagin and Clairece Booher Feagin, *Discrimination Amercian Style: Institutional Racism and Sexism* (Englewood Cliffs, NJ: Prentice-Hall, 1978), 157–163.
50. Adam Clymer, "Bush Assails 'Quota Bill' at West Point Graduation," *New York Times* (2 June, 1991), 32; Steven A. Holmes, "Quotas: Despised by Many, but Just What Are They?," *New York Times* (2 June, 1991), 32.
51. Catharine R. Stimpson, "Multiculturalism: A Big Word at the Presses," *New York Times* (22 September, 1991), Book Review Section, 27–29; Robert Reinhold, "Class Struggle," *New York Times* (29 September, 1991), Magazine Section, 26–30, 46–52; Arthur Schlesinger, "The Cult of Ethnicity, Good and Bad," *Time* (July 8, 1991), 21.
52. Barry D. Adam, *The Rise of a Gay and Lesbian Movement* (Boston: Twayne Publishers, 1987); John D'Emilio, *Sexual Politics, Sexual Communities* (Chicago: University of Chicago Press, 1983); Sandra J. Potter and Trudy E. Darty, "Social Work and the Invisible Minority: An Exploration of Lesbianism," *Social Work* 26 (May 1981): 187–192.
53. Feagin, *Racial and Ethnic Relations,* 178–205.
54. Alfred Kadushin, "The Racial Factor in the Interview," *Social Work* 17 (May 1972): 88–98.
55. Mary A. Young, "Cultural Factors and Family Case Work," *The Family* 19 (May 1938): 76–79; Maurine Boie, "The Case Worker's Need for Orientation to the Culture of the Client," National Conference of Social Work, *Proceedings* (1937); Leighninger, *Social Work: Search for Identity,* 162–163.
56. Rachel Morris, "The World is a Box of Crayons," *KnightLife* (March 30, 1988), Loy Norrix High School, Kalamazoo, MI. Identity issues for people with a mixed racial heritage are explored in Robert Anthony Watts, "Not Black, Not White, but Biracial," *The Atlanta Constitution* (12 December 1991), 1, 10.

C·H·A·P·T·E·R

six

Poverty—The Central Concept

The alarm woke Patty with its obnoxious buzz. She groaned as she slapped the bedside table in a wild attempt to shut it off before it woke the kids. Lying in bed, attempting to wake up but wishing she did not have to, Patty thought about her day—it was going to be a killer. Whoever said life on welfare was easy had never been there.

Patty Sanchez is a twenty-three-year-old divorced mother of two children, four-year-old Tina and two-year-old Ray. She has been receiving Aid to Families with Dependent Children for fourteen months, ever since her husband Ernesto deserted her. Ernie lost his job as a truck driver just about the time Patty discovered that she was pregnant with Ray. For a while, they lived on unemployment benefits and then they scraped by on what Patty's mother could spare (not much) and on what Ernie made from the few odd jobs he could get (also not much), and, after Ernie overcame his pride, they applied for and received food stamps. After he lost his job as a trucker, Ernie never did get a "real job." It was a horrible time. Patty was pregnant and sick, Tina was demanding and whiny, and they were evicted from their apartment. They were able to move into the dump where Patty still lives only because a local church helped them out. Finally, Ernie became depressed and began to abuse Tina.

After Ernie left, Patty and the kids began receiving AFDC and Medicaid in addition to their food stamps. Their name was at the top of the waiting list for a public housing apartment, and Patty had calculated that with low-cost housing she would finally be able to balance her budget. The prospect of going through a day without fear of the power being turned off or of creditors at the door seemed almost too good to be true.

Patty and Ernie's relationship had been unstable since before Tina's birth. Ernie's unemployment had been the "straw which broke the camel's back," and eventually he left the family. After Ernie left, Patty saw him around the neighborhood occasionally for a few months, but then he dropped out of sight. One of his friends told Patty that Ernie had gone to California because he had heard that they were hiring truckers, but Patty felt that he had left because he couldn't stand the embarrassment of seeing his family supported by welfare while he just sat around and did nothing.

Before waking the kids, Patty sat down with a cup of coffee and thought about her day. At 9:00 in the morning Chuck Patterson, a social worker with the child welfare office, would be coming by for the last time. In the months before he left, Ernie had begun to drink and to take out his frustration on his family, mainly on Tina. After one particularly bad incident, Patty had taken Tina to the emergency room to see if she had any broken bones. Tina did not, but the physician had called the hospital social worker, who had in turn called the child welfare office. Chuck Patterson was the social worker assigned to the case. At first, Patty had been very scared, thinking that her children would be taken away from her. It turned out that Mr. Patterson was very helpful, and he had spent a lot of time with Ernie helping him to develop better ways of dealing with anger and frustration. Now that Ernie was gone there was really no reason for the child welfare people to be involved, so this would be the last visit. Patty felt both happy and sad that she would no longer be seeing Chuck—happy because she felt that there were too many people involved in her life, but sad because with all of her responsibilities she could use all the friends she could get.

After Chuck Patterson leaves Patty plans to bundle up baby Ray and take him to the public health clinic for an evaluation. He has not been developing as quickly as he should and the doctors were afraid that there might be something wrong with him. Patty was afraid that his problems might be the result of the fact that she did not eat right and did not get any medical care during her pregnancy. Because they had so little money, her diet had consisted mainly of bread, rice, potatoes, and other cheap, starchy food. She had heard of a program called WIC (Women, Infants, and Children) that would have given her coupons to buy supplementary food during her pregnancy and Ray's infancy, but Ernie had been in his macho proud phase and had refused to even consider it. Now it looked as though little Ray was going to pay the price for his father's pride. At two, he was not yet walking, talking, or even responding very well when someone played with him.

At noon Patty has a group meeting at the community mental health center. After Ernie left she felt so bad that she spent most of each day in bed crying. Chuck Patterson had helped her join a support group at the center. The group is composed of eight other women who are undergoing life crises of various sorts, and they spend an hour each week just talking and comparing notes on how they cope. The group is led by a clinical social worker named Carol Crenshaw who gets the group going, occasionally makes a suggestion or interpretation of what is being said, and sums up at the end of the meeting; basically, the group runs itself. Patty thought of how much better she is doing now than when she first joined the group, and the thought of quitting entered her mind as it had frequently in the past few weeks. She decided that she would continue to go for a little longer because she enjoyed the fellowship of the group and felt that the other women needed her.

After the meeting at the community mental health center, Patty will rush home, feed the kids, and put them down for a short nap while she does her laundry and housework. At 2:30 she will wake the kids up and walk two blocks to the Learning Center, a local child care facility. At the Learning Center Patty drives the van that picks up kids after school, and then she supervises their play group until 6:00 when the last parents will pick up their children. Patty is only paid minimum wage for this job, but it includes child care for her own children as a benefit. She looked at other jobs, including full-time ones after Ernie left, but when she deducted child care expenses she would be left with almost nothing. Her welfare grant allows her to make a small amount of income and still keep her benefits, so this job improves her life a little bit and it strengthens her self-image a whole lot.

After work at the child care center Patty will rush home, feed her kids, and take them to her mother's house for the evening. While her mother cares for the kids, Patty will go to the local high school where she is enrolled in night classes. Patty had quit school when she was sixteen, shortly after she had met Ernesto. She had thought that she had it made. He had a good job and seemed to have lots of money, and Patty was sure he would take care of her forever. With a set-up like that, why did she need an education? "Well," she thought, "once again I learn the hard way." The course she is pursuing at the high school will not only lead to a high school diploma but will also get her a certificate in drafting. Patty has always been good in art, and the counselor at the school told her the salary and job prospects of drafters are very good. She likes school and plans to continue after she gets a job. Her dream is to eventually become a civil engineer.

With her coffee finished, Patty gets the kids up. Ray, who is sluggish at the best of times, is positively inert in the morning, and it will take the better part of an hour to feed him. Tina will want some attention, and the apartment needs to be straightened up before Chuck Patterson arrives. Facing two cranky kids, a messy apartment, and a schedule that is full until 10:00 PM, Patty thought, "Boy, being a welfare mother sure isn't all it's cracked up to be!"

The case of Patty Sanchez illustrates a number of key points that will be discussed in this chapter and the two that follow. The first point, and probably the most important, is that nearly all of the social welfare problems discussed in these chapters are closely related to poverty. Related to their poverty the Sanchez family has experienced unemployment and underemployment, marital breakdown, health problems, alcohol abuse, mental health problems, educational deficits, and child abuse. Some of these have contributed to their poverty and some have resulted from it; in most cases the relation has been circular—lack of education has led to poverty and poverty in turn has led to a lack of educational opportunity. That is why we are devoting three chapters to poverty and only one chapter to each of the other major social welfare problems. Scratch a social welfare problem, and underneath it you will find poverty.

The Sanchez family, following Ernesto's abandonment, consists of a woman and her children. This is typical and is becoming even more common. As will be discussed later in this chapter, two out of three poor adults are women, 50 percent of poor families are headed by females, and one-half of the children in female-headed families are poor. This trend has come to be identified by a phrase coined by Diana Pearce in 1978: "the feminization of poverty."

The next notable fact about the Sanchez family is that they belong to a minority group, in this case Hispanic American. This fits a popular stereotype about poor people in the United States—that they are mainly members of minority groups. This stereotype is not true—over half of the poor people in this country are white. However, it is true that minority groups are greatly overrepresented among the poor. One out of three African Americans in the United States lives in poverty, one out of four Hispanic Americans is poor, but only one out of ten whites falls below the poverty line. It is only because whites make up such a large majority of the population that they are numerically the largest group in poverty.

Another popular stereotype about poor people and welfare recipients is that they remain in this condition for an extended period of time, and that most likely their kids will inherit their poverty. Social workers and social scientists have been as guilty as laypeople of perpetuating this belief. Recent data provides a strong basis for refuting this idea and indicates that the case of Patty Sanchez may be fairly typical. A study that will be discussed in this chapter, the Michigan Panel Study of Income Dynamics, has found that only about one-half of people who are classified as poor during one year will be so classified the next, and only one-tenth of poor people will remain so for an extended period of time. Far more common are people like Patty Sanchez, who use welfare for a short period of time while they deal with problems in their lives and then go on to more prosperous futures.

In this chapter we discuss basic factors about poverty—what it is, how we define it, how we measure it, and whom it affects. In Chapter 7 we will look at characteristics of the poor, and theories and data about the causes and potential solutions to poverty. Finally, in Chapter 8, we will look at social responses to the problem of poverty— how we have historically dealt with it and how we deal with it now.

POVERTY: MAJOR ISSUES AND COMMON TERMS

The question and the answer are so familiar. You will hear them during almost any political campaign.

> *Reporter:* Ms. Porkbarrel, the figures recently released by the Census Bureau indicate that over the past ten years, roughly the period of time the Republicans have occupied the White House, the share of income of the richest people in this country has gotten significantly larger while the share of the poorest has become smaller. In fact the percentage of people living in poverty has increased nearly every year since 1980 and is now over 13 percent. So what we have is a situation with a small number of people spending money on second homes, European vacations, jewelry and the like, while an increasingly large number can't even afford the necessities of life. My question is, do you consider this to be a problem and, if so, what will you do about it if you are elected senator?
>
> *Candidate Porkbarrel:* "Well John, I'm glad you asked that question. Let me say this. First, I want to say that I firmly believe that the problem is the size of the pie, not how we cut it. I have an economic development program that will increase the size of the pie, and thereby deal with the people below the poverty level without cutting into the good life earned by hard working people. Second, I'm not sure that I agree with the figures released by the Census Bureau. I think that our poverty line is set at an unrealistically high level. Do you realize that a middle-income person in England has an income that would place him or her below our poverty line? Also, our poverty figures do not include all of the in-kind benefits we give poor people. We may have more people below the poverty line than we had in the 1960s, but these people have many benefits their 1960s counterparts did not have—benefits like food stamps and Medicaid, to name just two."

When listening to an exchange like this, we say, "Wait a minute. What does she mean that she would make the pie bigger rather than cutting it differently? What does she mean that the poverty line is too high? And what's all this business about in-kind benefits?" These are some of the major issues and common terms that come up in discussions of the problem of poverty. The size of the pie question refers to the distribution of income in our country. Some people believe that the rich are too rich, and they propose a kind of Robin Hood solution to poverty—you simply take from the rich and give to the poor. Others feel that this is not a good idea and that to reduce poverty, we must have economic growth. The other questions have to do with defining and measuring poverty. Discussion of these issues can, we realize, be somewhat tedious. However, to intelligently discuss poverty you must understand them. Even though on the surface the issues may seem rather dry, we hope that by the end of this chapter you will realize they have a very human face.

RICH COUNTRY, POOR COUNTRY

Poverty in third-world nations, such as Haiti or Bangladesh, is explainable in terms of the total wealth of the nation. If you were to take the total income of these nations

Poverty in the United States is different from poverty in the third world. We refer to our poverty as relative poverty because people in the United States are poor relative to other people in this country, but would not be considered poor in relation to the people who live in the community in this picture.

and divide it up evenly among the population, everyone in the country would be poor. This is not the case in the United States. In 1989 the Gross National Income (GNI) of the United States was $4,185,200,000,000 and the number of household units was 92,830,000.[1] By dividing the number of households into the amount of income, it can be seen that if income were distributed evenly, every household would have received $45,084.56 in 1989, an adequate amount of money by almost anyone's standards. However, income in the United States is not divided evenly. A few people have incomes greatly in excess of $45,000, and a larger number of people have incomes below this figure, with many far, far below it. The economist Paul Samuelson has given a particularly graphic description of the income distribution in the United States: "If we made an income pyramid out of a child's blocks, with each layer portraying $1,000 of income, the peak would be far higher than the Eiffel Tower, but most of us would be within a yard of the ground."[2]

To understand poverty in the United States, first we must understand economic inequality. In this section we will look at how inequality is measured, how income is distributed in this country, whether the income distribution is becoming more or less equal, and how the distribution of income is viewed from liberal and conservative perspectives.

The Measurement of Economic Inequality

The U.S. Bureau of the Census is one of the most highly regarded data collection agencies in the world. On a regular basis, the Census Bureau collects a wide range of information regarding the population in the United States. Among this data is information on income and wealth. For purposes of summary and comparison, the Bureau aggregates the data on income and wealth into quintiles (fifths) of the population. In this form we can see how much income and wealth is earned or held by the poorest fifth of the population, the next poorest fifth, and so on up to the wealthiest fifth. In addition, the Bureau also figures the income of the richest 5 percent and the wealth held by the top 1 percent and one-half percent of the population. This data is also broken down by racial and ethnic group and geographic region, and it is gathered and reported in a consistent manner so comparisons over time can be made. An example of Census Bureau data on income is presented in Table 6–1. The data in this table will be discussed later in this section.

Data such as that presented in Table 6–1 is useful and it tells us a few things, but it is not really very clear, particularly for the purposes of comparison. Imagine, for example, trying to compare two or three such tables which presented data for several points in time or for different geographic regions. To make better sense of this type

TABLE 6–1   **Money income of families—income at selected positions and percent of income received by each fifth and top 5 percent of families: 1987**

Item	All Families	Race			Region			
		White	Black and Other		Northeast	Midwest	South	West
			Total	Black				
Number								
(1,000)	65,133	56,044	9,089	7,177	13,382	15,905	22,846	13,000
Income at Selected Positions (dollars)								
Upper limit of each fifth:								
Lowest	14,450	16,057	7,514	6,800	16,308	15,001	12,833	15,606
Second	25,100	27,000	15,500	13,801	28,070	25,665	22,555	26,120
Third	36,600	38,200	25,500	22,590	40,100	36,300	34,200	38,200
Fourth	52,910	54,280	41,338	36,652	57,260	51,350	49,777	55,406
Top 5 percent	86,300	88,472	69,901	62,000	94,624	80,943	81,129	91,467
Percent Distribution of Aggregate Income								
Lowest fifth	4.6	5.1	3.2	3.3	4.7	4.9	4.3	4.8
Second fifth	10.8	11.2	8.5	8.7	11.4	11.4	10.5	10.7
Third fifth	16.9	17.0	15.3	15.5	17.4	17.4	16.7	16.5
Fourth fifth	24.1	23.8	24.8	25.1	24.1	24.2	24.3	23.7
Highest fifth	43.7	42.9	48.3	47.4	42.2	42.2	44.4	44.2
Top 5 percent	16.9	16.7	18.4	17.4	16.0	16.0	17.1	17.7

Source: U.S. Bureau of the Census, *Current Population Reports,* series P–60, No. 132 and 161.

of data, economists have developed two techniques, the Lorenz curve and the Gini coefficient. A *Lorenz curve* is a curve that "shows the percentage of total household incomes received by successively larger fractions of the population, starting with the poorest group."[3] The Lorenz curve traces out the share of total income held by different subgroups in the population. In the case of Census Bureau figures, it shows the income held by the lowest 20, 40, 60, 80, and 100 percent of the population. If income were distributed evenly, that is, if 20 percent of the population had 20 percent of the income, 40 percent of the population had 40 percent of the income, and so on, the Lorenz curve would be a straight line as shown in Figure 6–1. If, on the other hand, one person held all the income, the Lorenz curve would form a right angle as shown in Figure 6–2. It is obvious that neither situation actually occurs; the curve always falls somewhere between the 45° angle representing perfect equality and the 90° angle representing perfect inequality. Examples of two Lorenz curves, one for a very equal distribution of income and one for a very unequal distribution, are presented in Figure 6–3.

The Lorenz curve gives a nice graphic depiction of income structure, but it is still difficult to make comparisons over time and between countries. For these purposes, a summary statistic called the *Gini coefficient* is necessary. Using the situations depicted in Figure 6–3 as examples, the Gini coefficient is the area between the Lorenz curve and line OE, divided by the area of OEZ. As you can see, as the Lorenz curve approaches equality [curve (a)], the Gini coefficient approaches zero. As the Lorenz curve approaches inequality [curve (b)], the Gini coefficient approaches one. Thus, the Gini coefficient has possible values ranging from zero (perfect equality) to one (perfect inequality). The Gini coefficient makes comparisons very clear and easy. If country A has a Gini coefficient of .423 and country B has a Gini coefficient of .297, we can clearly see that country B has a more equal income distribution. Likewise, if the Gini coefficient for country A was .324 in 1960 and .423 in 1987, we can conclude that the distribution of income is becoming more unequal.

Now that we are familiar with some of the major sources of data and some of the tools used to study income and wealth, let's look at the situation in the United States.

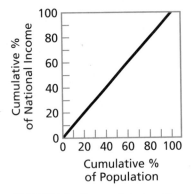

FIGURE 6–1   **Lorenz Curve for Absolute Income Equality**

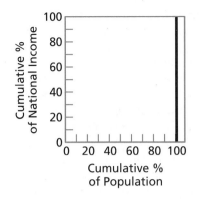

FIGURE 6–2 Lorenz Curve for Absolute Income Inequality

The Distribution of Income and Wealth in the United States

If you spend an hour driving around any city in the United States, it will be readily apparent that income and wealth are unequally divided. Within the space of a few miles you can see neighborhoods with houses valued at half a million dollars or more and neighborhoods with houses that most people would judge to be unfit for human habitation; you will see BMW dealerships next to Fast Freddie's Used Cars ("No credit, no problem—we tote the note"); you will see an Ethan Allen Furniture Gallery and a Salvation Army Thrift Store; we could go on and on, but there is no point in belaboring the obvious. What is not obvious, however, is just how unequal the distribution of income and wealth is.

The 1987 Census reported the data presented earlier in Table 6–1. A convenient and illustrative, although not precise, way to summarize this data is what we call the

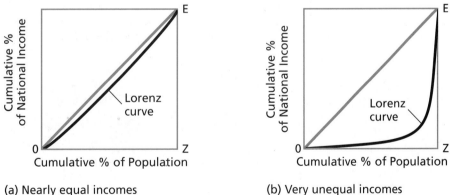

(a) Nearly equal incomes   (b) Very unequal incomes

FIGURE 6–3 Extreme Cases of the Lorenz Curve

Source: John Craven, *Introduction to Economics—An Integrated Approach to Fundamental Principles* (Oxford, England: Basil Blackwell, 1984), 100. Reprinted by permission.

Rich Country, Poor Country

20/5 principle. This principle states that in the United States the bottom 20 percent of the population receives approximately 5 percent of the income (actually 4.6 percent), and the upper 5 percent of the population receives approximately 20 percent of the income (actually 16.9 percent). The charts in Figure 6–4 illustrate this distribution. As can be seen, the bottom 20 percent of the population receives less than one quarter of its "share" and the top 5 percent receives more than three times its "share."

The most precise ways to illustrate the distribution of income are the Lorenz curve and Gini coefficient discussed earlier. The data in Table 6–1, summarized in a form from which a Lorenz curve can be drawn, is presented in Table 6–2. The Lorenz curve derived from this data is presented in Figure 6–5 on page 166. The Gini coefficient derived from this data is .393. We will return to this coefficient later when we look at trends in inequality in the United States over time and as compared to other countries.

We can see from the preceding data that the distribution of income in this country is very unequal. This is not the whole story, however. Income only refers to the amount of money coming in during a one-year period; it does not say very much about wealth. Income is the flow of money into a household; wealth is the stock of accumulated assets and includes things like houses, real estate, cars, jewelry, savings accounts, stocks, and bonds. Wealth is much harder to measure than income. Income must be reported each year on federal income tax returns, and although it is acknowledged that reporting is not precise, it is at least a pretty close estimate. The only required reporting of wealth occurs when estates must be reported to the federal government upon the death of the owner. Only a small proportion of estates are large enough to be affected by this requirement.

The distribution of wealth is even more unequal than the distribution of income. A study conducted by the University of Michigan's Institute for Social Research found that the vast majority of the total wealth in the United States is owned by one-tenth of the families. Even more astounding is the finding that the top one-half percent of the population owns 27 percent of everything in the country. Think about that—one two-hundredth of the population owns more than one-fourth of everything in the country.

The fact that some people are very rich is not in and of itself a problem. The popularity of TV shows such as *Life Styles of the Rich and Famous* attests to the fact that we all are fascinated by rich people. The problem is that while some people are

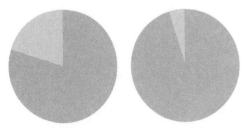

20% of all Americans receive
4.6% of the income

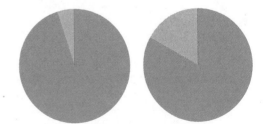

5% of all Americans receive
16.9% of the income

FIGURE 6–4   **Income Shares of the Poorest 20 Percent and the Richest 5 Percent of Americans**

TABLE 6–2	Income data from Table 6–1 prepared for presentation on a Lorenz Curve					
Point	Group	% of Population	Cumulative % of Population	Upper Limit of Group Income	% of National Income	Cumulative % of National Income
A	Poorest	20	20	14,450	4.6	4.6
B	Next poorest	20	40	25,100	10.8	15.4
C	Next	20	60	36,600	16.9	32.3
D	Next	20	80	54,280	24.1	56.4
E	Richest	20	100	—	43.7	100

very rich, others are very poor. About one-fourth of the population in the United States owns absolutely nothing of any value. As Ryan points out, for many, their wealth is actually negative—they owe more than they own.[4] The next one-fourth owns about 5 percent of all assets. Even this low figure probably makes this group seem better off than they actually are because a good deal of these assets are in the form of money in checking and saving accounts that will be spent for living expenses during the month and then replenished when the next paycheck or pension check comes in. Besides money for current living expenses, this group's primary asset is probably a car. The next 40 percent owns about 27 percent of all wealth. For this group, home ownership represents their primary means of acquiring wealth. James Smith of the Institute for Social Research says, "For many Americans owning a home is the *only* way to have net worth at all." And finally, of course, we get back to the upper 10 percent who own 68 percent of everything, including 90 percent of corporate stocks and business assets and 95 percent of bonds.[5]

Trends in the Distribution of Wealth and Income

Information that can be used to compare the concentration of wealth is available for the past sixty years. This data indicates that the concentration of wealth in the United States has been remarkably constant. The greatest concentration of wealth appears to have occurred during the late 1920s. This concentration declined because of the Great Depression, and the decline lasted until the end of World War II. Concentration of wealth increased into the mid–1950s and has remained constant ever since. James Smith of Michigan's Institute for Social Research says that only two factors have had any impact on the concentration of wealth. The first, a relatively minor factor, is government home loan programs, such as VA and FHA mortgages, which have enabled an increasing number of people to purchase homes since the end of World War II. The second, and major factor is the performance of the stock market. Smith says, "Severe disruption of the stock market is the only thing that can negatively affect the wealth of the richest of the rich, because they have so much invested in corporate stocks."[6]

Rich Country, Poor Country   **165**

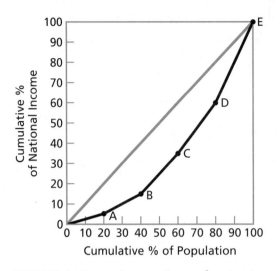

FIGURE 6–5   **Lorenz Curve showing income distribution for the United States in 1987**

The distribution of income is a different matter. A number of analysts using different methods have all concluded that the distribution of income has become more unequal in recent years. Representative Henry Reuss, Chair of the Joint Economic Committee, has used Census Bureau data to look at trends in income inequality. From his analysis of this data, Reuss contends that

> from 1929 to 1967 income distribution grew more equitable. Income shares of the lower four-fifths of American households went up during that period: the first two-fifths from 12.5 percent of total income to 14.2 percent; the third from 13.9 percent to 17.5 percent; the fourth from 19.3 percent to 24.8 percent. The top one-fifth declined, from 54.4 percent to 43.4 percent.[7]

Around 1969 the trend toward equality reversed. According to Reuss's analysis, the share of the lowest fifth has held constant, but the second and third fifths have steadily lost income, the fourth has held constant, and the income of the richest fifth has increased significantly, from 43.4 percent of total income to 45.2 percent.

An analysis of the most recent Census Bureau data on income distribution indicates that the pattern Reuss was concerned about in 1981 has continued and in some ways has grown worse. Table 6–3 displays the data on household income up to 1989. From this data it appears that all four lower income groups have lost income share between 1969 and 1989, while the top fifth, and especially the top 5 percent, made significant gains. You will note that the data used in the analysis by Reuss and in this table are slightly different than that presented when we discussed the 20/5 principle. The data used when discussing the 20/5 principle is based on family income, and the data used by Reuss and in Table 6–3 are based on household income, which is defined in a slightly different manner.

Earlier we described the Lorenz curve and Gini coefficient as methods that are useful for comparing inequality over time. The Census Bureau's Gini index for the United States from 1949 to 1989 is presented in Table 6–4. As can be seen, this method also indicates that inequality dropped from 1949 until 1969, and then it began to rise. It is clear from all the data presented here that inequality has increased in recent years. What this means is not clear, however; it is the subject of much debate between those with liberal and conservative perspectives.

Perspectives on Inequality

Liberals, conservatives, and radicals agree that equality is a basic part of the American creed and that greater equality is, at least theoretically, desirable. Liberals and conservatives also agree that economic inequality is a necessary fact of life. Even some radicals (although not all) will agree that some inequality is tolerable, for example, that a nuclear physicist may earn more than the person who sweeps out the physicist's laboratory. There is disagreement, however, about the degree and trend of inequality, the positive and negative effects of inequality, and how much inequality is desirable in our society.

First, let's look at the degree and trend of inequality. Looking at the data presented previously, liberals and radicals argue that we live in a very unequal, and therefore unjust, society. Further, they argue that inequality is rapidly increasing, especially since the Republican Party recaptured the presidency in 1980. Harrison, Tilly, and Bluestone say, "It now seems fairly clear that both family income and individual wages and salaries are being distributed more and more unequally among the working people of the United States."[8] Krugman observes, "Although the typical American family had about the same real income in 1988 as it did in 1978, this was not true of untypical families: the rich and the poor. The best-selling novel of 1988, Tom Wolfe's *Bonfire of the Vanities,* portrayed an America of growing wealth at the top, a struggle to make ends meet in the middle, and growing misery at the bottom. The numbers bear him out. During the 1980's the rich, and for that matter the upper middle class, became a great deal richer, while the poor became significantly poorer."[9]

The conservative interpretation of the data on inequality is, predictably, quite different. Using the Gini index presented earlier, Novak and Green argue that inequality

TABLE 6–3   **Share of aggregate income received by each quintile of households (in percent)**

	Quintile Share of Income					Top 5 Percent	Total
	1	2	3	4	5		
All families with children							
1969	4.1	10.9	17.5	24.5	43	16.6	100.0
1974	4.3	10.6	17.0	24.6	43.5	16.5	100.0
1979	4.1	10.2	16.8	24.7	44.2	16.9	100.0
1984	4.0	9.9	16.3	24.6	45.2	17.1	100.0
1989	3.8	9.5	15.8	24.0	46.8	18.9	100.0
Ratio 1989/1969 share	.93	.87	.90	.98	1.08	1.14	1.00

Source: Based on data in U.S. Bureau of the Census, *Money Income of Households, Families, and Persons in the United States: 1988 and 1989* (Washington, D.C.: U.S. Government Printing Office, 1991).

TABLE 6–4	United States Gini Index, 1949–1989	
	Year	**Gini Index**
	1989	.401
	1984	.383
	1979	.365
	1974	.356
	1969	.349
	1964	.361
	1959	.361
	1954	.371
	1949	.378

Source: U.S. Bureau of the Census, Current Population Reports, Series P–60, No. 156, *Money Income of Households, Families, and Persons in the United States: 1985* (Washington, D.C.: U.S. Printing Office, 1987) and U.S. Bureau of the Census, Current Population Reports, Series P–60, No. 172, *Money Income of Households, Families, and Persons in the United States: 1988 and 1989* (Washington, D.C.: U.S. Government Printing Office, 1991).

in the United States is similar to that in other western democracies. The heart of their argument is that inequality is caused less by unfairness than by the age structure of the labor force. Persons in the early years of their careers and those in retirement will have lower incomes than persons in their peak earning years. Thus, the same person will be at different positions along the Lorenz curve during different periods of his or her life. Novak and Green use this argument to interpret why statistical measures of inequality have increased during recent years. According to their argument, a greater number of people are now living in retirement due to increased life span, and the baby boom generation has been entering careers and setting up households in large numbers during the past decade. For these reasons, income figures in recent years include more people at low earning points in their careers. As this generation continues "its long trek through its lifetime positions along the Lorenz curve" presumably the Geni will decrease.[10]

Conservatives and liberals also differ on whether high inequality is a bad thing. Liberals believe that high, and especially increasing, inequality is a cause for great concern. They fear that if inequality is too great, social disruption will likely occur. Harrison, et al., observe ". . . the fear—expressed by a growing number of journalists and political analysts—that the frustrated expectations of significant numbers of younger workers unable to attain the living standards of their own parents could lead to potentially serious social unrest."[11] Reuss has said, "From a social standpoint, when whole classes feel themselves endangered, bloodshed and revolution have been the outcome, as in France in the 1790s and Germany in the 1930s."[12]

Conservatives argue that wage inequality is no particular cause for concern, and in fact it is actually desirable. George Gilder summarizes this argument:

Under capitalism, when it is working, the rich have the anti-Midas touch, transforming timorous liquidity and unused savings into factories and office towers, farms and laboratories, orchestras and museums—turning gold into goods and jobs and art. That is the function of the rich: fostering opportunities for the classes below them in the continuing drama of the creation of wealth and progress.[13]

Gilder argues that rich people (entrepreneurs to be more exact) serve a critical social function by being willing to risk their money on the hope that they will win great profits. When their risks pay off, they create new wealth for everyone in the form of jobs and economic growth. Thus, rich people are entitled to hundreds of times the income of regular people for two reasons: (1) they take great risks, often losing everything, and therefore they deserve great profits when their risks pay off, and (2) rich people use their money not for conspicuous consumption, but to create more wealth for us all. Gilder says

> the crucial role of the rich in a capitalist economy is not to entertain and titillate the classes below, but to invest: to provide unencumbered and unbureaucratized cash . . . Only a small portion of their money is consumed. Most of it goes to productive facilities that employ labor and supply goods to consumers. The rich remain the chief source of discretionary capital in the economy.[14]

It should be noted that Gilder provides virtually no empirical evidence to support his contentions. Nobel-prize winning economist Robert M. Solow, in his review of *The Spirit of Enterprise,* Gilder's sequel to *Wealth and Poverty,* remarked, "Only someone with a sense of humor could survive reading this book. And no one with any trace of a sense of humor could have written it."[15]

Finally, while liberals and conservatives agree that some inequality is necessary, they disagree on how much inequality is desirable. Conservatives, as can be inferred from the quotes from Gilder, are not really concerned with the amount of inequality. They agree that poverty is a bad thing, but they contend that poverty is not a result of inequality. They argue that the situation is really quite the opposite—when people make a lot of money we all benefit, so why should we care how rich some people are? If the average income of the wealthiest people in the country increased from, say, $5 million a year to $10 million a year, and as a result of their profit-seeking your income went up by $5 thousand, you would not be upset, right?

Liberals question this "trickle down" theory and argue that it does not follow that increased income for the rich results in increased income for other groups in society. They point out that as inequality in income has increased during recent years, the number of people below the poverty line has also increased. They believe that social efficiency (that is, providing enough reward to motivate the most highly qualified people to pursue the most difficult jobs) could be achieved with a much smaller amount of inequality than currently exists. Ryan, one of the most articulate spokesmen of this "fair shares" approach says

> I don't think many of us have strong objections to inequality of monetary income as such. A modest range, even as much as three or four to one, would, I suspect, be tolerable to almost everybody . . . The current range in annual incomes—from perhaps $3,000 to some unknown number of *millions*—is, however, intolerable, impossible to justify rationally, and plain inhuman.[16]

Most radicals would strongly agree.

No agreement about the effects, positive or negative, of increasing inequality has been reached, and our society has seemingly become willing to live with a high level of inequality. Krugman makes the rather discouraging observation:

> So income distribution, like productivity growth, is a policy issue with no real policy debate. The growing gap between rich and poor was arguably the central fact about economic life in America in the 1980's. But no policy changes now under discussion seem likely to narrow this gap significantly.[17]

POVERTY—THE DARK SIDE OF INEQUALITY

Most people would not consider inequality to be a problem if those on the low end of the distribution had at least enough income to live in a minimally adequate fashion. However, there is a large number of people who do not have this amount of income. We refer to the living condition of these people as *poverty*. In this section we will look at a number of aspects of poverty; we examine how it is defined, how the official poverty line is set, and some unresolved issues in measuring and defining poverty; and finally, we will look at liberal and conservative perspectives on poverty. We will not refer to a radical perspective in this section since radicals are more interested in the larger question of inequality than the way in which the poverty line is set.

The Definition of Poverty

We see the items in the newspaper frequently: "Poverty Rate Up By 2%," and "More Children Growing Up in Poverty Now than Any Year Since 1961." From these articles we assume that it is possible to measure poverty in a manner similar to measuring the annual rainfall—that there is some objective standard against which to measure poverty. But we also see headlines that say things like "Administration Questions Poverty Statistics," and "Aide Claims That If All Benefits Were Counted Poverty Level Has Declined by 3%." The question we are left with is, can we measure poverty and, if so, how accurately? The answer, as you will see, is that yes, we can measure poverty with a fairly high degree of accuracy, but there is widespread disagreement on what poverty is, what the best measure is, and what the immense quantity of data we have on poverty means.

The way we measure and define poverty is first dependent on which of two broad classes of definitions we employ. The first class of definitions is referred to as *economic definitions*; it basically defines poverty as a lack of money and other resources. The second class of definitions is known as *cultural definitions*; it defines poverty not only as a lack of money but also as a lifestyle composed of values, attitudes, and behaviors that are related to being poor. According to cultural definitions, important attributes of poverty include feelings of hopelessness, alienation, and matriarchal (mother dominated) family structure.[18] In this chapter we are dealing with poverty as an economic phenomenon and we will not concern ourselves with the cultural aspects. (They will be dealt with in the following chapter.) There are two broad categories that economic definitions of poverty fall into—absolute definitions and relative definitions.

Absolute Definitions[19]   An absolute definition of poverty is a relatively fixed level of income below which a person cannot function in a productive and efficient manner.

It is based on calculations derived from minimum costs of food, housing, clothing, and transportation. The emphasis is on *minimum* cost; no allowance is made for luxuries such as travel (even if it is for a purpose generally thought to be essential, such as visiting a sick relative) or entertainment. An absolute poverty line will increase along with the cost of living and as conditions in society change certain expenditures from nonessential to essential. For example, fifty years ago indoor plumbing was not considered essential and so the cost of sewer service was not included in poverty line calculations. Today an outdoor toilet is illegal within city limits, so the cost of sewer service has become essential and is therefore a part of poverty line calculations.

Mollie Orshansky, one of the people responsible for conceptualizing the official poverty line in the United States, has commented that there is no reason to count the poor, and hence no reason for defining poverty, unless you intend to do something about it.[20] It was not until the late nineteenth century that anyone even began to think that something could be done about poverty on a societal level, and this is when interest was first shown in setting a poverty line so the poor could be counted. The earliest attempts were made in England. In the 1890s, Liverpool businessman Charles Booth defined poverty in the following way:

> by the word "poor" I mean to describe those who have a sufficiently regular though bare income, such as 18s to 21s per week for a moderate family, and by "very poor" those who from any cause fall much below this standard. The "poor" are those whose means may be sufficient, but are barely sufficient, for decent independent life; the "very poor" those whose means are insufficient for this according to the usual standard of life in this country. My "poor" may be described as living under a struggle to obtain the necessaries of life and make both ends meet, while the "very poor" live in a state of chronic want.[21]

Booth arrived at these figures by observing thirty families who struck him as "poor" or "very poor" and using their expenditures as the basis for his poverty line.

Booth's definition was improved upon a few years later in a study by another Englishman, Seebohm Rowntree. Booth defined poverty using a subjective idea of the "necessaries of life." Rowntree wanted to be more scientific and to calculate the income necessary for "physical efficiency" as the dividing line between poverty and nonpoverty. To arrive at this figure he turned to the work of nutritionists who had conducted rigorous studies to determine how many calories were necessary for men to carry out "moderate muscular work." They had concluded that 3500 calories was the minimum intake required for physical efficiency. Using this as a standard, Rowntree developed a menu that would supply 137 protein grams of 3560 calories at the lowest possible cost. He then priced these items at the cheapest shops he could locate and calculated the lowest cost possible to feed a person at a level that would enable that person to work efficiently. Rowntree then added in the cost for the cheapest housing he could locate and an amount he considered adequate for "household sundries." By adding these figures together, Rowntree arrived at his poverty line.

There have been a number of attempts to develop better absolute poverty lines than those of Booth and Rowntree. Rowntree himself revised his calculations and methods in 1936 and again in 1950. The official U.S. government poverty line, which will be discussed later in this section, is based on a methodology similar to that of Rowntree. According to Holman, all of these absolute definitions share three elements. First, the poverty line is set at a level that will enable people to be physically efficient.

No allowance is made for enjoyment of life or for personal development of any sort. Of his poverty line Rowntree said, "It was a standard of bare subsistence rather than living." Second, the poverty line is based on calculations of utmost stringency. The only people considered poor are those whose lives, according to Booth, entailed ". . . a struggle to obtain the necessaries of life." Finally, absolute definitions of poverty are not related to the incomes of society as a whole. These definitions do not compare people with people, but attempt to compare people with an objective yardstick that only changes when the cost of living changes or when certain things, like sewer service, become necessary expenditures.[22]

The major advantage of absolute definitions and measures of poverty is that they provide a constant standard against which one dimension of the economic progress of a country can be measured. Using an absolute standard, we can look at the numbers and percentages of people living below the subsistence level at various points in history, and we can reach some conclusion about whether things are getting better or worse for the most disadvantaged segment of the population. We can also look at statistics over a shorter period of time and see if policies designed to help the poor are really having any effect.

There are some major problems with absolute definitions of poverty, however. The first and major problem is that absolute definitions are based only on physical needs and they assume that people will spend their money with absolute efficiency. These definitions ignore social and psychological needs and the fact that most people do not spend money with absolute rationality. Rowntree, for example, assumed that a family

> must never purchase a half penny newspaper or spend a penny to buy a ticket for a popular concert. They must write no letters to absent children for they cannot afford to pay the postage. They must never contribute anything to their church or chapel, or give any help to a neighbor which costs them money . . . the children must have no pocket money for dolls, marbles or sweets. The father must smoke no tobacco and must drink no beer.[23]

We all realize that this is not the way people actually spend their money. No one is so coldly efficient that he or she will refuse to call or write relatives, send a few Christmas cards, or occasionally go to a movie. Also, absolute definitions assume that people go to the cheapest stores and buy items at the lowest possible price. Not only do most poor people, like people in general, lack the knowledge to get the best bargains, but also the stores in their neighborhoods generally charge higher prices than those in more affluent areas.[24] Thus, the calculations used to set absolute definitions of poverty are based on assumptions that are false.

The second problem is a result of the first problem; because the assumptions on which absolute poverty lines are based are false, the lines are set at too low a level. Studies in both England and in the United States that ask the general population to set an absolute poverty line always result in figures much higher than the actual line. A 1981 study in England commissioned by London Weekend Television found that the general public set the poverty line at 33 percent higher than the actual line.[25] In the United States a 1981 Gallup poll found that Americans set the poverty line at 55 percent higher than the actual line.[26]

The final problem with absolute definitions of poverty is that they consider the wealth of the rest of society only as it influences the kinds of expenses a family has in order to get by at a subsistence level. We previously used sewer service as an example because everyone living in a city must pay for sewer service. Therefore, the poverty line in wealthy societies will be higher than in poor societies. However, beyond this the wealth of the rest of society is not considered. If the average income triples over a period of years and the cost of living stays the same, the poverty line will not increase. The reason that this is a problem with absolute definitions has to do with the concept of *relative deprivation*, which asserts that people feel rich or poor not in relation to some absolute yardstick, but rather in relation to the wealth of other people. Thus, even though people living at the poverty line are no poorer when the wealth of the rest of society increases, the fact is they feel poorer. This phenomenon is the reason some people argue that poverty should be defined not in absolute, but in relative terms.

Relative Definitions   Absolute definitions attempt to set an objective line that separates the poor from the nonpoor. Relative definitions see poverty as subjective; that is, it is a matter of opinion both on the part of the poor and the nonpoor as to what constitutes poverty. Poverty is viewed as relative to the wealth of the rest of society. According to relative definitions, a family with an income of $8,000 a year will consider itself, and be considered by others, as poor in a society such as the United States where the median annual income is over $25,000. However, this family would not be considered poor in a country such as Mexico where the median family income is much lower.

There are two main methods of setting relative poverty levels. One is to take an arbitrary percentage of the median family income and define this as the poverty level. The line in most countries is set at the 50 to 66 percent level.[27] In the United States the relative poverty line is set at 44 percent of the median income. The other method, best exemplified by the Townsend study in England, is to survey the general population to find out their opinion of where the poverty level should be.[28]

The major problem with relative definitions and measures of poverty is related to the fact that they are subjective. This problem is—what criteria do you use in setting the line? In setting an absolute line you have the criterion of physical efficiency, which can be ascertained by things like number of calories and the cost of a menu sufficient to obtain these calories. When setting a relative line there is no similar criterion. Desai proposes two principles to be used in setting a relative poverty line:

1. . . . . economic entitlement to an adequate living standard should be such that citizens can take full part in the political community.

2. . . . the level of the poverty threshold, i.e., the specific contents of the level of living flowing from a citizen's economic entitlement, must be determined by the community.[29]

The authors agree with Desai, but would broaden the first principle by eliminating the word *political*. Thus, when considering whether to include an item in a poverty line budget, the question would be asked, "Is this item necessary for full participation in the community?" rather than asking the absolute definition question, "Is this item necessary for physical efficiency?" For example, if you were considering whether to include the cost of a bicycle for a family with a ten-year-old child, using an absolute definition you would not include any money for this because the family can function with physical efficiency without a bicycle. However, using a relative definition you would include it because there is little doubt that a ten-year-old needs a bike in order to fully participate in the life of the community.

As you might expect, using a relative definition results in a much higher poverty line than an absolute definition, and consequently a much higher poverty rate. The London Weekend Television study in England and the Gallup poll in the United States cited earlier resulted in figures 33 and 55 percent over the official poverty line. The Townsend study in England resulted in a figure 50 percent over the official level. On the average the poverty line set by these groups was 90 percent greater than the official U.S. government level. Even when the very low relative poverty line figure of 44 percent of median income is used in the United States, the relative line comes out to be 10 percent higher than the absolute line.

Relative poverty measures have several advantages over absolute measures. The first and probably greatest advantage is that they are much more realistic than absolute measures. People do not live their lives according to the assumptions used for absolute poverty lines. They purchase toys for their children; they visit relatives; and they celebrate occasions such as anniversaries and birthdays. They generally do not manage their affairs with absolute efficiency. The second advantage is that relative definitions recognize that poverty is subjective. Poverty is a matter of feeling and opinion, both of the poor and the nonpoor, and relative definitions take opinions into account.

The major drawback of relative definitions is that they present a moving target, so to speak, for poverty policy and programs. One of the major reasons for defining poverty to begin with is to measure progress in our attempts to do something about it. Using absolute definitions, we can see over time what progress has been made. Using relative definitions, any change that occurs is likely to be as much a result of changing perceptions as it is a change in the level of well-being of the poorest section of the population.

Does a child in the United States actually *need* a bicycle? Using a relative definition of poverty, the answer is yes because a child cannot fully participate in the life of the community without one. Using an absolute definition, the answer is no because a bicycle is not necessary for health and efficiency.

A CLOSER LOOK

Poverty Definition Quiz

Do you think the following things are essential or nonessential?

1. For a ten-year-old child to have a bicycle.
2. For a family to have a car, even though it may be a "junker."
3. For a sixteen-year-old girl to have a formal dress, or a sixteen-year-old-boy to rent a tuxedo to attend the junior prom.
4. For a family to have enough food to be able to serve coffee and cookies, or beer and chips, when friends drop in.
5. For a family to have a television set in good working order.

If you answered that all, or most, of these things are nonessential, you are operating from an absolute definition of poverty. It is true that none of these things is necessary for life, or for efficiency. If you answered that all, or most, of these are essential, you are operating from a relative definition. There is little doubt that a family who does not have these things, as well as many others not listed here, is not able to fully participate in the life of our society.

The Official Poverty Line in the United States

Various government agencies in the United States have formulated definitions of poverty since the late nineteenth century. In 1907 the Bureau of Labor Statistics devised two budgets, one to meet "minimum standards" (an absolute measure), and one that was called a "fair standard" (a relative measure).[30] However, there was no "official" poverty line until the 1960s, when the U.S. government became serious about reducing poverty for the first time in its history. The official poverty line is defined as an attempt to "specify the minimum amount required to support an average family of given composition at the lowest level consistent with standards of living prevailing in this country."[31]

The first official poverty line in the United States was a crude measure developed in 1964 by the Council of Economic Advisors (CEA). This line used the same methodology that Rowntree had half a century earlier, which was based on the cost of food. The line was formulated using the *Engle's coefficient,* a technique that resulted in the conclusion that the average poor family spent one-third of its income on food. The Department of Agriculture (USDA) had developed menus to show what it cost families to eat at various levels, ranging from an economy budget to three higher cost budgets. Initially the line was set using the "low cost" menu and multiplying it by three (because food is supposed to take up one-third of a family's budget), which resulted in a poverty level of $3,995. This amount was deemed to be too high, so the CEA reformulated the line using the "economy budget," which resulted in a poverty level of $3,000. The main problem with this poverty line was that it only had two categories: families and single individuals. The poverty line was $1,500 for an individual and $3,000 for a family regardless of size, age of family members, or type of residence. Thus, a couple with no dependents and an income of $2,900 was considered poor, while a family of eight with an income of $3,100 was not.

Because of the problems with the CEA poverty measure, the Social Security Administration (SSA) decided to revise it in 1965. A panel was appointed to accomplish this task; Mollie Orshansky, a SSA statistician, was designated as the chairperson. The SSA panel decided to continue to use the Engle's coefficient and the USDA economy food plan as the base for its calculations because this method was thought to have resulted in a realistic poverty line for a nonfarm family of four. Beyond this, however, the panel felt that the method developed by the Council of Economic Advisors was too crude to differentiate among different family types and places of residence, as well as other factors. The result of this panel's work was a poverty table known as the "Orshansky Index."[32] The new index was based on two major changes in the method of computation. The first was that the Engle's coefficient was reformulated to reflect the fact that smaller families spend a smaller percentage of their incomes on food. For single individuals, the food budget was multiplied by a factor of 5.92; for couples, the factor was 3.88; and for all larger families, the factor was 3.0. The second was that the budget was reduced by 30 percent for farm families because it was presumed that they would grow a portion of their food. The resulting index differentiated among 124 different kinds of families, based on the sex of the head, the number of children under 18, the number of adults, and whether or not the family lived on a farm.

The poverty table developed by the Orshansky panel was updated each year based on changes in the price of food in the USDA economy food budget. In 1969 the Census Bureau adopted the index as its official measure of poverty and began to issue a statistical series on poverty. Over the years, the Census Bureau has made several changes in the index. The first is that they ceased updating it based on the cost of food and instead they began to update it based on changes in the Consumer Price Index (CPI). The second major change is that the differential between farm and nonfarm families has gradually been reduced until it was entirely eliminated in 1982. These changes, along with some other minor ones, have caused the current table to be simplified considerably. The official poverty table for 1991 is presented in Table 6–5. Because of the need for

TABLE 6–5	1991 poverty income guidelines for all states (except Alaska and Hawaii) and the District of Columbia
Size of Family Unit*	Poverty Guideline
1	$ 6,620
2	8,880
3	11,140
4	13,400
5	15,660
6	17,920
7	20,180
8	22,440

*For family units with more than 8 members, add $2,820 for each additional member.
Source: "Notices," *Federal Register,* Vol. 56, No. 34 (Wednesday, February 20, 1991): 6860.

TABLE 6–6	**Persons below the poverty line, 1959–1989**	

Year	Number (in millions)	Percentage of Total Population
1959	39.5	22.4
1960	39.9	22.2
1965	33.2	17.3
1968	25.4	12.8
1969	24.1	12.1
1970	25.4	12.6
1971	25.6	12.5
1972	24.5	11.9
1973	23	11.1
1974	23.4	11.2
1975	25.9	12.3
1976	25	11.8
1977	24.7	11.6
1978	24.5	11.4
1979	26.1	11.7
1980	29.3	13
1981	31.8	14
1982	34.4	15
1983	35.3	15.2
1984	33.7	14.4
1985	33.1	14.0
1986	32.4	13.6
1987	32.5	13.6
1988	31.7	13.0
1989	31.5	12.8

Source: Derived from U.S. Bureau of the Census, Current Population Reports, Series P–60, No. 161, *Poverty in the United States, 1987* (Washington, D.C.: U.S. Government Printing Office, 1989), 5 and U.S. Bureau of the Census, Current Population Reports, Series P–60, No. 168 *Money Income and Poverty Status in the United States, 1989* (Washington, D.C.: U.S. Government Printing Office, 1990), 56.

trend data the Census Bureau extrapolated the poverty line back to 1959. This trend data is summarized in Table 6–6.

The official U.S. government poverty line has been criticized for the same shortcomings as all absolute measures of poverty: it does not reflect how people actually spend their money, it ignores the fact that people have emotional needs which may be even more important to them than physical needs (parents may buy a child a birthday present even if it means that they do not have enough money left to pay the rent), and it is set at a level that is much lower than most people in our society would personally set it. These are shortcomings of all absolute poverty measures, not just of the specific line used in this country. There is, however, a hot debate between liberals and conservatives about how useful and accurate the line is, and just what it means. It is to this debate that we now turn.

Issues and Perspectives in Measuring and Defining Poverty

At first it sounds strange to speak of clashing perspectives and heated disagreements about something so seemingly dry and technical as the definition and measurement of poverty. However, as we shall see, these disagreements do occur and, while the matter may be dry and technical, it is certainly not unimportant. The definition of poverty is an inherently political act and one that has grave implications. The power to define poverty is the power to control statistics and, as Harrington has noted, ". . . the control of statistics is one of the critical functions of power in a democratic society. The numbers define the limits of the possible; they confer the awesome mathematical legitimacy of 'fact' upon some parts of reality and deny it to others."[33] Orshansky, the primary author of the official poverty line, is quite candid about the political nature of the line. She comments, "In the Social Security Administration poverty was first defined in terms of the public or policy issue: To how many people, and to which ones, did we wish to direct policy concern."[34] Orshansky and her committee wished to create a line that was politically credible. To be credible they felt that they had to select a figure that identified a group that was not so small that people would be tempted not to worry about it or so large that a solution would appear impossible.

You will recall from Chapter 1 that conservatives support the status quo and are generally opposed to government programs. Because of these views they tend to favor definitions that minimize the amount of poverty in America. If the level of poverty is shown to be low, this logically leads to the conclusion that society is working well (which supports the status quo) and that there is little need for more government programs. Liberals support change and are generally in favor of government programs that they believe will lead to an improvement in society. They favor definitions that maximize the amount of poverty because the existence of a large, and especially a growing, level of poverty logically leads to the conclusion that society is not functioning as well as it should be and that increased government intervention is called for.

In keeping with their respective agendas, liberals and conservatives hotly debate the official government poverty line. The debate revolves around four basic issues: Is the poverty line set at a realistic level? Do you count only cash as income or do you count other benefits? Are the Census Bureau figures upon which poverty estimates are based accurate? Should poverty be defined and measured using an absolute or a relative definition?

Is the Poverty Line Set at a Realistic Level?   Conservatives argue that the poverty line, $13,400 in 1991 for a family of four, is set at too high a level. The conservative economist Rose Friedman has argued that the Engle's coefficient used to estimate total needs from spending on food is incorrect. She asserts that low-income families spend a greater proportion of their income on food than average families and therefore the food budget should be multiplied by a number less than the three that is currently used. Friedman argues that the use of this incorrect coefficient has resulted in an overestimation of poverty by as much as 100 percent.[35]

Conservatives also argue that tying the poverty line to the Consumer Price Index (CPI) has further increased the already too-high poverty line. The CPI measures increases in the cost of living by figuring the cost of a specific "market basket" of goods. Butler and Kondratas say that this method ignores substitution of one commodity for another by households in order to keep the cost down. For example, if the price of soft drinks increased by 30 percent and the price of fruit juice did not increase at all, most consumers would substitute fruit juice for at least part of their soft drink consumption. This substitution would result in the actual cost of their "market basket" of goods increasing at a rate lower than the CPI. This is only one of several flaws in the Consumer Price Index that conservatives believe have artificially inflated the poverty line.

Liberals, to no one's surprise, take the opposite position and argue that the poverty line is too low. They point out that the Department of Agriculture, whose budgets are used as the basis of the poverty calculations, admits that the budgets are set at an unrealistically low level. USDA analysts have estimated that only about 10 percent of persons spending the amount allowed in the economy food budget are able to get a nutritionally adequate diet.[36] The USDA has also revised the Engle's coefficient. In 1965 an analysis by the department concluded that for poor families the coefficient should be 3.45 rather than 3.0. This increase would raise the poverty line by 15 percent and result in a large increase in the number of families defined as poor.

How Should Noncash Benefits Be Counted?   A good deal of assistance to poor families is given in forms other than cash. Poor people may receive food stamps, medical care, low-cost public housing, legal services, social services, and a number of other items and services. Although these items do not constitute income as such, it does cost money to provide them and they are of tangible benefit in improving the lives of the recipients. The current method of computing the poverty line counts only cash as income; no value whatsoever is given to in-kind benefits.

Conservatives argue that in-kind benefits should be counted as income. Butler and Kondratas point to the irony of not counting these benefits when they observe, "The federal government could give every poor person in America a free car, free housing and education, and free food for life, but as far as the official poverty definition is concerned, that would have no impact whatsoever on poverty."[37] They observe that the majority of the increases in benefits provided to the poor since the early 1960s have been in the form of goods and services rather than cash, and that if these benefits were counted, the poverty rate would greatly decrease. Martin Anderson, a leading conservative analyst on the subject of social welfare, has gone so far as to say, "The 'War on Poverty' that began in 1964 has been won. . . . Any Americans who truly cannot care for themselves are now eligible for generous government aid in the form of cash, medical benefits, food stamps, housing, and other services."[38] Anderson, using data from the Census Bureau and from a Congressional Budget Office study, estimates that largely because of the value of in-kind benefits, the number of people in poverty in 1978 was only one quarter of the official figure.

Liberals agree that in-kind benefits have value and should be considered when defining and measuring poverty. However, liberals believe that in-kind benefits are much more difficult to cost out than conservative analysts would lead one to believe. Harrington gives the following example of the problems involved.

> How does one evaluate the value of medical care that goes mainly to the aging poor? The Bureau of the Census gives an excellent case in point. In 1979, the market value of Medicaid coverage for an elderly person in New York State was estimated at $4,430. But this was almost $1,000 more than the poverty line for that person ($3,472). Clearly this $4,430 is "income" in a very special sense, since it cannot be spent on food, housing, or any other need (and it is indeed most unwelcome "income" since one has to be ill to get it). If one were to take that $4,430 at face value, then a person could enter the middle class, by virtue of having a long, expensive, subsidized terminal illness.[39]

A technical paper published by the Census Bureau in 1982 concluded that there were serious difficulties in "cashing out" in-kind benefits. This analysis concluded that counting in-kind benefits as income would reduce the poverty figures by only 12.2 percent rather than the 75 percent estimated by Anderson.[40]

Are the Census Bureau Figures Accurate?   The official poverty data does not come from someone actually going out and counting the poor. The Census Bureau selects a relatively small statistical sample of the population and requests that they fill out a detailed questionnaire on their financial situation. The fact that the data is derived from a sample rather than from a count of the whole population is not necessarily a problem. A count of everyone in the country would be impractical, and sampling techniques have become sophisticated enough that the data can be accepted as representative of the whole population with little question. However, the fact that the data is self-reported does bother some people, particularly conservatives.

Conservatives argue that people are very sensitive about their financial lives and as a result they do not report income data with a high degree of accuracy. Butler and Kondratas have said, "The known underreporting to the Census of even legal income reportable to the tax authorities is one of the most serious deficiencies of the poverty data. The Census Bureau's own estimates indicate underreporting of aggregate income of about 10 percent with welfare income underreported by as much as 24 percent."[41] Conservatives cite the Panel Study of Income Dynamics being conducted by the Survey Research Center at the University of Michigan, a generally liberal group, as supporting their contention. This survey, which uses techniques that are more accurate than those of the Census Bureau, estimated that in 1978 only 6.8 percent of the population had incomes falling below the poverty level, as compared to the official rate for that year of 11.4 percent.

Liberals challenge the idea that the poverty figures are artificially inflated because of underreporting of income by the poor. Beegley, for example, argues that the majority of underreporting occurs in upper income groups who gain substantial tax advantages by minimizing their income. Poor people have little, if anything, to gain by underreporting their income and, hence, they have no reason to do it. Beegley concludes that, "The notion that the number of poor people has not declined because of underreporting of income by the poor is false."[42]

Should Poverty Be Defined in Absolute or Relative Terms? This question is closely related to our earlier discussion of inequality. If you think for a few moments, you will realize that if you use a relative definition of poverty, the only way poverty will show a reduction is for the Gini coefficient to show a reduction. By way of example, let's use two rather improbable economic scenarios. In the first scenario, the economy enters a tremendous boom period with the result being that the income of everyone in the country doubles while prices remain the same. This means that a family of four that was living on $10,000 a year, a little below the poverty line, now is earning $20,000 a year, well above the poverty line. It also means that the family whose income was $250,000 a year, many times more than it needs, now has even more. If you apply an absolute definition of poverty to this scenario, poverty would almost disappear. However, if you apply a relative definition, the poverty level would be exactly the same because at the same time the median income doubled, the relative poverty line would also have doubled. Therefore, inequality would be the same, the Gini coefficient would be the same, and the poverty level would be the same, even though people would be twice as well off in absolute terms. The second scenario is the opposite. In this scenario, the country enters a tremendous depression and everyone's income takes a nosedive. However, let's suppose that the richer you are the harder you are hit. People in the bottom 20 percent (quintile) of the income distribution suffer a 30 percent reduction in income; people in the next quintile suffer a 40 percent reduction; the next quintile is reduced by 50 percent; the fourth quintile is reduced by 70 percent; and the richest 20 percent sees their income go down by 90 percent. This means that the family in the first scenario, whose income was $10,000 per year, now has an income of $7,000. The family whose income was $250,000 now has an income of only $25,000 per year. If an absolute definition of poverty were applied to this scenario, the poverty rate would skyrocket. However, if a relative definition were applied, the rate would drop dramatically. Before the crash, the income of the low-income family was only 4 percent of that of the high-income family. After the crash, it "improved" to 28 percent. This example is far-fetched but the point it illustrates is not—when using a relative definition, the only way to show a reduction in poverty is to reduce inequality.

As you know from the previous discussion of inequality, conservatives see no particular reason to reduce inequality and so they do not generally favor relative definitions. They believe that absolute definitions like the official poverty line, while not perfect, are satisfactory for the purposes they serve. Murray, for example, says

> The poverty definition has been attacked from all sides but continues to be used because, finally, it has a good deal of merit. The poverty line does not truly divide the "poverty-stricken" from the rest of us—the transition consists of a continuum, not a dividing line—but it gives us a common yardstick for talking about the issue. It is widely accepted, takes family size and inflation into account, and provides a consistent definition for examining income over time. Also, no one has proposed an alternative definition that has attracted widespread support.[43]

Liberals believe that the reduction of inequality would be a good thing and so they are more favorable toward relative definitions of poverty and more critical of absolute definitions. Rodgers, for example, criticizes the official poverty line because it has not kept up with the growth in personal income. He notes that in 1959 the poverty line was 53 percent of median income and that it is now only 38 percent. Rodgers believes that a relative definition is the only meaningful way of describing poverty and that the United States does not employ this method because the amount of poverty revealed would be embarrassing to the government.[44]

CONCLUSION

It has been said that statistics are problems with the tears wiped away. It is very important that we keep this in mind when discussing somewhat dry, technical subjects such as inequality and the definition and measurement of poverty. How we define and measure poverty has very real consequences for a large number of people. The eligibility requirements for many assistance programs are computed in some way based on the poverty line. Some housing assistance programs, for example, are open to people whose income does not exceed 125 percent of the poverty line. A revision of a few hundred dollars up or down in the poverty line will result in thousands of people becoming eligible or ineligible for a decent place to live. What the correct Engle's coefficient is may be puzzling to a student and fascinating to a professor, but it has very real consequences to a child who does not want to sleep with rats.

ENDNOTES

1. These figures are from the *Statistical Abstract of the United States: 1990,* 110th Edition (Washington, D.C.: U.S. Government Printing Office, 1990), Table No. 697, "National Income, By Sector: 1970 to 1988" and Table No. 55, "Households, Families, Subfamilies, Married Couples, and Unrelated Individuals: 1960 to 1989."
2. Paul A. Samuelson, *Economics,* 10th ed. (New York: McGraw-Hill, 1976), 84.
3. John Craven, *Introduction to Economics—An Integrated Approach to Fundamental Principles* (Oxford, England: Basil Blackwell, 1984), 99.
4. William Ryan, *Equality* (New York: Pantheon, 1981), 14.
5. University of Michigan Institute for Social Research, "Wealth in America," *ISR Newsletter* (Winter 1986–87): 3–4; Ryan, *Equality,* 14.
6. Quoted in University of Michigan Institute for Social Research, "Wealth in America," 3.
7. Henry Reuss, "Inequality Here We Come," *Challenge* (September–October 1981): 49–50.
8. Bennett Harrison, Chris Tilly, and Berry Bluestone, "Wage Inequality Takes a Great U-Turn," *Challenge* (March–April 1986): 32.
9. Paul Krugman, "The Income Distribution Disparity," *Challenge* (July–August 1990): 4.
10. Michael Novak and Gordon Green, "Poverty Down, Inequality Up?" *The Public Interest* (Spring 1986): 49–57.
11. Harrison, Tilly, and Bluestone, "Wage Inequality Takes a Great U-Turn," 27.
12. Reuss, "Inequality, Here We Come," 52.
13. George Gilder, *Wealth and Poverty* (New York: Basic Books, 1981), 63.
14. Gilder, *Wealth and Poverty,* 62.
15. Robert M. Solow, "The Entrepreneur As Hero," review of George Gilder, *The Spirit of Enterprise,* in *The New Republic,* October 22, 1984, 37–39.
16. Ryan, *Equality,* 30.
17. Krugman, "The Income Distribution Disparity," 6.
18. L.F. Hayes, "Non-Economic Aspects of Poverty," *Australian Journal of Social Issues 5* (February 1970): 41–54.
19. In actuality there is no such thing as an absolute definition of poverty. All definitions are relative because they occur in a certain social and economic environment. In the United States, for example, we consider a person poor if that person rarely can

afford to eat meat and fresh fruit, even if his or her nutritional intake is adequate, and he or she is getting needed protein and vitamins from other sources. In third world nations, this diet would not result in a person being classified as poor. Therefore, even an absolute definition is relative because it is only absolute in relation to the social, economic, and historical environment in which it occurs.

20. Mollie Orshansky, "How Poverty Is Measured," *Monthly Labor Review 92* (February 1969): 37.

21. Albert Fried and Richard M. Elman, eds. *Charles Booth's London: A Portrait of the Poor at the Turn of the Century, Drawn from His "Life and Labour of the People in London"* (New York: Pantheon Books, 1968), 10.

22. Robert Holman, *Poverty: Explanations of Social Deprivation* (New York: St. Martin's Press, 1978), 7–8.

23. Quoted in Holman, *Poverty*, 11–12.

24. David Caplovitz, *The Poor Pay More: Consumer Practices of Low Income Families* (New York: Free Press, 1967).

25. Joanna Mack and Stewart Lansley, *Poor Britain* (London: George Allen and Unwin, 1985).

26. "Family of Four Needs Record $277 Per Week," *The Gallup Report 185* (February 1981): 20–21.

27. Harrell R. Rodgers, Jr. "Limiting Poverty by Design: The Official Measure of Poverty," in *Applied Poverty Research*, Richard Goldstein and Stephen M. Sachs, eds. (Totowa, NJ: Rowman & Allenhead, 1984), 60.

28. Peter Townsend, *Poverty in the United Kingdom: A Survey of Household Resources and Standards of Living* (New York: Penguin Books, 1979).

29. Meghnad Desai, "Drawing the Line: On Defining the Poverty Threshold," in *Excluding The Poor*, Peter Golding, ed. (London: Child Poverty Action Group, 1986), 3–4.

30. Sharon M. Oster, Elizabeth E. Lake, and Conchita Gene Oksman, *The Definition and Measurement of Poverty, Volume 1: A Review* (Boulder, CO: Westview Press, 1978), 6.

31. Mollie Orshansky, "Measuring Poverty," *The Social Welfare Forum: Proceedings of the 92nd Annual Forum of the National Conference on Social Welfare* (New York: Columbia University Press, 1965), 214.

32. Orshansky, "How Poverty is Measured," 37–41.

33. Michael Harrington, *The New American Poverty* (New York: Holt, Rinehart and Winston, 1984), 71.

34. Orshansky, "How Poverty is Measured," 37.

35. Rose Friedman, *Poverty: Definition and Perspective* (Washington, D.C.: American Enterprise Institute, 1965), 36.

36. Orshansky, "How Poverty is Measured," 38.

37. Stuart Butler and Anna Kondratas, *Out of the Poverty Trap* (New York: The Free Press, 1987), 46.

38. Martin Anderson, *Welfare* (Stanford, CA: Hoover Institution, 1978), 15.

39. Harrington, *The New American Poverty,* 86.

40. U.S. Bureau of the Census, "Alternative Methods for Valuing Selected In-Kind Transfer Benefits and Measuring Their Effect on Poverty," cited in Harrington, *The New American Poverty,* 80.

41. Butler and Kondratas, *Out of the Poverty Trap,* 45–46.

42. Leonard Beegley, *Living Poorly in America* (New York: Praeger, 1983), 32.

43. Charles Murray, *Losing Ground* (New York: Basic Books, 1984), 271.

44. Harrell R. Rodgers, Jr., "Limiting Poverty by Design," in Goldstein and Sachs, *Applied Poverty Research,* 54.

C·H·A·P·T·E·R
seven

The Nature and Causes of Poverty

When I was a child, I lived with my family in Minneapolis. We lived on the south side of town, and our relatives lived on the north side where my father had grown up. We visited often. One Sunday afternoon in March we set off across town in our car and took a different route than usual. I think it had something to do with the construction of a new freeway which caused streets to be closed. Our new route took us through the middle of the area that would now be called the ghetto; then it was called the slums. This was new and foreign territory; I had never seen anything like it. I stared out of the window fascinated, horrified, and repulsed all at the same time. There were houses that had burned down and apparently had been abandoned; broken glass seemed to be everywhere; and the streets and yards were littered with paper and junk. Even more puzzling were the housing projects, which I could see were relatively new and modern structures, not unlike apartment houses in my neighborhood, but they looked little better than the old dilapidated buildings surrounding them. Their walls were covered with graffiti, there were cars up on blocks, and the yards were a series of lakes of mud separated by scraggly patches of grass.

Groups of children ran around and played; they did not look too different from the children I played with. They were a little ragged; some were wearing torn tennis shoes even though it was still cold, but otherwise they looked familiar. The groups of adults did not seem typical, however. They were standing around in small groups, looking tired and bored, and they lacked the appearance of purpose and command that I expected from the adults in my life.

"Who are these people?" I asked my parents. "Why are they here?" "What is this place?" "Do they like it?" "Why don't they leave?" My parents explained that these were poor people; they were here because they did not have enough money to go anywhere else; and most of them did not like it, but they probably did not know anything else. It was an unfortunate situation, but it was simply a fact of life. This explanation didn't really satisfy me because I knew poor people. My friend Mike was poor. Mike's father had been killed in the Korean War and his mother had some sort of chronic illness; people referred to her as frail. She was able to work only part-time answering the phone at the Lutheran church, and her salary from this, plus her small government check, provided very little income. Mike and his mother lived in a tiny two-room cottage in the backyard of a house two blocks down from where my family lived. The cottage had been built for the mother of the owner of the house, and when she died he rented it to Mike's mother for a small sum. Mike slept in the bedroom and his mother slept in a hide-a-bed in the living room. They did not have a car. Mike's mother had a basket that rolled on two wheels and could be folded up for easy carrying. She would carry this to the store, load her groceries in, and roll them home. They didn't have a TV set, even though the last holdout in the neighborhood (my father) had purchased one two years before. Like all of us, Mike worked, mowing lawns in the summer and shoveling snow in the winter. However, unlike us, he could not use his money for whatever he wanted. Whatever he earned he gave to his mother, who put it in the bank to be used for school clothes, Boy Scouts, and summer camp. Anything left over went into that mysterious black hole of youthful finance, the college fund.

As we drove out of the ghetto I thought that Mike was poor, but he was not like this. The only difference between Mike's family and mine was that we had more money.

This neighborhood appeared to be in another country, if not on another planet. Who were these people? Why were these people like this? It had to be more than simply money.

As an adult, I am still asking the same questions I asked as a child. They are the subject of this chapter. Who are the poor? Are they all the same? Why are they poor? Regarding the first two questions, as you will see, we know a good deal. We have massive amounts of statistical data to describe the poor. My youthful observation about the difference between my friend Mike and the people I observed in that Minneapolis ghetto was valid—poor people are not all the same and there is more to poverty than money, although obviously money is the most important part. The answer to the last question is not so clear. We have many theories about the causes of poverty, but no certain answers. The answers we do have are greatly clouded by our old friend political perspectives. These topics are the subject of this chapter.

WHO ARE THE POOR?

In this section we will present a statistical picture of the population in the United States who live below the poverty line. Two types of pictures will be presented. The first is the traditional means of describing this population based on statistical data gathered mainly by the Census Bureau as part of its series of Current Population Reports. This is the source of most of the figures that you will see on the evening news and that are referred to in statements by lawmakers and interest groups. This type of information has been referred to as "snapshot" data because it provides a series of statistical pictures at certain points in time, but it does not tell us much beyond a general description of the situation at that time. Poverty statistics show, for example, that the level of poverty in this country is fairly stable, running between 12 and 14 percent each year. However, these statistics do not tell us anything about the individual makeup of those figures at each point in time. Is the 12 to 14 percent composed of the same people this year as last year, or are different people poor each year? If the statistics describe a different population each year, how different is it? Are some people more likely to be part of the statistics for a short time while others are part of them for many years? To answer questions such as these a different type of data collection is needed. This type of data is called *longitudinal data,* which means that data is collected from the same persons at a number of points in time and questions such as the preceding ones can thereby be answered. We have only recently begun collecting longitudinal data, the best source currently being the Panel Study of Income Dynamics, conducted by the Survey Research Center at the University of Michigan. The first topic in this section, the statistical description of poverty, will rely mostly on snapshot data collected by the Census Bureau. The next section, types of poverty, will rely more on longitudinal data, mainly from the Panel Study of Income Dynamics.

Statistical Description of the Poverty Population

The Bureau of the Census periodically publishes a book which presents nearly 200 pages of statistics on the poverty population.[1] A few of the most interesting of these statistics for 1990 are summarized in Table 7–1 on page 189. As can be seen, nearly

Most people associate poverty with minority group members living in large cities. Actually, the majority of poor people are white, and those who live in rural areas are more likely to be poor than are city dwellers.

32 million Americans, 12.8 percent of the population, had incomes that were below the poverty level that year. The misery of poverty, however, was not evenly divided among the many groups of the population. The burden fell much more heavily on some than on others.

Race   The image of the poor in most people's minds is that of a minority, generally an African American person. As can be seen from this data, that image is both right and wrong. It is wrong in the sense that the majority of the poor, more than 58 percent, are white. However the image is correct in that a much greater proportion of minority group members fall below the poverty line. Only about one out of every ten white people in this country is poor, compared to nearly one out of three African Americans, and more than one out of four persons of Spanish origin. Whites make up the majority of the poor only because such a great majority of the population is white.

Age   The popular image of a poor person is of an able-bodied young adult. The Census Bureau data shows this image to be wrong. The largest group of the poor are, in fact, children who are too young to work and who thus cannot improve their own status. As people move into the productive adult years, the percentage in poverty rapidly declines. The percentage once again increases as people move into the older segment of the population.

Region   The distribution of poverty across the country is fairly even. There is a little more poverty in the south and a little less in the northeast. However, these differences

(handwritten: know how)

TABLE 7–1

TABLE 7–1   **Characteristics of the population below the poverty line**

Group	Number below Poverty Line (in thousands)	Rate (% below poverty line)
All Persons	31,528	12.8
Race		
White	20,785	10.0
Black	9,302	30.7
Spanish Origin*	5,430	26.2
Age		
Under 18 Years	12,590	19.6
18–24 Years	3,840	15.2
25–34 Years	4,782	11.1
35–44 Years	3,026	8.1
45–54 Years	1,883	7.4
55–59 Years	1,027	9.7
60–64 Years	1,017	9.5
65+ Years	3,363	11.4
Region		
Northeast	5,061	10
Midwest	7,043	11.9
South	12,934	15.4
West	6,487	12.5
Family Size		
2 Person	27,606	8.2
3 Person	15,353	9.8
4 Person	14,026	10.1
5 Person	5,938	13.5
6 Person	1,997	21.1
7 Person or more	1,170	32.3
Family Type		
All Families	6,784	10.3
Married Couple	2,931	5.6
Male Head, No Wife	348	12.1
Female Head, No Husband	3,504	32.2
Single Individuals		
All	6,766	19.2
Male	2,539	15.7
Female	4,227	22.3

*Persons of Spanish origin may be of any race.

Source: Derived from U.S. Bureau of the Census, Current Population Reports, Series P–60, No. 168 *Money Income and Poverty Status in the United States* (Advance Data from the March 1990 Current Population Survey) (Washington, D.C.: U.S. Government Printing Office, 1990), various tables.

Who Are the Poor?

probably reflect the greater proportion of the population in the south who live in rural areas.

Family Size   Another popular stereotype of the poor is that they generally have very large families. As can be seen from Table 7–1, this is false. The average size of families below the poverty line is only slightly larger than the average family in the United States. This difference can probably be explained by the fact that families below the poverty line are younger than the average and thus have more members at home, rather than actually being larger. However, the stereotype of the large poor family is correct in one sense. A far greater proportion of large families than small families fall below the poverty line. Only 8.2 percent of two-person families are living in poverty, while 32.3 percent of families with seven or more members are poor. The reason for this, we should note, is not that large families earn less money than small families, but that they need more money to live adequately. In 1991 the poverty line for a two-person family was $8,880, while the line for a eight-person family was $22,440.

Family Type   As will be discussed later in this chapter, researchers are finding a great deal of evidence that points to family type as the most important determinate of economic status. The basis for this line of thinking can be found in Table 7–1. Families where there is both a husband and a wife have a poverty rate of only 5.6 percent. For families with a male head and no wife present, the rate more than doubles to 12.1 percent. For families with a female head and no husband present, the rate is six times that of intact families and three times that of single male-headed families, 32.2 percent. Interestingly, single-person households appear to do rather poorly in economic life. The overall rate of poverty for single individuals is 19.2 percent; for single males the rate is 15.7 percent; and for single females it is 22.3 percent.

The Feminization of Poverty   You have probably noticed in all the data being reviewed that women appear to be doing poorly in relation to men. This is an accurate observation and not one that has gone unnoticed by researchers and policy makers in recent years. In fact, a term was coined in 1978 to describe this problem—*the feminization of poverty.*[2] This problem has become even more severe in recent years because of the rapid and steady increase in the number of families headed by women. The percentage of families headed by women increased from 10.1 percent in 1950 to 14 percent in 1976, an increase of almost 40 percent in only one generation.[3] By 1984 this number had increased further to 16 percent, a 14 percent increase in only eight years. In our society, because women are generally the parent who provides the bulk of child care, this trend contributes to the great number of children living below the poverty line.

Combinations of Characteristics   Characteristics related to high poverty rates tend to combine in an additive fashion. For example, 21 percent of six-person families are poor, 30.7 percent of African American families are poor, and 32.2 percent of female-headed families are poor. If we combine these characteristics, we find that 50.8 percent of African American, female-headed families are below the poverty line, and an almost unbelievable 68.5 percent of six-person, African American, female-headed families fall into this category.

FIGURE 7–1

Source: Copyright, 1987 *Boston Globe*. Distributed by Los Angeles Times Syndicate. Reprinted by permission.

Different Types of Poverty

While it is very useful for giving us a general description of the characteristics of the poor, the preceding data is static. That is, it just tells us what the population looks like at various points in time and says little, if anything, about differences other than demographic ones within the population. Sociologists have long known that the poverty population is not homogenous, and recent studies, notably the Panel Study of Income Dynamics, have added greatly to our understanding of the many differences within the poverty population.

Three Levels of Poverty   In their 1981 study of poverty, Segalman and Basu posited the existence of three different segments in the poverty population: the transitional poor, the marginal poor, and the residual poor.[4] The transitional poor are those people whose experience of poverty is only temporary and is usually brief. Poverty for this group is generally the result of some life change or misfortune. Examples of situations likely to result in transitional poverty are a person returning to school to finish a degree and living on a bare bones budget while doing it; a person unemployed because of a plant closing being unable to find a new job and finally moving to a more economically prosperous area; a person who has an extended illness; and a widow for whom it takes a year or so to adjust to the new realities of her situation, including entering or reentering the job market. Segalman and Basu say that new immigrants, such as the wave of Southeast Asians who entered this country during the 1970s, generally go through a period of transitional poverty before learning the many things necessary to compete in the job market. The key characteristics of transitional poverty are that it is brief, temporary, and generally related to specific events in the life of the person experiencing it.

The marginal poor are the group often referred to as the working poor. They generally have jobs, but because of low educational levels and few skills, or because of discrimination, the jobs they have are low paying and insecure. These people are nearly always at the margin of the poverty line and, depending on luck and the economy, they may be on one side or the other. When the oil crisis was at its peak, many of the marginal poor in oil-producing states like Texas and Louisiana were earning near middle-class incomes because of the great amount of work and overtime available. Now that the demand for oil has decreased, most of these folks are back below the poverty line. The main difference between the transitional poor and the marginal poor is that the transitional poor are experiencing a brief episode of poverty, they may never experience another, and they may quickly rise well above the poverty line. For the marginal poor, rising out of poverty and sinking back into it is a long-term pattern, and it is doubtful for most that they will ever rise much above the poverty level.

The residual poor are a group who remain in poverty over an extended period of time. They are generally dependent on welfare benefits for their daily living, and their poverty may well be intergenerational. This group has received a good deal of attention in recent years, and they have come to be referred to as "the underclass."[5] Most references to the problem of poverty in the United States, or to the corollary welfare problem, are generally referring to the residual poor. This is the group that is hard to reach and often seems almost immune to help; this group is thus very frustrating to a society that likes to find rapid solutions to problems.

Data on Different Types of Poverty and Poverty Patterns   The preceding discussion of different types of poverty is based on Census Bureau data which, as discussed earlier, is of somewhat limited usefulness because it consists of statistical "snapshots" taken at various points in time. The data does not answer questions related to the proportion of the poor that are residual, the extent to which families and individuals move out of or remain in poverty, and, consequently, the factors that are related to escaping poverty. To make up for this deficiency in the data about poverty, a group of social scientists at the Survey Research Center at the University of Michigan began a long-term study in 1968 entitled the "Michigan Panel Study of Income Dynamics."[6] For this study a random sample of over 5,000 families was selected, and repeated annual interviews have been conducted with the families each year since 1968. There is now over twenty years of data on these families and the data has been, and is still being, subjected to intensive analysis; the study promises to greatly increase our understanding of poverty. In this section the major findings of the Panel Study are summarized. In the following section on causes of poverty, this data will be utilized to examine some of the major theories on causes of the poverty problem.

The official poverty rate in the United States remains fairly steady at between 11 percent and 15 percent; the rate in 1990 was 12.8 percent. With regard to this rate, the Panel Study contains both bad news and good news. The bad news is that during the decade from 1968 to 1978 a percentage of the population much larger than 12.8 percent was in a state of poverty for at least one year. Nearly one quarter of the population (24.4 percent) fell below the poverty line for at least one year. The group we have called the residual poor, or the underclass, is called the *persistently poor* by

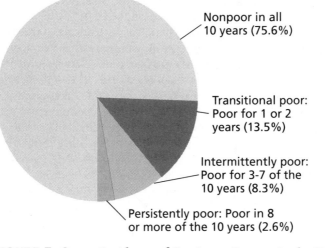

Nonpoor in all
10 years (75.6%)

Transitional poor:
Poor for 1 or 2
years (13.5%)

Intermittently poor:
Poor for 3-7 of the
10 years (8.3%)

Persistently poor: Poor in 8
or more of the 10 years (2.6%)

FIGURE 7–2   **Incidence of Persistent Poverty in the United States,
1969–1978**

Source: Adapted from: Greg J. Duncan, et al., *Years of Poverty—Years of Plenty: The Changing Economic
Fortunes of American Workers and Families* (Ann Arbor, MI: Institute for Social Research, The University of
Michigan, 1984), 42.

the Panel Study researchers. The researchers define this group as people whose incomes
were below the poverty line for at least eight of the ten years. The good news from
the Panel Study data is that it shows that only 2.6 percent of the population were
persistently poor.* The group Segalman and Basu call the marginal poor is called the
intermittently poor by the Panel Study researchers. They define this group as people
who were poor for three to seven of the ten years studied, usually with no predictable
pattern to the years. They found that 8.3 percent of the population fell into this category.
Thus, to summarize, 2.6 percent of the population was found to be persistently poor,
an additional 8.3 percent was intermittently poor, and an additional 13.5 percent was
poor for only one or two years. This data is summarized in the chart in Figure 7–2.

When comparisons are made between the transitionally poor and the persistently
poor using Panel Study data, the demographic differences are even more striking than
those found using the Census Bureau one-year data. The Panel Study found an overwhelmingly disproportionate representation of African Americans and women among
the ranks of the persistently poor. The data shows that during the study period, 62
percent of the persistently poor were women (only 19 percent of the population lived
in families headed by women in 1978) and 58 percent were African American (African
Americans made up only 12 percent of the population in 1978). The largest proportions
of the temporarily poor were found to be composed of whites and males. Thus, it
appears that poverty for minorities and women tends to be of the long-term variety,
while poverty for males and whites is generally of the temporary variety.

---

*We use the term "only 2.6 percent" advisedly, being fully aware that this encompasses more than six million
people.

Who Are the Poor?   **193**

There is one additional finding of the Panel Study data that is interesting to note here. The popular image of the poor in the United States is of a group of people living in large, northern, industrial cities. This is particularly true of the image of the permanent, or residual poor. A 1980 Manpower Demonstration Research Corporation report, for example, refers to "a group of people, largely concentrated in [this country's] principal cities, who live at the margin of society. . . . They are simultaneously the source and the victims of urban decay."[7] The Panel Study data indicates that this stereotype is not true. The data shows that among the persistently poor, 50 percent live in the south (30 percent of the total population live in the south) and 24 percent live in rural areas (15 percent of the population live in rural areas). One-third of the persistently poor live in cities with populations over five hundred thousand, a percentage closely reflecting the percentage of the population living in large cities. The remainder of the persistently poor is found in cities with populations between ten and five hundred thousand.

WHY ARE THE POOR, POOR?

Imagine that a social scientist randomly sampled 1000 people from across the United States and lined them all up along a long, straight road in Nebraska or somewhere. The people would be lined up according to income, with the poorest people on the left, progressing toward the richest on the right. The social scientist would then actually paint a line to represent where the poverty level began, with people to the left being those in poverty and people to the right being those out of poverty. Assuming that the poverty rate was 12.8 percent, 128 people would be to the left of the line and 872 to the right of it. The social scientist would then stand back and ask "What is different about the 128 people to the left of the line? Why are *they* there and not the other 872?" Some differences would be obvious to the social scientist or to anyone else observing the line. A much greater percentage of the people to the left of the line would be members of minority groups, many more would be women, and more would be old and young. To the right of the line a disproportionate percentage would be white, male, and in the early and middle adult years.

This simple visual inspection of the people would give us a hint as to the causes of poverty—it has something to do with race, sex, and age—but it would not give us a complete answer because of two broad questions. The first question has to do with what statisticians call *between-group variance*. We can see that more members of the female group are poor than members of the male group. However, we do not know the source of this variance. Are more women poor because there is something in our society that systematically discriminates against them and prevents them from an equal chance at well-paying jobs? This is known as a *structural explanation;* in other words, the source of the problem is in the social structure. Or, are more women poor because there is something genetic or cultural that makes women less competitive in the job market, factors such as desire to stay home and have children, or a fear of competition? This is known as an *individual explanation.* The second question has to do with what statisticians call *within-group variance.* This question deals with the fact that while a disproportionate number of women and African Americans are in poverty, not all are, and while most whites are not in poverty, some are. What are the differences among the members within these groups?

The question of the causes of poverty is very complex and controversial; answers are very incomplete, and yet the question is extremely important. Proposed solutions to poverty based on different explanations often will be diametrically opposed. If you propose a program based on a structural explanation, the focus of the program will be on changing society. If you propose a program based on individual explanations, the focus will be on changing individuals. In this section we will take a close look at three different broad explanations of poverty. The first is the explanation that views poverty as being the result of individual characteristics. The second views poverty as being the result of the poor holding fundamentally different values than the rest of society, values which prevent them from escaping poverty and make it likely that their children will follow them into lives of poverty, an explanation known as the *culture of poverty thesis*. The third explanation sees the poor as victims of society, and thus it explains their poverty as the result of impersonal economic forces or of discrimination and oppression which are mainly institutional; these are the structural explanations referred to earlier.

Poverty as the Result of Individual Characteristics

In previous chapters we have discussed the belief among Americans, especially conservative ones, in individualism. The aspect of this belief most important for understanding social welfare is that it tends to attribute the cause of problems to the individuals affected by the problems. Thus, it is natural in our society to assume that the primary cause of poverty is to be found in some defect in the individuals affected. Holman notes that, "The analyses do not necessarily allocate blame to individuals who are poor, but they do regard poverty as stemming from the limitations, maladjustments or deficiencies of individuals."[8]

Individualistic explanations of poverty can be divided into three main types, which have emerged in rough chronological order. The explanation with the longest history is that people are poor because of inferior genetic quality, especially, but not limited to, intellectual ability. This explanation is still occasionally expounded, but it has been largely discredited. The view that replaced this was that the poor were not necessarily genetically inferior, but that they suffered from psychological problems that inhibited their ability to compete for good jobs. This view continues to have some influence; in its most recent form it is known as the *expectancy model*. The current favorite theory of those who insist on individual explanations of poverty is known as *human capital theory*. This is the notion that poor people do not have the knowledge, skills, and attributes (human capital) that make them valuable to employers. These three individualistic explanations are discussed in detail next.

Genetic Inferiority   People in the United States at one time attributed poverty almost entirely to genetics. Behavior was often described as being "in the blood." The Irish immigrants were poor because they drank heavily and had bad tempers, the Italians were hot-blooded Mediterraneans, and African Americans were fun-loving and childlike. All were suspected of having low intelligence. As various groups have entered the mainstream of American life and have competed successfully for jobs and income, these theories of innate genetic inferiority have generally been dropped. They have been replaced by a much more sophisticated theory based on the science of psychological measurement, specifically the development of the IQ test. This theory argues that intelligence is inherited (that is, it is genetically determined) and that economic success is closely related to intelligence.

The originator of the IQ test and of the idea that intelligence was a measurable quality was the French psychologist Alfred Binet. Binet developed the test in the early 1900s for the use of Paris public school administrators who desired a way to identify children in need of special education. Binet developed a test that served this purpose, and he was quite specific about its limitations. He insisted that the test should be used only to identify children in need of special help and it should not be used to classify normal children. Binet strongly asserted that the tests did not measure anything innate or permanent and that, "Low scores shall not be used to mark children as innately incapable."[9]

Binet's ideas of testing intelligence were quickly snapped up by H.H. Goddard and Lewis M. Terman in the United States and by Sir Cyril Burt in England. They chose to ignore Binet's statements about the limitations of intelligence tests, and, in fact, they advanced quite the opposite idea. They insisted that intelligence was heritable (passed down from generation to generation) and immutable (could not be changed). Therefore, a person who is born to parents with low intelligence is doomed to a life of failure and probably misery. The result of the work of these men and a number of similar thinkers was what has come to be called the *eugenics movement*. This movement, which will be discussed in greater detail in Chapter 10, was based on the idea that not only is intelligence genetic but also those with very low intelligence (at that time called the feeble-minded) reproduce at rates far greater than the more intelligent segments of the population. Thus, the human race was seen as being in danger of becoming overrun by people of low intelligence.[10]

Although eugenics fell into disrepute following World War II, the notion that intelligence is hereditary and that poverty can be largely explained by inherited low intelligence has persisted. The most influential modern advocate of the notion that intelligence is an innate quality and is inherited is the Berkeley psychologist Arthur Jensen.[11] Jensen argues that modern genetic research has firmly established that about 49 percent of the variance in IQ scores can be explained by heritability. After reviewing the work of seventeen geneticists and behavioral geneticists, Jensen concludes, "With such general agreement among scientists, it is all the more amazing how the popular media have so often promoted the notion that the genetic inheritance of intelligence is a highly controversial issue."[12]

The most influential modern exponent of the idea that social class, and by extension poverty, is related to inherited intelligence is Richard Herrnstein. Herrnstein states his question in the form of a syllogism:

1. If differences in mental abilities are inherited, and
2. If success requires those abilities, and
3. If earnings and prestige depend on success,
4. Then social standing (which reflects earnings and prestige) will be based to some extent on inherited differences among people.

Herrnstein argues that a strong case can be made for removing the "ifs" in his syllogism. He argues that the differences in intellectual ability between social classes is becoming greater as barriers to the upward mobility of gifted people are removed, thus removing them from the gene pool of the lower classes. Because people tend to marry within their class, Herrnstein believes that eventually most of the superior genes will be in the upper classes and inferior genes will be in the lower strata of society. He concludes, "The biological stratification of society looms . . . "[13]

The idea that intelligence is an inherited trait and that success is the result of high intelligence and lack of success is the result of low intelligence has been the subject of severe, and often emotional, criticism. The arguments are technical and complex and we do not have room to go into them in detail. However, basically the critics of Jensen and Herrnstein argue that we do not really know what intelligence is, and that whatever it is, it is doubtful that intelligence tests measure it. It is argued that the tests are culturally biased. That is, items selected for the tests are based on what is familiar to white and middle-class people, and minorities and lower-class people are less likely to be familiar with them. For example, one test item calls for the test taker to be familiar with the word "symphony." It is argued that this item is much more likely to reflect whether the child taking the test has ever been to a symphony than any real measure of intelligence. It is, of course, much more likely that a middle-class child will have been to a symphony. Block and Dworkin, for example, argue

> that it does not seem likely that IQ tests measure mainly intelligence. The evidence suggests that there is no good reason to believe IQ tests *do* measure mainly intelligence and that a number of other quantities (such as sociocultural background and personality-motivational-temperamental factors) appear to have as good a claim to be measured to some degree by IQ tests as intelligence does.[14]

This controversy has never been resolved, but it has died down in recent years.

Poverty as the Result of Psychological Problems   The idea that a large proportion of the poor are that way because they are suffering from some psychological problem gained popularity throughout the 1950s, peaked and even gained legislative support during the 1960s, and then rapidly lost influence. Especially popular was the idea that the poor live in "multi-problem families" that have an almost insatiable appetite for social services. Buell, for example, in a study of social services in St. Paul, Minnesota, found that 6 percent of families receiving services consumed over half of the total services provided.[15] The basic idea of this theory is that poor people do not have their developmental needs met as children; as a result they are immature, and consequently they are unable to meet the needs of their own children who then grow up immature, and the cycle goes on and on. The British social worker Elizabeth Irvine contends that among the poor

> There is impulsiveness and lack of control in various spheres, including those of sex and aggression. Often there is a compulsive need for oral satisfaction whether in the form of sweets, cigarettes or drink. In some instances the usual inhibitions on anal interests have not been developed, children are not toilet trained and faeces lie about on the floor or are stored away in tin baths or cupboards. . . . These characteristics seem to add up to a picture of extreme immaturity; is not most of this behavior the sort of thing one would

expect from a two-year-old, three-year-old or four-year-old left without adult guidance or control?[16]

The theory that poverty is largely caused by psychological problems among the poor hit its high point in 1962 when it was incorporated into the amendments to the Social Security Act popularly known as the social service amendments. These amendments were based on the idea that the poor "needed not just, or even primarily, financial aid but rather psychological assistance and other forms of counseling; they had to 'adjust' to being single parents or to life in the city; they needed instruction on how to keep house and manage their meager resources in order to make ends meet; they needed to learn how to make friendships and develop self-esteem . . ."[17] The amendments provided a large sum of money to enable states to hire social workers trained in psychological techniques to go out and help people solve psychological problems that were preventing them from being self-supporting.

The social service amendments proved to be the undoing of the theory that psychological maladjustment was a major dynamic in poverty. Social workers went out armed with their new therapeutic skills and quickly discovered that these had little relevance for dealing with the harsh realities of impoverished families. Congress also quickly lost its enthusiasm for this approach when the welfare rolls did not go down. In fact, just the opposite happened; following the passage of the social service amendments, the welfare caseloads skyrocketed. This approach has continued to lose influence, and there are currently very few people who seriously argue that psychological maladjustment is a major factor in understanding poverty.

A new version of the psychological explanation of poverty has recently emerged that does not assume pathology but, rather, explains the problem of poverty in social psychological terms. This theory is known as the *expectancy model*. This model is based on the theory that there is a relationship between confidence, sense of control, and success. Those who are successful gain confidence and this leads to a sense of control over their lives, which in turn results in more success. On the other hand, those who fail lose confidence, begin to feel out of control of their lives, and this leads to further failure. Poverty results when people lose a sense of control over their lives, when they begin to expect failure, and when they cease to believe that they can ever escape poverty. Ellwood observes that, "People who are frustrated by their lack of control may be observed to exhibit two almost opposite kinds of responses: either an aggressive and potentially antagonistic response or a very passive and sedate one. People become overwhelmed by their situation and lose the capacity to seek out and use the opportunities available."[18]

The Human Capital Approach   This is an economist's approach to explaining the individual's contribution to his or her own poverty. Human capital is defined by Thurow "as an individual's productive skills, talents, and knowledge. It is *measured* in terms of the value (price multiplied by quantity) of goods and services produced."[19] In other words, the human capital approach looks at how much an individual's labor is worth. People who have a large amount of skill obtained by experience, education, and training are going to be worth more on the labor market than those who have not invested in these things. Some aspects of the value of human capital are, of course, natural abilities that cannot be acquired. Most aspects, however, are acquired or enhanced by human actions.

The human capital approach views poverty as the result of individuals having low amounts of human capital. Thurow notes, "Efforts to eliminate poverty and the income gap between white and black have focused attention on the factors that produce individual incomes of human capital . . . If individuals are paid according to their productivity, then individual skills, talents, and knowledge determine earnings. A wide dispersion in the distribution of human capital creates a wide dispersion in the distribution of earnings. Many factors, such as discrimination, play a role in determining the shape of the income distribution, but the distribution of productive investments is certainly one determinant."[20]

The human capital approach is a very straightforward approach to poverty. It says, in essence, that people are poor because they lack the knowledge and skills necessary to get good jobs that will provide above-poverty-level incomes. There is no doubt that this is one factor in understanding poverty. However, the human capital approach does not account for a number of factors, including discrimination. Traditionally female jobs requiring a college degree (in other words, a large amount of human capital), such as elementary school teaching, will often pay much less than jobs traditionally held by men and requiring much less human capital—for example, the job of electrician. Be that as it may, for our purposes the human capital approach merely substitutes one definition of poverty for another. Thurow says, "One of the advantages of thinking in terms of human capital is that it immediately focuses attention on the production problem. What factors create human capital? What is the most efficient method of combining these factors?"[21] These are interesting questions, but they take us back to the question with which we began this chapter—why are some people poor and others not? The human capital approach merely substitutes the question, "why do some people possess low amounts of human capital?" for the question "why are some people poor?" and this takes us back to where we began.

Cultural Explanations of Poverty

The individual explanations of poverty discussed previously tend to appeal to conservatives because of the conservative focus on the individual's responsibility for his or her own situation. Structural explanations, which are discussed in the next section, locate major responsibility for personal problems within the social structure in which the individual finds himself or herself. These explanations tend to be favored by liberals and radicals because of their belief in the strength of the environment in shaping individuals' lives. Between these two types of explanations are the cultural explanations. These have been, and continue to be, very influential because, as we shall see, they mix individual and structural factors in such a way that both conservatives and liberals feel comfortable subscribing to them.

Cultural explanations, like individualistic explanations, locate the proximate cause of poverty as being individual characteristics. Individuals who are poor are seen as being in this situation because they are not motivated to succeed, they do not value work, they demand immediate gratification of their needs, and they do not value marriage or education. However, unlike individualistic explanations, cultural explanations do not view these individual characteristics as being caused by any innate quality of the individual affected, such as low intelligence or some form of psycho-pathology. Individuals are viewed as possessing these characteristics because of the social situations they were born into, and in which they were reared and educated. Thus, cultural explanations are more hopeful than individual explanations because these factors are more easily "corrected" than low intelligence or psychological disorders. There are two slightly different versions of cultural explanations: the culture of poverty theory and the cultural deprivation theory.

Culture of Poverty   The concept of a *culture of poverty* was first suggested by an-thropologist Oscar Lewis in his 1959 book *Five Families: Mexican Case Studies in the Culture of Poverty*.[22] The concept won almost immediate acceptance by social scientists, journalists, and policy makers who were struggling with ways to deal with poverty in the 1960s. Michael Harrington made extensive use of the concept in his 1962 book *The Other America,* Frank Riessman related the concept to education in his 1962 book *The Culturally Deprived Child,* and Daniel Patrick Moynihan used the concept in his controversial but influential Department of Labor report *The Negro Family.*[23] The mas-sive antipoverty programs of the Kennedy administration and Lyndon Johnson's War on Poverty programs were greatly influenced by the culture of poverty idea.

Lewis set out to apply basic ideas of anthropology to the study of poverty. He looked at poverty as a "subculture with its own structure and rationale, as a way of life which is passed down from generation to generation along family lines." He pro-posed that poverty was not only something negative—want and deprivation—but also that it includes positive aspects, some rewards without which the poor could not carry on. The culture of poverty develops, according to Lewis, as a reaction by the poor to their marginal position in society and it "represents an effort to cope with feelings of hopelessness and despair which develop from the realization of the improbability of achieving success . . .[24]

The culture of poverty, according to this theory, consists of a set of values, behavior patterns, and beliefs among the poor which are different from those of the larger society. Once this culture comes into effect, it is passed from one generation to another. Lewis identified seventy separate elements of the culture of poverty, which he lumped into four groups. The first is a number of characteristics which reflect that the poor are not effectively integrated into the major institutions of the larger society. For example, they do not participate in unions, political parties, or voluntary groups. In fact, they show a basic distrust of many of the basic institutions of society—the police, government offices, and even the church. They are poorly integrated into the job market, and this is a main reason that they control very little wealth. Banfield, a popularizer of culture of poverty theory whose version is much more conservative than that of its originator, comments that the poor person "feels no attachment to community, neighbors, or friends . . . resents all authority (for example, that of policemen, social workers, teachers, landlords, employers), and is apt to think that he has been 'railroaded' and to want to 'get even.' "[25]

The second group of elements of the culture of poverty is related to the communities in which poor people live. In these communities, there is little organization beyond the level of the extended family. Occasionally, temporary groupings and voluntary organizations emerge, and sometimes even a sense of community, but this does not last long.

The third group of elements of the culture of poverty are those related to the family. According to Lewis, major traits of family life are "absence of childhood as a specially prolonged and protected stage in the life cycle, early initiation into sex, free unions or consensual marriages, a relatively high incidence of the abandonment of wives and children, a trend toward female- or mother-centered families and consequently a much greater knowledge of maternal relatives, a strong predisposition to authoritarianism, lack of privacy, verbal emphasis upon family solidarity which is only rarely achieved because of sibling rivalry, and competition for limited goods and maternal affection."[26] Banfield asserts that the child rearing style of the mother is impulsive, and once children have passed infancy they are likely to be neglected or abused.[27]

Finally, there are those elements which are related to the individual. People in the culture of poverty supposedly have strong feelings of marginality; that is, they do not feel that they really belong to anything in society. They are also characterized by strong feelings of helplessness, dependence, and inferiority. There is a high incidence of maternal deprivation, weak ego structure, and confused sexual identity. Poor people are viewed as having poor impulse control, a strong present-time orientation with little ability to defer gratification and to plan for the future, and a corresponding sense of resignation and fatalism. Banfield says, "At the present-oriented end of the scale, the lower-class individual lives from moment to moment. If he has any awareness of a future, it is of something fixed, fated, beyond his control: things happen *to* him, he does not *make* them happen . . . whatever he cannot use immediately he considers valueless."[28]

Lewis argues that these elements represent characteristics of a culture, or more accurately, a subculture. They are social, psychological, and economic traits that are passed on from one generation to another. They represent beliefs, attitudes, and values

Culture of poverty theory asserts that people are poor and remain poor because they do not share major American values essential for success, for example deferral of gratification and marriage before parenthood.

that are fundamentally different from those of the larger society. Lewis says, "People with a culture of poverty are aware of middle-class values, talk about them and even claim some of them as their own, but on the whole they do not live by them. Thus it is important to distinguish between what they say and what they do. For example, many will tell you that marriage by law, by the church, or by both, is the ideal form of marriage, but few will marry." A key point in understanding the culture of poverty theory is the argument that these cultural elements survive and are passed down from generation to generation because they are functional for people living within a poverty situation. Lewis continues the example on marriage, "To men who have no steady jobs or other sources of income . . . free unions and consensual marriage makes a lot of sense. Women will often turn down offers of marriage because they feel it ties them down to men who are immature, punishing and generally unreliable."[29]

According to culture of poverty theorists, these characteristics of the poor make it very unlikely that they will be able to escape their poverty. To get out of poverty, one has to participate in social institutions, especially school; one has to form stable relationships, mainly two-parent families; and perhaps most important of all, one must be willing to defer gratification of immediate wants in order to gain greater rewards at a future date. For example, we all realize that going to college requires that a young person delay a large number of desires. It generally involves putting off buying a nice car, getting married, and traveling for at least four years. Going to college costs a lot in terms of deferring a number of things people want. However, most people realize that if they put these things off for four years, they will reap large rewards over the remainder of their lifetime. Culture of poverty theorists assert that poor people are unable to see this far ahead and so they do not defer gratification in order to get an education, among other things; thus, they hurt, or destroy, their chances to escape poverty.

Three additional points need to be made about the culture of poverty theory. The first is that this theory is not meant to apply to all poor people. The group being discussed is the group we identified earlier as the residual poor. This group represents only a small percentage of the poor, but receives much attention because of the seemingly intractable nature of their poverty. The second point is that culture of poverty theory views the lives of the residual poor as containing a kind of an irony. That is, the beliefs, attitudes, and behavior patterns that help make life in poverty bearable are the same patterns that prevent people from escaping poverty. For example, for a teenage boy in the ghetto, belonging to a gang and selling drugs is going to provide much more pleasure and status among his peers than being on the honor roll and working afternoons at McDonalds for minimum wage. However, going to school and working at a straight job is likely to result in a person escaping poverty, while belonging to a gang and selling drugs is probably going to result in a downward spiral. The third point is that because poverty constitutes a subculture, it involves more than money. According to this theory, if members of the poverty culture were given enough money to adequately meet all their needs, their lives would not change greatly. They would most likely "squander the money" to gratify immediate needs and wants, and they would end up just as miserable as before.

Cultural Deprivation   While culture of poverty theory is based on research in anthropology and focuses on the concept of culture, cultural deprivation theory is based on research in education and focuses on the concept of socialization. Cultural deprivation theory does not assert that the poor have *different* values, beliefs, and knowledge than the nonpoor; it posits that they are deprived of the opportunity to develop the knowledge, beliefs, and values of the larger society. Cultural deprivation theory has been mainly focused on low educational achievement among poor children, which in turn results in poor life chances. The theory argues that differences in educational achievement between poor and nonpoor children are explained by differences in home background. Ryan, a critic of this approach, summarizes it as follows, "Uneducated parents, crowded living quarters, absence of books, family disinterest in education—all combine to handicap the poor black child as he enters the school system. There is a specific denial of any *innate* inferiority; rather there is perceived a *functional* inferiority that is attributable to the depressing and stultifying effects of living in poverty, which is, of course, condemned as bad and unjust."[30] According to cultural deprivation theory, poor children do not *dis*value education, they have simply never been taught (or more accurately, socialized) to value it. According to Holman, "If the child-rearing practices are deficient, then the children will not develop into adults who can fit into the prevailing culture with all its opportunities for education and advancement. (Again, a contrast can be made with the culture of poverty thesis in which the children are adequately socialized but into a culture which accepts poverty.)"[31]

Critique of the Cultural Explanations

Cultural explanations of poverty are extremely popular for two major reasons. The first is that they appeal to both liberals and conservatives. The second reason is that to the average person on the street, as well as to academics and professionals, these theories just seem to make so much *sense*. However, when subjected to close scrutiny, cultural explanations do not make nearly as much sense. There are several criticisms of cultural theories, mainly directed at the more influential culture of poverty theory and its intellectual heir, underclass theory. The first criticism is directed at the research upon which the theory is based, and the second stems from other research which has failed to support major aspects of the theory. The third, aimed at the recent popular interest in the underclass, asserts that cultural explanations of poverty are really a modern attempt to define a portion of the poor as "undeserving." In this section we will briefly address these critiques,we will discuss a major and influential theory called "blaming the victim" that rejects cultural explanations, and finally we will look at alternative explanations of the characteristics of the poor that have been attributed to cultural differences.

Culture of Poverty Theory is Based on Methodologically Flawed Research
Although culture of poverty theory has been expounded by an enormous number of authors, very few have conducted original research to test whether the theory is correct. Nearly all applications of the theory are based on the anthropological studies of Oscar Lewis, notably *Five Families: Mexican Case Studies in the Culture of Poverty; The Children of Sanchez;* and *La Vida: A Puerto Rican Family in the Culture of Poverty—San Juan and New York.* The method Lewis employed in writing these books is simple and straightforward. He begins with a description of the attributes of the culture of poverty as discussed previously. He then records an immense quantity of biographical data about

people whom he believes characterize the culture of poverty. According to one of his critics, Charles Valentine, "The principal purpose of this design is evidently to convey the impression that the biographical evidence supports and validates the theoretical abstraction which is labeled the 'culture of poverty.'" Valentine argues that Lewis's research does not validate the culture of poverty concept because of the following flaws:

> Lewis met with the subjects of his research in his office rather than in their own environment.

> Lewis employed a "directive" approach, guiding the respondents to material he wanted them to cover.

> Lewis edited the material and, according to Valentine, "often reorganized the material, selected some portions of the testimony, and eliminated others."

> The most serious flaw, according to Valentine, is that the subjects selected may not have been representative of the group being studied. For example, in the Rios family, the subjects of *La Vida,* prostitution is very important in the lives of the women. This is not typical of poor Puerto Rican families and indicates that the family is a poor basis for generalization.[32]

Valentine concludes that, "The scientific status of the 'culture of poverty' remains essentially a series of undemonstrated hypotheses. With respect to many or most of these hypotheses, alternative propositions are theoretically more convincing and are supported by more available evidence."[33] These alternative propositions will be discussed later in this section.

Research Fails to Support Elements of Cultural Explanations   Criticisms of weakness in the design of research by Lewis are supported by the fact that studies looking at various characteristics of people who are supposedly members of the culture of poverty have almost uniformly failed to verify the existence of these characteristics. Culture of poverty theory asserts that one of the reasons poor people do badly in the job market is that they do not value work. Two studies by Goodwin, based on a sample of over 4,000 adults, found just the opposite to be true. These studies found that work was just as essential to the self-esteem of poor people as it was to the nonpoor.[34] Ethnographic studies by anthropologists have resulted in the same conclusion—the poor want to work just like the middle class; that is, there is no cultural difference on this variable.[35]

A cornerstone of cultural theories, particularly cultural deprivation theory, is that the poor do not value education and so they are not motivated to strive for an education. The research evidence also casts doubt on this proposition. A study by Sears, Maccoby, and Levin found that the poor were even more concerned that their children do well in school than were middle-class parents.[36] Similarly, Riessman found that lower-class parents regretted their own lack of education and were strongly motivated to see that their children did better.[37]

We could go on and on discussing research that casts doubt on cultural explanations of poverty. The proposition that lower-class children are less verbal than middle-class children has been challenged.[38] Valentine has demonstrated that, counter to the assertion that lower-class people do not participate in community organizations, community organization exists even among shanty town dwellers.[39] The belief that poor people hold sexual attitudes and values that are different from the rest of the population has been challenged by research by both Rainwater and Bogue.[40] However, there is still one problem: even though research has demonstrated that the poor do not really hold values significantly different from the rest of the population—that is, they do not have a separate culture—there are still some differences in their lifeways that must be explained if cultural explanations are rejected. For example, it has been demonstrated that the poor are less likely to defer gratification than the middle class; poor kids are less likely to continue their educations; and poor women are more likely than nonpoor women to have children outside of marriage. How do we explain these things?

Cultural Definitions Really Refer to the "Undeserving Poor." The well-known sociologist and urban planner Herbert Gans points out that the original use of the term *underclass* was as a purely economic concept to describe people who were chronically unemployed or underemployed as a result of the emerging post-industrial economy. These people were poor for purely structural reasons. In recent years, however, there has been a gradual change in the use of the term. *Underclass* has come to refer more and more to people who are viewed as attitudinally and behaviorally deviant. Gans believes that it is not coincidental that those defined as members of the underclass are almost entirely African American and Hispanic American. Thus, the term, according to Gans, has become a codeword for the old concept of the *undeserving poor*. It has become the most recent of a long line of concepts that permit us to maintain harsh attitudes and hard hearts toward the poor because it defines their poverty as their own fault. Gans says, "The *first* danger of the term is its unusual power as a buzzword. It is a handy euphemism; while it seems inoffensively technical on the surface, it hides within it all the moral opprobrium Americans have long felt toward those poor people who have been judged to be undeserving. Even when it is being used by journalists, scholars, and others as a technical term, it carries with it this judgmental baggage . . . A *second* and related danger of the term is its use as a racial codeword that subtly hides anti-black and anti-Hispanic feelings."[41]

Alternative Explanation for the Lifeways of the Poor At the risk of seeming re-petitive, we need to emphasize that the main idea of the cultural explanations of poverty is that the lifeways, or behaviors, of the poor are caused by a set of *values* existing among poor people that are fundamentally different from those of the larger society. Poor people often have children out of wedlock because, supposedly, they do not value marriage; poor people do not work, the theory contends, because they do not value work and do not feel any stigma from being supported by welfare; poor children do not do well in school, it is argued, because they have not been taught to value education and its related components, such as paying attention and reading books. There is a different explanation for these lifeways of poor people. That is, poor people have the same values as the rest of society (this has been supported by the research cited earlier), but they behave differently because within the limited range of choices available to them those behaviors are the ones that make the most sense. Sociologists refer to this as the *situational adaptation interpretation* and economists call it the *choice model*.[42]

Let's illustrate this interpretation with an example of two young couples: James and Vivian, and Cindy and Dave. Each couple has had a relationship for about one year. Vivian and Cindy each become pregnant and both are strongly opposed to abortion as a solution. Here the similarity ends.

James and Vivian have grown up in the ghetto, and they are the children of welfare mothers. Vivian finished the eleventh grade and then dropped out of high school. She has worked fairly steadily in a series of minimum-wage jobs, mainly in fast food restaurants. James dropped out of school in his senior year when the high school graduation exam revealed that he could barely read or write and school personnel said he would be required to take remedial work before he could earn his diploma. Since he left school, he has worked only sporadically, usually in temporary manual labor jobs.

In contrast, Cindy and Dave are both juniors at a large state university. They grew up in the suburbs, and they are the children of middle-class professional parents. Dave is majoring in engineering and is an officer candidate in army ROTC. Cindy is majoring in accounting.

Upon learning of their respective pregnancies, what do the two couples do? James and Vivian do not even consider marriage. Vivian applies for welfare and food stamps shortly after the baby is born; she had to quit her job because she could not afford day care on the salary she was earning. James hung around for a few months and contributed whatever money he could for the baby's support, but he eventually drifted away. Vivian basically reproduced her own childhood for her baby.

Dave and Cindy approached the situation differently. When they learned that Cindy was pregnant, they immediately decided to get married. They both took part-time jobs, and this income combined with Dave's ROTC stipend plus some help from their families provided enough income for them to survive until Dave graduated and was commissioned a second lieutenant in the army. Cindy took a year off to be with the baby, then went back to school and earned her degree.

How do we explain the different behaviors of these two couples? Cultural theories would say that their behaviors reflect the fundamentally different values that the two couples have learned in their respective social environments. James and Vivian come from environments that have taught them that single parenthood is acceptable, perhaps even preferable, to marriage. They do not really value work and achievement and so welfare is viewed as an acceptable way to rear their child. Fathers are not considered to be important to the well-being of children and so no one is too concerned when James drifts away. Cindy and Dave hold different values. For them it is of paramount importance that a child have parents who are married; the concepts of work and self-support are also extremely important to them.

The situational adaptation interpretation provides a different explanation. This perspective argues that the values of the two couples are probably similar, but they are existing in very different situations that make their choices different. Both couples value marriage and work, but these are realistic choices only for Cindy and Dave. James and Vivian realize that there is no bright future for them as a couple. There is no commission in the army followed by a good engineering job for James and there is no period of full-time motherhood followed by a professional career with good day care supports for Vivian. They realize that what lies in their future is a series of low paying jobs interspersed by long periods of unemployment. To make matters worse, by getting married Vivian would lose eligibility for some types of aid. Thus, both couples are making rational choices based on the opportunities available to them. The difference is that the opportunities available to Cindy and Dave are in line with major American values—marriage, job, and a two-parent family. For James and Vivian, violating these norms makes far more sense because as a single mother at least Vivian will not be tied to an unemployed man, and James will not be constantly frustrated by obligations he has no way of fulfilling.

If poor people like James and Vivian hold basically the same values as the rest of society, but they are forced to violate these values in order to make rational decisions, how do they cope with the frustration that must result? Rodman argues that they do this through a process he calls the "lower class value stretch." This is a process through which poor people "come to tolerate and eventually evaluate favorably certain deviations from middle class values."[43] This is a process closely related to what psychologists call *rationalization* or the "sweet lemon effect." For example, when Vivian and James do not get married, one might very well hear Vivian saying something like, "I don't want to be tied down to one man anyway. This way I can be a mother and still be able to party and have fun." When James can only secure manual labor jobs, he might say something like, "I'd really hate to be cooped up in an office all day and be forced to wear a tie. Only suckers do that. I want to be working outside with the real men. Sure, the boss can fire me any time he likes because my job is only temporary, but the other side of that coin is that anytime I want I can tell him to take this job and shove it. I don't have to take grief from anyone!" The point Rodman emphasizes is that poor people share the same basic values as the rest of society, but because of their limited opportunity to make these values work for them, they "stretch" the values to fit the opportunities they do have.

With all the criticisms of the cultural theories, why do they continue to exert so much influence? These theories were first formulated and exerted tremendous influence in the 1950s and 1960s. They largely went out of vogue in the 1970s with the landslide of contradictory data. Like the mythological Phoenix they have arisen from the ashes and once again have a grip on our collective imagination, this time under the new and catchy label "the underclass." The reemergence of cultural theories is in no way related to any new data, but this appears to bother only a few people. One of these is the economist David Ellwood, who sees value in cultural theories but recognizes that they remain largely untested. Even Ellwood, a hard-nosed, empirically oriented (and incidentally liberal) economist, is willing to assign some credence to cultural theories, arguing "that [cultural] theories are hard to test and interpret is not a legitimate basis for ignoring them in empirical work or policy discussion. The way welfare recipients are treated, the way they perceive the world, and the way the world interacts with them must have profound influences."[44] Why do cultural theories continue to exert so much influence in the face of so little solid empirical support? And why have so few people even shown any inclination to seek empirical support, instead relying on the assumption that these theories are valid? The answer, perhaps, lies in a tendency in American society that psychologist William Ryan calls "blaming the victim."[45]

Blaming the Victim   Because of our strong belief in individualism, we tend to place responsibility for problems, as well as credit for successes, squarely on the shoulders of the individual affected. This approach sometimes makes perfectly good sense, but we often carry it to ridiculous extremes. A woman is raped and some people will ask, "Why was she wearing such suggestive clothes? Had she been drinking? What was she doing unescorted in a bar? Had she been flirting with her attacker?" The implication of these questions is that she somehow was responsible for her own attack. This tendency is so deeply ingrained that we even do it to ourselves. When a person's car is stolen, you will often hear the person saying things like, "I should have known better than to park it in that lot," or "I knew I should have ridden the bus to work; this neighborhood is no place to leave a car." The point is the woman did not rape herself and the person did not steal his own car. These things were done to them; yet we still tend to place much of the blame on the person who was victimized.

Ryan asserts that because of our tendency to blame people for their own problems, we naturally look for reasons that the poor are responsible for their own poverty. The earliest explanations were that the poor were in some way morally or genetically inferior. However, these explanations always seemed harsh, at least to liberals, and they did not last long against the weight of experience with the poor. So, according to Ryan, we developed new theories that still placed the responsibility for poverty on the poor themselves, but seemed to be more scientific and more humanitarian. When trying to explain why poor children do less well than middle-class children in school we ask

> What is wrong with the victim? . . . The shorthand phrase is "cultural deprivation," which, to those in the know, conveys what they allege to be inside information: that the poor child carries a scanty pack of cultural baggage as he enters school. He doesn't know about books and magazines and newspapers . . . They say that if he talks at all . . . he certainly doesn't talk correctly . . . If you can get him to sit in a chair, they say, he squirms and looks out the window . . . In a word he is "disadvantaged" and "socially deprived," they say, and this of course, accounts for his failure (*his* failure, they say) to learn much in school . . . In pursuing this logic, no one remembers to ask questions about the collapsing buildings and torn textbooks, the frightened, insensitive teachers, the six additional desks in the room, the blustering frightened principals, the relentless segregation, the callous administrator, the irrelevant curriculum, the bigoted or cowardly members of the school board, the insulting history book, the stingy taxpayers, the fairy tale readers, or the self-serving faculty of the local teachers' college. We are encouraged to confine our attention to the child and to dwell on his alleged defects.[46]

Ryan argues that cultural explanations of poverty are so powerful and they have lasted so long precisely because they allow us to continue to explain problems as being the fault of the individuals affected, but to do so under the cloak of liberal humanitarianism and concern. The old conservative notion of intrinsic or hereditary defect is replaced by an emphasis on environmental causation

> The new ideology attributes defect and inadequacy to the malignant nature of poverty, injustice, slum life, and racial difficulties . . . But the stigma, the defect, the fatal difference—though derived in the past from environmental forces—is still located *within* the victim, inside his skin. With such an elegant formulation, the humanitarian can have it both ways. He can, all at the same time, concentrate his charitable interest on the defects of the victim, condemn the vague social and environmental stresses that produced the defect (some time ago), and ignore the continuing effect of victimizing social forces (right now). It is a brilliant ideology for justifying a perverse form of social action designed to change, not society, as one might expect, but rather society's victim.[47]

Ryan's belief is, of course, that the individual is not responsible for his or her own poverty, and cultural explanations are just sophisticated attempts to cover up the real reasons for poverty. These reasons are not defects in the individual, but defects in the structure of society. It is to this explanation of poverty that we now turn.

Structural Explanations of Poverty

Structural explanations argue that poverty is not a result of individual or cultural factors that can be changed by working with individuals on a one-to-one basis. Rather, poverty is viewed as the result of social factors that act upon individuals, causing them to exhibit the characteristics that the other theories state are the result of individual or cultural shortcomings. To significantly reduce poverty, according to the structural perspective, the basic fabric of society will need to be changed. Obviously, this is a perspective that appeals to liberals and radicals and one that conservatives generally find unacceptable.

What are these structural factors that are purported to have so much influence over the life chances of people? One of the clearest explanations of these factors is presented by the sociologist Leonard Beeghley. Beeghley classifies structural factors that contribute to poverty into four main groups:

- The way in which the correlates of poverty create a vicious circle that often traps the poor and prevents them from changing their situation.
- The way the class system reproduces itself over time.
- The organization of the economy.
- The continuation of institutionalized discrimination against African Americans and women.[48]

Recently sociologist William Julius Wilson added another structural factor which he argues causes poverty, particularly the rapidly increasing concentration of poverty among inner city African Americans. This factor is:

- The increasing social isolation of the ghetto.

These five factors are discussed next.

Poverty as a Vicious Circle   Once people are caught in poverty, it becomes a trap from which it is very difficult to escape. There are a number of elements in this poverty trap. The first is the public assistance system which, although it seeks to make people self-supporting, often perversely contributes to their inability to escape welfare and poverty. One aspect of the welfare system that traps people in poverty is the fact that people must be so destitute before they become eligible for assistance that they no longer have the resources to obtain employment. Before people can get welfare, they have often lost their home, furniture, and car; and their clothes are old and worn. Obviously, if you don't have a nice outfit to wear to a job interview, if you can't afford to take a trip to another town to look for work where the opportunities may be better, if you don't have a phone for prospective employers to call or even an address to which they can write, and if you do not have a dependable car to go to work, your chances of obtaining a good job and escaping poverty are slim.

Another element of the vicious circle is crime and the criminal justice system. Poor people are much more likely to be the victims of crime than are people in higher income brackets. They must spend much more time and energy defending themselves against crime than other citizens, time and energy that might otherwise be devoted to escaping poverty. One of the authors once worked in a community school in the inner city area of St. Louis. The school provided a number of educational programs to help people develop marketable job skills. A number of people did not take advantage of the school because it was at night and they were afraid to walk in that neighborhood after dark. In a very real sense, these folks were trapped in their own homes by their poverty. The other side of this element is what happens to poor people when, as defendants, they come in contact with the criminal justice system. When higher income people are arrested for some crime, they post bail and go about their lives more or less as usual. When tried, they are represented by competent lawyers who will often strike a bargain for them that allows them to stay out of jail. By contrast, poor people will often not be able to afford bail. Thus, when arrested, they will stay in jail, which means they will lose their jobs, be evicted from their homes or apartments, and lose anything they are making payments on. When a poor person goes on trial, he or she will probably not be able to afford the best lawyer, will have no influence with the judge, and will probably be given a prison term with all its predictable economic consequences.

The next element in the vicious circle of poverty is ill health and the health care system. By almost any measure available, the health of the poor is significantly worse than that of the population in general.[49] Poor health is both a cause and an effect of poverty. If a person has a health problem, particularly a chronic one, it is going to adversely affect that person's ability to make a living. Once a person is poor, his or her access to healthy conditions becomes limited. Poor people cannot afford to eat the most healthy foods, they live in conditions which are hot in the summer and cold in the winter, and their homes are more prone to infestations by disease-carrying pests such as rats. Illness also has a more immediate economic effect on the poor than on the general population. When poor people become ill for more than a few days, it is very likely that they will lose their jobs and it is very unlikely that they will have insurance to cover either the cost of medical care or the lost income from missing work. The health care system in the United States, as will be discussed in a later chapter, is designed to primarily serve the middle class, and it does not do a very good job serving the health care needs of the poor. So, once poor people become sick, they will most likely have a hard time obtaining efficient, high-quality medical care.

There is an old saying that it takes money to make money. A corollary of this saying related to the vicious circle of poverty is that it takes money to save money. It is a hard fact of economic life that the poor pay more. If poor people need to borrow money, they pay much greater interest rates than the nonpoor. Stores in ghetto areas charge higher prices than stores in the suburbs. You must have extra money to take full advantage of sales. For example, middle-income parents often refuse to buy disposable diapers at regular price. They wait until they go on sale, at discounts as much as two or three dollars a box, and then they stock up on several weeks, or even months, worth of diapers. Poor parents who do not have the forty or fifty dollars to take advantage of the sale end up paying much more than the higher income parents for the same diapers.

There are a number of other elements to the vicious circle of poverty that we could discuss. The poor lack political power and so they rarely get their way when decisions are being made that could benefit them. Low-income people tend to get married earlier and have children earlier; they thereby increase the chance that their children will grow up poor and in turn marry early and have children early. The educational system tends to define poor children as low achievers, to put them into remedial classes, and thereby to increase the probability of this becoming a self-fulfilling prophecy. The main point is that the very condition of being in poverty decreases a person's chances of getting out of poverty. These conditions, over time, tend to wear a person down and cause many of the characteristics that Lewis identified as the culture of poverty.

Does the Class System Reproduce Itself?   Beeghley, among others, argues that one of the causes of poverty is that the class system tends to reproduce itself. He discusses the status attainment process in the United States and concludes, "The result is that the class structure reproduces itself over time and a stratum of impoverished persons is continually recreated."[50] What he means is that the children of wealthy parents, through various mechanisms such as inheritance and family connections, themselves grow into wealthy adults; children of middle-class parents become middle-class adults; and children of poor parents, as a result of the socially disadvantaged position into which they are born, are almost automatically doomed to lives of poverty. Does this actually happen? The answer is that no, the class system does not totally reproduce itself, but yes, the lowest and highest classes do.

Research on stratification and social mobility is one of the most highly developed areas in contemporary sociology.[51] This area seeks to understand how people obtain and change their positions in the social structure. We all like to believe that the United States is the land of opportunity, that our class structure is open, and that people often rise out of poverty into wealth, as in the famous Horatio Alger stories. Research results indicate that the class system in the United States is open for most people; that is, parents' status has relatively little effect on the status of their children. Featherman and Hauser, building on earlier research by Blau and Duncan, found that only about 7 percent of variation in socioeconomic status could be attributed to family background. A much larger percentage of the variance (36 percent) was explained by education, which itself is highly influenced, but not completely determined, by family background. This is the good news. The bad news is that the researchers found that for the top and, more importantly, for the bottom of our society, the socioeconomic status of one's parents is by far the most important determinant of a person's own status.[52] Thus, the American dream is alive and well for most people in the country, but for poor people, being born into poverty generally means living out one's life in poverty. For the poor, the class structure does indeed reproduce itself.

The Organization of the Economy   This element of the structural explanation of poverty asserts that the organization of the economy is such that a number of people are forced into poverty. There are two versions of this, the radical version and the liberal version. The radical version is derived from the work of Marx and Engels and claims, basically, that the labor market of capitalist economies cannot provide sufficient employment at above-poverty-line wages to prevent poverty. Behind this problem is the assertion that capitalist economies are organized so the owners of the means of production (the capitalists) get wealthy by exploiting the workers.[53] This perspective further asserts that the welfare system is designed to force people into starvation-level jobs when they are available, but to provide enough support when jobs are not available to prevent workers from organizing and overthrowing the capitalist system.[54] The basic contention is that in capitalist economies, poor people are poor because this is a necessary condition for others to be rich. In other words, poverty is intentional; it is designed into the fabric of the economy.

The second version of the assertion that the organization of the economy forces people into poverty is the liberal version. This version claims that there are two labor markets operating in our society, the primary and the secondary labor markets, sometimes called the *core* and the *periphery*. The primary, or core, labor market is the one in which most Americans work. Jobs in this labor market pay well; they include benefits such as insurance, sick leave, a retirement plan, and paid vacation; and they are generally secure. The secondary, or peripheral, job market is made up of jobs which do not pay well; they generally include few benefits, and they offer little security. Jobs in the primary labor market are found in government and in industries dominated by large, capital-intensive, and oligopolistic firms. Jobs in the secondary labor market are found in small, labor-intensive, highly competitive firms. These are businesses that unions have not been able to organize because of their small size, that cannot pay well because they have to keep costs down to remain competitive and do not offer benefits for the same reason, and that do not offer job security because of the basic instability of their position in the market. The job skills and training (human capital) of workers in the secondary labor market are not much different from those of workers in the primary labor market. It is just a matter of luck and sometimes geographic location that determines whether a person gets a job at the new General Motors Saturn plant in east Tennessee and consequently enjoys a life of economic security and a secure retirement, or spends her life in a series of minimum-wage jobs at fast-food restaurants in the Kentucky boondocks or some inner city in the rustbelt.[55] Beeghley says, "Regardless of the skills people have, the nature of the jobs available to them decisively influences the likelihood of their living poorly."[56]

Racial, Sexual, and Age Discrimination   Prejudice and discrimination appear to be a major structural component of poverty. As the data reviewed earlier clearly indicates, a disproportionate number of minorities, women, and the elderly are found among the ranks of the poor. Beeghley identifies three mechanisms that he believes account for the large proportion of minorities and women among the poor. These are recruitment procedures used by employers that work to the advantage of white males and to the disadvantage of other groups; divorce laws that usually grant custody of children to the mother, but often do not grant enough child support to adequately care for them or, if adequate child support is ordered, do not strongly enforce its payment; and, finally, child rearing patterns that tend to guide women into lower paying careers or to create the expectation that women should be dependent on a husband, thus putting a woman in a bad position when her marriage breaks down and she has to support herself.

The Increasing Social Isolation of the Ghetto   A recent structural explanation of poverty that is gaining a wide following is the social isolation hypothesis of University of Chicago sociologist William Julius Wilson. This explanation is especially popular among liberals who are anxious for an alternative to the extreme culture of poverty interpretation of conservatives such as Edward Banfield. Wilson argues that much of poverty in the United States can be explained by the fact that poor people are geographically and, consequently, socially isolated. That is, they are largely confined to housing projects and inner city ghettos where they are denied contact with the wide variety of influences and opportunities the rest of society enjoys.

Wilson contends that the rapid increase in poverty, particularly among inner city blacks, and in the growth of what is now referred to as the underclass, has been an ironic by-product of the success of the civil rights movement. The ghetto, Wilson states, used to be characterized by vertical integration of different segments of the urban African American population. Lower-, middle-, and upper-class African Americans used to live in the same communities, largely because neighborhood segregation provided few options for the higher income groups. The presence of these economically better off segments of the population resulted in a high degree of social organization in the neighborhoods, "including a sense of community, positive neighborhood identification, and explicit norms and sanctions against aberrant behavior."[57] Today, because of the success of the civil rights movement, middle- and upper-class African American professionals have moved out of the inner city areas, leaving these areas almost totally populated by the unemployed, welfare recipients, drug addicts and alcoholics, the mentally ill, and other problem-ridden segments of the population. The result has been that these communities have lost their stability, crime and violence have increased, unemployment has increased, female-headed families have become the norm, welfare is the standard form of support, leadership has disappeared, children have few role models, and the inner city has become characterized by a tangle of pathology.

Social isolation means several things to the residents of inner city areas. First, it means that these communities are characterized by a high concentration of poverty and its associated problems, which Wilson refers to as *concentration effects*. It also means that the residents lack contact or sustained interaction with individuals or institutions that represent mainstream society; Wilson refers to this as a *social buffer*. Because of this social buffer, the residents of these areas are unlikely to develop good work habits—if you don't know anyone who gets up each morning to go to work, it is unlikely that you will develop this habit yourself. Also, because businesses have left inner city areas along with the higher income groups who were their best customers, very few jobs are left for inner city residents; the only ones available are generally undesirable and likely to alienate the people who do them. According to Wilson, "the combination of unattractive jobs and lack of community norms to reinforce work increases the likelihood that individuals will turn to either underground illegal activity or idleness or both."[58]

The results of social isolation look very much like the attributes of the poor that culture of poverty theorists attempt to explain—low work ethic, a high degree and favorable evaluation of welfare dependency, female-headed families, and inability to defer gratification. Wilson admits that these cultural traits exist, but contends, in opposition to culture of poverty theorists, that they do not result from unique, ghetto-specific values. Culture of poverty theory "places strong emphasis on the autonomous character of the cultural traits once they come into existence. In other words, these traits assume a 'life of their own' and continue to influence behavior even if opportunities for social mobility improve." By contrast "social isolation does not mean that cultural traits are irrelevant in understanding behavior in highly concentrated poverty areas;

rather it highlights the fact that culture is a response to social structural constraints and opportunities."[59]

Wilson's social isolation hypothesis is very similar to the situational adaptation thesis and the choice model discussed earlier. You will recall that these theories contend that the differences in behavior between poor and nonpoor people are not a result of different values, but rather are caused by the different situations in which people find themselves. The value of marriage is functional for two people who have reasonable expectations of a secure future; it makes much less sense to people who know that life will be hard enough on their own and who expect that for a married couple it will only be harder. Wilson's hypothesis deals with the rapid rise of inner city poverty in recent years and contends that the situation to which poor people have to adapt has gotten quite a lot worse for a large number of people because of social isolation, concentration effects, and social buffering.

Wilson's social isolation hypothesis has great implications for social policy regarding inner city poverty. Using this approach instead of the currently prevailing cultural explanations would mean shifting the focus of our policies and programs from attempting to change subcultural traits (by means of classes on family life for poverty teenagers, counseling sessions aimed at developing an appreciation of the benefits of deferring gratification, and work habits classes) to attempting to change the structure of constraints and opportunities in which inner city dwellers find themselves. In other words, the social isolation approach to inner city poverty would involve changing social structures rather than changing individuals.

Critique of Structural Explanations

As you might imagine, structural explanations of poverty are not well received by conservatives. These explanations are diametrically opposed to nearly all of the major components of the conservative belief system discussed in Chapter 1. Conservatives believe in individual responsibility; the structural perspective rejects this and says the social and economic environment is largely responsible for poverty. Conservatives believe in minimum government; the structural perspective logically leads to the conclusion that governmental intervention is necessary to correct the structural flaws which are causing poverty. Conservatives believe in the free market; the structural perspective argues that the market is not really free. Thus, it is obvious that conservatives will be critical of this perspective.

Probably the most influential critique of the structural perspective in recent years is the book *Losing Ground* by Charles Murray. Murray argues that the huge growth of social programs which occurred during the 1960s was based on a structural explanation of poverty. He says that, according to the designers of the antipoverty programs, "Poverty was not a consequence of indolence or vice. It was not the just deserts of people who didn't try hard enough. It was produced by conditions that had nothing to do with individual virtue or effort. *Poverty was not the fault of the individual but of the system.*"[60] Murray believes that poverty is indeed caused by all of the individual failings structural explanations reject. He reviews what he believes to be the catastrophic failure of the social programs that have been implemented in the last quarter century and lays the blame for this failure squarely at the feet of structural explanations of poverty. Murray argues that the result of structural explanations has been to remove responsibility for self-support from individuals and to make it more profitable to be on welfare than to work; this in general has made "it profitable for the poor to behave in the short term in ways that were destructive in the long term."[61]

Murray's critique of structural explanations of poverty can itself be criticized on a number of points. There have been a number of responses which criticize Murray's use and interpretation of data, as well as the logic of his arguments.[62] Murray cites a great deal of research that he claims demonstrates that programs were failures, but fails to even mention research that did not reach these conclusions.[63] The most serious shortcoming of Murray's argument, however, is that very few people have ever believed that the social programs developed during the 1960s were based on a structural explanation of poverty. Most, even Murray's fellow conservatives like Butler and Kondratas, have interpreted the programs as being based on the culture of poverty theory. This theory, as reviewed previously, gives lip service to structural factors, but still lays responsibility for poverty at the feet of the poor person. Thus, as far as being a critique of structural explanations of poverty, Murray's argument is really of the straw man variety.

C O N C L U S I O N

If you find the preceding discussion a little confusing, do not be surprised, because it is. Obviously there is no consensus on what causes poverty and so, as we will see in the next chapter, there is no agreement on what to do about it. What you believe causes poverty is heavily influenced by your political perspective. If you are conservative, you are likely to believe either in individual factors or in the individual components of cultural factors. If you are liberal, you will most likely believe in structural explanations and/or in the social components of the cultural explanations. If you are radical you will concentrate on structural factors.

How do we make sense out of all of this uncertainty? The first thing we need to do is to recognize the complexity of poverty. Anyone searching for a simple, single-variable explanation of poverty is going to be frustrated. To say poverty is a multivariate problem is to understate the situation. Each individual case of poverty involves hundreds of variables, including age, sex, race, health, geographic location, family background, friends, and luck—the list goes on and on. When you multiply these variables by millions of individuals, you see the complexity of the situation. There are some commonalities among individuals, however, and so

it is possible to discover some generalizations, even though they are imperfect.

If you will recall, at the beginning of this chapter we spoke of within-group variance and between-group variance. We think that it is probably safe to say that different types of explanations probably better explain the different types of variation. For example, if you take a sample of people who are carefully matched on as many characteristics as possible—they are all of the same race, sex, social class background, and from the same geographic location—and then compare the members of the group on the variable of economic status, it would be a good hypothesis that differences were largely caused by individual characteristics. Those who were more intelligent, energetic, focused, and motivated would probably be found to be doing better. However, the statistics reviewed earlier reveal that a large part of poverty falls into the between-group variance. Being a minority, old or young, female, a member of a single-parent family, rural, or an inner city dweller all greatly increase the likelihood of being in poverty. It is very difficult to explain poverty related to these variables using anything but a structural explanation.

1. U.S. Bureau of the Census, Current Population Reports, Series P-60, No. 168, *Money Income and Poverty Status in the United States.* (Washington, D.C.: U.S. Government Printing Office, 1990).

2. Diana Pearce, "The Feminization of Poverty: Women, Work, and Welfare," *Urban and Social Change Review* 11 (February 1978): 28–36.

3. Pearce, "The Feminization of Poverty," 29.

4. Ralph Segalman and Asoke Basu, *Poverty in America—The Welfare Dilemma* (Westport, CT: Greenwood Press, 1981), 10–12.

5. Gunner Myrdal, *The Challenge of World Poverty* (New York: Vintage, 1970); Ken Auletta, *The Underclass* (New York: Random House, 1982); Christopher Jencks and Paul E. Peterson, eds., *The Urban Underclass* (Washington, D.C.: The Brookings Institution, 1990).

6. The Panel Study of Income Dynamics has resulted in numerous publications. Information in this chapter, unless otherwise noted, comes from Greg J. Duncan, et al., *Years of Poverty, Years of Plenty—The Changing Economic Fortunes of American Workers and Families* (Ann Arbor, MI: Survey Research Center-Institute for Social Research, The Univeristy of Michigan, 1984).

7. Quoted in Auletta, *The Underclass,* 25.

8. Robert Holman, *Poverty—Explanations of Social Deprivation* (New York: St. Martin's Press, 1978), 54–55.

9. Stephen Jay Gould, *The Mismeasure of Man* (New York: W.W. Norton & Company, 1984), 155.

10. Walter I. Trattner, *From Poor Law to Welfare State—A History of Social Welfare in America,* 4th ed. (New York: The Free Press, 1989), 180–182.

11. Arthur R. Jensen, "How Much Can We Boost IQ and Scholastic Achievement?" *Harvard Education Review* 33 (1969): 1–123; Arthur R. Jensen, *Bias in Mental Testing* (New York: The Free Press, 1979); Arthur R. Jensen, *Straight Talk About Mental Tests* (New York: The Free Press, 1981).

12. Jensen, *Straight Talk About Mental Tests,* 103, 105.

13. Richard J. Herrnstein, *I.Q. in the Meritocracy* (Boston: Little, Brown and Company, 1971), 197–198, 221.

14. N.J. Block and Gerald Dworkin, "Heritability and Inequality," in *The I.Q. Controversy—Critical Readings,* N.J. Block and Gerald Dworkin, eds. (New York: Pantheon Books, 1976), 411.

15. Bradley Buell, and associates, *Community Planning for Human Services* (New York: Columbia University Press, 1952).

16. Elizabeth Irvine, "The Hard to Like Family," *Case Conference 14* (1967): 54.

17. Trattner, *From Poor Law to Welfare State—A History of Social Welfare in America,* 292.

18. David T. Ellwood, "The Origins of 'Dependency': Choices, Confidence, or Culture," *Focus 12* (1989): 9.

19. Lester C. Thurow, *Investment in Human Capital* (Belmont, CA: Wadsworth Publishing Company, 1970), 20.

20. Thurow, *Investment in Human Capital,* 11–12.

21. Thurow, *Investment in Human Capital,* 13.

22. Oscar Lewis, *Five Families: Mexican Case Studies in the Culture of Poverty* (New York: Basic Books, 1959).

23. Michael Harrington, *The Other America: Poverty in the United States* (New York: Penguin Books, 1962); Frank Reissman, *The Culturally Deprived Child* (New York: Harper and Row, 1962); Daniel Patrick Moynihan, *The Negro Family* (Washington, D.C.: U.S. Department of Labor, 1965).

24. Oscar Lewis, *La Vida: A Peurto Rican Family in the Culture of Poverty—San Juan and New York* (New York: Random House, 1965), xliii–xliv.

25. Edward C. Banfield, *The Unheavenly City Revisited* (Boston: Little, Brown and Company, 1974), 62.

26. Lewis, *La Vida,* xlvii.

27. Banfield, *The Unheavenly City Revisited,* 62.

28. Banfield, *The Unheavenly City Revisited,* 61.

29. Lewis, *La Vida,* xlvi.

30. William Ryan, *Blaming the Victim* (New York: Pantheon Books, 1971). Copyright 1971 Pantheon Books, a Division of Random House, Inc.

31. Robert Holman, *Poverty—Explanations of Social Deprivation* (New York: St. Martins Press, 1978), 112.

32. Charles A. Valentine, "The 'Culture of Poverty': Its Scientific Significance and Its Implications for Action," in *The Culture of Poverty: A Critique,* Eleanor Burke Leacock, ed. (New York: Simon and Schuster, 1971), 194–197.

33. Valentine, "The 'Culture of Poverty': Its Scientific Significance and Its Implications for Action," 193.

34. Leonard Goodwin, *Do The Poor Want To Work?* (Washington, D.C.: Brookings Institution, 1972); Leonard Goodwin, "How Suburban Families View

the Work Orientations of the Welfare Poor," *Social Problems* 19 (1972): 337–348.

35. See, for example, Elliot Liebow, *Tally's Corner* (Boston, MA: Little Brown, 1967); Joseph T. Howell, *Hard Living on Clay Street* (New York: Anchor Books, 1973).

36. Robert Sears, Eleanor Maccoby, and Harry Levin, *Patterns of Child Rearing* (New York: Row Peterson, 1957).

37. Riessman, *The Culturally Deprived Child.*

38. See, for example, Vera P. John, "Language and Educability," in Leacock, *The Culture of Poverty: A Critique,* 41–62.

39. Charles Valentine, *Culture and Poverty* (Chicago: University of Chicago Press, 1968), 55–56.

40. Lee Rainwater, "The Problem of Lower Class Culture and Poverty-War Strategy," in *On Understanding Poverty,* Daniel Moynihan, ed. (New York: Basic Books, 1968), 229–259; Donald Bogue, "A Long-Term Solution to the A.F.D.C. Problem: Prevention of Unwanted Pregnancy," *Social Service Review* 49 (1975): 539–552.

41. Herbert J. Gans, "Deconstructing the Underclass; The Term's Danger as a Planning Concept," *APA Journal* 56 (Summer 1990): 271–277.

42. Leonard Beeghley, *Living Poorly in America* (New York: Praeger, 1983), 122; Ellwood, "The Origins of 'Dependency': Choices, Confidence, or Culture?," 6–9.

43. Hyman Rodman, "The Lower Class Value Stretch," *Social Forces* 42 (December 1963): 205–215.

44. Ellwood, "The Origins of 'Dependency': Choices, Confidence, or Culture?," 13.

45. William Ryan, *Blaming the Victim.* Copyright 1971 Pantheon Books, a Division of Random House, Inc.

46. William Ryan, *Blaming the Victim,* 4. Copyright 1971 Pantheon Books, a Division of Random House, Inc.

47. William Ryan, *Blaming the Victim,* 4. Copyright 1971 Pantheon Books, a Division of Random House, Inc.

48. Beeghley, *Living Poorly in America,* 133.

49. Beeghley, *Living Poorly in America,* 108–115.

50. Beeghley, *Living Poorly in America,* 141.

51. David Featherman, "Stratification and Social Mobility: Two Decades of Cumulative Social Science," in *The State of Sociology: Problems and Prospects,* James F. Short, Jr., ed. (San Francisco, CA: Sage Publications, 1981), 79–100.

52. David Featherman and Robert Hauser, *Opportunity and Change* (New York: Academic Press, 1978); Peter Blau and Otis D. Duncan, *The American Occupational Structure* (New York: John Wiley, 1967).

53. Karl Marx and Friedrich Engels, *Manifesto of the Communist Party* (1848), reprinted in Lewis S. Feuer, ed., *Marx and Engels: Basic Writings on Politics and Philosophy* (Garden City, NY: Doubleday, 1959), 1–41.

54. Francis F. Piven and Richard A. Cloward, *Regulating the Poor: The Functions of Public Welfare* (New York: Pantheon Books, 1971).

55. E.M. Beck, Patrick M. Horan, and Charles M. Tolbert, "Stratification in a Dual Economy," *American Sociological Review* 43 (October 1978): 704–720.

56. Beeghley, *Living Poorly in America,* 155.

57. William Julius Wilson, *The Truly Disadvantaged: The Inner City, the Underclass, and Public Policy* (Chicago, IL: The University of Chicago Press, 1987), 3.

58. Wilson, *The Truly Disadvantaged,* 61.

59. Wilson, *The Truly Disadvantaged,* 137, 61.

60. Charles Murray, *Losing Ground: American Social Policy, 1950–1980* (New York: Basic Books, 1984), 29.

61. Murray, *Losing Ground,* 9.

62. See, for example, Rino Patti, Mimi Abramovitz, Steven Burkhardt, Michael Fabricant, Martha Haffey, and Rose Starr, *Gaining Perspective on Losing Ground* (New York: The Lois and Samuel Silberman Fund, 1987).

63. For example, Murray argues that the Negative Income Tax (NIT) experiments ". . . validated not the sponsors' hopes but their fears. The results were more or less what the popular wisdom said they would be." (p. 150) He ignores research that did not reach this conclusion, such as Sonia Wright, "Work Response to Income Maintenance: Economic, Sociological, and Cultural Perspectives," *Social Forces* 53 (June 1975): 553–562. Wright found that, contrary to "popular wisdom," no work disincentives were found.

C·H·A·P·T·E·R

eight

The Development of Antipoverty Programs

The authors have heard the stories dozens of times. We have heard them at parties, from colleagues, and over coffee with friends; and we hear at least one version each time we teach the introductory social welfare course. The stories we are referring to are those of the welfare Cadillac and of the food stamp Lincoln. The stories go like this:

> A person known to the teller of the story is standing in line at the bank. The woman ahead of him or her cashes a welfare check. Having only a brief transaction, the storyteller's acquaintance follows the person out of the bank and in the parking lot observes the person getting into a brand new Cadillac.

> A person known to the storyteller works as a checker in a food store or is standing in line at the food store. A woman comes through the line and pays for her groceries with food stamps. The woman is then observed going out to the parking lot and driving away in a brand new Lincoln.

These stories often vary in terms of the details and the amount of embroidery added. Sometimes the type of car is different; a BMW or a Mercedes Benz are popular alternatives. Sometimes the welfare recipient acts in a haughty or highhanded manner. In some versions the food stamp recipient purchases an extremely extravagant basket of groceries. A large number of kids, often obviously neglected, is another popular variation. However, the main details of the story are always the same. The teller gets the story from an absolutely reliable source, such as an aunt or a good friend. Bank and food store personnel also are good sources because they have about them the mantle of experts, seeing much of such things. The subject of the story always demonstrates in some way that he or she is receiving some form of public aid. Finally, the person always demonstrates that he or she does not deserve such aid by driving away in some type of extravagant car.

The stories of the welfare Cadillac and the food stamp Lincoln are examples of a phenomenon that folklorists (scholars who specialize in the collection and analysis of folk traditions) have labeled *urban legends*. They are, according to Brunvand, "an integral part of white Anglo-American culture and are told and believed by some of the most sophisticated "folk" of modern society—young people, urbanites, and the well educated. The storytellers assume that the true facts of each case lie just one or two informants back down the line with a reliable witness, or in a news media report."[1] An important aspect of urban legends is that the teller believes them to be absolutely true, and he or she generally believes this with a great deal of conviction. The secretary of one of the authors once recounted the story of the welfare Cadillac to him and then communicated in no uncertain terms that she considered him to be somewhat less than bright when he tried to explain to her that the story was not true; he even went so far as to show her the welfare department regulations limiting the value of a car a person can own and still be eligible for benefits.

Urban legends tell us something about our society. According to Brunvand "like traditional folklore, the stories do tell one kind of truth. They are a unique, unselfconscious reflection of major concerns of individuals in the societies in which the legends circulate."[2] What do the stories of the welfare Cadillac and the food stamp Lincoln tell us about the major concerns of our society? They indicate several things. First they point out that we are very concerned with the problem of financial dependency. They tell us that we are uneasy that the people, or at least some of the people, receiving help do not really deserve it. They point to a fear that the people who are managing the programs to aid the poor are either incompetent or else they are such bleeding-heart liberals that they give money to undeserving people. Finally, and probably most importantly, they reflect a very strong undercurrent of resentment about welfare programs.

In this chapter we will look at the historical development of welfare programs and attempt to gain some perspective on why the concerns cited earlier have developed. It would actually be more accurate to say why they have *persisted* because concerns such as these have existed since the very first attempts to help the needy.

HISTORICAL PERSPECTIVE ON ANTIPOVERTY EFFORTS

The eminent social welfare historian Walter Trattner has written

> The basic tenets and programs of any social welfare system reflect the values of the society in which the system functions. Like all other social institutions, social welfare systems do not arise in a vacuum; they stem from the customs, statutes, and practices of the past. Therefore, one cannot understand current efforts to help the needy without first comprehending the foundations on which they were built. And since the practice of assisting people in need as we know it in America did not originate in this country but was transplanted from the Old World to the New during the colonial period, we must go back in time . . . to . . . study social welfare.[3]

In Chapter 4 we discussed ancient developments in social welfare. In this chapter we will go back to fourteenth century England to begin our story.

We should note before we begin that we will be dealing with a very narrow slice of history. We begin in England and then rapidly move to the United States. In the United States the history we will be discussing is mainly related to urban areas, and it usually focuses on majority group members. This approach leaves out quite a lot of interesting history. It largely skirts the history of Native Americans, African Americans, and other minority groups; it does not give much credit to other areas of the world that made major advances in the area of social welfare; and it does not pay attention to the unique problems of rural areas. However, for better or for worse, this is the history of the development of the major antipoverty programs in this country. A direct line can be drawn from England to the colonies, and straight up to the present time. Until very recent years this line did not include much concern for minority groups and, often unfortunately, social welfare traditions other than the Anglo-Saxon have had very little influence on developments in this country. So bear in mind when reading this that there is a much broader social welfare history than we are reporting here. However, our major purpose is to gain perspective on our current poverty programs, and the relevant history of these programs is the rather narrow one described here.

Finally, we should note that histories of social welfare developments present different political perspectives on those developments. Although historians strive for objectivity, they, like all of us, are members of a particular society and social and economic class. Therefore, their work reflects the sorts of attitudes about social welfare discussed in Chapter 1. The historical approach in this chapter generally represents a liberal point of view.

In this historical survey you will notice that there are themes and issues that recur over the 600-plus years we are discussing. Among the more prominent of these themes is the issue of compassion or protection as the chief motivator for public assistance efforts. Are we engaging in these efforts because we are concerned with human suffering, or are we doing so because we fear adverse consequences, such as crime, revolution, or begging, if we do not?[4] Another issue is the regulation of labor. Social welfare reforms are often preceded by periods of either labor unrest or labor shortage, and the welfare reforms appear to be primarily for the purpose of either settling the labor force down or driving it toward certain types of employment. A third issue that appears throughout history is a fear of strangers who may become dependent, criminal, or both. In earlier years the fear was actually of strangers—people from outside one's own geographic area. In modern history this seems to have been replaced by a fear of people who are different, primarily members of minority groups. Finally, the history of social welfare is a history of cycles. For a period of years the approach to people who are dependent will be positive and progressive and then the pendulum will swing back to an approach that is harsh and punitive.

At the end of the last chapter we concluded that structural explanations appear to be the only way to explain much of poverty. The following historical survey will further support this argument. For each period in history that poverty has greatly increased, it can be clearly seen, in hindsight, that the increase was related to structural factors. The decline of feudalism and the rise of the wool industry, plague, famine, industrialization, urbanization, immigration, and economic depression have all been major contributors to the economic woes of individuals. Interestingly, at each point in history in which poverty has increased, the powers-that-be have attempted to attribute the problems to individual deficiencies and thus they have attempted to evade structural (public) responsibility for a structural problem. Michael Katz has said that history "shows that many popular ideas about welfare are myths. It points to the stale, repetitive, and self-serving character of ideas about poor people in American social thought . . . There is an American style of welfare. It is old. It is no cause for pride or satisfaction."[5]

English Roots

Historians would probably be horrified at such a broad generalization, but we're going to make it anyway: Up until the fourteenth century, the social life in the world had been relatively constant. People the world over generally lived in rural settings; they usually lived by means of a combination of subsistence farming and gathering; they lived with their extended families as part of a clan or tribe; and they were born, lived, and died within a radius of a few miles. By the eleventh century the form of social organization dominant in England, as well as most of Europe, was the feudal system. Under this system the continent was divided into a number of fiefdoms, and each of these was divided into a number of what were basically tenant farms. The structure was hierarchal; a monarch would give control of a fief to the church or to a nobleman in return for taxes and help in obtaining recruits for his army when needed. The church or noble would then assign the land to serfs who were the tenant farmers in return for a share of their produce as well as their service in the monarch's army if needed.

Under the feudal system, at least in theory, people's basic needs were met. People who lived on feudal manors were extremely poor, but they were at least protected by their masters from extremes of want caused by sickness, unemployment, becoming orphaned, and old age. Basically, in return for their service to their master, the serfs were provided with a primitive form of social insurance. They were not free to leave the land at will, but then they could not be driven off it either. A woman had the right to remain on the land after her husband's death, and children had the right to take over the farming of their parents' land. Serfs were poor but secure. The small proportion of the population who were not serfs generally lived in the few cities and towns, and they made their living as craftsmen of various sorts. Security was provided for these people by the development of craft guilds, which were mainly mutual protection societies that provided insurance against disability, old age, and widowhood. The few people who did not come under the feudal or the guild system were provided a little protection by the church, which in England at this time was the Catholic Church. The church ran monasteries and hospitals which cared for the sick, the lame, and distressed travelers. Finally, people who fell between the cracks were under the charge of the bishop of their diocese; each bishop had the responsibility for feeding and protecting the poor within his district.[6]

In the fourteenth century things began to change. Initially the changes stemmed from purely negative events. The Swiss historian J.C.L.S. de Sismonde summarized the century very simply when he said that it was "a bad time for humanity."[7] Tuchman has said that the disorders of the fourteenth century "cannot be traced to any one cause; they were the hoofprints of more than the four horsemen of St. John's version, which had now become seven—plague, war, taxes, brigandage, bad government, insurrection, and schism in the church."[8] The most important events for the student of social welfare were a series of calamities that befell the land in rapid succession—crop failures, famine, pestilence, and finally the bubonic plague which swept across Europe from 1348 to 1349 and killed almost one-third of England's population. By this time the feudal system had begun to break down and the tenant farming and guild systems were rapidly being replaced by a system of wage labor. The black death (as the plague was also known) created a labor crisis in that so many workers were killed that an extreme labor shortage was created. This resulted in a situation in which workers could come and go as they pleased, travel where they wanted, and demand much higher wages than in the past. Needless to say, the owners of the farms and businesses which employed them were not at all pleased with this situation.

The travails of the fourteenth century resulted in what is generally recognized as the first step in the development of a social security system in England, and by extension, in the United States. This was the passage of a law in 1349 called the *Statute of Laborers*. This act sought to solve the labor problem by setting a maximum wage, compelling unattached workers to work for whoever wanted them, forbidding laborers from traveling, and making it illegal for able-bodied men to beg. The reader may legitimately wonder why this act, which is completely repressive and clearly in the interest of the well-to-do rather than in the interest of the poor, is presented as the first step on the road to social security. There are two reasons. The first is that even though this act was itself repressive and had little to do with welfare, successive reforms of it eventually led to the passage of true social security legislation. The second reason is probably more important. This act is the beginning of a long history, which is still going on in the United States, of linking labor problems to problems in the public welfare system. Karl de Schweinitz says of the Statute of Laborers, "The King and his lords saw begging, movement and vagrancy, and the labor shortage as essentially the same problem, to be dealt with in one law."[9] Problems since this time have very rarely included a shortage of labor, but we have consistently passed public welfare laws with the fear that they will result in people taking advantage of the system rather than supporting themselves through honest work. Handler has noted that ". . . the central, overarching goal of the relief policy, at least as far back as the Great Plague, has been to control the supply of labor—in a word, to make sure that those who *could* work *would* seek work rather than welfare. This central idea explains the enormous continuities in welfare policy through the ages."[10] The current emphasis on workfare is the latest development in this regard.

The Statute of Laborers illustrates one additional point. That is, whenever we have a problem of labor or dependency in our society, our first reaction is to deal with it in a repressive manner. Thus, this law did not attempt to deal with the problems of labor shortages and begging by setting fair wages and by attending to the problems of those who were for legitimate reasons so poor that they had to resort to begging for survival; rather, it set maximum wages, it made it illegal to travel and to beg, and it set severe punishments for those who defied these provisions.

Following the fourteenth century, the pace of change in England quickened, and many of the changes were part of what we generally think of as progress. As the feudal system declined mercantilism arose, trade routes opened, new industries developed, the New World began to open up, and in general the potential for greater prosperity was everywhere. However, along with progress, these developments brought with them tremendous problems. The major problems had to do with the supply of labor and the growing insecurity of life. When the majority of people had been serfs they were poor, but at least they had a form of security. No matter how hard times were, the serfs at least had the land and whatever sort of shelter they had erected upon it. With the coming of industrialization and the accompanying urbanization, most people no longer had any right either to the land they lived on or to their dwellings. The feudal system had, for the common person, been replaced by the wage system. The majority of people were one payday away from destitution. This led to a continuation of the perception of a threat to social order that had begun with the labor shortage following the black death. However, the threat rapidly came to be perceived not as a shortage of laborers, but rather as an excess of unemployed and unattached people who wandered the roads begging and stealing. This situation was made worse by the Protestant Reformation of 1536 when Henry VIII expelled the Catholic church from England. This act basically kicked most of the social welfare provisions out of England along with the church, because it was the church that had been given the primary responsibility for caring for the old, the sick, travelers, and the poor in general.

A number of laws were passed, following the Statute of Laborers, that attempted to deal with the problems of labor, begging, and crime. These various acts were finally collected together in one major piece of summary legislation, the *Elizabethan Poor Law* of 1601. This law is especially significant because it represented a compilation and refinement of all the antipoverty legislation of the previous 250 years and, even more importantly, it was to remain the basic social welfare law in England and the United

States for an additional 250 years. The Elizabethan Poor Law was a combination of provisions that were both harsh and progressive. One of the harsh aspects of the law was that people were responsible for their children and parents up to three generations. Thus, a person could be legally forced to support his or her parents and grandparents in one direction, and his or her children and grandchildren in the other. The law was especially harsh in regard to vagrants. A person convicted of vagrancy could be whipped, branded, jailed, stoned, or put to death.

The harsh features of the Elizabethan Poor Law are not surprising, for this was a harsh age. What is more significant are the constructive features of the law. Of major importance is the fact that the law clearly indicated that the state had a responsibility to relieve want and suffering and to insure the maintenance of life. It proceeded from the assumption that not only did the state have a responsibility to help the needy but also the needy had a right to such help.[11]

The Elizabethan Poor Law also had some administrative aspects that were to have great influence; some are still in evidence in our contemporary public welfare system. The law established three broad categories of poor people—the vagrant, the involuntary unemployed, and the helpless—and set down different ways of dealing with each group. Vagrants were to be punished, the unemployed were to be set to work, and the helpless were to be apprenticed in the case of children and given assistance in the case of the aged or disabled. The law established the principle that the smallest unit of government, the Parish, was the unit responsible for poor relief. If a person became destitute away from home, he or she would be returned to the home parish to receive assistance. The Parish was also given the power to levy taxes to support poorhouses, to provide assistance to the helpless poor in their own homes, and to purchase materials necessary to provide work for the involuntarily unemployed.[12]

The Elizabethan Poor Law reflected a basic shift in attitudes toward poverty in the western world. Karl de Schweinitz says

> After two centuries of attempts to control poverty by repressive measures, government slowly and reluctantly came to accept a positive obligation for the help of people who could not provide for themselves. The experience of the years between 1349 and 1601 had convinced the rulers of England of the presence of a destitution among the poor that punishment could not abolish and that could be relieved only by the application of public resources to individual need.[13]

Colonial Years and the Era of the American Revolution

The situation in the colonies was, of course, much different from that in England. The population was sparse and there was an abundance of resources in the New World that was not in evidence in the old. In England, because of certain factors, such as the enclosure movement that converted farm land to pasture land for sheep, many people had been dislocated from their land. Although the developing textile and mining industries were providing an increasing number of jobs, the number of jobs created lagged behind the number of dislocated people, thus causing unemployment. In the colonies there were more resources, and there was a labor scarcity rather than a labor surplus. However, life in the new world was very hard. The people who emigrated from Europe were generally not very well-to-do to begin with. Many were sick when they arrived because of the harsh conditions on their long voyage. Even those who arrived in good health and with some resources found life to be very hard because of the harsh weather, problems with Native Americans who often did not take kindly to foreigners settling on their land, and the general risks of pioneering. Thus, a new set of problems was substituted for the old ones, with the result being that dependency rapidly became a problem for the colonists just like it was for the people who remained in the Old World.

At a very early date each colony was faced with the problem of caring for the old, the blind, the disabled, the widowed, and the orphaned, as well as for the seasonally unemployed. When confronted with these problems each colony in turn adopted the Elizabethan Poor Law. Plymouth Colony was the first, adopting the law in 1642, followed by Virginia in 1646, Rhode Island in 1647, Connecticut in 1673, and Massachusetts in 1692. Eventually all of the colonies adopted the Poor Law. True to the English law on which they were closely modeled, the colonial poor laws stressed public responsibility for the dependent, local responsibility, legally enforceable family responsibility, and legal settlement (a person could not receive assistance except in the place in which he or she had established legal residence).

Although the colonies leaned heavily on the English experience in shaping their approach to the problem of poverty and dependency, a unique American approach began to emerge very early. In England the vast majority of poor relief was furnished under the public poor law, supplemented by a small amount of aid from the church. In America a dual welfare system developed from the very beginning. Responsibility was divided between public and private sectors, with a strong preference for the private sector. Along with the passage of the poor laws, private organizations emerged, such as the Scots Charitable Society established in Boston in 1657, the Friends Almshouse opened in Philadelphia in 1713, the Boston Episcopal Society formed in 1724, and the Society House of Carpenters organized in New York in 1767.[14]

The colonial approach to poor relief was characterized by another idea that reflected the development of a unique culture in the New World. This was the tremendous importance attached to the idea of work. The belief in the importance of work stemmed from two sources—economic and cultural. The economic reasons are fairly clear and straightforward. In the colonies there was a shortage of both labor and wealth. In order to survive and to develop a store of excess wealth it was of paramount importance that everyone who could possibly work do so. The cultural factors are related to what later came to be called the *protestant ethic,* or simply the *work ethic.* This is the very strong belief that work is innately good and that hard work indicates a person of quality—hard work may even be useful for earning salvation. The other side of this coin is the belief that idleness, laziness, and sloth are sin. The belief in work and the fear of idleness were reflected in the colonial poor laws. The laws called for children to be apprenticed and the able-bodied set to work; they even supported the development of home industry, mainly related to linen spinning, for women and children who would otherwise become public charges.[15]

A strong preference also developed in the colonies for what came to be called *indoor relief.* This meant that help was offered to people in the various categories of need, but rather than being given assistance in the form of cash or cash equivalents such as food or fuel, people were cared for by being taken into some form of custodial care. Thus, in return for being helped, a person was forced to give up a great degree of freedom. This care was at first provided in private homes at public expense. In some townships a poor person was sent "round the town" meaning that each citizen, in turn, would care for the person in his home for a period of two weeks. In other towns a kind of a reverse auction was held; at a town meeting townspeople bid against each other to determine who would provide care for a person at the lowest cost.[16] This form of indoor relief was rapidly replaced by the development of large-scale institutions.

Poor relief was not an issue in the American Revolution, so the revolution had little immediate effect on antipoverty efforts in this country. However, the type of government set up as a result of the revolution has resulted in a number of long-range effects. The first effect has to do with the fact that a federal form of government was set up. The idea was that the states were to remain as independent as possible, with a relatively weak central government. This has meant that in contrast to European democracies, which have strong central governments, no strong central welfare system has ever developed in the United States. Rather, we have fifty separate systems with some loose central coordination. The wide discrepancies among the state systems can be easily illustrated by looking at benefit levels for the Aid to Families with Dependent Children (AFDC) program, where levels of assistance varied in 1988 from a low of $113.83 per month in Alabama to a high of $598.59 per month in Alaska. Another significant effect of the form of government set up is a result of the separation of church and state. The fact that no central church was created has led to a proliferation of religious bodies, and most have devoted significant time and resources to social welfare activities.[17]

The standard historical interpretation has been that the colonial and Revolutionary War era was one of humanitarianism. This, it is argued, carried over into people's attitudes toward the poor and led to a general willingness to help the poor in a remarkably nonjudgmental way. Historians describing this positive attitude explain it as the result of three factors. The first is the Great Awakening, which was a religious movement that rejected the Calvinistic notion of predestination (the belief that a person is either saved or damned at birth and what he or she does in this life will have no effect on this destiny) and substituted for it the belief that salvation was earned through good works. Thus, the poor were no longer viewed as necessarily damned and the nonpoor could earn points toward their own salvation by aiding them. The second factor contributing to the supposed positive attitude toward the poor was the Enlightenment. This was the rise of a faith in science and a belief that all, or nearly all, problems, including social problems like poverty, could be studied and solutions could be found. The third reason was the revolution itself which, supposedly, led to a kind of group solidarity and a general spirit of change.[18]

As appealing as this idea might be—that our forebears were humanistic and accepting of the poor—recent research has cast doubts on this interpretation. In a study of colonial poor relief records from Somerset County Maryland, Guest concludes that

> The Somerset records make it clear that it was not generosity and solicitude but at best indifference that, in the main, characterized the colonists' attitudes towards their dependent poor. [Historians] misread these attitudes because they fail to examine home [outdoor] relief. In home relief there were no intermediaries, allowances were given directly to paupers, hence one is much better able to discern what it was thought a pauper deserved (as opposed to what was considered appropriate to compensate a householder for keeping a pauper). Evidently in Somerset, the Court did not think that paupers receiving home

relief were worthy of much. Payments to them were grudgingly made and allowances were so small that they must have resulted in semi-starvation.[19]

By the time the American Revolution was fought, poverty and poor relief had become issues of major size and importance. Between 1700 and 1715 the amount of money spent on poor relief by the city of Boston quadrupled; it then doubled again by 1735; and it increased by an additional 250 percent by 1753. Similar patterns occurred in other cities, such as New York and Philadelphia. By the time of the revolution it has been estimated that somewhere between 10 and 35 percent of municipal budgets were being expended for poor relief.[20] Among the reasons for this growth were the large number of immigrants streaming into large cities; the seasonal nature of many jobs, such as fishing and shipbuilding; the number of refugees from the Indian wars; and the many widows and orphans who were left when breadwinners died, as they frequently did in a land and in occupations often fraught with danger. Another factor contributing to poverty was a rather high out-of-wedlock birth rate. We generally think of our forebears as rather prudish people with regard to sex. This was not the case at all. Collier and Collier write that the colonists "were, moreover, a far more openly sexual people than we are likely to think. . . . In 1787 sex during the engagement was customary in some places: in one New England county, supposed to be typical, half the brides were pregnant on their wedding day during the Revolutionary era."[21] It appears that more than a few women were left standing at the altar—according to some estimates, as many as one-third to one-half of all first births were to unwed mothers.

Thus it can be seen that even in the earliest years of the country, poverty and poor relief were already rearing their heads as major problems. During the next era the problem really began to heat up.

Early Years of the Republic, 1781–1860

The years between the ratification of the Constitution and the beginning of the Civil War were a formative period for antipoverty policies and programs in the United States. This was a period of rapid and immense population growth. The first United States census, taken in 1790, found the population to be a little under 4 million. By 1860, the population had increased by more than eight times to 31.5 million. This population growth was accompanied by the triple threat of social problems: urbanization, industrialization, and immigration. In 1800, only about 6 percent of the population lived in urban areas; by 1860, 20 percent were city dwellers. The period of rapid industrialization was yet to come, but early industries were beginning to develop and the urban growth was partially a result of the opportunities these industries presented. Finally, a large part of the population growth was a result of immigration, particularly after 1830. In the 1830s, 538,381 people immigrated to this country and in the 1840s, 1.5 million people immigrated; immigration set a record at 2.8 million in the 1850s.[22]

The relation of these factors to poverty should be obvious. Urbanization results in people being separated from the resource of the land which rural dwellers can generally fall back on for some support during hard times. Urban dwellers also generally do not have the close relations with neighbors that are common in rural settings and so, when they are faced with a problem, they are on their own. Industrialization results in people being dependent on a paycheck for support, and thus they are one check away from destitution. Immigrants generally arrive with few resources, few skills, and often with the barrier of a different language and customs.

Ideas about the Causes of Poverty   These rapid social changes brought on a great increase in poverty. The concern generated by this increase brought on a new development—an interest in the causes of poverty and a desire to do something about it. The prevailing social beliefs about the causes of poverty concentrated almost entirely on individual defects, usually moral defects, as the major explanation. For example, in 1818, the New York Society for the Prevention of Pauperism listed the causes of poverty as: ignorance, idleness, intemperance (this was the most important), want of economy, imprudent and hasty marriages, lotteries, pawnbrokers, houses of ill fame, and charitable institutions themselves.[23] Some recognition was given to factors outside the individual which might result in poverty, and as a result a distinction was made between the "worthy" and the "unworthy" poor, an idea that has lasted until the present time. The worthy poor were those whose destitution was a result of some factor that was clearly not under their control, such as misfortune, old age, sickness, or some other adversity. The unworthy poor were those whose poverty was believed to be a result of some moral defect.

It is interesting, perhaps even contradictory, that while the causes of poverty were almost universally considered to be individual defects, the cause of these defects, and hence their cure, was strongly believed to be environmental. As Axinn and Levin note, "The economic growth, geographic expansion, and extension of political democracy that had created a world of opportunity had also created a world of change, insecurity, and temptation. A society making claim to a belief in human perfectibility but given to the creation of environmental and human disorders must provide order—and cure—for both."[24] This cure for poverty, as well as for a number of other defects such as mental illness, was seen to lie in the creation of large institutions. Thus, during this era the poorhouse rose, and fell, as the solution to poverty.

The Growth of Indoor Relief   Generally, indoor relief, as the poorhouse was known, gained favor because of the belief during this era of the desirability of institutions as the answer to all sorts of problems. Specifically, the poorhouse gained favor because it was perceived to be the most effective way of alleviating and preventing poverty. There was a belief that if people were given assistance in their own homes, they would soon come to prefer this over work and they would become permanent public charges. If placed in a poorhouse they could have a regular routine imposed upon them that would be beneficial to them in developing habits of industry and they could be given work that would contribute to their own support.

Life in the poorhouse was purposely hard. Men and women were separated (and thus families were broken up), the food was poor, and residents' lives were tightly regulated. Thus an additional benefit of this approach was that the specter of the poorhouse looming overhead would be a spur to people to maintain self-support and not to become dependent in the first place. Supporters of indoor relief felt that the ideal situation would be for the poorhouse to be the only recourse for those experiencing poverty.

The movement toward indoor relief was given focus in 1823 when the New York Legislature asked the Secretary of State to conduct a study of the poor laws in New York. The report, submitted by Secretary Yates in February of 1824, recommended the adoption of the "poorhouse plan." This plan called for the establishment of one or more poorhouses in every county in the state. These were to be houses of employment in which paupers might be "maintained and employed . . . in some healthful labor, chiefly agricultural, their children to be carefully instructed, and at a suitable age, to be put to some useful business or trade." The Yates Report gained national attention and resulted in the poorhouse becoming the major approach to poverty in the United States. By 1860, New York had more than 55 poorhouses, Massachusetts had 219, Pennsylvania had 31 county and numerous local poorhouses, and Maryland had a poorhouse in every county except one.[25]

By 1860, the fascination with the poorhouse had begun to decline. There were several reasons for this, generally having to do with the clash of theory with reality. The poorhouses in theory, at least as described in the Yates report, were supposed to be positive, humane environments that would contribute to the reform of paupers. However, in actuality they were more often than not places so bad as to be scandalous. Poorhouses were supposed to set people to work so they could contribute to their own support. In reality most of the inmates in poorhouses were unable to work for the same reasons most welfare recipients today are not able to work—they were generally old, very young, sick, or disabled in some way. The idea of a vast sea of able-bodied paupers who needed to be set to work was then, as now, largely a myth.

Outdoor Relief   Even though indoor relief was the preferred method of providing for the poor during this era, outdoor relief never really died out. For example, in New York, which was one of the states most enthusiastic about the potential of the poorhouse, between 34 and 50 percent of all expenditures for poor relief between 1830 and 1860 went for relief to people in their own homes. Because it was less expensive to provide outdoor relief, it is estimated that three to four times as many people were on outdoor relief as were in the poorhouses.[26] In the South, outdoor relief made up an even greater proportion of the total relief picture, "doubtless because the Calvinistic principle of 'work hard, don't idle' was less pressing in the Anglican religion, the dominant religion in the South, and because the Southern landed gentry had developed a strong sense of noblesse oblige. This was in contrast, of course, to New England and New York, where Calvinism underlay many attitudes toward the poor."[27]

By the late 1850s, public officials were taking a position that was almost the opposite of the one officials had taken a generation earlier. They were arguing that the poorhouse did not encourage independence and thrift among the poor. In 1857, the mayor of Philadelphia, a city that had a few years earlier constructed one of the largest poorhouses in the country, Old Blockley, expressed his preference for outdoor relief. Sending people to the poorhouse would, he argued, reduce the self-reliance of persons in temporary need. In the same year, the President of the Board of Guardians of the Poor expressed his feeling that outdoor relief was more humane and less expensive than institutional care.

Private Antipoverty Organizations   There were two major economic depressions during the early years of the republic, one from 1815 to 1821 and another from 1837 to 1845. During these depressions there was widespread unemployment, and a good deal of social unrest manifested itself through mass meetings and a number of riots. These events appear to have alarmed the well-to-do about the situation of the poor and to cause them to worry that perhaps America was developing a permanent class of paupers similar to that in Europe. The result was the formation of two large organizations for the purpose of studying poverty and seeking its cure. These were the Societies for the Prevention of Pauperism, which flourished in the 1820s, and the longer lasting Associations for Improving the Conditions of the Poor (AICP), which emerged during the 1840s.[28] These organizations were based on several ideas that have continued to wield considerable influence in antipoverty efforts. The first, and probably the most important idea, is that poverty, except in the most extraordinary situations, is an individual problem and the result of individual shortcomings, rather than a social and economic problem. Individual shortcomings were generally believed to be moral (such as bad habits and laziness), and so giving assistance, particularly public assistance, was viewed as dangerous and counterproductive. If a person learned he could live without working, then, it was believed, the natural thing for the person to do was to take advantage of the help and no longer work. Because the cause of poverty was personal and not structural, the solution proposed by these organizations was to give as little material assistance as possible—preferably none. In its place was to be substituted moral uplift—teaching the poor person industry, sobriety, and thrift. Finally, these organizations were opposed to public aid. Public aid smacked of the notion that financial assistance was a right, and this was thought to be dangerous. These organizations felt that assisting the poor was a civic and Christian duty, but to even hint that to be supported was a right was to encourage the very pauperism that the societies were seeking to cure.*

Government Antipoverty Efforts   True to the poor law principle of relief being the responsibility of the smallest unit of government, most public anti-poverty efforts during this era were sponsored by state and local governments. One attempted departure from this came in the 1850s when Dorothea Dix was successful in her efforts to get the U.S. Congress to pass legislation to appropriate federal lands to be used for the support of mental institutions. President Pierce vetoed the bill in 1854 with the now famous message that, "I cannot find any authority in the Constitution for making the Federal Government the great almoner of public charity throughout the United States." Although the bill before him dealt specifically with the mentally ill and not with the poor as such, Pierce saw no difference, saying, "If Congress have power to make provision for the indigent insane without the limits of this District, it has the same power to provide for the indigent who are not insane; and thus to transfer to the Federal Government the charge of all the poor in all the States." Pierce felt that the inevitable result of this would be that, "the fountains of charity will be dried up at home, and the several States, instead of bestowing their own means on the social wants of their own people, may themselves, through the strong temptation, which appeals

---

*In this context the meaning of the term *pauper* is interesting. As the term was originally used, a pauper was not just a very poor person, but a poor person who had been forever ruined by the indiscriminate giving of charity. A person who had been "pauperized" was one who had learned that he or she could live without working and was, consequently, never willing to work again.

to states as to individuals, become humble suppliants for the bounty of the Federal Government, reversing their true relation to this Union . . ."[29] This veto set a precedent that was to effectively block any large-scale federal intervention against poverty for eighty years.

Attitudes of the Nonpoor   Perhaps the most important aspect of this era for our purposes is not so much the events we have been reviewing but rather the attitudes they reflect. In earlier years attitudes toward the poor may not have been highly positive, but at least there was some modicum of understanding. In the years 1781 to 1860 these attitudes changed, and the changes have proven to be fairly permanent. According to Trattner

> conditions had changed. Industrial capitalism, urbanization, greater poverty, higher taxes, and the laissez-faire philosophy had made the pursuit and accumulation of wealth a moral virtue and dependency a vice.[30]

In England, prime minister Benjamin Disraeli remarked that it had become "a crime to be poor." In the United States, the attitude appears to have been just as bad.

The most interesting aspect of this attitude change is that it signaled the beginning of a stubborn, almost intentional, resistance to understanding poverty. All the data available, all the requests for aid, and presumably most people's contacts with the poor, clearly showed that the vast majority of the poor were the old, the very young, the sick, the disabled, and the seasonally unemployed. In other words, they were people who were poor through no fault of their own and whose poverty could not readily be "cured." However, reports, speeches, legislation, and newspaper accounts portrayed the poor as being able-bodied people who were simply unwilling to work. Thus, the favorite solution to poverty, the poorhouse, was intended to discourage these people from ever applying for aid, and if they did, to teach them habits of thrift and industry so they would not apply again. This solution, like every solution we have tried since then, did not work because it was based on a faulty understanding, early urban folktales.

Social Transformation, Reform, and Reaction, 1860–1930

Although for our purposes we are treating the years from 1860 to 1930 as one period, they really encompass three separate historical eras. The years from 1860 until near the turn of the century were years that witnessed the rapid transformation of American society from what Leiby has termed the "rural democracy" into a country that was clearly on its way to becoming an urban industrial giant.[31] This was a period of rapidly developing social problems, but there was not much recognition of how serious they were nor was there any general acceptance of social responsibility for their solution. The years from roughly 1898 until 1918, between the assassination of President McKinley and the end of World War I, are known as the *Progressive Era* and were a period marked by a wholesale spirit of reform aimed at finding solutions to these social problems. The years between 1918 and 1930, the end of the war and the beginning of the Great Depression, are popularly known as the *Roaring Twenties* and represent an era characterized by people's efforts to forget about social problems, to avoid responsibility, and to enjoy life. This was a time of great political conservatism.

Collectively, the years between 1860 and 1930 were a period of massive changes in American society. Between 1860 and 1900, the population more than doubled, going from 31.5 million to 76 million. By 1930, the population had increased to 123 million. Much of the population growth came from immigration. Almost 14 million immigrants arrived in the United States between 1860 and 1900; another 13.7 million arrived by 1915; and 5.6 million more came by 1930. Most of the immigrants arrived with very few resources and they generally settled in the large cities along the eastern seaboard, causing great urban problems. The country became much wealthier during this period, with the Gross National Product increasing from $6.7 billion in 1860 to $16.8 billion in 1900 and to $104 billion in 1929. The flow of wealth was not constant, however; the country suffered deep depressions from 1873 to 1878 and from 1893 until 1898; and finally the Great Depression began in 1929. The great increase in wealth was largely caused by the continuing process of industrialization. In 1860, 58 percent of the population were employed in agriculture and only 18 percent in manufacturing and construction; in 1900, the number employed in agriculture had shrunk to 37 percent and the number in manufacturing and construction had increased to 28 percent; by 1930, the number in agriculture had decreased to 21 percent, the number in manufacturing and construction had only increased to 29 percent, but other urban occupations, such as finance and other professions, had increased by 15 percent. In addition, the extent of urbanization continued to increase at a rapid rate. In 1860, there were only 9 cities with populations over 100,000. By 1900, there were 38 such cities and by 1930, there were 93.[32]

Changing Attitudes toward the Poor   During the years 1860 to 1930, Americans' attitudes toward poverty underwent a major change. During the latter half of the nineteenth century, the American attitude was, in Bremner's words, "a somewhat incongruous composite of two sharply contrasting points of view." On the one hand, there was the traditional Christian view that poverty was a result of God's incomprehensible but beneficent will. Poverty was a blessing in disguise because it gave the nonpoor an opportunity to demonstrate their goodness by performing acts of charity toward the poor. On the other hand, there was the view that poverty was unnecessary in this land of plenty, that there was enough work for all, and that anyone who wanted to badly enough could lift himself up by his own bootstraps. Therefore, poverty was undesirable, it was totally the fault of the individual affected, and rather than being a blessed state, it was the obvious result of sloth and sinfulness. These two views were combined into a creed that went, according to Bremner, as follows

> Poverty is unnecessary (for Americans), but the varying ability and virtue of men make its presence inevitable; this is a desirable state of affairs, since without the fear of want the masses would not work and there would be no incentive for the able to demonstrate their superiority; where it exists, poverty is usually a temporary problem and, both in its cause and cure, it is always an individual matter.

This individualistic interpretation of poverty was based on a radical American idea, namely that work was not an onerous task falling mainly on the lowborn, but rather it was a positive thing, an end in itself, a means that anyone could use to get ahead. "The promise of America was not affluence, but independence; not ease, but a chance to work for oneself, to be self-supporting, and to win esteem through hard and honest labor."[33]

This stress on self-support and honest labor was further bolstered in the late nineteenth century by new ideas about society put forth by the English social theorist Herbert Spencer and reinforced by the work of Charles Darwin. Spencer compared society to a biological organism and incorporated Darwin's theories about evolution and survival of the fittest into his perspective. *Social Darwinism,* as this approach came to be called, held that the concept of survival of the fittest applied to the marketplace as well as to the jungle. The foremost proponent of Social Darwinism in the United States was William Graham Sumner. Sumner argued that economic competition helped weed out those individuals and families who could not successfully adapt to life in industrial America. Government intervention to help people with economic and social problems would only delay the natural workings of the law of evolution. Social Darwinism thus contributed to individualistic interpretations of poverty in its stress on individual survival in a competitive world.

During the latter years of the nineteenth century and the early years of the twentieth century this individualistic view of poverty began to be substantially modified, although it never entirely died out. Rugged individualism was perhaps functional during the earlier era when the United States was still a frontier society, but as the frontier was replaced by the city and the farm by the factory, it became increasingly apparent that people's troubles were more often than not caused by circumstances over which they had no control. Although it was difficult to accept, Americans began to suspect that in a complex economy, individuals were no longer the independent agents they had been in the recent past. Josephine Shaw Lowell noted in 1893 that the causes of the distress of the poor were "as much beyond their power to avert as if they had been natural calamities of fire, flood, or storm."[34]

In the Victorian era, there was an ever-increasing concern for the poor and the beginning of a more positive and realistic attitude toward poverty, but there was not very much in the way of hard information available on the problem. One of the hallmarks of the Progressive Era which followed was an almost insatiable desire for tangible facts about society. This was the age of muckraking journalism and of the large-scale social survey. People wanted the inside scoop on politics, crime, corporations, labor, and perhaps most of all, poverty. For the first time in history a body of valid, reliable knowledge began to accumulate about the life and problems of the poor. Government researchers made several attempts to survey the conditions of immigrants. Settlement house workers conducted careful block-by-block surveys of impoverished neighborhoods. A number of journals which were devoted to promoting social research began publication, the most notable being *The Survey,* published by Paul U. Kellogg. Schools of social work began to open and the Russell Sage Foundation gave generous grants to five of them to open social research departments. From 1907 to 1909, a large group of researchers and social workers conducted the Pittsburgh survey, which was the first attempt made in the United States to survey at close range the conditions under which working people existed in a large industrial city.

The massive amount of data collected during the Progressive Era provided a clear picture of poverty for the first time in history. This picture was considerably different from the image many people still had of the poor as being a basically lazy, shiftless lot, who were to blame for their own poverty. This research found that the lot of the poor was generally overwork; underpay; pitiful living conditions usually caused by the fact that they couldn't afford better ones on the wages available; and exploitation by greedy landlords, merchants, and employers.

Old attitudes die hard. Although during the Progressive Era much was learned about poverty and, as will be discussed in the following section, many programs were instituted to attempt to alleviate it, the spirit of reform faded during the conservative years of the Roaring Twenties. Those years were prosperous and Americans believed that the problem of poverty was well under control. The prevailing belief was that the conditions revealed by surveys like that in Pittsburgh had been corrected and now the nation was working the way it was supposed to. Thus, once again, the attitude became dominant (if it had ever actually lost dominance) that if a person were poor it must be because of some personal failure.

Private Antipoverty Efforts   By the Civil War a clear division of labor had developed in American antipoverty efforts—public agencies could provide indoor (poorhouse) relief for people who simply could not make it on their own, but outdoor relief was considered to be the exclusive jurisdiction of the private sector. There were several reasons for the belief that it was not proper for public agencies to dispense outdoor relief. The first was that public agencies were considered to be corrupt and inefficient, and therefore incapable of managing efficient and effective relief programs; thus, the effect of public programs was to pauperize recipients. Secondly, this was the high point of laissez-faire economics and the belief was that if public monies were given to people in their homes, it would threaten the economy. Nineteenth century leader in philanthropy Louisa Lee Schuler, speaking about the economic effects of public outdoor relief upon New York City, said that, "The wisest and safest course would be ultimately to abolish all official outdoor relief, to improve and enlarge the accommodations in the institutions, and to throw the responsibility of providing for the wants of the poor entirely on existing private charity."[35] The third reason that private aid was preferred over public aid was that private charity gave people a chance to develop the virtue of charity, something that did not happen if they were taxed for the expense of charity and had no choice in the matter. The final reason was that it was firmly believed that it was morally wrong to take money from one person in the form of taxation and to give it to another in the form of charity. Another philanthropic leader, Josephine Shaw Lowell, said of this

> Every dollar raised by taxation comes out of the pocket of some individual, usually a poor individual, and makes him so much the poorer, and therefore the question is between the man who earned the dollar by hard work, and needs it to buy himself and his family a day's food, and the man who, however worthy and suffering, did not earn it, but wants it to be given to him to buy himself and his family a day's food. If the man who earned it wishes to divide it with the other man, it is usually a desirable thing that he should do so, and at any rate it is more or less his own business, but that the law, by the hand of a public officer, should take it from him and hand it over to the other man, seems to be an act of gross tyranny and injustice . . . The less [public relief] that is given the better for everyone, the giver and the receiver.[36]

This anti-public-aid bias became so strong that by 1880, public outdoor relief had been outlawed in New York City, Brooklyn, Buffalo, Indianapolis, Philadelphia, and Chicago, as well as in a number of smaller cities.

The private charities that emerged and became dominant during this era at the outset reflected the belief in the individual and moral causes of poverty and the pernicious effects of "indiscriminate alms giving" which it was believed encouraged "indolence and beggary."[37] Although a number of antipoverty agencies emerged during this era, the largest and most important were the Charity Organization Societies which began in Buffalo, New York in 1877 and spread to virtually every city of any size within a few years. As discussed in Chapter 3, the COS movement addressed itself to urban destitution, the increase in poverty, and the potential for conflict between social classes. It held that destitution could be reduced, hardship ameliorated, and mendicancy prevented by instituting a system of scientific charity, abolishing public relief, and replacing the existing chaos in almsgiving with a systematically coordinated private philanthropy. The social philosophy of the COS reflected that of the country as a whole. The COS rejected the influence of the environment on the lives of people. It was felt that people were free agents who could control their destinies commensurate with their abilities and moral fiber. Any lapse into dependency was a result of intemperance, improvidence, indolence, ignorance, or some other personal defect. Thus, charity had to be dispensed very carefully, on a strictly individualized basis, by trained volunteers or paid staff. Only a private organization utilizing the principles of scientific charity could do this; it was a task clearly beyond the capability of public officials.

By the time the twentieth century began, the COS and other private agencies had amassed considerable experience in dealing with poor people. Because of this contact, in addition to the information gathered by the researchers mentioned earlier, the COS began to abandon its cherished belief that poverty was the result of personal moral shortcomings. The movement's leaders realized that the causes of poverty were social, economic, and psychological rather than the result of personal moral failure. However, one principle that was not abandoned was that charity was the business of the private sector and that government should stay out as much as possible.

Government Antipoverty Efforts   Although the years prior to the onset of the Great Depression were characterized by a near-total dominance of charity by private organizations, some things were beginning to stir that paved the way for the large-scale government programs enacted in the 1930s. These events revolved around the newly emerging concept of *social insurance*. A few people were beginning to consider social insurance to be an attractive alternative to charity. Insurance was not based on the notion of charity or sympathy, but on self-interest and on shared risk. Most of the advocates of social insurance were not benevolent altruists, but prudent businessmen. They understood the concept of rationalizing risks through insurance.[38]

The concept of social insurance was first called *workingman's insurance*. Leiby says

> it was supposed to meet the special needs of the urban industrial worker. Peasant or yeoman farmers were largely self-sufficient on their land, and family and neighbors could help out in emergencies. The urban worker had no garden and his family and neighbors were usually less reliable. He was vulnerable to any interruption in pay, in which case he was likely to fall on charity. Already by 1880 it was possible to identify the main risks to steady pay. The breadwinner could not work if (1) he was sick or (2) he had an accident (on the job, most likely); (3) if there was a slack in the demand for labor (high unemployment); (4) if he grew too old or feeble to work; or (5) if he died.[39]

People who were familiar with the concept of insurance, already well developed for the purpose of smoothing out the risks of business, began to conceive of insurance as a way of smoothing out the economic risks of urban industrial life.

Social insurance was conceived as being government sponsored or assisted insurance for urban industrial workers. The first type to be proposed and implemented was workman's compensation, which was designed to deal with the problem of people disabled from work-related accidents. The first workman's compensation law was passed in Maryland in 1902; the federal government passed a law to protect its own employees in 1908; and by 1920, 43 states had passed such legislation.

Shortly after the campaign for workman's compensation insurance, movements began for other types of social insurance that stretched the concept a bit. These were proposals for social insurance for mothers with young children, the elderly, and the blind. The concept was stretched because these were not insurance programs by any reach of the imagination. Basically, they were outdoor relief programs that simply proposed to give a cash grant to people in these categories. The significant point is that these were categories of the needy who were defined as being worthy poor. Mothers were thought to be rendering a service to society (rearing children) for which they should be compensated, and the elderly were assumed to have rendered service and to thus deserve continuing support. The blind, presumably like the other two groups, were clearly poor through no fault of their own. The first mothers' pension law was passed in Illinois in 1911, and 18 states had followed suit by 1913. Old age pensions were a little slower in coming because states feared that they would increase the cost of doing business and make the state less competitive. Pennsylvania, Montana, and Nevada passed old age pension laws in 1923 and four others did so by 1927. The first legislation authorizing pensions for the blind was passed in Ohio in 1898; Illinois passed such a law in 1903, Wisconsin passed a similar law in 1907, and a number of other states passed laws after 1915.[40]

Private Domination of Social Welfare   Although some headway had been made by advocates of public responsibility for the impoverished in the form of social insurance schemes, when the Great Depression hit in 1929, social welfare was clearly dominated by private agencies. Social workers in these agencies continued to oppose public programs. They felt that pensions were just another form of outdoor relief (which in fact they were), and as such, were susceptible to all the abuses that social workers had criticized these programs for in the past. The second objection social workers had to pension programs was that these programs assumed that the only problem poor people had was a lack of money, and that a pension would solve this problem. Social workers believed that poverty was symptomatic of other problems that required treatment and that this could only be provided by private agencies. Finally, social workers believed that pensions were a distraction from the real problems, which were structural issues like why there were so many widows in the first place (poor public health and industrial accidents). In any case, public pension plans only aided a very small proportion of the poor, a select group for whom it could be clearly demonstrated that their destitution was no fault of their own. The remainder of the poor had to rely on the often questionable sympathies of private agencies and existed, in Michael Katz's words, in the shadow of the poorhouse.[41]

Seeds of the Reluctant Welfare State, 1930–1940[42]

The 1920s in the United States was a time of unprecedented prosperity: factories sought to turn out goods fast enough to meet demand; every month avid investors snapped up hundreds of millions of dollars in new securities; and colleges and movie theaters were jammed. In this atmosphere President Hoover was able to say, "we in America are nearer to the final triumph over poverty than ever before in the history of any land." But this triumph was not to come, for abruptly in October of 1929, the stock market crashed. By the end of 1929, the value of securities had shrunk by $40 billion. Hundreds of thousands of families lost their homes, millions of unemployed walked the streets, and tax collections fell to such a low that school teachers could not be paid in many areas. The United States had faced depressions before, but these had lasted only a few years. The Great Depression of 1929 was to last a full decade.[43]

President Hoover reacted to the depression with faith that natural forces in the economy would correct the situation if government did not interfere. He did not entirely repudiate the responsibility of the national government to act, but he did hold firmly to the English Poor Law principle that relief was exclusively the concern of local government, and preferably of private charity. Hoover's philosophy regarding the desirability of the federal government's engaging in welfare activities was summed up in his statement that, "You cannot extend the mastery of government over the private lives of people without at the same time making it the master of their souls and thoughts." He therefore limited national government response to pumping money into businesses in the form of contracts for roads, public buildings, loans and so forth, thinking this would stimulate the economy and aid the natural forces of recovery. His tactic for dealing with the crisis was graphically illustrated in December of 1930 when he approved an appropriation of $45 million to feed the livestock of Arkansas farmers, but opposed an additional $25 million to feed the farmers. The natural forces that Hoover placed so much faith in did not work. By 1932, the number of unemployed was over twelve million, five thousand banks had closed, thirty-two thousand businesses had failed, and national income had declined from $80 billion to $40 billion.

By the time Franklin Roosevelt entered office in 1933, the economic situation was so bad that people were questioning whether the American system was viable any longer. Disorder was spreading and threats of revolution were heard. Roosevelt quickly repudiated Hoover's doctrine of government nonintervention in the area of welfare. In the place of Hoover's doctrine Roosevelt substituted the philosophy he had developed as governor of New York and had implemented in that state under the Wicks Act. This philosophy held that people in need have a right to governmental aid because this aid is financed out of tax dollars which they paid when they were employed. Thus, receiving welfare payments was no different than sending children to public school or asking for police protection. Under this philosophy, with social worker Harry Hopkins as his assistant, Roosevelt implemented a wide range of public welfare programs beginning with the 1933 Federal Emergency Relief Act (FERA) and culminating in the 1935 Social Security Act—a beginning, if incomplete, attempt of the federal government to assume cradle-to-grave security for the citizens of the nation.

The Social Security Act—as it finally emerged after many compromises—was designed to alleviate financial dependency through two lines of defense: contributory social insurance and public assistance. Its main insurance feature was a program that

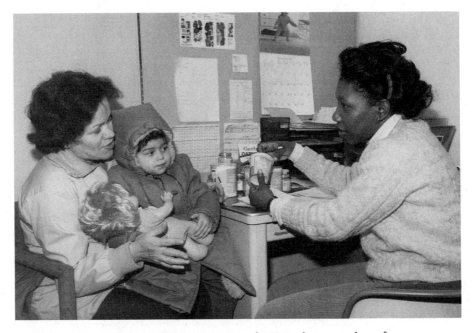

With the passage of the Social Security Act of 1935 a large number of
social workers became employed in public agencies.

provided protection for workers from poverty caused by old age or disability, and for
children and widows from poverty caused by the death of the breadwinner. This is
the Old Age Survivors and Disability Insurance (OASDI) that is paid partially out of
the paycheck of workers and partially by employer contributions. The second insurance
feature was unemployment insurance. Four categories of public assistance were set up
under the Social Security Act. Old Age Assistance (OAA) provided support for the
elderly who for some reason were not protected under OASDI. Aid to the Blind (AB)
and Aid to the Permanently and Totally Disabled (APTD) provided support for those
who could not support themselves because of physical disabilities. Finally, Aid to
Families with Dependent Children (AFDC) was established to serve basically the same
group that state widows' pension laws were helping—single mothers with small children.

When the depression hit, the majority of poor relief came from private donations
and it was administered through private family service agencies. Aid was distributed
on a highly individualized basis according to the old notion that economic dependency
was a symptom of some basic individual deficiency requiring treatment. The coming
of the depression had two rapid and profound effects on the private agencies that had
traditionally dominated welfare in the United States. The first was that when private
money ran low, as it quickly did, local governments began contributing money to these
private organizations to support their relief giving programs. In less than a year after
the crash, well over half of the aid distributed by private agencies came from public
funds. The second was that the depression shocked the social workers who administered
these agencies and who had historically opposed public welfare into realizing that social

and economic forces were at the root of many of the problems with which they were dealing. As Paul Kellogg, editor of *The Survey* said, "You cannot deal effectively with an inferiority complex on an empty stomach."[44] His message was clearly that social workers needed to concentrate on social, political, and economic issues, as well as on understanding the psychology of the individual.

When the Federal Emergency Relief Act was passed in 1933, it changed the structure of social services in the United States. Immediately upon assuming office, Harry Hopkins, administrator of the act, formulated Regulation Number 1, which stated that public money was to be administered by public agencies. Another provision of the FERA was that each local administrator was to employ at least one experienced social worker and at least one qualified supervisor for every twenty employees. The major effect of this regulation, and similar regulations in the 1935 Social Security Act, was to quickly and decisively end the domination of welfare by private agencies and to move it firmly into the public sector.

Attitudes toward the Poor   The Great Depression in the United States, in a period of only ten years, witnessed significant changes in attitudes both toward the poor and toward antipoverty programs. In this brief span of time, the welfare system in this country was converted from one that was almost totally private to one that was dominated by public agencies. The massive size of the problem of economic dependency in modern industrial society was brought home with a vengeance and the country generally came to realize that the private sector simply could not handle it. More important, however, was the change in attitude toward poverty and the poor themselves. The huge amount of unemployment made it clear to nearly everyone that poverty in most, if not all, cases was more a result of structural factors than of personal failings. The social commentator Clinch Calkins concluded

> As the reader has seen over and over again, not perseverance, nor skill, education, and health, nor a long and excellent work-record, stand the breadwinner in any certain stead when the bad word is handed down from directors to executive to foreman. To be sure, the best man may be the last to be discharged. But even he has no assurance of security. Laziness, incompetence, and shiftlessness determine the incidence but not the quantity of unemployment. . . . Because labor has been regarded as, if not a commodity, at least the most flexible and easily replaced element in production, the general run of business has long taken an attitude toward its labor supply which it would be too thrifty to take toward raw materials . . . [Whether] protection is arranged by individual management, by the trade as a whole, or through public action, as in [workman's] compensation laws, the burden of unemployment should not be allowed to fall solely on the family of the worker.[45]

Unfortunately, this positive attitude toward the poor did not signal any permanent change. People had come to understand unemployment in bad times like the Great Depression, but they still had no understanding of it during good times. The Aid to Dependent Children program, for example, was considered a temporary program that would wither away and eventually become insignificant when the economy improved. The fact that it has not, and the fact that it has grown steadily larger have proven to be the primary bones of contention in our contemporary welfare situation.

The Return of Prosperity, 1940–1960

The Second World War brought an end to the depression that Roosevelt's New Deal programs had succeeded in ameliorating but not ending. In 1940, the gross national product (GNP) increased to a level equal to the boom year of 1929. Between 1940 and 1960, the GNP increased fivefold. Population growth, which was minimal during the depression, also boomed. In the 1940s, the population grew by twenty-one million and in the 1950s it grew by an additional thirty million, with most of the increase caused by the birthrate. Generally the era was characterized by optimism and prosperity, which was unfortunately accompanied by complacency and conservatism.

The country was characterized during this era by a pulling back from large social issues such as public welfare. There were many reasons for this trend. Most people, including most social workers, felt that after the passage of the Social Security Act, the problems of poverty were being adequately addressed. More important was the general perception of mass prosperity. Experts, such as social workers and economists, who should have known better, believed that poverty was fast becoming a minor problem. In his best-selling book *The Affluent Society,* published in 1958, economist John Kenneth Galbraith argued that America was close to solving the problems of scarcity and poverty. This belief tended to make the poor invisible and it made concern about them seem remote and almost antiquarian.

Ironically, at the same time that Americans were perceiving that poverty was fast becoming a thing of the past, welfare rolls were rising at rapid rates and attitudes toward the poor, which had become more positive during the depression years, were once again becoming harsh. Communities throughout the nation were following the lead set by the city fathers in Newburgh, New York, and attempting to discourage people from applying for public assistance by making receipt of aid as unpleasant as possible. Samuel Mencher reported on the methods used in Newburgh. These were: give as much assistance as possible in-kind rather than in cash so recipients would have no choice of what they consumed; threaten prosecution of people who, intentionally or unintentionally, receive more assistance than that for which they are technically eligible; frequently reevaluate eligibility of recipients; provide assistance only for a temporary period of time; make illegitimate children ineligible for aid; and, finally, threaten parents with the removal of their children. Of the situation in Newburgh, Mencher commented, "The opposition to public assistance shows that though our society has greatly changed, the ideas and values affecting public assistance have hardly budged from their earliest beginnings."[46]

Reform and Reaction, 1960–1988

By the end of the 1950s the country was feeling restless and ready for change. John F. Kennedy was campaigning for the presidency on the assertion that the country was stagnating, and he promised that he would get it "moving again" toward "new frontiers." Shortly after his election, the 1960 census was completed; it revealed that the country clearly needed to get moving again. The census data revealed that the New Deal and the Second World War had not eliminated poverty as had been generally believed. In addition, the data indicated that poverty was not restricted to people living in certain deprived areas or to members of certain groups, as Galbraith had asserted, but that it was common and widespread. A number of books based on the new data made clear the extent of poverty; the most influential was Michael Harrington's *The Other America: Poverty in the United States*. In light of this " rediscovery of poverty," the federal government attempted to attack the problem from three different approaches under three different presidents during the sixties.

The approach of the Kennedy administration was embodied in Public Law 87–543, known as the Social Service Amendments, signed into law on July 25, 1962. This law grew out of the recommendations of the Ad Hoc Committee on Public Welfare appointed by Health, Education, and Welfare Secretary Ribicoff in May 1961, and on a report by George Wyman at about the same time. Wyman was an administrator with experience in a wide variety of social welfare agencies including local, state, and federal agencies as well as voluntary agencies. The Committee's and Wyman's recommendations were heavily influenced by advice from social workers and other experts who contended that providing intensive social services would rehabilitate and bring financial independence to the poor. The act provided increased federal support (75 percent) to the states to enable them to provide social services to recipients of public assistance. In reality the act represented a very old approach—providing individual services to help people lift themselves out of poverty, with little attention directed toward altering the social conditions that caused the poverty.[47]

The Social Service Amendments rapidly increased the number of social workers in public welfare settings. Recommendation number 12 of the Ad Hoc Committee stated, "To make possible the rehabilitative services so strongly advocated [by the committee], the goal should be established that one third of all persons engaged in social work capacities in public welfare should hold master's degrees in social work." Money was allocated for welfare departments to send employees to graduate school in social work, and these schools began to incorporate additional public welfare content into their curricula.

When social workers advocated providing professional services to welfare recipients, they did so in the belief that these services would improve recipients' lives and would be judged on this basis. Unfortunately, Congress supported the services in the belief that they would help people become self-supporting, thereby reducing the welfare rolls, and judged them on this basis. After the passage of the amendments, the welfare rolls rose at a faster rate than ever, making social workers suspect in policy makers' eyes and causing them to look for a new approach.

The new approach came in 1964 when, in his State of the Union message, President Johnson called upon Congress to enact a thirteen-point program that would declare "unconditional war on poverty." In July of 1964 the Economic Opportunity Act established the Office of Economic Opportunity. The Act also created Volunteers In Service To America (VISTA), the Job Corps, Upward Bound, the Neighborhood Youth Corps, Operation Head Start, and the Community Action Program (CAP).

There were a number of reasons behind President Johnson's War on Poverty. One was pressure from the civil rights movement for an attack on hunger and poverty. An example of the intensity of this pressure was a march for "jobs and freedom" that brought two hundred thousand people to Washington, D.C. and culminated in a historic speech by Martin Luther King, Jr. The major reason, however, was probably the growing awareness of the extent of poverty in the United States and the continued growth of the welfare rolls, despite the Social Service Amendments. A significant new development in the War on Poverty programs was that they made a concerted effort to include input from the poor themselves into the design and administration of the programs; this was done under the Economic Opportunity Act's provision for "maximum feasible participation" of the poor, which encouraged participation of low-income people on boards and staffs of community programs.

If anything, the War on Poverty programs were even less successful than the Social Service Amendments. Congress and taxpayers stuck to reducing welfare rolls as the primary criterion for success, and far from shrinking, the rolls increased at a record rate, with more than one million persons being added between 1963 and 1966. In addition, the War on Poverty drew severe criticism for other reasons: mayors were upset because the federal government was funding programs over which they had no control; members of Congress were upset by lawsuits brought against government agencies by government-funded legal services; and citizens were upset by the aggressiveness and hostility of the poor, who had found a voice through the "maximum feasible participation" concept. As a result of these criticisms, the Economic Opportunity Act of 1966 sharply curtailed community action.

Two War on Poverty programs that perhaps have had little effect on reducing welfare rolls, but have had an immense impact on improving the lives of the poor were the 1964 Food Stamp Act and the 1965 Medicare and Medicaid amendments to the Social Security Act. The Food Stamp Act replaced the commodities program that had provided nutritional assistance for the poor by making surplus agricultural produce available to them. While better than nothing, the commodities program provided no choice; the type of food available largely depended on the commodities of which there was a surplus. The Food Stamp Program provides vouchers that can be used just like cash for the purchase of food and so they permit recipients the same range of choice that anyone else has in his or her weekly shopping. The Medicare program for the first time made medical care available to the impoverished elderly and the Medicaid program did the same for children and mothers receiving support under the AFDC program.

Toward the end of President Johnson's term in office, the mood of the country began to drift to the right. In 1966, on the same day the new Economic Opportunity Act was signed into law, the Republicans gained fifty-one seats in Congress, mostly replacing liberal Democrats. In 1968 the Republicans added the White House to their list of victories. With the conservative mood of the country, sentiment grew for limiting "soft" services, such as social services and community action, and for emphasizing "hard" services, such as day care and work training programs. The Social Security Amendments of 1967 reflected this mood, setting up the Work Incentive Program, which required all AFDC recipients with no children under six to register for work or for job training and to accept employment or training as soon as it became available. The purpose of this program was to once again attempt to force welfare recipients to stop being lazy and get to work. True to the experience of all such programs in the past, the number of welfare recipients who expressed a desire for the jobs or training promised by the program far exceeded the ability of state job service offices to supply work or training. Another part of the amendments instituted a formula whereby a welfare recipient's grant was reduced by only a percentage of earned income when that person became employed. Also funded was daycare for welfare recipients who were employed or in training.

Following the failure of these programs to reduce the welfare rolls, in spite of the fact that they undoubtedly improved the lives of many poor people, the country lost interest in antipoverty programs. In 1969 President Nixon unveiled his Family Assistance Plan, which was intended to replace existing cash assistance programs with one unified, if stingy, minimum guaranteed annual income. The plan placed a premium on work and little emphasis on social services. It immediately ran into controversy and was eventually defeated except for one part: the Supplemental Security Income program (SSI) that was enacted in 1972 and went into effect on January 1, 1974. Under this program financial assistance for the elderly, the blind, and the disabled became 100 percent federally funded and administered. This program is managed by the Social Security Administration and once more implies that these groups are somehow more deserving than mothers with dependent children and that they should receive a "pension" rather than "welfare."

President Carter attempted a major public welfare reform when he unveiled the Jobs and Income Security Program on August 6, 1976, proposing that it become effective in October 1980. The plan proposed the sweeping abolition of the existing welfare system with its patchwork of benefits, including AFDC, food stamps, and SSI. These would be replaced with a two-tier system—a job program for those who were able to work and an income maintenance program for those who were not. The proposal called for the creation of 1,400,000 job slots for persons who were able to work but unable to find jobs. The schedule of benefits was designed so that those who found work in the private sector would always be better off than those who worked in public service jobs. Those unable to work, regardless of the reason, would receive benefits from a single program. Unfortunately, President Carter became so quickly mired in political problems that his Jobs and Income Security Program was placed on the back burner, where it remained until he left office.

When Ronald Reagan entered office in 1980, his strategy for reducing poverty could be described as new wine in old bottles. Although he called his approach "supply-side economics" it was really just the old conservative trickle-down theory with a new name. Basically, this approach argues that to improve things for the poor you must first improve things for the rich. The rich will then use their extra money to expand businesses, which will hire more people, and the benefits will "trickle down" to the poor.

To stimulate the supply side of the economy, one of Reagan's goals was to reduce federal spending. To do this he proposed, among other things, to reduce welfare programs while leaving a basic "safety net" of benefits and services in place. A 1984 study by the Southern Regional Council reported that cutbacks by the administration had reduced the welfare rolls by 4 million people. This group included 3.2 million who had lost food stamps, 330,000 dropped from AFDC, 300,000 dropped from Medicaid, and 108,000 dropped from Supplementary Security Income.[48] To make up for these losses Reagan called on the churches and the voluntary sector to resume their "historic mission" of caring for the poor.

True to the predictions of critics, including George Bush, who referred to it as "voodoo economics," Reagan's supply-side approach did not work. It led neither to rapid economic growth nor to a reduction in poverty. In fact, as discussed in Chapter 6, poverty rapidly increased under the Reagan administration. Fortunately, although it did some damage, Reagan's attack on the welfare system also failed. Reagan admirers Stuart Butler and Anna Kondratas comment

> in the fifth year of the Reagan presidency, . . . Johnson's legacy was showing every sign of withstanding the strongest attack ever mounted against it. . . . the former Johnson staffers could feel understandably confident that the essential foundations of the Great Society would outlast Ronald Reagan. With practically a full term ahead of it, the Reagan Administration onslaught [on welfare programs] was clearly stalled . . . such confidence is still [in 1987] well founded.[49]

A New Era for Antipoverty Policy

Following strong recommendations from the 1987 Governors' Conference, in 1988, Congress finally passed a welfare reform bill. This bill, entitled the Family Support Act, was described by Representative Thomas Downey (D-NY) as the first "significant change in our welfare system in 53 years," and by Senator Daniel Patrick Moynihan (D-NY) as legislation which "redefines the whole question of dependency. This is no longer to be a permanent circumstance. It is to be a transition to employment." Moynihan predicts that the program will "bring a whole generation of young American women back into the mainstream of American life."[50] Is this new law really a significant change in the welfare system and will it improve the life chances of a large number of welfare recipients? The answer to this question is, unfortunately, no. As will be described next, the act contains a few positive provisions, but nothing which will result in any radical, or even significant changes in the lives of a great number of poor people. The act is, however, significant for another reason. This is that, however ineffectual it may turn out to be, the act represents a major and forceful reformulation of the basic philosophical underpinnings of our welfare system, and in what ways and to what extent we consider ourselves to be a welfare state.

The Family Support Act In 1987 a major welfare reform bill was introduced into each house of Congress—HR1720 in the House of Representatives and S1511 in the Senate. These bills emerged from the conference committee and were signed into law during October of 1988. The centerpiece of the bill is an employment and training program which is called JOBS (for Job Opportunities and Basic Skills). The purpose of this program, commonly called "workfare," is to provide the resources (education, training, and child care) necessary to enable welfare recipients who are capable of doing so to work, and it includes provisions requiring them to take advantage of these resources. Major provisions of the law are:

> Two-parent families will be eligible for welfare assistance in all 50 states and territories. Prior to the act only 23 states had provisions for providing assistance to two-parent families, a program known as AFDC-U (U for Unemployed parent).

> Effective October 1, 1993, at least one parent in two-parent families receiving assistance must engage in unpaid work for at least 16 hours per week in what is to be called the Community Work Experience Program.

> By 1995, states will be required to have a minimum of 20 percent of family assistance recipients (minus certain exempt groups such as women with very young children) in jobs or job training.

The policy of linking the receipt of benefits to work, trumpeted by supporters of the 1988 Welfare Reform Act as a new and innovative concept, is really nothing new. Welfare has been linked to labor since the earliest attempts to deal with poverty.

States must withhold court-ordered child support from the wages of non-custodial parents.

Recipients who become self-supporting will be allowed to keep Medicaid and day care benefits for one year after leaving the welfare rolls.

Criticisms of the Family Support Act Aside from the enthusiastic endorsements that the act has received from the members of Congress who supported it, analyses of the Family Support Act from both liberals and conservatives have concluded that it will likely have little, if any, effect on the overall problems of poverty and welfare dependency. Liberals point out that a major problem of the bill is that it appropriates a ridiculously small amount of money to achieve its aims. The estimated cost of the bill is $3.34 billion over a five-year period, which seems like a lot of money. However, this "works out to $20.62—exactly twenty dollars and sixty-two cents—for every man, woman and child living in poverty in the United States of America."[51] It seems obvious that a program which only plans to spend about four dollars per year per person over a five-year period is unlikely to have much effect on the problem of poverty.

The main target of liberal criticism of the Family Support Act is its centerpiece, the JOBS program. The theory behind this program is sound, namely that when people receive welfare assistance it should be given in such a way as to not create dependency, and the way to prevent this is to be sure recipients stay connected to the labor market. Liberal critics argue that the act's provisions are unlikely to accomplish this end for several reasons. The first is that the proposed jobs do not pay enough to raise a family above the poverty line. At the current minimum wage, a person working full time, 52 weeks a year, earns only $8840, well below the poverty line of $13,400 for a family of four. The second criticism is that due to labor market conditions, it is predicted that in instances where program participants are able to move out of subsidized jobs into jobs in the general economy it is likely that the jobs they move into will pay low wages, few benefits, and be very unstable. Thus, few will actually be able to move into long-term self-support. Finally, critics point out that the JOBS program is very similar to previous employment programs such as the 1962 Manpower Development and Training Act (MDTA): the Comprehensive Employment and Training Act (CETA); Jobs Training Partnership Act (JTPA), and the Work Incentive Program (WIN), and that these programs were not successful. Gideonse and Meyers observe, "These earlier manpower training programs made little headway in providing the hard-core unemployed with marketable skills so that working could be a route out of poverty. Positive effects were at best modest: Participants . . . who became employed generally found jobs little or no better than their previous ones . . . Many in WIN returned to welfare after short-term jobs . . . [workfare] jobs usually turn out to be a poor route to good unsubsidized jobs."[52] Thus, many liberals and some radicals suspect that the work provisions of the new law are largely a sham. They point out that the current unemployment rate of 6 percent is the level that most mainstream economists, and most policy makers, consider to be the optimum level. If we go below this figure the general belief is that we will pay for it with higher inflation. Thus, the suspicion is that policy makers do not really want to lower unemployment and so the bill will not actually put more people to work (the unemployment-inflation tradeoff is discussed in greater detail in Chapter 13).[53]

Conservatives also have serious concerns regarding the Family Support Act. While they applaud the intent of the bill—to put people to work—they are concerned that its effect may be to actually encourage rather than discourage economic dependency. The major concern of conservative policy analysts such as Charles Murray has to do with the provision of the act which allows recipients to retain day care and Medicaid benefits for one year after leaving the welfare rolls. Murray expresses several reservations regarding this provision. First, he argues that people will quit work when their day care and Medicaid benefits expire in order to go back on the welfare rolls to reestablish eligibility for these benefits. The second concern expressed by Murray is that the new law makes the welfare system more attractive to people not already on assistance, and it may well result in people going on welfare who otherwise would have remained independent. He says that, "there is no way to make it easier to get off welfare without also making it more attractive to get on welfare in the first place." Perhaps Murray's greatest fear is that the law will further expand our nation's concept of entitlement by making free day care and medical care a *right* for all, or nearly all, working mothers. About this he says, "Within a few years it will become politically intolerable that women lose these benefits just because they have been off welfare for more than a year, and both benefits will become entitlements for all women up to the borders of the middle class."[54]

The New Philosophy of Antipoverty Policy   Regardless of whether or not one thinks the Family Assistance Act will result in a reduction in poverty, one thing is clear. The act represents a fundamental change in this country's approach to the problem of poverty and public dependency. The AFDC program, as it was originally formulated as part of the 1935 Social Security Act, was based on the premise that dependent

Welfare Reform Does Not Address the Basic Problem: Poverty

The welfare system and its participants are once again in the news as the Senate prepares to debate Daniel Patrick Moynihan's welfare reform package. Such debates have a long history behind them. Commissions study the issue, policy makers cast their votes and editorials appear across our newspapers. No one can deny that there are problems with the current system of public assistance in the United States. But we have lost sight of the real problem, which is poverty itself, not welfare. As long as reform focuses on the outcome of poverty and not on its underlying causes, we will not make real and lasting headway.

In spite of the potential modifications to the welfare system, the problem of poverty remains largely untouched. It has become all too popular to claim that welfare creates dependency and ultimately poverty. The truth is quite the opposite— poverty creates the need for public assistance.

People Receiving Welfare Want to Work

People turn to welfare because they are poor. The causes of that poverty are complex, including downturns in the economy, more and more single parent families and too many people without skills that make them eligible for decent-paying jobs. It is clearly easier to blame the welfare system than to unravel the problems of poverty.

Research consistently shows that individuals receiving welfare want to work and want to get off public assistance. The problem is that viable opportunities are not available to everyone. Our society is plagued by a shifting industrial base, low-paying and part-time jobs, and no reasonable child care. It is almost impossible for a single woman in a low-paying job to support her children.

Certainly there are people who abuse the welfare system. These are the cases that quickly find their way into politicians' speeches, newspapers or television talk shows. Yet such recipients are in the minority. You rarely hear people talk about the typical welfare case: a family trying its best to survive on a day-to-day basis, clearly wanting to reestablish economic independence by getting off public assistance.

Study after study shows that the vast majority of welfare recipients turn to public assistance as a last resort, that once on they want to get off the welfare rolls, and often do so after several years. Very few individuals on welfare become complacent and lazy.

Furthermore, living on welfare is anything but easy. Surviving in poverty and on public assistance is indeed extremely difficult. Many families are forced to go hungry or to substantially alter their diet near the end of the month when their checks run out. It is quite common for families to live on soup and bread during the final week in a month.

It is not a question of budgeting money wisely —the payments are simply so low that it is impossible for a family to make it through an entire month on a reasonable diet with the support available to them.

As one woman told me, "I'm not knocking the welfare program. It's a lifesaver—it's there. Because you've got a roof over your head and you're not out in the street. But on the other hand, as far as my own situation is concerned, it's pretty rough living this way. I can't see that anybody would ever settle for something like this, just for the mere fact of getting a free ride, because it's not worth it!"

Nevertheless, critics continue to argue that the welfare recipient simply needs to develop the right attitude, the incentive to go out and get a decent-paying job. The truth is, most welfare recipients would like nothing better than to have that job. While Sen. Moynihan's education and job training proposals may help, the fundamental problem is the limited number of those adequately paying jobs.

An individual in a three-person household with a head working full time at the minimum wage will still find himself below the poverty line for the year. Fast food, clerical and cleaning positions are the kind of low-paying jobs available for people struggling to find a way out of poverty. None of these pays enough to keep a family above the poverty level.

Treating Symptom Rather than Illness

In short, while welfare reform is debated and enacted, the underlying problem of poverty continues to exist. It will not go away by changing or modifying welfare requirements. Adopting workfare programs or other requirements is simply inade-

quate. To use a medical analogy, policy makers are dealing with the symptom, rather than treating the illness. People turn to welfare as a result of being in poverty. Welfare does not create poverty, poverty creates the need for welfare.

It is easier to modify public assistance programs than to address the more difficult and disturbing fact that 32 million people in the United States live below the poverty line. As a result, the welfare system is the all-too-easy scapegoat. Yet we delude ourselves into thinking we are addressing the problem, when we fail to even see what the problem is.

Source: Mark Rank, "Welfare Reform Does Not Address the Basic Problem: Poverty." Reprinted with permission.

people, mainly women with children, were poor largely due to circumstances beyond their control, and that it was in society's interest for them to stay home and take care of their children.

The Family Assistance Act represents a new approach to the problem of public dependency. First, it is based on the theory that we are now dealing with a new and different type of poverty than we have dealt with in the past. Senator Daniel Patrick Moynihan, one of the architects of the new law, argues that we are dealing with a new, "emergent form of dependency: the kind associated with *post*-industrial society." A principal factor in this new kind of dependency is a major change in family structure, resulting in what Moynihan calls the "post-marital" family. By this he is referring to the massive increase in single-parent families and the known correlation between this family form and poverty. Moynihan frankly admits that we have a very poor understanding of this phenomenon, but emphasizes that it is absolutely essential that antipoverty policy address it.[55] The provisions in the new law for collecting child support from absent parents is one attempt to address this problem. A second major change in antipoverty policy represented by the new law is that the law reflects society's changing expectations for women. It is clear from the provisions of the act that poor women, even those with children, are now expected to work.

We have no problem with features of welfare reform that emphasize work and family. What we do have concern with is the fact that discussions of welfare have recently taken on a highly moralistic tone reminiscent of an earlier and harsher era. We seem to be returning to an approach characterized by what we previously described as "blaming the victim." The conservative social critic James Q. Wilson has observed, favorably we might add, that the most important change in recent American social policy is the "deepening concern for the development of character in the citizenry." In regard to this concern, Schwartz has noted that, "Recent attempts to cope with poverty have been particularly marked by this shift: increasingly, measures are being proposed and implemented that explicitly present the restoration of moral order as a key to the reduction of poverty . . . [recent] policies . . . are premised upon an old-fashioned idea: if the poor are to escape poverty, they must somehow be encouraged to take responsibility for themselves—to hold jobs, to marry, and to obey the law."[56] To us this new approach sounds very much like the nineteenth century Charity Organization Society belief that the solution to poverty was to teach the poor about diligence, abstinence, and thrift. The approach of placing total responsibility on the poor for their own poverty didn't work then, and it undoubtably won't work now.

CONCLUSION

One of the main characters in the 1988 movie *Crossroads* is an old black man who has been confined to a mental hospital since before the civil rights movement. During the course of the movie, he and a young friend are walking across Mississippi, essentially as vagrants. They are stopped by the local sheriff in one rural county. This man fits all the negative stereotypes of the southern sheriff—he is loud and overbearing, he has a pot belly, and he is wearing mirror sunglasses. He fits all the stereotypes except one—he is black. The sheriff escorts the old black man and his young friend to the county line and tells them to leave; he warns that if they return they will be in for big trouble. The old man looks at the sheriff and says, "Yes sir, sheriff, things certainly have changed. But then again, they certainly have stayed the same." This statement precisely sums up our conclusion on the history of antipoverty programs in the United States—things certainly have changed. But then again, they certainly have stayed the same.

How have things changed? As we have seen in this chapter, over the years our society has come to realize that people need some form of protection against the insecurities that come part and parcel with an urban, industrial existence. We have accepted the fact that this protection is the duty of government. We have not yet accepted the idea that people have a right to assistance, but we absolutely believe in our responsibility to help those in need. These are, for the most part, relatively recent developments, with most coming in the current century.

How have things stayed the same? This is the discouraging part of the picture. Now, just as in

the fourteenth century, we are afraid that an adequate welfare system will encourage people not to work, even though every work program that has been tried has failed because not enough jobs and training were available—not because the poor refused to participate. The history of job programs is that they have been overrun with applicants. The myth persists that there is a huge number of able-bodied poor who are on welfare because they are lazy. The current emphasis on workfare is the latest example of the power of this myth. We are saying that we are going to make people work for the assistance they get. What we will discover, once again, is that many more poor people will show up wanting the promised work than we will be able to accommodate. We will also learn, once again, that those who do not show up fail to do so not because they are lazy, but because they are old, very young, mothers with young children and no day care, or sick or disabled.

Once again we are looking at the increase in poverty and attempting to explain it as a result of individual shortcomings. Yet, once again, it is becoming clear that the major factors are structural, and not individual. Michael Harrington points out in his book *The New American Poverty* that the poverty we are currently experiencing is different from twenty-nine years ago when Lyndon Johnson launched the War on Poverty. Harrington writes

> Now there are new structures of misery. In the winter of our national discontent in 1982–83, when there were more jobless Americans than at any other time in almost half a century, a young worker walked through the milling, sometimes menacing men on East Third Street in Manhattan and asked

the City of New York for a bed at the Municipal Shelter. One of the reasons he was there was that there are steel mills in South Korea. That is, the poor—and the entire American economy—are caught up in a crisis which is literally global. . . . The great, impersonal forces have indeed created a context in which poverty is much more difficult to abolish than it was twenty years ago. But it is not the South Koreans—or the Japanese, the West Germans, or anyone else—who have decided that the human costs of this wrenching transition should

be borne by the most vulnerable Americans. We have done that to ourselves.[57]

Concern with the poor is once again increasing. That is good. Attitudes toward the poor are still negative and largely based on beliefs that are untrue. That is bad. It is, perhaps, inevitable—a result of some flaw in the American character—that those concerned with social welfare will have to deal with the same urban folktales each time America attempts to improve the condition of the poor.

E N D N O T E S

1. Jan Harold Brunvand, *The Vanishing Hitchhiker— American Urban Legends and Their Meanings* (New York: W. W. Norton, 1981), xi.

2. Brunvand, *The Vanishing Hitchhiker,* xii.

3. Walter I. Trattner, *From Poor Law to Welfare State: A History of Social Welfare in America,* 3rd ed. (New York: The Free Press, 1984), 1.

4. Ralph Pumphrey, "Compassion and Protection: Dual Motivations in Social Welfare," *Social Service Review* 33 (1959): 21–29.

5. Michael B. Katz, *Poverty Policy in American History* (New York: Academic Press, 1983), ix.

6. Trattner, *From Poor Law to Welfare State,* 4–5.

7. Quoted in Barbara Tuchman, *A Distant Mirror: The Calamitous 14th Century* (New York: Alfred A. Knopf, 1978), xiv.

8. Tuchman, *A Distant Mirror,* xiii.

9. Karl de Schweinitz, *England's Road to Social Security* (New York: A. S. Barnes & Company, 1943), 6.

10. Joel F. Handler, "The Assault on the Ablebodied," *Reviews in American History* September (1987): 394.

11. Trattner, *From Poor Law to Welfare State,* 9–12.

12. Blanche D. Coll, *Perspectives in Public Welfare: A History* (Washington, D.C.: U.S. Government Printing Office, 1969), 5.

13. de Schweinitz, *England's Road to Social Security,* 29.

14. June Axinn and Herman Levin, *Social Welfare: A History of the American Response to Need,* 2nd ed. (New York: Longman, 1982), 17.

15. Axinn and Levin, *Social Welfare: A History of the American Response to Need,* 18–19.

16. Trattner, *From Poor Law to Welfare State,* 19.

17. Trattner, *From Poor Law to Welfare State,* 41–43.

18. Trattner, *From Poor Law to Welfare State,* 37–38.

19. Geoffrey Guest, "The Boarding of the Dependent Poor in British Colonial America," *Social Service Review* 63 (March 1989): 107.

20. Trattner, *From Poor Law to Welfare State,* 31–32.

21. Christopher Collier and James Lincoln Collier, *Decision in Philadelphia: The Constitutional Convention of 1787* (New York: Ballantine Books, 1986), 28.

22. Axinn and Levin, *Social Welfare: A History of the American Response to Need,* 38–39.

23. John Griscom, chairman, *The First Annual Report of the Managers of the Society for the Prevention of Pauperism in the City of New York* (New York: Printed by J. Seymore, 1818), 12–22, reprinted in Ralph Pumphrey and Muriel Pumphrey, *The Heritage of American Social Work: Readings in its Philosophical and Institutional Development* (New York: Columbia University Press, 1961), 60.

24. Axinn and Levin, *Social Welfare: A History of the American Response to Need,* 49.

25. Axinn and Levin, *Social Welfare: A History of the American Response to Need,* 57.

26. Handler, "The Assault On The Ablebodied," 395.

27. Coll, *Perspectives in Public Welfare: A History,* 30.

28. Blanche D. Coll, "Social Welfare: History," *Encyclopedia of Social Work,* 17th ed. (Washington, D.C.: National Association of Social Workers, 1977), 1506.

29. "President Franklin Pierce's veto of the bill resulting from Miss Dix's efforts," *Congressional Globe,* Thirty-third Congress, 1st sess. May 3, 1854, 1061–1063, reprinted in Pumphrey and Pumphrey, *The Heritage of American Social Work,* 132–134.

30. Trattner, *From Poor Law to Welfare State,* 52.

31. James Leiby, *A History of Social Welfare and Social Work in the United States* (New York: Columbia University Press, 1978), 6–12.

32. These statistics are all from United States Bureau of

the Census, *The Statistical History of the United States from Colonial Times to the Present* (New York: Basic Books, 1976).

33. Robert H. Bremner, *From the Depths: The Discovery of Poverty in the United States* (New York: New York University Press, 1956), 16–17.

34. Josephine Shaw Lowell, "Methods of Relief for the Unemployed," *The Forum,* XVI (1893–1894): 659, cited in Bremner, *From the Depths,* 22.

35. Quoted in Robert H. Bremner, *The Public Good: Philanthropy and Welfare in the Civil War Era* (New York: Alfred A. Knopf, 1980), 200.

36. Josephine Shaw Lowell, "The Economic Effects of Public Outdoor Relief," *Proceedings of the National Conference of Charities and Corrections, 1890* (Boston 1890): 81–82.

37. Roswell B. Mason quoted in Bremner, *The Public Good,* 192.

38. Leiby, *A History of Social Welfare and Social Work,* 191–192.

39. Leiby, *A History of Social Welfare and Social Work,* 196.

40. Leiby, *A History of Social Welfare and Social Work,* 210–215.

41. Michael Katz, *In the Shadow of the Poorhouse: A Social History of Welfare in America* (New York: Basic Books, 1986).

42. Much of this section was published earlier in Philip R. Popple, "Contexts of Practice," in *Handbook of Clinical Social Work,* Aaron Rosenblatt and Diana Waldfogel, eds. (San Francisco: Jossey-Bass, 1983), 81–84.

43. Allen Nevins and Henry Steele Commager, *A Short History of the United States* (New York: Alfred A. Knopf, 1966), 470–471.

44. Trattner, *From Poor Law to Welfare State,* 278.

45. Clinch Calkins, *Some Folks Won't Work* (New York: Harcourt Brace, 1930), 160–162.

46. Samuel Mencher, "Newburgh: The Recurrent Crisis of Public Assistance," *Social Work* 7 (January 1962): 3–11.

47. Trattner, *From Poor Law to Welfare State,* 300.

48. William E. Schmidt, "Study Says Reagan's Cuts in Aid to Poor Affected South the Most," *New York Times,* 15 March 1985.

49. Stuart Butler and Anna Kondratas, *Out of the Poverty Trap: A Conservative Strategy for Welfare Reform* (New York: The Free Press, 1987), 1–2.

50. David Stoesz and Howard Jacob Karger, "Welfare Reform: From Illusion to Reality," *Social Work 35* (March 1990): 144; Sarah K. Gideonse and William R. Meyers, "Why the Family Support Act Will Fail," *Challenge* (September–October 1989): 33.

51. George P. Brockway, "Reality and Welfare Reform," *The New Leader* (28 November, 1988): 14–16.

52. Gideonse and Meyers, "Why the Family Support Act Will Fail," 34.

53. Brockway, "Reality and Welfare Reform," 16.

54. Charles Murray, "New Welfare Bill, New Welfare Cheats," *Wall Street Journal* (13 October, 1988), A22.

55. Daniel Patrick Moynihan, "Toward a Post-Industrial Social Policy," *The Public Interest 96* (Summer 1989): 16–27.

56. Joel Schwartz, "The Moral Environment of the Poor," *The Public Interest 103* (Summer 1991): 21–37.

57. Michael Harrington, *The New American Poverty* (New York: Holt, Reinhart, and Winston, 1984), 1–2.

C·H·A·P·T·E·R

nine

Child Welfare

Y ou can find the stories in the newspaper of any large city. Sometimes they are in the headlines and sometimes they are buried in the back pages, but read the paper for a few weeks and you will find them.

- A two-year-old child is left with his young mother's intoxicated boyfriend while she goes to work. The child won't stop crying and the boyfriend, in a fit of rage, hits him with a cast iron skillet, killing him.

- A twelve-year-old girl goes to the school nurse complaining of itching and burning sensations. She is referred to a public health clinic, where she is diagnosed as suffering from genital herpes. A social worker for child protective services investigates and finds that the girl has been sexually abused by her stepfather, a man who has served five years in prison as a result of a rape conviction and who is currently free on parole. The mother tearfully told the social worker, "He told me he had been framed on that rape charge and I believed him."

- Responding to the call of a neighbor, the police go to an apartment to find three children ages two, three, and five staying by themselves. The apartment is a shambles, the children are dirty, and the only evidence of food is an empty peanut butter jar, a warm jug of milk, and a few nearly empty boxes of dry cereal. When interviewed by the police, the five-year-old stated that their mother no longer lived with them and their father had not been home for several days. The father showed up two days later, stating, "Those kids can take care of themselves every now and then. Why heck, that Cindy is just like a little mother. She's sure better than their real one ever was."

- In an area of town known to local residents as the "meat market," a man is arrested after approaching an undercover vice officer and offering to arrange a "date" for him with a thirteen-year-old girl. Upon investigation it was learned that the girl was the man's daughter and that she had been used to support his drug habit for over a year. The child's mother had supported her husband's drug habit by working as a prostitute and apparently had managed to protect her daughter. However, two years ago she died from appendicitis and the man turned to his daughter for support. An outraged judge and jury sentenced the man to fifty years in prison and the state child welfare agency was called upon to attempt to restore some of the girl's childhood.

The family is the social institution we rely on for the care, protection, and nurturance of children. We believe that every child has a right to grow up in a warm, loving family group. Perhaps because our society provides so little support for families, they break down and fail to provide even the most basic requisites for a healthy childhood far more often than we care to believe. Because Americans tend to distrust government and to strongly believe that parents have a right to rear their children in their own manner and to the best of their abilities, we are hesitant to intervene on the behalf of children. However, there is a vague line below which we feel we must intervene to protect the child. When child care sinks to this point, society looks to the field of social work known as child protective services, an important part of child welfare, to deal with the problem.

The family is the social institution we rely on to provide for the care and nurturance of children.

DEFINITION

In a broad sense, *child welfare* refers to all the aspects of society essential for the well-being of children. Included are day care, education, medical care, parks and recreation, and public safety. Child welfare as an area of social welfare and a field of social work has a somewhat more limited focus. In this more limited context, child welfare has generally been concerned with the special needs of children and their families when parental functioning is impaired; when the family lives in such poverty that effective parenting is impossible; or when the child, because of developmental, emotional, or behavioral problems may not be able to function within his or her own family.

Child welfare, according to the Child Welfare League of America, involves providing social services to children and young people whose parents are not able to adequately fulfill their child-rearing responsibilities, or whose communities fail to provide resources and protection that families and children require.[1] Kadushin and Martin expand on this definition

> Child welfare services are those services required when parents or children are either incapable of implementing or unwilling to implement (or both) their respective role requirements, or when a serious discrepancy arises between the role expectations of the community and the individual's performance.[2]

They list seven problems of role functioning in the parent-child-community network that are likely to lead to a need for child welfare services:

1. *Parental role unoccupied.* For any of a large number of reasons, one or both parents are not present in a child's life. In many single-parent families, the one parent is able to adequately fulfill all necessary roles and the child has no unusual problems. However, the absence of one parent greatly increases the risk of problems, for example, in the case of the Brown family.

Child Protective Service was called by a neighbor who reported that the five Brown children, ages three to nine, were being left at home alone. The social worker who investigated the case found this to be true. Mr. Brown is a single father trying to rear five children by himself following his wife's desertion of the family. He told the social worker, "I know these kids shouldn't be left alone; it just worries me to death. But I've got to work, and day care even for just the three little ones will eat up nearly all my pay." The social worker helped Mr. Brown arrange day care in a subsidized center which he could afford. She recommended that the case remain open because of the likelihood of Mr. Brown needing ongoing support in adequately fulfilling all parental roles.

2. *Parental incapacity.* The parent is present and may want to fulfill his or her role requirements, but is prevented from doing so by physical, mental, or emotional inadequacy, or by a lack of knowledge or training. A threat to a child's safety resulting from parental incapacity is illustrated by the Valdez case.

The night intake worker was called to the public hospital emergency room one evening by the resident physician. The mother of seven-month-old Maria Valdez had brought her in with severe scalding burns on her legs and torso. The resident had also called the police and, diagnosing the situation as intentional child abuse, demanded that the mother, Juanita Valdez, be arrested. When the social worker met Ms. Valdez in the hospital waiting room, he met not the monster described by the resident, but a sweet, loving woman whom he estimated to be functioning intellectually on the level of a seven-year-old.

Over the next few days he was able to piece together what had happened. Ms. Valdez was in the habit of placing Maria in the bathtub of her old apartment and turning on the hot water tap. The water would come out lukewarm because the water heater was so old it barely worked. She would then go to the kitchen and begin dinner while Maria's bath ran. Just prior to Maria's injury, the apartment owner had replaced the water heater and had sent a note to that effect to all the tenants. Ms. Valdez was unable to connect the fact that there was a new water heater with the necessity to change Maria's bath routine. The result was that Maria was seriously injured.

3. *Role rejection.* The parent, often because he or she did not want a child in the first place, either consciously or unconsciously rejects the parental role, resulting in varying degrees of failure in role performance. An example of this is the Murphy case.

Anna Nelms brought one-year-old Cecily Murphy to the Children's Emergency Center early on a Monday morning. She reported that she had been the child's day care provider since Cecily was three months old. Cecily had been placed in day care because her mother Elizabeth was a single parent and had gone to work full time. Ms. Nelms reported that Ms. Murphy had dropped the child off at her house as usual on Friday morning but had never returned to pick her up. The social worker called Ms. Murphy's work number and found that she was at work and she agreed to meet him at her home that evening. When he went for the meeting, she was not there. The next day he went to the hospital where Ms. Murphy worked as a medical secretary and insisted on speaking with her. Ms. Murphy was a very attractive and apparently intelligent nineteen-year-old who appeared to be overwhelmed with the demands of parenthood. She told the social worker that since she became pregnant with Cecily her life had been miserable. She said, "Two years ago I was a carefree kid and now I'm well on my way to being an old hag."

The social worker made another appointment to meet with Ms. Murphy and begin working on her problems. Once again, she missed the appointment. This became a pattern over the next two months, with the social worker tracking Ms. Murphy down, Ms. Murphy making commitments to meet with him or with other resources and then not following through. Finally Ms. Murphy was contacted and told that a court hearing had been set asking for permanent custody of her child so that she could be placed for adoption. Her rights were explained to her and she was told that if she would like to work to regain custody of her child, the agency was still open to helping her. Ms. Murphy did not show up for the hearing, an omission interpreted by the court as a clear statement that she was rejecting the role of parent. The court terminated Ms. Murphy's rights and Cecily was placed in an adoptive home and at last word was doing well. Ms. Murphy has never contacted the agency to inquire about Cecily.

4. *Intrarole conflict.* In this type of situation the parents are in conflict regarding role definition. They fail to reach agreement about who is supposed to do what, for, and with, the child.

> The school social worker was contacted by the principal of Lincoln Elementary School. She reported that the Andrews twins, Billy and Becky, were frequently complaining in their first grade class that they had not had breakfast. When the social worker contacted the parents, he found a rather prosperous couple. Both had demanding careers and were unable to agree on who had responsibility for certain household and parental tasks. Each felt the other should feel very guilty about not getting breakfast for the twins. The parents were referred for family counseling, and the level of child care was greatly improved.

5. *Interrole conflict.* This is the situation in which a person is unable to adequately discharge parental responsibilities because of the interference of other social roles. Recent social changes which increase the likelihood of both parents having demanding careers outside of the house often leads to interrole conflict, as the following situation illustrates.

> Whitney, the twelve-year-old daughter of Drs. Stephen and Barbara Bradford, has been in counseling with a clinical social worker for over a year. The counseling was a result of a number of behavior problems exhibited by Whitney that appeared to be increasing as she approached adolescence. The social worker attributes most of Whitney's problems to the fact that she receives inadequate attention from her parents, who have deferred most child-rearing duties to the family's maid. The parents realize that they should devote more time to their daughter, but have not been successful in this effort. Stephen and Barbara are family physicians who have a clinic in an underserved, impoverished area of the city. They work twelve to eighteen hours a day, often seven days a week, and still do not reach all the people in need of medical care. When they did tear themselves away to spend an hour talking to Whitney's social worker, Barbara lamented, "What are we to do? I feel as though we're between a rock and a hard place. If we don't start spending more time with Whitney, she'll probably be screwed up for the rest of her life. But if we do cut down on our hours to be with her, people are going to die from lack of medical care."

6. *Child incapacity and/or handicap.* An exceptional child places exceptional demands on parents. Even the most capable, organized, and well-adjusted parents are greatly taxed by the needs of a child with a physical handicap or emotional disturbance. Parents or caretakers whose abilities and resources are marginal will often be unable to cope, as is illustrated by the Costa case.

> Sam and Gena Costa came to the child welfare office requesting that their two-year-old, Stanley, be placed in an institution. The Costas were barely functioning as parents to their

three older kids, and when they learned that Gena was pregnant with Stanley, they didn't see how they would cope with a fourth child. A problem became a disaster when it turned out that Stanley was seriously hyperactive. The Costas stated that they were at the end of their rope and felt that they could adequately parent the other three children only if Stanley were placed in an institution or foster home. After a good deal of work by the social worker, including finding day care for Stanley and training for the parents on managing a hyperactive child, placement was prevented.

7. *Deficiency of community resources.* Parents are sometimes unable to adequately implement their roles because of a lack of community resources. For example, if both parents need to work but there is no day care available, they are caught in a double bind. They have a choice of either quitting work and thereby failing in the role of breadwinner, or leaving the children unattended and failing in the role of caretaker. Or, as in the following situation, children are often placed in foster care because less drastic alternatives are not available.

> Susan Dobbins, a child welfare worker, sits back and sighs with frustration: "John Ryals has been in three foster homes during the past three years and he doesn't need to be. He needs to be home with his mother. She's really a great mother but she occasionally goes into deep, black depressions. When she does, she gets sent to the state mental hospital and Johnny to a foster home. If we had better community mental health service for Mrs. Ryals and homemaker service to come in and help with Johnny when Mrs. Ryals is depressed, she wouldn't have to go into the hospital and he wouldn't have to go to a foster home. I'll tell you another thing, it would cost a whole lot less!"

Therefore, in keeping with the definition, discussed in Chapter 2, of social welfare as the management of dependency in society, child welfare is defined as those services provided when dependency is created by problems in functioning in the parent–child–community role network. The child may be considered dependent because he or she is lacking parental care, and the parent may be considered dependent on society for help in fulfilling his or her expected roles. Dependency can also result from a lack of service and support available in the community. Child welfare services are nearly always provided on a residual basis (see Chapter 2); that is, they come into play only after the institution considered to be primary, the family, has broken down. This is unfortunate, because there is no area in which institutional services are more needed. In today's fragmented, fast-moving society, in which more and more families are finding it essential for both parents to work, even the most capable people are finding it difficult to adequately fulfill all parental roles.

The preceding discussion of definitions of child welfare is well and good, but it does not differentiate child maltreatment from acceptable child-rearing behavior. Just what types of acts toward children are considered to represent a role breakdown serious enough to warrant intervention? After reviewing a number of definitions of child maltreatment from the perspective of the medical, legal, and social work professions, Faller and Russo identified four requirements for a situation to be defined as child maltreatment:

1. First, there must be some definable parental behavior directed toward the child. This may be an act of commission (abuse) or omission (neglect), and it can be either physical or mental.

2. Second, there must be some demonstrable harm to the child. This may be a physical injury or condition, or it may be evidence of psychological damage, or both.
3. Third, a causal link needs to be established between parental behavior and the harm to the child.
4. Finally, the social worker needs to feel that the maltreatment is sufficiently serious to warrant intervention.[3]

STATISTICAL PROFILE

In this section we will concentrate on child maltreatment, which is the area of child welfare in which most social workers are involved. Unfortunately, we do not have precise statistics regarding child maltreatment. Because of the lack of a uniform definition, what one source reports as abuse or neglect another does not. Also maltreatment, like crime, is private, so people attempt to cover it up and thus avoid becoming part of the statistics. For these reasons, plus the historic lack of attention to the problem, it has only been recently that much effort has been expended to discover the dimensions of the problem of child maltreatment.

From 1974 to 1986 an excellent source of data regarding child maltreatment was the annual *National Study of Child Neglect and Abuse Reporting* (referred to hereafter as the National Study) conducted by the American Humane Association and funded by the federal Children's Bureau. Unfortunately this project was funded for only a very reduced study in 1987 and has not been funded since. The National Study consisted of a nationwide compilation of data derived from official reports of child maltreatment documented by state child protective service agencies. A more limited study has been conducted since 1982 by the National Committee for Prevention of Child Abuse (referred to hereafter as the NCPCA Study). The most recent data from the NCPCA Study is for the 1989/90 fiscal year. The major shortcoming of both the National Study and the NCPCA Study is that they compile *reports* of abuse and neglect rather than *incidence*. In other words these studies consist only of those cases known to officials and it is uncertain if these represent 80 percent of all cases, 50 percent, 25 percent, or whatever. In order to estimate the actual incidence, a number of studies have been conducted based on statistical samples. Notable among these are Gil,[4] and Straus, Gelles, and Steinmetz,[5] which will be discussed later.

Researchers have been frustrated in their effort to find clear patterns among the data. Pelton notes

> I was often warned by experienced social workers that abuse and neglect problems are so varied that they defy generalizations. As a social scientist, I expect to discover generalizations. Unfortunately, I found that the cases conformed more closely to their advice than to my optimism.[6]

Therefore, the following data should be regarded as rough estimates.

Number of Children Involved   The NCPCA Study for the 1989/90 fiscal year estimates that 2,508,000 children were reported to state protective service agencies as victims of maltreatment. These figures work out to a rate of about 39 children per 1000 United States child population.

Because the NCPCA Study consists only of cases actually reported to child protective agencies, it is an underrepresentation of the actual incidence. Several studies based on statistical samples have attempted to ascertain the actual incidence. Gil estimated the incidence of abuse alone to range from 2,500,000 to 4,070,000.[7] Straus, Gelles, and Steinmetz, who limited their study to abuse and to children between the ages of three and seventeen, estimated that between 1.4 and 1.9 million were subjected to abuse during a one-year period.[8] Thus, while figures are inadequate to reach many solid conclusions, it is clear that the problem is immense.

Type of Maltreatment The NCPCA Study data on "Type of Maltreatment" is summarized in Table 9–1. As can be seen by inspecting the table, neglect is by far the most frequently reported type of maltreatment.

Sex The National Study found that reports of maltreatment were fairly evenly divided between boys and girls. In 1986, 46.5 percent of reports involved boys and 53.5 percent involved girls. The proportion of reports involving girls has been increasing in recent years, up from 51.1 percent in 1983, because of the increase in sexual abuse referrals, which predominantly involve female victims.

Social Class While it is true that child maltreatment occurs in all social classes, the data indicates that it is most common among families in lower socioeconomic levels. In a survey of abusive families, Gil found that nearly 60 percent had been on public

TABLE 9–1   Type of maltreatment[a]

Data from Those States with Comparable Classification Systems for the Four Major Types of Maltreatment[b]	Physical Abuse %	Sexual Abuse %	Neglect %	Emotional Maltreatment %	Other[c] %
Average percentage breakdown for all cases (n = 22 states)	27	15	46	9	4
Breakdown for reported cases only (n = 11 states)	28	15	45	9	3
Breakdown for substantiated cases only (n = 11 states)	25	14	47	9	5

[a]Total percentages may add to more than 100 due to rounding.
[b]Excludes Arizona which classified 50% of reports as other.
[c]In many cases, "other" includes abandonment and dependency.
Source: The National Center on Child Abuse Prevention Research, Current Trends in Child Abuse Reporting and Fatalities: The Results of the 1990 Annual Fifty State Survey (Chicago, IL: National Committee for Prevention of Child Abuse, 1991), 13.

assistance at some time and that slightly more than 34 percent were receiving welfare at the time of the report.[9] The National Study data for 1986 found that 48.9 percent of the families reported for child maltreatment were receiving public assistance. Pelton surveyed child protective service records in New Jersey and found that 79 percent of the families had incomes below the poverty line. These figures have often been rejected, based on the theory that poor people are more susceptible to being reported to public agencies than middle-class people, and thus the figures reflect reporting bias rather than an actual relationship between socioeconomic class and child maltreatment. However, social scientists now conclude that while poor people may be slightly overreported, it is very probable that a greater proportion of poor children are maltreated.[10]

Race   All studies of child maltreatment have found that minority groups are overrepresented. The 1986 National Study found that minority groups represented 36.1 percent of reports of child maltreatment. Minorities make up about 18 percent of the United States population. However, it is generally thought that these figures represent differences in social class rather than race. One study conducted by the American Humane Association found that when income was controlled for, rates for nonwhite children were actually slightly lower than for white children.[11]

Age   The 1983 National Study collected the data in Table 9–2 on pages 262–263 regarding type of maltreatment and age of involved children. Although maltreatment occurs throughout childhood, it should be noted that clearly the younger a child is, the greater the danger of serious harm.

Trend   Probably the most significant finding of the National Study is not the absolute level of reporting, but the extent to which reporting has increased over time. This information is presented in Figure 9–1 on page 264. The overall reporting levels have increased by 274 percent between 1976 and 1990. It is doubtful that these figures represent anywhere near this large an increase in the actual numbers of children being maltreated. Rather, they mostly reflect factors that increase the likelihood of incidents being reported. These factors, as given by the authors of the National Study, include: the allocation of more federal money for reporting; the strengthening of state reporting laws (physicians, teachers, social workers, and other professionals who work with children are now required to report in all states); the redesign of state social service department intake systems; the implementation of 24-hour hotline systems; and the massive public awareness campaigns in the 1970s.

In 1969 when David Gil estimated that the incidence of child abuse was somewhere between 2.5 and 4.07 million, he was severely criticized. Straus's 1980 estimate of 6.5 million has also been criticized. These numbers were, and still are, mind-boggling. If true, they mean that between 4 and 10.4 percent of all children in the United States are victims of abuse. Because we know that physical abuse accounts for only about one-third of all maltreatment (neglect and sexual abuse account for about two-thirds), these figures mean that between 12 and 31.2 percent of children are subjected to some form of maltreatment. Recent findings regarding sexual abuse lend credence to these alarming figures. According to the best estimates available, somewhere between 9 and 54 percent of women and between 3 and 9 percent of men were sexually abused as children.[12] The steadily increasing numbers of actual reports compiled by the National

TABLE 9–2   Type of maltreatment and age of involved child ($N = 381,168$)

Age	Major or Major with Minor Physical Injury ($N = 8,800$)	Minor or Unspecified Physical Injury ($N = 71,884$)	Sexual Maltreatment ($N = 27,714$)	Deprivation of Necessities ($N = 192,223$)
0–5	64.1%	37.3%	24.8%	48.6%
6–11	19.8%	32.6%	34.3%	33.2%
12–17	15.9%	30.0%	40.6%	18.2%
Total	100%	100%	100%	100%

Source: American Association for Protecting Children, *Highlights of Official Child Abuse and Neglect Reporting* (Denver, CO: American Humane Association, 1985), 16.

Study and the NCPCA Study indicate that these figures may be more accurate than we dared imagine.

DYNAMICS

Faced with the staggering statistics on child abuse and neglect, the question that demands an answer is, "Why do people do such things?" The most obvious answer, and the one that dominated thinking until recently, is that parents who abuse and neglect their children are psychologically sick, or perhaps even evil. Steele and Pollack[13] refer to abusive parents as a "gold mine of psychopathology"; Kempe and his associates[14] describe the abuser as the "psychopathological member of the family"; Young[15] says that "neglecting parents tend to wear blinders imposed by their own unsatisfied needs," and refers to abusive parents as "parents who hate"; and finally, Eisenberg refers to abusive parents as having "cancer of the soul."[16] A great deal of research has been done on this question in recent years. The general consensus that has emerged is that the dynamics of abuse and neglect are much too complex to be adequately explained by a simple psychopathological model. It is now thought that abuse and neglect result from the interaction of three types of factors: individual-parent factors, family factors, and environmental factors. The following discussion of these factors is based on an essay by Faller and Ziefert.[17]

Individual-Parent Factors   While the majority of parents who maltreat their children have no diagnosable psychopathological condition, researchers and practitioners have identified a number of personality traits and social attributes that are frequently found among the parents. Among the more common are:

- *Feelings of low self-esteem.* These parents often feel they are worthless, incompetent, and bad. Neglectful parents often neglect themselves as well as their children.
- *Excessive dependency.* Neglectful and abusive parents look to others to fulfill needs; mature adults take care of themselves.

Emotional Maltreatment (N = 24,808)	Other Maltreatment (N = 15,917)	Multiple Maltreatment (N = 39,822)	Percent of All Involved Children (N = 717,315)	Percent of All U.S. Children (N = 62,580,000)
34.0%	47.0%	41.5%	43.3%	34.5%
34.2%	26.8%	31.7%	32.5%	30.7%
31.9%	26.2%	27.0%	24.1%	34.7%
100%	100%	100%	100%	100%

- *Serious difficulty coping with the demands of parenting.* They often expect their children to parent them rather than vice-versa.
- *Impulsivity.* Everyone has impulses to do things that are improper. These range from mild things like going to the beach instead of going to work on a nice day, to more serious things like striking someone when they frustrate or irritate us. Part of maturing is learning to control these impulses, or in Freudian terms, developing a superego. Maltreating parents often have not done this.
- *Rigid personalities.* Maltreating parents often have fixed ideas about the way things should be and they are unable to tolerate their children deviating from these ideas.
- *Deficient consciences.* These parents often demonstrate an inability to sympathize with their children and a great ability to rationalize their own behavior. Therefore, they feel little remorse when they maltreat their children.
- *Childhood deprivation.* Often, maltreating parents are repeating child-rearing patterns they experienced as children.
- *Social isolation.* Maltreating families are often cut off from their social environment. They avoid, and in turn, are avoided by, neighbors. They rarely participate in church or community activities, and they are often alienated from their extended families.

A small proportion of parents who maltreat their children do have diagnosable personality disorders. Among these are:

- *Psychopathy.* A true psychopath is a person who, because of severe deficiencies in his or her own nurturing, has developed a grossly distorted superego. These people do not have deficient consciences; they have *no* consciences. Thus, when they harm a child, they feel no remorse at all. This is a very rare condition and accounts for less than 5 percent of abusive parents.
- *Depression.* This is probably the most common personality disorder among maltreating parents, particularly neglectful parents. These people feel so bad that they find it impossible to get up the energy to care for their children.
- *Psychosis.* A psychotic parent is one who suffers from a distorted sense of reality. They may think that strangers are trying to kill them, they may hear the voice of

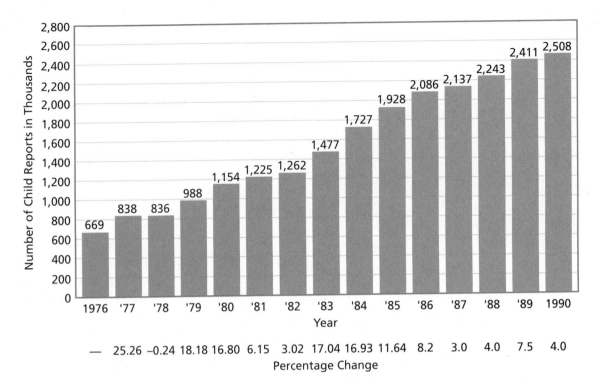

	1976	'77	'78	'79	'80	'81	'82	'83	'84	'85	'86	'87	'88	'89	1990
Number of Child Reports in Thousands	669	838	836	988	1,154	1,225	1,262	1,477	1,727	1,928	2,086	2,137	2,243	2,411	2,508
Percentage Change	—	25.26	–0.24	18.18	16.80	6.15	3.02	17.04	16.93	11.64	8.2	3.0	4.0	7.5	4.0

FIGURE 9–1   **National Estimates of Child Abuse and Neglect Reports 1976–1990**

Source: American Association for Protecting Children, *Highlights of Official Child Abuse and Neglect Reporting* (Denver, CO: American Humane Association, 1988), 7; Deborah Daro and Karen McCurdy, *Current Trends in Child Abuse Reporting and Fatalities: The Results of the 1990 Annual Fifty State Survey* (Chicago, IL: The National Committee for Prevention of Child Abuse, 1991), 6.

God, or they may think that their child is possessed by the devil. Although only about 5 percent of parents who mistreat their children are psychotic, these children are in great danger.

- *Mental retardation.* Mentally retarded parents can be caring and nurturing. However, they often lack the knowledge and skill to rear children adequately (without help) and thus have difficulty adequately protecting their children.
- *Substance abuse.* Drug addiction and alcoholism contribute to child maltreatment in two ways. One way is that the alcohol or drugs can lower a parent's impulse control, and he or she may express underlying anger by injuring the child. The second way is that children are often neglected because the parent is unable to perform everyday tasks while under the influence of alcohol or drugs.

Family Factors   When a case of child maltreatment comes to light, there are a number of questions to be answered. The most disturbing questions relate to the role of family members other than the victim and the perpetrator. If a child is abused by one parent, we ask, "Where was the other parent during all this? Why didn't he or she protect the child?" "Where were the brothers and sisters? If they were older, why didn't they intervene? If they were younger, why didn't they tell someone?" In neglect situations, we ask questions such as, "How could the whole family have ignored the need for medical treatment? How could both parents have been so careless?" The answers to questions such as these lie in the realm of family dynamics. Although we do not yet fully understand these answers, some of the important dynamics we are learning about are:

- *Parental collusion.* Although one parent may be the active perpetrator in abuse cases, or the parent most obviously failing in his or her role responsibilities in neglect cases, it is rare that the other parent does not play some part in the maltreatment. The passive parent is generally aware of what is happening and gives covert permission and support to the active parent.
- *Scapegoating.* Often one child becomes the focus for anger and aggression present in family relations. Other family members "take out" their rage and aggression on the designated child.
- *Single parent status.* Single parents are heavily overrepresented among protective service cases. Single parents often lack adequate resources, including financial resources, for raising children and our society is not particularly generous in its assistance to them.
- *Adolescent parents.* Young parents are overrepresented in child welfare caseloads. Late adolescence and early adulthood are stressful times without the added burden of parenthood—often single parenthood.
- *The extended family.* The extended family is considered a primary source of support during times of stress. Parents who maltreat their children are frequently found to not have this source of support.
- *Factors related to the child.* Children often play a significant part in their own maltreatment in the sense that they place greater demands on their caretakers than the caretakers are able to cope with. A very active child places more stress on parents and is therefore more likely to be a target for abuse. A passive child places fewer demands on parents and is at greater risk of neglect. A child who is different in some way—mentally retarded, handicapped, or hearing impaired—has been found to be at greater risk of maltreatment.

Environmental Factors   A time-honored bit of practice wisdom among social workers is that child maltreatment results from internal stress combined with external press. Internal stress refers to the individual parent and the family factors discussed previously. The external press refers to factors in the environment that overload the abilities of individuals and families to cope with difficulties in healthy ways. Major types of environmental factors that relate to child maltreatment are:

- *Chronic stressors.* These are long-term problematic conditions with which a family must cope. Simply being a parent is a chronic stressor, especially for parents who are too young, ignorant, or not ready for the responsibilities of having children. Having a family member who is chronically ill, either physically or mentally, is another great stress on a family. Probably the most persistent chronic stressor is poverty. Rearing children is much easier for parents who can afford babysitters, summer camps, music lessons, nice houses, and innumerable other things. When you can never financially afford a break from your kids, and when you can never say yes to their desires, parenthood can be a hard road indeed.
- *Situational stressors.* These are changes in a family's social situation, generally, but

A CLOSER LOOK

Incidents Defined as Child Maltreatment

Specifically, what type of incidents are considered to be sufficiently serious to warrant intervention? A useful list was developed as part of the *National Study of the Incidence and Severity of Child Abuse and Neglect.* The forms of maltreatment identified are:

Physical Assault with Bodily Injury

1. Assault with implement (knife, strap, cigarette, etc.)
2. Assault without implement (hit with fist, bit, etc., or means of assault unknown)

Sexual Exploitation

3. Intrusion (acts involving penile penetration—oral, anal or genital; e.g., rape, incest)
4. Molestation with genital contact
5. Other or unknown

Other Abusive Treatment

6. Verbal or emotional assault (threatening, belittling, etc.)
7. Close confinement (tying, locking in closet, etc.)
8. Other or unknown

Refusal of Custody

9. Abandonment
10. Other (expulsion, refusal to accept custody of runaway, etc.)

Inattention to Remedial Health Care Needs

11. Refused to allow or provide needed care for diagnosed condition or impairment

12. Unwarranted delay or failure to seek needed care

Inattention to Physical Needs

13. Inadequate supervision
14. Disregard of avoidable hazards in home (exposed wiring, broken glass, etc.)
15. Inadequate nutrition, clothing, or hygiene
16. Other (e.g., reckless disregard of child's safety: driving while intoxicated, etc.)

Inattention to Educational Needs

17. Knowingly "permitted" chronic truancy
18. Other (repeatedly kept child home, failed to enroll, etc.)

Inattention to Emotional/ Developmental Needs

19. Inadequate nurturance/affection (e.g., failure-to-thrive)
20. Knowingly "permitted" maladaptive behavior (delinquency, serious drug/alcohol abuse, etc.)
21. Other

Other

22. Involuntary neglect (due to hospitalization, incarceration, etc.)
23. General neglect (more than two of codes 13–16)

Source: Children's Bureau, U.S. Department of Health and Human Services. *Study Findings, National Study of the Incidence and Severity of Child Abuse and Neglect,* Appendix A, "Data Forms for Child Protective Service Agencies," (Microfiche, September 1988), 50.

not always, for the worse. Situational stressors to which the family may be unable to accommodate include unemployment, moving, divorce, homelessness, death, birth of a new baby, a promotion, and the mother going to work. These stressors produce tension and often a role overload which may be instrumental in abuse or neglect.

- *Precipitating stressors.* These are incidents that immediately trigger an incident of maltreatment. They are, in Faller and Ziefert's words, "the straws which break the camel's back."[18] Precipitating stressors are most commonly identified in cases of abuse, but they sometimes lead to neglect in the form of abandonment or withdrawal from parenting responsibilities. The most common form of precipitating stressor is actual or perceived child misbehavior.

Additional Factors   Two additional factors need to be considered in order to understand the dynamics of child maltreatment. These are our culture's general ambivalence about violence, and subcultures that approve of violence to a greater degree than the rest of society.

Although we in the United States consider ourselves to be a peace-loving people, we exhibit a degree of approval toward physical violence. The success of movies such as "The Last Boy Scout," "Robocop," and martial arts films of all types demonstrate this. Further, we sanction a level of violence directed toward children that is considerably higher than we do toward adults. Imagine what would happen if a supervisor rapped a bookkeeper on the knuckles with a ruler because his work was late, or if an executive struck his secretary with his belt because her work was sloppy. Everyone would be horrified, and the perpetrators would likely end up in court on criminal or civil charges. However, if a parent, or even a teacher, were to do these things to a child they would generally be considered to be acting in a perfectly acceptable manner. Gil asserts that the culturally sanctioned approval of physical violence toward children is the "basic dimension upon which all other factors [contributing to child abuse] are imposed."[19]

The final dynamic related to child maltreatment is the existence of subcultures within society that sanction the use of a greater degree of violence toward children than does society in general, or who hold greatly different standards regarding appropriate care. Although the relationship between social class and use of violence is complex and not fully understood, there is evidence that lower-class parents are more likely to condone the use of violence than middle-class parents.[20] In recent years there have been a number of highly publicized cases of religious groups who practice what most of us would consider to be child abuse in the name of proper, biblically supported child rearing. There are also a number of subgroups within our society who for religious or other reasons do not believe in modern medical care. When a child in one of these groups becomes critically ill, intervention becomes necessary to protect the child. With our tradition of religious freedom, this is a very touchy area.

HISTORICAL PERSPECTIVE

The earliest known provision for the protection of children in this country was a statute passed in Massachusetts in 1735 which provided that when parents "were unable, or neglected to, provide necessaries for the substance and support of their children . . . and where persons bring up their children in such gross ignorance that they do not know, or are not able to distinguish the alphabet, or twenty-four letters, at the age of six years, the overseers might bind out such children to good families for a decent

Poverty is one of the most common chronic stressors of parents with young children.

Christian education."[21] This law, however, was an anomaly. We do not find evidence of widespread, serious concern for child protection until well into the nineteenth century.

The Emergence of Concern for Children

Why is it that our society did not exhibit much concern about the welfare of children until one hundred fifty years ago? There are three general, interrelated reasons: the lengthening of childhood, the breakdown of the ability of the family and the church to manage child dependency, and a gradually changing conception of childhood.

The Lengthening of Childhood   Prior to the Industrial Revolution, childhood was relatively short because in a rural agricultural setting, children became economically useful and began to fulfill adult roles at young ages. On a farm, where most children grew up, a five- or six-year-old would be a productive part of the family, gathering eggs, weeding the garden, and bringing lunch to the workers in the fields. Children's economic value quickly exceeded their cost. Higgeson wrote in his 1629 *New England's Plantation* that, "little children here by setting of corne may earne much more than their own maintenance."[22] Bossard and Boll note "that children, little children, worked hard. But adults worked hard too. Hard work was a colonial necessity for both. The struggle for existence in the New World was a stern reality."[23] Children who did not grow up on farms were often apprenticed at an early age, and thus they became productive and assumed adult functions. Childhood as a lengthy period of immaturity and dependence prior to assuming adult responsibilities, which is how we think of it today, did not exist until well into the nineteenth century.

The Breakdown of the Ability of the Extended Family and the Church to Manage Child Dependency Prior to the Industrial Revolution, which in the United States really took hold during the mid-nineteenth century, family and child problems were more or less adequately dealt with by the basic social institutions of the extended family and the church. If a child were orphaned, he or she would generally be taken in either by a member of the extended family or by a church family. If a child were being neglected or treated cruelly by his or her family, informal social pressure would be exerted on the family, hopefully resulting in an improvement in the level of care. If parents were mentally or physically ill, the extended family, church, or community would step in to assure that the child's care did not sink too far below an adequate level. With the onset of heavy industrialization, the family, the church, and the community no longer were able to handle child dependency. An ever-increasing number of people lived in cities far from their extended families; they were marginally involved in church; and many had little knowledge of, or concern for, their neighbors. The first visible symptom of the breakdown in the ability of the family and the church to handle child dependency was a vast and rapid increase in the number of homeless children. Fry notes

> the numbers were *immense*. At a time when New York City's population was around five hundred thousand, the police estimated that there were ten thousand homeless children wandering about. Later, after close observation [social workers] came to the conclusion that the number ran as high as thirty thousand.

This large number of homeless children was, of course, cause for concern. Fry continues

> Ragged, verminous, barefoot, the vagrant children slept where they could: in doorways, under stairways, in privies, on hay barges, in discarded packing boxes, and on piles of rubbish in alleys and littered back yards. The older boys often became members of street gangs who terrified respectable citizens when they weren't bashing one another's heads in; many of the girls were accomplished streetwalkers by the time they were twelve or thirteen years old.[24]

In the latter half of the nineteenth century, social services rapidly evolved to deal with the massive problem of homeless children. Part of the reason for the development of services was, of course, humanitarian concern for the well-being of the children. Probably a greater reason was fear that these children represented a threat to social stability. One of the leading child welfare figures of the time, Charles Loring Brace, referred to homeless children as the "dangerous classes," and described his efforts to remove the children from the city and place them in rural foster homes as a "moral and physical disinfectant."[25]

The Development of a Changed Conception of Children and Childhood
Before the nineteenth century children were viewed, at best, as miniature adults and more likely as products of original sin, possessed of evil impulses, who would run wild if not strictly controlled.[26] Childhood was viewed by adults as an inconvenient period that people had to get through before they began the real business of living as adults. Children were not thought to have special needs or to require any special care. As a result of this perception, children were generally treated poorly. DeMause found in his research on the history of childhood that

A child's life prior to modern times was uniformly bleak. Virtually every childrearing tract from antiquity to the modern century recommended the beating of children. We found no examples from this period in which a child wasn't beaten, and hundreds of instances of not only beating, but battering, beginning in infancy.[27]

Williams notes

> Since time immemorial children have been treated with incredible cruelty . . . Children have been tortured, burned, worked to death, terrorized, and flogged daily in order to "discipline" them, dipped in icewater and rolled in the snow in order to "harden" them, and buried alive with their dead parents.[28]

Few people felt that children needed protection or that they had any right to protection. Children were considered to be the property of their fathers. In Roman law, the power of a father over his children was absolute—he could kill, sell, or offer them as sacrifices if he so chose. English common law progressed a little from this, setting forth the duties of parents to support and educate their children. However, common law recognized these duties as "imperfect," which means they were considered to be unenforceable.

In nineteenth century America, a marked change in attitude toward children began, which evolved into a conception of children as beings who had unique needs and the right to have these needs fulfilled to a reasonable extent. Williams identified three factors contributing to the evolution of a more positive attitude toward children.

1. Humanitarianism was increasing and its application to the plight of children was much in evidence in the writings of poets and novelists. Americans had come to accept the theories of John Locke, who speculated that children were not depraved, but that "the souls of the newly born are just empty tablets afterwards to be filled in by observation and reasoning."
2. A more complicated reason was the strong ideological vision of a classless, participatory democracy in the United States. Persons holding this vision felt that it could only be implemented if child labor were prohibited and a system of compulsory education implemented, so that future citizens would be literate. A literate citizenry was deemed essential to the achievement of the dream of a classless, participatory democracy.
3. People were beginning to feel that parents did not always provide the best examples for children. There was a growing desire to protect children against the deviance and immorality of their parents.

The changing view of children, combined with the enlightened view of jurists that parental rights result from the carrying out of their duties to their children, created an atmosphere where laws and programs to protect children were possible.[29]

These three factors converged and interacted during the nineteenth century to create a need and demand for child welfare services. Industrialization contributed to a lengthening of childhood by greatly postponing the age at which a person became economically useful; the combination of industrialization and urbanization led to such a number of homeless children that they were perceived as threats to social stability; and people began to view children as beings with unique needs and certain rights to have these needs fulfilled.

The Development of Child Welfare Services

There were a few child welfare facilities in the United States prior to the nineteenth century, notably a home for girls established in New Orleans by the Ursuline Sisters in 1729; the Bethesda House for Boys, founded near Savannah, Georgia, in 1740; and the Charleston Orphan House, established in 1790.[30] However, services did not develop to any great extent until well into the nineteenth century. Most children who could not be cared for by their parents (dependent children) during the colonial years and early years of the republic were either placed in private families and put to work or bound out as apprentices.[31]

The Development of Children's Homes   As the apprenticeship system declined and the number of dependent children increased during the early nineteenth century, the first response was to treat dependent children in the same manner as other dependent people, and thus to place them in county poorhouses. A report submitted to the Senate and Assembly of New York in 1823 found 2,604 children growing up in poorhouses in that state.[32] There children grew up in the company of elderly, alcoholic, sick, insane, and feeble-minded people. A visiting committee of the New York State Charities Aid Association described the plight of children in the Westchester County poorhouse in 1873 as follows

> The children, about sixty in number, are in the care of an old pauper woman, whose daughter and whose daughter's child, both born in the poorhouse, make her one of three generations of paupers. The daughter assists in the care of the children. She has a contagious disease of the eyes, which is, apparently, communicated to them. The children are neither properly clothed nor fed; but saddest of all is to see the stolid look gradually stealing over the faces of these little ones, as all the joy of their lives is starved out of them.[33]

With conditions such as these, it is not surprising that a call for reform began. The Charities Aid Association report continues

> to think what these children must grow up to, what they must become, if they are not soon removed from this atmosphere of vice . . . Alas! We know only too well what becomes of children who live and grow up in the poorhouse.[34]

The people of New York State felt so strongly about this problem that in 1875 an Act to Provide for the Better Care of Pauper and Destitute Children was passed. This act made it unlawful for any child over three and under sixteen years of age to be committed to a county poorhouse "unless such child be an unteachable idiot, an epileptic or paralytic, or . . . otherwise defective, diseased, or deformed, so as to render it unfit for family care."[35]

The obvious shortcomings of the poorhouse as a solution to the problem of dependent children resulted in the development of specialized children's institutions. In 1800, there were 3 children's institutions, by 1851 there were 77, and by 1860 there were 124.[36] Although the children's homes were a great improvement over county poorhouses, they had many shortcomings. They were large, impersonal, rigid, authoritarian, and generally antifamily. One of the leading critics of institutional care, Charles Loring Brace, felt

The impersonal custodial care of an institution . . . not only stunted children, it destroyed them. . . . The regimentation did little to build self-reliance, to prepare the child for practical living . . . institutional life, like charity handouts, perpetuated pauperism, and that both were dismal failures when it came to helping people to learn to stand on their own.[37]

In addition to the charge that children's institutions were not appropriate places for rearing children, other problems quickly began to seriously erode the unquestioned acceptance they had enjoyed. One problem was that in spite of the great growth in the number of institutions, the number of dependent children was growing at a much faster pace. The overflow either ended up in county poorhouses or, more likely, became "street arabs" living on their own. Another problem resulted from the fact that institutions were designed to take care of children for a relatively short period of time "during which education and reeducation for orderly living were provided. Having satisfactorily completed this period of rehabilitation, the male child was placed out by the institution as an apprentice in a particular trade or occupation; the female child was indentured as a domestic servant."[38] The spread of compulsory public education and the decline of the apprentice system greatly lengthened the period of time dependent children needed care. This further increased the pressure on already overcrowded institutions because as children stayed longer, fewer children could be cared for.

The Idea of Foster Family Care   The problems of children's institutions and their inability to handle the problem of caring for dependent children led to the notion of placing children with private families to be cared for as a member of the family. While probably not the originator of the concept, the first person to effectively put it into practice was the Reverend Charles Loring Brace, who founded the New York Children's Aid Society in 1853. Brace's basic idea was to take homeless children from the streets of New York—where they had few options other than begging, crime, and vice, and therefore were a serious social problem—and transport them to rural regions of the country to be placed with farm families where they would be an asset, because even small children are useful on a farm. Brace and his associates advertised their plan and found the response to be immediate and astounding.

He later recalled

Most touching of all was the crowd of little ones who immediately found their way to the office. Ragged young girls who had nowhere to lay their heads; children driven from drunkards' homes; orphans who slept where they could find a box or a stairway; boys cast out by stepmothers or stepfathers; newsboys whose incessant answer to our question, "Where do you live?" rang in our ears—"Don't live nowhere!" . . . All this motley throng of infantile misery and childish guilt passed through our doors, telling their simple stories of suffering and loneliness and temptation.[39]

The technique of the Society was to gather together homeless children in shelters in New York City and, when a large enough group was gathered, to send them by train to towns in the west. Agents of the Children's Aid Society would precede the train into each town, organize a local placement committee of prominent citizens, and advertise the location and the date the children would be available for placement. When the day arrived, local families would inspect the children, and families who were deemed suitable by both the Society's agent and the local committee could select one or more children. The prospective parents promised to take good care of the child and to provide him or her with a "Christian home" and an education. No money was exchanged between the parents and the Society.

In terms of numbers alone, the Children's Aid Society was a tremendous success. By 1873, the Society was placing more than 3,000 children a year. Its peak year was 1875, when a total of 4,026 children were placed. However, in terms of policies and techniques, the Society was the object of some well-deserved citicism. A major concern was that if a child had living parents, the Society made no attempt to work with them so that the child could return home. The Society worked from the assumption that parents who were unable to care for their children were somehow morally inadequate, and it saw its role as rescuing the child from them. Another criticism was raised by Catholics, who felt that the Children's Aid Society, founded and run by Protestants, was snatching Catholic children off the streets and sending them west to be reared as Protestants. Many of the states receiving children soon lost their enthusiasm for the Society's work. Many of the children—one study estimated nearly 60 percent—became sources of trouble and public expenditure when their placements failed to work.[40] Finally, the most serious criticism was the lack of study, the generally casual nature of the placement process, and the almost total absence of follow-up supervision after a placement was made.

Although the Children's Aid Society's program had many flaws, the basic idea of placing dependent children in a family setting caught on and had a tremendous impact on child welfare practice. Toward the end of the nineteenth century, members of the newly emerging social work profession, notably John Finley of the New York State Charities Aid Association, Charles Birtwell of the Boston Children's Aid Society, and Homer Folks of the Children's Aid Society of Pennsylvania, began to develop systematic and sound administrative procedures for child placement. These procedures included placement of the child in his home community, if possible; thorough study of the child and the prospective foster home; some financial support for the child; and careful supervision of the placement. With these new procedures, foster care for children spread rapidly. By the turn of the century foster care had replaced institutional placement in a number of cities. In 1909, the report of the first White House Conference on Children gave support to the foster care movement with the recommendation that "it is desirable that [children] should be cared for in families whenever practicable. The carefully selected foster home is for the normal child the best substitute for the natural home."[41] The spread of foster care has continued until the present time, when placement in an institution is considered appropriate only for special needs children.

The Development of Protective Services   At the same time nineteenth century America was wrestling with the problem of what to do with the children left homeless in the wake of industrialization, another child welfare problem was emerging—the abuse and neglect of children. Interestingly, the awareness and concern regarding this problem was slightly preceded by concern with the abuse and neglect of animals. In 1866 Henry Bergh founded the Society for the Prevention of Cruelty to Animals. He quickly succeeded in getting laws passed prohibiting neglect and abuse of animals and deputizing the Society's agents, giving them power to actually make arrests and issue subpoenas.

It was to Bergh and his society that a charity worker turned with her concern about the treatment of Mary Ellen Wilson, an eight-year-old girl who was being abused and neglected by her step-parents.[42] Bergh directed his attorney, Elbridge T. Gerry, to seek custody of the child and prosecution of the step-parents. Gerry did this and, amidst much publicity, was successful. Media coverage of the Mary Ellen Wilson case caused a flood of public opinion resulting in the passage in New York in 1875 of "an Act of the incorporation of societies for the prevention of the cruelty to children."[43] In a manner similar to the SPCA, agents of these new societies were empowered to "prefer a complaint before any court or magistrate having jurisdiction for the violation of any law relating to or affecting children . . ." In 1877, the American Humane Association was incorporated. By 1900, its membership was composed of one hundred fifty anticruelty or humane societies throughout the country, most dealing with both child and animal protection, but about twenty restricting their activities to protection of children only.[44]

The Societies for the Prevention of Cruelty to Children viewed themselves as child rescue agencies. In a manner similar to law enforcement agencies, which for all practical purposes they were, the societies investigated cases of abuse, neglect, and exploitation. If the complaint were substantiated, they would initiate criminal charges against the perpetrators and file for custody of the child. The 31st Annual Report (1907) of the American Humane Association stated that the societies were never intended to reform children or families; they were

> a hand affixed to the arm of the law by which the body politic reaches out and enforces the law. The arm of the law seizes the child when it is in an atmosphere of impurity, or in the care of those who are not fit to be entrusted with it, wrenches the child out of these surroundings, brings it to the court, and submits it to the decision of the court.[45]

Once they had gained custody of the child, they would place the child in a home or institution and close the case. Only in cases of lost or kidnapped children did the society ever consider returning them to their parents.

Thus, by the turn of the century the seeds of our current child welfare system had been planted. The beginning of our current foster home system was in place in the form of state children's aid associations, and the current protective service system was beginning in the local societies for the prevention of cruelty to children. The final step in putting the current system in place was to merge the two elements and put the programs under public auspices. In 1914, the Secretary of the Pennsylvania SPCC, addressing a conference of the American Humane Association, said

> This thing we are doing is, after all, the job of the public authorities. The public ought to protect all citizens, including the children, from cruelty and improper care. As speedily as conditions admit, we should turn over to the public the things we are at present doing.[46]

C. C. Carstens, director of the Child Welfare League of America, found both developments well under way when he addressed the National Conference on Social Work in 1924. He observed that in many areas of the country, "the children's protective and children's aid functions are being combined under one society," and that in some areas "public departments have been given the power and to some extent the equipment to take over the whole of the children's protective service."[47] The government on all levels was showing an ever-increasing willingness to become involved in providing social welfare services, particularly those involving children. The 1909 White House Conference resulted in the establishment in 1912 of the U.S. Children's Bureau located in the Department of Commerce and Labor. The Bureau was charged with investigating and reporting upon "all matters pertaining to the welfare of children and child life among all classes of our people."[48] In 1918 the Infancy and Maternity Bill was passed, which set up infant and maternal health centers administered by state health departments. In 1935, child welfare services became a predominantly public function with the passage of the Social Security Act which, under Title IV B, mandated that all states provide services for dependent children and provided funding for these services.

The Rediscovery of Child Abuse and Neglect The basic structure of the child protective services system was in place with the passage and implementation of Title IV B of the Social Security Act of 1935. Following this landmark legislation there was a period of nearly three decades of apathy regarding child welfare. Although child protective services were officially a responsibility of government, the services were spotty and poorly funded. Three states had no child protective services at all. In the states that did have services, an American Humane Association survey found "that much of what was reported as child protective services was in reality non-specific child welfare services or non-specific family services in the context of a financial assistance setting."[49] In addition, the survey found that services provided by private agencies had undergone a long-term decline. In the late 1950s and early 1960s, the problem of child maltreatment was rediscovered and greatly increased resources were directed toward its resolution.

Perhaps the major reason for the rediscovery of child maltreatment was the belated recognition of the problem by the medical profession. In the late 1940s and early 1950s, radiologists began to recognize injuries that we now know to generally result from abuse and neglect, but they tended to view the causation as accidental. In 1960, a social worker at Children's Hospital in Pittsburgh published an article regarding the resistance of physicians to diagnosing child abuse; the article attributed this resistance to both a repugnance to the problem and a difficulty in assuming an objective attitude with abusive parents.[50] Kempe, the physician instrumental in overcoming this resistance, recalls

> When I saw child abuse between 1956 and 1958 in Denver, our housestaff was unwilling to make this diagnosis [child abuse]. Initially I felt intellectual dismay at diagnoses such as "obscure bruising," "osteogenesis imperfecta tarda," "spontaneous subdural hematoma."[51]

In 1960, Kempe used his prerogative as program committee chair of the American Academy of Pediatrics to plan a plenary session on child abuse. The rest of the committee agreed, provided he could come up with a catchy name for the session. The name Kempe coined was "the battered child syndrome." Shortly after the meeting, Kempe, with the assistance of a psychiatrist and a radiologist, published an article with the same name in the *Journal of the American Medical Association*. As Williams notes, "The speed of public and professional response, enhanced by media coverage, was incredible."[52] In 1962, the U.S. Children's Bureau held a conference to draft model child welfare legislation. That same year the Social Security Act was amended to require all states to develop a plan to provide child protective services in every political subdivision. In 1963, eighteen bills were introduced to Congress dealing with child abuse and eleven of them passed. By 1967 all states had passed laws requiring professionals to report child abuse. Also in 1967, Title XX of the Social Security Act was passed. Part of this act made protective services mandatory for all states, and it provided a large amount of federal money to pay for these services. In 1972, the National Center for the Prevention and Treatment of Child Abuse and Neglect was established with the help of federal funds. This center publishes a newsletter, engages in research on child protection, and provides training for professionals concerned with child maltreatment. In 1974, the Federal Child Abuse Prevention and Treatment Act was passed. This act provides direct assistance to the states to help them develop child neglect and abuse programs; it also provides support for research mainly through the establishment of the National Center for Child Abuse and Neglect within the Children's Bureau. The center supports research and acts as a clearinghouse for information on public and private programs in the area of child protection. Congress authorized $15 million to finance implementation of the act, and this has since been increased to $22 million. Finally, in 1980, the Adoption Assistance and Child Welfare Act was passed. (This act will be discussed in the next section on permanency planning.)

CURRENT ISSUES AND TRENDS

The rediscovery of child abuse and neglect by first the medical profession and then the general public led to an explosive growth in the size of the child protective service system and in the number of children in foster care. In recent years, social workers and the courts, alarmed at the immense number of children in out-of-home placements, have been taking a careful look at our approach to the problem of children in need of protection and have been making some fundamental changes in the way we respond to the problem. As a result, there have been three significant developments: an emphasis on permanency planning, an emphasis on family-based services, and a tendency by the courts to order states to upgrade services to children in need of protection.

Emphasis on Permanency Planning

The roots of child protective services are in the Societies for the Prevention of Cruelty to Children, which engaged in "child rescue" work. They viewed their role as removing the child from a bad environment, going to court to gain custody and prosecute the parent, finding a new living situation for the child, and then moving on to another child in need of rescue. They did not view their role as working with either the child's family of origin or the child after placement. In the 1920s, as child protective services became a part of the profession of social work, people in the field began to question the wisdom of this approach, which wrote off a child's family and consigned him or her to a life in limbo. De Francis notes that

> They began to question this approach in terms of asking, "Is it truly beneficial to the child to rescue the child from a bad home? Would it not make better sense if we provided services so that we made responsible parents out of irresponsible people?"[53]

This approach of keeping the family together if possible, and working to return the child quickly if not, has become the guiding philosophical principle of child protective services.

The current emphasis on permanency planning began in 1959, with a study by Henry Maas and Richard Engle, published under the title *Children in Need of Parents*. This study, still considered a landmark in the field, looked at foster care in nine representative communities. The authors found that there were about 260,000 children in foster care in the United States at the time of the study. They estimated that in no more than 25 percent of the cases was it probable that the child would return to his or her own home. Further, the researchers found regular parent-child contact in fewer than half the cases. They concluded "that there are roughly 168,000 children today who are in danger of staying in foster care throughout their childhood years."[54] Thus, far from being a temporary haven for children while their family problems were being corrected, foster care was found to be a permanent arrangement for a huge number of children. Even worse, because the placement was considered temporary, no long-term plans were made for these children to either (1) return them to their own homes, (2) legally free them for adoption, or (3) define their foster home as permanent so they could develop a permanent bond with their foster families. Because of this lack of planning, many of these children would grow up, not in one foster home, but in a whole series of homes.

Concern about children "adrift" in foster care stimulated by Maas and Engle's study and a number of more recent works, notably *Beyond the Best Interests of the Child* by Goldstein, Freud and Solnit, has led to the development of one of the guiding principles of child protective services—permanency planning.[55] According to Meezan

Permanency planning takes as its major premise the idea that the child's "well-being" must be paramount in any service delivery plan. In order to insure this, children must have a home in which they feel a sense of belonging and permanent membership. . . . Permanency planning thus suggests that the biological family is primary to the care and upbringing of a child. Here an initial sense of belonging is developed, and here family memberships initially lie. Disrupting this tie is a major decision—one that must be based on evidence that serious harm will come to the child if left at home. . . . If the situation is serious enough to warrant the child's removal from home, it is incumbent upon the agency to provide an alternative for the child in which these needs can be met. Restorative work with the biological family must be ongoing . . . if restorative work is not successful and the biological family cannot resume care of the child, a home intended to last indefinitely must be found. This can be accomplished either through the termination of parental rights and the placement of the child in an adoptive home or through *planned* long-term foster care in a single home, which allows the child to develop substitute parental ties.[56]

Meezan enunciates seven principles which must be followed for permanency to fulfill its promise.

1. There must be early identification of cases in which family dysfunction can lead to the placement of the child.
2. There must, whenever possible, be work with parents and children in their own homes to prevent entry into the placement system.
3. Removal of a child from home must be based on specific guidelines and should occur only after it has been determined that the parents, with agency supports, cannot remediate the situation with the child in the home.

4. Prior to or shortly after the removal of the child from home, there must be an examination of the various placement alternatives, and the child must be placed in the least detrimental alternative available.

5. There must be established for children and their families a time-limited casework plan designed to achieve, as soon as possible, an appropriate permanent placement. Appropriate services must be provided to establish and carry out this plan.

6. There must be established a consistent set of guidelines regarding the termination of parental rights, which can be implemented if children cannot return to their homes.

7. There must be sufficient resources available for the child who cannot return home to insure that a permanent substitute home can be arranged.[57]

Increased knowledge regarding problems in the foster care system and the development of the principles of permanency planning led to the passage of P.L. 96–272, the Adoption Assistance and Child Welfare Act of 1980. This act directs federal fiscal incentives toward permanency planning objectives—namely the development of preventive and reunification services and adoption subsidies. In order for states to be eligible for increased federal funds, they must implement a service program designed either to reunite children with their families or to provide a permanent substitute home. They are required to take steps, such as the establishment of foster placement review committees and procedures for regular case review, which ensure that children enter foster care only when necessary, that they are placed appropriately, and that they are returned home or else are moved on to permanent families in a timely fashion. The act also creates fiscal incentives for states to seek adoptive homes for hard-to-place children, including children who are handicapped, older, or minority group members.[58]

Meezan has analyzed the child protective services system in the United States in relation to the principles of permanency planning. He concludes that the system falls short in a number of ways but, because permanency planning is relatively new, the system should be viewed as being in transition. He finds that the system performs well for most children and that "it is this record of achievement that gives us confidence that current deficiencies can be corrected."[59]

Emphasis on Family-Based Services

Contrary to the optimism about permanency planning, the population of children in foster care has continued to grow at an alarming rate. Between 1977 and 1982, the foster care census experienced a sharp decline, but then began to increase rapidly. The number of children in foster care rose from 242,000 in 1982, to almost 500,000 currently, and is projected to increase to 850,000 by 1995.[60] A major reason for this increase was identified by the Edna McConnell Clark Foundation as that in this country "children are separated from their families by default. Too few alternatives are available to help [families] stay together safely."[61] With significant financial backing from the Clark Foundation, a new model of services has begun to emerge in child welfare to address this problem. These services go by various names, but are generically referred to as *family-based services.*

The main idea behind family-based services is to prevent children from ever entering the foster care system by providing services of varying intensity to protect children while keeping them in their own homes. As Allen has noted, "Many of us have talked for years about a family's own home being the best permanent placement for children."[62] An additional idea behind family-based services is that many of the families who are referred for child protective services may not be amenable to conventional office-based clinical or educational services and so a new approach to helping them is needed.[63]

The Child Welfare League of America classifies family-based services into three levels. These are:

1. *Family resource, support, and education services.* These are services which are provided on an institutional basis (see Chapter 2) to all people in a community to assist and support adults in their role as parents. Examples are telephone crisis and support services, "mother's day out" programs, parenting classes, emergency financial and food services, and the like. The key is that these services should be widely available to prevent crises which cause the removal of children from ever developing.

2. *Family-centered services.* These services are provided on a residual basis to families who are demonstrating serious problems in functioning. They include services such as case management, counseling/therapy, education/skill building, advocacy, and/or the provision of concrete services.

3. *Intensive family-centered services.* These services are provided to families in crisis, generally when a point is reached where removal of a child appears imminent. Intensive family-based services are generally short-term, lasting from four to twelve weeks; family focused, occurring in the family's home with all family members participating; and intensive, involving eight to ten hours of service per family per week.[64] Most intensive family-based service programs are based on a pilot project named the *Homebuilder's* model developed in Tacoma, Washington in 1974. The Edna McConnell Clark Foundation has invested considerable funding in the development and promotion of this model at various sites in the country.

Family-based services enjoy considerable public and professional support for several reasons. First, they emphasize keeping families together, which appeals to the American value of the family as sacred and government intervention in the family as bad. Second, they are viewed as a cost-effective alternative to foster care or institutionalization of children. Finally, family-based services are compatible with public policy mandates to preserve families as spelled out in Public Law 96–272, and to treat children in the least restrictive environment. For these reasons, family-based service programs have expanded rapidly, growing from 20 programs in 1982 to 269 in 1988.[65]

There is an additional reason why many states are embracing the concept of family-based services, which is related to the final trend in child welfare services. One state after another is facing class action lawsuits on behalf of children in the foster care system demanding that the states fully fund and implement the provisions of Public Law 96–272.

Class Action Lawsuits on Behalf of Children in Foster Care

Public Law 96–272, discussed earlier, was intended to be a "major restructuring of Social Security Act programs for the care of children who must be removed from their own homes . . . to lessen the emphasis on foster care placement and to encourage greater efforts to find permanent homes for children either by making it possible for them to return to their own families or by placing them in adoptive homes."[66] Unfortunately, the experience in the 1980s has been characterized by a huge increase in child welfare caseloads, coupled with a decrease in budget and staff in most agencies. For example, in Kansas, a fairly typical state:

- Children and youth in SRS (the agency responsible for child welfare) custody rose 18 percent in the 1980s—and 28 percent from 1985 and 1991;
- Child abuse and neglect reports rose from 17,500 in 1980 to 23,400 in 1990;
- The number of social service field staff decreased by 24 percent during the 1980s.[67]

As a result services to children in foster care have actually deteriorated during this decade.

In response to the problem of the foster care system being unable to meet the spirit or letter of the law as written in P.L. 96–272, in the late 1970s the American Civil Liberties Union began the Children's Rights Project. In Missouri in 1983, in the case of *G.L.* v. *Zumwalt,* the ACLU was able, for the first time, to get children in foster care recognized as a class and to get the court to order relief for the whole class. Since this time, the ACLU has successfully pursued cases in Kansas, Connecticut, Washington, D.C., Pennsylvania, New Mexico, New York, Kentucky, Louisiana, and Massachusetts, and is preparing cases in a number of other areas. The project has developed an impressive body of case law which includes:

- Foster children in state custody can now file federal lawsuits through community members acting as their "next friends," over any objections of their legal custodian, the state.
- Foster children now have the right to seek relief that entails reorganization of entire foster care systems at a city, county, or state level, and to seek this relief for all foster children through class action suits in either state or federal court.
- Foster children are now entitled to sue, for monetary damages, state officials who violate state or federal rights.
- Foster care reform can now be litigated in the federal courts, over the objections of our opponents, who had claimed that foster care is exclusively a state concern to be addressed on a case-by-case basis instead of systemically.[68]

The judgments won by the ACLU in these states order the state governments to upgrade the child welfare system to make it able to meet the requirements of P.L. 96–272. Orders typically require the states to greatly increase the number of social workers in the child welfare system, hire more professionally trained (both BSW and MSW level) social workers and supervisors, increase the level and quality of in-house staff training, decrease case loads by as much as two-thirds, increase training of foster parents, provide special therapeutic foster homes for seriously disturbed children, and develop permanent placement plans for children within six months of their entry into the system.

The Children's Rights Project, as well as efforts by other interested parties who have filed suit in other states, is drastically altering the child welfare system. States are no longer able to excuse poor care for foster children with the argument that they cannot afford the staff and other resources necessary to do better. The courts, using the doctrine of "the right to freedom from harm," have recognized foster children as a class with constitutional rights to quality services, and the states will have no choice but to come up with the necessary resources.[69]

---

not necessary

At first look, it is hard to imagine that there are liberal and conservative perspectives on child maltreatment. It is true that no sane and decent person, liberal or conservative, advocates the maltreatment of children or ignores children in need of protection or assistance. However, there are still some substantial areas of disagreement. The main areas of disagreement are conceptions of which behaviors constitute appropriate discipline and which are inappropriate; theories of the causation of maltreatment; and beliefs concerning the rights and responsibilities of parents, children, and the state.

Conceptions of Appropriate Discipline

Conservative Perspective   While conservative philosophy does not advocate abusing children, it accepts a certain level of physical discipline.[70] This acceptance is rooted in the conservative's generally pessimistic view of human nature. People are innately bad and thus early, firm discipline is necessary for them to become productive members of society. The conservative belief in individual responsibility for behavior and in the importance of respect for authority also contributes to the belief that physical punishment is appropriate for effective child rearing. One of the most influential experts currently involved in parent training is the conservative psychologist James Dobson. Dobson has this to say about discipline

> The issue of respect can be a useful tool in knowing when to punish and how excited one should get about a given behavior . . . In my opinion, spankings should be reserved for the moment a child (age ten or less) expresses a defiant "I will not!" or "You shut up!" When a youngster tries this kind of stiff-necked rebellion, you had better take it out of him, and pain is a marvelous purifier.[71]

Dobson provides a number of biblical citations to support his belief in corporal punishment.

Liberal Perspective   While liberals do not always condemn spanking, they are much less enthusiastic about it than conversatives. They base this on their belief that human nature is innately good and that it is acceptable, and sometimes even desirable, to question authority. They tend to believe that violence teaches violence and that physical punishment does more to make the child feel angry and resentful toward the parent than it does to make him or her a responsible citizen. Dr. Spock notes that "We have all seen children who were slapped and spanked and deprived plenty, and yet remained ill-behaved."[72] Those who take a radical view believe that the social sanction of physical violence toward children, in the form of approval of spanking, is the basic underlying cause of all child abuse. Gil, for example, argues

> Whenever corporal punishment in child-rearing is sanctioned, and even subtly encouraged by a society, incidents of serious physical abuse and injury are bound to happen, either as a result of deliberate, systematic, and conscious action on the part of perpetrators, or

under conditions of loss of self-control. In either case, but especially in the latter, physical attacks on children tend to relieve tensions and frustrations experienced by the perpetrators. Clearly, then, these attacks are carried out to meet the emotional needs of the perpetrators rather than the educational needs of the victims, as is often claimed by advocates of corporal punishment.[73]

Analysis and Synthesis   In many ways the differences between the conservative and liberal perspectives are not as great as they initially appear. The conservative psychologist Dobson states, "One of my greatest concerns in recommending corporal punishment (spanking) is that some parents might apply the thrashings too frequently or too severely."[74] He is adamant that teenagers should never be spanked because "teenagers desperately want to be thought of as adults, and they deeply resent being treated like children. Spanking is the ultimate insult."[75] On the other hand, the liberal pediatrician Spock feels there has been an over-reaction against spanking, saying, "I'm not particularly advocating spanking, but I think it is less poisonous than lengthy disapproval, because it clears the air, for parent and child."[76] Even so, the main difference is clear— generally conservatives feel corporal punishment is acceptable, and even desirable ("spare the rod and spoil the child") for teaching respect and maintaining discipline. Liberals, most of whom would agree with Spock and hesitate to condemn a parent for spanking, nonetheless think that corporal punishment is not the most desirable way to discipline children, even though it may occasionally be justified. Liberals feel that respect does not always mean absolute obedience and that when corporal punishment is necessary, discipline has already broken down. They advocate withdrawal of privileges, time outs, and extra chores as being more desirable forms of punishment.

There are two areas where conceptions of whether corporal punishment is acceptable directly impact on child protective services. The first is the definition of child abuse. If our society were to take a stand, as Sweden has, that corporal punishment is wrong, the definition of abuse would be much easier. If a child were beaten to the point of leaving marks of any kind, this would constitute evidence of abuse and the case would be "open and shut." Using the conservative idea, as our society does, that spanking is acceptable, we have no clear basis for definition. Is it spanking to hit a child with your hand, but abuse to use a belt? Is it spanking to hit a child with a belt, but abuse to leave bruises? Is it spanking to leave bruises below a child's waist, but abuse to bruise above? If corporal punishment is acceptable in any form, these become questions of individual opinion. For example, one of the authors began his career as a child welfare worker in a large city which had two juvenile court judges, one liberal and one conservative. All of the child welfare workers knew that unless an abuse case was very severe, they should work to get it placed on the docket of the liberal judge. The conservative judge was likely to dismiss a case with the admonition that "you can't blame a man for whipping his boy."

The second area where conceptions of the appropriateness of corporal punishment impact on child protective services is the causation of child abuse. A frequent cause of abuse is a spanking "gone wrong." A parent begins with the intention of administering a mild spanking and loses control and carries it to excess, or attempts to hit the child on the bottom and misses, hitting the child's eye or ear, resulting in far more pain and injury than was intended.

The Causation of Maltreatment

In the section on the dynamics of maltreatment, we discussed the three types, or levels, of causative factors: individual-parent, family, and environmental. Conservatives and liberals differ on the amount of emphasis they place on each level.

Conservative Perspective   Conservatives, with their belief in autonomy as governing behavior, place almost total blame for child maltreatment on individual-parent factors. If parents abuse or neglect their child, it is because they choose to do so. They may choose to do so because they are lazy, ill-tempered, or perhaps even evil. If this is the case, then the proper societal response is to see that they are arrested, prosecuted, and punished for their unacceptable behavior. On the other hand, they may choose to maltreat (or choose to not adequately care for) their children because they are mentally ill. If this is the case, the proper societal response is to provide appropriate psychological services in an attempt to "cure" them. This is the perspective which defines a social problem in terms of individual illness, which is called the *medical model*. This is the model strongly advocated by the pediatricians and psychiatrists who formed the battered child team at the University of Colorado School of Medicine. They attribute child abuse to parent factors, with some contribution by child factors, and they assert that individual psychiatric treatment is the appropriate response because "it deals in the most humanitarian and constructive way we know with a tragic facet of people's lives."[77] Underlying this explanation is the conservative assumption that society is functional and everyone has the opportunity to adequately fulfill all roles, in this case that of parent, if they work at it and, if necessary, receive help.

Liberal Perspective   Liberals as well as radicals place much greater stress on the role of environmental factors in child maltreatment. They point out that research has failed to conclusively demonstrate that psychopathology exists in a greater proportion of child protective services clients than in the general population.[78] They assert that the really important causative factors are the environmental conditions that lead to stress and frustration, such as poverty, overcrowded and dilapidated neighborhoods, large numbers of children, single-parent households, and alienating work. Also, liberals argue that regardless of how adequate individual parents are, the whole society is guilty of child maltreatment because it does not provide adequate schools, safe neighborhoods, high quality affordable child care, and adequate welfare support, and because it sanctions corporal punishment in schools. According to this perspective, programs to help individual parents, while necessary, only treat the symptoms, and not the disease. Gil, coming from a radical perspective, says, "There simply is no way of escaping the conclusion that the complete elimination of child abuse on all levels of manifestation requires a radical transformation of the prevailing unjust, inegalitarian, irrational, competitive, alienating, and hierarchical social order into a just, egalitarian, rational, human, and truly democratic, decentralized one."[79] Underlying the liberal view of the cause of child maltreatment is the belief that individuals are not autonomous and that society, as it is presently structured, is not functional for large numbers of people.

Analysis and Synthesis   The liberal, radical, and conservative perspectives on the causation of child maltreatment are truly a case of the blind men examining different parts of the elephant. As discussed earlier, child maltreatment is a phenomenon with several levels of causation. It is undoubtedly true, as the liberal and radical perspectives assert, that the only way to significantly reduce child maltreatment is to change the many social and economic factors that oppress and frustrate people. We know, for example, that when the unemployment rate declines, child abuse declines. As Gil notes, "If one's priority is to prevent all child abuse, one must be ready to part with its many causes, even when he is attached to some of them, such as the apparent blessings, advantages, and privileges of inequality."[80]

The conservative emphasis on the individual level of causation also has several strong points. We have generally used our criterion of pragmatism to argue for the liberal perspective, but in this case the conservative view is, perhaps, more pragmatic. When dealing with a specific case of child maltreatment, it does little good to point out that the family is the victim of environmental pressures beyond its control. What must be focused upon is how the family members respond to those pressures and how they can improve their ability to cope.

Although conservatives are most comfortable emphasizing the individual causes of child maltreatment and liberals and radicals like to emphasize the environmental causes, nearly everyone will admit that the problem needs to be addressed on all levels. As social workers, many of us are expected to work on the individual level, but it is our professional responsibility to also make time to combat the environmental factors. For example, social workers responding to referrals of young children being left at home alone in a community without adequate day care are failing in their professional duties if they only help parents, on a case-by-case basis, find child care. In addition to helping individual families, they should work to have adequate, affordable, accessible, day care established so parents won't have to leave their children alone in the first place.

Rights of Children, Parents, and the Government

Child rearing in our society is based on beliefs and assumptions regarding the rights and responsibilities of a triad—children, parents, and the government. These beliefs and assumptions are not the same for liberals and conservatives.

Costin and Rapp state that "an essential question in any formulation of family social policy is the extent to which children have their own rights and interests independent of parents, with a claim to their recognition and enforcement."[81] There have been numerous formulations of children's rights over the years, such as the "Children's Charter" adopted by the 1930 White House Conference on Children and the "Children's Charter for the Seventies" presented at the White House Conference on Children in December, 1970. These documents give as children's rights things such as understanding and guarding his/her personality; prenatal care for the mother; a safe, sanitary, and wholesome place to live; recognition of and help for handicapping conditions; when "in conflict with society the right to be dealt with intelligently as society's charge, not society's outcast"; and an adequate standard of living. The 1970 document added as rights freedom from pollution, freedom from racism, and freedom from fear. As Costin points out, these statements are really statements of children's "needs" as defined by current knowledge about the physical, psychological, and social development of the child, rather than "rights," which are based on a legal definition and carry a claim or an "entitlement" and are enforceable. Public education is a right because if it is denied a child, that child can force the community to provide it by court action. An adequate standard of living is a need, but it is not a right. Millions of children in our society live well below what the government defines as an adequate level (the poverty line), but they are not entitled to a better living standard under current law.

Parents in our society are given almost total responsibility for the care and up-bringing of their children. As long as the level of child care does not sink below a minimal standard demanded by the community, parents are given a large number of rights. Among these rights are the rights of guardianship; the right to determine the "living pattern" and standards of everyday conduct; the right to select the religion (or lack of religion) of the child; and the right to determine the kind and extent of the child's education, the quality and type of health care given to the child, and the place where the child will live. If a child's parents move him to a new city during his last year of high school, if they select an academic curriculum when both the child and the school prefer a vocational one, if they bring him to the Unitarian Church every Sunday when he would like to attend the Church of Christ, if they buy him slacks and oxford cloth dress shirts when he would like to wear blue jeans and T-shirts, the child and the community might object, but they would have little power to oppose the parents because these decisions are theirs by right.

Society has the general responsibility to promote the welfare of children and it has certain rights necessary to carry out this responsibility. The legal term for this is *parens patria,* which means that ultimately the state is the parent to all children. The state exercises its rights and responsibilities in three broad ways:

- *Regulatory powers.* For the general protection of children, the state formulates regulations which govern all persons dealing with children. Examples are compulsory school attendance laws which require communities to provide free public education and require parents to send their children to school, and employment laws which forbid hiring children below a certain age or for jobs considered harmful or dangerous. "The intent of the state's use of its regulatory authority is to represent society's interest in all children through the application of broad powers to set standards which apply to children generally, or all parents generally, or other adults acting in relation to children."[82]
- *Power to intervene in the relationship between parent and child.* When the level of care provided a child falls below a certain level, or when a child's behavior violates the law, the state has the right to intervene to either protect or correct the child. This may, in serious cases, involve the removal of the child from the home and his or her placement in a foster home or institution.
- *Power to legislate for the development of child welfare services.* The state has the right to collect revenue via taxation and to spend it on any of a number of services to benefit children. Costin and Rapp state that the importance of this power cannot be overemphasized. "How successfully children are helped often depends upon the extent to which the statutes of a state reflect modern knowledge about children and their changing world, respect for their rights, and readiness to tax and appropriate money for professional services and facilities to meet the needs of children."[83]

Conservative Perspective   Conservatives, with their fear and disapproval of government and their belief in tradition and authority, emphasize the rights of parents and the responsibilities of parents and children, and they deemphasize the rights and responsibilities of government. They feel that government should intervene in the relationship between parents and children only in serious cases, and then the intervention should be subject to sharp controls. They point to examples of the danger of excessive government power in this area, such as the following reported in *Woman's Day,* a popular, large-circulation magazine.

> On May 7, 1985, Elene Humlen of Whittier, California, lost custody of her nine-year-old son, Chris, and her 16-month-old daughter when Chris went to school with a black eye received when he was struck by a tennis ball while playing near his home. Discounting the boy's explanation, school and CPS officials suspected abuse and hastily placed both Humlen children in foster homes. On July 22, after losing her job and spending $10,000 in legal fees, Humlen regained permanent custody of her children when a judge dismissed the charges. Surprising as it seems, these actions were perfectly legal. Although police must have a warrant to invade the sanctity of a home when pursuing thieves, rapists and murderers, they need only uncorroborated suspicion to come in and take a child. "When you're charged with abusing a child," says Stanley Hodge [an attorney], "everyone assumes you're guilty until you prove your innocence."[84]

Conservatives argue that excessive government power will inevitably lead to abuses such as the one reported in this incident. Wald has analyzed state statutes regarding neglect and concludes that the language is so broad and vague that the statutes give almost unlimited power to state officials. He recommends greater protection of parent rights by writing laws that focus less on vague standards of parental behavior and more on evidence of specific harm to the child.[85]

Conservatives feel as strongly as anyone that children should be well cared for. However, they feel that the philosophical basis for this care is not the right of children to demand it, or the right of government to enforce it, but the moral duty of parents to provide it.

Liberal Perspective   Liberals are much more sympathetic to the notion of rights of children, less sympathetic to the rights of parents, and more willing to support governmental intervention. They feel that there should be no difference between needs and rights of children. They are comfortable with government intervention in the relationship between parents and children to enforce children's rights. The Polanskys, for example, think that we are too hesitant to intervene in families exhibiting low levels of child care. They think that the state fails to protect children far more often than it needlessly intrudes. They endorse an approach by government in which social, medical, and legal actions are "authoritative, intrusive, and insistent."[86] Liberals believe that parents have too many rights, and children and the state have too few. As Costin and Rapp have summarized the situation from a liberal point of view:

> The right of children to be dealt with as individuals, continues to be given insufficient attention in the law, which is weighted in the favor of the rights of adults and which seems to make them owners of children rather than trustees who have a duty to care for and protect all children, not just their own.[87]

Analysis and Synthesis   Conservatives and liberals agree that children should be adequately cared for. Conservatives argue that this care is the moral duty of parents and liberals argue that it is the right of children. The main difference between conservatives and liberals is their opinion about the right, or wisdom, of government intervention in parent-child relations when child care falls below a certain level. Conservatives fear that when government is given power to intervene, it will use this power to the maximum and "snatch" children from their homes and place them in foster care when there is no compelling need. The research evidence gathered on this matter indicates that this fear is unfounded. In 1972, approximately 3 million children received child welfare services and only 14 percent were in foster care. In 1969, 1972, and 1975, the Child Welfare League of America conducted a census of requests for child welfare services. They found that in 26 percent of the cases, the parents themselves were requesting foster home placement, but the agency complied in less than one-fourth of the instances. The other three-quarters were given in-home services. A survey of child abuse referrals in Wisconsin between 1969 and 1975 found that 72 percent of the children were given services in their own homes. Further, the data indicated that the percent placed in foster care was decreasing over time. Therefore, there appears to be little justification for the fear that government will frequently overstep its bounds and remove children from their homes when removal is not justified.[88]

SOCIAL WORK ROLES

Child protective services is one of the most challenging and important areas of social work practice. It is also one of the largest. In 1978 it was estimated by the Bureau of Labor Statistics that 350,000 people held the job title of social worker. Of these it was estimated that about 25 percent were involved in child welfare services. With the recent trend toward courts ordering states to upgrade the number and qualifications of child welfare staff, it is predicted that the number of social work positions in child welfare agencies will steadily increase.

The major reason for the importance of child protective services as an area of social work practice is that child welfare is the only institution in which social work is considered the principal profession responsible for its operation. In most other areas of practice, social workers are located in *host institutions,* where some other profession is central to the institution and social workers provide an ancillary service. Even financial assistance, which many people associate with social work, is actually dominated by public administration, with proportionately few social workers employed. But child welfare is clearly social work's field and this perception is shared by the general public.

Another important attribute of child protective services is that it is the field of social work practice that enjoys the most public support. As Kadushin observes

> Public attitudes toward a profession are shaped in part by the attitudes toward the client groups with which the profession is associated. . . . To what extent can one expect that the situation will change and the client will become a productive citizen? On both these counts, children are regarded as "acceptable" clients.[89]

A study by Carter, Fifield, and Shields found that 80 percent of 9,346 respondents would spend "however much is necessary" to help welfare children become productive adults. The respondents were also asked to rank their willingness to support seventeen different social services. Four of the top six ranked services were child welfare services: foster-home care, protective services, adoption, and day care.[90] In a study of the New York State legislature's reaction to social service bills, Howe found that child welfare bills were given the highest priority. Bills concerned with child abuse, neglect, foster care, and adoption were more likely to be approved than bills concerned with the handicapped, the indigent, and the aged.[91]

The majority of opportunities in child welfare are with state social service agencies. These used to be called departments of public welfare, but in recent years most states have changed the name to something that sounds more modern. Common names are department of social services, department of family and children's services, department of human resources, and department of human services. These departments will have a division called either the child welfare or the child protective services division. A smaller, but still significant number of child welfare social workers are employed by private agencies. Child protective services in these agencies is discussed as a separate category.

Direct Services in Public Child Welfare

Child protection agencies organize their direct service staff in a large number of configurations depending on the size and philosophy of the agency. Regardless of organization, workers in all agencies will fill the following general roles: intake and assessment, services to children and families with children at home, services to children and families with children in foster homes, recruitment and supervision of foster homes, and adoption services. In a small office in a rural area, one worker will often fill all of these roles. In a large urban office there may be a whole unit of six or seven social workers who perform only one role, for example foster home recruitment.

Intake and Assessment   The intake worker is responsible for responding to reports of child maltreatment received by the protective service agency. The worker makes contact with the family involved and with all parties who are involved and/or have pertinent information. A decision is then made to accept or not accept the case for services. If the case is accepted for services, the assessment process begins. The assessment process is aimed at making an accurate estimate of the client's problems. This is the most important stage in the history of a case. As Meyer notes, an accurate assessment

> at the outset in the career of a case is the best guarantee of successful outcome. The need for staff that is the most competent, best trained, and at the highest level of professional education in direct practice to enact the central decision-making role at the point of access to services, cannot be exaggerated.[92]

At the end of the intake/assessment process, the case is either closed or opened for ongoing services with the child in either his or her own home or in a foster home. In many agencies, it is at this point that the case is transferred to another social worker for long-term services.

Services to Children and Families with the Child at Home   In many cases, the assessment process will find a family in which standards of child care and discipline are below those demanded by the community, but where the children are in no danger of serious harm. In these situations the case is opened for agency supervision for purposes of assisting the parents to improve the level of child care. If the parents realize there is a problem and are willing to work with the agency to try to solve it, no court action is necessary. If the parents are unwilling to deal with the problem voluntarily, sometimes the court will assign legal custody of the children to the agency, but leave physical custody with the parents on the condition that they accept services. Social workers in this role must carefully monitor the home to be sure that child care does not further deteriorate; they must find supplemental services (such as tutoring or recreation) to compensate for deficits in the home; and they must work with the parents, often with the assistance of other professionals, such as psychologists and vocational rehabilitation counselors, to help them resolve problems and learn skills necessary for successful parenting.

Services to Children and Families with the Children in Foster Care   There are two general circumstances when the decision at assessment will be to place the child in foster care. One is when the parent is not physically present or able to provide care because of such factors as illness, imprisonment, or desertion. The other is when the parents are present and physically capable, but in the judgment of the social worker, who is backed up by a court order, the level of danger to the child is too great to leave him or her in the home. The emphasis in working with children in foster care is to quickly make a permanent plan for the child, for return to the parents if possible, or, if not, to move to terminate parental rights and place the child in an adoptive home. Sometimes one social worker works with the biological family and another works with the foster family and child. Sometimes one works with all three, but this is not as common. Important professional functions in this role are: making and frequently updating a plan for the child; engaging the biological family in the work of repair in order to return the child as quickly as possible; engaging the foster parents in the work of ongoing responsibility for the child, being particularly active at points of change in the foster family's and child's circumstances; and helping the child cope with problems of identity and change.

Recruitment and Assessment of Foster Homes   The number of children requiring foster home care has increased from about 175,000 in 1961 to about 500,000 in 1977. During the same years, the literature indicates a dwindling supply of families willing to assume the responsibilities of foster parenthood.[93] The combination of these two trends has made effective recruitment and assessment of new foster parents, as well as support for existing ones, among the most critical roles in child protective services. The recruitment process generally begins by working with the media to obtain newspaper publicity (classified ads and feature stories) as well as radio and television announcements; making speeches to community groups; and working with community leaders to encourage persons from groups they represent to apply. When a pool of interested persons is formed, the social worker will schedule a meeting to present information and answer questions about foster parenting. Studies of foster home recruitment show a very high rate of attrition among people who express initial interest. Between 80 and 90 percent drop out before they are licensed, the greatest number withdrawing following the initial meeting.[94] If a couple still expresses interest after the initial meeting, a social worker is assigned to do a detailed assessment of the family. The assessment is based on objective criteria outlined in state licensing standards (for example age and health of couple and size of home) and on socioemotional factors that are considered desirable in a foster home (for example motivation for becoming foster parents, potential effect on natural children, and the history of the marriage and current marital interaction). A decision is then made whether or not to license a couple as foster parents. Regarding this decision, Kadushin notes that agencies seek to be flexible, often waiving requirements regarding mother's employment, age of foster parents, and need for religious affiliation. However, "agencies still, for the most part, prefer to select what is considered a 'typical' family—a nuclear, heterosexual couple living in fairly comfortable economic circumstances and espousing middle-class values. The greater the extent to which families deviate from this model—by being homosexual or single for example—the more reluctant and anxious agencies are about selecting them as homes for children."[95] Following recruitment, selection, and approval, an agreement is signed and the family is licensed.

Adoption   When parents do not wish to have responsibility for their children, as in the case of many unwed mothers and in instances of desertion, or in situations which are so severe that there is little hope the parents will ever be able to adequately care for their children, the agency and the courts terminate parental rights and seek to create a new family for the child through adoption. This is considered to be among the most serious tasks social workers perform, largely because of the life-long implications. Because of this, the social workers assigned to the adoption function are usually the best-trained and most experienced in the agency. Important parts of the role of the adoption worker include counseling biological parents, terminating biological parents' rights, making the decision to place for adoption, preparing the child for adoption, selecting adoptive parents, handling "failed placements," and working with the courts and other agencies. In recent years the number of prospective parents wishing to adopt healthy infants has far exceeded the number of infants available. Because of this, agencies, particularly in the public sector, have begun to concentrate on placing "special needs" children, that is, those who are not easily adoptable because of age, race, handicap, or medical problems.

Private Agencies

Although by far the largest number of child welfare social workers are employed in public agencies, a number work in private settings. Among the private agencies employing child welfare social workers are private, often church-affiliated adoption agencies; child guidance clinics; children's homes; private, usually therapeutic, foster care agencies; children's hospitals; and day care centers. Social workers in these settings usually have graduate training and occupy therapeutic roles.

CONCLUSION

For a number of reasons it can be said that child protective service is the most central area of the social work profession. It is the largest field of practice, it is the one area in which social work is the host profession, it has grown the most rapidly, and it enjoys the highest level of public support. Child protective service is also one of the most professionally and personally satisfying areas of social work practice. As Kadushin has written

> The Talmud, emphasizing the importance of each individual life says, "If during the course of your

own life, you have saved one life, it is as if you have saved all mankind." Few occupations give us the opportunity of participating in the saving of a life. The everyday work of the child welfare worker is concerned with just that—reclaiming a child for life. It is to be expected that such a task would be very difficult. It is also to be expected that there are few, if any, tasks that offer the same degree of satisfaction and the same sense of accomplishment.[96]

ENDNOTES

1. Council on Social Work Education, "Child Welfare," in *Description of Practice: Statements in Fields of Social Work Practice* (New York: CSWE, 1959, mimeo), 5.
2. Reprinted with the permission of Macmillan Publishing Company, Inc. from *Child Welfare Services,* fourth edition by Alfred Kadushin and Judith A. Martin. Copyright © 1987 by Macmillan Publishing Company.
3. Kathleen Faller and Sally Russo, "Definition and Scope of the Problem of Child Maltreatment," in *Social Work with Abused and Neglected Children—A Manual of Interdisciplinary Practice,* Kathleen Coulborn Faller, ed. (New York: The Free Press, 1981), 103.
4. David Gil, *Violence Against Children: Physical Abuse in the United States* (Cambridge, MA: Harvard University Press, 1970).
5. Murray Straus, Richard Gelles, and Susan Steinmetz, *Behind Closed Doors: Violence in the American Family* (New York: Anchor Press, 1980).
6. Leroy H. Pelton, "Child Abuse and Neglect and Protective Intervention in Mercer County, New Jersey," in *The Social Context of Child Abuse and Neglect,* Leroy H. Pelton, ed. (New York: Human Sciences Press, 1981), 103.
7. Gil, *Violence Against Children,* 59.
8. Straus, Gelles, and Steinmetz, *Behind Closed Doors,* 64.
9. Gil, *Violence Against Children,* 112.
10. Leroy H. Pelton, "Child Abuse and Neglect: The Myth of Classlessness," in Pelton, *The Social Context of Child Abuse and Neglect,* 23–38; Leroy H. Pelton, *For Reasons of Poverty* (New York: Praeger, 1989), 37–42.
11. Pamela D. Mayhall and Katherine E. Norgard, *Child Abuse and Neglect—Sharing Responsibility* (New York: John Wiley & Sons, 1983), 101.
12. David Finkelhor, "How Widespread is Child Sexual Abuse?" *Children Today 13* (July–August, 1984): 18–20.
13. Brandt F. Steele and Carl B. Pollock, "A Psychiatric Study of Parents Who Abuse Infants and Small Children" in *The Battered Child,* Roy E. Helfer and C. Henry Kempe, eds. (Chicago, IL: The University of Chicago Press, 1968), 103.
14. C. Henry Kempe, Frederic N. Silverman, Brandt F. Steele, William Droegemueller, and Henry K. Silver. "The Battered Child Syndrome," *Journal of the American Medical Association 181* (July 1962): 17–24.
15. Leontine Young, *Wednesday's Children—A Study of Neglect and Abuse* (New York: McGraw-Hill, 1964): 17–24.
16. Cited in Helfer and Kempe, *The Battered Child,* 170.
17. Kathleen Faller and Majorie Zeifert, "Causes of Child Abuse and Neglect," pp. 32–52. Reprinted with permission of The Free Press, a division of Macmillan from *Social Work with Abused and Neglected Children—A Manual of Interdisciplinary Practice,* Kathleen Coulborn Faller, Editor. Copyright © 1981 by The Free Press.
18. Kathleen Faller and Marjorie Zeifert, "Causes of Child

Abuse and Neglect," p. 49. Reprinted with permission of The Free Press, a division of Macmillan from *Social Work with Abused and Neglected Children—A Manual of Interdisciplinary Practice,* Kathleen Coulborn Faller, Editor, Copyright © 1981 by The Free Press.

19. Gil, *Violence Against Children,* 135.
20. Urie Brofenbrenner, "Socialization and Social Class Through Time and Space" in *Readings in Social Psychology,* 3rd ed., Eleanor E. Maccoby, Theodore M. Newcomb, and Eugene L. Hartley, eds. (New York: Holt, Rinehart and Winston, 1958), 400–425; Howard S. Erlanger, "Social Class and Corporal Punishment in Child Rearing—A Reassessment" in *Child Abuse and Violence,* David Gil, ed. (New York: AMS Press, 1979), 494–515.
21. Homer Folks, *The Care of Destitute, Neglected and Delinquent Children* (New York: Macmillan, 1911), 167.
22. Higgeson, *New England's Plantation,* cited in James Bossard and Eleanor Stoker Boll, *The Sociology of Child Development* (New York: Harper and Brothers, 1960), 613.
23. Bossard and Boll, *The Sociology of Child Development,* 614.
24. Annette Riley Fry, "The Children's Migration," *American Heritage* 26 (January 1974): 4–10, 79–81.
25. Walter I. Trattner, *From Poor Law to Welfare State—A History of Social Welfare in America,* 3rd ed. (New York: The Free Press, 1984), 115.
26. Ross W. Beales, "In Search of the Historical Child: Miniature Adulthood and Youth in Colonial England," *American Quarterly* 27 (October 1975): 379–398.
27. Lloyd DeMause, "Our Forebears Made Childhood a Nightmare," *Psychology Today* (April 1975): 85–88.
28. Gertrude J. Williams, "Child Abuse and Neglect: Problems of Definition and Incidence," in *Traumatic Abuse and Neglect of Children at Home,* Gertrude J. Williams and John Money, eds. (Baltimore, MD: The Johns Hopkins Press, 1980), 9.
29. Gertrude Williams, "Protection of Children Against Abuse and Neglect: Historical Background," in Williams and Money, *Traumatic Abuse and Neglect of Children at Home,* 47–51.
30. June Axinn and Herman Levin, *Social Welfare—A History of the American Response to Need* (New York: Dodd, Mead & Co., 1975), 45–46.
31. Trattner, *From Poor Law to Welfare State,* 111.
32. Axinn and Levin, *Social Welfare,* 43.

33. Robert H. Bremner, ed., *Children and Youth in America—A Documentary History,* Vol. II: 1886–1932 (Cambridge, MA: Harvard Univeristy Press, 1971), 250–251.
34. Bremner, *Children and Youth in America,* 251.
35. Axinn and Levin, *Social Welfare,* 95.
36. Folks, *The Care of Destitute, Neglected and Delinquent Children,* 52–55.
37. Fry, "The Children's Migration," 6.
38. Axinn and Levin, *Social Welfare,* 95.
39. Charles Loring Brace, *The Dangerous Classes of New York and Twenty Years Work Among Them* (New York: Wynkoop and Hallenbeck, 1872), 88–89.
40. Trattner, *From Poor Law to Welfare State,* 118.
41. Trattner, *From Poor Law to Welfare State,* 118, 202.
42. For an excellent discussion of the Mary Ellen case and the beginning of the Society for the Prevention of Cruelty to Children see Sallie A. Watkins, "The Mary Ellen Myth: Correcting Child Welfare History," *Social Work* 35 (November 1990): 500–503.
43. Williams and Money, *Traumatic Abuse and Neglect,* 77.
44. Bremner, *Children and Youth in America,* 201.
45. Bremner, *Children and Youth in America,* 214.
46. Bremner, *Children and Youth in America,* 217.
47. Bremner, *Children and Youth in America,* 220.
48. Trattner, *From Poor Law to Welfare State,* 205.
49. Vincent DeFrancis, "Protecting the Abused Child," Hearings before the Subcommittee on Children and Youth, 93rd Congress, on the Child Abuse Prevention Act (S1191), 1973, 323–331.
50. Elizabeth Elmer, "Abused Young Children Seen in Hospitals," *Social Work* 5 (1960): 98–102.
51. C. Henry Kempe, "Child Abuse—The Pediatrician's Role in Advocacy and Preventive Pediatrics," *American Journal of Diseases in Children* 132 (1978): 255–260.
52. Gertrude Williams, "Cruelty and Kindness to Children: 1874–1974," in Williams and Money, *Traumatic Abuse and Neglect of Children at Home,* 86.
53. DeFrancis, "Protecting the Abused Child," 323.
54. Henry S. Maas and Richard E. Engles, Jr. *Children in Need of Parents* (New York: Columbia University Press, 1959), 380.
55. Joseph Golstein, Anna Freud, and Albert J. Solnit, *Beyond the Best Interest of the Child* (New York: The Free Press, 1973).
56. Reproduced by permission of the publisher F.E. Peacock Publishers Inc., Itasca, Illinois from William Meezan, "Child Welfare—An Overview of the Is-

sues," in Brenda G. McGowan and William Meezan, eds. *Child Welfare: Current Dilemmas—Future Directions.* Copyright © 1983, p. 12.

57. Reproduced by permission of the publisher F.E. Peacock Publishers Inc., Itasca, Illinois from William Meezan, "Child Welfare—An Overview of the Issues," in Brenda G. McGowan and William Meezan, eds. *Child Welfare: Current Dilemmas—Future Directions.* Copyright © 1983, p. 13.

58. Mary Lee Allen and Jane Knitzer, "Child Welfare: Examining the Policy Framework" in McGowan and Meezan, *Child Welfare: Current Dilemmas—Future Directions,* 120–123.

59. Reproduced by permission of the publisher F.E. Peacock Publishers, Inc. Itasca, Illinois from William Meezan, "Child Welfare: An Overview of the Issues," in Brenda G. McGowan and William Meezan, eds. *Child Welfare—Current Dilemmas—Future Directions.* Copyright © 1983, p. 36.

60. Thomas D. Morton, *Interpersonal Helping Skills Resource Guide* (Atlanta, GA: Child Welfare Institute, 1992), 5; Select Committee on Children, Youth, and Families, U.S. House of Representatives, *No Place to Call Home: Discarded Children in America* (Washington, D.C.: U.S. Government Printing Office, 1990).

61. Quoted in Peter J. Pecora, Mark W. Fraser, and David A. Haapala, "Client Outcomes and Issues for Program Design," in Kathleen Wells and David E. Biegel, eds., *Family Preservation Services—Research and Evaluation* (Newbury Park, CA: Sage Publications, 1991), p.4.

62. Mary Lee Allen, "Family-Centered Services in the National Policy Arena," in Alvin L. Sallee and June C. Lloyd, eds., *Family Preservation—Papers from the Institute For Social Work Educators,* (Riverdale, IL: National Association for Family-Based Services, 1991), p. 67.

63. James Whittaker, "The Leadership Challenge in Family-Based Practice: Implications for Policy, Practice, Research, and Education," in Alvin Sallee and June C. Lloyd, eds., *Family Preservation,* p. 1.

64. Child Welfare League of America, *Standards for Services to Strengthen and Preserve Families with Children* (Washington, D.C.: Child Welfare League of America, 1989), pp. 13–33.

65. David E. Biegel and Kathleen Wells, "Introduction," in Kathleen Wells and David Biegel, eds., *Family Preservation Services,* p. xiv.

66. S. Rep. No. 336, 96th Cong., 2nd Sess. Quoted in Marcia Lowry, "Derring-Do in the 1980's: Child Wel-

fare Impact Litigation After the Warren Years," *Family Law Quarterly 20* (Summer 1986), 259.

67. Bill Craven, "Increased funding of SRS necessary to settle lawsuit concerning children," *The Topeka Metro News* (7 February, 1992), 7.

68. Quoted from Jean Carey Bond, "The A.C.L.U. Helped Put My Family Together Again," (New York: Department of Public Education of the ACLU, 1988), pp. 5–6.

69. Michael B. Mushlin, Louis Levitt, and Lauren Anderson, "Court-Ordered Foster Family Care Reform: A Case Study," *Child Welfare 65* (March–April 1986), 145.

70. Russell Eisenman and Henry B. Sirgo, "Liberals vs. Conservatives: Ego Control, Child Rearing Attitudes, and Birth Order/Sex Differences," (Unpublished manuscript, McNeese State University, 1990).

71. James Dobson, *Dare to Discipline* (Wheaton, IL: Tyndale House, 1971), 27.

72. Benjamin Spock, *Baby and Child Care, New and Revised Edition* (New York: Hawthorne Books, 1968), 336.

73. David Gil, "Unraveling Child Abuse," in Gil, *Child Abuse and Violence,* 11–12.

74. Dobson, *Dare to Discipline,* 60.

75. Dobson, *Dare to Discipline,* 61.

76. Spock, *Baby and Child Care,* 338.

77. Steele and Pollock, "A Psychiatric Study of Parents Who Abuse Infants and Small Children," 145.

78. Leroy H. Pelton, *For Reasons of Poverty; A Critical Analysis of the Public Child Welfare System in the United States,* (New York: Praeger, 1989), 27–29.

79. Gil, "Unraveling Child Abuse," 16.

80. Gil, "Unraveling Child Abuse," 17.

81. Lela B. Costin and Charles A. Rapp, *Child Welfare: Policies and Practice,* 3rd ed. (New York: McGraw-Hill, 1984), 6.

82. Costin and Rapp, *Child Welfare: Policies and Practice,* 9.

83. Costin and Rapp, *Child Welfare: Policies and Practice,* 10.

84. Glenn P. Joyner, "False Accusation of Child Abuse—Could It Happen to You?" *Women's Day* (May 1986), 30–40.

85. Michael S. Wald, "State Intervention on Behalf of "Neglected" Children: A Search for Realistic Standards" in *Pursuing Justice for the Child,* Margaret K. Rosenheim, ed. (Chicago, IL: Univeristy of Chicago Press, 1976), 246–278.

86. Norman A. Polansky and Nancy F. Polansky, *The*

Current Status of Child Abuse and Neglect in This Country, Report to the Joint Commission on Mental Health for Children, February, 1968.

87. Costin and Rapp, *Child Welfare Policies and Practice,* 8.

88. Alfred Kadushin, "Children in Foster Families and Institutions" in *Social Service Research: Review of Studies,* Henry Maas, ed. (Washington, D.C.: National Association of Social Workers, 1978), 91–92.

89. Alfred Kadushin, *Child Welfare Services,* 3rd ed. (New York: Macmillan, 1974), 679.

90. Genevive W. Carter, Lilene H. Fifield, and Hannah Shields, *Public Attitudes Toward Welfare—An Opinion Poll* (Los Angeles, CA: Regional Institute on Social Welfare, UCLA, 1973).

91. Elizabeth Howe, "Legislative Outcomes in Human Services," *Social Service Review 52* (June 1978): 173–185.

92. Carol H. Meyer, "Staffing Issues in Child Welfare," in McGowan and Meezan, *Child Welfare—Current Dilemmas—Future Directions,* 479–502.

93. Delores Taylor and Phillip Starr, "Foster Parenting: An Integrative Review of the Literature," *Child Welfare 46* (July 1971): 372.

94. J.E. Vick, "Recruiting and Retaining Foster Homes," *Public Welfare 25* (July 1967): 229–234.

95. Reprinted with the permission of Macmillan Publishing Company, Inc. from *Child Welfare Services,* fourth edition by Alfred Kadushin and Judith A. Martin. Copyright © 1987 by Macmillan Publishing Company (p. 336).

96. Reprinted with the permission of Macmillan Publishing Company, Inc. from *Child Welfare Services,* fourth edition by Alfred Kadushin and Judith A. Martin. Copyright © 1987 by Macmillan Publishing Company (p. 697).

C·H·A·P·T·E·R

ten

Crime and
Criminal Justice

It was not the message I wanted to receive the first thing Monday morning as I entered my office at the county child welfare agency. The message said that the supervisor of the Children's Emergency Shelter had called and I was to call her as soon as I got in. This message meant trouble. Either one of the children in my caseload who was in the shelter was sick, had run away over the weekend, or else had caused some serious disruption. Although I was prepared for trouble when I returned the call, I was not prepared for the kind of trouble I encountered. Bobby Garrett was no longer in the shelter; he was now locked up in the county juvenile detention center.

Bobby Garrett, age 14, his two sisters, Ann, 12, and Amy, 11, and his brother Peter, 9, had been on my mind a lot lately. The four had been placed in the emergency shelter when their mother, Barbara Garrett, had been arrested and jailed for armed robbery. It would be an understatement to say that Barbara Garrett's life had not gone well. Everything she had ever done turned out badly. Every time she found a lover, he would eventually beat her up; Bobby and his siblings had been in foster care twice when Mrs. Garrett was in the hospital recovering from injuries from the beatings of boyfriends. Every time she found a job, she was fired; the children were in foster care once when Mrs. Garrett had been fired, was evicted from her apartment, and ended up living on the street. And now it appeared that Mrs. Garrett was even going to fail as a criminal—her lawyer informed me that she would be lucky to be out of jail in three years. There was one thing, however, that Mrs. Garrett had done right. In spite of all her troubles she had somehow reared four beautiful, healthy, and remarkably strong children. The four seemed to realize at an early age that there was not much they could count on, so they had better be able to count on each other. When Mrs. Garrett was incapacitated, the four functioned as a very strong family unit with Bobby as the head. When they had been placed in the shelter, Bobby had informed me that they did not care where they were placed, but that they had to be together. I agreed to this, but had been searching in vain for a place for all four of them for six weeks. Meanwhile, they had been living in our emergency shelter, which was a perfectly good place for a brief stay, but it was not designed for long-term living. The shelter was located on a major industrial boulevard, in the middle of a huge concrete parking lot, with only a tiny area to play in, and it had few recreational facilities. I had been doing the best I could to provide activities for the kids, but I knew they were becoming bored, anxious, and unhappy.

I was surprised by the message because Bobby Garrett was the last kid in my caseload that I would expect to be in trouble with the law. Red headed, freckle faced, five feet tall if he stretched, with a sharp mind and an infectious smile, Bobby was one of the most remarkable kids I had ever known. Under his leadership, Bobby and his siblings all did well in school, and they were well adjusted, well liked, and rarely in trouble. I could not imagine why he would be locked up.

I asked the shelter supervisor what had happened. She related to me that Bobby had seemed very restless over the weekend, like "a tiger in a cage." Late Sunday night, after lights out, Bobby and one of his friends had sneaked out of a window in the back of the shelter. They had wandered around for awhile, and finally they ended up by the public hospital down the street where a new wing was under construction. They climbed a ten-foot high chain-link fence to get inside the construction area. Once inside, they looked at all the machinery and discovered that the keys had been left in a huge dump truck. The boys decided that it would be fun to take a ride. The gate was locked, but this was no problem for the truck—Bobby just drove it right through. They had not gone two blocks when a police officer spotted them and, figuring that a five-foot tall fourteen-year-old probably had no business driving a dump truck at two in the morning, he pulled up behind them and turned on his red lights. Bobby figured that if he ignored the policeman perhaps he would go away. When the truck did not pull over, the policeman pulled alongside the truck and gestured for Bobby to pull over; Bobby continued to ignore him. Finally, in what had to be one of the worst law enforcement decisions of the century, the officer sped about a block ahead of the truck, pulled his cruiser sideways in the street to block all lanes, got out, and stood beside it with his arm out, palm raised, in a gesture guaranteed to get the truck to stop. Unfortunately, the officer did not know that Bobby was not too sure how to stop the truck. At the last possible moment, the officer jumped into a ditch as Bobby and the dump truck turned the police cruiser into two tons of junk. Amazingly, no one was hurt and Bobby and his friend were arrested, booked, and locked up in the juvenile detention center.

I phoned the Juvenile Department and was horrified to learn that Howard Jordan was the juvenile officer assigned to Bobby's case. I had worked with Mr. Jordan before and did not care for his approach to his job. Mr. Jordan was hard-nosed and rigid, and he had a wide and deep punitive streak. He viewed his job as protecting the public from juvenile lawlessness, and he believed that locking kids up was the best way to accomplish this task. Mr. Jordan had once told me that in his estimate at least 50 percent of teenagers would benefit from a stay in the state training school. I resolved to deal with Mr. Jordan in as positive a manner as possible, and I made an appointment to see him later that day.

When the time for my meeting with Mr. Jordan arrived, I began by stating that although Bobby had acted badly, we had to keep in mind the context of his actions. The system had not been as responsive to Bobby as we might desire and his actions were a result of boredom and frustration. We had to keep in mind that our overriding concern was the welfare of Bobby and his siblings. Therefore, if Mr. Jordan would be so kind as to go and get Bobby for me, I would take him back to the shelter and we would increase our efforts to find an appropriate placement for Bobby and his siblings.

After one look at Mr. Jordan's face, I knew that my entreaties had fallen on deaf ears. He informed me that my analysis of the situation was wrong. Bobby was a juvenile delinquent—a criminal and a felon. His actions had resulted in the destruction of over $8,000 worth of government property. He would like to see Bobby tried as an adult, but failing that, he assured me that he would see to it that Bobby was sent to the state training school until he was eighteen years old. Bobby's mother was a criminal, he told me, and in a burst of insight, he advised me that "the apple does not fall far from the tree."

I went to my supervisor and asked for suggestions as to who would be a good lawyer for Bobby—someone who would work for nothing. She called a friend who agreed to take the case and said she would speak to all the parties involved and would call me the next morning. The lawyer we had gotten Bobby, Rita Sanchez, was a radical. She was mainly a labor lawyer and had once been a candidate for the city council on the Socialist Party ticket. She was not popular with either the police or the district attorney's office, but she had a reputation as a strong client advocate.

The next morning Ms. Sanchez phoned me as she had promised. She told me that yes, the juvenile officer had been right when he said serious crimes were involved here. I told her I was surprised to hear her say that because I really could not think of Bobby as a criminal. She said, "Bobby's the only one in this situation who isn't a criminal. Your department, the Child Welfare Division, is guilty of criminal child neglect for leaving these kids in the shelter for six weeks. The construction company that owns the dump truck is guilty of criminal misconduct for leaving the keys in an attractive nuisance like that truck. The police department is guilty of public endangerment for parking that police car across the road in front of a truck driven by what the officer could clearly see was not a qualified operator. The Juvenile Department is guilty of criminal child abuse for the conditions in their detention facility. Finally, the probation officer, Howard Jordan, is guilty of being a jackass. The only reason that Bobby's in jail rather than the actual guilty parties is because he's the only one without the power to define things as crimes."

Following her conversation with me, Ms. Sanchez phoned the director of the juvenile department, the juvenile court judge, the police chief, and the editors of several local newspapers. I was not surprised when, later that day, I received a call from Mr. Jordan informing me that they had decided to not pursue the case and requesting that I come and get Bobby and return him to our emergency shelter, preferably before the reporters arrived. I did this, and within a few days, the foster home unit had located a home to take Bobby and his siblings. The last I heard they were still in the home and were doing well.

This case illustrates a number of issues about crime and delinquency that we will be discussing in this chapter. One issue is the definition of crime. Are crimes acts that constitute innate threats against the social order, or are crimes simply actions that are defined as such by the powerful forces in society? Another issue is the age of the offender. At what age do people become totally responsible for their behavior and how should we handle persons who are below this age? Another issue has to do with social welfare and crime. Which offenders, which acts, and which parts of the processing of offenders should come under the scope of the criminal justice institution, and which are more appropriate targets for the social welfare institution? Then there is the question of why people commit crimes. Do they do so because there is something wrong, or even evil, about their nature—they are "criminal types" so to speak? Or do people commit crimes because they come from an environment which has corrupted them, or even because they are the victims of an unjust social system? Finally, there is the closely related question of what society's reaction to crime should be. Should we be concerned with retribution against those who commit criminal acts, or should we view these acts as symptoms of some personal maladjustment or social problem and seek to correct the causes?

The order in which topics are covered in this chapter will be slightly different from the others. Perspectives will be covered at the beginning of the chapter rather than at the end because of their centrality to the topic of criminal justice. It is impossible to discuss any aspect of criminal justice without reference to political perspectives. In fact, the perspectives become almost parodies of themselves with the "hang-them-high" judge and the "bleeding-heart-liberal" social worker or civil rights lawyer. Therefore, we will begin with a discussion of perspectives and then discuss the other aspects of criminal justice.

PERSPECTIVES ON CRIMINAL JUSTICE

The conservative, liberal, and radical perspectives on criminal justice are so firmly embraced by their advocates that Walker prefers to describe them as "crime control theology." He says that, "Thinking of crime control policy as theology helps us explain the dogged tenacity of various ideas."[1] In this section we will briefly describe the most basic tenets of these perspectives; considerable elaboration will be given in following sections.

The Conservative Perspective

Basic Beliefs   Conservatives believe that individuals are fully responsible for their own actions and this includes the breaking of laws. The individual is not a passive pawn of external forces, but rather has free will and can make choices between right and wrong. When the individual makes these choices, he or she does so fully aware of the consequences and so he or she should be ready to suffer the penalties for wrong choices. Conservatives believe in a world of discipline and self-control in which people exercise restraint and subordinate their personal passions for the common good. It is a world of limits, and criminal law is an important set of limits.

Because conservatives believe that human nature is basically negative and that human behavior can be largely explained using a pleasure–pain calculus, they have a strong belief in the effectiveness of punishment. People who violate rules should be punished. Punishment teaches a good lesson; it teaches criminals that breaking rules has unpleasant consequences, and thus they learn to obey rules in the future. Punishment also serves as an example to everyone else that they should continue to follow rules or they will also suffer unpleasant penalties. To conservatives, rules are terribly important.

The conservative approach to crime advocates punishment as the most effective and just social response.

Conservatives believe in tradition and authority. Walker says, "The world of conservative crime control is modeled after an idealized image of the patriarchal family. Criminal sanctions resemble parental discipline. Minor misbehavior is greeted with a gentle warning; a second misstep earns a sterner reprimand. More serious wrongdoing is answered with severe punishment . . . . Conservative thinking about crime is closely related to conservative ideas about the problem of 'permissiveness' in child rearing."[2]

Major Issues[3]   According to Miller, conservatives are concerned about five major issues in criminal justice. The first is a belief that our system is characterized by excessive leniency toward lawbreakers. Conservatives believe that swift and sure punishment is the only way to prevent crime, and they therefore get very upset when they think an offender has escaped paying the full price for his or her actions. The full price according to conservatives is generally very high.

The second issue is a belief that the system tends to favor the rights and welfare of lawbreakers over the rights and welfare of their victims, of law enforcement personnel, and of the general public. Conservatives become very upset about things like the Miranda rule which requires that people be advised of their rights when they are arrested; the fact that illegally obtained evidence cannot be used; and the fact that prisoners must have individual cells. Conservatives are strongly in favor of recent developments that promote the rights of victims of crimes, such as rulings that victims must be advised of, and permitted to testify at, parole hearings.

The third issue conservatives are very concerned about is what they believe to be a general erosion of both discipline and respect for duly constituted authority. This is referred to by Miller as an "ancient concern," and centers around the behavior of youth who are generally considered to constitute the worst generation ever. Interestingly, we are currently at a rare point in history where many conservatives believe the current generation of young people is far superior to any in recent memory. One now hears the liberals complaining about the sorry state of youth who are perceived as being self-centered, overly materialistic, and entirely too willing to conform to discipline and authority.

The fourth issue on conservatives' minds is the cost of crime. This issue is somewhat less passionately held than the others, but it is still a major concern. Conservatives resent the large amount of money which must be spent on law enforcement and criminal processing. A particularly sore spot in this concern is the money spent for programs that enhance the welfare of criminals, providing such things as free legal counsel, prison recreation, improved food, and individual cells with the possibility of prisoners having their own televisions. The question conservatives ask is, "Why should hard working, law abiding citizens pay for luxuries for criminals?"

The final issue, related to the others, is excessive permissiveness. This is seen by conservatives as being a, if not *the,* basic flaw in our social order. It is believed that there has been an erosion of discipline, excessive leniency, and abdication of responsibility by authorities. The problem is seen as a continuum beginning with too much permissiveness at home, leading to excessively lenient schools, and finally resulting in a lax criminal justice system. The result is perceived as a society of people who do not suffer the appropriate consequences for improper behavior and therefore are increasingly predisposed to engage in such behavior.

The Liberal Perspective

Basic Beliefs   You will recall from Chapter 1 that a central belief of the liberal world view is that human nature is basically good and that if people behave badly, as in breaking laws, it is because they have somehow been corrupted by their social environment. This is the cornerstone of the liberal perspective on criminal justice. While conservatives attribute lawbreaking to individual moral failure, liberals place the responsibility on social influence. People commit crimes because of bad influences in the family, the peer group, or the neighborhood, or perhaps because of broader social influences such as unemployment or general lack of economic opportunity.

Because liberals believe that human nature is basically good, they place their faith in education and individual reform as the basis for the criminal justice system. As Walker has said, "If conservatives view the world as a large family, liberal crime control theology views it as a big classroom. Rehabilitation, the core liberal policy, involves instructing the criminal offender in the ways of correct behavior."[4] Liberals firmly believe that people who have been corrupted by a bad environment can be reshaped, and once this is done, they will follow their natural inclination to behave properly.

Major Issues   The major criminal justice issues of concern to liberals revolve around the aspects of society which they believe adversely influence people, sometimes leading to their committing crimes. The first issue is labeling and stigmatization. This will be discussed in some detail in the section on dynamics and so will only be identified here. Basically, liberals argue that the main thing that makes a person a criminal is the fact that he or she is labeled as one. Thus, they argue that we should do everything possible to keep people out of the criminal justice system because by assigning labels the system itself creates criminals.

The second issue which concerns liberals is overinstitutionalization. Liberals believe that we lock up too many people and that this does more harm than good. Based on their belief in the power of the environment to shape behavior, liberals argue that by locking people in prisons we create "crime colleges" where offenders learn new and better criminal techniques and become more favorably disposed toward committing crimes. Liberals believe we would accomplish more by placing more people on probation and into community-based treatment programs. Only dangerous people should be locked up.

The third issue of concern to liberals is their belief that there is a discriminatory bias to the system. They point to evidence that supports this belief, such as the fact that given the same crime, a member of a minority group is much more likely to be sent to prison than a white person, and the fact that the murderer of a minority person is much less likely than the murderer of a white person to be given the death sentence. Liberals charge the system with being racist, sexist, oppressive, and brutal toward minorities and low-income people.

The final major criminal justice issue of concern to liberals is overcriminalization. Liberals believe that too many things in our society are defined as crimes, and therefore, one quick way to reduce crime is to decriminalize acts that are viewed as not having a victim. Gambling, prostitution, and homosexual behavior are examples of the kinds of acts many liberals would like removed from the legal statutes. Probably the hottest example right now is drug use. The argument for all these issues is that they are against the law because some people think they are immoral; however, they really do not hurt anyone other than the person who engages in them and that is, after all, his or her own business. Interestingly, this is an issue on which some conservatives, mainly libertarians, agree with liberals.

The Radical Perspective

Basic Beliefs   The basic position of radicals is that the criminal justice system is one of the primary tools that the capitalist ruling class uses to dominate and exploit the rest of the population. A concise statement of the basic position is given by Spitzer, who argues that populations in capitalist societies become

> eligible for management as deviant when they disturb, hinder or call into question any of the following: (1) capitalist modes of appropriating the product of human labor (e.g., when the poor "steal" from the rich), (2) the social conditions under which capitalist production takes place (e.g., those who refuse or are unable to perform wage labor), (3) patterns of distribution and consumption in capitalist society (e.g., those who use drugs for escape and transcendence rather than sociability and adjustment), (4) the process of socialization for productive and non-productive roles (e.g., youth who refuse to be schooled or those who deny the validity of "family life") and (5) the ideology which supports the functioning of capitalist society (e.g., proponents of alternative forms of social organization).[5]

By this Spitzer means that acts that are perceived as threatening the interests of powerful people in society are defined as crimes; acts that do not threaten the interests of powerful people, even though they may be harmful, are not defined as crimes.

Major Issues   The major criminal justice issue for those of the radical persuasion is the redefinition of crime. Radicals believe that many of the acts which are currently defined as crimes could more accurately be defined as legitimate political acts by people attempting to battle an oppressive social system, or as understandable actions of people for whom all legitimate avenues of opportunity have been blocked. On the other hand, they believe that many acts which are now considered to be perfectly legal should be redefined as crimes. Schwendinger and Schwendinger, for example, argue that human rights violations, imperialism, war, racism, sexism, and allowing poverty to exist, are all forms of crime.[6] Radicals believe that these forms of crime are allowed to exist under capitalism because they are necessary for its survival.

DEFINITION

We will narrow our definition into two broad areas—legal definitions of crime and the definition of crime as a social welfare concern.

Legal Definitions of Crime

A good definition of crime from a legal perspective was written a number of years ago by Michael and Adler.

The most precise and least ambiguous definition of crime is that which defines it as behavior which is prohibited by the criminal code. The criminal law describes many kinds of behavior, gives them names such as murder and arson and rape and burglary, and proscribes them. If crime is defined in legal terms, the only source of confusion is such ambiguity as may inhere in the legal definitions of specific crimes. It is sometimes difficult to tell whether specific conduct falls within the legal definition, whether, for example, a specific homicide is murder or what degree of murder, as that offense is defined by law. But even so, the legal rules are infinitely more precise than moral judgments or judgments with regard to the antisocial character of conduct. Moreover, there is no surer way of ascertaining what kinds of behavior are generally regarded as immoral or antisocial by the people of a community than by reference to their criminal code, for in theory, at least, the criminal code embodies social judgments with respect to behavior and, perhaps, more often than not, fact conforms to theory.[7]

Thus, crime is defined, from a legal standpoint, as any behavior which is against the law.

In Whose Interest Is Criminal Law?   The problem with defining crime as any behavior which is against the law is that it leaves a number of important questions unanswered. The major question is what and whom these laws represent. There are two major viewpoints on this question. The first is the consensus (sometimes called functionalist) perspective subscribed to by conservatives and some liberals. The other is the conflict perspective accepted by some liberals and all radicals. The *consensus perspective* starts with the assumption that there is fundamental agreement (consensus) about basic social values. We are all supposedly in agreement about certain issues, such as that it is all right for people over the age of 21 to drink liquor, but it is not all right for them to use cocaine. From this perspective, law reflects the basic values and norms of the majority of people in our society. Hall states the basic position of the consensus perspective as, "Criminal law represents a sustained effort to preserve important social values from serious harm and to do so not arbitrarily but in accordance with rational methods directed toward the discovery of just ends."[8] The problem with this perspective is that we can all think of examples of laws that clearly do not represent the values of most people, but rather represent special interests. For example, in many states it is illegal to cremate a body without a casket. Most people resent paying for a casket which will only be burned and thus suspect that the only group that values this law is the funeral industry which then does not lose a commission on a casket sale when someone chooses cremation rather than burial.

The other perspective, the *conflict perspective,* provides an explanation as to why some laws are clearly to the benefit of certain groups, sometimes very small groups. This perspective argues that the assumption that a consensus exists in a large, heterogeneous society such as ours is incorrect. Diversity in our society is so great as to make cooperation difficult, if not impossible. There are a number of groups in society; each is pursuing its own self-interest. Laws do not represent a consensus, but rather they are the outcomes of struggles between groups to control the machinery of government for their own purposes. Thus, according to the conflict perspective, if abortion is once again outlawed, this will not mean that a consensus exists in society that abortion is wrong, but it will mean that conservative religious groups have managed to wield enough power to get their definition of morality imposed on everyone.[9] Ms.

Sanchez, Bobby's attorney in the vignette at the beginning of the chapter, was illustrating a conflict perspective when she said that the only reason Bobby was charged with the crime is that he was the only one without enough power to define things as crimes.

When looking at the question of what and whom laws represent, we should note that legal scholars generally classify crimes into two general categories. The first is offenses that are *mala in se* (evil in themselves). These are acts that are presumably understood by everyone to be bad, acts such as murder, rape, arson, assault, and robbery. These acts are banned in virtually every human society. The other category of crimes is acts that are *mala prohibita*. These are acts that are crimes only because they are defined as such by legislation; there is nothing inherently evil about them. Acts that are *mala prohibita* include drug use, prostitution, gambling, and homosexual conduct. In some societies these acts are perfectly legal—in fact, they are sometimes considered desirable—but in others they constitute criminal behavior. Regarding acts that are *mala in se,* a consensus view of law makes a good deal of sense; it is clear that there is near universal agreement about these laws. Regarding acts that are *mala prohibita,* a strong argument can be made for a conflict model. It is doubtful that a consensus exists in our society that marijuana should be illegal and that alcohol should be legal. However, it is clear that powerful interests support the manufacture and sale of alcoholic beverages and this same support is not present for marijuana.

Children as a Special Case   People who have not yet reached the age of majority are treated differently by the criminal justice system in a number of ways. With regard to the definition of crime, one of the ways that children are treated differently from adults is that there is a whole set of acts that are *mala prohibita* only for nonadults. These are generally known as *status offenses* and include things such as truancy, running away, being incorrigible, drinking liquor, and, in some areas, it is even illegal for a child to be on the streets after a certain hour. These acts are all perfectly legal for an

Prostitution is an act which is *mala prohibita,* that is, it is a crime only because it is against the law, not because it is inherently harmful to individuals or society. Many liberals, and libertarian conservatives, argue that we should cease worrying about acts like prostitution and concentrate only on crimes like murder and robbery which are *mala in se*—evil in themselves.

adult, but a child can be arrested and adjudicated for them. Thus, the definition of crime is much broader for children than for adults.

Another way that the definition of crime is different for children is that children are generally not considered responsible enough for their own behavior to be defined as criminals. Rather, children who commit acts that would be considered crimes for adults are defined as delinquents rather than as criminals. The definition of *juvenile delinquent* varies from state to state, but it generally refers to a person who has not reached the age of majority, which is eighteen in most cases, and who has either committed an act that would be considered a crime if he or she were an adult, or who has committed a status offense. Juvenile delinquents are considered to be the responsibility of the social welfare system rather than the criminal justice system; the goal is clearly rehabilitation rather than retribution, and once the person passes his or her eighteenth birthday the records are generally sealed and the act for which the person was arrested becomes as though it never happened.

Crime as a Social Welfare Problem

In order to understand crime as a social welfare problem we must first look at two major ideas about what the response of society to crime should be. The first idea is that society's response to crime should simply be to punish the offender; the second, and somewhat more ambitious, idea is that society should do something to rehabilitate the offender.

The Punishment Approach This approach is based on the idea that the function of the criminal justice system should simply be to exact a penalty from the wrongdoer and to do whatever is possible to right any wrong that has been done. There are several variations to the punishment approach which are advocated either alone or in conjunction with one another. The first is known as *retribution* and is based on the old eye-for-an-eye philosophy; it advocates punishment as an end in itself. The belief is that criminal acts are inherently wrong and therefore they should be punished; the punishment serves no other purpose. The second variation on the punishment approach is known as *restitution* and it is based on the belief that the punishment of the wrongdoer should somehow pay the victim back for the pain and suffering or loss he or she experienced as a result of the crime. The third variation is *incapacitation.* This is centered around the idea that punishment should not only punish the offender but also should shield society from him or her for as long as possible. Advocates of this approach believe in long prison sentences for convicted criminals. The argument is that in prison, antisocial people can only prey on each other and they will be forced to leave the rest of us alone. Finally, there is an updated version of the retribution approach known as *"just deserts."* This approach, also known as the *justice model,* seeks to set more precise penalties for various crimes than we now have; it seeks to insure that retribution can be justified because it is done in a fair way. Central to this model is the idea of determinant sentences; in other words, there would be no "time off for good behavior" because every person convicted of a certain crime would serve the same sentence.[10]

The aims of the punishment approach are rather modest and limited. Gelman refers to this as the "moralist approach" because he says that the criminal justice system "is one in which the system is seen as upholding the morals and values of society."[11]

The purpose of the criminal justice system is to affirm the values of society by punishing those who violate the values which have been deemed important enough to be codified into criminal law.

The only claim that the punishment approach makes other than affirming the values of society is that some advocates argue that it reduces crime through specific and general deterrence. *Specific deterrence* means that lawbreakers will be deterred from further crimes by the suffering that society puts them through for their acts. *General deterrence* is the idea that people other than the person being punished will be deterred from committing crimes because they will witness the suffering of the lawbreaker and they will not want to risk such a fate for themselves. At one time in England, it was not uncommon for parents to take their children to a public hanging and then to beat the children to impress upon them the lesson that crime brings pain and perhaps even death; in other words, they sought to amplify the general deterrent aspects of the event.

The Rehabilitation Approach   The rehabilitation approach to criminal justice views lawbreakers not as bad people in need of punishment but rather as people who are demonstrating a very serious adjustment problem. Even though they may not realize it themselves, lawbreakers are in need of help. This is the point at which criminal justice becomes a social welfare concern. In keeping with our definition of social welfare given in Chapter 2, people who get in trouble with the law are having difficulty fulfilling their role as citizens, and they are dependent on society to help them become able to fill this role and become interdependent actors in society. In nearly all cases, people who are subjected to rehabilitation are defined as dependent by someone else, generally the criminal justice system, and they are, at least initially, involuntary clients. The rehabilitation approach, or perhaps we should say criminal justice as a social welfare concern, involves four basic types of services: diversion, probation, correctional services, and parole, which is also called *correctional casework* or *aftercare*.

Diversion is one of the newest reforms in the criminal justice system; it gained great popularity during the 1960s and 1970s. The objective of diversion programs is to get people out of the criminal justice system as quickly as possible. Generally people are diverted at two points, either prior to arrest or prior to prosecution. At either point the suspect, rather than being subjected to further prosecution by the criminal justice system, is diverted into a treatment program. The idea behind diversion programs is that processing by the criminal justice system often works against the goal of rehabilitation in two ways. The first is that the system labels the person as a criminal and this often becomes a self-fulfilling prophecy—the child whom people think is a thief begins to act like a thief. The second is the old notion of jails as "crime colleges." Once a person is put in close association with criminals, he or she tends to learn all sorts of new crimes, as well as justifications of why they are acceptable.

> Missy Long, 24, was arrested at the mall for shoplifting. She had gone into the dressing room with her two-month-old son in a baby carrier. While in the dressing room, she had wrapped a skirt around the baby, wrapped his blanket around this, and had then walked out of the store. She tearfully told the arresting officer that since she became pregnant and quit work, she and her husband never had money for anything but necessities. She said "I don't know why I took the skirt. The impulse came over me and I just couldn't resist."

Finding that she had no previous criminal record and that she appeared to be going through a very stressful life phase, and believing that no good would come from subjecting her to prosecution, the social worker from the district attorney's office asked if she would be willing to participate in a diversion program. He explained that this would mean that she would need to sign an agreement to fully participate in a program of treatment at the county mental health center. If she dropped out of the program or did not fully cooperate, the shoplifting charges would be reactivated and she would be prosecuted. If she completed the program, all charges would be permanently dropped. Mrs. Long entered the program, which eventually involved individual counseling for her, marriage counseling for her and her husband, and a referral to the state employment service to help her find a part-time job. After one year she completed the program and has had no trouble with the law since.

Probation intervenes in the criminal justice system at a later date than diversion. Under the probation system a person is arrested, convicted, and sentenced to a term in prison or, in the case of a juvenile, is declared to be a delinquent. At this point the person's sentence is suspended and he or she is instead given conditional freedom for a period generally equal to the jail sentence, under the supervision of a probation officer. The conditions of probation include a lengthy list of rules forbidding the probationer to engage in activities such as going to bars and associating with known criminals. The rules also require the probationer to regularly report to the probation officer and get permission to travel out of town, among other things. In the case of juveniles, the rules usually include regular school attendance, and they sometimes even specify the grades he or she must earn in order to stay out of detention. Probation rarely involves any form of treatment and the vast majority of probation officers are neither trained adequately to provide treatment nor do they have time to do so.

At age 15, John Story had been arrested five times for offenses ranging from truancy to auto theft. The fifth arrest was for selling drugs to kids at his school. This time he was prosecuted, declared delinquent, and placed on probation for an indeterminate period. John resented probation and resented his probation officer, about whom he said, "It's like having another father, only worse." He continued to skip school and finally he ran away from home, hopping a freight train with a friend and ending up in California. When he returned several weeks later, his probation officer recommended that his probation be revoked and that he be sent to state training school. This was done and John remained in the training school until his eighteenth birthday.

Correctional services involve the provision of social work services to people who have actually been imprisoned. There are two major types of correctional services. The first involves the provision of counseling/therapy to inmates in an attempt to help them adjust to prison life, resolve personality problems which contributed to their difficulty in living a "straight" life, and plan for their life following release. The other type of services involves helping families of inmates adjust to the many problems that they face. The following example is from England.

Pete appeared in the Crown Court and was sentenced to three years' imprisonment for jointly stealing a lorry-load of jeans. Perhaps unrealistically he had not anticipated being sent to prison and so family affairs were in a real mess the day he was taken down to the cells. He left behind a wife, Rose, and five children aged between ten years and twelve months. Andy [the social worker] called a few days later. He found a mountain of work to be done. Finances needed to be juggled as cleverly as possible, and Rose needed advice over visiting. The children were upset and confused about their father's absence and Rose was distraught.

Andy tried to help during the prison sentence but became aware that his efforts were small compared to the family's needs. [Welfare] levels were pitifully inadequate. Andy helped out with a hamper and toys from a local charity at Christmas, and second-hand clothes at other times. He hated giving "charity," especially when he saw how embarrassed Rose was at needing to accept it. The children missed their father and began playing up; Rose missed her husband but managed to cope with the kids' distress. She became ill through worry and not eating enough, and was slow to recover. The washing machine broke down and the kids were wetting the beds.

Andy gave what he called "support." He argued with obstinate gas board officials and awkward [welfare department] officers on Rose's behalf. One time her [welfare check] didn't arrive. The [welfare department] said it was in the post and refused payment although she was broke. Rose was at the end of her tether and tearfully told Andy she was going down to smash their windows. He calmed her down and arranged a small loan to tide her over until the [check] arrived.

Pete began to wonder if Rose was having an affair—not because he had any evidence, it was just that so many other men had received "dear John" letters. Visits became strained as Pete aggressively questioned Rose about her movements. Anxiety about parole increased the tension. Andy tried to calm Pete and Rose's worries and submitted a parole report emphasizing the positive aspects of circumstances at home. Secretly he doubted whether Pete would get parole.[12]

Parole is the situation in which a person is released from prison before the end of his or her sentence to serve the remainder of the sentence under conditions similar to probation. Violation of any of the many conditions of parole will result in the person being returned to prison to complete the remainder of the sentence. Parole, like probation, generally involves little treatment and often involves little more than loose supervision. The roles of parole officer and probation officer are often combined.

Sandy had run away from home at age 15 and had supported herself as a prostitute. By age 19 she had developed a cocaine habit that was so expensive that she began robbing her clients to get enough money to support it. One night a client resisted and she stabbed him, nearly killing him. She was arrested for attempted murder and, with her history of drug and prostitution busts, was lucky to get the 5 to 20 year sentence that she did. In prison Sandy was a model inmate, getting over her drug habit, earning a high school diploma, and working as a typist in the chaplain's office. After seven years Sandy was released on parole. She was fortunate to be assigned to Martha Stewart, a probation officer who was a trained social worker with over ten years experience. With Martha's help Sandy entered counseling at the local United Way counseling agency, got a job as a typist at the welfare department, and entered secretarial school with a Pell grant to pay her tuition and books. Things are not perfect (Martha suspects that Sandy still occasionally returns to her old profession when times get tough), but with a little luck and continued work she has a chance for a reasonably happy and productive life.

STATISTICAL PROFILE

There are shortages of many things in the world, but criminal justice statistics is not one of them. The *Sourcebook of Criminal Justice Statistics* published annually by the Department of Justice contains more than 500 pages of tables on various aspects of crime and justice; the *Uniform Crime Report* published annually by the FBI adds another 350 pages; the Bureau of Justice Statistics supplements these with numerous reports released periodically. The volume of crime statistics is not a matter of debate; however, the usefulness of them is.

Problems with Crime Statistics

Criminologists claim that there are serious flaws in official crime statistics that make them of highly questionable validity and reliability. Major criticisms include

- The statistics are collected in a fragmented and uncoordinated manner. The agencies collecting the data have no official power to make local agencies report and they have no methods of ascertaining the accuracy of the reporting.
- The crimes reported are not representative of the actual amount and pattern of offenses. Only a fraction of the crimes committed are ever reported to the police. For many crimes, less than half of the actual incidences are ever reported.
- The definitions used vary among jurisdictions and often change from one year to another. The official statistics aggregate data from 50 different states, each with its own criminal code. Thus, in one state an offense committed by a 17-year-old may enter the statistics as a juvenile offense, while in another it is reported as an adult crime.
- The official statistics may be subject to outright fraud and manipulation. These statistics are often used to judge the performance of organizations, such as police departments, or of elected officials, such as district attorneys. These people will often manipulate the statistics to exaggerate the amount of crime if they are seeking a budget increase, or to minimize the crime rate if they wish to make their organizations appear effective.[13]

The point is, when you are looking at criminal justice statistics, including those presented here, do so with a critical eye. While the statistics probably reflect reality, they are not a perfect representation of reality. Also, it is not always clear what reality they reflect. For example, the large increase in drug arrests in recent years is generally interpreted as a reflection of increasing drug use. This may be so, but a large part of the increase may be because of increased drug law enforcement rather than increased use.

Patterns of Crime

In this section we will look at data on the amount of crime and the characteristics of persons arrested.

Volume of Crime   Figure 10–1 and Table 10–1 are presented to give a very rough idea of the amount of crime in the United States. Figure 10–1 is the crime clock which is published annually by the FBI as the most aggregate representation of data in the *Uniform Crime Report*. It is a very rough measure, but it does serve to effectively illustrate that there is a tremendous amount of crime. Table 10–1 on pages 312–313 is a more detailed presentation. Perhaps the most important aspect of Table 10–1 is the section

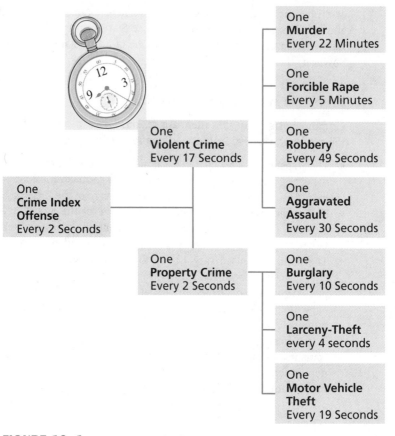

FIGURE 10–1   Crime Clock 1990

Source: Uniform Crime Reports, *Crime in the United States* (Washington, D.C.: U.S. Department of Justice, Federal Bureau of Investigation, 1990), 7.

showing the percent change in the number of offenses. You will note that most of the items have increased, with the most dramatic increase being in the area of violent crimes. Between 1977 and 1989, violent crime statistics recorded an increase of 39.5 percent. The accuracy of this figure is not important for our purposes here. What is important is that it is generally perceived to be accurate and it contributes to the attitude, to be discussed later, that we are experiencing a crime wave and that we need to get tough with criminals.

Sex   Crime is an overwhelmingly male activity. In 1984 in the United States, 83.3 percent of all arrests made were of males. There are a few areas of crime in which female arrests come close to or exceed those of males—30.2 percent of arrests for larceny-theft; 33.7 percent of arrests for forgery and counterfeiting; 40.4 percent of embezzlement arrests; 36.9 percent of arrests for buying, receiving, or possessing stolen property; and 69.9 percent of arrests for vice (mainly prostitution).[14]

Age   Criminal behavior tends to be highly concentrated among the younger age groups. As can be seen in Table 10–2 on page 314, the vast majority (70 percent) of arrests are of people between the ages of 13 and 34. After age 34 the tendency toward criminal behavior drops sharply and after age 40 it becomes relatively rare. These figures form much of the support for the position of those who argue that the function of the criminal justice system should be incapacitation. They argue that if a criminal is incapacitated by being locked up for a long enough period of time, then he or she will most likely "grow out" of his or her criminal tendencies.

Race   As can be seen by inspecting Table 10–3 on page 315, whites and Asians are underrepresented in the crime statistics. African Americans and Native Americans are overrepresented, particularly in the area of violent crime. There are four reasons which account for these differences. The first is the age structure of various subgroups of the population. Minority groups tend to be younger than whites—particularly African Americans, whose average age is seven years less than that of whites. Because crime is concentrated among the young, this partially accounts for the difference in crime rates. The second reason is that minorities are more heavily concentrated in urban areas where more opportunities for both crime and apprehension by the police exist. The third reason is selective enforcement. Police tend to patrol minority neighborhoods more heavily than they do white neighborhoods, thereby increasing the chance of a minority lawbreaker being arrested. The final explanation is economic opportunity. In the section on dynamics we will discuss theories of crime that explain crime as being largely a result of people lacking legitimate opportunities for success. As we discussed in the section on poverty, minorities are far more likely than whites to be poor. Therefore, according to strain and opportunity theories, they are more likely to turn to crime as a means of achieving goals to which the legitimate channels of achievement are blocked.

Social Welfare and Crime

The statistics discussed earlier are interesting, but they are of secondary importance for our purposes here. What is of primary importance is how these statistics grind through the criminal justice system and become input for the social welfare system.

Juveniles   Because children are not considered to be responsible for their actions, rehabilitation is almost always chosen over punishment as a response to juvenile crime. Less than 2 percent of all juvenile arrests result in waiver to criminal court; the rest are handled either informally or else in the more treatment-oriented juvenile court.[15]

Tables 10–4 and 10–5 present breakdowns of the placement of juveniles. Table 10–4 on page 316 shows the types of offenses and placements of the young people placed outside their homes. Table 10–5 on page 317 shows that the average length of stay was relatively short, considerably less than one year. Worthy of note is the fact that only 25,704, slightly less than 46 percent of the total placed, were in public, long-term, institutional facilities, generally known as reform or training schools, also colloquially called "junior jails." Thus, out of a beginning number of 1.3 million arrests, only about two-tenths of one percent end up in what is generally considered a pun-

TABLE 10–1   Index of Crime, United States 1977–1989

Population	Crime Index Total	Total Violent Crime	Total Property Crime	Violent Crime Murder and Nonnegligent Manslaughter
Number of Offenses:				
1977–216,332,000	10,984,500	1,029,580	9,955,000	19,120
1980–225,349,264	13,408,300	1,344,520	12,063,700	23,040
1983–233,981,000	12,108,600	1,258,090	10,850,500	19,310
1986–241,077,000	13,210,800	1,488,140	11,722,700	20,610
1989–248,239,000	14,251,400	1,646,040	12,605,400	21,500
Percent change: number of offenses				
1989/1986	+7.8	+10.6	+7.5	+4.3
1989/1983	+17.7	+30.8	+16	+11.3
1989/1980	+6.3	+22.4	+4.4	−6.6
1989/1977	+29.7	+59.9	+26.6	+12.4
Rate per 100,000 inhabitants				
1977	5,007.6	475.9	4,601.7	8.8
1980	5,950.0	596.6	5,353.3	10.2
1983	5,175.0	537.7	4,637.4	8.3
1986	5,479.9	617.3	4,862.6	8.6
1989	5,741.0	663.7	5,077.9	8.7
Percent change: rate per 100,000 inhabitants				
1989/1986	+4.8	+7	+4.4	+8.9
1989/1983	+10.9	+23.4	+9.5	−5.5
1989/1980	−3.5	+11.3	−5.1	−2.3
1989/1977	+14.6	+39.5	+10.3	

Source: Adapted from Kathleen Maguire and Timothy J. Flanagan, *Sourcebook of Criminal Justice Statistics—1990* (Washington, D.C.: U.S. Department of Justice, Bureau of Justice Statistics, U.S. Government Printing Office, 1991), 353.

ishment facility. This figure clearly illustrates the point that crime among juveniles is considered to be a more proper subject for rehabilitation by the social welfare institution than for punishment by the criminal justice system.

Adult Corrections   The statistics for the adult correctional population are summarized in Table 10–6 on page 318. The fact that over one-half of the population is on probation, which means they are supervised in the community instead of serving any prison time, indicates that even in the area of adult crime we still have faith in the rehabilitative ideal and turn to the social welfare institution for dealing with the problem of crime.

Forcible Rape	Robbery	Aggravated Assault	Property Crime		
			Burglary	Larceny-Theft	Motor Vehicle Theft
63,500	412,610	534,350	3,071,500	5,905,700	977,700
82,990	565,840	672,650	3,795,200	7,136,900	1,311,700
78,920	506,570	653,290	3,129,900	6,712,800	1,007,900
90,430	542,780	834,320	3,241,400	7,257,200	1,224,100
94,500	578,330	951,710	3,168,200	7,872,400	1,564,800
+4.5	+6.5	+14	−2.2	+8.5	+27.8
+19.7	+14.2	+45.7	+1.2	+17.3	+55.3
+13.9	+22	+4.5	−16.5	+10.3	+38.3
+48.8	+40.2	+78.1	+3.1	+33.3	+60
29.4	190.7	247.0	1,419.8	2,729.9	451.9
36.8	251.1	298.5	1,684.1	3,167.0	502.2
33.7	216.5	279.2	1,337.3	2,868.9	430.8
37.5	225.1	346.1	1,344.6	3,010.3	507.8
38.1	233.0	383.4	1,276.3	3,171.3	630.4
+1.6	+3.5	+10.8	−5	+5.3	+24.1
+13	+7.6	+37.3	−4.6	+10.5	+46.3
+3.5	−7.2	+28.4	−24.2	+.01	+25.5
+29.6	+22.2	+55.2	−10.1	+16.2	+39.5

DYNAMICS

When we look at explanations of crime, we are confronted with a bewildering array of theories. There are three major groups of theories that attempt to explain the dynamics of crime—control theories, cultural theories, and social victim theories.

Control Theories

Control theories proceed from the conservative assumption that human nature is basically bad and that society must control people's natural antisocial nature. Ernest van den

TABLE 10–2	Percent distribution of total U.S. population and persons arrested for all offenses by age group, United States, 1989	

Age Group	U.S. Resident Population	Persons Arrested
Age 12 and younger	19.1%	1.7%
13 to 15	4.0	6.3
16 to 18	4.3	12.4
19 to 21	4.5	13.6
22 to 24	4.6	11.9
25 to 29	8.7	18.4
30 to 34	8.9	14.1
35 to 39	7.9	9.0
40 to 44	6.8	5.3
45 to 49	5.4	3.0
50 to 54	4.6	1.7
55 to 59	4.3	1.1
60 to 64	4.4	0.7
Age 65 and older	12.5	0.7

Source: Timothy J. Flanagan and Kathleen Maguire, eds., *Sourcebook of Criminal Justice Statistics, 1990,* (Washington, D.C.: U.S. Department of Justice, Bureau of Justice Statistics, U.S. Government Printing Office, 1991), 414.

Haag, for example, argues that "For the most part, offenders are not sick. They are like us. Worse, we are like them. Potentially, we could all be . . . criminals."[16] These theories explain crime as the result of people failing to control their natural antisocial impulses. They may be unable to control their impulses because they are inherently incapable of controlling themselves, because they are psychologically incapable of self-restraint, because they have been improperly socialized, or because the costs and benefits of crime result in a more favorable outcome than the costs and benefits of self-control.

Biological Control Theory The earliest theories of crime were *biological control theories,* which Empey refers to as "kinds-of-people" theories. These theories assert that criminals are innately inferior people who have not inherited the ability to control their aggressive impulses and behave in responsible ways.[17] The first biological control theorist was the nineteenth century Italian physician Cesare Lombroso. Lombroso believed that criminals were physically different from noncriminals and he set out to test his hypothesis by performing an extensive series of physical measurements on convicts and comparing these measurements to those of nonconvicts. Lombroso published his findings in 1876 in a book entitled *The Criminal Man.* In this book Lombroso reported his conclusion that criminals are "atavistic types"; that is, they are born

TABLE 10–3	Distribution of arrests by race, 1989			
Group	% of Population	% of Total Crime	% of Violent Crime	% of Property Crime
White	78	67.3	50.8	63.9
Black	11	30.8	47.7	34
Asian	1.4	.8	.7	1.1
Native American	.6	1	.7	1

Source: Adapted from Timothy J. Flanagan and Kathleen Maguire, eds., *Sourcebook of Criminal Justice Statistics–1990,* (Washington, D.C.: Department of Justice, Bureau of Justice Statistics, U.S. Government Printing Office, 1991), 424.

law-breakers who are subhuman throwbacks to an earlier, more primitive stage of human evolution. Criminal types could, Lombroso claimed, be identified by physical features that are characteristic of an earlier form of evolutionary development. These characteristics are: imbalanced regions of the brain, an asymmetrical face and skull, an abnormal nose, fleshy protruding lips, excessively long arms, abundant wrinkles, abnormal sex organs, a high tolerance for pain, and other physical anomalies. Lombroso argued that people who possess five or more of these characteristics will lack self-control and be predisposed to crime.[18] Simply put, according to Lombroso criminals are cavemen in our midst.

Following Lombroso, there have been a number of theories and studies which have attempted to explain crime as somehow related to innate characteristics which render the individual incapable of controlling his or her antisocial impulses. Probably the most influential is the work of William Sheldon, who argues that people are innately predisposed to criminal behavior and that this predisposition can be detected by an examination of body types. Sheldon conducted a study of the physical measurements of 200 boys in a school for delinquents and compared these with measurements of 200 college boys. Based on the data he collected, he divided young men into three distinctive body types. The first he called *endomorphs,* who are fat and round; the second are *mesomorphs,* who are large-boned and muscular; and third are *ectomorphs,* who are lean and delicate. Sheldon argues that these body types are genetically determined and that each produces a different personality and temperament. Mesomorphs are aggressive and insensitive, they are quick to translate impulse into action, and they are inherently deficient in internal controls. Sheldon concludes that because of these characteristics, mesomorphs are predisposed to criminal behavior.[19]

Biological control theories died out in the liberal years of the 1960s and were generally thought to be so wrong-minded that they were often treated in texts and in criminology classes as subjects of humor. However, with the resurgence of conservatism in the 1980s, these theories have found new advocates and are once again the subject of serious academic debate and research. In their 1985 book *Crime and Human Nature,* political scientist James Q. Wilson and psychologist Richard J. Herrnstein, both of Harvard University, devote five chapters to the relation of constitutional factors to criminal behavior. They forcefully conclude that the work of Lombroso and Sheldon,

TABLE 10–4   Number of juveniles in custody by reasons held and by type of public facility: 1989

	All Facilities	Short-term Facilities			Long-term Facilities		
		Total	Institutional	Open	Total	Institutional	Open
Total juveniles	56,123	19,967	19,146	821	36,156	25,704	10,452
Total detained	17,612	16,885	16,349	536	727	402	325
Delinquent offenses[a]	16,277	15,670	15,516	154	607	378	229
Status offenses[b]	1,008	929	701	228	79	21	58
Abuse/neglect[c]	249	212	62	150	37	3	34
Offenses unknown[d]	78	74	70	4	4	0	4
Total committed	38,209	3,014	2,762	252	35,195	25,291	9,904
Delinquent offenses	36,760	2,847	2,664	183	33,913	24,927	8,986
Status offenses	1,237	140	77	63	1,097	355	742
Abuse/neglect	177	14	8	6	163	7	156
Offenses unknown	35	13	13	0	22	2	20
Voluntarily admitted	302	68	35	33	234	11	223

[a]Offenses that would be criminal if committed by an adult.

[b]Offenses that would not be criminal for adults, such as running away, truancy, or incorrigibility.

[c]Also includes dependency, emotional disturbance, and mental retardation.

[d]Includes unknown or unspecified acts.

Source: Terence P. Thornberry, et. al., eds., *Children in Custody—1987; A Comparison of Public and Private Placement Facilities* (Washington, D.C.: U.S. Department of Justice, Office of Juvenile Justice and Delinquency Prevention, U.S. Government Printing Office, 1989), 43.

among others, was too quickly dismissed and that it should be taken seriously. Their work comes under the heading of neoclassical control theory, which will be examined later in this section.

Psychological Control Theory   Heavily based on the theories of Freud, *psychological control theories* locate the causes of criminal behavior within the psychological development of the individual rather than in his or her genetic makeup. Freud asserts that people are born with a set of primitive, antisocial instincts, which he labeled the *id*. Freud wrote that "The primitive, savage, and evil impulses of mankind have not vanished in any individual, but continue their existence, although in a repressed state."[20] The basically antisocial instincts of people are repressed by the socialization process of children, which results in the development of what Freud called a *superego,* generally known as a conscience. Advocates of psychological control theory claim four major insights about the causes of crime: (1) criminal behavior is neurotic behavior; (2) criminal behavior is the result of a defective superego; (3) the superego is defective because of faulty childhood socialization; and (4) criminal behavior represents a search for gratification to compensate for deprivations in childhood.[21] Thus, like biological control theory, psychological control theory shares the belief that human beings are basically antisocial and will naturally commit crimes unless they are controlled in some

TABLE 10–5	Average lengths of stay in public and private facilities, 1986		
Average Length of Stay (days)			
Short-term facilities			
Institutional	16	14	30
Open	34	33	34
Long-term facilities			
Institutional	265	225	317
Open	267	159	290
All facilities	210	109	261

Source: Barbara Allen-Hagen, *Public Juvenile Facilities, Children in Custody, 1989* (Washington, D.C.: U.S. Department of Justice, Office of Juvenile Justice and Delinquency Prevention, U.S. Government Printing Office, 1991), 5.

way. Unlike biological theory, psychological control theory does not believe that some people are predisposed to crime at birth; rather it asserts that we are all equally predisposed and what happens during the early years of childhood socialization explains which of us follow our natural tendencies and become criminals and which of us are able to overcome these tendencies and become law-abiding citizens.

Although psychological control theory shares biological control theory's pessimism about human nature, it is more optimistic about what can be done about it. The problem of crime is seen as an unconscious response to a combination of antisocial instincts and poor parental practices. Therefore, the problem of criminal behavior is viewed as being treatable just like any illness or adjustment problem. The whole rehabilitation approach in corrections, especially the juvenile court, is based on psychological control theory. The premise is that if some form of treatment can be delivered to criminals that will compensate for their faulty upbringing and help them develop self-control through developing their superego, they will become productive citizens.

Social Control Theory Like the other control theories, *social control theory* starts with the belief that human nature is inherently antisocial. A leading proponent of social control theory, Travis Hirschi, says that "we are all animals, and thus all naturally capable of committing criminal acts." Hirschi says that the question of "why do people commit crimes?" needs no answer. People commit crimes because it is their nature to do so. The question that really needs an answer is "why do most people *not* commit crimes?"[22]

Hirschi asserts that most people do not commit crimes because there is a bond between them and society. People internalize the norms of the society in which they live and in so doing they become moral beings sensitive to the needs of others. The social bonds identified by Hirschi include: the ties of respect and affection that develop between children and key people in their lives, such as parents, teachers, relatives, and friends; commitment to social norms of behavior and to success in regard to such values as getting a good education, a good job, and being successful; involvement in

TABLE 10–6	Adults involved in the criminal justice system, 1989	
	Probation	2,520,479
	Parole	456,797
	Jail	393,303
	Prison	683,367
	Total	4,053,946

Source: Adapted from data in Steven Dillingham, *Correctional Populations in the United States, 1989* (Washington, D.C.: U.S. Department of Justice, Bureau of Justice Statistics, U.S. Government Printing Office, 1991), 6.

activities because the more activities a person is involved in, the less time he or she will have to get into trouble; and finally the fact that most persons are brought up to believe in and respect the law.

Social control theory basically views criminal behavior as a result of people not being adequately attached to the society in which they live. Hirschi says, "If a person does not care about the wishes and expectations of other people—that is, if he is insensitive to the opinion of others—then he is to that extent not bound by the norms. He is free to deviate."[23] The family is viewed as the major place where attachments, and therefore commitment to norms, develop. Thus, social control theory advocates the strengthening of families as a major crime control strategy.

Neoclassical Control Theory   Partly in response to the fact that the crime rate has continued to rise in spite of numerous rehabilitation and crime prevention programs, and partly in response to the general growth of conservatism in recent years, a resurgence of control theories has occurred. *Neoclassical control theories* are based on the belief that rehabilitation programs are totally without merit and that the criminal justice system should return to the practice of responding to crimes, not criminals. There are two versions of neoclassical theory—utilitarian theory and just deserts theory.

The primary proponents of *utilitarian theory* are James Q. Wilson, Richard Herrnstein, and Ernest van den Haag.[24] Utilitarian theorists contend that people commit crimes for basically practical reasons; they do so because they can get away with it and because they know that if they do get caught, the price they pay will not be severe. In other words, crime is viewed as having a favorable cost/benefit ratio. People commit crimes because they make a rational calculation that the potential profit from a crime exceeds the potential cost.

Utilitarian theory is based on two basic beliefs. The first is that punishment deters crime. Because people commit crimes for practical reasons involving costs and benefits, a high risk of severe punishment will increase the cost of doing crime and therefore it will discourage this behavior. The second belief is that punishment vindicates the social order. Utilitarians believe that in a just society, debts must be paid if people are to take the society seriously and to believe in its basic fairness. When a person commits a crime, he or she must be punished in order to square accounts. Ernest van den Haag says, "Laws threaten, or promise, punishments for crimes. Society has obligated itself by threatening. It owes the carrying out of its threats. Society pays its debt by punishing the offender, however unwilling he is to accept payment."[25]

The other brand of neoclassical control theory is the *just deserts theory*. This approach has been characterized by Empey as "a remarkable expression of the despair and pessimism that characterize currently popular views of American justice."[26] The main idea of the just deserts philosophy is that rehabilitation does not work, which is an idea shared with utilitarian theory, but it goes further and argues that punishment does not work either. The sole purpose of the criminal justice system, according to this theory, should be to insure that offenders are punished to a degree consistent with the severity of their offense—no more, no less. The just deserts approach is very concerned with due process issues. Its adherents would like to remove as much discretion as possible from the process and make the justice system mechanized.

Summary of Control Theories   The four versions and several subversions of control theory that we have reviewed all share a very conservative, pessimistic view of human nature. Humans are viewed as being aggressive, self-serving, and amoral by nature. People will all commit crimes unless somehow they are controlled. Basically these theories are all pessimistic about the potential for rehabilitating law violators, and they are therefore generally hostile to a social welfare approach to crime. The one exception to this is psychological control theory, whose adherents are sympathetic to the idea of therapy for criminals.

Cultural Theories

Cultural theories of crime are closely related to cultural theories of poverty discussed in Chapter 7. These theories reject the assumption of control theories that human nature is inherently antisocial and that control mechanisms are necessary to prevent people from committing crimes. Rather, cultural theories assume that human nature is inherently social and crime is a result of people becoming involved with deviant subcultures that value crime over law-abiding behavior. According to these theories, a criminal is a person who is behaving in accordance with the values and norms of the particular groups with which he associates. There are three major variants of cultural theories of crime: cultural deviance, differential association, and strain theory.

Cultural Deviance   *Cultural deviance theory* began with the work of Clifford R. Shaw and Henry D. McKay in Chicago in the 1920s. Shaw and McKay, who were trained as demographers, were originally interested in two questions related to juvenile delinquency. The first was, "How are delinquents geographically distributed in the city?" They studied this by simply plotting on city maps the addresses of all juveniles officially declared to be delinquent by Chicago courts. What they found was that delinquency rates were consistently higher in inner city, impoverished neighborhoods. Looking at delinquency rates over time they found a very interesting thing. The delinquency rates for neighborhoods remained remarkably constant over time *even though the population of the neighborhood often completely changed.* A neighborhood might be Italian for a number of years, then change to mainly Irish, and then gradually change until it was almost completely black, yet the delinquency rate stayed constant. The delinquency rate of the group which moved out, generally to a better neighborhood, by contrast, dropped to a rate that mirrored the rate of the new neighborhood.

Shaw and McKay's findings on the geographic distribution of delinquency led to their second question, "What are the social conditions associated with high delinquency neighborhoods?" They found that prominent among these conditions were physical deterioration; economic segregation; racial and ethnic segregation; a high incidence of social ills, such as infant mortality, mental illness, unemployment, divorce and desertion; and a high rate of dropping out of school.

Shaw and McKay developed cultural deviance theory in an effort to explain the findings of their research. They assert that crime is more closely related to characteristics of the neighborhoods in which people live than it is to any innate characteristics of the people who commit crimes. The process works basically as follows: deteriorated areas (generally known as slums or ghettos) produce social disorganization characterized by inadequate family life, poverty, physical deterioration, and ineffective religious, educational, and recreational organizations. This social disorganization leads to a lack of effective social controls over children; lack of effective social controls from family, church, and school causes children to form into street gangs, which develop deviant social controls; and finally, the deviant social controls developed by street gangs are then passed from one generation to another.[27]

Walter Miller, an anthropologist, updated cultural deviance theory in 1958 into a form that is closely akin to Oscar Lewis's culture of poverty theory.[28] Miller argues that the lower class is characterized by a distinctive culture with its own norms and standards of behavior. In contrast to Shaw and McKay, Miller argues that lower-class communities are not disorganized; they just have different values than the larger society. He says that "there is emerging a relatively homogeneous and stabilized native American lower-class culture."[29] The values that Miller describes as characterizing this subculture are very similar to those described by Lewis in his books on culture of poverty: female-dominated families; marginal roles for men; focal concerns of trouble, smartness, fate, and autonomy; and the belief that deferred gratification and hard work are for suckers. In this culture, according to Miller, crime is considered to be acceptable and even desirable; conformity to middle-class standards is deviant.

The major idea of cultural deviance theories is that people who commit crimes are not deviants whose basically antisocial nature is not adequately controlled. Rather, criminals are individuals who are conforming to a set of social norms just like anyone else; however, their set of norms is different from that of the majority of society. Crime, in other words, is a product of the environment, not the individual.

Differential Association Theory *Differential association theory* began with the work of Edwin H. Sutherland in 1939.[30] The assumption of this theory is that both human nature and the social structure are plastic; a person's behavior and values are constantly changing in response to the group that he or she is interacting with, and groups are constantly changing in response to the people who participate in them. Furthermore, everyone participates in a number of groups, and the roles and expectations may be very different, and sometimes even conflicting, in different groups. All people, according to this theory, are exposed to deviant as well as conformist influences.

Differential association theory explains crime as learned behavior. People learn criminal behavior through the groups with which they associate. If a person associates with more groups that define criminal behavior as acceptable than groups that define criminal behavior as unacceptable, the person will probably engage in criminal behavior. On the other hand, if a person mostly associates with groups that do not define crime as acceptable, the person will probably not commit crimes.

Differential association theory provides a strong argument against imprisoning people convicted of crimes. According to this theory, putting a person in prison removes him or her from association with groups that do not define crime in favorable terms and it puts the person exclusively in contact with groups who possess definitions favorable to crime. Thus, a person spending time in prison will only develop a more positive attitude toward crime and a more negative definition of law-abiding behavior.

Strain Theory The final variety of cultural theory, *strain theory,* is based on the work of Robert Merton, and it has been further developed by Albert Cohen, Richard Cloward, and Lloyd Ohlin.[31] Strain theory rejects many of the arguments of cultural deviance theory that crime is a result of a deviant lower-class subculture, and of differential association theory that criminal behavior occurs when a person associates with more groups who favor crime than groups who do not. Both these theories assert that people become criminals because they have values which are different from those of the larger society. Strain theory, in contrast, argues that people who commit crimes have basically the same values as everyone else. Primary among these values is an emphasis on achievement and success. According to this theory, the avenues for the achievement of success are greatly restricted for people in the lower class. Thus, they are faced with a cruel dilemma: either they abandon the major American values of success and prosperity or they abandon another—obedience of the law. According to Merton, "A cardinal American virtue, 'ambition,' promotes a cardinal American vice, 'deviant behavior.' "[32]

Strain theory has been mainly applied to juvenile delinquency among lower-class boys. The central idea is that these young people share the value of success with the larger culture, but because of inadequate socialization they are unable to effectively compete. This produces strain which they seek to resolve. In Cohen's version of the theory, the boys respond to this strain by adopting one of three general roles. The first role is what he calls the "corner boy." This person adapts to his sense of frustration and failure by accepting his lower-class status, removing himself from competition for success, and withdrawing into a sheltering group of boys who have also resigned themselves to failure. The name for this role is derived from the fact that these are the type of people one sees aimlessly hanging around street corners. The second role is what Cohen calls the "college boy." This person, who is relatively rare according to Cohen, accepts the challenge of middle-class society and chooses to compete on middle-class terms. Finally there is the "delinquent boy." This person accepts middle-class standards of material success but rejects middle-class means of acquiring success; he turns to crime as a means of achieving valued goals.

Summary of Cultural Theories The three general types of cultural theories discussed here share the view that human nature is basically social and that criminal behavior can be best explained by looking at environmental influences on individuals. Cultural deviance theory asserts that lower-class communities produce a deviant subculture that is relatively favorable to crime. In these communities, a person who commits crimes is considered normal and one who strongly opposes crime is considered abnormal.

Differential association theory argues that people become criminals not because they live in deviant subcultures but because they associate with more groups that favor crime than groups that oppose crime. A strength of this theory over the others is that it makes it possible to explain people in lower-class neighborhoods who are law abiding as well as people in middle- and upper-class areas who engage in criminal acts. The final version, strain theory, argues that lower-class people have the same values as people in the rest of society—mainly that they value success—but they lack access to legitimate channels for achieving success. Therefore they turn to crime as a means of pursuing the American dream.

Social Victim Theory

Social victim theories, as a group, proceed from the liberal assumption that human nature is basically good and that if a person becomes a criminal it is because society has somehow corrupted him or her. Empey observes that social victim theory "represents the culmination of a line of social thought which has progressively led away from the notion that delinquent tendencies are inherent in individuals and toward the notion that such tendencies are inherent in the way society makes rules, enforces those rules, and selectively punishes some people and not others."[33] Two major types of social victim theories will be discussed, labeling theory and radical theory.

Labeling Theory *Labeling theory* makes the assertion that committing a crime is not what makes a person a criminal. Studies indicate that the vast majority of people have committed at least one, and often many, acts that are against the law. Yet most people are not criminals. Labeling theorists argue that what makes a person a criminal is getting *caught* committing a crime and then being publicly identified as a criminal. In other words, it is the label that makes a person into a criminal, not the act itself. Howard Becker, one of the leading proponents of labeling theory says

> Social groups make deviance by making the rules whose infractions constitute deviance and by applying these rules to particular people and labeling them as outsiders. From this point of view, deviance is *not* a quality of the act a person commits, but rather a consequence of the application by others of rules and sanctions to the "offender." The deviant is one to whom that label has successfully been applied; deviant behavior is the behavior that people so label.[34]

The theory goes on to argue that if a person is unlucky enough to get caught, and thereby become labeled as a criminal, then people will respond to the person as a criminal, the person will begin to think of himself or herself as a criminal, and the person will then internalize this socially imposed self-image and begin to act in ways in which we expect a criminal to behave. In other words, what occurs is a self-fulfilling prophecy—society expects a person to act like a criminal and the person lives up to the expectation. As you will learn in Chapter 11 a similar process can be described for those labeled mentally ill.

Labeling theorists argue that labels are very selectively applied. Not everyone who is caught is labeled. The labeling depends on a number of factors that are not related to the act a person has committed, including who they are, what class they are, what race they are, and whether they treat the police with the proper respect. Members of low-power groups, it is argued, are much more likely to be labeled when caught committing a crime than are members of higher status groups. Thus, there are more poor, young, and minority group criminals because we are more likely to assign the label of criminal to members of these groups and hence to make them criminals.

Radical Criminology   *Radical criminology* is based on the assumption that human nature is essentially good and, although people may occasionally act in selfish ways, if they actually become criminal it is because they are responding to a repressive and corrupting society. This approach rejects all attempts to understand crime as a result of individual characteristics and it advocates radical social change as the only real way to reduce crime. One of the leading advocates of radical theory, Richard Quinney, has summarized the theory's main ideas in the following six propositions

- American society is based on an advanced capitalist economy.
- The state is organized to serve the interests of the dominant economic class, the capitalist ruling class.
- Criminal law is an instrument of the state and ruling class to maintain and perpetuate the existing social and economic order.
- Crime control in capitalist society is accomplished through a variety of institutions and agencies established and administered by a governmental elite, representing ruling class interests, for the purpose of establishing domestic order.
- The contradictions of advanced capitalism . . . require that the subordinate classes remain oppressed by whatever means necessary, especially through the coercion and violence of the legal system.
- Only with the collapse of capitalist society and the creation of a new society, based on socialist principles, will there be a solution to the crime problem.[35]

Radical theory sees little difference between the punishment and rehabilitation approaches to dealing with crime. Both are viewed as means by which society blames the victims of capitalist repression for problems for which they are not responsible. The only real solution to the problem of crime, according to these theorists, is to abandon the approach of working with individuals altogether and to instead focus on the real source of crime, the oppressive and repressive social and economic system.

A BRIEF HISTORY OF CRIMINAL JUSTICE

Historian Blake McKelvey subtitled his study of corrections in America "A History of Good Intentions." McKelvey makes the point that generation after generation of reformers have attempted to make prisons into something constructive, and time after time, their efforts have had poor and often tragic results.[36] Unfortunately, McKelvey's pessimistic analysis of prisons can be generalized to all efforts to deal with the problem of crime in our society. All efforts to make something constructive out of criminal justice programs, from the development of prisons right through to the recent emphasis on diversion programs, have started out with high hopes and great expectations, but have generally turned sour. As Rothman has observed, the pride of one generation becomes the shame of another.[37]

Prisons—The First Reform

Because it is hard for us to imagine a society without prisons, it is therefore surprising to realize that the idea of the prison has a fairly recent origin. Prior to the late 1700s there were no prisons that were places where people were incarcerated for long periods of time for either punishment or rehabilitation. As Dershowitz has said, "The concept of rehabilitation would have been entirely alien to the early colonists . . . Society's duty was simply to punish the offender swiftly, publicly and often quite harshly."[38] Rothman explains that the colonists' nearly exclusive use of corporal or capital punishment and their total lack of concern with reforming lawbreakers was a natural result of their view of human nature. He says that given the colonists' "conception of deviant behavior and institutional organization, they did not believe that a jail could rehabilitate or intimidate or detain the offender. They placed little faith in the possibility of reform. Prevailing Calvinist doctrines that stressed the natural depravity of man and the powers of the devil hardly allowed such optimism. Since temptations to misconduct were not only omnipresent but practically irresistible, rehabilitation could not serve as the basis for a prison program."[39] Given this orientation, jails existed only as places where people accused of crimes could be detained while awaiting trial and, if convicted, punishment. Punishments consisted of fines for those able to pay and/or some inconvenience or abuse of the offender's body, such as stocks, pillory, flogging, branding, or mutilation, and, for many offenses, death.

The establishment of prisons in eighteenth century America was a result of two developments—the Enlightenment and the American Revolution. Enlightenment thinking, as espoused in the works of philosophers such as Montesquieu, Rousseau, and Voltaire, stressed that man was a rational creature and that the world was guided by rational principles which man could discover and ultimately control through the use of his intelligence. This philosophy was applied to criminal justice by Cesare Beccaria, an Italian who published *On Crimes and Punishments* in 1764. Beccaria made three main points regarding how society should react to crimes: punishment should be proportional to the severity of the crime; punishment should be certain and should be just severe enough so the cost of committing a crime exceeds the benefits derived from it; and excessively severe penalties undermine the authority of the courts and the deterrent effect of punishment.[40] The American Revolution, for its part, contributed to an atmosphere in which everything English was viewed with suspicion. The brutal criminal justice system which the new republic inherited from the colonies was clearly of English origin and thus it was considered ripe for reform. The works of Enlightenment thinkers such as Beccaria provided the rationale for the reform.

The process of criminal justice reform began almost immediately after the end of the American Revolution. It had two major components. The first was the elimination of the death penalty for crimes other than first-degree murder or a handful of serious crimes such as treason. This reform was based on Beccaria's idea that punishment should not be overly severe for the crime in question. People had frequently been found not guilty of crimes by juries who thought them guilty but were unwilling to impose the death penalty for a relatively minor crime. Thus, the overly severe punishment resulted in people not being punished at all. The second component, related to the first, was the development of the concept of incarceration in prison for long periods of time as a substitute punishment for death and the usually grotesque corporal punishments previously applied. This was related to Beccaria's idea that punishment should be proportional to the seriousness of the crime. The length of prison sentences could be precisely tailored to fit crimes of any degree of seriousness: for a minor crime, a person could be imprisoned for as little as a few days; for a major crime, he or she could be imprisoned for life. Prison construction proceeded at a fast pace with the first, the Walnut Street Jail, being built in Philadelphia in 1790, Newgate state prison built in New York in 1796, the New Jersey penitentiary completed in 1797, prisons in Virginia and Kentucky built in 1800, and facilities completed within a few years in Vermont, New Hampshire, and Maryland.[41] Thus, in a remarkably short time, the criminal justice system in the United States had been reformed from a system based on a Calvinistic notion of punishment to one based on an enlightened notion of rehabilitation with the prison as its central feature.

The assumption behind the first wave of criminal justice reform which resulted in the construction of prisons was that the legal system itself was the cause of crime. Because it was arbitrary, uncertain, and brutal, the system was believed to increase rather than control crime. When the system was reformed and prisons were constructed, the new system in which sentences were fair and certainty of punishment was high would, in itself, be sufficient to control crime. Thus, prisons were constructed with a serious problem built in; no one had really given much thought as to what to do with convicts once they were there. As Rothman has noted, "A repulsion from the gallows rather than any faith in the penitentiary spurred the late-eighteenth century construction. Few people had any clear idea what these structures should look like or how they should be administered—or even addressed themselves seriously to these questions."[42]

The Indeterminate Sentence and Parole

The correctional philosophy of the early prison reformers and administrators was highly simplistic. They believed that crime was a result of disorder in society and so the reformation of criminals was simply a matter of placing them in a well-ordered environment where they would learn orderly habits and develop the moral fiber necessary to resist the corrupting influences of a disorderly society. Therefore, the emphasis in prisons was on routines, silence, and reading the Bible. This was accomplished by isolating and regimenting the prisoners as much as possible. The ideal was to have each person confined to his cell almost all of the time, with only a Bible for companionship. By the middle of the nineteenth century people began to realize that this approach to penology was not working. The failure of the system was considered to be due to the fact that prison administrators were having to devote almost all of their energy to maintaining order. In an 1867 report to the New York legislature, E. C. Wines and Theodore Dwight stated that prisons no longer had rehabilitation as their central goal. They said that "There is not a state prison in America in which the reformation of the convicts is the one supreme object of the [institution] to which everything else must bend." By the standard of reformation "there is not a prison system in the United States, which . . . would not be found wanting. There is not one, we feel convinced . . . which seeks the reformation of its subjects as a primary object

. . . They are all . . . lacking in the breadth and comprehensiveness of their scope; all lacking in the employment of a wise and effective machinery to keep the whole in health and vigorous action."[43]

Critics argued that the major failing of the correctional system was that prisoners had no incentive to cooperate in their own rehabilitation. They were given "flat" or "determinate" sentences by the courts, which meant that they knew exactly how long their sentences were and nothing they did, short of committing a new criminal offense, would have any effect on the length. Reformers in the last half of the nineteenth century began to advocate *indeterminate sentences,* in which a person was sentenced to serve a range of years, say three to ten; by cooperating with prison authorities the person could serve the shorter length of time, and by not cooperating, he would serve the maximum length of time. As one prison reformer said, "The prisoner's destiny should be placed, measurably, in his own hands; he must be put into circumstances where he will be able, through his own exertions, to continually better his own conditions. A regulated self-interest must be brought into play, and made constantly operative." Another said, "When a man keeps the key to his own prison, he is soon persuaded to fit it to the lock."[44]

The concept of the indeterminate sentence was first applied at Elmira Reformatory in New York in 1876. A person who was set free before the expiration of his term was required to serve out the remaining time on parole. The parolees were supervised by volunteer citizens, known as *guardians.* The parolee was required to report to the guardian the first day of each month, and a written report had to be submitted to the prison signed by both the guardian and the parolee's employer. The parole concept spread slowly but steadily. By 1901 twenty states had parole statutes and by 1944 every American jurisdiction had some form of provision for indeterminate sentences and parole.

The indeterminate sentence became the centerpiece for an approach to corrections known as the *new penology.* Other aspects of this approach were the ideas that convicts should be treated humanely and should be given meaningful and productive work to occupy their time, and that juveniles, women, and first-time offenders should be housed separately from older, hardened criminals. The overall focus of this approach was that rehabilitation rather than punishment and vengeance should be the aim of the correctional system. Cullen and Gilbert observe that the new penology did not stir any immediate and major reforms in the American correctional system, stating that "Nevertheless, it must be recognized that the champions of the new penology played a large role in bolstering the legitimacy of rehabilitative ideology at a time when it appeared vulnerable to being discredited and swept aside."[45]

Probation

English common law, which forms the basis for the American legal system, recognizes the power of courts to suspend sentences. This means that a person is found guilty and is assessed a punishment, but the court orders that the punishment not be carried out, providing that the person stays out of trouble. This power was used in the United States as early as 1830.[46] In the mid-1800s, the shortcomings of the prison system which led to the development of the indeterminate sentence and parole, combined with the fact that a number of convicted criminals were being given suspended sentences which did not require any supervision, gave impetus to the development of the concept of *probation*. The first person to apply the concept of probation, also the first person to use the word, was a well-to-do Boston shoe manufacturer, John Augustus. Beginning in 1841, supported at first by his own funds and later by donations of well-wishers, Augustus would go to the Boston court, interview the prisoners awaiting trial, and intervene with the judge in the case of those he thought were good candidates for reformation. As recounted by Moreland

> It was Augustus' practice to bail, after his conviction, an offender in whom there was hope of reformation. The man would be ordered to appear before the court at a stated time at the expiration of which Augustus would accompany him to the courtroom. If the judge was satisfied with Augustus' account of his stewardship, the offender, instead of being committed to the House of Correction, would be fined one cent and costs. The one cent and costs, which amounted generally to from three to four dollars, Augustus paid.[47]

In 1878 Massachusetts honored Augustus's innovative work by becoming the first state to pass a probation law. It remained the only state with such a law until 1897, when other states began passing probation laws in rapid-fire succession. By 1920, probation was permitted in two-thirds of the states for adults and in every state for juveniles.

The Concept of Delinquency and the Juvenile Court

Since the earliest years of our country, the courts have treated children differently than adults. There have been two main areas of difference. The first is that children have not generally been considered responsible for their actions. Traditionally, a child below the age of seven has been assumed to not be responsible; a child between seven and fourteen was considered responsible only if it could be proved that he or she was aware that the act committed was wrong. The second area of difference is that children have not been guaranteed the same rights as adults. Because children have not been considered to be responsible for their actions, they have been defined as dependent people, the same as the mentally defective or insane. Consequently, principles of due process did not apply. Rather, under the principle of *parens patriae* (the state as parent), it was believed that authorities required broad discretionary powers to act on behalf of children. Even though children were recognized as being different under the law, prior to the late nineteenth and early twentieth centuries, they were tried in the same courts as adults, they were subjected to basically the same procedures, and they were often locked up in the same jails awaiting trial and the same prisons following trial. In the reform years around the turn of the century, which is known as the *progressive era*, these practices became the prime targets of reformers.

The concept of delinquency and the juvenile court both emerged during the early years of this century. The juvenile court was first developed in Chicago as a result of the efforts of the Chicago Women's Club. In the late 1800s, the club adopted as a project the general improvement of jail conditions in Cook County. While engaged in this effort, the members of the club were shocked to find that children were locked up with adults, and they soon came to the conclusion that there was no way to really improve conditions for these children as long as they were in the adult criminal justice system. In 1895, the members of the club drafted a bill providing for a completely separate court to handle the cases of juveniles. When they submitted the bill to their legal advisor he questioned its constitutionality, believing that the bill was too broad and that it lacked procedural safeguards. Consequently, the club dropped the bill. It was picked up two years later by the Illinois Conference of Charities, where it gained the support of the Chicago Bar Association and was passed by the legislature. The bill created a juvenile court with jurisdiction for all legal matters pertaining to children under the age of sixteen. It provided for a special judge, a separate courtroom, and the maintenance of separate records. Perhaps the most important aspect was that it called for court hearings to be informal rather than formal.

The juvenile court was based on the concept of *delinquency*, which had as its object the decriminalizing of antisocial behavior in youth. The basic approach was succinctly stated in an address given to the American Bar Association in 1909 by Julian W. Mack, a juvenile court judge in Chicago

> Why isn't it just and proper to treat these juvenile offenders as we deal with the neglected children, as a wise and merciful father handles his own child whose errors are not discovered by the authorities? Why isn't it the duty of the State instead of asking merely whether a boy or a girl has committed the specific offense, to find out what he is, physically, mentally, morally, and then, if it learns that he is treading the path that leads to criminality, to take him in charge, not so much to punish as to reform, not to degrade but to uplift, not to crush but to develop, not to make him a criminal but a worthy citizen.[48]

The invention of the concept of delinquency and the creation of the juvenile court represented the zenith of the rehabilitation movement. Children were not to be defined as criminals and moral deviants; rather, they were to be thought of as misguided people who needed firm but kindly parenting to get them back on the right track. The idea caught on quickly. Ten years after Illinois created the first juvenile court, such courts had been established in twenty states and in the District of Columbia; within twenty years only three states lacked separate juvenile courts; and by the middle of the century all states and territories, as well as many foreign countries, had passed juvenile court laws.

Criminal Justice Reform—Rhetoric and Reality

Our brief survey has described how, between the American Revolution and about 1930, the philosophy of the criminal justice system in America underwent a complete philosophical transformation from an emphasis on punishment and retribution to an emphasis on reform and rehabilitation. Unfortunately, the reality of the situation has never closely approximated the philosophy. Treatment of inmates behind prison walls, both by officials and by other prisoners, has often been as brutal as the corporal punishments that prisons were supposed to replace. Programs to help prisoners resolve problems and thus to help them reform have almost never been adequately staffed by people qualified to meet the objectives of the programs. For example, in 1954 there were only 23 full-time psychiatrists employed to provide treatment to 161,587 inmates in state and federal prisons.[49] Probation and parole officers are expected, under the rehabilitation ideal, to help offenders resolve life problems and make a better adjustment to society, but a "normal" caseload consists of 100 cases and caseloads can run as high as 250 or more.[50] The juvenile court, which was supposed to replace the cold impersonality of the adult court with an approach resembling that of a kindly parent, has often worked just the opposite, ignoring due process and basic rights, and often punishing juveniles for acts that are not even crimes for adults, as well as assigning penalties far more severe than adults would receive for the same acts.

CURRENT ISSUES

The major current issues in criminal justice relate to the effectiveness of the rehabilitation ideal which has dominated thinking since the early years of the last century. Untold millions of dollars are spent annually on prison counseling programs, parole supervision, juvenile programs, and the newest reform—diversion programs. Many critics in recent years have argued that not only are these programs not doing much good but also they may actually be doing harm. The criteria used to evaluate the effectiveness of criminal justice programs are generally the overall crime rate and the recidivism rate (the percentage of people convicted of one offense who go on to commit another). As we discussed in the statistics section, the rates have skyrocketed in recent years and so the critics have plenty of ammunition for their attacks.

Prisons

Since the early 1970s, treatment programs in prisons have been almost universally criticized. Criminologist Donald Cressey has written that treatment programs in prisons are "both farces and failures."[51] Walker notes that "As instruments of rehabilitation, American prisons are an obscene joke."[52]

Suspicion regarding the effectiveness of prison treatment programs began in the early 1960s with the rising crime rates. Many people believed that much of the increase in crime could be attributed to people who had been released from prison who were committing second or even third crimes. This suspicion was reinforced in the 1960s by a number of studies that confirmed that the programs were having no measurable effect. In 1966, Bailey published a review of reports on the effectiveness of one hundred treatment programs and concluded that very few could be said to have any demonstrable effect.[53] In 1974, Martinson published another review that looked at studies of correctional treatment programs from 1945 to 1967. Like Bailey, Martinson came to the conclusion that virtually no treatment program had been found to work.[54] In 1980, Gottfredson and Gottfredson published a study which found that 56 percent of released prisoners were eventually convicted and sent to prison again.[55] Dozens of other studies concluded that the prison treatment system was having little or no effect.

At about the same time, an additional criticism of treatment programs emerged. This one, which generally came from the left end of the political spectrum, charged that the whole purpose of treatment programs was suspect. Treatment programs, it was argued, served the function of coercion and control of prisoners, not of really helping them to resolve problems. Typical of these critics is journalist Jessica Mitford, who in 1973 published an exposé of the prison system, *Kind and Usual Punishment*. Mitford quotes a former prison psychiatrist, who says of modern, treatment-oriented prisons, "In good prisons, like those in California, physical degradation is replaced by psychological degradation. I call these pastel prisons; they look good, shiny, sanitary. But inmates will tell you thousands of ways in which they are psychologically degraded." She concludes her discussion of treatment

> For the prison administrator, whether he be warden, sociologist, or psychiatrist, "individualized treatment" is primarily a device for breaking the convict's will to resist and hounding him into compliance with institution demands, and is thus a means of exerting maximum control over the convict population. The cure will be deemed effective to the degree that the poor/young/brown/black captive appears to have capitulated to his middle-class/white/middle-aged captor, and to have adopted the virtues of subservience to authority, industry, cleanliness, docility. Subtle methods are, of course, preferable if and when they work. If and when they do not, there are cruder ones in the closet: the club, such products of an advanced chemistry as tear gas and Mace, and, in the last analysis, the gun.[56]

The dominant current opinion is that the concept of treatment is simply not compatible with the concept of imprisonment. Walker says, "many experts believe that there is something inherently contradictory in prison and rehabilitation and that prisons are unreformable."[57] Similarly, Morris argues that cure cannot be coerced; rehabilitation cannot take place in the punitive environment of the prison.[58] Critics point out that a pitifully small percentage of prison budgets is devoted to treatment, usually well under 10 percent. The argument is that in modern prisons, just like prisons two hundred years ago, the major function and the major priority of the administration and staff is custody. This goal is always successful at bending any attempt at treatment to its will.

Parole

Parole has become the whipping boy in the current age of frustration over the ineffectiveness of the criminal justice system. Conservatives attack parole because they believe that it results in criminals being released before they should be and thus it is partially responsible for the increase in crime. Liberals attack it because they believe that the decisions of parole boards are arbitrary and based on no reliable data, and that the hope of parole is used to coerce prisoners into participating in treatment programs that they really don't desire. Parole survives however, because prison administrators still believe that it is necessary for the orderly administration of prisons, and because prisons are so overcrowded that if parole were abolished they would burst at the seams.

Is parole effective? The answer depends on how its goals are defined. There is little doubt that parole is effective in making prisons more manageable. Under our system of indeterminate sentencing, early release on parole has become the "carrot" to induce inmates to cooperate with prison authorities. It is also effective in reducing the prison population. Only South Africa and the former USSR rival the United States in the extreme length of sentences given to persons convicted of crimes. Parole is necessary to mitigate the extreme length of these sentences and thus to keep the prison population at a manageable level. Whether the actual practice of parole (sometimes called *correctional casework or aftercare*) is effective as a helping process that assists parolees in improving their lives and preventing further difficulties with the law is a somewhat more doubtful proposition.

Like the studies of correctional treatment, the scientific studies of parole supervision have had universally negative results. Probably the best study to date is *4000 Lifetimes* conducted by the National Council on Crime and Delinquency, which studied 104,182 men paroled between 1965 and 1970. A subsample of 1,810 was studied for a period of eight years. The study found that only 30 percent of the sample stayed completely out of trouble for the whole period; 40 percent were convicted for another serious crime; and 30 percent were convicted of a minor offense and/or violated parole. Most of the failures were found to occur during the first two years of parole.[59]

Operating on the theory that parole was not working because it was not intensive enough, California developed and evaluated a Special Intensive Parole Unit (SIPU). Parole officers in this unit had much lower caseloads than regular officers so they would be able to offer much more help and supervision to their charges. The evaluations of this program found that intensive supervision and treatment produced no meaningful improvement in the behavior of parolees.[60]

Probation

Probation is the one form of correctional treatment that appears to be effective, but it succeeds, according to Walker, "for reasons that are not particularly comforting to the correctional establishment." The great majority of persons placed on probation do not commit another offense, and the majority who commit a second offense do not commit a third. The success of probation, however, appears to be unrelated to any treatment that is provided to the probationer. Most people who are placed on probation go on to rehabilitate themselves. Walker explains, "Job, marriage, or simply getting older leads many young offenders away from crime. Probation supervision, in fact, is essentially a myth. The supervision amounts to little more than bureaucratic paper shuffling . . . probation officers call on their clients (push doorbells) and fill out the required reports. This process provides little if any substantive assistance to the client."[61]

It has often been theorized that probation could have a much more positive effect if probation officers were given caseloads which allowed them time to be more than "doorbell pushers." This theory was tested in the 1960s in what came to be called the San Francisco Project. In this project, offenders granted probation were randomly assigned to probation officers who had four different sizes of caseloads. One group of officers had only 20 cases each, one group had 40 cases each, one group had a more typical caseload of 70 to 130 cases each, and one group had caseloads of several hundred each. An evaluation of the results of the differing levels of probation treatment found no differences among the various groups.[62]

Diversion

Diversion programs, which became popular in the late 1960s, are based on the work of labeling theorists who argue that if we can prevent people from being labeled as criminals, we can reduce the probability that they will become criminals. The technique of diversion programs is to intervene in the criminal processing system before a person is charged and indicted for an offense and to "divert" the person into a treatment program of some type which is outside of the formal criminal justice system. Thus, the person will get the help he or she needs without being labeled as a criminal. During the 1970s, approximately 1,200 diversion programs were set up; they were funded by the federal Law Enforcement Assistance Administration, as well as numerous programs funded on the state and local level.

Diversion programs have lost popularity because they have generally been judged to be ineffective. The reason for their ineffectiveness is what has come to be called the "expanding net syndrome." This means that diversion programs have not served the population for whom they were originally designed—people who would normally be booked and prosecuted. These people, it has been found, are still booked and prosecuted. The people who are referred into diversion programs tend to be people who, prior to the existence of the diversion program, would have been freed without being charged anyway. In other words, what has been discovered is that an informal diversion program has always been in existence. The police officer on the beat and the district attorney have always made judgments resulting in a fair number of people being released with only a warning. With the advent of diversion programs, it is these people, rather than people who would otherwise be prosecuted, who are referred into the formal programs.

Do formal diversion programs achieve better results than the old informal methods? The answer, unfortunately, is no. A model diversion project, the Des Moines Adult Diversion Project, was evaluated and was found to have little impact on reducing recidivism among people referred to the program as compared to people handled the traditional way. An evaluation of a juvenile diversion program found that the recidivism rate was lower for kids placed in the program as compared to those processed by the juvenile court, but higher than those diverted in the traditional way, that is, turned over to their parents with a warning.[63]

Abandoning Rehabilitation?

Following the publication of the negative results of evaluation studies of rehabilitation, especially Robert Martinson's 1974 article, which concluded that, "with few and isolated exceptions, the rehabilitative efforts that have been reported so far have had no appreciable effect on rehabilitation," the calls for reform once again intensified.[64] However, these new calls have been different because they generally have called for deemphasizing, if not completely eliminating, any pretense of rehabilitation from the system.

Conservatives have always been critical of the rehabilitation model, believing that, because human nature is basically bad, treatment is a waste of time. Conservatives have always believed that the only proper response to crime was to be sure offenders are caught and then adequately punished. What is new is that it is now liberals who are calling for an end to attempts to rehabilitate offenders. Calling their approach the *justice model,* these reformers argue that the efforts of past liberals to reform criminals must be abandoned and the impossibility of helping people in a coercive situation must be admitted. The goal of liberal reform should not be for the state to "do good" for offenders, but rather to reduce state intervention and to compel the state to "do justice." The emphasis of the criminal justice system under this approach should be to assure due process, equity, and fairness. The primary components of the reformed criminal justice system under the justice model would be specific penalties for specific crimes (all people convicted of a certain crime, manslaughter for example, would receive exactly the same penalty), the return of determinate sentences, and the abolition of probation and parole. Liberal scholars Willard Gaylin and David Rothman advocate the justice model but say, "still we are not happy. Our solution is one of despair, not hope . . . under the rehabilitative model we have been able to abuse our charges, the prisoners, without disturbing our consciences. Beneath this cloak of benevolence, hypocrisy has flourished, and each new exploitation of the prisoner has inevitably been introduced as an act of grace."[65] They advocate, therefore, that the goal of the criminal justice system should not be to do good, but rather to do as little harm as possible.

As we move into the final section of this chapter, we find ourselves in a peculiar position. The subject of the section is social work roles, but before we even begin the discussion we must first, in light of the material presented earlier, deal with the question of whether social workers should even be involved with the criminal justice system.

SOCIAL WORK ROLES

The social work profession has always had highly ambivalent feelings about involvement in the criminal justice system. Originally this ambivalence was caused by the question of whether social work values and techniques were appropriate for work in an involuntary setting. Fox states that the major problem historically for social workers in corrections was "the doctrine of self-determination, which meant that social workers help people help themselves. Since corrections is coercive through enforcement and confinement, 'self-determination' is automatically excluded from the field of professional social work, which cannot function in an authoritative setting." Fox, among others, believes that social work can and should be involved in corrections, and he argues that it is a disservice to clients—perhaps even unethical—for social workers to refuse to be involved with corrections because they believe the clients to be unmotivated. He rejoices in the fact that, "There are now professional social workers who can talk about 'aggressive casework,' 'hard-to-reach groups,' 'reaching out,' and motivating people 'to help themselves.' "[66]

The problem is different now, however. Social workers no longer question the appropriateness of working with unmotivated or involuntary clients. As we have discussed in other chapters, clients in a number of settings, such as child welfare and mental health, are, at least initially, involuntary. The problem now is based on the research cited in the previous section, which has universally found that efforts at rehabilitation within the criminal justice system are ineffective. Worse yet is the belief of many that social workers who become involved in the criminal justice system quickly become coopted, losing sight of treatment goals and embracing the punitive goals of the system. Mitford quotes a former prison psychiatrist who says that, "Those [treatment personnel] who do not fit in will be eliminated and those who do fit in will stay on."[67] By "fitting in" he means that the person must adopt the correctional system's attitude that offenders are a "special form of humanity" who are not worthy of the trust and respect of decent people.

Does this mean that there is no place for social workers interested in the problem of crime in society? Certainly not. While we believe that caution should be exercised by anyone who actually wants to work within the system in the traditional roles of prison social worker, juvenile officer, probation officer, and parole officer, just as caution should be exercised by those working within public welfare and mental hospitals, we are not suggesting that these roles be avoided. There is, after all, something to the argument that if good people refuse to work in these systems, then the systems will become even worse. There are also some less traditional roles within the general area of criminal justice that are emerging and in which we believe social workers can have a particularly positive impact. A discussion of these roles follows.

Treatment Programs Outside of the Criminal Justice System

The studies of rehabilitation programs have concentrated on traditional programs run within the criminal justice system—prison treatment, probation, parole, and diversion. For people whose initial problem is law violation, there are a number of programs which are run outside of the system in community mental health centers, schools, and community centers. The results of these programs have sometimes been encouraging. An example is the Group Integration Project run in the Jewish Community Centers Association in St. Louis. This project was based on labeling theories and on theories of group influence. The basic approach was to take juveniles who had been identified as being in some way antisocial and to place them in the normal recreation and socialization groups which the Center runs in great numbers. The groups were led by trained social workers, some of whom used "the traditional social group work method taught at many graduate schools of social work." Other social workers used "the group-level behavior modification method, based essentially on the principles of social learning theory and applied behavior analysis." The project was rigorously evaluated and the approach was found not only to be effective but also to be very inexpensive—in 1983, about $150 per participant was spent. This project, as well as others, convincingly demonstrates that it is possible for social workers interested in working with antisocial individuals to do so within humane and effective environments.[68]

Victim Assistance

A recent development in the criminal justice system is *victim assistance programs,* which address the needs of the victims of crimes. Roberts observes, "One of the most overlooked areas of justice social work has been services for victims. Historically, victims of crime have been ignored by the courts, social welfare policymakers, and those in social work practice."[69] In recent years the victim has become a concern for social workers in the criminal justice system. There is a wide variety of services now provided to victims of acts such as rape, family violence, and child abuse, as well as assault and robbery. The programs provide counseling and support; they help the victim seek restitution for losses sustained and social services to meet other needs; and they frequently support the victim through the often long and traumatic proceedings involving pressing charges against an assailant.

> Seventy-nine-year-old Hattie Meadows suffered a broken arm when her purse was snatched by a man while she was returning to her apartment in the Oak Lane Housing Projects. The police took Mrs. Meadows to the hospital and while being treated she was visited by Harry Carstairs, a social worker from the city Victim Assistance Bureau. Mr. Carstairs helped Mrs. Meadows replace the food stamps that were in her purse. He then went with her to the housing project office to request that the locks on her doors be replaced because her keys were in her purse. The housing project manager said that there was a fee for

changing the locks and Mr. Carstairs arranged to have this paid for by the Victim Assistance fund. Later that week the perpetrator was arrested while trying to use Mrs. Meadows's food stamps. Mr. Carstairs visited her and told her that he would stay with her throughout the process if she decided to press charges and testify.

Supported by a large amount of money provided by federal agencies, such as the Law Enforcement Assistance Administration, the National Center for the Prevention and Control of Rape, Community Development and ACTION grants, as well as state, local and private sources, victim assistance programs proliferated during the 1970s. Cutbacks in federal funds have severely restricted these programs in recent years, but most have survived in some form.

Dussich has provided a useful list of primary, secondary, and tertiary functions of victim assistance programs:

Some primary functions include:

- Taking immediate responsibility for the victim
- Ensuring that the victim is provided with emergency medical or social services . . .
- Addressing the client's family needs . . .
- Following up on the delivery of public assistance to clients

Some secondary functions include:

- Helping victims in their role as witnesses
- Providing advice to reduce the victim's risk of revictimization
- Establishing volunteer efforts to augment victim service units
- Rendering aid to victims and their families with aftermath arrangement, such as funerals, insurance, and victim compensation . . .
- Arranging with victims convenient times for court appearances
- Maintaining a victim-witness courtesy center where victims can wait for their court appearance . . .

Some tertiary functions include:

- Studying individual victimizations for use in preventive planning
- Developing public awareness programs for target hardening [making oneself and one's home less vulnerable to criminal violation.]
- Developing victim awareness throughout the community . . .
- Setting up periodic victim-awareness seminars for middle and upper management criminal justice personnel . . .
- Publishing a community services directory tailored to victim needs . . .
- Assisting in developing restitution and compensation programs[70]

Social workers in victim assistance programs work in a number of settings. Common settings are rape crisis centers, domestic violence shelters, programs that provide counseling and support to crime victims while the case is being tried, and victim restitution programs.

A specialized type of victim assistance work is the emerging specialty of police social work. The police social worker is a victim assistance specialist who works within the police department so as to be able to immediately render services to people with whom the police have come in contact. Roberts states that the police social worker is a person who is knowledgeable about police procedures and who is assigned the following responsibilities: "(1) to establish solid working relationships with agencies providing emergency medical, psychiatric, and social work services in the community; (2) to provide the initial diagnostic assessment of clients referred to them by police officers, make appropriate referrals to local agencies, and follow-up to ensure that service was rendered; (3) to provide police officers with in-service training in crisis intervention techniques; and (4) to be on the job twenty-four-hours-a-day to serve as a back-up resource for the policemen and policewomen on patrol."[71] The job of police social worker is not yet common, and whether or not it will become so in the future is not yet clear.

Police Work as Social Work

There is an irony in the law enforcement profession that has long been obvious to criminologists: the image of the police held both by themselves and by the public is that of a super crime fighter. However, task analyses of the actual work of the police indicate that the great majority of what they do could more accurately be described as social work; this work really calls for social work skills rather than the skills concentrated on at the police academy. Only 20 to 30 percent of all calls to police involve crimes, even in areas with the highest crime rates.[72] The majority of calls are requests for help with problems not involving any law violation: a woman whose husband is drunk and she cannot get him into the house; a store owner who finds a disoriented old person in front of his business and does not want to turn the person out into the street but does not know what else to do; a person whose neighbors are having a loud fight which he fears may become violent; a woman who finds a toddler wandering around a busy street and cannot find anyone who knows the child or his parents; or a homeless family which has set up a tent in a public park. During the typical tour of

Criminologists have observed that the vast majority of the work police officers actually do could more accurately be classified as social work than as crime fighting. Here a police officer conducts a drug education program for a fifth grade class.

duty a police officer does not arrest a single person, and during a career of from twenty-five to thirty years in length most never even fire a shot.[73]

Even though crime fighting is a relatively minor part of the actual work of the police, it is this aspect on which both they and the public concentrate. The police envision themselves as "the thin blue line" standing between citizens and crime. On the other hand, citizens are suspicious and fearful of the police. As Empey has written, "Dressed in jodhpurs and boots, wearing a helmet and dark glasses, with a pistol and club strapped to their belts, their approach creates a tinge of panic in even the most innocent of citizens."[74] Even though 70 to 80 percent of a police officer's job involves activities which could be classified as social work rather than crime fighting, the police choose largely to reject this part of their role. Ennis quotes a Philadelphia police inspector as saying, "Once a police officer becomes a social worker, he isn't any good anymore as a policeman."[75]

Our view, as you might guess, differs from that of the Philadelphia police inspector. We believe that a job which involves 70 to 80 percent social work functions should be filled by people who are trained as social workers. Therefore, while not a typical choice, we believe that the job of police officer is an appropriate choice for a person with social work training.

CONCLUSION

When discussing criminal justice as a social welfare area and considering the role of social work within it, it is all too easy to fall into the trap of accepting the reduction of the crime rate as the major goal of the activity. If this is taken as the goal, it is hard to be optimistic because, as Walker has noted, "the best criminological minds of our time do not have anything practical to offer. Neither liberals nor conservatives are any help. The intellectual and programmatic bankruptcy is truly nonpartisan."[76]

In spite of his pessimism, Walker believes that scholars do have a pretty good understanding of the causes of crime, but as a society we are unable, or perhaps unwilling, to seriously address these causes. We know factors which are associated with a low rate of criminality: a sense of self-worth; a sense of achievement and the actual experience of achievement even if it is modest; and a belief that the future, for one's children if not for oneself, will be better than today. These things can only be accomplished through social change which opens up opportunities for all people in our society. It is interesting to note that conservative scholars agree that the real causes of crime are in the social struc-

ture, but they argue that crime can be dealt with without dealing with the causes. Murray, for example, states that, "In problems other than crime . . . the professionals commonly devise effective cures without doing anything at all about causes. . . . And yet when it comes to the problem of using correctional programs [jail] to reduce crime, many have assumed that something has to be done about the root causes before changes will occur in behavior."[77] Murray believes that even though the cause of crime may be an unjust social and economic system, it is all right to ignore this and simply to toughen up the criminal justice system, so that we in effect are telling people, "Your life may be bad now, but it's nothing compared to how bad it'll be if you break the law." However, in spite of Murray's optimism, an increase in the sureness, swiftness, and harshness of penalties has had no greater effect on the crime rate than attempts to rehabilitate the offender. We have to conclude, along with Walker, that if we want to reduce crime we have to work for social justice.

In the meantime, while waiting for our efforts to result in a truly just society (which may be a long wait) what do we conclude about crime and social welfare? The first thing is that we should fight the idea that the reduction of crime is our job. While reducing crime would be nice, we must accept that it is beyond our abilities, just as it is beyond those of everyone else, given our current social and economic structure. We should substitute for this an understanding of the fact that crime in our society is both the result and the cause of a large amount of pain. The job of social welfare in relation to crime should be to reduce the pain of both the victims of crime and the victims of the criminal justice system. If a social worker is working with a man who is on probation and the man commits another crime, under current evaluative standards, the social worker is generally considered to have failed. We believe, however, that if the social worker has helped the man's son to stay in school and graduate, and if he or she has helped the man's wife get a good job, find an affordable place to live, and generally put her life back together, the social worker certainly has not failed. We must be clear that our goals are not to reduce crime, but to reduce the pain resulting from crime.

E N D N O T E S

1. Samuel Walker, *Sense and Nonsense about Crime: A Policy Guide,* 2nd ed. (Monterey, CA: Brooks/Cole, 1989), 13.

2. Walker, *Sense and Nonsense about Crime,* 13.

3. The major issues for all three perspectives closely follow the discussion in Walter B. Miller, "Ideology and Criminal Justice Policy: Some Current Issues," *Journal of Criminal Law and Criminology,* vol. 64, no. 2 (1973): 141–162.

4. Walker, *Sense and Nonsense about Crime,* 16.

5. Steven Spitzer, "Toward a Marxian Theory of Deviance," *Social Problems* 22 (June 1975): 638–651.

6. Herman Schwendinger and Julia Schwendinger, "Defenders of Order or Guardians of Human Rights?" *Issues in Criminology* 5 (Summer 1970): 123–157.

7. Jerome Michael and Mortimer J. Adler, *Crime, Law and Social Science* (New York: Harcourt, Brace and Company, 1933), 2.

8. Jerome Hall, *General Principles of Criminal Law* (Indianapolis, IN: Bobbs-Merrill, 1947), 1.

9. William J. Chambliss, *Criminal Law in Action* (Santa Barbara, CA: Hamilton Publishing, 1975), 6.

10. Warren Netherland, "Corrections System: Adult," *Encyclopedia of Social Work,* Vol. 1, 18th ed. (Silver Springs, MD: National Association of Social Workers, 1987), 354.

11. Sheldon R. Gelman, "Correctional Policies: Evolving Trends," in *Social Work in Juvenile and Criminal Justice Settings,* Albert R. Roberts, ed. (Springfield, IL: Charles C. Thomas, 1983), 49.

12. Hilary Walker and Bill Beaumont, *Probation Work: Critical Theory and Socialist Practice,* (Oxford, England: Basil Blackwell, 1981), 4–5.

13. Thomas J. Sullivan, Kenrick S. Thompson, Richard D. Wright, and Dale R. Spady, *Social Problems: Divergent Perspectives* (New York: John Wiley & Sons, 1980), 574–577.

14. Timothy J. Flanagan and Edmund F. McGarrell, eds., *Sourcebook of Criminal Justice Statistics—1985* (Washington, D.C.: U.S. Department of Justice, Bureau of Justice Statistics, 1986), 418.

15. Howard N. Snyder, Terrence A. Finnegan, Ellen H. Nimick, Melissa H. Sickmund, Dennis P. Sullivan, and Nancy J. Tierney, eds., *Juvenile Court Statistics—1984* (Pittsburgh, PA: National Center for Juvenile Justice, 1987), 15.

16. Ernest van den Haag, *Punishing Criminals: Concerning a Very Old and Painful Question* (New York: Basic Books, 1975), 118.

17. LaMar T. Empey, *American Delinquency: Its Meaning and Construction* (Homewood, IL: Dorsey, 1982), 163.

18. Edwin H. Sutherland and Donald R. Cressey, *Criminology,* 9th ed. (Philadelphia, PA: J.B. Lippincott, 1974), 53.

19. William H. Sheldon, *Varieties of Delinquent Youth* (New York: Harper and Row, 1949), 14–30.

20. Sigmund Freud, *An Outline of Psychoanalysis* (New York: W. W. Norton, 1963), 14; quoted in Empey, *American Delinquency: Its Meaning and Construction,* 171.

21. David Feldman, "Psychoanalysis and Crime," in *De-*

linquency, Crime and Social Process, Donald R. Cressey and David A. Ward, eds. (New York: Harper and Row, 1969), 433–442.

22. Travis Hirschi, *Causes of Delinquency* (Berkeley, CA: University of California Press, 1969), 31–34.

23. Hirschi, *Causes of Delinquency,* 18.

24. James Q. Wilson, *Thinking about Crime* (New York: Vintage Books, 1975); James Q. Wilson and Richard Herrnstein, *Crime and Human Nature* (New York: Simon and Schuster, 1985); Ernest van den Haag, *Punishing Criminals: Concerning a Very Old and Painful Question.*

25. van den Haag, *Punishing Criminals,* 15.

26. Empey, *American Delinquency,* 461.

27. Clifford R. Shaw and Henry D. McKay, *Juvenile Delinquency and Urban Areas,* revised ed. (Chicago, IL: University of Chicago Press, 1969).

28. Walter Miller, "Lower-class Culture as a Generating Milieu of Gang Delinquency," *Journal of Social Issues 14* (Summer 1958): 5–19.

29. Walter Miller, "Implications of Urban Lower-class Culture for Social Work," *Social Service Review 33* (September 1959): 225.

30. Edwin H. Sutherland and Donald Cressey, *Principles of Criminology,* 5th ed. (Philadelphia, PA: J. B. Lippincott, 1955).

31. Robert Merton, *Social Theory and Social Structure,* enlarged ed. (New York: Free Press, 1968); Albert Cohen, *Delinquent Boys: The Culture of the Gang* (New York: Free Press, 1955); and Richard Cloward and Lloyd Ohlin, *Delinquency and Opportunity: A Theory of Delinquent Gangs* (New York: Free Press, 1960).

32. Merton, *Social Theory and Social Structure,* 146.

33. Empey, *American Delinquency,* 423.

34. Howard S. Becker, *Outsiders: Studies in the Sociology of Deviance* (New York: Free Press, 1963), 9.

35. Richard Quinney, *Criminal Justice in America* (Boston, MA: Little, Brown, 1974), 23–25.

36. Blake McKelvey, *American Prisons: A History of Good Intentions* (Montclair, NJ: Patterson Smith, 1977).

37. David J. Rothman, *Conscience and Convenience: The Asylum and its Alternatives in Progressive America* (Boston, MA: Little, Brown, 1980), 17.

38. Alan M. Dershowitz, "Background Paper," in Twentieth Century Task Force on Criminal Sentencing, *Fair and Certain Punishment* (New York: McGraw-Hill, 1976), 83; quoted in Francis T. Cullen and Karen E. Gilbert, *Reaffirming Rehabilitation* (Cincinnati, OH: Anderson Publishing Co., 1982), 46.

39. David J. Rothman, *The Discovery of the Asylum: Social Order and Disorder in the New Republic* (Boston, MA: Little, Brown, 1971), 53.

40. Cesare Beccaria, *On Crimes and Punishments* (Indianapolis, IN: Bobbs-Merrill, 1963; reprint of original from 1764), 42–44.

41. Rothman, *The Discovery of the Asylum,* 61.

42. Rothman, *The Discovery of the Asylum,* 62.

43. Quoted in Rothman, *The Discovery of the Asylum,* 240–242.

44. "Declaration of principles promulgated at Cincinnati, Ohio, 1870," in *Prison Reform,* Charles R. Henderson, ed. (Dubuque, IA: Brown Reprints; originally published in 1910), 39; quoted in Cullen and Gilbert, *Reaffirming Rehabilitation,* 67; Alexander Maconochie, quoted in Snell Putney and Gladys J. Putney, "Origins of the Reformatory," *Journal of Criminal Law, Criminology, and Police Science 53* (December 1962), 439.

45. Cullen and Gilbert, *Reaffirming Rehabilitation,* 72.

46. Paul F. Cromwell, Jr., George G. Killinger, Hazel B. Kerper, and Charles Walker, *Probation and Parole in the Criminal Justice System,* 2nd ed. (St. Paul, MN: West Publishing Co., 1985), 10.

47. John Moreland, "John Augustus: The First Probation Officer," paper read at the 35th Annual Conference of the National Probation Association, Boston, MA, May 29, 1941, reprinted in Cromwell, et al., *Probation and Parole in the Criminal Justice System,* 21.

48. Julian Mack, "The Juvenile Court as a Legal Institution," in *Preventive Treatment of Neglected Children,* Hasting H. Hart, ed. (New York: Russell Sage, 1910), 296–297; quoted in Empey, *American Delinquency,* 67.

49. Cullen and Gilbert, *Reaffirming Rehabilitation,* 81.

50. Alexander B. Smith and Louis Berlin, *Introduction to Probation and Parole* (St. Paul, MN: West Publishing Co., 1976), 190.

51. Donald R. Cressey, "Foreword," in Cullen and Gilbert, *Reaffirming Rehabilitation,* xix.

52. Walker, *Sense and Nonsense about Crime,* 218.

53. Walter Bailey, "Correctional Outcome: An Evaluation of 100 Reports," *Journal of Crime, Law, Criminology, and Police Science 57* (1966): 153–160.

54. Robert Martinson, "What Works?—Questions and Answers about Prison Reform," *The Public Interest 35* (Spring 1974): 22–54.

55. Michael R. Gottfredson and Don M. Gottfredson, *Decision-Making in Criminal Justice: Toward the Rational Exercise of Discretion* (Cambridge, MA: Ballinger, 1980).

56. Jessica Mitford, *Kind and Usual Punishment* (New York: Alfred A. Knopf, 1973), 99, 116–117.

57. Walker, *Sense and Nonsense about Crime,* 218.

58. Norvel Morris, *The Future of Imprisonment* (Chicago, IL: University of Chicago Press, 1974).

59. Gottsfredson and Gottsfredson, *Decision-Making in Criminal Justice,* 250–257.

60. William P. Adams, Paul M. Chandler, and M.G. Neitherland, "The San Francisco Project: A Critique," *Federal Probation,* vol. 35, no. 4 (1971): 45–53.

61. Walker, *Sense and Nonsense about Crime,* 210–212.

62. J. Banks, A.L. Porter, R.L. Rardin, T.R. Silver, and V.E. Unger, *Evaluation of Intensive Special Probation Projects: National Evaluation Program, Phase I* (Washington, D.C.: U.S. Government Printing Office, 1971).

63. Thomas G. Blomberg, "Widening the Net: An Anomaly in the Evaluation of Diversion Programs," in *Handbook of Criminal Justice Evaluation,* Malcolm W. Klein and Katherine S. Teilman, eds. (Beverly Hills, CA: Sage, 1980), 572–592.

64. Martinson, "What Works? Questions and Answers About Prison Reform," 22.

65. Willard Gaylin and David J. Rothman, "Introduction," in *Doing Justice: The Choice of Punishments,* Andrew von Hirsch. (New York: Hill and Wang, 1976), xxxiv–xxxix.

66. Vernon Fox, "Introduction," in *Social Work in Juvenile and Criminal Justice Settings,* Albert R. Roberts, ed. (Springfield, IL: Charles C. Thomas, 1983), xi–xii.

67. Mitford, *Kind and Usual Punishment,* 101.

68. Ronald A. Feldman, Timothy E. Caplinger, and John S. Wodarski, *The St. Louis Conundrum: The Effective Treatment of Antisocial Youths* (Englewood Cliffs, NJ: Prentice-Hall, 1983).

69. Albert R. Roberts, ed., *Social Work in Juvenile and Criminal Justice Settings* (Springfield, IL: Charles C. Thomas, 1983), 119.

70. J.P.J. Dussich, "Evolving Services for Crime Victims," in *Perspectives on Crime Victims,* B. Galaway and J. Hudson, eds. (St. Louis, MO: C.V. Mosby, 1981), quoted in John T. Gandy, "Social Work and Victim Assistance Programs," in Roberts, ed. *Social Work in Juvenile and Criminal Justice Settings,* 122–123.

71. Albert R. Roberts, "The History and Role of Social Work in Law Enforcement," in Albert R. Roberts, ed., *Social Work in Juvenile and Criminal Justice Settings,* 101.

72. Elaine Cumming, Ian Cumming, and Laura Edell, "Policeman as Philosopher, Guide, and Friend," in *The Ambivalent Force: Perspectives on the Police,* Arthur Niederhoffer and Abraham S. Blumberg, eds. (San Francisco, CA: Rinehart Press, 1973), 186.

73. Albert J. Reiss, Jr., *The Public and the Police* (New Haven, CT: Yale University Press, 1971), 15.

74. Empey, *American Delinquency,* 311.

75. Philip H. Ennis, *The Police and the Community,* Vol. 2 (Washington, D.C.: U.S. Government Printing Office, 1966), 139, quoted in Empey, *American Delinquency,* 315.

76. Samuel Walker, *Sense and Nonsense about Crime* (Monterey, CA: Brooks/Cole, 1985), 221.

77. Charles A. Murray and Louis A. Cox, Jr., *Beyond Probation; Juvenile Corrections and the Chronic Delinquent* (Beverly Hills, CA: Sage Publications, 1979), 174.

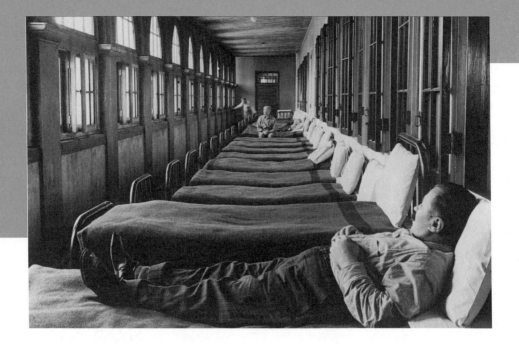

C·H·A·P·T·E·R

eleven

Mental Health
and Developmental
Disability

"When the doctor told us Michael had cerebral palsy and would be severely retarded, we were devastated," Mrs. Polanski told the social worker at Family Social Services. "This has never happened to anyone in our family. My friends sympathized, but they didn't know how to help. The doctor wanted us to put him in an institution right away—but somehow, we couldn't do it. He's our son. It hasn't been easy keeping him at home—especially at first, because we tried to do it all ourselves. We felt guilty about having other people, like my mother or my neighbor, help us. But this babysitting co-op that Family Services has organized for people like us is just great. I'm glad we got talked into joining. It's not just that it gives us a break away from caring for Mike—it's the first time ever that I've been around other parents with kids who have handicaps. They *know* what it's like. And the ones with older kids are real helpful about things like telling us what to expect when he goes to school."

Ed was born with a development disability. He lives with his parents in the suburbs. He has traveled by special van to school or to the sheltered workshop all his life. Recently, he enrolled in a Supported Employment Program and got a job at a Taco stand, where he fills paper cups with salsa and sour cream. His Job Coach drove him to work but now that he has learned the job and no longer needs his Job Coach every day, he has learned to ride the bus to work. It takes an hour and a half and requires two changes. A group home was proposed in the neighborhood near his job, but the neighborhood's residents opposed its construction. So Ed continues to ride the bus. Waiting at the transfer points in the winter is unpleasant, but he values his new independence, income, and friends.

The Unit III resident-staff meeting at Urban Community Mental Health Center's Inpatient Division is called to order by the division administrator, a psychiatric nurse. The main item of discussion is how to handle the behavior of Vida, a resident recently admitted to the center. Vida has frequent outbursts of angry shouting directed at no one in particular. She has also run off the ward five times in the last two days. The last time, she was found in the middle of the main street by the Center, daring drivers to hit her. The residents and the staff discuss their concerns for Vida's safety. One resident suggests, "Why don't we lock the ward doors for a couple of days, just until she calms down?" Other residents and staff agree. A vote is taken, and the decision is made to lock the ward doors for forty-eight hours. (This means that to leave the ward, residents will have to find a staff person with a key.) The rest of the meeting time is spent planning the week's recreational activities, including arranging transportation for residents to go to the shopping mall.

"I don't belong in that group home," my neighbor tells me. "The other people living there are OK, although most of them have much worse mental handicaps than I do. But I've had it with that director. First he wouldn't give me my spending money. Now that my social worker helped me straighten that out, he's leaning on me about coming back home at nine o'clock every night. If I'm late, he makes my life miserable. The worst thing is meals—if I don't get there to eat at six o'clock, he doesn't let me have any dinner at all. And with my crutches and my forgetfulness, it's easy for me to miss a bus and be late. It's not fair."

Howard is a twenty-four-year-old man in Chicago who has spent the last six years of his life moving back and forth between a nearby state mental hospital, homeless shelters, and occasionally the streets. His family lives in a Chicago suburb. When his schizophrenia was first diagnosed, they tried to help him at home; however, his erratic behavior and occasional violent episodes have now made this impossible. When Howard feels his "sickness" coming on again, he goes to the hospital intake division and tells them he feels suicidal. As he explains to a new worker at the shelter, "If I don't say that, they won't let me back, and I know I can't get any help out here."

"You know, I don't understand it," says a new mental health aide gazing out the window of the state psychiatric hospital. "That's the third black person I've seen brought in handcuffs to the hospital by the police. But when the police bring whites in here, they never have handcuffs on." "I know," answers his supervisor, "It's been like that all the time I've been here."

The preceding scenes illustrate a variety of themes and issues in society's responses to mental illness and developmental disability. They also suggest some of the needs and concerns of affected individuals and their families. These themes include (1) society's desire to protect and at the same time be protected from those labeled mentally ill or developmentally disabled; (2) the question of whether the best approach to such situations is community placement or institutionalization; (3) the challenge of how to develop humane and effective services; and (4) the problem of ongoing discrimination in the system. From the point of view of individuals with mental illness or developmental disability and their families, relevant issues also include the individual's desire for control over his or her life and the need for support from programs and from other people. This chapter will explore such issues, describe the fields of mental health and developmental disability, and take a look at social work's role in these important areas of practice.

Although mental illness and developmental disability constitute two different phenomena, we have chosen to discuss them in the same chapter because responses to them tend to be administratively linked in our social welfare system. We will analyze the definitions, dynamics, and history of each field separately, but will note important similarities in issues and practice related to the two.

ISSUES IN DEFINITION

You may have noticed that in our opening paragraph we referred to people being "labeled" mentally ill or developmentally disabled. That is because mental illness and developmental disability can be seen both as actual conditions in their own right and as constructs, or labels, developed in particular ways within particular societies. That is, while we might accept that mental illness is a "real" condition, characterized broadly as being out of touch with reality and responding inappropriately to events and to other people, we can also argue that society plays a major role in defining mental illness and deciding just who is "mentally ill." For example, a wealthy older woman who sometimes thinks she is the reincarnation of Cleopatra may simply be regarded

Individuals who exhibit behavior or expressions which seem "different" from those of other people are often labeled *deviant* by society.

as "eccentric." A bag lady who talks to herself as she roams the streets of New York may well be called "crazy."

Developmental disability, which includes mental retardation, seems to be a more tangible concept than mental illness. After all, it can be defined and measured in seemingly objective ways, through intelligence tests and behavioral assessments. Yet we also know that the label of "retardation" can be assigned to children with cultural backgrounds different from our own or to individuals who have serious communication difficulties. The child who is clumsy or slow to learn may soon be called "retard" by other kids. The issue of labeling is an important consideration, then, in discussions of definitions of mental illness and developmental disability.

Labeling theory, or the idea that society labels certain people as different from the norm, is an approach used by a number of sociologists in examining deviance.[1] This approach rejects the idea that deviant, or undesirable, acts are the same in all societies, and that they can be defined easily and consistently over time. Instead, labeling theorists argue that deviance is socially defined. What is acceptable in one society or time period may be considered deviant in another. In the 1990s, women who seek careers outside the home are not seen as abnormal. In the 1890s, they were often considered deviant.

The notion of what constitutes an illegal, immoral, or inappropriate act is thus decided upon by certain individuals or groups in society. The people making these decisions do so based on their own particular interests and values. Activities that don't fit with these values are labeled deviant, along with the people who engage in them. For example, assertive behavior by minority students in a public school classroom might be defined as delinquent activity by teachers and administrators who are anxious to maintain a quiet and well-regulated atmosphere.

Labeling theorists argue that people become what we call them. If we say an assertive student suffers from a behavioral disorder, she may begin to accept that judgment. If we say often enough that a student who speaks nonstandard English is retarded, he may begin to act like it.

Some theorists put particular stress on the importance of power in labeling deviants. They state that those with more authority in society are the ones who can impose their images and rules on others.[2] For example, it is not infrequent in the United States for influential politicians and their backers to successfully discredit members of various protest groups by labeling them "unAmerican."

Another group of theorists, who follow a functionalist perspective, look at labeling and deviance in a somewhat different light. They see the source of labeling not in specific powerful groups, but in the community as a whole. They argue that deviant behavior refers to conduct which the people of a community "consider so dangerous or embarrassing or irritating that they bring special sanctions to bear against the persons who exhibit it."[3] The act of defining and condemning such conduct draws the community together and reminds people about the acceptable boundaries of behavior. One learns what is "right" to do by seeing what is "wrong." One knows who "belongs" in the community by discovering who does not. The theorists' stress here is not on power, but rather on the need for social cohesiveness and the reinforcement of community norms. A good example of this idea is the sort of labeling teenagers use to define who is part of the in group and who is not.

Another example of this concept of the function of deviance is a study by sociologist Kai T. Erikson. Erikson looked at the ways in which Puritans in the Massachusetts Bay Colony used ideas about sin to reaffirm community values and to define acceptable behavior. Individuals and groups who questioned the church and existing political arrangements were accused of worshipping the Devil and they were punished accordingly. Activities like the celebrated Salem witch trials drew together a community troubled by both political uncertainty and a loss of religious purpose.[4] The same phenomenon occurs today, although the labels and values have changed. As psychiatrist Thomas Szasz notes, "In the past, men created witches; now they create mental patients."[5]

Underlying both the labeling theory and the functionalist approaches to deviance is the notion that what constitutes deviance is not inherent in an individual, but is defined by others. This idea lends a helpful perspective to the following discussion of the various definitions of mental illness and developmental disability. The phenomenon of mental illness, in particular, has drawn a good deal of attention from deviance theorists. Of course, to view mental illness as being socially determined does not mean one has to deny the reality of certain behaviors, such as delusions, hallucinations, and depression, which have been exhibited in a variety of cultures and time periods. What is important is how these behaviors are labeled and interpreted, which aspects of them have been stressed, and how they have been treated by different societies.

DEFINITIONS OF MENTAL ILLNESS

The phenomenon of mental illness has been defined in various ways in our society. Currently, there exist several approaches to definition: mental illness as the absence of mental health, as sickness, as difficulty in social adaptation, or as "troublesome" behavior which *others* label as insanity. Of these four approaches, the idea of mental illness as disease predominates. The power of this particular conceptualization reflects the strong attraction of medical and scientific ideas in twentieth century America.

Mental Illness as the Absence of Mental Health

Perhaps the simplest approach to defining mental illness is to view it as being the opposite of mental health. Yet this idea poses difficulties. What, after all, is mental health? While several criteria for mental health have been proposed, including the degree of an individual's self-actualization, autonomy, and mastery of the environment, experts have yet to agree on a definitive description.[6] Lacking a generally accepted definition of mental health, "absence of mental health" is not a particularly helpful measure of mental illness.

Mental Illness as Disease

A far more potent definition of mental illness is the disease or medical model. Not only is it more specific in its idea of insanity but also it fits with our society's widespread acceptance of a medical interpretation of social problems. As the United States and other modern industrial societies have become more complex, the definition of deviant behavior has changed from religious to legal to medical-scientific interpretations. Alcoholism, for example, used to be seen as immoral or sinful; now it is regarded as an illness.

In part, such changes relate to the growth in the prestige and authority of the medical profession. In the United States particularly, doctors have come to dominate the organization of health care and to lay "first claim to jurisdiction over the label illness and *anything* to which it may be attached."[7] Alcoholism, child abuse, mental disorders, and marital problems—all have come, to a greater or lesser degree, under the authority of the physician. As many of our TV commercials testify, "Doctors know best" about the best brand of aspirin, about the cure for hemorrhoids, and, by extension, about the most effective way to deal with personal and emotional problems.

The medical model has the following components: (1) People who behave strangely are "sick"; (2) They are not responsible for their sickness and they are entitled and even obligated to be helped; (3) That help or treatment should come from the medical profession, particularly psychiatrists, and allied personnel—nurses, psychiatric social workers, and psychologists; and (4) Treatment should be carried out in mental institutions or in private psychiatric offices or clinics. The model sees mental illness as stemming either from organic conditions or from elements in an individual's psychological development.

In many ways, the move to view mental problems as illnesses to be treated can be considered a humane advance over the practices of punishing the mentally ill or treating them as outcasts. Yet this approach can carry its own, more subtle forms of control. People who are labeled mentally ill may not "know what's best for them" and they are thus subject to the authority of physicians and others in the health system. In addition, the medical model, when strictly adhered to, roots the problem in the individual and ignores the social context in which it occurred. Social and economic factors in mental illness are given little consideration.[8]

The most widely utilized document based on the medical approach to mental illness is the *Diagnostic and Statistical Manual of Mental Disorders* (now in a revised third version), published by the American Psychiatric Association.[9] This 567-page manual, fondly referred to as the "cookbook" by psychiatric residents and hospital

A CLOSER LOOK

Diagnostic Criteria for 313.00 Overanxious Disorder

A. Excessive or unrealistic anxiety or worry, for a period of six months or longer, as indicated by the frequent occurrence of at least four of the following:

(1) Excessive or unrealistic worry about future events

(2) excessive or unrealistic concern about the appropriateness of past behavior

(3) excessive or unrealistic concern about competence in one or more areas, e.g., athletic, academic, social

(4) somatic complaints, such as headaches or stomachaches, for which no physical basis can be established

(5) marked self-consciousness

(6) excessive need for reassurance about a variety of concerns

(7) marked feelings of tension or inability to relax

B. If another Axis I* disorder is present (e.g., Separation Anxiety Disorder, Phobic Disorder, Obsessive Compulsive Disorder), the focus of the symptoms in A are not limited to it. For example, if Separation Anxiety Disorder is present, the symptoms in A are not exclusively related to anxiety about separation. In addition, the disturbance does not occur only during the course of a psychotic disorder or a Mood Disorder.

C. If 18 or older, does not meet the criteria for Generalized Anxiety Disorder.

D. Occurrence not exclusively during the course of a Pervasive Developmental Disorder, Schizophrenia, or any other psychotic disorder.

*Axes refer to different classes of information used in the DSM III R (Axis I = Clinical Syndromes)

Source: American Psychiatric Association: *Diagnostic and Statistical Manual of Mental Disorders, Third Edition, Revised,* Washington, D.C., American Psychiatric Association, 1987.

admissions staff, gives a detailed classification of mental problems, including neurotic disorders, schizophrenia, paranoia, eating disorders, anxiety states, and so on. While the manual brings a broad variety of behaviors under the title of mental disorder, this labeling process does not operate in a vacuum. It can be affected by nonmedical groups. Thus, the designation of homosexuality as mental disease was eliminated from the manual in 1973, in part because of the concerns expressed by organizations representing people who are homosexual.[10]

Mental Illness as Reaction to Life's Problems

Some social scientists and mental health professionals have defined mental illness as "problems in living" or "difficulties in social adaptation," partly as a reaction against the medical model. While not denying the existence of anxiety, depression, and other such conditions, Thomas Szasz, Erving Goffman, and others view these states not as illnesses, but as understandable reactions to life's difficulties. Goffman notes that many of the "most spectacular and convincing of [psychiatric] symptoms in some instances . . . signify merely a temporary emotional upset in a stressful situation, however terrifying to the person at the time."[11]

Definitions of Mental Illness

Mental Illness as a Label Assigned by Others

The conception of mental illness as "problems in living" is intended as a way of thinking about mental disorders that does not cast affected individuals into a passive, patient role. This concept is related to our final definition: mental illness is primarily a social construct created by others, or a social role which those labeled must play. According to this definition, people labeled mentally ill have actually "broken rules"—that is, they have behaved in a way that violates certain community or group norms. A simple example of rule breaking is the individual who, in "normal" conversation, fails to keep eye contact or stands too close or too far away from the other person. More extreme examples include withdrawing, displaying violent anger, or choosing to sleep in the street rather than in a home. Once this rule breaking has led to a person's designation as mentally ill, that individual begins to play out the expected social role. As sociologist Thomas Scheff observes, the more you define people as mentally ill, the more they define themselves in that manner.[12]

Thus, there are a number of ways of thinking about mental illness. While the disease model is the predominant approach in our society, the ideas of the labeling theorists and others who study deviance remind us that the act of calling someone "mentally ill" is not necessarily a scientific and objective process. People may receive this title because of behavior that is frightening or unacceptable to others. In addition, some of this "crazy" behavior might in fact be an understandable reaction to life's problems.

DYNAMICS OF MENTAL ILLNESS

The preceding definitions of mental illness are linked to ideas about its causes. We will discuss four schools of thought about the dynamics of mental disorder: the physiological approach, the psychological-developmental approach, the behavioral approach, and the sociological approach. While these theories are not mutually exclusive, each emphasizes a different element in the human experience. Each also leads to different ways of dealing with mental illness.

Physiological Explanations

The belief in physiological causes of madness has a long history. In ancient Greece, "mental abnormality was considered a disease . . . caused in the same way as a disease of the body."[13] In the Middle Ages and later, mental illness among women was attributed to disorders of the reproductive organs. By the late 1800s, scientists had uncovered the connection between syphilis and mental deterioration. Interest in physiological factors received additional emphasis in the 1950s, with the discovery of psychotropic drugs (tranquilizers and antidepressants). More recently, researchers have been exploring the possibilities of genetic and chemical causes of mental illness as well as the effects of physical abnormalities in the brain.

In the attempt to uncover genetic factors in schizophrenia, scientists have studied children whose schizophrenic parents gave them up for adoption at birth, and they

"On Being Sane in Insane Places"

In the early 1970s, D. L. Rosenhan, a psychologist, conducted an experiment to test whether mental health personnel could accurately determine whether a person is sane or insane. Rosenhan asked the basic question: Do the characteristics that lead to psychiatric diagnoses "reside in the patients themselves or in the environments and contexts in which observers find them?" In other words, how much are diagnoses based on the way people behave and communicate, and how much are they colored by the environment in which that behavior and communication takes place? To explore this question, Rosenhan chose eight "normal" people (that is, people who had never suffered symptoms of serious psychiatric disorders), all of whom were to gain secret admission to a mental hospital. The eight "pseudopatients" were admitted to a variety of mental institutions, located in five different states. The length of their hospitalization ranged from seven to fifty-two days. Each person came to the hospital complaining that he or she was hearing voices. In giving details about life history, marital status, and so on, the pseudopatients were completely truthful. Each was subsequently admitted to the hospital, and all but one was diagnosed schizophrenic. Once on the ward,

the pseudopatients acted normally, although each took notes, generally openly, of the experience.

Their experience was that hospital personnel, including psychiatrists and nurses, continued to regard them as mentally ill. Behaviors such as note-taking were sometimes seen as symptoms of mental illness. One nurse's record read: "Patient engages in writing behavior." Life histories were interpreted as confirming or explaining the existence of such illness. When the individuals were discharged from the hospitals, it was generally with the diagnosis of "schizophrenia, in remission." Interestingly, many of the other patients saw through the experiment, making comments like "You're not crazy. . . . You're checking up on the hospital."

From this experiment, Rosenhan concluded that, "a psychiatric label has a life and an influence of its own." Hospital staff expected to see mental illness in people admitted to the institution, and so that is what they saw. Subsequent researchers have questioned whether Rosenhan's study does indeed test the hypothesis that mental health professionals are unable to distinguish sanity from insanity. Yet the study remains a powerful reminder of the attitudes and responses prompted by the label "insane."

Sources: D. L. Rosenhan, "On Being Sane in Insane Places," Science 179 (January 1973): 250–258; Robert Spritzer, "On Pseudoscience in Science, Logic in Remission, and Psychiatric Diagnosis: A Critique of Rosenhan's 'On Being Sane in Insane Places,' " Journal of Abnormal Psychology 84 (October 1975): 442–452.

have also examined the incidence of schizophrenia among the siblings (including twins) and other relations of those diagnosed with the disorder. Generally, these studies have confirmed the existence of a genetic component which may predispose people to schizophrenia. However, the genetic factor is sufficient to ensure development of the condition. Similarly, while it is not now generally accepted that schizophrenic conditions are also accompanied by biochemical and structural changes in the brain, researchers still do not know whether these changes are the result or the cause of schizophrenia. Thus, although progress is being made in the study of biological elements in mental illness, these processes are complex and, so far, incompletely understood.[14]

Psychological Explanations

The psychological-developmental model of mental illness views mental disorder as an outgrowth of an individual's personality development. Spurred particularly by Sigmund Freud, this approach looks at how past experiences affect current functioning. The stress on individual personality rather than on social causes of illness fits well with American tenets of individualism. Freudian psychology has been embraced much more strongly in the United States than in Europe. Terms like "Oedipal complex" and "transference" have filtered into our everyday language. While the idea that the development of a man's adult psyche depends to a good deal on his infant infatuation with his mother and jealousy of his father is no longer fashionable, the concept that early childhood experiences shape future behavior is commonly accepted.

Later theorists have expanded on Freud's ideas and have included more emphasis on social factors. Ego psychology, as developed by Anna Freud, Erik Erikson, and others, focuses on the role of defenses in personality development throughout the life cycle, rather than just during the early years. Social workers have found Erikson's theories particularly useful. Erikson looks at human development as a series of life stage crises to be resolved. Positive resolutions of these crises lead to an integrated and healthy personality; lack of resolution can lead to emotional problems in the future.[15]

Behavioral Explanations

Behavioral approaches to mental illness do not concern themselves with the inner processes of personality or "workings of the mind." Instead, they concentrate on behavior and view it as a set of learned responses resulting from a combination of rewards and punishments. The "symptoms" of mental illness are really dysfunctional behaviors, such as hallucinating in public places. The behavioral therapist rewards behaviors to be maintained and punishes behaviors to be changed. For example, while a Freudian therapist might view a child's "uncontrollable" temper tantrums as being the result of some problem in his early development, a behavioral therapist would see them as a behavior which has been reinforced. The behaviorist would then look for the reinforcement (such as parental attention) and work to remove it, thus extinguishing the behavior.

Sociological Explanations

While the preceding explanations of mental illness focus on individual development within a fairly limited social context, a final set of ideas, loosely labeled "sociological," emphasizes broad social factors in the occurrence of mental disorder. Mental illness is seen as being rooted in an individual's social experience. One version of the sociological viewpoint is the idea that various life stresses, particularly those caused by poverty, racism, and sexism, can lead to mental illness. Studies of African Americans, for example, have found a high correlation between stress and mental health status.[16]

Individuals from low-income and minority groups are particularly apt to encounter stressful life situations. One study of women and depression tells the story of a low-income woman who was worried about her son's dyslexia and emotional problems

She tried and failed to get him an early learning abilities evaluation through his school and tried and failed to have him placed in a Big Brother program, in after-school day care, and in a special school for the learning disabled. Unable to obtain the help she needed, through no failure of effort or imagination on her part, she felt guilty and inadequate as a mother . . . . These coping failures occurred not because of any fault in the woman's coping strategy but simply because powerful institutions declined to respond.

The kind of stress and hopelessness arising from such situations, and the feeling of not being in control, can be seen as increasing the anxiety and depression that are a part of mental illness.[17]

As we discussed in our earlier section on labeling theory, some social scientists have taken another approach in relating mental illness to the individual's social experience. Goffman, Scheff, and others have described mental illness as a social role created by society for the "disturbed" person. From this perspective, the initial behavior triggering the label of *mentally ill* can be described as one of three things: "rule breaking," an understandable reaction to stress, or a reasonable response to a "crazy world." (The novel *Catch 22* gives a vivid example of the eccentric but basically sane behavior brought on by the irrationality of war: Air Corps bombadier Yossarian sitting naked in a tree at the funeral of a crew mate.) The mental illness in these situations *follows* the initial behavior, as people are forced into "careers" as mental patients. Once hospitalized as a schizophrenic, for example, a person faces pressure from hospital staff and relatives to accept the role of a mentally ill person. Even other patients reinforce the role, as in this hospital ward conversation reported by Scheff:

New patient: "I don't belong here. I don't like all these crazy people. When can I talk to the doctor? I've been here four days and I haven't seen the doctor. I'm not crazy."
Another patient: "She says she's not crazy." (Laughter from patients.)
Another patient: "Honey, what I'd like to know is, if you're not crazy, how did you get your ass in this hospital?"
New patient: "It's complicated, but I can explain. My husband and I. . . ."
First patient: "That's what they all say." (General laughter.)[18]

Essentially, this view argues that the cause of mental illness lies in the reaction of others.

By and large, our society tends to emphasize psychological explanations for mental illness. However, theories of mental illness have begun to move from unitary explanations to multifactor models, which include a sociocultural perspective. One such model might look something like this:

1. Certain factors, such as physiological characteristics, may predispose an individual to mental illness.
2. Precipitating stresses and conditions, such as life changes and persistent tension, can lead to the onset of psychiatric disorders.
3. But mediating factors, including personal and extrapersonal resources and labeling by others, can affect the individual's ability to successfully cope with the precipitating condition.[19] (See Figure 11–1.)

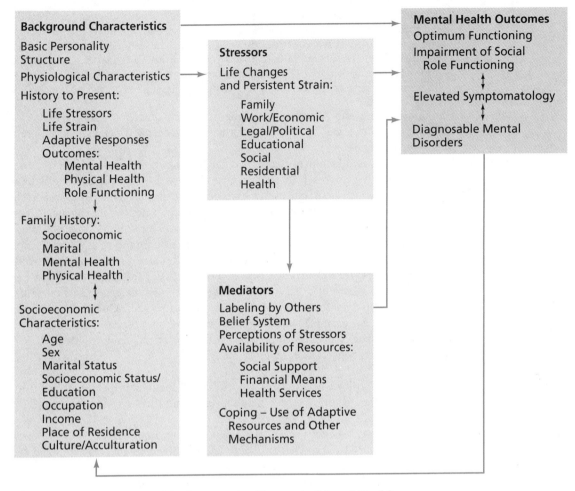

Background Characteristics

Basic Personality Structure

Physiological Characteristics

History to Present:
    Life Stressors
    Life Strain
    Adaptive Responses
    Outcomes:
        Mental Health
        Physical Health
        Role Functioning

Family History:
    Socioeconomic
    Marital
    Mental Health
    Physical Health

Socioeconomic Characteristics:
    Age
    Sex
    Marital Status
    Socioeconomic Status/
    Education
    Occupation
    Income
    Place of Residence
    Culture/Acculturation

Stressors

Life Changes and Persistent Strain:
    Family
    Work/Economic
    Legal/Political
    Educational
    Social
    Residential
    Health

Mediators

Labeling by Others
Belief System
Perceptions of Stressors
Availability of Resources:
    Social Support
    Financial Means
    Health Services

Coping – Use of Adaptive Resources and Other Mechanisms

Mental Health Outcomes

Optimum Functioning

Impairment of Social Role Functioning

Elevated Symptomatology

Diagnosable Mental Disorders

FIGURE 11–1   A Model of Interactive Factors in Mental Health

Source: Adapted from William A. Vega and Manuel R. Miranda, *Stress and Hispanic Mental Health: Relating Research to Service Delivery* (Rockville, MD: U.S. Department of Health and Human Services, 1985), 4.

STATISTICAL PICTURE OF MENTAL ILLNESS

Mental illness, although difficult to measure, is a widespread phenomenon in our society. Current estimates suggest that at any one point in time, about 20 percent of the adult population may be suffering from an emotional or psychological disorder. In a 1988 survey of five U.S. cities, almost a third of the respondents reported having had a mental disorder at some time during their life.[20] Estimates of mental illness are made in a variety of ways. Some studies base their figures on interviews with sample populations, using either self-reports by subjects or assessments by interviewers of the respondents' mental status. These surveys try to report both treated and untreated incidents of mental disorder. Another more limited, but more concrete way to measure mental illness is to concentrate on the numbers of people being treated. In 1986, for example, almost four million people were admitted to some kind of mental health program in the United States.[21] The number of people being treated in mental health programs is lower than the total number of individuals with a mental disorder because some will seek informal help from family physicians, relatives, or friends, and others will not seek help at all.

The statistics on mental illness also show interesting links between mental disorder and various social factors. The most potent connection has been shown for socioeconomic class status. The classic work in this area is August B. Hollingshead and Frederick C. Redlich's *Social Class and Mental Illness,* published in 1958. Looking at the distribution of treated mental illness among all social classes in New Haven, Connecticut, Hollingshead and Redlich found that class constituted a significant factor in the distribution of mental patients in the population. Specifically, "the lower the class, the greater the proportion of patients."[22] (See Table 11–1.) Subsequent studies have generally upheld these findings. As Table 11–2 on page 354 shows, a summary of results from forty-one studies of the relationship between socioeconomic class and psychopathology suggests that the average rate of mental illness in the lowest socioeconomic classes is 2.73 times that reported for the highest class.[23]

It is not clear whether these findings mean that more lower class people become mentally ill (due perhaps to greater life stresses) or that more of them are *labeled* mentally ill. The same questions relate to data on mental illness among minorities and women. Here, although the figures are less conclusive, connections are found between gender, race, ethnic background, and mental illness. For example, a recent study of

TABLE 11–1	Class status and the distribution of patients and nonpatients in the population	
	Population, %	
Class	Patients	Nonpatients
I	1.0	3.0
II	7.0	8.4
III	13.7	20.4
IV	40.1	49.8
V	38.2	18.4
	$n = 1891$	236,940
	$\chi^2 = 509.81$, 4 df, $p < .001$	

Note: This table shows one test of a possible interrelation between class status and mental illness. Class I is the highest socioeconomic class, Class V the lowest. Class I individuals constitute 3 percent of the total nonpatient population, but only 1 percent of the patient population. Therefore, Class I has only one-third as many patients as might be expected if Class I individuals were distributed in the same proportion in the patient population as in the nonpatient population. The difference is particularly striking for Class V. Here, the percentage of patients is more than double the percentage of Class V individuals in the general population.

Source: August B. Hollingshead and Frederick C. Redlich, *Social Class and Mental Illness.* (New York: John Wiley and Sons, 1958), 198–199.

TABLE 11–2	Comparison of rates reported for all types of psychopathology in highest and lowest social classes		
Study Site	Number of Studies in which the Rate is Higher for		Average Ratio Low-High Class
	Lowest Class	Highest Class	
N. America and Europe	17	3	2.59
U.S.	5	1	2.37
Non-U.S.	13	2	2.73

This table summarizes the findings of 41 studies investigating the relationship between socioeconomic class and psychopathology.

Source: Richard Neugebauer, et al, "Formulation of Hypotheses about the True Prevalence of Functional Psychiatric Disorders among Adults in the United States," in *Mental Illness in the United States,* Bruce P. Dohrenwend, et al. (Praeger Publishers, 1980), 56. Copyright © 1980 by Praeger Publishers, an imprint of Greenwood Publishing Group, Inc. Reprinted with permission of Greenwood Publishing Group, Inc.

mentally ill patients in state psychiatric hospitals in the Chicago area found well over half of these patients to be African American men. In addition, African American men are more likely to be labeled paranoid-schizophrenic than white men. Class background is often a related variable. Thus, proportionately more African Americans in the lower socioeconomic classes appear to become psychiatric patients than do whites in these classes. The way a mental illness displays itself may also be related to racial and ethnic background. African Amercians and Hispanic Americans tend to exhibit more hallucinations, hostility, and delusions than whites, while whites show more depression and guilt. Psychiatric symptoms and diagnoses also differ by gender. The most frequent diagnosis for men aged eighteen to sixty-four is alcohol abuse and dependence; for women of all ages, it is phobia. Finally, women tend to utilize mental health facilities more than men, and they are disporportionately labeled depressed.[24] (See Table 11–3.) Differences in rates, diagnoses, and utilization of services by sex, race, and ethnic group raise a number of issues. These include the degree to which biases in labeling and treatment are occurring and the applicability of the medical definition of mental illness to women and minorities.

DEFINITIONS OF DEVELOPMENTAL DISABILITY

A social work student in a public school setting describes a recent home visit to his field instructor: "You know, Mrs. Watson seemed willing to get her daughter to the doctor, but somehow she hasn't been able to pull it off. I don't think she knows how to use the bus system, even though she's lived here all her life. I tried to explain the schedule to her, but I had the feeling she really couldn't read it. It's not just that, though—she just seems kind of slow in general—smiles a lot but doesn't talk much, and doesn't seem to understand me when I explain why her daughter needs the

TABLE 11–3   Inpatient: Persons from minority races as a percent of the under care and admission populations in inpatient psychiatric services, by sex and type of inpatient psychiatric service: United States, 1986

Sex	Total, All Inpatient Services	Inpatient Psychiatric Service				
		State and County Mental Hospitals	Private Psychiatric Hospitals	VA Medical Centers	Non-Federal General Hospitals	Multiservice Mental Health Organizations
Under care April 1, 1986						
Total, both sexes	28.7%	34.6%	11.7%	23.7%	23.6%	19.0%
Male	33.4	40.5	11.2	24.3	27.7	26.0
Female	21.9	25.8	12.2	—	19.8	10.0
Admissions during 1986						
Total, both sexes	24.5%	33.5%	14.6%	26.3%	23.6%	19.4%
Male	27.1	33.9	16.6	26.8	27.7	18.4
Female	21.0	32.8	12.5	12.3	19.8	20.8

Source: National Institute of Mental Health, *Mental Health, United States, 1990,* Ronald W. Manderscheid and Mary Anne Sonnenschein, eds. DHHS Pub. No. (ADM) 90–1708 (Washington, D.C.: U.S. Government Printing Office, 1990), 141.

inoculations before she can start kindergarten. But otherwise she seems to be taking good care of her daughter."

His supervisor responds: "Well, we'd have to know more specifically about her IQ level, but I'd say you're dealing with a woman with a developmental disability— she's probably slightly retarded."

Defining developmental disability appears a more straightforward task than the delineation of mental illness. The signs of arrested intellectual and social development seem clearer than those of mental illness, more easily measured and observed. Yet even here, cultural components play a part in the definition process.

Developmental disability is a relatively new term, and many people think it is synonymous with mental retardation. However, it refers not only to retardation but also to a variety of conditions, occurring before age twenty-two, which hinder development. These include cerebral palsy, epilepsy, autism, and fetal exposure to drugs. The definition was developed as part of legislation addressing the needs of those whose severe disabilities, occurring during the maturing years, affect their total development. It is thus more of a planning tool than a clinical definition, since it was designed by those interested in providing services to particular groups of disabled children and adults.

The fullest description of developmental disability appears in the Rehabilitation, Comprehensive Services, and Developmental Disabilities Act (PL 95-602) of 1978

> Developmental disability means a severe, chronic disability of a person which is "attributable to a mental or physical impairment or combination of mental and physical impairment and

Definitions of Developmental Disability

- is manifest before twenty-two years of age
- is likely to continue indefinitely
- results in substantial functional limitations in three or more of the following areas of major life activity:
  - self care
  - receptive and expressive language
  - learning
  - mobility
  - self-direction
  - capacity for independent living
  - economic self-sufficiency

and reflects the person's need for a combination and sequence of special, interdisciplinary, or generic care, treatment or other services which are of lifelong or extended duration and individually planned and coordinated."[25]

Mental retardation is the largest category within developmental disability, and it is the area we will focus on in this chapter. Its definition raises a number of issues. Chief among these is the question of whether to base the definition on level of intelligence or level of functioning in daily life. Mental retardation as a state of "backwardness" was acknowledged from early cultures on up through the nineteenth century.[26] Yet it was not until the development of intelligence testing in the early 1900s that experts were able to base the diagnosis of mental retardation on a person's score on an IQ (intelligence quotient) test. With refinement of the Stanford Binet and other intelligence scales, it became possible to define mental retardation in terms of standard deviations from the mean (or degree of difference of scores from the average intelligence score on a normal distribution curve). Thus, a person with mental retardation can be characterized as having an IQ score that is more than two standard deviations below the mean. Levels of retardation, from profound to mild, can be categorized according to the actual number of deviations. Of course, such classifications will vary according to the particular intelligence test used.[27] (See Table 11–4.)

TABLE 11–4	Level of retardation indicated by IQ range obtained on measure of general intellectual functioning		
	Intelligence Test Scores		Educational Classification
Level of Mental Retardation	Stanford-Binet	Wechsler	
Mild	52–68	55–69	Educable
Moderate	36–51	40–54	Trainable
Severe	20–35	25–39	Dependent
Profound	>20	>25	Dependent
Standard Error of Measurement	3	4	
Standard Deviation	16	15	

Source: Duane F. Stroman, Mental Retardation in Social Context (University Press, Lanham Maryland, 1989), 24.

A father interacts with his son, who has Down's Syndrome. They are taking part in a special Father-Infant-Toddler Program for children with developmental disabilities.

The view that mental retardation can be defined exclusively in terms of cognitive ability has increasingly been questioned. Critics have pointed to the inadequacy of intelligence testing and its potential for cultural bias. They have urged that the individual with retardation be regarded as a whole person within a total life environment. This has led to a functional assessment of retardation which bases diagnosis not simply on intelligence but also on how well "the individual meets the standards of personal development and social responsibility expected from his or her age and cultural group."[28] The stress is on social adaptation and being able to carry out basic tasks of living: feeding and dressing oneself, performing household tasks, learning an occupation, and entertaining and visiting friends. A widely accepted version of a definition with functional elements is the 1983 description used by the American Associaton on Mental Deficiency: "Mental retardation refers to significantly subaverage general intellectual functioning existing concurrently with deficits in adaptive behavior and manifested during the development period."[29] The advantage of the functional approach is that it focuses on an individual's strengths and limitations, and looks at the whole person over a series of different developmental stages.

Just as with mental illness, however, retardation or developmental disability can be viewed as a social construct or a culturally determined label. Judgments of intelligence level or learning ability in particular might relate to the expectations of a social system. A person can be considered retarded in one system and normal in another. For example, a child who is a slow learner growing up in a family with high educational expectations may be seen as mentally retarded. A similar youngster in a family with low educational expectations may be considered normal by family members.[30]

The judgment of retardation also varies from culture to culture. In simple, agrarian societies, developmental deficiencies may not matter because skills for daily living are less complex than those in advanced technological societies. As we discussed in the section on labeling theory, a particular society's values, such as a stress on intellectual competence, affect the type of attributes seen as deviant.

Definitions of Developmental Disability

DYNAMICS OF DEVELOPMENTAL DISABILITY

Each condition included under developmental disability has its own etiology. Cerebral palsy is a disability caused by brain damage before or during birth, which results in a loss of muscular coordination and control. Epilepsy refers to a variety of conditions causing seizures. Some stem from known organic pathology, such as lesions in the brain, but the causation of others is not known. Epilepsy affects an estimated 2 percent of the total population.[31] Childhood autism, the least understood type of developmental disability, is characterized by an individual's inability to relate to and perceive the environment in a realistic way. It appears to be linked with perceptual disorders.

Mental retardation presents a particularly complex and diverse picture of causation. There is a long list of organic triggers of the condition. These include infectious diseases of the mother, for example, German measles, or of the child, such as encephalitis; the effects of drugs and alcohol on the fetus; metabolic disorders, such as phenylketonuria (PKU), caused by a recessive gene; biochemical and nutritional disorders, including maternal malnutrition; chromosomal abnormalities, such as that producing Down's syndrome; and physical or traumatic damage during or after birth, for example, deprivation of oxygen.[32]

Socioeconomic factors may interact with organic ones to cause mental retardation. Poverty is a major element here. Low-income women, for example, are more likely to be malnourished and to lack proper medical care both before and during pregnancy. A pregnant woman on welfare, especially if she lives in a rural area, may not be scheduled to see a physician until the seventh or eighth month of pregnancy, if then.

Researchers have also postulated that environmental conditions can by themselves lead to retardation. Of particular interest is the quality of family and community life, including relationships between parents and children, child rearing practices, educational opportunities, and degree of sensory, verbal, and mental stimulation offered to the child. Disadvantaged children are sometimes denied opportunities to learn and to explore "because of large family size or closely spaced births that overwhelm the capacities of . . . parents. Neglect and abuse are not uncommon in parents preoccupied with their own survival, but most frequently, the limited parent lacks the communication skills to stimulate the child's acquisition of language and cognitive development."[33] In addition, community resources, such as day care and early childhood education, may be inadequate or nonexistent. Although these situations can occur in middle- and upper-income families and communities, they are more prevalent in low-income areas.

STATISTICAL PICTURE OF DEVELOPMENTAL DISABILITY

Researchers have had difficulty estimating the number of individuals with developmental disabilities in the United States, particularly because the functional definition of developmental disability is hard to operationalize. Widely accepted criteria for measuring such life skills as "self-direction" and "capacity for independent living" do not yet exist, although some are being developed. Most studies rely on figures for the individual diagnostic categories, such as cerebral palsy and mental retardation, even though there is not an exact fit between these older categories and developmental disability. For example, not all individuals with mental retardation can be defined as being developmentally disabled. Current estimates of the prevalence of developmental disability range from 1.5 to 2.4 percent of the total population.[34]

Estimates of mental retardation, the largest category within developmental disability, generally vary from 1 to 3 percent of the population. Roughly 90 percent of these individuals have mild retardation. They will probably be able to achieve a fifth to eighth grade education by their late teens and to acquire the skills necessary for independent living. More seriously retarded individuals represent much smaller amounts of the total, with profound retardation accounting for less than 2 percent of all those in the category. Individuals with profound retardation often have physical impairments as well, such as blindness, deafness, and orthopedic problems. They are generally highly dependent on others for care.[35]

Class and minority status appear to affect the prevalence of mental retardation, although this has been less well-documented than in the case of mental illness. Economically depressed areas in the United States, both rural and urban, have relatively high percentages of individuals with retardation. A disproportionate number of children from minority groups and poverty settings are categorized as being mildly retarded. More severely retarded persons seem to be distributed fairly evenly throughout the population.[36] The greater incidence of mild retardation in poor, often minority communities may reflect inadequate health care, greater rates of malnutrition, and other problems. It also suggests the use of culturally determined labels by a dominant group, based on their own values and expectations of behavior.

HISTORICAL PERSPECTIVES ON MENTAL ILLNESS

The phenomena of mental illness and mental retardation have long histories, reaching back into the ancient world. While similar issues arise in each history—cultural influences on definitions, variation in societal responses to these conditions over time, and the changing nature of institutions—there are important differences as well. In this section and in the next, we will analyze these separate but related histories, and will concentrate primarily on their development in the United States.

Americans in colonial society responded to the mentally ill with ideas imported from eighteenth century Europe. These ideas were tempered by life in a frontier world. The religious teachings of the Protestant church dominated the ways in which people thought about poverty, mental illness, and other human problems. Colonial Americans saw the insane as simply one group among many needy people. Because they believed in a divinely created social order, they viewed the existence of poverty and dependence "as natural and just, and its relief as necessary and appropriate." The presence of dependent individuals—the madman, the widow, the blind child—provided men and women with a God-given chance to do good.[37]

Relief of the dependent was not only an individual concern but also a matter of public responsibility. The Elizabethan Poor Laws, transported to America with the colonists, held that care of the needy was both a family obligation and the duty of the local parish. Relatives were responsible for dependent family members, but if these individuals could not be cared for at home, the local authority would provide relief. In colonial America, if you were judged mentally ill, your family generally kept you at home. If you lacked family or were uncontrollable, the public authorities provided other alternatives. You might be boarded out to another household, placed in an empty attic or cellar in a local almshouse, or even confined in a shack or hut constructed for this purpose on the town commons. An important consideration in a frontier world of isolated settlements was the matter of residency. The community was prepared to take care of its own, including the insane, but non-resident dependent people were expelled and sent back to their towns of origin if possible.[38]

Community care of the dependent at home or in small, informal institutions came to seem less reasonable and practical in the new nation emerging after the American Revolution. Population increased, cities grew, and factories began to develop. The close-knit small community became less important in the political and social scheme of things. Increasingly, the state became a significant unit of government. In addition, Enlightenment ideas, which stressed the improvability of man, challenged earlier Protestant notions about the predetermination of dependency. Optimism about scientific and humane treatment of the mentally ill seemed in keeping with the development of the new republic.

These factors contributed to the growth of a new, institutional response to mental illness—the insane asylum. Hospitals for the care of the mentally ill emerged in the 1700s. But the real growth of the asylum began in the 1830s, and by 1860, twenty-eight of the thirty-three states had public institutions for the mentally ill.[39]

The reasons for the rise of the asylum were complex. New fears of the insane played a part; by 1800 concentrations of population in growing cities made people more aware of "queer" or deviant behavior. At the same time, physicians and reformers promoted the idea that madness could be cured through special treatment in an institution. Finally, as David Rothman, social historian, has argued, the "discovery of the asylum" reflected the desire for social order in an increasingly turbulent world. The Jacksonian era was a time of great social change, and traditional ideas and practices seemed outmoded. The rise of the asylum, along with other institutions for dependent individuals, constituted an effort "to insure the cohesion of the community in new and changing circumstances." Not only did the asylum provide an orderly environment for the treatment of mental illness but also it presented a model of stability for the outside world to follow.[40]

Other historians have questioned Rothman's stress on the dominance of the asylum. They observe that many mentally ill individuals remained with their families or were sent to poorhouses.[41] However, although it was not the only vehicle for the care of the insane, the new institution marked a major shift in society's responses to this dependent group.

What did this new institution look like? First, it was removed from the community and set in pastoral surroundings. Second, it was built differently. The earliest asylums were simple structures, often like large houses. The institutions of the 1830s and later were good-sized, orderly, symmetrical buildings. Internal space was regimented and carefully divided, "giving a uniform and repetitious appearance floor after floor." Separate wards existed for men and women. Inmates' daily lives were regimented, and regular work of some sort played an important part in the program. In a hospital in Pennsylvania, for example, patients rose at 5:00, received their medicines at 6:00, ate breakfast at 6:30, and then went to work or to some other form of exercise. At 12:30

they ate their main meal and then resumed work or other activities until 6:00 when everyone joined for tea. They passed the evening indoors, and all were in bed by 9:30.[42]

The orderly life of patients in the mental institution was seen not as punishment, but as a major part of treatment. Work, discipline, and support by hospital staff would overcome the confusion and turmoil in the minds of the insane. Such turmoil often stemmed from the demands of a rapidly changing, socially mobile society, where people felt challenged to move beyond the achievements and life patterns of their parents. Removal of the mentally ill from family and community meant that patients could be isolated from the strains and temptations of this new world, and thus they might be cured. Madness was no longer considered an act of God, as colonial Americans had believed, but as a treatable disease caused largely by social, economic, and political conditions.[43]

The treatment ideal was promoted by the psychiatrists who served as medical superintendents of the new institutions, and by reformers like Dorothea Dix. Dix promoted state responsibility for the care of those with mental illness. In her campaign, Dix went from town to town, noting the poor conditions in which the mentally ill were kept and developing allies among local philanthropists and physicians. She then lobbied state legislatures to create special institutions for the insane, arguing that such programs were beyond the resources of local communities. All told, Dix was instrumental in founding or enlarging thirty-two mental hospitals in the United States and abroad.[44]

To Dix, the medical superintendents, and other reformers, the new state hospital held forth the promise of humane treatment and eventual cure. Sadly, it would be a promise unfulfilled. While the institution aimed to bring order and stability into patients' lives, it offered a regimentation and repressiveness more like the factory of the day than the traditional community it sought to restore. In addition, hospitals were understaffed and often ill-equipped to deal with the more violent patients. Hoped-for cures did not materialize and the continued influx of patients strained facilities to their limit. Gradually, the therapeutic institution became an organization for long-term, custodial care.

From the 1870s on, state institutions went into dramatic decline. Carefully ordered routines broke down; unruly patients were increasingly subjected to restraints and punishments; the nature of the patient population changed from acute to aged and chronic; and institutions became holding places run by psychiatrists whose primary goals had changed from treatment to administration. Part of the decline stemmed from factors such as underfunding and the difficulties in "curing" mental disease. An additional element was the changing attitudes toward deviance in American society.[45]

In a rapidly industrializing society, many Americans became fearful about crime, the possible violence of the newly organizing working class, and particularly, the effects of the great influx of immigrants from poor backgrounds in southern and eastern Europe. A number of these immigrants found their way to mental institutions, where they were resented for drawing on the public purse. In this uneasy atmosphere, the ideas of Social Darwinists like Charles Sumner attracted a wide audience. Dependency came to be seen more and more as individual defect, which was often hereditary, rather than as the product of social forces. The idea of punishment, or at least isolation from society, often replaced the treatment goal.

Deterioration in the state institutions eventually helped promote another round of reform. The mental hygiene movement, a product of changes within psychiatry as well as of exposés by former mental patients, grew rapidly in the first twenty years of this century. With its stress on prevention and community-based psychiatry, the movement introduced important ideas that would be more fully developed in the community mental health programs of the 1960s.

The best-known catalyst for this new approach was the publication in 1908 of a book called *A Mind that Found Itself*, written by Clifford Beers. Beers had spent three years in mental institutions. In his influential account of these years, he exposed the mistreatment suffered by mental patients and proposed "a call for action to inaugurate a new beginning in the institutional care and treatment of the mentally ill." While Beers initially sought to improve existing institutions, he broadened his approach after joining forces with Adolf Meyer, a prominent psychiatrist. Meyer suggested enlarging the campaign to include a major focus on the promotion of mental health, or, as it was then called, mental hygiene. In 1909, the two men organized the National Committee for Mental Hygiene. The organization's goals included not only the reform of state institutions but also the establishment of outpatient clinics and aftercare programs and the "general dissemination of knowledge regarding . . . the causes and prevention of mental disorders."[46]

Social workers played an important role in the development of the mental hygiene movement. Julia Lathrop, of the Hull House circle, served on the executive committee of the National Committee for Mental Hygiene and helped Meyer become more aware of the social aspects of mental illness. Early psychiatric social workers, including Meyer's wife, Mary Potter Brooks Meyer, stressed an environmental approach to mental disorder; this approach became part of the broader mental hygiene movement.[47]

The mental hygiene movement established several significant new programs for the treatment of mental illness: aftercare programs, the psychopathic hospital, and the child guidance clinic. Aftercare programs, such as that set up by the New York Charities Aid Association in 1906, provided trained agents (often social workers) who kept in contact with released mental patients and helped them in their economic and social readjustment into the community. The aftercare concept led to experiments with "boarding out," or family care, in which hospital patients could be released to the care of families in the community.

Psychopathic hospitals sought to reach individuals *before* they were committed to mental institutions. These were well staffed, urban-based facilities which attempted to provide careful diagnoses of mental problems, and to treat acute, rather than chronic patients. Structured as research and training centers, such hospitals hoped to provide effective, short-term treatment which would prevent confinement in the chronic wards of the state institutions.

Child guidance clinics carried the preventive goal even further. These outpatient clinics were designed to deal with the mental health problems of children. They provided consultation to community agencies like the schools and offered therapy to children and their parents. Such therapy, it was hoped, would prevent the continuation of behavioral and emotional problems into adult life.[48]

Clifford W. Beers: *A Mind that Found Itself*

Clifford Beers was born in New Haven, Connecticut, in 1876. His father was in the produce business, and Beers himself aspired to a career in business. He attended Yale University, and after receiving a Ph.D. degree, he moved to New York City to work as a clerk. Although he later described his boyhood as relatively normal, Beers was also a sensitive and introspective child. When he was a young man preparing for college, his older brother experienced what was thought to be an attack of epilepsy. Upon the brother's death six years later, the doctors concluded that he had in fact suffered a brain tumor. The family, and particularly Clifford, was devastated. Beers, then working in New York, developed a morbid fear of a similar fate. He eventually broke down mentally and attempted suicide. Suffering from hallucinations and delusions, he was admitted to a private mental institution. Over the next three years, he lived in three different institutions, including a state hospital. When his condition shifted to a manic, excitable phase, he was consigned to the "violent ward." Four years after he was finally discharged, Beers wrote a unique account of his experience of madness and his treatment in mental institutions. The following excerpts suggest the power of the book which helped initiate the modern mental health movement.

On his experience in a private institution:

Choice of a sanatorium by people of limited means is, unfortunately, very restricted. Though my relatives believed the one in which I was placed was at least fairly well conducted, events proved otherwise. From a modest beginning made not many years previously, it had enjoyed a mushroom growth. About two hundred and fifty patients were harbored in a dozen or more small frame buildings. . . . Outside the limits of a city and in a state where there was lax official supervision, . . . the owner of this little settlement of woe had erected a nest of veritable fire-traps in which helpless sick people were forced to risk their lives. This was a necessary procedure if the owner was to grind out an exorbitant income on his investment.

. . . To guard me at night while the . . . attendant slept, my hands were imprisoned in what is known as a "muff." A muff, innocent enough to the eyes of those who have never worn one, is in reality a relic of the Inquisition. . . . The muff I wore was made of canvas and [had an] inner partition, also of canvas, which separated my hands. . . . At either end was a strap which buckled tightly around the wrist and was locked.

On his consignment to a violent ward in the state hospital:

Few, if any, prisons in this country contain worse holes than this cell proved to be. . . . It was about six feet wide by ten long. . . . A heavily screened and barred window admitted light and a negligible quantity of air, for the ventilation scarcely deserved the name. The walls and floor were bare, and there was no furniture. . . . Worst of all, winter was approaching and these, my first quarters, were without heat. . . . To be half-frozen, day in and day out . . . was exquisite torture.

. . . Thus day after day, I was repressed in a manner which probably would have driven many a sane man to violence. Deprived of my clothes, of sufficient food, of warmth, of all sane companionship and my liberty, I told those in authority that so long as they should continue to treat me as the vilest of criminals, I should do my best to complete the illusion.

Source: Excerpt from *A Mind That Found Itself* by Clifford Beers. Copyright 1907, 1917, 1921, 1923, 1931, 1932, 1934, 1935, 1937, 1939, 1940, 1942, 1948, 1953 by the American Foundation for Mental Hygiene, Inc. Reprinted by permission of Doubleday, a division of Bantam Doubleday Dell Publishing Group, Inc. (pp. 41, 46–47, 151–152, 178–179)

The mental hygiene movement fit nicely with the reformist mood of the Progressive era. Its proponents pictured mental disease as the product of environmental, hereditary, and individual psychological deficiencies. Its cure required scientific knowledge and administrative action. To promote this cure, mental hygienists "launched a broad-based crusade to create a better society."[49]

While the mental hygiene campaign introduced ideas and programs with long-range implications, its immediate effects were disappointing. State institutions had become so entrenched by the turn of the century that they ended up dominating the mental health scene despite the development of new programs. The psychopathic hospital, conceived as a treatment facility for acutely ill patients, evolved into an arm of the large state institutions. Quickly overwhelmed by the number of patients it received, the psychopathic hospital was unable to offer effective treatment, and it soon turned into a funnel through which patients moved into the state hospital. These larger hospitals proved resistant to change. While some medical superintendents supported ideas such as aftercare and special facilities for the acutely ill, most sought rationales for maintaining the power and centrality of the institutions they headed. A major rationale was the provision of long-term care for those who were labeled chronically mentally ill.[50]

Thus the large state hospitals increasingly became facilities for the poor and aged chronically mentally ill. As states took over more and more responsibility for mental illness, local governments diverted the dependent elderly, particularly those labeled "senile," from old age homes to state care. During this forty-year period, approximately 40 percent of mental institution patients were fifty years old and over. Most patients came from low income groups. Particularly in the 1920s, a large proportion were foreign-born. African Americans had separate and inferior facilities. Patient stays were lengthy, and sometimes life-long. This was the world of the "back ward," with patients spending endless hours in bleak day rooms, punctuated only occasionally by an organized party or film show run by volunteers, or a visit to the psychiatrist's office. Excitable patients were put in strait jackets or "packed" in cold sheets. More manageable residents were engaged in "work therapy," cleaning bathrooms or pushing floor waxers down endless halls.

While the large state hospital dominated the mental health picture, the smaller network of services developed under the mental hygiene movement managed to survive. This network operated primarily in the private sector. Its scientific and therapeutic thrust was strengthened during World War I, when psychiatrists were called upon to deal with cases of shell shock and the war-related emotional problems of servicemen and their families. It was this mental hygiene arena within which social work established a presence as one of the mental health professions. Social workers had been key staff people in the early aftercare programs. Later they collaborated with psychiatrists in the development of child guidance clinics. In these clinics, the division of labor between the two professions called for psychiatrists to provide therapy to children and social workers to carry out "social studies" of their development by interviewing parents. Mary Jarrett, an early psychiatric social worker, helped establish the first social services department in a psychiatric hospital in 1913. There, as in the child guidance clinic, social workers became indispensable assistants to psychiatrists. They provided essential information on the patient's family and community environment. The emergence of psychiatric social work as a specialty received a particular boost when the National Committee on Mental Hygiene helped to create the Smith College School of Social Work in 1918. This program trained students exclusively in the new clinical focus. By the 1920s, psychiatric social workers had established their own professional group, the Association of Psychiatric Social Workers.

The late 1940s brought the first glimmerings of both a powerful challenge to the predominance of state institutions and a broader development of the ideas of short-term, community-based treatment and prevention. The culmination of this challenge was the community mental health movement, which drew upon two bodies of innovation: changes in the mental hospital and ideas about community practice.

World War II encouraged both types of innovation. Military data brought the problem of mental illness once more to public attention. Twelve of every one hundred men examined for service were rejected for psychiatric reasons. Almost 40 percent of all those discharged for disability had psychiatric diagnoses. The disorders which developed during combat and the adjustment problems faced by soldiers and their families led mental health workers to experiment with early, intensive, and brief treatment approaches. After the war, Veterans Administration Hospitals promoted increased staff training and better patient–staff ratios, and expanded their outpatient work.[51]

New awareness of mental illness as a national issue was reinforced by a series of exposés, in the tradition of Clifford Beers, which called attention to the terrible conditions of mental hospitals. These conditions had worsened because of neglect during the war and depression years. Mary Jane Ward's novel *The Snake Pit,* for example, gave a chilling picture of survival in a large mental hospital. The culmination of this new concern was the National Mental Health Act of 1946, which gave grants to states for the development of mental health programs outside the state hospitals. The act also established the National Institute of Mental Health. The goals of this federal program were to support research into the causes of mental illness, to further training of needed mental health personnel, and to aid states in building programs and facilities to serve the mentally ill.[52]

One of the single most important factors in the movement toward the community mental health ideal was the discovery of the first *psychotropic drugs* in the mid–1950s. These drugs, which include tranquilizers and antidepressants, were able to alter feeling states without apparently impairing an individual's ability to perceive and think. Although the overuse of drugs would later be blamed for creating "zombie-like" patients, these medications were heralded early on for their ability to make patients more amenable to treatment and more capable of being discharged from long-term hospitalization to community programs.

A new treatment idea, the *therapeutic community,* also contributed to changes in hospital practices. Developed by Maxwell Jones, a British psychiatrist, this was an attempt to modify hospital culture, as experienced by patients on the ward, and to reconstitute this culture as a total treatment environment. Often called *milieu therapy,* the approach suggested that much of mental illness stemmed from faulty learning of how to relate to people. By promoting open communication between patients and staff, a more normal atmosphere, and the involvement of patients in their own treatment, milieu therapy would help people learn new, more successful interpersonal behaviors. The hallmarks of the therapeutic community were patient–staff "unit" meetings, open

A CLOSER LOOK

The Snake Pit

Mary Jane Ward wrote *The Snake Pit,* a story of life in a mental hospital, in the mid–1940s. Ward was born in Indiana in 1915. Her first interest was music, but after her marriage to a statistician who wrote plays and painted, she turned to writing. Her early works met with limited literary and financial success. For three years she and her husband lived the life of poor artists in New York's Greenwich Village. In 1941, Ward suffered psychiatric problems and spent nine months in a mental hospital. Several years later, she wrote a poignant novel based on this experience. The main character's name is Virginia—she is a gentle, bewildered young woman who finds herself in a confusing environment.

They lined up in front of the dining-room. When the door was unlocked they marched out. . . . They marched up the brown hall and stopped at the door at the end of it. Miss Hart unlocked the door and they went into the waiting room. They crossed that room and paused at another door. Miss Hart unlocked the door. They went into another hall. They stopped at another door. When it was unlocked they went into a room that was stunningly different.

It was a large light room. There was tile on the floor, tiny octagonal pieces of tile charmingly fitted together. . . . The walls had the two-color [brown] paint job, but they seemed more cheerful. It was a lovely room. Virginia studied the floor as if it was an exceptional mosaic and she thought suddenly of her beautiful Kelim rug and had then to suppress a ridiculous and unexpected sob. Don't be a baby. Suppose you had to stay here.

If I had to remain in this prison I would choose this room, she thought. But presently her enthusiasm waned. There were four booths. The women stood and waited their turn. . . . None of the booths had a door.

When at last it was her turn she discovered that an even more vital accessory was missing. There was no wooden seat and the old joke about not falling in was in this case no joke. But she forgot how frightful this was when she saw there was no toilet paper . . . She was about to call to her next neighbor, but then she remembered the cleansing tissues in her handbag.

When she left the booth she peered at the walls of the other three. None of them had paper. This must be reported.

As a rule she held back and let others do the reporting but now she was angry and she went to Miss Hart to say what is the idea of not providing these women with toilet paper. When she reached Miss Hart she saw that the woman was providing toilet paper. Miss Hart was the dispenser. If you required paper you asked her for it in advance and she doled it out to you. She was the judge of how much you needed. It was a curious and humiliating procedure. Hadn't they gone deep enough into a woman's privacy when they removed the doors from the booths?

Source: From *The Snake Pit,* by Mary Jane Ward. Copyright © 1946 by Mary Jane Ward. Reprinted by permission of Random House, Inc. (pp. 33–34); "Mary Jane Ward," in *Current Biography,* Anna Rothe, ed. (New York: H.W. Wilson, 1947), 623–624.

---

wards, patient government, and street clothes rather than uniforms for hospital personnel.[53] Rather than becoming institutionalized, the patient was being readied for discharge into the "regular" world.

Drugs and other innovations like milieu therapy made shorter hospital stays possible. The thrust toward community-based programs continued. A Joint Commission on Mental Health and Illness, created by Congress in 1955, called for the development of outpatient programs and the use of front-line workers, such as clergy, family physicians, and teachers, in combatting mental illness. Finally, in 1963, President John F. Kennedy addressed Congress on the topics of mental health and mental retardation, the first time a United States president had done so. Referring to the Joint Commission's work, he called for "a bold new approach," the creation of a new type of facility, the community mental health center. This facility would provide a complete, community-based range of care, with a strong emphasis on prevention. Eight months later Congress adopted legislation authorizing federal matching funds to states for the construction of "comprehensive community mental health centers."[54]

Thus, the community mental health movement took its place among the other social programs of the 1960s. It proceeded from the assumption that much of mental illness stemmed from social and economic forces, which needed to be dealt with within a community setting. Centers were established across the country. By federal requirement, each provided at least five types of service: (1) inpatient services—generally short-term; (2) outpatient services; (3) partial hospitalization, such as day programs; (4) emergency services; and (5) consultation and education services for community agencies and professional personnel. The community mental health movement also gave rise to halfway houses, which offered a bridge between state facilities and independent living.[55]

In New York, Syracuse Psychiatric Hospital presented a typical picture of a community mental health facility in the 1960s. It was housed in a medium-sized three-story building near the center of the city. Each floor constituted an unlocked patient ward, or unit, which related to a geographical "catchment area" in the city of Syracuse. Average maximum patient stays were two weeks. Some people came only for day treatment, and then returned home at night. Patients, or "residents," engaged in psychodrama (a type of therapy using role play), recreational activities, and group therapy, as well as individual treatment sessions. They also participated in frequent unit meetings with staff, such as the one described at the beginning of this chapter.

Unit personnel included mental health aides, nurses, social workers, occupational and recreational therapists, psychologists, and psychiatrists. None wore uniforms. A staffing concept called *role blurring* was practiced, in which all staff were seen as contributing to the therapeutic community. A member of any one of the staff groups, including aides, could be assigned as a patient's "chief therapist." Unit administrators were generally social workers or nurses, rather than psychiatrists. The democratic atmosphere was such that professional staff mopped their own office floors.

The hospital offered outpatient services and consultation to local schools and agencies. Units tried to develop close relationships with their catchment areas, which included low-income and minority populations. One unit operated a "Neighborhood Referral Service" in a one-room storefront; this was staffed by a hospital social worker, along with a mental health aide who lived in the area and was familiar with its problems. The referral service offered help with obtaining housing, employment, welfare, and other services. The service also provided informal counseling for personal and family difficulties. It served as a link between the psychiatric hospital and the community. For example, when a young Puerto Rican woman was ready to be discharged from the hospital, the referral service worked with leaders of the local Puerto Rican community to find a family that would take her in.[56]

The use of psychotropic drugs and the development of the community mental health movement made possible a dramatic decline in the population of state hospitals. In 1955, patients in state and county mental hospitals had numbered 559,000. Twenty years later, these institutions housed only 215,000 patients.[57] At that point, some five hundred federally funded community mental health centers were in operation. The original community mental health center plans called for a decreasing proportion of federal funds and an increasing amount of local and state support, but by the early 1970s, a number of local communities began abandoning the programs as their share of the costs increased. At the same time, states still faced large overhead expenditures for the state hospitals. Thus, even while state hospitals continued to discharge patients, the necessary community programs received less and less governmental support. As we shall see in the section on "Current Issues and Trends," federal funding for community mental health was drastically curtailed in the early 1980s. The community mental health movement, which began with such optimism, had stalled.

Interestingly, each era of reform in mental health—the rise of the asylum, the mental hygiene movement, and the development of community mental health—has gone through similar periods of innovation, peaking, criticism, and retrenchment. Such a history suggests that mental illness is a complex phenomenon, with no single magical answer or cure.

HISTORICAL PERSPECTIVES ON DEVELOPMENTAL DISABILITY

Developmental disability, particularly mental retardation, presents a historical picture similar to that of mental illness. Yet overall, those with mental retardation attracted fewer champions and excited fewer large-scale attempts at institutional development and reform. The frequent neglect of this segment of the population relates in part to the perceived nature of the condition. Unlike mental illness, mental retardation has generally been viewed as a life-long affliction, with no hope of cure. While there have been movements recognizing the potential for growth, change, and even independence among people who are retarded, the most typical response has been one of low expectations, often resulting in consignment to life-long custodial care.

A bright spot in the history of the treatment of those with mental retardation was the development of special training schools in the United States in the mid–1850s. Prior to this experiment, people with mental handicaps were generally cared for by their families or were placed in poorhouses. Their treatment thus resembled that of the mentally ill. In the years just prior to the Civil War, however, a small group of reformers set out to show that if reached early enough, children who were retarded could be trained to live fulfilling and productive lives.

These reformers were inspired by new discoveries in Europe. One, in the early 1800s, was the famous case of the "wild boy" of Aveyron. A French physician, Jean-Marie-Gaspard Itard, carried out an ambitious educational program with an abandoned deaf-mute child who roamed the woods and foraged in people's gardens for food. Victor, as he was subsequently named, was caught, diagnosed as an "idiot," and entrusted to Itard's care. Theorizing that the boy's lack of speech and intellectual skills stemmed from isolation and the absence of human stimulation, Itard spent five years developing Victor's senses, mental processes, and manners. Relatively successful in several of these areas, Itard failed to achieve his ultimate goal of teaching the boy to speak. Nevertheless, his conviction that the condition of idiocy could be altered through training inspired the work of his student, Edouard Seguin, who became a major figure in the development of education for the retarded.[58]

Seguin, trained as a physician, headed schools for children with retardation first in France and then, after 1848, in the United States. He believed that every individual with retardation had abilities that could be cultivated. He established a broad treatment and training program that stressed the creation of a positive relationship between pupil and teacher. Seguin's system included physical and sensorimotor exercises, a sound diet, and group learning experiences. The system was subsequently adopted in almost every American and European institution dealing with mental retardation.[59]

In the United States, Seguin's methods helped to stimulate the establishment of a number of facilities for the care and treatment of individuals with retardation, beginning in the late 1840s. Psychiatrists and experts in the education of the handicapped convinced legislatures in New York, Massachusetts, and other states to provide funding for experimental training schools. The reformers won lawmakers over through presentations of statistics on the prevalence of retardation, warnings of its spread through generations of families, and evidence of the inadequacy of care in almshouses and homes. A major figure in this movement, Samuel Gridley Howe, argued that idiocy was a disease of society. Parents who violated certain natural and physical laws through ignorance and sin passed mental retardation down to their children. However, despite this pessimistic view, Howe stressed that those who were mentally retarded could be rehabilitated.[60]

In 1848, Howe, a physician, became director of the Massachusetts Experimental School for Teaching and Training Idiotic Children. The mission of the Massachusetts school and others that followed was to give students' "dormant faculties the greatest practicable development" and then to return these pupils to their families and communities. The schools intended to teach the occupational, intellectual, and social skills necessary for reasonably self-sufficient lives. Unlike the new mental asylums of the same period, they did not separate their charges from family and community. They encouraged ongoing family contacts through frequent visits and even summer vacations at home. On no account were the training schools to be seen as custodial institutions; instead, their "graduates" would lead productive lives in the outside world.[61]

By 1876, twelve state residential schools for the retarded had been established. In that year, on Seguin's suggestion, the superintendents of these schools formed an organization which was the forerunner of the American Association on Mental Deficiency. The organization's founding heralded a professional commitment to research the causes of retardation and to further develop training for those with mental deficiencies.[62]

In their initial years, the training schools maintained their sense of mission and enjoyed a degree of success. Yet it gradually became apparent that their founders had been overly optimistic. A number of students did not improve to the point expected. Others, who were capable of discharge, found that their families were unable and sometimes unwilling to take them back. In order to ensure the school's success, selective admissions policies had concentrated on young, less seriously retarded individuals. This meant that large numbers of people with more severe mental handicaps remained outside of the system. Disillusioned about the potential for rehabilitation and faced with pressures to handle the more seriously retarded, training school administrators

The Mismeasure of Man

In 1927 Oliver Wendell Holmes, Jr., delivered the Supreme Court's decision upholding the Virginia sterilization law in *Buck* v. *Bell*. Carrie Buck, a young mother with a child of allegedly feeble mind, had scored a mental age of nine on the Stanford-Binet. Carrie Buck's mother, then fifty-two, had tested at mental age seven. Holmes wrote, in one of the most famous and chilling statements of our century:

> We have seen more than once that the public welfare may call upon the best citizens for their lives. It would be strange if it could not call upon those who already sap the strength of the state for these lesser sacrifices. . . . Three generations of imbeciles are enough.

(The line is often miscited as "three generations of idiots. . . ." But Holmes knew the technical jargon of his time, and the Bucks, though not "normal" by the Stanford-Binet, were one grade above idiots.)

Buck v. *Bell* is a signpost of history, an event linked with the distant past in my mind. The Babe hit his sixty homers in 1927, and legends are all the more wonderful because they seem so distant. I was therefore shocked by an item in the *Washington Post* on 23 February 1980—for few things can be more disconcerting than a juxtaposition of neatly ordered and separated temporal events. "Over 7,500 sterilized in Virginia," the headline read. The law that Holmes upheld had been implemented for forty-eight years, from 1924 to 1972. The operations had been performed in mental-health facilities, primarily upon white men and women

considered feeble-minded and antisocial—including "unwed mothers, prostitutes, petty criminals and children with disciplinary problems."

Carrie Buck, now seventy-two, lives near Charlottesville. Neither she nor her sister Doris would be considered mentally deficient by today's standards. Doris Buck was sterilized under the same law in 1928. She later married Matthew Figgins, a plumber. But Doris Buck was never informed. "They told me," she recalled, "that the operation was for an appendix and rupture." So she and Matthew Figgins tried to conceive a child. They consulted physicians at three hospitals throughout her childbearing years; no one recognized that her Fallopian tubes had been severed. Last year, Doris Buck Figgins finally discovered the cause of her lifelong sadness.

One might invoke an unfeeling calculus and say that Doris Buck's disappointment ranks as nothing compared with millions dead in wars to support the designs of madmen or the conceits of rulers. But can one measure the pain of a single dream unfulfilled, the hope of a defenseless woman snatched by public power in the name of an ideology advanced to purify a race. May Doris Buck's simple and eloquent testimony stand for millions of deaths and disappointments and help us to remember that the Sabbath was made for man, not man for the Sabbath: "I broke down and cried. My husband and me wanted children desperately. We were crazy about them. I never knew what they'd done to me."

Source: Reprinted from *The Mismeasure of Man* by Stephen Jay Gould, by permission of W.W. Norton & Company, Inc. Copyright © 1981 by Stephen Jay Gould. (pp. 335–336)

acquiesced by expanding their facilities and transforming them into institutions for custodial care.[63]

In the late 1800s, the move to custodial care received further impetus from changing attitudes toward those with mental retardation. This change was part of the same fear of "dependent and defective" populations which had brought forth negative responses to the mentally ill. Increasingly, individuals with retardation came to be seen as "potential sources of social disruption who required isolation and control." Social welfare professionals and even some superintendents of institutions for those with retardation warned of the "menace of the feeble-minded" and suggested a causal link between retardation and crime, prostitution, and poverty. These notions found reinforcement in a new set of ideas about heredity: the eugenics movement.[64]

The eugenics movement, which we discussed in Chapter 7, postulated that a number of social problems, including delinquency, alcoholism, poverty, mental illness, and mental retardation, were interrelated and could be traced to hereditary sources. As we have seen, a major tool in the research supporting this idea was the intelligence test developed by Alfred Binet. Using this test among prostitutes, criminals, and juvenile delinquents, researchers concluded that large percentages of these groups were, in fact, mentally retarded. Such retardation, they theorized, was genetically determined. The nail which drove the argument home was the 1912 publication of an influential study, *The Kallikak Family: A Study in the Heredity of Feeble-Mindedness*. Written by Henry H. Goddard, a psychologist and head researcher in the Vineland, New Jersey Training School, the book traced the descendants of the family of Deborah Kallikak, an eight-year-old resident in the Vineland School. Goddard found that while a number of family members had been normal, law-abiding citizens, those descending from the union of Deborah's great-great-grandfather and a "promiscuous tavern maid" constituted "an almost unbroken line of degeneration: 143 feeble-minded, only 46 normal, 36 illegitimate, 33 immoral persons, 24 alcoholics, 8 pimps, and a total of 82 who died in infancy." Rejecting notions of social causes—all family members, after all, "lived in the same environment"—Goddard decided that most of these deficiencies were inherited.[65]

The belief in eugenics fostered by such studies continued into the 1920s. The movement supported the idea of permanent custodial care of the retarded. Since the condition appeared to be genetically caused, and IQ was seen as being fixed, there seemed little point in trying to educate those who were labeled retarded. In addition, eugenicists promoted the development of marriage-restriction laws and even the use of sterilization for those with retardation. By 1917, fifteen states had a eugenical sterilization law on the books.[66]

Although the eugenics movement had lost most of its credibility by the late 1920s, large-scale institutions for those labeled retarded remained in place. Their populations continued to grow. Like those who were considered mentally ill, many people diagnosed as retarded languished in custodial facilities up through the 1950s. While many institutions maintained a small training component, their major purpose was to remove those with retardation from the "normal" world. At best, they promoted a goal of self-sufficiency within the institution. At worst, they offered bleak, unstimulating, and even abusive environments.[67]

It is important to remember, however, that throughout this period institutions housed only about 5 percent of people deemed mentally defective. And, as in the case of mental illness, a number of programs kept alive ideas of rehabilitation and early intervention. These focused on preschool training, special education classes for children in the public schools, and vocational training for young adults. Professionals tried new approaches, such as milieu therapy and behavioral techniques, which brought promising results in the socialization and education of people with retardation.

In addition, the parents of children with mental retardation had begun to organize. High birth rates and medical advances in the care of infants after World War II, which resulted in fewer retarded infants dying at birth, led to increased numbers of young, severely retarded children in institutions. Parents sought improved conditions for this group, as well as expanded services in the community for those with less serious retardation. Parental concerns led to the formation of the Association for Retarded Children (later changed to Retarded Citizens) in 1950. Parents' pressures for improved programs gathered strength with the development of the civil rights movement in the 1950s and its promotion of the equality of all citizens. A series of first-hand reports on the harmful conditions in institutions for the retarded and mentally ill added to the fervor of parents and others seeking fair and effective treatment for these two groups.[68]

The campaign for improvement in the lives of those with retardation found a champion in President John F. Kennedy. One of Kennedy's own sisters had been diagnosed as mentally retarded. Soon after his election, he created a Presidential Panel on Mental Retardation. The panel's report in 1962 called for research into retardation and a system of services to provide a continuum of care. The panel found a high correlation between retardation, deprivation, and low socioeconomic status. It consequently recommended a program of social action to alleviate the effects of poverty. Kennedy's 1963 address to Congress on mental health included the plight of the retarded and called for community-based programs providing educational, health, rehabilitation, and employment services. The 1963 Community Mental Health Centers Act also allocated funds for research and new clinical facilities for treating persons with retardation. With these new programs, Kennedy predicted, "reliance on the cold mercy of custodial isolation will be supplanted by the open warmth of community concern and capability."[69]

As we shall see, Kennedy's prophecy has only partly been realized. Large institutions for the retarded remain, although with different and reduced populations. The process of deinstitutionalization has created its own set of problems. Yet although the record is mixed, exciting and effective new programs are changing the lives of both those with retardation and their families.

CURRENT ISSUES AND TRENDS

In this section we will comment on issues and trends common to both mental illness and developmental disability. We will also analyze problems, responses, and current programs in each field.

No doubt the single most significant phenomenon currently affecting the lives of people with mental illness and developmental disability is deinstitutionalization—the movement out of the institution and into community living. Although it was begun with high hopes in the 1950s and 1960s, deinstitutionalization has come to carry negative connotations of neglect, exploitation, and abandonment of vulnerable people. It has been particularly problematic for those with mental illness. As we will describe in Chapter 14, individuals discharged from state mental institutions have helped swell the ranks of the homeless. Some observers contend that the failures of deinstitutionalization stem from faulty ideas about mental illness and developmental disability and show that institutionalization of special populations will always be necessary. Other argue that the idea of community placement is a sound one; the major difficulties relate to implementation, and particularly to the shockingly low level of public resources allocated to community care.

The process of deinstitutionalization, which began in the early 1960s, expanded substantially in the 1970s and 1980s. Between 1970 and 1989, the number of psychiatric beds in nonfederal psychiatric hospitals dropped over 60 percent. Almost all of the decrease occurred in state and county hospitals. The field of retardation witnessed similar changes. Between 1970 and 1988, the number of residents in state institutions decreased by over 88,500 persons. The greatest percentage of reductions took place among those with mild retardation. More and more parents have been raising these children at home, leaving an institutional population of those with the most severe physical and mental handicaps.[70]

There are many reasons for the wholesale shift away from institutions. Court rulings regarding the civil rights of those with mental illness or developmental disabilities provided one impetus. The landmark *Wyatt* vs. *Stickney* case of 1972 involved a class action suit brought against the Alabama Department of Mental Hygiene by residents of two mental hospitals and a school for the mentally retarded. The federal judge hearing the case declared the right of those in institutions to treatment. He ruled that it was a violation of due process to deprive a person of his or her liberty for therapeutic reasons and then to fail to provide such therapy. In addition to legal considerations, economic motives played a part in the move to empty the large institutions. During the fiscal crises of the 1970s, politicians and officials in a number of states argued that decreasing the patient census would allow state governments to save large amounts of money.[71]

Advocates for community placement of those with developmental disabilities used two powerful new rationales in their campaigns: "normalization" and the right to treatment "in the least restrictive setting." *Normalization,* a concept imported from Sweden, holds that individuals who are developmentally disabled should be given the opportunity to live as normal a life as possible. Such a life includes becoming as self-sufficient in daily living skills as one can, using community facilities for education and recreation, and, in the area of employment, receiving a salary equal to that of an average person doing the same work.[72] Normalization is made possible by placing people in settings posing as few restrictions as possible, such as small group homes in the community, rather than residential schools, for example. These concepts, which were widely adopted by professionals in the field of developmental disability, offered a strong philosophical justification for the movement of clients into the community. In addition, important legislation was passed to combat discrimination against the developmentally disabled in the community. For example, the Rehabilitation Act of 1973 barred discrimination against handicapped individuals in both public and private agencies that receive federal aid.

Probably the greatest push toward deinstitutionalization, however, resulted from important changes in federal aid to persons with disabilities. In 1962, the Department of Health, Education, and Welfare decided to allow federal matching funds to be used by state public assistance programs for the support of people released from mental institutions. Then the development of the Supplemental Security Income program (SSI) in 1972 provided direct federal assistance to those blind, aged, and disabled persons who were still poor even after receiving regular Social Security payments. Most importantly, people in public institutions were not eligible for SSI payments. The funds went to individuals as direct cash grants, which could be used to pay for care in boarding homes and other community residences. States took this opportunity to shift individuals out of state-funded institutions and into less expensive facilities, where costs could be carried either in large part or entirely by the federal government. Such residences did not initially require any monitoring by welfare agencies. The result was the creation of a market for private, for-profit boarding homes, adult foster care homes, "single room occupancy" (SRO) residential hotels, and other facilities whose owners were not required to provide any services beyond room and board to their residents.[73] Many states opted not to provide such services either, partly because of growing financial problems.

The results were the dark side of the deinstitutionalization picture. Thousands of chronic long-term mental patients, particularly the elderly, as well as those with developmental disability, were discharged into private boarding homes, nursing homes, and welfare hotels. While some of these facilities provided decent care, lack of regulations all too often led to unsanitary and unsafe living conditions, inadequate medical care, and poor nutrition. Communities became alarmed about the congregation of "ex-mental patients" in downtown parks and other public areas. Federally funded community mental health programs were insufficient to fill the gap in services. People discharged from state institutions simply had nothing to do and no place to go. In fact, while first-time hospital admission rates fell, readmission rates rose. This indicated the difficulty of surviving "on the outside."[74]

The severity of the situation led to several federal initiatives for change. In 1977, legislation was passed that allocated federal funding to assist states in setting up community-based programs for individuals who were mentally ill. Such "community support programs" would provide housing, case management, treatment, advocacy, and other services. Two years earlier, similar legislative mandates had been established for increased community support and rehabilitation for adults with developmental disabilities. In the early 1980s, federal legislation mandated that states establish and enforce standards for community residences that use SSI payments, such as group homes.

The partnership between federal and local governments in the provision of services to the mentally ill was broken, however, by the passage of President Reagan's Omnibus Budget Act in 1981. This act created a system of state block grants, which ended direct federal funding to community mental health centers and other health and human services programs. States now receive a lump sum for various social and mental health services, which gives them much greater discretion as to how to spend the money. These block grants bring states less money than was previously provided in the areas of health care, social services, and mental health. The amount that states earmark for mental health varies from state to state. As a result, the type and amount of services offered also varies. Community Support Programs for those with mental illness were not explicitly included in the Budget Act and their direct federal funding has been drastically diminished. In general, then, less public money is being spent for services for those with mental illness. The field of developmental disability has fared somewhat better, with a continuing, moderate amount of federal funding.[75]

States and localities now provide the major initiative for services for the mentally ill. Funding comes largely in the form of state revenues, federal block grant funds, and

A CLOSER LOOK

Influx of Ex-Mental Patients Upsetting Long Beach

In hotels and rooming houses once built for the well-to-do who came to spend their vacations along the sea, hundreds of former mental patients now sit, heads sunk into their hands, oblivious to grim, often filthy surroundings.

It is estimated that there are 300 to 800 former mental patients in Long Beach, which has a population of 34,000. And many residents worry about the growing numbers.

Rumors multiply daily here about new incidents involving supposed former mental patients, although most officials say they are usually heavily sedated and docile, however bizarre their behavior may appear.

Among those most disturbed are the aged, who got here first and whose simple, well-ordered lives are disrupted when former mental patients move in down the hall.

Of the 39,000 patients in the state's 20 mental hospitals, more than one-third are in the five state hospitals on Long Island. New drugs and new medical and legal concepts about mental illness have drastically reduced the stays of the patients. And the hospitals' social-service departments help those without homes find single rooms.

However, residents of New York City have said that their local facilities are unsuitable for former mental patients, and Long Beach landlords, with sparsely filled buildings on their hands, have made their vacancies known to the social-service departments.

The influx has meant more stress for the former mental patients and also for Long Beach's aged tenants, said Carleton Reo, director of social service for Long Beach Memorial Hospital.

"The impact of taking a block of people like this from an institution and throwing them into a facility where there is no counterbalancing force of hospital personnel builds up a kind of pathological milieu," Mr. Reo said. "They also tend to put people who are under stress, like our elderly and those never made for the world, under more stress, so that we've seen people—little old ladies who were formerly managing with their ongoing associations—ending up in our mental-health clinic."

Mr. Reo said the community's hostility added to the former patients' feelings of isolation, but he said the community had the right to determine its own make-up. He said Long Beach had 2,500 of the 3,500 licensed beds in Nassau County approved by the New York State Department of Social Services for all types of adult care. In addition, Long Beach has 500 unlicensed beds in hotels and boarding houses, where some of the worst conditions prevail.

State's Help Sought

Mr. Reo said the state should provide more money and workers to develop facilities, preferably family facilities, outside of Long Beach to reduce the concentration here, which he said was "destroying the network of the community."

The city has pressed enforcement of its building and zoning codes. The practice of locking some tenants in their rooms or locking the back doors at night to keep the tenants in has apparently been stopped after the practice was uncovered during a fire in one of the rooming houses, where two former mental patients were trapped in a locked room.

James Nagourney, City Manager of Long Beach, said he had succeeded in stopping a plan to place 200 mental patients being released from a New York City hospital in one of Long Beach's old hotels. He said he had talked with officials of the state's Department of Mental Hygiene to get the hospital to drop the plan.

"The policy of releasing former mental patients is as much a financial policy as it is a medical one," Mr. Nagourney said. "In the mental hospitals, the state pays for 100 per cent of their care. If they are released and put on the welfare rolls [as disabled], the county pays 25 per cent, the state pays 25 per cent and the Federal Government pays 50 per cent."

(continued)

Safety Rules Issued

However, a spokesman for the Department of Mental Hygiene said it usually cost more to support a former mental patient in the community than in a mental hospital.

The 14 facilities in Long Beach certified by the state's Social Services Department receive rules about safety, sanitation and program requirements. They usually offer bingo games, television and card games.

Source: The New York Times (December 9, 1973), 50. Copyright © 1973 by The New York Times Company. Reprinted by permission.

SSI payments to individuals. State and county mental hospitals continue to function, although on a smaller scale. In 1970 there were 310 such hospitals; in 1989, there were only 258. Other facilities serving those with mental illness include community mental health centers (numbering 691 in 1986), outpatient programs sponsored by a variety of organizations, private psychiatric hospitals, psychiatric units in general hospitals, and community support programs. In recent years, the number of psychiatric units in general hospitals has grown at a greater rate than any other mental health organization. These units almost doubled in number between 1970 and 1986, and constitute 42 percent of all inpatient organizations. (See Figure 11–2.) They tend to deal with acute patients and to use an active treatment focus to keep hospital stays short.[76]

The decline in state mental institutions and the rise in private hospital treatment of those with acute mental illness has left a gap in care for an increasingly important group, the chronically mentally ill. These are individuals who have a serious mental disorder, such as schizophrenia, and whose illness is of long duration. While the group includes older individuals with mental illness who were discharged into the community as a result of deinstitutionalization in the 1960s and 1970s, the more challenging contingent is the growing number of younger people with mental disorders. Some of these individuals have never been institutionalized. Others, like the young man in the vignette at the beginning of the chapter, alternate between brief hospital stays and life in the community. Living with their families, in community-based housing facilities, or on the streets, they have had freer access to street drugs and alcohol, which may exacerbate their problems, and they often resist treatment. While their housing is generally under private auspices, the mental health services that they use tend to be public.[77] Growing concern about the homelessness, substance abuse, and other problems faced by younger chronically mentally ill persons has led a number of states and local communities to embrace the community support program model initiated by the federal government in the late 1970s. This approach relies on a case manager who establishes a long-term personal relationship with the individual and who links that person with various community services, such as housing, financial resources, and protection of legal rights. Often, the case manager will attempt to engage the family as a partner in helping the client, thus viewing the family as a resource rather than as the "cause" of the relative's problem. While this community-based model has met with a good degree of success, it has received much less funding than that for inpatient services.[78]

Another important element in mental health services is the growing trend toward "privatization," or the rise in programs that are privately funded. Many of these private

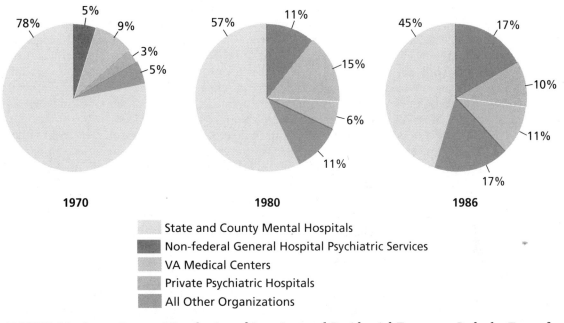

FIGURE 11–2 **Percent Distribution of Inpatient and Residential Treatment Beds, by Type of Mental Health Organization: United States, 1970, 1980, and 1986**

Source: National Institute of Mental Health, *Mental Health, United States, 1987,* Ronald W. Manderscheid and Sally Barrett, eds., DHHS Pub. No. (ADM) 87-1518 (Washington, D.C.: U.S. Government Printing Office, 1987), 16; National Institute of Mental Health, *Mental Health, United States, 1990,* Ronald W. Manderscheid and Mary Anne Sonnenschein, eds. DHHS Pub. No. (ADM) 90-1708 (Washington, D.C.: U.S. Government Printing Office, 1990), 31.

institutions are run for profit. Private for-profit nursing homes now care for many elderly individuals formerly institutionalized in state mental hospitals. Private psychiatric hospitals are admitting increasing numbers of patients. Many of these hospitals are part of chains run by for-profit corporations. Much of the community housing for those with developmental disability and mental illness is offered by private, for-profit providers. Private boarding homes and group homes are now the most frequently used placement for individuals discharged from state and county mental hospitals. These homes have paid managers and generally house from six to twenty people. While regulations governing such housing facilities have improved, the primary focus for many remains providing a bed rather than rehabilitation. Although there are a number of well-run private housing and treatment programs, scandals periodically emerge not only about poor care in private community housing, but also about insurance fraud and patient mistreatment in for-profit psychiatric hospitals.[79]

Privatization in the field of mental health has raised issues about the relative effectiveness and fairness of government and private services. The supporters of privatization see private programs as more innovative, efficient, and cost effective. They can point to research which shows that public mental health services are indeed more expensive than private ones. People critical of private initiatives argue that private programs help strengthen a dual system of mental health services, in which poorer individuals are underserved. This argument is supported by studies indicating that private facilities are "more likely to screen out nonpaying patients than are government-owned providers." Low income patients—including the unemployed and marginally employed—are more apt to be referred to public facilities for care; these facilities may have lower levels of staffing and other resources.[80] People with higher incomes can take advantage of mental health services (often called *employee assistance programs*) where they work, and they comprise the clientele not only for private inpatient programs but also for an expanding array of for-profit counseling services.

The private/public and dual-track debates seem less relevant in the field of developmental disability. New initiatives for improved care have arisen in both private and public arenas. Issues of equity have been more directly addressed, particularly in the area of education. Major changes took place in this area during the 1970s. The most important of these, the federal Education for all Handicapped Children Act of 1975, uses federal funding to encourage states to offer public education to all handicapped children aged three to twenty-one. Many states have mandated such an education. Following federal guidelines, these programs reflect a philosophy of *mainstreaming*, in which students are integrated into regular schools and even into regular classrooms wherever possible.

The idea of mainstreaming has recently been extended to the area of employment. The Rehabilitation Act of 1973 helped to pave the way by promoting nondiscriminatory hiring and employment policies for those with handicaps. "Supported employment" of the handicapped is a new, federally funded approach. It has developed in part as a reaction against the sheltered workshop system, in which workers are generally paid less than minimum wage and rarely move on to competitive employment. In contrast, supported employment programs place people with disabilities directly into regular work settings. In some cases they are part of a unit of similar workers under the supervision of an on-site staff person who provides support, encouragement, and training. In other situations, an individual works directly alongside workers without disabilities. Necessary support is provided by a job coach.[81] For example, Hank Thomas, a thirty-year-old man with Down's Syndrome, works in a research department in a large university. He makes coffee, delivers mail, and is being trained by his job coach to run the copy machine. He is a regular paid staff member of the department, he joins other staff in coffee breaks and social events, and he shows obvious pride in the job he is doing.

Respite care services provide another important support for the maintenance of individuals with developmental disabilities in the community. These services are often developed by private organizations, and they are particularly relevant for both children and adults with profound disabilities who are cared for at home. Such services offer "respite" to families for short periods on a regular basis or for weekends or vacations. Families might bring their children to a special center for care over a weekend, for example, or a trained worker might come to the home for two hours a day to allow parents the chance to run errands or visit friends. The babysitting cooperative mentioned at the beginning of this chapter is another type of respite care which is set up by parents to take turns sitting each other's children. (See Figure 11–3.)

Educational reforms, supported employment programs, and respite care services represent positive new developments in the area of family and community care. Yet

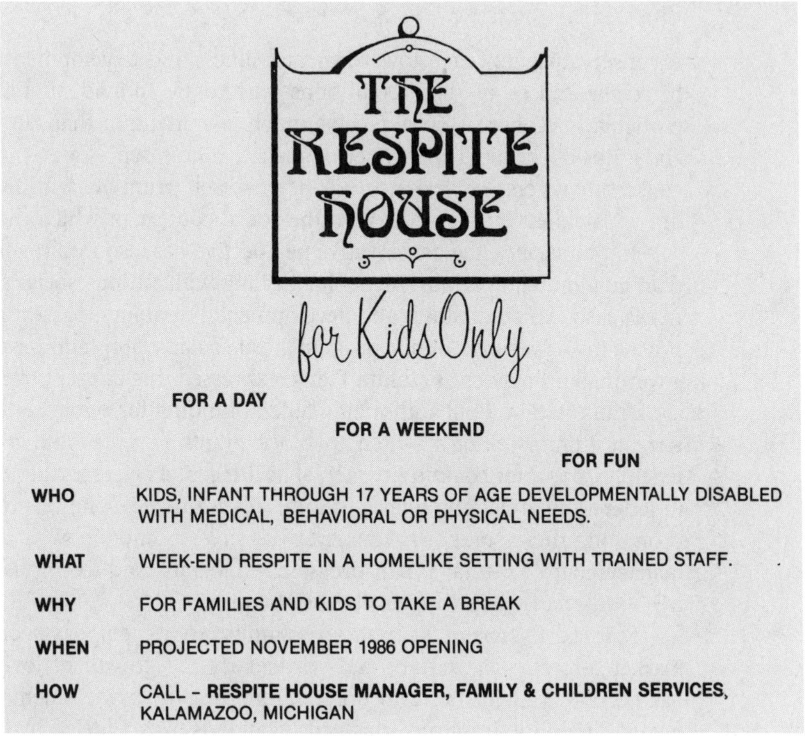

THE RESPITE HOUSE
for Kids Only

FOR A DAY

FOR A WEEKEND

FOR FUN

WHO	KIDS, INFANT THROUGH 17 YEARS OF AGE DEVELOPMENTALLY DISABLED WITH MEDICAL, BEHAVIORAL OR PHYSICAL NEEDS.
WHAT	WEEK-END RESPITE IN A HOMELIKE SETTING WITH TRAINED STAFF.
WHY	FOR FAMILIES AND KIDS TO TAKE A BREAK
WHEN	PROJECTED NOVEMBER 1986 OPENING
HOW	CALL – **RESPITE HOUSE MANAGER, FAMILY & CHILDREN SERVICES**, KALAMAZOO, MICHIGAN

FIGURE 11–3

about half of those with developmental disability still live in institutions of sixty-four or more residents. In addition, since people with developmental disability now live much longer, parents who have taken care of their developmentally disabled children all their lives are beginning to struggle with the problem of finding alternative living situations for their children when they are no longer around. Creating new housing arrangements will continue to be a challenge for people with developmental disability and their advocates.[82]

PERSPECTIVES

Political perspectives on mental illness and developmental disability are complex. They apply both to how people interpret the causes of these conditions and to what they see as the appropriate responses or solutions. They also vary over time, so that what might be considered a "liberal" approach to mental illness in one period—for example, the creation of the large asylum—becomes the "conservative" answer to the problem in the next. However, certain broad distinctions between conservative, liberal, and radical viewpoints can be described.

The Conservative Perspective

A conservative approach toward mental illness and developmental disability tends to place the causes of these conditions within the individual. Environmental factors, particularly economic ones, receive much less attention than do individual behaviors and values. The medical model of mental illness represents a good example of the conservative perspective, since it concerns itself primarily with the individual and his or her "sickness" rather than with the social context in which the person lives.

In our society, the conservative perspective has also meant a faith in private rather than governmental arrangements for dealing with various social and economic needs. In the case of mental illness and developmental disability, conservatives generally stress private initiatives over public programs, particularly programs developed by the federal government. President Franklin Pierce expressed this concept over one hundred years ago in his veto of a bill authorizing federal funding for public mental institutions. The Reagan administration's switch to block grants to states and its cessation of direct federal support for community mental health centers were further examples of a distrust in federal initiatives and a faith in local, often private, solutions to social problems. In promoting these solutions, conservatives stress economic goals and efficiency in the management of mental health programs. (Liberals tend to emphasize social goals like freedom, security, and especially social equity.)

Spurred by recent Republican administrations' emphases on the importance of market forces, privatization, and particularly the growth of for-profit organizations, has become a major trend in programming for those with mental illness or developmental disability. Ironically, this privatization is in fact fueled by federal resources. SSI payments, for example, are used to maintain individuals with developmental disability in private, for-profit boarding homes.

The Liberal Perspective

The liberal perspective does not completely reject private responses or the medical model of mental illness. However, it tends to view mental illness and developmental disability as relating to a combination of individual and social causes. Liberal policy-makers in the 1960s stressed the links between mental illness and poverty, discrimination, and lack of educational opportunity. The community mental health center, in its melding of psychiatric and environmental approaches to dealing with mental illness, represents an excellent example of a liberal response to the problem.

The community mental health center was federally funded and its program was federally designed. This, too, fits the liberal approach. While not ruling out the usefulness of private programs, liberals look to the government to provide direction and resources for dealing with social problems. In the case of developmental disability, they have promoted federal legislation to regulate treatment and to expand opportunities for affected individuals. The federal law encouraging public education for children with developmental disability is a good example.

The Radical Perspective

Radical perspectives on mental illness and mental handicap take a much stronger stance regarding the social determinants in these situations. One approach, as seen in the work of Thomas Szasz, is to view terms like "mental illness" as inappropriate labels for what are basically problems in living. They may even be seen as labels used to oppress minorities and the poor. A related set of ideas explains mental illness and developmental disability almost entirely in terms of environmental factors. This approach looks particularly at social class and power differentials in our society. Thus, the lives of discharged mental patients can be described as lacking in social and economic resources and characterized by oppression, domination, and manipulation by professionals and for-profit providers of services. Radicals sometimes speak of the political economy of mental illness (or the intersection of politics and economics), and they point to the ability of private entrepreneurs to influence mental health policy.[83]

Radical solutions focus on challenging or drastically changing existing institutions. This might be accomplished through major changes in economic and social institutions aimed at eradicating poverty and equalizing the distribution of power in our society. Yet broad societal restructuring is a tall order. More manageable strategies are the continued promotion of effective, publically financed community services and the use of advocacy/empowerment models such as the one developed by Stephen Rose and Bruce L. Black. Rose and Black deplore existing services for those discharged from mental institutions, seeing these services as "rarely [acknowledging] the world of poverty, inadequate housing, landlord domination, inaccessible health services . . . and related problems that comprise the daily life of former patients." They propose a response to these difficulties which stresses advocating for and with clients for their rights to fair treatment and adequate services. The advocacy/empowerment approach includes, for example, legal challenges to private group home administrators who withhold residents' personal living allowances provided through SSI payments. The approach is based on a conflict perspective which assumes that clients and care providers have different interests and goals, and concentrates on helping clients increase their power and their access to community resources.[84]

SOCIAL WORK ROLES IN MENTAL HEALTH AND DEVELOPMENTAL DISABILITY

The mental health service system has long been a major area for social work practice. The field of developmental disability has drawn less interest, but it also offers many opportunities for social work involvement. Both fields call on social workers to interact with a number of other professionals, so it is best to begin by differentiating their various roles.

A fair amount of overlap has developed among the different disciplines in the field of mental health. Psychiatrists, psychologists, social workers, and psychiatric nurses all can function as individual or group therapists. In addition, however, each group has areas of specialization. Psychiatrists, as physicians, are the only professionals who can prescribe medications. They, like nurses, also tend to be more in tune with the physiological aspects of a client's condition. Psychiatric nurses can administer medications, and they are generally concerned with the relationship between an individual's physical and mental well-being. Clinical psychologists are trained in the administration and interpretation of psychological tests, such as the Rorshach projective test and the Minnesota Multiphasic Personality Inventory, (MMPI), which are used to assess clients' emotional functioning. Social workers have particular competence in two areas relevant to mental health services. They have a solid working knowledge of community resources and they are trained in referring clients for specific services and monitoring the results. They also specialize in assessing the family and community context of mental illness, which enables them to write up social studies of client situations and to make recommendations regarding environmental changes. These include shifts in an individual's job situation or living arrangements.

Social workers also utilize these skills in the field of developmental disability. Here their sensitivity to family interaction often leads to direct work with the families of children who are disabled. Their involvement in this field brings them in contact not only with psychologists, who conduct intelligence tests, but also with special education teachers. Such teachers have received specialized training in the techniques of educating students with developmental gaps. An overlap between teachers and social workers lies in the teaching of daily living skills, such as shopping, personal hygiene, and using public transportation.

Mental health social workers use their skills in a variety of settings. Some maintain their own offices as full or part-time private therapists. Most, however, work primarily in organizational settings. These include state, county, and private mental hospitals; VA hospital psychiatric programs; psychiatric units in general hospitals; aftercare services; residential treatment centers for emotionally disturbed children; outpatient clinics; community mental health centers; and community support programs. Social work is a highly visible profession within these settings. After nurses, social workers make up the largest professional group staffing mental health facilities. (See Table 11–5.)

The field of developmental disability also offers a large number of practice areas. These include state institutions, community residences, public schools, respite care programs, advocacy organizations such as the Association for Retarded Citizens, sheltered workshops, supported employment programs, and case management services. Although social work has not yet established a major presence in the field, innovative services for those with developmental disability are expanding rapidly and they present a challenge for social work involvement.[85]

Social workers carry out many different roles within the mental health and developmental disability systems. In both systems, they can operate as case managers. In this role, they assess clients' needs, refer clients to services and programs to meet these needs, and follow up to make sure clients receive appropriate resources or other help. Case managers can be found in aftercare and community support programs for those discharged from mental institutions. They serve individuals with developmental disability in community-based services such as Centers for Independent Living, which refer people to a variety of community supports that can help them live reasonably independently.

The case manager role often includes the function of advocacy for client rights. This means making sure that individuals receive all the services to which they are entitled. As Rose and Black point out in their work on advocacy and empowerment, this function calls for courage and commitment on the part of social workers, because it is all too easy to support existing service arrangements, even when they do not meet client interests.[86]

Other roles which social workers carry out in both fields are planning, administration, and supervision. Social workers help formulate policies and plan programs for

TABLE 11–5 Number and percent distribution of full-time equivalent staff in mental health organizations, by discipline: United States, selected years, 1972–86[1]

Staff Discipline	1972	1978	1984	1986
	Number of FTE Staff			
All staff	375,984	430,051	440,925	494,515
Patient care staff	241,265	292,699	313,243	346,630
Professional patient care staff	100,886	153,598	202,474	232,481
Psychiatrists	12,938	14,492	18,482	17,874
Other physicians	3,991	3,034	3,485	3,868
Psychologists[2]	9,443	16,501	21,052	20,210
Social workers	17,687	28,125	36,397	40,951
Registered nurses	31,110	42,399	54,406	66,180
Other mental health professionals (B.A. and above)	17,514	39,363	48,081	56,245
Physical health professionals and assistants	8,203	9,684	20,571	27,153
Other mental health workers (less than B.A.)	140,379	139,101	110,769	114,149
Administrative, clerical, and maintenance staff	134,719	137,352	127,682	147,885
	Percent Distribution of FTE Staff			
All staff	100.0%	100.0%	100.0%	100.0%
Patient care staff	64.2	68.1	71.0	70.1
Professional patient care staff	26.9	35.8	45.9	47.0
Psychiatrists	3.4	3.4	4.2	3.5
Other physicians	1.1	0.7	0.8	0.8
Psychologists[2]	2.5	3.8	4.8	4.1
Social workers	4.7	6.5	8.2	8.3
Registered nurses	8.3	9.9	12.3	13.4
Other mental health professionals (B.A. and above)	4.7	9.2	10.9	11.4
Physical health professionals and assistants	2.2	2.3	4.7	5.5
Other mental health workers (less than B.A.)	37.3	32.3	25.1	23.1
Administrative, clerical, and maintenance staff	35.8	31.9	29.0	29.9

[1]For 1984 and 1986, some organizations had been reclassified as a result of changes in reporting procedures and definitions. For details, see text.

[2]For 1972–78, this category included all psychologists with a B.A. degree and above; for 1984 and 1986, it included only psychologists with an M.A. degree and above.

Source: National Institute of Mental Health, *Mental Health, United States, 1990,* Ronald W. Manderscheid and Mary Anne Sonnenschein, eds. DHHS Pub. No. (ADM) 90-1708 (Washington, D.C.: U.S. Government Printing Office, 1990), 39.

both populations, focusing particularly on programs for those who have been deinstitutionalized. They advocate for legislation and program changes to ensure client rights and to improve services. They also supervise other workers, administer programs, and head agencies. They carry out advocacy work on two levels: promotion of the rights of individual clients and advocacy for legislation and program changes to ensure the rights of the total client population.

Within mental health, social workers have long acted as therapists or counselors. In this role, they conduct intake interviews, make assessments of individuals' situations, and provide individual, marital, family, and group counseling. They have traditionally been assigned to work with the families of those who have been diagnosed as mentally ill. The more up-to-date version of this work is to serve as a link between client, family, and community.

When working with people who are developmentally disabled, social workers tend to concentrate on case management, although they may do individual and family counseling. New and challenging roles include working as resource persons for parents' groups, for example, helping parents to develop respite care services, and functioning as job coaches in supported employment programs. These two areas of work are particularly exciting, as they stress helping clients and their families to develop their own skills and to gain a greater ability to fulfill their own needs.

CONCLUSION

The fields of mental health and developmental disability present many opportunities and challenges for social work. Difficult problems, such as the lack of community resources for the deinstitutionalized and the need to find an effective balance between private and governmental efforts, call upon planning and political skills for their resolution. Innovative approaches, including supported employment programs and community services for those with chronic mental illness, necessitate learning new roles and expanding expectations of clients' abilities. Both fields are in the process of change and expansion, and both offer social workers a chance to participate in these changes in a meaningful and positive way.

ENDNOTES

1. See for example, Howard S. Becker, *Outsiders: Studies in the Sociology of Deviance* (New York: Free Press, 1963); Erving Goffman, *Asylums* (New York: Anchor Books, 1961); Thomas Scheff, *Being Mentally Ill* (Chicago, IL: Aldine, 1966); Edwin M. Lemert, *Human Deviance, Social Problems, and Social Control* (Englewood Cliffs, NJ: Prentice-Hall, 1967).

2. Peter Conrad and Joseph W. Schneider, *Deviance and Medicalization: From Badness to Sickness* (St. Louis, MO: C.V. Mosby, 1980), 1–2.

3. Kai T. Erikson, *Wayward Puritans* (New York: John Wiley and Sons, 1966), 3–6. Erikson bases his ideas on the work of Emile Durkheim.

4. Erikson, *Wayward Puritans,* 67–159.

5. Thomas S. Szasz, *The Manufacture of Madness* (New York: Delta, 1970), xx.

6. Marie Jahoda, *Current Concepts of Mental Health* (New York: Basic Books, 1958), 10, 23–65.

7. Conrad and Schneider, *Deviance and Medicalization,* 32–37; Eliot Freidson, *The Profession of Medicine* (New York: Dodd, Mead, and Co., 1970), 251.

8. Conrad and Schneider, *Deviance and Medicalization,* vii; Thomas S. Szasz, *The Myth of Mental Illness* (New York: Hoeber-Harper, 1961), 37–45.

9. *Diagnostic and Statistical Manual of Mental Disorders,* 3rd ed. rev. (Washington, D.C.: American Psychiatric Association, 1987).

10. *Diagnostic and Statistical Manual of Mental Disorders,*

3rd ed. (Washington, D.C.: American Psychiatric Association, 1980), 380.

11. Goffman, *Asylums,* 131–132; Szasz, *The Myth of Mental Illness,* 296–308.

12. Scheff, *Being Mentally Ill,* 24–54.

13. George Rosen, *Madness and Society* (New York: Harper Torchbooks, 1969), 72–74.

14. Eda G. Goldstein, "Mental Health and Illness," *Encyclopedia of Social Work,* Vol. I (Silver Spring, MD: National Association of Social Workers, 1987), 105; K.S. Kendler, "The Genetics of Schizophrenia and Related Disorders," in *Relatives at Risk for Mental Disorders,* D.L. Danner, E.S. Gershon, and J.E. Barrett, eds. (New York: Raven Press, 1988), 247–263; Roberta Sands, *Clinical Social Work Practice in Community Mental Health* (New York: Merrill, 1991), 21, 58–59; Ursula Gerhart, *Caring for the Chronic Mentally Ill* (Itasca, IL: F.E. Peacock, 1990), 18–20.

15. Erik H. Erikson, *Childhood and Society* (New York: W.W. Norton and Co., 1963), 247, 270–273.

16. Diana Dill and Ellen Field, "The Challenge of Coping," in *Lives in Stress: Women and Depression,* Deborah Belle, ed. (Beverly Hills, CA: Sage, 1982), 187–188, 194–195; Goldstein, "Mental Health and Illness," 108–109; William A. Vega, Richard L. Hough, and Manuel R. Miranda, "Modeling Cross-Cultural Research in Hispanic Mental Health," in *Stress and Hispanic Mental Health: Relating Reserach to Service Delivery,* William A. Vega and Manuel R. Miranda, eds. (Rockville, MD: National Institute for Mental Health, 1985), 1–21; W.W. Dressler, "Extended Family Relationships, Social Support, and Mental Health in a Southern Black Community," *Journal of Health and Social Behavior 26* (March 1985): 39–48.

17. Dill and Field, "The Challenge of Coping," 189–190.

18. Scheff, *Becoming Mentally Ill,* 86.

19. Vega, et al., "Modeling Cross-Cultural Research in Hispanic Mental Health," 3–5.

20. David A. Rochefort, "Mental Illness and Mental Health as Public Policy Concerns," in *Handbook on Mental Health Policy in the United States,* David A. Rochefort, ed. (New York: Greenwood Press, 1989), 3; U.S. Department of Education, *Chartbook on Disability in the United States* (Washington, D.C.: National Institute on Disability and Rehabilitation Research, March, 1989), 7.

21. National Institute of Mental Health, *Mental Health, United States, 1990,* Ronald W. Mandersheid and Mary Anne Sonnenschein, eds., DHHS Pub. No. (ADM) 90–178 (Washington, D.C.: Superintendent of Documents, U.S. Government Printing Office, 1990), 154.

22. August B. Hollingshead and Frederick C. Redlich, *Social Class and Mental Illness* (New York: John Wiley and Sons, 1958), 216–217.

23. See, for example, Leo Srole, et al., *Mental Health in the Metropolis* (New York: McGraw-Hill, 1962); John Schwab, et. al., *Social Order and Mental Health: The Florida Health Study* (New York: Brunner/Mazel, 1979); Richard Neugebauer, et al., "Formulation of Hypotheses about the True Prevalence of Functional Psychiatric Disorders among Adults in the United States," in *Mental Illness in the United States: Epidemiological Estimates,* Bruce P. Dohrenwend, et al. (New York: Praeger, 1980), 55–60; Christopher G. Hudson, "The Social Class and Mental Illness Correlation: Implications of the Research for Policy and Practice," *Journal of Sociology and Social Welfare 15* (March 1988): 27–31.

24. Dan A. Lewis, Stephanie Riger, Helen Rosenberg, Hendrik Wangenaar, Arthur J. Lurigio, and Susan Reed, *Worlds of the Mentally Ill* (Carbondale, IL: Southern Illinois Press, 1991), 25–33; B.E. Jones and B.A. Grey, "Problems in Diagnosing Schizophrenia and Affective Disorders among Blacks," *Hospital and Community Psychiatry 37* (January 1986): 61–65; James S. McNeil and Roosevelt Wright, "Special Populations: Blacks, Hispanics, and Native Americans," in *Social Work and Mental Health,* James W. Callicut and Pedro J. Lecca, eds. (New York: The Free Press, 1983), 183, 195; Nancy Felipe Russo, "Women in the Mental Health Delivery System: Implications for Research and Public Policy," in *Women and Mental Health Policy,* Lenore E. Walker, ed. (Beverly Hills, CA: Sage, 1984), 27–35; Evelyn J. Bromet and Herbert C. Schulberg, "Special Problem Populations: The Chronically Mentally Ill, Elderly, Children, Minorities, and Substance Abusers," in Rochefort, *Handbook on Mental Health Policy in the United States,* 75–78; National Institute of Mental Health, *Mental Health, United States, 1985,* Carl A. Taube and Sally A. Barrett, eds., DHHS Pub. No. (ADH) 85-1378 (Washington, D.C.: U.S. Government Printing Office, 1985), 5.

25. William E. Kiernan and Jack A. Stark, eds. *Pathways to Employment for Adults with Developmental Disabilities* (Baltimore, MD: Brooks Publishing Co., 1986), 12–15.

26. R.C. Scheerenberger, *A History of Mental Retardation* (Baltimore: MD: Brooks Publishing Co., 1983), 3–87.

27. Eveline D. Schulman, *Focus on the Retarded Adult* (St. Louis, MO: C.V. Mosby, 1980), 9–11.

28. Kiernan and Stark, *Pathways to Employment for Adults with Developmental Disabilities,* 11; Schulman, *Focus on the Retarded Adult,* 10–11.

29. Duane F. Stroman, *Mental Retardation in Social Context* (Lanham, MD: University Press of America, 1989), 17–18.

30. Schulman, *Focus on the Retarded Adult,* 22; Martha Ufford Dickerson, *Social Work with the Mentally Retarded* (New York: The Free Press, 1981), 20–22.

31. Harriett C. Johnson and Edward J. Hart, "Neurological Disorders," in *Adult Psychopathology: A Social Work Perspective,* Francis J. Turner, ed. (New York: The Free Press, 1984), 78–79.

32. Dickerson, *Social Work with the Mentally Retarded,* 24–25.

33. Michael J. Begab, "Issues in the Prevention of Psychosocial Retardation," in *Psychosocial Influences in Retarded Performance,* Vol. 1, Michael J. Begab, H. Carl Haywood, and Howard L. Garber, eds. (Baltimore, MD: University Park Press, 1981), 9–12.

34. Lynn McDonald-Wikler, "Disabilities: Developmental," *Encyclopedia of Social Work,* Vol. II, 425; Paul J. Castellani, *The Political Economy of Developmental Disabilities* (Baltimore, MD: Paul H. Brookes, 1987), 87–88.

35. Dickerson, *Social Work with the Mentally Retarded,* 32–38.

36. Dickerson, *Social Work with the Mentally Retarded,* 31; Scheerenberger, *A History of Mental Retardation,* 221.

37. David J. Rothman, *The Discovery of the Asylum* (Boston: Little, Brown, and Co., 1971), 1–7.

38. Rothman, *The Discovery of the Asylum,* 11–13, 43–45; Murray Levine, *The History and Politics of Community Mental Health* (New York: Oxford University Press, 1981), 15–16; Nancy Tomes, "The Anglo-American Asylum in Historical Perspective," in *Location and Stigma: Contemporary Perspectives in Mental Health and Mental Health Care,* Christopher Smith and John A. Giggs, eds. (Boston: Unwin Hyman, 1988), 3–4.

39. Rothman, *The Discovery of the Asylum,* 43–45, 130.

40. Levine, *The History and Politics of Community Mental Health,* 16; Rothman, *The Discovery of the Asylum,* xviii.

41. Michael B. Katz, *In the Shadow of the Poorhouse* (New York: Basic Books, 1986), 99.

42. Rothman, *Discovery of the Asylum,* 153; Pennsylvania Hospital, *First Annual Report,* summarized in Rothman, 145.

43. Levine, *The History and Politics of Community Mental Health,* 16–19.

44. James Leiby, *A History of Social Work and Social Welfare in the United States* (New York: Columbia University Press, 1978), 66–68.

45. Rothman, *The Discovery of the Asylum,* 265–295; Gerald N. Grob, *Mental Illness and American Society, 1875–1940* (Princeton, NJ: Princeton University Press, 1983), xi–xii, 8–15.

46. Grob, *Mental Illness and American Society,* 150–153; David J. Rothman, *Conscience and Convenience: The Asylum and its Alternatives in Progressive America* (Boston: Little, Brown and Co., 1980), 316–318.

47. Sands, *Clinical Social Work Practice in Community Mental Health,* 36–39; Norman Dain, *Clifford W. Beers: Advocate for the Insane* (Pittsburgh, PA: University of Pittsburgh Press, 1980), 112–121.

48. Roy Lubove, *The Professional Altruist* (New York: Atheneum, 1969), 93–100.

49. Grob, *Mental Illness and American Society,* 145; Rothman, *Conscience and Convenience,* 319–375.

50. Rothman, *Conscience and Convenience,* 324–335.

51. Levine, *The History and Politics of Community Mental Health,* 38–41; *The Community Mental Health Center* (Washington, D.C.: American Psychiatric Association, 1964), 3–4.

52. Levine, *The History and Politics of Community Mental Health,* 39–44.

53. Maxwell Jones, *Social Psychiatry in Practice* (Baltimore, MD: Penguin Books, 1958), 85–117.

54. Levine, *The History and Politics of Community Mental Health,* 46–47; *Action for Mental Health,* Final Report of the Joint Commission on Mental Illness and Health (New York: John Wiley and Sons, 1961), vii–xxxiii; *The Community Mental Health Center,* 1–7.

55. *The Community Mental Health Center,* 7.

56. Syracuse Psychiatric Hospital had originally been a psychopathic hospital. Reminiscences by Leslie Leighninger, 1967–1969.

57. Levine, *The History and Politics of Community Mental Health,* 45.

58. Peter L. Tyor and Leland V. Bell, *Caring for the Retarded in America* (Westport, CT: Greenwood Press, 1984), 3–6.

59. Tyor and Bell, *Caring for the Retarded in America,* 8–10; Scheerenberger, *A History of Mental Retardation,* 55–56, 68–70.

60. Tyor and Bell, *Caring for the Retarded in America,* 10–14.

61. Scheerenberger, *A History of Mental Retardation,* 101–104; Tyor and Bell, *Caring for the Retarded in America,* 21–15.

62. Schulman, *The Retarded Adult,* 39; Tyor and Bell, *Caring for the Retarded in America,* 51.

63. Tyor and Bell, *Caring for the Retarded in America,* 34–41.

64. Tyor and Bell, *Caring for the Retarded in America,* 45.

65. Tyor and Bell, *Caring for the Retarded in America,* 108–114.

66. Wolf Wolfensberger, *The Origins and Nature of Our Institutional Models* (Syracuse, NY: Center on Human Policy, 1974), 53–61; Tyor and Bell, *Caring for the Retarded in America,* 118–120.

67. Scheerenberger, *A History of Mental Retardation,* 241–243.

68. Tyor and Bell, *Caring for the Retarded in America,* 123–142; Schulman, *The Retarded Adult,* 43–45. Examples of these reports include Goffman's *Asylums,* D.J. Vail, *Dehumanization and the Institutional Career* (Springfield, IL: Charles C. Thomas, 1967), and Burton Blatt, *Christmas in Purgatory* (Boston: Allyn and Bacon, 1966).

69. Tyor and Bell, *Caring for the Retarded in America,* 144–146; Scheerenberg, A History of Mental Retardation, 247–249.

70. American Hospital Association, *Hospital Statistics: A Comparative Study of U.S. Hospitals, 1990–1991* (Chicago, IL: AHA, 1990), 3; U.S. Bureau of the Census, *Statistical Abstract of the United States: 1991* (Washington, D.C.: 111th Edition, 1991), 113.

71. Tyor and Bell, *Caring for the Retarded in America,* 149; Bruce L. Black, "Institutional Context and Strategy," in *The Organization of Community Mental Health Services,* W. Richard Scott and Bruce L. Black, eds. (Beverly Hills, CA: Sage, 1986), 243–244.

72. Tyor and Bell, *Caring for the Retarded in America,* 147–149; Wolf Wolfensberger, *The Principle of Normalization in Human Services* (Toronto: National Institute on Mental Retardation, 1972), 7–54.

73. Paul Lerman, *Deinstitutionalization and the Welfare State* (New Brunswick, NJ: Rutgers Univeristy Press, 1982), 89–101; Levin, *The History and Politics of Community Mental Health,* 70–72.

74. Black, "Institutional Context and Strategy," 246–247; Lerman, 4–12; Steven P. Segal, "Deinstitutionalization," *Encyclopedia of Social Work,* Vol. II, 378.

75. David Braddock, *Federal Policy Toward Mental Retardation and Developmental Disabilities* (Baltimore, MD: Paul H. Brookes, 1987), 25–28; Richard C.

76. Tessler and Howard H. Goldman, *The Chronically Mentally Ill* (Cambridge, MA: Ballinger, 1982), 193–195.

76. AHA, *Hospital Statistics,* 202; NIMH, *Mental Health, United States, 1990,* 27–28.

77. Gerhart, *Caring for the Chronic Mentally Ill,* 17–30; Sands, *Clinical Social Work Practice,* 186–187; Steven P. Segal and Jim Baumohl, "No Place Like Home: Reflections on Sheltering a Diverse Population," in Smith and Giggs, *Location and Stigma,* 249–263.

78. Sands, *Clinical Social Work Practice,* 210–280; David Goodrick, "Mental Health System Strategic Planning," in Rochefort, *Mental Health Policy in the United States,* 457–458.

79. Mark Schlesinger and Robert Dorwart, "Ownership and Mental Health Services: A Reappraisal of the Shift Toward Privately Owned Facilities," *New England Journal of Medicine 311* (October 11, 1984): 959–965; Richard Blake, "Boarding Home Residents: New Underclass in the Mental Health System," *Health and Social Work 12* (Spring 1987): 85–90; Peter Kerr, "Mental Hospital Chains Accused of Much Cheating on Insurance," *New York Times* (24 November 1991), 1, 20.

80. Schleslinger and Dorwart, "Ownership and Mental Health Services," 959–962.

81. G. Thomas Bellamy, et al., "Supported Employment," in Kiernan and Stark, *Pathways to Employment for Adults with Developmental Disabilities,* 129–137.

82. Stroman, *Mental Retardation in Social Context,* 227; Tamar Lewin, "As the Retarded Live Longer, Anxiety Grips Aging Parents," *New York Times* (28 October 1991), 1, 13.

83. Phil Brown, "Recent Trends in the Political Economy of Mental Health," in Smith and Giggs, *Location and Stigma,* 58–80; Stephen M. Rose and Bruce L. Black, *Advocacy and Empowerment: Mental Health Care in the Community* (Boston: Routledge and Kegan Paul, 1985), 55.

84. Rose and Black, *Advocacy and Empowerment,* 16, 57–69. See also Steven Wineman, *The Politics of Human Services* (Boston: South End Press, 1984), 43–47, 79–87.

85. Lynn Wikler and Maryanne P. Keenan, eds. *Developmental Disabilities: No Longer a Private Tragedy* (Silver Spring, MD: National Association of Social Workers, 1983); Charles R. Horejsi, "Developmental Disabilities: Opportunities for Social Workers," *Social Work 24* (January 1969): 40–43.

86. Rose and Black, *Advocacy and Empowerment,* 31–32.

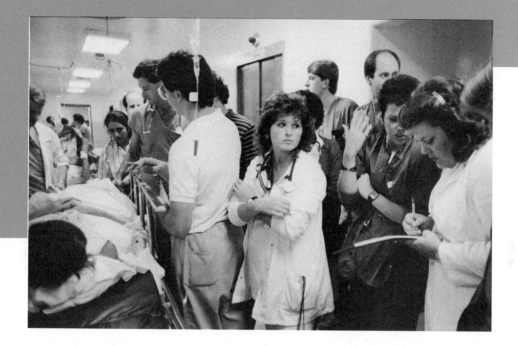

C·H·A·P·T·E·R
twelve

Health Care

Emily Rensor, a hairdresser, talks about her health problems with a customer: "I finally got to my doctor yesterday, and it's not great news. He's been watching my fibroid condition, and he says that now they've started to grow rapidly. I guess that explains the bleeding and the pain I've been having lately. He thinks I ought to have a hysterectomy—and soon. He's probably right, but I just can't afford it. You know, there's some health insurance with this job, but it doesn't cover everything. For one thing, there's a big deductible. And on top of that, I don't have disability coverage. I certainly can't afford to take six weeks off work. I could ask my ex-husband for help, but I don't think that'll get me anywhere. I guess I'll just wait and see if it gets worse."

Jeff Waite, a social worker in a private hospital in a rural community, is working on a proposal for a new hospital service—a place for relatives of out-of-town patients to stay while their family member is being treated. "Hospitality House" will be an alternative to a more expensive motel. It will provide both housing and emotional support to parents of sick children, men or women whose spouses have been hospitalized, or any other person helping a loved one through a hospital stay. As he prepares his proposal, Jeff is careful to show how his idea will enhance the hospital's standing in nearby communities, and thus contribute to hospital admissions and revenues. Knowing that the hospital board is concerned with marketing the institution's services, Jeff refers to the new program as a "product line."

Mr. and Mrs. Giamanco are in their late seventies. Until recently, they managed fairly well in their small apartment in an older residential area of the city. No longer comfortable driving, they could walk to nearby stores and to visit friends. Social Security payments and Mr. Giamanco's small pension from his bookkeeping job provided a reasonably adequate income. All this changed several months ago, when Mrs. Giamanco suffered a stroke. Bedridden and partly paralyzed, she needs constant care. Mr. Giamanco, depressed and frightened by his wife's situation, is finding it harder and harder to shoulder the burden of household chores and nursing care. The couple's daughter lives in another state and is unable to leave her job and family to come help out. Medicaid-funded home health services would be ideal, allowing the Giamancos to stay together in their apartment. But because of Mr. Giamanco's pension, their income level is too high for them to qualify for the program, and they can't afford to pay for a home health aide on their own. Much as Mr. Giamanco dreads the decision, he feels that his only other option will be to place his wife in a nursing home. Since the Medicare program for Social Security recipients does not cover long-term nursing home care, the Giamancos will have to use up their modest savings. Then, finally, Medicaid will pick up the costs.

Two faculty members are discussing the university's recent decision to restrict smoking to private offices and a few designated areas in campus buildings. "I think it's a great idea," one tells the other. "My dad died of cancer two years ago, after a lifetime of smoking. I'm convinced that all the doctors and medical treatments in the world won't make a difference with cancer. We've got to tackle it by changing the main causes—lifestyle and environment."

"It was such a hard thing to do," Grace O'Neal explains to the other students in her social work field placement seminar. "My supervisor was out of town so I was on my own in the Emergency Room last night. A sixteen-year-old boy was brought in after his motorcycle was hit by a van; he died just before his parents got to the hospital. I was just sitting there with them after the nurse told them, in case they wanted to talk with someone. Then the doctor and nurse came back in and started asking them about donating their son's organs for transplants. I know they have to work fast, but it was awful—those poor people had hardly accepted the fact that he was dead. I stayed and acted as a go-between; I got the medical staff to wait a little while, and I talked with his folks about how they felt and about the organ donation process. After about an hour, they decided that they would give permission for the donation, and they left. I went home and cried with my roommate."

Today's health care system reflects great progress, but it faces many problems. As the preceding scenarios suggest, we now live in a world where organ transplants are commonplace and new health care programs continually emerge. In addition, average life expectancies have steadily increased and the rates of many major diseases have fallen dramatically. Yet the system is plagued with gaps and inequities. Medical costs are soaring. A number of people lack medical insurance. We do not provide adequate services for the home-bound chronically ill. The system does not treat everyone equally; women, minorities, and the elderly face particular difficulties in getting appropriate and adequate care. A rapidly growing marketplace approach to medical care reinforces America's two-track scheme of health services: one for low-income groups and the other for the more well-to-do. Those in the bottom track include people who are not welfare recipients but whose low wages or inadequate health insurance make them medically poor. A large body of research reveals that many of our health problems are environmentally caused, yet we are reluctant to carry out the preventive measures this suggests. Finally, as in the relationship between grief-stricken parents and a hospital staff anxious to save other lives, we are frequently caught in conflicts between social and medical needs. This chapter describes the history and present state of health and health care in America, analyzes current issues and problems in the system, outlines different ideological perspectives on promoting health, and depicts the roles carried out by social workers in health care settings.

DEFINITIONS OF HEALTH AND ILLNESS

There are a variety of ways to define both health and illness. These definitions vary from society to society, for as sociologists point out, conceptions of health, illness, and appropriate treatment are to a large degree culturally determined.[1] Even different groups within a single society may view disease in diverse ways. For example, in our country, Navajo Indians sometimes define illness as a disharmony with nature, while groups attracted to a health food philosophy may see illness largely as a matter of poor nutrition and the ingestion of chemical additives.

Although there are a number of definitions of health and illness in the United States, the major ones are based on a biomedical model. Derived from molecular biology, this model describes disease as a deviation from a biological norm. Disease is perceived as a discrete entity, independent of the social context in which it occurs. Health is characterized as the absence of disease. The biomedical model stresses technical, medical treatment as the appropriate response to illness.[2]

The biomedical model has been criticized as presenting too narrow a picture of health and illness. To remedy this, an important variation of the biomedical definition adds psychosocial factors. The World Health Organization, for example, defines health as "a state of complete physical, mental, and social well being, and not merely the absence of disease or infirmity." Elfrieda Schlesinger, who writes about social work in health care, further broadens this definition by suggesting that one can lead a healthy, rewarding life even when disease is present. She stresses that health involves the ability to cope, both physically and psychologically, with various discomforts and infirmities.[3] A 55-year-old man with diabetes, for example, who manages this condition with diet and insulin and notes no other change in his daily activities, could thus be considered a healthy individual.

Another set of definitions of health and illness comes from the ecological and general systems perspectives. These approaches put even greater emphasis on environmental factors in disease. The *ecological,* or *holistic approach* looks at a variety of elements which bring about ill health, including environmental, socioeconomic, physiological, and psychological factors. Health is based on "positive self-image, plus the resources necessary to cope with the environment and its pressures." Health indicates a person's ability to function in the fullest and most positive way.[4]

General systems theory contributes an explanatory framework for these ideas. The systems approach views human beings in terms of a hierarchy of interrelated, natural systems. These systems range from subatomic particles to molecules and tissues, and on up through families, communities, and cultures. A problem in one system can spread to others. A person's well-being is related to the overall functioning and harmonious interaction of all these systems. Poor health thus stems from disruption of the interaction of natural systems, "to the point where one or more system levels are malfunctioning."[5] While this picture may seem abstract, the basic point of the ecological and systems model is that health relates to the many interconnected elements in an individual's life. Health promotion and disease prevention measures should therefore not be limited to the physiological realm.

STATISTICAL PICTURE OF HEALTH CARE

The most striking statistics about health care today are those relating to its cost. A frequent topic in the media and in current political debates, the rising cost of medical services has alarmed both policy makers and the public. The visit to the doctor that was $20 ten years ago may now cost twice as much. One day's stay in the hospital jumped from an average of $81 in 1970, to $127 in 1980, and to $315 in 1990. The coronary bypass that cost an average $18,000 in 1979 now costs about $49,000. In 1989, one in ten families had to allocate more than 10 percent of its income for health care.[6]

The United States spent well over $700 billion on health care in 1991, topping the annual defense budget. Health expenditures presently constitute about 13 percent of the Gross National Product. Their continued increase is particularly alarming. Medical costs rose at an average annual rate of 12 percent from the 1970s through 1983. Although the rate of increase fell in the mid-1980s, it has again begun to climb. National health expenditures were 10.5 percent higher in 1990 than in 1989. If this situation continues, the nation's medical bill will more than double in the next 10 years. Ironically, while the United States spends more on health than any other country in the world, our life expectancy is not appreciably greater, and our infant mortality rates are worse than those of most industrialized nations.[7] (See Figure 12–1 and Table 12–1.)

How are our health costs being covered? The answer is a complicated combination of private insurance (generally connected with employment), federal and other governmental expenditures, and out-of-pocket payments by individuals. In 1990, 43 percent of all health spending was covered by state, local, and federal government sources, 33 percent by private insurance companies, and 20 percent by consumers. The federal government accounts for almost a third of all health expenditures, with the major portion of this money going to the Medicare and Medicaid programs for the poor and elderly. While approximately 85 percent of the population has health insurance of some type through private or public sources, such insurance varies in what it covers. Fifteen percent of all Americans, including an estimated 8 million children, have no health insurance at all. The number of uninsured has increased 24 percent since 1980. And just as health costs increase, so do the costs of insurance. Average increases in private insurance premiums reached 18 percent in 1989. Monthly premiums paid by individuals on Medicare continue to rise much faster than inflation. Even business bears its share of growing insurance and health care costs; in 1990, companies spent anywhere from 25 to 50 cents of each dollar of profits on health care.[8]

Have increasing expenditures made a difference in the health of Americans? This is a complicated question, especially because, as we will see, medical care is a relatively minor factor in the overall changes in disease rates. However, it is helpful at this point to have a general picture of the health of the nation.

In 1989, in an annual national survey of self-assessed health status, over two-thirds of the U.S. population reported that their health was either excellent or very good. This assessment varied according to race. Seventy-one percent of white persons reported good or excellent health, compared to only 55 percent of African American

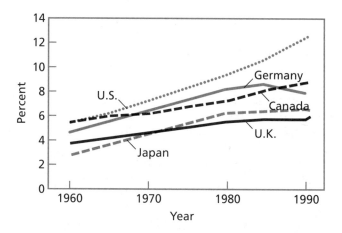

FIGURE 12–1   **The Cost of Health Care**

Source: Tom Morganthau, "Health Care: Cutting Through the Gobbledygook," *Newsweek* (February 3, 1992), 24. © 1992, Newsweek, Inc. All rights reserved. Reprinted by permission.

Statistical Picture of Health Care   **393**

TABLE 12–1	Infant mortality rates: selected countries, 1982 and 1987 (Infant deaths per 1,000 live births)	

	Infant Mortality Rate	
Country	1982	1987
Japan	6.6	5.0
Sweden	6.9	5.7
Switzerland	7.7	6.9
Canada	9.1	7.3
Netherlands	8.3	7.6
France	9.5	7.8
German Federal Republic	10.9	8.2
Australia	10.3	8.7
German Democratic Republic	11.4	8.8
United Kingdom	10.8	9.2
Italy	13.0	9.8
United States	11.5	10.1
Israel	13.9	10.7

Source: National Center for Health Statistics, *Health, United States, 1990,* DHHS Pub. No. (PHS) 91-1232, Public Health Service (Washington, D.C.: U.S. Government Printing Office, 1990), 73.

respondents. Another assessment of health is the rate of hospital admissions in the United States. Between 1980 and 1989, this rate declined by 13 percent (although the use of outpatient facilities increased).[9]

Improvement has also taken place in two major indicators of health: life expectancy and infant mortality, or death rates. Life expectancy for Americans has increased substantially since 1900. The majority of Americans born today can expect to live into their mid-seventies. Much of this increase has occurred between 1970 and the present. White females have the longest life expectancy (about 79 years), followed by African American females (74 years), white males (73 years), and African American males (65 years). This is an increase of about 6 years for men and over 7 years for women since 1950.[10] (See Figure 12–2.)

In addition, infant mortality has steadily declined, from 29.2 deaths per 1000 live births in 1950 to 9.7 deaths per 1000 in 1989. Yet, as we have noted, the United States continues to lag behind most other industrialized nations in its infant mortality rate. In addition, infant deaths vary by race, ethnic group, and socioeconomic class. For example, the mortality rate for Native American infants is about 40 percent higher than that for whites, and African American infant mortality is twice that of white infants. An African American infant born in Washington, D.C. or the state of Michigan is more likely to die before its first birthday than a child born in Jamaica.[11] (See Figure 12–3 on page 396.)

Death rates for many, but not all diseases, have also declined. One major change

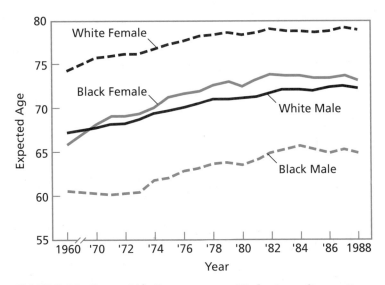

FIGURE 12–2   Life Expectancy at Birth, According to Race and Sex: United States, 1960 and 1970–88

Source: National Center for Health Statistics, *Health, United States, 1990,* DHHS Pub. No. (PHS) 91-1232, Public Health Service (Washington, D.C.: U.S. Government Printing Office, 1990), 12.

since the early 1900s has been the control of infectious diseases. In 1900, about 40 percent of all deaths could be attributed to eleven major infectious diseases, such as tuberculosis and scarlet fever. By the 1970s, these same eleven illnesses accounted for only 6 percent of all deaths. Chronic diseases, such as heart disease, cancer, and stroke, now make up a much larger part of the medical picture than acute or infectious conditions. In fact, these three are the leading causes of death in the United States today. (See Figure 12–4 on page 397.) It is estimated that half of the population has one or more chronic conditions. The death rates for heart disease and stroke have dropped in the last thirty years; on the other hand, deaths from lung cancer, which is caused chiefly by cigarette smoking, have markedly increased.[12]

Of particular concern in the last decade has been the rising toll of deaths due to AIDS, or Acquired Immune Deficiency Syndrome. Physicians first became aware of the existence of AIDS in the gay community in 1981. Since then, the disease has reached epidemic proportions. An estimated one million people in the United States are HIV-positive; of these, almost 200,000 have developed AIDS. Nearly 65 percent of these individuals have died of the disease. Once seen as an affliction of men who are gay, AIDS is now widespread in poor, African American and Hispanic American inner city communities, particularly among intravenous drug users and their sexual partners and babies. (See Figure 12–5 on page 398.) While the rate of contraction of AIDS among homosexual men has leveled off, its spread among poor African American and Hispanic American heterosexuals continues to increase. Drug users and their partners and babies now account for over one quarter of all AIDS cases. With possibilities for prevention, but as yet no cure, AIDS constitutes a major public health emergency.[13]

Statistical Picture of Health Care   **395**

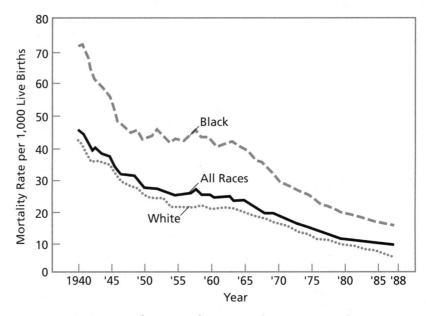

FIGURE 12–3   **Infant Mortality Rates* by Race, United States, 1940 to 1988**

*Rate per 1,000 live births.

Source: Adapted from *Metropolitan Life Statistical Bulletin* (April–June 1988), 5. Courtesy *Statistical Bulletin,* Metropolitan Life Insurance Company; U.S. Bureau of the Census, *Statistical Abstract of the United States: 1991* (Washington, D.C.: 111th Ed.), 78.

Health and Socioeconomic Factors

Studies of health and illness in the United States indicate definite relationships between disease and social class, race, ethnicity, gender, and age. Particularly notable is the correlation between disease and poverty. People with lower incomes are much less likely to report good health than those who are relatively well-off. In 1989, for example, about 19 percent of individuals with family incomes of $14,000 or less reported fair to poor health. In contrast, only 6.9 percent of those making between $25,000 and $34,999, and fewer than 4 percent of those with incomes above $50,000 saw their health status in those terms.[14]

Rates of chronic and acute disease—often called *morbidity rates*—generally show strong differences by socioeconomic status. For example, diabetes and tuberculosis have much higher morbidity rates among low-income individuals. People with low incomes are also more likely than high-income individuals to be restricted in activities because of illness or injury. In 1989, for example, individuals with an income below $10,000 took an average of 27 "disability days," compared to 10 such days for people with incomes of $35,000 or more.[15]

Race and ethnicity are also powerfully related to health status (see Figure 12–6 on page 399). As we have observed, both infant mortality and life expectancy rates indicate major differences between the experiences of whites and African Americans. The chronic disease picture shows similar variation. Rates of heart disease, diabetes,

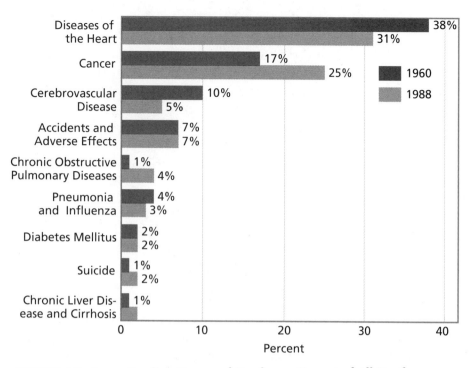

FIGURE 12–4   Leading Causes of Death as a Percent of All Deaths:
United States, 1960 and 1988

Source: U.S. Department of Health and Human Services, 1991.

and most forms of cancer are higher for African Americans than for whites. Blacks in the United States have twice the rate of high blood pressure as whites, and about five to seven times the rate of severe hypertension. Finally, blacks are twice as likely as whites to become disabled. Among individuals 65 and over, African American women are particularly likely to have some major limitation in daily activities. Similar kinds of differences can be found for other minority groups. AIDS is the second leading cause of death for Hispanic Americans between the ages of 25 and 44, but only the fifth leading cause of death for whites in that age range. Among older Native Americans, the death rate for liver disease and cirrhosis is three times that for whites. While the higher percentage of minority groups with low incomes accounts for a proportion of these differences, variations in health status remain even when the variable of class is controlled for.[16]

Gender plays an equally important role in health and illness. Women report more sickness than men, and yet they live longer. Men and women have different rates of chronic disease and a different mortality picture. For example, death rates from heart disease are substantially higher for men than for women. Breast cancer is the leading cause of cancer deaths among women; lung cancer is a major factor in cancer deaths among men (however, because of the increasing prevalence of cigarette smoking among women, the death rate for lung cancer among females has risen rapidly in recent years—see Figure 12–6). While women are less likely to have a chronic health con-

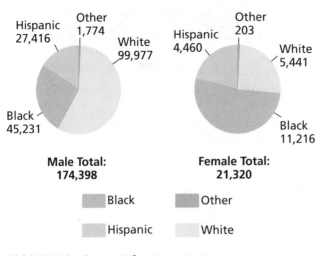

Male Total:
174,398

Female Total:
21,320

▨ Black   ▨ Other

▨ Hispanic   ▨ White

FIGURE 12–5   **Who Has AIDS**

Source: *New York Times* 17 November 1991, Sec. 4, p. 3. Copyright © 1991 by The New York Times Company. Reprinted by permission.

dition, they report a greater number of acute complaints than do men. In addition, as Schlesinger notes, they "spend more time in bed when ill . . . or otherwise restrict their activities to a greater extent."[17]

Age is also a factor in an individual's health status. As age increases, the number of those reporting fair or poor health rises. Acute health conditions decline and chronic health problems increase. Ten percent of those age 65 and over report being unable to carry on major activities because of chronic illness or impairment. In the general population, only 4 percent describe such limitations. However, we should be careful not to equate old age with ill health and disability. It is important to note that well over two-thirds of those 65 and over view their health as good to excellent.[18]

The health picture of the nation is thus complex and fluid. Costs are rising and they are covered by a diversity of sources. Many health indicators have improved, yet these improvements vary according to social class, race, age, and gender. Finally, chronic, or long-term disease has surpassed the infectious diseases as our major health problem.

DYNAMICS OF HEALTH AND ILLNESS

In order to deal with health problems, we need to understand the causes of disease and illness. Although this appears simple, there are in fact a number of models that seek to describe the dynamics of poor health. We will explore two major models in this section, the medical model and a social/environmental model. We will then discuss corresponding approaches to dealing with illness.

The *medical model* of illness focuses on disease and its treatment. It assumes that poor health is primarily caused by genetic malformations, internal chemical imbalances, and the attacks of viruses, bacteria, and other agents on our bodies. Diagnosis and

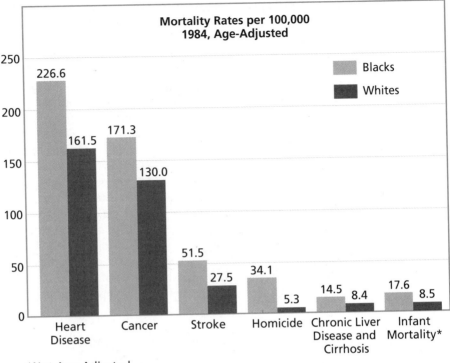

Mortality Rates per 100,000
1984, Age-Adjusted

Blacks
Whites

Heart Disease — Blacks 226.6, Whites 161.5
Cancer — Blacks 171.3, Whites 130.0
Stroke — Blacks 51.5, Whites 27.5
Homicide — Blacks 34.1, Whites 5.3
Chronic Liver Disease and Cirrhosis — Blacks 14.5, Whites 8.4
Infant Mortality* — Blacks 17.6, Whites 8.5

*Not Age-Adjusted

FIGURE 12–6   Six Fatal Inequalities

African Americans are afflicted with more than their share of mortal diseases, a disparity responsible for 59,000 "excess deaths" each year.

Source: Adapted from *Newsweek on Health* (Winter 1988), p. 29; U.S. Bureau of the Census, *Statistical Abstracts of the United States: 1991* (Washington, D.C.: 111th Ed., 1991), 78, 81.

treatment, or healing, occur only after the person becomes ill. The physician, a highly trained expert, decides which treatment is needed. Most often, drugs or surgical procedures are chosen to combat illness and to restore the individual to the equilibrium known as health.[19] A physician following a strictly medical model, for example, might prescribe coronary bypass surgery for a patient suffering from a heart ailment, rather than stressing changes in diet and lifestyle.

The medical orientation to illness focuses primarily on the individual, and has relatively little concern for social context. Yet many people, including an increasing number of physicians, would argue that it is this social context—involving cultural, economic, and environmental factors—which shapes health and disease. For example, there is a growing consensus that between 70 and 90 percent of human cancers are environmental in origin. The causative agents include industrial chemicals; carcinogens in our air, food, and water; and tobacco smoke. Cigarette smoking has been called "the single most avoidable cause of death in the United States." Smoking accounted for 22 percent of all deaths among men and 11 percent of deaths among women in the United States in 1985. The high risk of cancer in certain occupations is equally appalling; about 50 percent of all long-term asbestos-insulation workers die of the disease, while some 30 percent of all premature deaths in uranium miners is caused by lung cancer. Thus cancer, like many other chronic diseases, demonstrates the interrelationships among environment, occupation, habits and lifestyle, and illness.[20]

A *social/environmental model* of disease has many components. In its attempt to understand health and illness, the model looks at the interaction between human biology and socioeconomic status, psychological state, racial and ethnic background, gender, lifestyle, occupation, and environmental elements such as housing, nutrition, and exposure to certain chemicals. A large body of research indicates numerous ties between these factors and disease. The childhood heart ailment of rheumatic fever, for example, has been linked to overcrowded living conditions. Similarly, marital status has been found to be an important indicator of health, with married persons generally demonstrating better health than those who are divorced.[21]

Poverty, race and ethnic group, and gender are three major, often interrelated elements in the dynamics of disease. While cause and effect are often unclear, in each situation a variety of intervening factors seems to be at work. These factors include socialization, lifestyle, exposure to stress, and access to medical services. For example, African Americans have a much higher rate of elevated blood pressure than do blacks in Africa. Most scientists believe that environmental factors such as diet, smoking, and stress play an important role in triggering the condition in blacks who have a genetic vulnerability to it.[22]

Stress seems to be a particularly important contributor to poor health, although the exact way in which this works is not well understood. However, researchers have found that people who are exposed to many difficult life events are more frequently ill. Stress may contribute directly to specific illnesses, or it may change relevant behavior patterns.[23] For example, a low-income single parent who has just lost her job may develop poor eating habits and difficulty in sleeping. Poor nutrition and lack of rest might then make her more susceptible to disease.

People in low-income groups have higher morbidity and mortality rates for almost every disease or illness. This occurs in part because of the connections between poverty and poor nutrition; inadequate housing; lack of medical care; social stress; and exposure to environmental hazards, infections, and parasites. In addition, those living in chronically deprived life situations may lack the coping capacity and sense of confidence which can enhance good health.[24]

Lack of access to adequate health care is an important contributor to health problems among low-income Americans. Novelist Harriet Arnow presents a vivid picture of the difficulties poor people can face in obtaining appropriate medical treatment. In *The Dollmaker*, Arnow describes the experiences of Appalachian farm families transplanted to Detroit to work in war industries during the 1940s. When children in these families were diagnosed as needing tonsillectomies, only outpatient operations were provided. The families then had to take their children home within hours of the operation. In the following passage from the novel, Gertie Nevels, the book's main character, is helping her neighbors, Sophronie and Whit Meanwell, care for their two boys, who have just had tonsillectomies.

Gertie . . . saw that the battered Meanwell car was back. She saw Whit go alone up the walk in a kind of staggering run, as if drunk. She hurried out to help, and Sophronie, pale, but no longer shaking, explained that the overpowering fumes of ether in the closed car had made Whit sick to his stomach. Gertie carried in both boys, squinching her eyes a little against the dripping blood, the strong smell of ether, the vomit-spewing, blue-lipped mouths.

Sophronie turned a shade whiter each time one spat blood, and if either lay still an instant she was bending over him, listening to the heart beat. However, they seemed gradually to improve, and breathed more slowly and spat less blood, though when time came for Sophronie to go to work, she lingered with them too long, and then had to run, looking over her shoulder, entreating Gertie, "You'll watch em good, now won'tcha?"[25]

Class and poverty help to account for the relationship between racial or ethnic background and disease. In other words, if proportionately more Hispanic Americans are poor, then it is not surprising that their morbidity rate for certain diseases is higher than that of white Americans, who are proportionately better off. Yet social class does not explain all the variation between majority and minority groups. An additional causative element may be the stress brought on by encounters with racism in our society. Institutionalized racism also affects health by limiting access to quality medical care and by forcing many African Americans and other minorities to live in segregated, and often crowded housing situations.[26]

Recognition of environmental factors in disease leads to responses different from the exclusively curative measures of the medical model. In other words, pills and operations cannot solve the problems of overcrowded housing, institutional racism, or stress. True, many physicians recognize the interrelationship of social and biological factors in disease, and they do discuss changes in patients' diets and lifestyles. Another, more institutionalized method of dealing with environmental factors in disease is the public health approach.

The *public health approach* stresses prevention rather than treatment of diseases already acquired. In order to carry out preventive measures, public health researchers study the epidemiology of illness. That is, they look carefully at how and why diseases are distributed within a community. This entails investigation of the kinds of social and environmental factors described earlier. Then three levels of prevention can be carried out: (1) primary prevention, which entails intervening in the social environment to keep diseases from occurring in the first place; (2) secondary prevention, which involves early detection and treatment of disease; and (3) tertiary prevention, or responding to acute and chronic health problems through rehabilitation and other measures. Public health activities include maternal and child health measures (such as monitoring the progress of low-birth-weight babies), mass immunization against infectious diseases, health education, diet and weight control programs, and improvements in sanitation and other environmental problems.[27]

Another approach to dealing with illness from a social and environmental perspective is the *holistic health model*. As you may recall from our earlier description of the holistic definition of health, this definition emphasizes the interrelationship of psychological, biological, and environmental systems in the creation of health or illness. Holistic medicine thus calls for a systems-based, "biopsychosocial" approach to healing. While it recognizes broad environmental factors in the etiology of disease, holistic medicine differs from the public health model in its focus on the individual, rather than on large groups or the environment in general. Practitioners of holistic medicine promote a balance between a person's body, mind, spirit, and environment. They emphasize the patient's capacity for healing, and unlike traditional medical practitioners, they regard patients as active partners in, rather than passive recipients of health care. Holistic practitioners suggest the following kinds of treatment: modifications in diet and eating patterns, exercise programs, meditation, relaxation and biofeedback techniques, and changes in attitude toward illness.[28] Recently, the holistic and public health models have been combined in the "health promotion" approach, in which employers make various preventive and health education programs (such as weight-loss, stress reduction, and smoking cessation workshops) available to their employees.

The medical and social/environmental models of disease and its treatment both have long histories. The following section will explore their development and will also look at the history of social work's involvement in health care.

HISTORY OF HEALTH CARE

Today's health care system is a complex entity. It includes a wide array of organizations: physicians' offices, individual hospitals, large medical centers, free-standing emergency care and other outpatient facilities, public health and planning agencies, professional associations, and health insurance and pharmaceutical companies. It has been dominated by a strong medical profession, which stresses scientific medicine, specialist practice, and research. More recently, government and corporations have also become important forces in the structure of our health care. Surprisingly, this complex system has emerged relatively recently. Medical practice and the settings in which it took place were quite different only 100 years ago.[29]

During much of the 1800s, both in the United States and Europe, disease was thought to be the product of an imbalance in the body—an idea essentially unchanged since the time of Hippocrates. The ways of treating disease included drugs and chemicals, bloodletting, and exposure to the elements. Often, as health care analyst Howard S. Berliner has observed, these procedures "were largely irrelevant to the process of healing." Sometimes they were downright harmful. A medical case from 1833, for example, describes a pregnant woman who had convulsions as her delivery time approached. The doctors bled her of eight ounces of blood and gave her a purgative. When she suffered more convulsions the following day, they drew twenty-two ounces of blood. Continued symptoms led to more bloodletting, emetics to cause vomiting, ice packs on the head and mustard plasters on the feet. Eventually, the woman delivered a stillborn child.[30]

A good deal of health care was common sense "domestic medicine," with wives and mothers often in charge of healing. On the more formal level, medicine was practiced by a wide variety of individuals who had different degrees and types of training. Some were lay healers, such as herbalists; some were "regular" physicians whose training ranged from a European medical school degree to a course of lectures; and others were homeopathic doctors, with varying backgrounds, who stressed both the spiritual aspects of disease and the uses of small doses of drugs in its cure. People from all races and walks of life had access to some form of medical training and practice. Women were especially active as midwives, giving prenatal care and delivering babies. Much medicine was practiced in people's homes. Hospitals tended to be places of last resort for poor and elderly ill people; they were often viewed as places where one went to die.[31]

All of this changed in the late 1800s, because of revolutionary changes in sanitary practice and the growth of the germ theory of disease, which in turn fostered the rise of scientific medicine. Sanitary reforms in the United States in the 1860s and later drew on important public health developments in England, which had passed a Public Health Reform bill in 1848. These developments included changes in drinking water, sewage disposal, housing, and work conditions. They were based on new theories about the social and environmental causes of disease. The U.S. Public Health Service, America's oldest federal welfare agency, was founded in 1912. The agency enthusiastically adopted the new theories in its work with immigrants and others in crowded United States cities. Public health measures, along with improvements in diet, led to a dramatic and long-term reduction in morbidity and mortality rates.[32]

The Rise of Scientific Medicine

At about the same time, several events precipitated the rise of scientific medicine in the United States and Europe. Edward Lister's discovery of antiseptic technique in 1867, along with previous developments in the use of anesthesia, led to the growth of safer and more effective surgery. A new germ theory of disease evolved from the work of Pasteur and others, who isolated the bacteria responsible for the major infectious diseases. This made the creation of vaccines possible. Such discoveries bolstered not only the public health movement (which could now, for example, launch mass inoculation campaigns against diseases like typhoid and tetanus), but also helped create a new, scientific approach to medicine. This "scientific medicine," or the medical model of health care prevalent up through much of the present century, assumes that all disease is caused by discrete agents, like bacteria, and that treatment will generally be a surgical or chemical procedure performed on a passive patient by a highly trained physician.[33]

The period between 1880 and 1910 in the United States witnessed the gradual establishment of the notion of a scientific medicine practiced by a highly trained medical elite. Germ theory and improvements in surgery favored the growth of a formally educated, research-oriented medical profession. This growth was further encouraged by increasing faith in science and technology during the Progressive Era. This was a time, after all, of exciting innovations: the discovery of electromagnetic waves and their use in radio, the building of the automobile, and the perfection of the lowly light bulb. As sociologist Paul Starr notes

> The less one could "believe one's own eyes"—and the new world of science continually prompted that feeling—the more receptive one became to seeing the world through the eyes of those who claimed specialized, technical knowledge, validated by communities of their peers.[34]

Prior to the late 1800s, physicians had been a relatively powerless group. Although states had created medical licensing laws early in our history, they rejected these laws as undemocratic in the mid-1800s. Medical practitioners were too divided to lobby either for the reenactment of the laws or for standardized training. "Regular" physicians

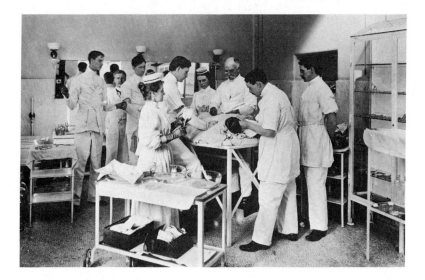

A surgical operation at Roosevelt Hospital in New York City, 1901.
The discovery of antiseptic technique and developments in the use of
anesthesia had brought about a new "scientific medicine" in the
United States and Europe.

had to compete for patients and public recognition with lay practitioners, homeopathic
doctors, female midwives, and others. By the end of the century, however, the new
acceptance of the expert enabled regular physicians to gain dominance over other
medical groups. Physicians were able to reestablish state licensing in a stronger form.
Such laws excluded lay practitioners from medical practice. In a movement well-
documented by feminist historians, physicians also succeeded at last in a long campaign
to push women out of the field of baby delivery. They created obstetrics as an important
medical specialty, practiced almost exclusively by men.[35]

Concurrent with these developments, the modern hospital emerged as an efficient,
scientific center for the treatment of illness. Hospitals shed their reputation as institutions for the poor and elderly, and they grew at a rapid rate in the 1800s. The
medical profession was gradually able to restrict the right to practice in hospitals to
those in their own ranks. In addition, because they supplied patients to hospitals,
physicians achieved a fair amount of control over hospital policies.[36]

An important turning point in the growth of the medical profession's exclusivity
and power came in 1910, when an extensive investigation of medical training was
commissioned by the doctors' professional organization, the American Medical Association. Although today we think of the AMA as a highly influential group, it was weak
and ineffective for many years after its founding in 1846. However, as doctors gained
strength, so did the AMA. By 1910, half of all MDs in the United States belonged to
the organization, and the AMA felt confident enough to embark on major changes in
medical education. Medical education at that time was of uneven quality; most of it
did not take place on the graduate level, and many schools had been unable to keep
up with new technologies.

The AMA commissioned Abraham Flexner, a prominent educator, to survey the field and make recommendations. (This is the same Flexner who was later invited to a national social welfare conference to discuss whether social work was a profession.) The Flexner report criticized many schools and suggested a radical weeding out of "inferior" programs. Along with tighter licensing laws and new standards from the AMA, the Flexner report led to widespread closing of medical schools. Many of these were located in the South and a number of them served a black student body. Only one in seven black schools survived into the 1920s. In addition, most of the schools serving women students were shut down.[37]

Gradually, the medical profession was becoming an exclusive and powerful body, composed primarily of white, middle- to upper-class men. Medical schools now established quotas limiting women to about 5 percent of admissions. Schools also discriminated against African Americans and Jews. At the same time, scientific medicine was becoming institutionalized as the dominant mode of medical practice in the United States.[38]

The medical profession solidified its position in the health care system from the 1920s through the 1950s. Improvements in clinical medicine and surgical techniques; new forms of technology, such as the electrocardiograph; and exciting discoveries in the area of pharmaceuticals, such as the Salk vaccine against polio, led to increasing public faith in the wonders of medicine. People tended to credit doctors with the dramatic and continuing fall in morbidity and mortality rates, even though much of this decrease could actually be traced to environmental reforms begun in the late 1800s. As medicine became more complex, doctors tended to choose specialized practice. The family general practitioner was increasingly replaced by the specialist—the internist or the heart surgeon—who commanded more prestige and a higher salary. Faith in the expert and awe at the increasing sophistication of medical care caused people to become more and more dependent on physicians. Of course, other groups, such as nurses and physical therapists, played a role in health services, but they were generally kept firmly under the authority of the physician. Nurses had difficulty in establishing an autonomous profession; through the 1940s, their training was largely controlled by hospitals.[39]

The high status of physicians in American society led to their growing influence in areas other than strictly medical ones. Some observers have termed this the "medicalization" of social issues. One example, discussed in a previous chapter, was the conversion of "insanity" into "mental illness," a "disease" to be treated by medically trained psychiatrists. Doctors, as an organized group, became particularly powerful on the political scene. Although not all doctors belonged to or subscribed to the views of the AMA, the organization came to speak with authority for the entire medical profession. The AMA constituted a potent lobby against governmental measures which threatened to undercut physicians' authority. As early as the 1920s, the group helped to repeal a nationally funded, state administered program of maternal and child health services. This program had drastically reduced infant mortality, birth defects, and maternal deaths. However, the AMA argued that such public programs constituted a dangerous experiment in state medicine.[40]

The power of the AMA to influence health policy became particularly evident in the 1930s. President Roosevelt had contemplated adding a national health care program to his package of Social Security benefits. Yet he and his advisors were dissuaded from doing so because of their awareness of the AMA's powerful opposition to such a scheme. Nevertheless, the Social Security Act did reinforce the legitimacy of government activity in the health field. Title VI of the act, for example, gave the U.S. Public Health Service additional resources and authority to support state and local government efforts in the area of public health.

While doctors were increasing their dominance in the medical arena, hospitals were strengthening their position as a major setting for health care. Hospital expansion was particularly notable after World War II. The federal system of Veterans' Administration hospitals, already the largest hospital system before the war, underwent revitalization and increased growth. In 1946, nongovernmental, nonprofit hospitals, often called *community hospitals,* received a particular boost from a hospital construction act known as the Hill-Burton program. The program provided federal funds for new hospital construction. In promoting funding of hospitals, federal policy makers opted to steer public financing away from areas like national health insurance or outpatient medical services. In addition, the Hill-Burton program forbade the federal government from interfering with hospital policy. In a move which would be repeated in subsequent years, the government took on a major financial responsibility for health care, but it did not gain accompanying control.[41]

Medical Social Work

Medical social work was a professional specialty which developed largely in conjunction with the expansion of hospitals and the rise of the medical profession. Although some social workers were involved in the public health measures of the late 1800s and early 1900s, particularly through their work in settlement houses, medical social work as a scientific entity first appeared in the hospital setting. A number of its first practitioners were, in fact, nurses. The establishment of hospital social work allowed these individuals to pursue a more autonomous professional status, one that was more independent of physicians than nurses were able to be.

In 1905, Dr. Richard Cabot set up the first medical social services department at Massachusetts General Hospital. Before coming to Massachusetts General, Cabot had directed the Boston Children's Aid Society. Impressed with the work of caseworkers at the Society, he felt there was a place for their services in the hospital context. Social workers could be particularly helpful in overcoming the depersonalization of the hospital and its tendency to ignore the social and environmental roots of disease. They could assist in the process of medical diagnosis by providing a study of the patient's social and economic situation; they could organize community resources, particularly to help hospital outpatients and those with physical handicaps; and they could investigate the role of environmental factors in causing disease.

Although medical social workers had an uphill battle convincing the bulk of MDs of the usefulness of their skills, over the next several decades they found a place for their practice in many large city hospitals. The goals established by Cabot—humanize the impersonal hospital and provide insights into the social aspects of disease—remain part of the basic core of medical social work today.[42]

The new specialty soon developed its own training programs—the Boston School of Social Work set up the first medical social work course in 1912—and its own professional organization, the American Association of Hospital Social Workers (1918).

It contributed prominent theorists, practitioners, and educators to the social work profession. These included Ida M. Cannon, who was an early director of Massachusetts General's Social Service Department, and Harriett Bartlett, who wrote widely on the goals and functions of medical social work and was active in professional development in both medical social work and the field of social work as a whole in the 1940s and 1950s. Up until the 1940s, when it was eclipsed by psychiatric social work, medical social work was considered by many to be the most prestigious area of the profession. Part of this standing stemmed from an emphasis on a high degree of training. In addition, medical social workers absorbed some of the status ascribed to physicians, although they had to work hard to develop some measure of autonomy within a system dominated by MDs.[43]

While medical social work—direct practice with clients and consultation with physicians, generally in hospital settings—was the dominant mode of social work in health care, a small number of social workers pioneered in the area of health policy. Julia Lathrop and Grace Abbott were important figures in this endeavor. As successive directors of the U.S. Children's Bureau from 1912 to 1933, they promoted state and federal programs in the area of child and maternal health. Abbott was responsible for development of such programs under the Sheppard-Towner Act. The act established federal financing for state efforts to reduce the incidence of maternal and infant mortality by providing health services to pregnant women and children. When the act's appropriation was up for renewal in 1927, Abbott and other social workers fought for its reinstatement against the bitter opposition of a variety of groups, including the AMA. These critics warned of the "international control of children" and the "imported socialistic scheme" inherent in the act. Those who attacked the maternal and child health programs did so to protect special interests and issues, such as states' rights, a conservative fiscal policy, antifeminism, and the authority of the medical profession. This last factor was crucial in the act's defeat.[44]

The strength of the medical lobby took its toll on social work's involvement in health policy issues. Although many social workers saw a need for federally sponsored health measures in the 1930s and later, their awareness of opposition from the medical profession helped to negate most organized efforts at reform. However, social work's interest in health policy revived in the 1960s, when the War on Poverty promoted greater public attention to the need for government involvement in health planning and services.

Health Care in the 1960s and 1970s

The 1960s and 1970s brought new challenges and changes in the health care system. Lack of access to medical care, particularly for the elderly and poor, had become an increasing problem as medical costs rose after World War II. President Truman had attempted to deal with these problems in the 1950s, but when he pushed for federal health insurance, the AMA responded with cries of "socialized medicine." Organized labor also fought the program, fearing that government insurance would usurp the union role in providing health benefits through negotiations with employers.[45]

The 1960s "discovery" of the existence of poverty and racism in the United States led to heightened awareness of the connections between poverty and ill health, and of the ways in which discrimination against minorities affected access to adequate

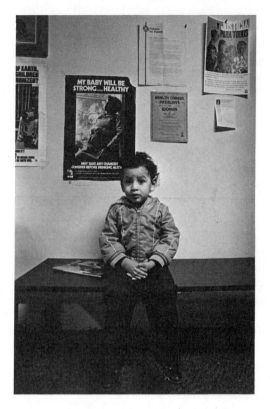

The development of community health clinics in urban and rural areas has brought quality health care to many individuals with low incomes.

health care. This awareness reawakened the call for government intervention. At that point, the United States might have chosen a publicly funded system of medical services for all, such as the system adopted in other industrialized nations. However, many factors, including a tradition of individualism, the fear of "big government," and the ongoing opposition of the organized medical profession, made such a move unthinkable. The next likely scheme, a program of national health insurance, still met with ardent disapproval from the AMA.

The AMA favored private insurance offered by commercial companies and the quasi-public Blue Cross/Blue Shield system developed by hospitals in the 1930s and 1940s. In Blue Cross plans, hospitals agreed to provide service based on prepaid premiums from participants. Special legislation exempted these plans from the usual state taxes paid by insurance companies. Blue Shield plans were a similar scheme applied to services provided by doctors in their offices. Both Blue Cross/Blue Shield and commercial insurance were often tied to employment. Those unable to participate in such group plans—the elderly, the unemployed, and those whose jobs did not offer insurance—were often unable to pay the higher premiums of the individual subscriber.

The inadequacies of existing insurance, rising medical costs, and the gathering force of the War on Poverty finally forced some solutions. In 1965, Congress passed legislation establishing the Medicare and Medicaid programs. Medicare provided comprehensive, federally financed medical insurance for the elderly and others receiving Social Security. Medicaid, which was to be jointly financed by the state and federal governments and administered by the states, extended health insurance to low-income groups. Significantly, no cost controls were built into these measures. Under Medicare, for example, the government would pay whatever hospitals charged.

At the same time, federally funded community health centers were added to the antipoverty programs of the 1960s. These centers "embodied ideas that had been espoused by health care reformers since the early twentieth century, including concepts of comprehensive health care, social medicine, and community participation." Generally located in low-income urban neighborhoods, the centers offered health care and preventive services in an outpatient setting. Policy makers hoped that the centers would decrease reliance on hospitalization and the use of crowded emergency rooms. The centers thus had several goals: to offer high quality health care to the poor, to experiment with changes in health care delivery, and to serve as a model for the reorganization of health care services for the public as a whole. In the 1970s, the community health center idea was extended to rural communities, in recognition of the fact that more than half of the medically underserved lived in rural areas.[46] (See Figure 12–7 for a description of a rural health center in the 1990s.)

WELCOME TO THE HEALTH CENTER

The Health Center is a general family clinic designed to make health care and health education more readily available to area residents.

The Health Center operates as a private health practice, offering complete, coordinated, and individualized health care to people of all ages; from babies to grandparents. In this sense, we try to fill the role of the old-time family doctor.

We have designed our Health Center to include the most modern approaches to health care. We provide a one-stop location for many of your family's health needs, including primary medical care, laboratory tests, and a variety of other programs geared to "health maintenance" — the prevention of illness.

Our staff will work with you to treat you when you are sick, and to keep you healthy when you are feeling well.

OUR SERVICES

MEDICAL CARE:
The Health Center provides general health care for all ages, including pediatrics, adult medicine, and care for the elderly.

Treatment of Acute Illnesses: colds, earaches, minor injuries, etc.

Treatment of Chronic Illnesses: arthritis, heart disease, high blood pressure, etc.

Physical Examinations: work, annual, comprehensive, school, insurance, camp, etc.

Pediatric Care: common illnesses, well child care, immunizations, etc.

Women's Health: pelvic exams, Pap smears, breast exams, birth control.

Our physicians are also on staff at Copley Hospital in Morrisville. If you have to be admitted to the hospital, you can be seen by your physician from the Health Center.

LABORATORY:
Many laboratory tests can be performed at the Health Center. This is often less expensive and more convenient for you. Those tests for which we do not have the necessary equipment are sent out to licensed commercial laboratories.

Tests we provide at the Health Center include: premarital blood tests, pregnancy tests, throat cultures, VD tests, cardiograms, urinalysis, etc.

There are no x-ray facilities at the Health Center.

Each health center has a local Board of Directors. These people decide health center policies and make sure the services the people in the area want and need are being provided.

The Hardwick HEALTH CENTER

High Street
Hardwick, Vermont
472-3300

FIGURE 12–7

Source: Hardwick Health Center, Hardwick, Vermont.

History of Health Care

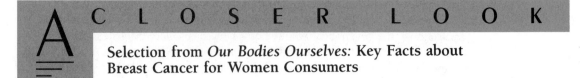

Selection from *Our Bodies Ourselves*: Key Facts about Breast Cancer for Women Consumers

1. Women are still their own best protection against a fatal breast cancer. We are in the best position to find suspicious lumps, through breast self-examination, and to report them. Over 90 percent of diagnosed breast cancers are found by women, not doctors.

2. Most lumps are benign, close to 90 percent of those biopsied. Lumps that don't disappear in one or two menstrual cycles are probably benign, but without tests neither you nor your doctor can tell for sure by examination alone.

3. A biopsy should be performed and the results carefully explained to you before any treatment decision is made. General anesthesia is not always necessary for a biopsy. Be sure your physician is qualified to treat you.

4. Cancer is not the leading cause of death of women in the United States, but breast cancer kills more women than any other cancer—over 33,000 annually—and it is the leading cause of death for all women age thirty-seven to fifty-five. Many of these deaths are preventable through early diagnosis and treatment.

5. Radical mastectomy (removal of the breast) is not the only treatment for breast cancer and has yet to be proven better than other treatments.

Breast cancers are not all the same and call for individual treatment or, increasingly, for combined treatments (surgery, radiation and chemotherapy).

6. Whenever removal of a breast (or any other organ or body part) is recommended it is wise to seek another opinion, from a specialist in breast cancer, in this case, preferably affiliated with a different hospital than your doctor. A university (teaching) hospital staff physician's opinion should be available to you before you decide anything.

7. You have a legal right to be told all the advantages and disadvantages of any treatment recommended; what all the alternatives and known outcomes are; and what the risks may be, including those of having no treatment.

8. You have a right to refuse any treatment or procedure at any time.

9. Make sure you have someone with whom you can talk out your feelings. Most doctors and nurses are too busy and may have different ideas from yours about what is important. If possible, get someone you trust to act as an advocate for you. Even the strongest of us needs familiar support at a time of crisis.

Source: The Boston Women's Health Collective, *Our Bodies Ourselves* (New York: Simon and Schuster, 1979), 135. Copyright © 1974, 1975, 1976 by The Boston Women's Health Collective, Inc. Reprinted by permission of Simon & Schuster, Inc.

The holistic health and hospice movements constituted other forces for change in the traditional health system. Each generated alternative programs. Holistic health centers stressed preventive measures and patient involvement in health care. The hospice movement, which promoted supportive multidisciplinary care for the dying patient, often outside of the hospital, offered yet another alternative to traditional practices.[47] The growth of new kinds of outpatient care, along with the decline in acute diseases and the overbuilding of hospital facilities, contributed to a growing surplus of hospital beds. This set the stage for increased competition between hospitals in both the 1980s and 1990s.

The 1960s and 1970s also brought increased criticism of the medical profession. The egalitarian ideals and social critiques of the 1960s caused many to question the power and elitism of professional groups, including doctors. Minority groups raised issues about access to medical education. The women's movement was a particularly potent force in challenging the medical establishment. The movement criticized the medical profession for its predominantly male composition and its reliance on male interpretations of women's health problems. Feminists questioned male doctors' conceptualization of childbirth as a traumatic medical event, rather than as a natural occurrence. Alternative women's clinics and books like *Our Bodies Ourselves* encouraged women to become more involved in their own health care.[48]

These challenges led to reforms in both the medical profession and the larger health care system. More women and African Americans were admitted to medical schools. By 1991, over a third of all medical students were women.[49] African Americans and other minorities fared less well. While minorities as a whole constituted 26 percent of medical students, African Americans made up only 7 percent of the student total. (See Figure 12–8 on page 412.)

Partly because of the influence of the women's movement, medical practices regarding women began to change in many communities. For example, in 1970 the hospital in the small town of Oswego, New York did not allow prospective fathers to be with their partners during labor. Two years later, men not only could accompany their partners in the labor room but they could be present at the actual delivery of their babies. In addition, local doctors no longer discouraged women from breastfeeding, and some physicians had begun to recommend classes in prepared childbirth to their patients.

The health system still contained problems in the 1970s, however. Inflation fueled higher health costs. Fears grew that America faced a "health care crisis." The situation was greatly exacerbated by the fact that Medicare and Medicaid were "open-ended" programs, in which increases in health charges could be passed along directly to the government. Access to health care for the poor and minorities had improved because

More women are entering the health professions and more women are seeking their services.

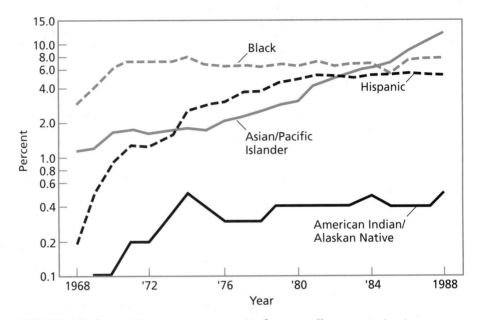

FIGURE 12–8   **First-Year Minority Student Enrollment in Schools of Medicine, According to Race/Ethnicity: United States, 1968–88**

Note: Excludes schools of osteopathic medicine.

Source: National Center for Health Statistics, *Health, United States, 1990*. DHHS Pub. No. (PHS) 91-1232, Public Health Service (Washington, D.C.: U.S. Government Printing Office, 1990), 36.

of Medicaid and the new Neighborhood Health Centers. However, partly because of rising medical costs, government support for health centers was drastically reduced in 1978. Two more measures to deal with cost and access issues emerged in the 1970s and 1980s—the first was an effort at broad health planning, and the second was support for Health Maintenance Organizations or HMOs.

Health planning legislation in 1974 created a network of federally funded local health planning agencies. It also mandated state agencies charged with implementing the results of the planning process. The planning agencies included consumer participation, and they were to look into problems such as duplication of services, lack of access, and unnecessary costs. At the same time, hospitals introduced "utilization reviews" in an attempt at self-evaluation.

Health Maintenance Organizations, which were first developed in the 1930s, are a form of prepaid medical service. For a fixed monthly fee, subscribers in a particular HMO can obtain preventive and acute health care. This care is either provided directly or arranged by physicians in the program. HMOs seek to contain costs and provide effective medical care by operating on a fixed fee and by stressing prevention. Unlike many traditional insurance policies, for example, the HMO fee covers regular medical check-ups. The Nixon administration passed legislation supporting HMO growth in 1971 and forecast a widespread move toward this form of financing and delivering health care.[50] President Reagan continued this stress on HMOs as a way to contain costs in the 1980s.

However, these attempts to improve the system met with serious setbacks. AMA opposition to HMOs and diminished support in Congress led to a variety of requirements which made it difficult for health maintenance plans to compete with conventional insurance. In addition, as part of a movement to reduce the role of the federal government, the Reagan administration ended the funding of health planning agencies. From the 1980s on, Americans have been faced with profound and continuing deficiencies in health care provision.

CURRENT ISSUES AND TRENDS

The preceding history of health care indicates the complexity of the American system. Many players crowd the field, including physicians and other health care workers, government policy makers, hospitals, insurance companies, private corporations, and consumers. Sponsorship of care includes government bodies, private nonprofit groups, and for-profit organizations. Finally, health care in the United States is delivered in a variety of settings, ranging from physicians' offices to hospitals to "health and wellness" programs run on holistic health principles. This complexity offers certain advantages, such as greater choice of services for many consumers. Yet it also creates confusion (who provides the best service, and where?) and presents problems in coordination.

As the U.S. medical system has grown in complexity, it has also developed serious flaws. These flaws exist despite the fact that the health of Americans has improved greatly over the years. Four interrelated issues dominate discussion of these deficiencies: (1) rising costs, (2) increased specialization on the part of physicians, (3) the development of commercialization in health care, and (4) increased inequities in health delivery, leading to two health systems, one for the well-off and another for the poor. Widespread concern over these problems has led to numerous proposals for health care reform in the 1990s.

Rising Costs

As we have seen, health costs have been rising steadily in the last thirty years, increasing most spectacularly during the 1970s and 1980s. Medicine has become more expensive because of new technology, the rise in long-term chronic diseases, and the needs of an aging population. In addition, costs inevitably grow because of the way in which we organize the system and its financing. The United States does little overall national planning for health care, and thus faces duplication of services and the lack of a comprehensive program of prevention. In addition, our insurance arrangements, both private and public (for example, Medicare), have paid hospitals and doctors on a cost or fee-for-service basis. In other words, "the more hospitals have spent, the more money they have received; the more services doctors perform, the more money they make."[51] The resulting costs hurt all of us. High Medicare and Medicaid expenditures eat into public tax money. Rapidly rising insurance premiums deplete the pockets of individuals as well as large corporations. The Chrysler Corporation, for example, pays so much for employee health care that Blue Cross/Blue Shield has become the company's largest supplier. Finally, of course, the poor and the uninsured are hurt. Either they do without medical care or they receive what is all too often an inferior level of service.

New attempts to cut costs initiated by the Reagan administration have been continued under President Bush. On the federal level, two methods have been pursued: greater pressure on insured individuals to shoulder a part of their medical expenses and a change in the way hospitals are reimbursed for their services to those on Medicare. In the first situation, the federal government increased the amount of money Medicare recipients must pay toward their health care. For example, the Medicare deductible, or cost of the first sixty days of hospital care, was raised from $304 to $520 in the mid-1980s, and to $652 in 1992. Of course, such a measure may represent a shifting of cost to the consumer rather than an actual cut. Yet a higher copayment will cut costs if it encourages people to seek less expensive alternatives to hospitalization wherever possible.

The second approach, introduced in 1983 by the Reagan administration, constitutes a more direct attack on the traditional fee-for-service method of financing health care. The new system utilizes Diagnostic Related Groups, or DRGs, to set fixed fees for Medicare reimbursement to hospitals. Once a patient has been diagnosed, the hospital is paid a set fee, reflecting the average cost of treating that particular condition. The hospital keeps the difference if the cost is lower than average, but must absorb the extra expense if the patient uses more services or takes a longer than average time to treat. In 1992, a similar reimbursement system was adopted for physicians.

The new incentive to keep expenses under control at first brought promising results. From 1983 to 1984, Medicare costs underwent their smallest increase (8.6 percent) since the start of the program. In the next year, the rate of increase fell to 5.5 percent. National health spending increases dropped as well. However, beginning in 1986, these trends reversed themselves, with yearly increases again on the rise. (See Figure 12–9.) In addition, the use of DRGs has stirred worries over whether hospitals now release patients sooner than is medically advisable. Periodically, newspaper accounts surface regarding elderly patients who die shortly after what appears to have been a premature hospital discharge. So far, there is little evidence to indicate a dangerous pattern, but it is clear that many patients are released to nursing home facilities rather than to their own care.[52] Nursing home facilities are not reimbursed by Medicare, so these costs are shifted elsewhere. All in all, however, DRGs mark an important inroad into a system where providers, in this case hospitals, have up to now had a good deal of power over medical fees.

Rising medical costs have also led to experiments with new arrangements for delivering care. Hospitals have developed "same-day surgery" plans, where patients have blood tests and other procedures done ahead of time. They then check in for surgery in the morning and thus avoid expenses for the previous night. In addition, many surgical procedures are being carried out on an outpatient basis, either in regular hospitals, physicians' offices, or in freestanding "surgicenters." Now you can have a cataract removed in the doctor's office, rather than spending several days in the hospital.

Most recently, large employers have entered the cost-cutting arena in an attempt to counteract rising expenditures on health insurance for their employees. These large-scale purchasers of health services constitute a new and important force in shaping health care provision. Their ability to make inroads into the powers of physicians and hospitals is suggested in a headline in the newsletter of the Midwest Business Group on Health: "Employers Taking Control of Health Marketplace." Corporations are pursuing a wide variety of measures to cut costs, including raising employee insurance

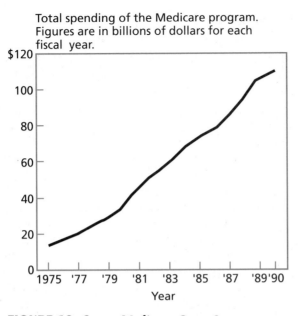

Total spending of the Medicare program. Figures are in billions of dollars for each fiscal year.

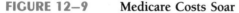

Year

FIGURE 12–9   Medicare Costs Soar

Source: New York Times, 10 March, 1991, Sec. E., p. 4. Copyright © 1991 by The New York Times Company. Reprinted by permission.

premiums and setting up comprehensive "wellness" or health promotion programs. A number of employers have also instituted measures which collectively are known as "managed care." These approaches include mandating second opinions on the need for certain surgical procedures, sending workers to particular HMOs or physicians' plans, and negotiating with hospitals for flat fees for high-cost procedures such as heart bypass operations. Finally, some employers have simply dropped employee health insurance altogether.[53]

Increased Specialization

Rising specialization within the medical profession creates another set of difficulties. The concept of specialization began in the earlier years of this century. Now 70 percent of all physicians are specialists.[54] Because of their claim to a particular expertise, specialists can charge more than general practitioners. "My son, the heart surgeon," carries more prestige than "my son, the doctor." The growing dominance of specialized over general practice has meant a lessening of attention to the whole patient. Many consumers find themselves consulting a variety of physicians, with little ongoing or consistent relationship with any one of them.

The medical profession has attempted to deal with this problem through the creation of family practice physicians. These physicians take a more holistic view of health care, and they serve as the primary medical care giver for all members of the family. Although this is a promising development, family physicians still constitute a small portion of the profession and they do not command the status of the specialist.

The Business of Health Care

In a famous article in the *New England Journal of Medicine* in 1980, editor Arnold S. Relman coined the phrase "the medical-industrial complex." Relman was referring to "a large and growing network of private corporations engaged in the business of supplying health-care services to patients for a profit." As Relman has observed

> Health insurance and third-party payment, coupled with increased specialism and the technology explosion, have been largely responsible for the rapid rise in health care expenditures, and have created a new climate for medical practice in which there are virtually irresistible incentives for doctors to become entrepreneurial and profit seeking in their behavior.

This climate for entrepreneurial practice has been enhanced by the stress in the 1980s and 1990s on the market economy as a major force for solving social problems. Both doctors and medical institutions have become involved in medicine as "big business." Relman warns that this growth of medicine as a business venture raises issues about the potential conflict between the profit motive and the basic right to health care.[55]

The most striking evidence of the move toward corporate medicine is the expansion of for-profit hospitals, particularly in multihospital chains. While most hospitals are still owned by nonprofit entities, the number of private hospitals has increased dramatically. Between 1980 and 1988, the number of state and local government hospitals declined over 15 percent and private nonprofits by 2.4 percent, but the number of private hospitals grew by about 8 percent. The profits of investor-owned hospital chains increased by 75 percent in 1990. We are all familiar with the achievements of the Humana Heart Institute in Louisville, Kentucky, which placed an artificial heart in the chest of patient William J. Schroeder in 1984. We may be less aware of the fact that publicity about such spectacular feats helps strengthen a giant chain of almost 80 for-profit hospitals owned by Humana. Chains such as Humana and the Hospital Corporation of America own not only medical hospitals, but also medical supply companies, psychiatric hospitals, clinical laboratories, nursing homes, and group health insurance plans. Thus many for-profit chains have become conglomerates, managing a diverse package of health care programs. This phenomenon is not limited to the for-profit chains. Nonprofit hospitals have begun to develop or buy up other health care programs, such as breast cancer screening clinics located in shopping centers. These subsidiaries may even be for-profit ventures.[56]

The growth of multihospital systems and medical chains on both the profit and nonprofit level creates increasing concentration of ownership and control of health services. Decisions about medical care—the type, the cost, and who will be served—begin to emanate from national corporate boardrooms rather than from regional sources. This type of medical provision, as Starr notes, begins to take on a fast-food image, with a standard product offered nationwide. For example, chains of emergency surgical and urgent care centers are springing up all over the country, especially in the Sunbelt and affluent suburban areas. Such centers (jokingly referred to as Docs in a Box) could be called the medical equivalent of McDonalds or 7-11 stores.[57]

Recent studies indicate that competition between hospitals can actually lead to higher costs (partly because of offering expensive new technologies) and longer patient stays. In addition, the climate of profit making and the competition for a declining number of hospital patients means that large sums of money are spent on medical advertising. Hospitals and physicians' groups now send glossy brochures to prospective clients and place appealing advertisements in magazines and newspapers. Money for advertising is money lost to patient care. The pharmaceutical industry, which is the second most profitable industry in the United States, spends more on sales and marketing than on research and development.[58]

Doctors are becoming part of this growing corporate movement. Some physicians are entrepreneurs in their own right. They own ambulatory health care centers and other medical programs. In Florida, for example, doctors own 78 percent of the radiation-therapy centers and 60 percent of the clinical labs, leading to possible conflict-of-interest situations.[59] Other physicians have become the salaried employees of medical "businesses." While physicians will probably always maintain a certain amount of autonomy based on their skills and expertise, the move to salaried positions within medical programs decreases physicians' control over practice.

It would be unfair to blame the entrepreneurial approach for all the ills of health care today. Competition between health providers may in fact sometimes lead to reduced costs or more effective services. Physician domination over health care decisions may not be better than corporate control or centralized government control, although the latter is generally more open to public scrutiny. Yet the rise of "big business medicine" appears to many to be reinforcing a dual-track medical system, in which the more well-off receive good service, while the poor receive increasingly inferior care.

Inequities in Health Care

The following stories suggest a disturbing trend toward increased inequities in health care in the United States.

> William Jenness, a 27-year-old California man, was severely injured in a 1984 auto crash. As *Newsweek* reports "Jenness was taken to Memorial Hospital Medical Center of Modesto, a nonprofit. When officials discovered he had no insurance and could not post a $1,000 down payment, they transferred him to Scenic General Hospital, a public facility, despite the fact that he was badly wounded. As a result, surgery on Jenness did not commence until four hours after the crash. Jenness died on the operating table; the autopsy report noted almost a quart of blood in his chest cavity."[60]

> The Humana chain believes in treating all emergency cases. Yet, if patients are uninsured, Humana then transfers them to public institutions for ongoing care. One such patient died after being transferred within one day of suffering a heart attack. As a Humana official explained "These freebies cost $2,000 or $3,000 a day. Who's going to pay for them?"[61]

As these examples indicate, the increasing financial problems of private nonprofit hospitals and the growth of for-profit chains have led to the phenomenon of dumping— the transfer of poor patients to other institutions. In Florida, where for-profit hospitals make up about 50 percent of all hospitals, these hospitals accounted for only 4.2 percent of the state's care for the poor in 1985. Most of the nation's poor are now cared for in teaching hospitals, Veterans Administration hospitals, and public hospitals, which are often located in the inner cities. Staggering under the pressure of the AIDS epidemic, drug abuse, and problem pregnancies, these institutions can barely cope.[62] Patient dumping, however, is only the tip of the iceberg. There are other long-term inequities in American health care.

The Medicare and Medicaid programs were established in the 1970s in an attempt to deal with inequities faced by the poor and elderly. They did improve access to medical care. However, even before the cuts of the Reagan administration, Medicare covered less than one-half of the medical expenses of the elderly. Medicaid is even more problematic, particularly because not all low-income individuals qualify for the program. Individual states determine who can receive Medicaid. Some states include in the program the "medically indigent"—those not receiving public welfare, but too poor to afford medical care. Other states restrict Medicaid recipients to those on the welfare rolls. Thus those at the poverty borderline are often unprotected.

People who receive Medicaid still face difficulties. As the federal government has reduced its matching funds to states for Medicaid programs, some financially strapped states have lowered reimbursements to doctors and/or have increased the amount of copayment the individual recipient must make. Because Medicaid generally pays doctors less than their regular charges, an increasing number of physicians have refused to take Medicaid patients.[63] Nursing homes sometimes refuse Medicaid patients for the same reason.

Medicare and Medicaid were designed in part to fill gaps and reach groups not covered by private insurance. However, 15 percent of Americans have neither public nor private insurance. Almost 80 percent of them are employed or are the dependents of employed individuals. They tend to work for themselves or for small companies that do not provide health coverage. Age and race play an important role in determining coverage. In 1988, one-half of those lacking health insurance were under 25 years old. Twenty percent of African Americans and 26 percent of Hispanic Americans were uninsured, compared with 12 percent of whites.[64] (See Figure 12–10.)

Class, plus racial or ethnic background also influence people's use of health care and the type of services available. Researchers have documented lower utilization of health services by the poor and minorities, although access for these groups has mark-

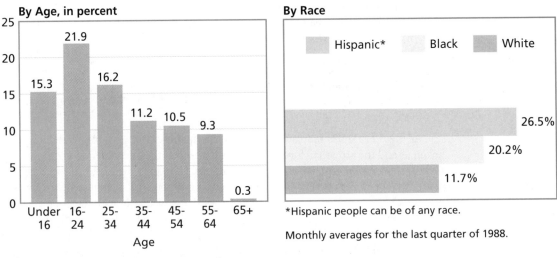

*Hispanic people can be of any race.

Monthly averages for the last quarter of 1988.

FIGURE 12–10   **Who's Uninsured**

Source: New York Times, 9 January 1992, 1. Copyright © 1992 by The New York Times Company. Reprinted by permission.

edly improved since the introduction of Medicare and Medicaid in the 1960s. However, the problem of the type of service utilized remains. Many low-income areas lack adequate health facilities. All too often, poor and minority individuals rely on emergency room treatment. (See Table 12–2.) Their other resources include "Medicaid mills," factory-like inner city private clinics offering inferior care, or overcrowded and understaffed city and county public hospitals.

Health care in rural areas presents additional problems. Most physicians choose to practice in urban and more populated areas, leaving rural communities, particularly poor ones, underserved. The rural South suffers particularly from the maldistribution of health care. In addition, a large proportion of hospital closures in recent years have been in rural areas.

Sometimes the inadequacies of Medicaid and the scarcity of doctors interact to create a crisis situation. Such a situation was headlined in the *St. Louis Post-Dispatch*: "State's Rural Poor Lack Prenatal Care." According to the article,

> The availability of prenatal care for poor women and Medicaid recipients has declined dramatically in rural Missouri over the last year, forcing hundreds of pregnant women to do without medical supervision, jeopardizing their health and their babies.

A combination of rising malpractice insurance costs and "woefully inadequate" Medicaid reimbursements by the state have caused many obstetricians, some quite reluctantly, "to cut Medicaid patients from their practices or stop delivering babies altogether, leaving some communities entirely without such medical services." The only recourse

TABLE 12–2	Source of physician care by race and income, 1989		
	Source or Place of Care[1]		
Category	Doctor's Office	Hospital Outpatient Department (percentage of visits)	Telephone
All	59.6	13.2	12.3
Race			
White	60.9	12.2	12.9
Black	50.6	20.4	9.3
Family income			
Less than $14,000	48.5	18.0	10.8
$14,000–$24,999	58.9	14.3	12.9
$25,000–$34,999	61.0	12.1	12.4
$35,000–$49,999	63.1	12.1	12.9
$50,000 or more	63.4	10.7	13.6

[1]Includes hospital outpatient clinic, emergency room, and other hospital contacts.
Source: Adapted from National Center for Health Statistics, *Health, United States, 1987,* DHHS Pub. No. (PHS) 88-1232, Public Health Service (Washington, D.C.: U.S. Government Printing Office, 1988), 103; *Health, United States, 1990,* 137.

for women in these cases is to show up in a hospital emergency room once labor has begun.[65]

Children are perhaps the greatest victims of health care inequities. They have been the hardest hit by decreases in Medicaid; that program covers only one-third of all poor youngsters. Children are also affected by cuts in nutrition programs and in school lunch plans. As one writer notes, "Even with inadequate data, a disturbing picture is already emerging of the deteriorating health status of children, child-bearing women, and adults with chronic disease. . . . The health of poor Americans is getting worse."[66]

Many observers of the health care scene fear that the rise of for-profit facilities will add to these problems. Whether dumping will become a widespread practice is not yet clear. Many for-profit chains commit themselves to the treatment of a certain number of indigent people. Yet their need to make a profit, and the nonprofit hospitals' need to stay financially solvent, prompts both groups to ask, "Who is responsible for the poor?"[67]

Ethical Issues

Many of the elements in health care today—new technologies, increased longevity, and inequities in provision of care—lead to profound ethical dilemmas for our society. As our population ages, for example, questions of when to remove terminally ill individuals from life support systems will become increasingly important. The cost of $2000 a day for intensive care for premature infants raises doubts about continuing such care for severely disabled babies. Progress in the area of organ transplants leads to the problem of how to ration these sophisticated and expensive procedures. In order to maintain a comprehensive health care program, for example, the state of Oregon is developing a system of financial triage, or a formula for deciding questions such as who will receive transplants. The Oregon system proposes that a child on Medicaid may receive a liver transplant, while a chronic alcoholic may not. These are just a few of the ethical issues that health care practitioners, and society as a whole, must deal with in the years to come.[68]

Health Care Reform

Calls for reform of the U.S. health system now come from virtually all the affected sectors: business, physicians, hospitals, government, and the public. Health care proposals were critical issues in the 1992 presidential campaign. However, while dissatisfaction with the current system is high, there is no general consensus regarding the best solution. (See Tables 12–3 and 12–4.) As suggested in an editorial in the *Journal of the American Medical Association,* the multitude of recommended programs can be categorized into four major types:

1. A compulsory, employer-based private insurance program, with the government insuring nonworkers and the poor;
2. A plan that requires employers to provide their employees with health insurance or pay a tax [the "pay or play" plan];
3. A program of income-related tax credits for individuals; and
4. An all-government insurance system.[69]

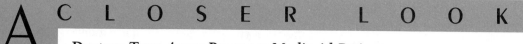

Doctors Turn Away Pregnant Medicaid Patient

When Kim Huggins of Branson, Mo., has her third child in the next few days, it will be under conditions that are far from ideal.

Like hundreds of other women in southwestern Missouri in the last year, Huggins—an unemployed, unmarried woman on Medicaid—was unable to find an obstetrician to provide her with prenatal care. Nor could she get the hospital in her hometown to allow her to deliver there. That's because she's on Medicaid and high-risk: she needs a Caesarean section because her pelvis structure is too small to safely deliver a child.

So when she goes into labor, Huggins will travel the 38 miles from her parents' home in Branson to Lester E. Cox Medical Center in Springfield, where a doctor she's never met, with no knowledge of her medical history, will operate on her to deliver her child.

Were she a private physician's paying patient, she likely would already have delivered the child in a scheduled operation; that's the preferred, safe way for a woman who knows in advance that she must have a C-section. But that option was unavailable to Huggins, because no physician will take responsibility for her care until she's ready to deliver.

When Huggins, 27, began looking for a doctor to take care of her, she ran into problems: The three doctors in the Branson area who deliver babies would not see her because she's on Medicaid. Nor would doctors 45 miles away in Berryville, Ark., or 38 miles away in Springfield, or anywhere in between.

"I called all over," she said. "I did everything but get down on my knees and beg. They told me the only thing I could do was wait until I went into labor, and go to the emergency room."

Huggins' baby is due in about a week. Three times in the last three weeks, she's gone into false labor. The first time, she went to Skaggs Hospital in Branson and was turned away. The second time she went to Cox, one of only two hospitals in the region that will accept "walk-in" Medicaid patients for delivery. Nurses there diagnosed her condition and promised her good care when she goes into actual labor.

On Friday, Huggins went into what turned out to be false labor again. This time she stayed home, waiting to see what would happen, reluctant to make another trip to the hospital and saddle Medicaid with an additional bill.

Huggins is apprehensive about what lies ahead. "It scares me to death," she said Friday. "The risks of having a C-section after you've already gone into labor are so great. I worry about whether the baby is going to be OK. If I were able to pay a private physician, there's no way he'd let me go into labor if I'm going to have a C-section."

When she comes out of the hospital, Huggins says she wants to "do whatever I can to make sure no one else has to go through this."

"What good does it do to be on Medicaid if no doctor will take it?" Huggins asked. "All I want to do is do what's right for my baby, and I can't. It's terrible."

Huggins has been luckier than many other Medicaid recipients in her area in that she was able to persuade a general practitioner in Branson to examine her periodically through her pregnancy. Many other Medicaid patients in the area get no prenatal care, authorities say.

Bonnie Thomas, a social worker at Cox, says cases like Huggins' frustrate her. "I don't like telling people I don't know what they can do," she said. "I think about how scared I would be if I was pregnant and couldn't get in to see a doctor. It's really frightening."

Source: Martha Shirk, "Doctors Turn Away Pregnant Medicaid Patient," *St. Louis Post-Dispatch,* March 22, 1987.

TABLE 12-3	Public satisfaction with health care system and with own medical care in four nations	
Country	Very Satisfied with Own and Family's Care, %	Satisfied with Current Health Care System,* %
United States	55	10
Canada	60	56
Great Britain	39	27
(West) Germany	45	41

*Believed that only minor changes were needed.
Source: Robert J. Blendon and Jennifer N. Edwards, "Caring for the Uninsured, Choices for Reform," *Journal of the American Medical Association* 265 (May 15, 1991): 2563. Copyright 1991, American Medical Association.

The American Medical Association has produced a plan, "Health Access America," which outlines an employer-based private insurance program. In order to provide affordable health care coverage to all Americans, the plan calls for an expansion of Medicaid to meet the needs of the poor and requires that employers provide health insurance for all full-time employees and their families. In an alternate "play or pay" proposal, the National Leadership Coalition for Health Care Reform, a group of big companies and labor unions, suggests that all employers be required either to provide health insurance or to pay a 7 percent federal payroll tax to fund public coverage. Both kinds of plans have built-in tax incentives or other supports to help businesses, particularly small ones, to participate. George Bush's prescription for the nation's health care system is an example of the third type of approach. It includes tax credits for the purchase of medical insurance and incentives for people to enroll in prepaid group health plans. It also stresses increased use of HMOs.[70]

You will note that the preceding proposals combine elements of the existing system and do not cast the federal government in a dominant role. In contrast, the fourth alternative, which was embraced by several Democratic presidential candidates, calls for full-blown, government-funded national health insurance. Proponents of this approach often point to Canada as an instructive example. In Canada, the government provides health insurance for all through a form of taxation; the government holds down costs by maintaining careful control over the organization and use of health care services. While the Canadian system has its share of critics in the United States, it costs far less than health care in America; also, a recent study finds no evidence that such higher expenditures lead to better care.[71]

PERSPECTIVES

Proposals for health care reform reflect different ideological assumptions. The political perspectives described here address the issue of responsibility for the poor as well as

TABLE 12–4 Preferences for universal health insurance systems

System Option	Corporate Executives, %	Labor Union Leaders, %	Public, %
Favor an all-government national health plan	27	58	46
Favor a compulsory private insurance plan, with government providing for the unemployed	35	28	33
Favor no change in the present system	35	10	19

Source: Robert J. Blendon and Jennifer N. Edwards, "Caring for the Uninsured, Choices for Reform," *Journal of the American Medical Association* 265 (May 15, 1991): 2565. Copyright 1991, American Medical Association.

the question of who should control the medical system: consumers, corporations, physicians, or the government?

The Conservative Perspective

In its purest sense, the conservative point of view would call for an unfettered free-market approach to health care. That is, there would be no government interference in the provision of services. Individuals, or consumers, would pay for care with their own funds or private insurance. Medical programs would compete freely for their dollars. Adequate health care would not be considered a right for all citizens.

Such a point of view has little acceptance in the United States today. Instead, conservatives generally present a modified market approach to health care delivery. This approach is based on the idea that the government is inherently incompetent at certain tasks, and that public policies and programs cannot be sensitive enough to variations in individual preferences and local conditions. Conservatives argue that the market is a much better mechanism for responding to such preferences and conditions. However, the explosion in health costs, especially for businesses, has now led many conservatives to agree that the government needs to play a somewhat larger role in the health care system. This role might include controlling costs by regulating "suppliers" (hospitals and physicians), expanding the basic medical "safety net" for poor people, and requiring businesses to provide health insurance provision for all employees.[72] Although they accept the idea of limited federal insurance programs like Medicare (which, after all, supplies revenues to private for-profit hospitals), conservatives are highly critical of a government-sponsored national insurance scheme such as the one developed by Canada.

Conservative health care proposals often stress the element of choice, suggesting tax credits or incentives for purchasing private health insurance or enrolling in a qualified health plan of one's own choosing, such as an HMO or a doctors' group practice. Critics of this approach argue that the "informed consumer" of medical care is largely a myth. Health care has become so complex that few of us can really know for sure whether a particular operation is warranted or which surgeon will perform it best. A seemingly straightforward matter like a runner's stress fracture is not so easy to diagnose—X-rays may not differentiate between a fracture and tendinitis, and they may not show the condition at all if the equipment is not positioned appropriately. After diagnosis, treatment suggestions vary—"stay off the leg for eight weeks," "run as soon as it stops hurting," or "wear special supports in your shoes." In this confusing situation, one can't expect that the runner, or consumer, knows best and will be able to choose the best doctor or the most effective treatment.[73]

The Liberal Perspective

Liberals generally stress the right of all people to adequate health care. They see government as a major enforcer of this right. They also emphasize the importance of consumer participation in health care planning. Not all of these ideas are antithetical to what radicals and conservatives believe. What makes liberals different is the mechanisms they adopt to achieve these goals.

Liberals generally believe in specific reforms rather than in the overhaul of the entire health system. They tend to follow a regulatory model, which puts the federal government in charge of enacting reforms to make health care more equitable. For example, they would probably be comfortable with regulations specifying that doctors must serve a certain percentage of Medicaid patients. Liberals also see the government's role as supplementing, rather than supplanting, the private health care system, in order to smooth out inequities in health insurance and health services. For example, in the 1960s, liberals supported the creation of federally subsidized community health centers in poor, often minority neighborhoods. Medicaid and Medicare are another part of the liberal approach—with government providing insurance subsidies to needy populations. Finally, a nationwide program of health insurance for all, like that developed in Canada, has long been a liberal goal. Such a program would change the financing of the health care system, but not the actual delivery of services.

The Radical Perspective

The radical approach rejects the market model entirely and argues for a complete restructuring of health care in America. Such restructuring is necessary to redistribute power over health care planning and provision from the few to the many. In their analysis of our present health care system, radicals assert that this system mirrors social class divisions in the United States. That is, the owners, controllers, and producers of services in health institutions—physicians, hospital board members, and pharmaceutical company executives—are predominantly upper-class, white males. These powerful individuals and their organizations often act together to preserve their authority. For example, in the 1970s, community organizers in St. Louis tried to help residents of poor neighborhoods campaign against the existence of poisonous lead paint in many of their apartments. A number of the absentee landlords, who owned large amounts of these properties, refused to remove the harmful paint. When organizers and residents approached St. Louis hospitals for help in this preventive health campaign, their requests were rejected. The reason, they discovered, was that many of the same landlords sat on the hospital boards.[74]

The radical approach to health care states that dominance of the health field by the rich and powerful leads to denial of effective and accessible care to minorities, women, and the poor. In addition, radicals follow an environmental model regarding the causes of disease and suggest that much of today's poor health stems from poor working conditions, unemployment and other economic disruptions, and industry's abuse of the environment.[75]

Radicals propose many solutions to these problems, including strong environmental controls and the development of a national health system such as the systems found in England and the Scandinavian countries. (A number of liberals would agree with these proposals.) Most importantly, radicals stress the need to move to community and citizen control over health care planning and delivery. As Ehrenreich and Ehrenreich conclude

> The only way to fundamentally change the health system so that it provides adequate, dignified care for all is to take power over health care away from the people who now control it.[76]

SOCIAL WORK ROLES

Health care social workers often function as mediators between the health care system and its clients. As this system has become more complex and problematic, the mediator role has increased in importance. Health care social work is generally carried out in host institutions—the hospital, group medical practice, HMO, or neighborhood clinic—and these host institutions, as we have seen, are part of a complex network of health services and health care financing. (See Figure 12–11.) A large portion of the social worker's job consists of helping clients negotiate that large network, as well as obtain needed and appropriate services from the individual health care institutions. And, as you might expect, health care social workers also help people and their families deal with issues of health and illness on a personal level.

A hospital social worker, for example, might assist the children of an elderly parent in their attempts to acquire understandable and comprehensive information from the physician about their parent's condition. That same social worker might also explain the intricacies of Medicaid eligibility and referral for nursing home care and help the family arrange for such care and its financing. Finally, the social worker might develop a counseling relationship with the elderly client, helping him or her deal with feelings about the upcoming move and assisting the client in playing an active role in decisions about nursing home care or other alternatives.

As they work in the health care system, social workers interact with a number of other disciplines. Physicians generally see social workers as knowledgeable about the psychosocial aspects of health and illness. For example, they call upon a social worker for help when clients seem emotionally troubled, when family or personal problems seem to be interfering with treatment plans, or when clients need help in handling the financial aspects of illness or planning discharge. Social workers also work alongside occupational therapists, physical therapists, nurses, and medical aides in promoting

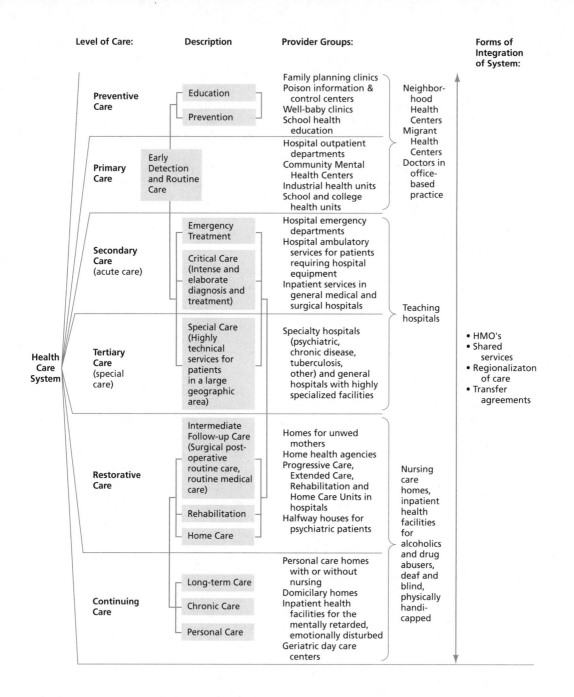

FIGURE 12–11   **Network of Health Care Services**

Source: U.S. Department of Health, Education and Welfare, *Trends Affecting U.S. Health Care System,* Publication no. 76-14503 (Washington, D.C.: January 1976).

client health. Social workers and occupational therapists share an interest in the environmental factors in illness and disability, and they place emphasis on building clients' coping abilities. For example, both a social worker and an occupational therapist are working with Mrs. Kasselbaum, who has become a wheelchair user because of an auto accident which injured her spine. The occupational therapist is helping Mrs. Kasselbaum learn how to dress herself, cook, and carry out other daily living activities from a wheelchair. Soon, she will be assisting Mrs. Kasselbaum in her return to her former job as a high school guidance counselor. The social worker is meeting regularly with Mrs. Kasselbaum and her family, to support them as they come to grips with both the emotional and practical impact of her disability on all of their lives. Although each worker has distinct functions in this situation, both are concerned with helping Mrs. Kasselbaum deal with practical realities, and with reinforcing her coping abilities and those of her family.

Perhaps the greatest role overlap exists between nurses and social workers. Each has specific areas of expertise; nurses, for example, can attend knowledgeably to physical needs and conditions, and they are skilled in helping patients and families adapt to life-threatening diseases. Social workers, for their part, are particularly experienced in using community resources (a skill they share with public health nurses) and in helping with discharge and financial planning. Yet both professions stress the building of sensitive, client-centered relationships which help people cope with the implications of illness. Nursing, as a field, is expanding in the areas of administration, research, and psychiatric work, all areas in which social workers are also active. While the overlap with nurses and other professions can be confusing, especially for the novice health care social worker, the mixture of shared skills and goals, along with specialized areas of expertise, enhances a teamwork approach which health care professionals often use in working with clients.[77]

As you can see from the preceding examples, health care social work is practiced in a variety of settings and it involves a number of different functions. The hospital, where medical social work as a specialty began, is still the major place in which health care social work is carried out. About 50 percent of United States hospitals have social service departments. The roles of hospital social workers, as described by Schlesinger, include:

1. Counseling patients and families about the internal and external stresses that may interfere with the effectiveness of medical treatment;
2. Establishing relationships with community groups and developing community resources, including developing new programs for people whose needs are not met by established programs; and
3. Helping people with diverse ethnic and cultural backgrounds whose needs for care may not be met by prevailing programs.[78]

Recently, discharge planning has become a major function for hospital social workers. This entails working with patients and their families to ensure that discharge back home or to another facility is smoothly carried out. Much of this work takes place with elderly clients, and it includes referring patients to nursing homes as well as arranging supportive community services for those patients returning home.[79]

Because a hospital is a complex bureaucratic setting, with specialized staff, many rules and regulations, and often an air of impersonality, hospital social workers can be particularly effective as patient advocates. A social worker, for example, might help the mother of a young child obtain special permission to stay overnight in her sick child's hospital room. The same social worker might also advocate for a change in hospital policy and the creation of facilities to accommodate parents on pediatric wards on a regular basis. Social workers also interact with the bureaucracy of hospital life in their involvement on various policy and planning committees. Often, hospital social workers contribute to decision making involving complex ethical issues, such as a decision by parents to terminate a problem pregnancy.

A much newer location for health care social work is in a physicians' group practice. Often, this is a family medicine practice. In a small but growing trend, physicians either hire social workers directly or establish collaborative relationships with social workers in social service agencies or private practice. The physicians can then consult with social workers regarding patients' family problems and other social and environmental issues. They may also refer patients to social workers for counseling or for linking up with various community services.[80]

Social workers have traditionally played a role in public health settings. There they become involved in preventive work. They may screen cases and plan outreach services in the areas of maternal and child health, alcoholism, and victims of sexually-transmitted diseases. They may also conduct health education groups and assess a community's social and health needs.[81]

Other health settings in which social workers are active include rehabilitation programs, publicly funded community health centers, and family planning clinics. Social workers even teach in medical schools, where they discuss the psychosocial aspects of health and illness. Social workers participate in planning health services and developing health policy, either in specialized planning agencies or in the other settings discussed earlier. Most importantly, because they are first-hand observers of the effects of the health care system on individuals, social workers can publicize problems and inequities and promote reform. As an example of involvement in legal and ethical issues surrounding health care, social workers assisting persons with AIDS and their families have supported strong social protections to combat discrimination against affected individuals. Social workers bring to all these activities their broad perspective on the whole range of physical, emotional, and environmental factors that influence people's health and well-being.[82]

CONCLUSION

As Americans grapple with the need to improve health care in order to make it more affordable, humane, and equitable, social workers can play an important part. They can promote the changes in lifestyle and environment that are so crucial to good health and longevity. They can help broaden the medical model through their understanding of the psychosocial and cultural context of health and illness. They can advocate for client involvement in system changes. Finally, they can become directly involved in the planning process, bringing to bear their dual emphasis on the individual and the surrounding social, economic, and political environment.

1. See, for example, David Mechanic, *Medical Sociology* (New York: The Free Press, 1968), 52–57.

2. Elfriede G. Schlesinger, *Health Care Social Work Practice* (St. Louis, MO: Times Mirror/Mosby, 1985), 78–80; Alfred Katz, "Future Directions in Health Policy," in *Social Work and Health Care Policy,* Doman Lum, ed. (Totowa, NJ: Allanheld, Osmun and Co., 1982), 194–195; Mechanic, *Medical Sociology,* 90–95.

3. Schlesinger, *Health Care Social Work Practice,* 78–79.

4. Katz, "Future Directions in Health Policy," 195–196.

5. Henrik L. Blum, *Expanding Health Care Horizons* (Oakland, CA: Third Party Publishing Co., 1983), 6–23.

6. Leonard J. Marcus, "Health Care Financing," *Encyclopedia of Social Work,* Vol. 1 (Silver Spring, MD: National Association of Social Workers, 1987), 697; Janice Castro, "Condition: Critical," *Time* (November 25, 1991), 34; U.S. Bureau of the Census, *Statistical Abstracts of the United States: 1991* (Washington, D.C.: 111th Ed., 1991), 108.

7. Katharine R. Levit, Helen C. Lazenby, Cathy A. Cowan, and Suzanne W. Letsch, "National Health Expenditures, 1990," *Health Care Financing Review,* Vol. 13, Fall, 1991 (Washington, D.C.: U.S. Department of Health and Human Services, Health Care Financing Administration, October, 1991), 30, 46; Castor, "Condition: Critical," 34; Tom Morganthau, "Health Care: Cutting through the Gobbledygook," *Newsweek* (February 3, 1992), 24–25.

8. Sally T. Sonnefeld, Daniel R. Waldo, Jeffrey A. Lemieux, and David R. McKusick, Projections of National Health Expenditures through the Year 2000," *Health Care Financing Review,* Vol. 13, Fall, 1991 (Washington, D.C.: U.S. Department of Health and Human Services, Health Care Financing Administration, October, 1991) 1, 6, 13; Castro, "Condition: Critical," 36; Philip J. Hilts, "Say Ouch: Demands to Fix U.S. Health Care Reach a Crescendo," *The New York Times* (19 May, 1991), sec. 4, p. 1; Robert J. Blendon and Jennifer N. Edwards, "Caring for the Uninsured," Editorial, *Journal of the American Medical Association* 265 (May 15, 1991): 2563; Emily Friedman, "The Uninsured: From Dilemma to Crisis," *Journal of the American Medical Association* 265 (May 15, 1991): 2493.

9. National Center for Health Statistics, *Health, United States, 1990,* DHHS Pub. No. (PHS) 91-1232, Public Health Service (Washington, D.C.: U.S. Government Printing Office, 1990), 123; American Hospital Association, *Hospital Statistics: A Comparative Study of U.S. Hospitals, 1990–1991* (Chicago, IL: American Hospital Association, 1990), 2.

10. *Health, United States, 1990,* 67.

11. *Health, United States, 1990,* 68; Jacqueline Teare, "State's Black Infant Death Rate One of Worst," *Kalamazoo (Michigan) Gazette* (9 March, 1989), 2.

12. John B. McKinlay and Sonja M. McKinlay, "Medical Measures and the Decline of Mortality," in *The Sociology of Health and Illness,* Peter Conrad and Rochelle Kern, eds. (New York: St. Martin's Press, 1981), 18–24; *Health, United States, 1990,* 80.

13. Kevin Anderson, "AIDS-Related Firms' Focus Could Change," *USA Today* (11 November, 1991), sec. B, p. 1; Steve Findlay, "Speaking of the Plague," *US News and World Report* (June 17, 1991): 20–22.

14. *Health, United States, 1990,* 123.

15. *Statistical Abstracts: 1991,* 117.

16. *Statistical Abstracts: 1991,* 81; Warren E. Leary, "Black Hypertension May Reflect Other Ills," *New York Times* (22 October, 1991), 136; "Older Americans' Health," *Metropolitan Life Statistical Bulletin 69* (April–June, 1988): 13; *Health, United States, 1990,* 14–15; Sadye M. L. Logan, Edith M. Freeman, and Ruth G. McRoy, *Social Work Practice with Black Families* (New York: Longman, 1990), 239–248.

17. Schlesinger, *Health Care Social Work Practice,* 101–102.

18. *Health, United States, 1990,* 121, 123.

19. Herbert H. Hyman, "National Health Policy," in *Social Work and Health Care Policy,* 39; Mechanic, *Medical Sociology,* 50–52, 90–94.

20. Samuel S. Epstein, "The Political and Economic Basis of Cancer," in *Sociology of Health and Illness,* 75–79; *Health, United States, 1990,* 30; U.S. Department of Health and Human Services, "Reducing the Health Consequences of Smoking: Twenty-five Years of Progress," A Report of the Surgeon General, DHHS Pub. No. (CDC) 89-8411 (Washington, D.C.: U.S. Government Printing Office, 1989), 47–48, 159.

21. David Mechanic, *From Advocacy to Allocation: The Evolving American Health Care System* (New York: The Free Press, 1986), 90–91.

22. Warren E. Leary, "Black Hypertension May Reflect

Other Ills," *New York Times* (22 October 1991), sec. B, p. 6.

23. Schlesinger, *Health Care Social Work,* 118; Mechanic, *From Advocacy to Allocation,* 115.

24. S. Leonard Syme and Lisa F. Berkman, "Social Class, Susceptibility, and Sickness," in *Sociology of Health and Illness,* 36; Mechanic, *From Advocacy to Allocation,* 90.

25. Harriet Arnow, *The Dollmaker* (New York: Macmillan Publishing Co., 1954), 277. Ironically, one of the novel's characters explains that the doctors performed outpatient tonsillectomies so that they could collect insurance money from those patients who had it and split this with the hospital.

26. Schlesinger, *Health Care Social Work,* 22; Wornie L. Reed, "Suffer the Children: Some Effects of Racism on the Health of Black Infants," in *Sociology of Health and Illness,* 314–327; Peter L. Schnall and Rochelle Kern, "Hypertension in American Society: An Introduction to Historical Materialist Epidemiology," in *Sociology of Health and Illness,* 110–111.

27. Milton Wittman, "Application of Knowledge about Prevention to Health and Mental Health Practice," in *Social Work in Health Care,* Neil F. Bracht, ed. (New York: Haworth Press, 1978), 203; Schlesinger, *Health Care Social Work Practice,* 128–131; Peter Hookey, "Primary Health Care," in *Social Work and Health Care Policy,* 114–115.

28. James S. Gordon, "Holistic Health Centers in the United States," in *Alternative Medicines,* J. Warren Salmon, ed. (New York: Tavistock Publications, 1984), 230–233; Phyllis H. Mattson, *Holistic Health in Perspective* (Palo Alto, CA: Mayfield Publishing Co., 1982), 9–12.

29. Paul Starr, *The Social Transformation of American Medicine* (New York: Basic Books, 1982), 24–28.

30. Howard S. Berliner, "Scientific Medicine Since Flexner," in *Alternative Medicines,* 31; Richard W. Wertz and Dorothy C. Wertz, "Notes on the Decline of Midwives and the Rise of Medical Obstetricians," in *Sociology of Health and Illness,* 178–179.

31. Berliner, *Alternative Medicines,* 34–35; Starr, *The Social Transformation of American Medicine,* 32–37, 51–54, 93–99; Charles E. Rosenberg, *The Care of Strangers* (New York: Basic Books, 1987).

32. Berliner, *Alternative Medicines,* 31–32; James Leiby, *A History of Social Welfare and Social Work in the United States* (New York: Columbia University Press, 1978), 286–287; Walter Trattner, *From Poor Law to Welfare State,* 3rd ed. (New York: Free Press, 1984), 135–154.

33. Berliner, *Alternative Medicines,* 31–33; Starr, *The Social Transformation of American Medicine,* 134–140.

34. Starr, *The Social Transformation of American Medicine,* 19.

35. Barbara Ehrenreich and Deirdre English, *Witches, Midwives, and Nurses: A History of Women Healers* (Old Westbury, NY: The Feminist Press, 1973), 33–34; Wertz and Wertz, *Sociology of Health and Illness,* 171–177.

36. Starr, *The Social Transformation of American Medicine,* 146–179.

37. Starr, *The Social Transformation of American Medicine,* 116–125; Ehrenreich and English, *Witches, Midwives, and Nurses,* 30–33.

38. Starr, *The Social Transformation of American Medicine,* 124.

39. Barbara Melosh, *The Physician's Hand: Work Culture and Conflict in American Nursing* (Philadelphia: Temple University Press, 1982), 37–76.

40. Lela B. Costin, *Two Sisters for Social Justice: A Biography of Grace and Edith Abbott* (Urbana, IL: University of Illinois Press, 1983), 130–146.

41. Edward Berkowitz and Kim McQuaid, *Creating the Welfare State* (New York: Praeger, 1980), 129–132; Starr, *The Social Transformation of American Medicine,* 349–350.

42. Roy Lubove, *The Professional Altruist* (New York: Atheneum, 1969), 24–30.

43. Harriett M. Bartlett, *Social Work Practice in the Health Field* (New York: National Association of Social Workers, 1961); Leslie Leighninger, *Social Work: Search for Identity* (Westport, CT: Greenwood Press, 1987), 186–187; "Ida Maud Cannon," *Encyclopedia of Social Work,* vol. 2, 919.

44. Costin, *Two Sisters for Social Justice,* 134–146.

45. Starr, *The Social Transformation of American Medicine,* 249.

46. Alice Sardell, *The US Experiment in Social Medicine: The Community Health Center Program, 1965–1986* (Pittsburgh: University of Pittsburgh Press, 1988), 3–4, 111–117.

47. Linda J. Proffitt, "Hospice," *Encyclopedia of Social Work,* vol. 1, 812–816.

48. Erica Bates, *Health Systems and Public Scrutiny* (New York: St. Martin's Press, 1983), 157–159; The Boston Women's Health Collective, *Our Bodies Ourselves* (New York: Simon and Schuster, 1979).

49. Paul Recer, "Feminists Want to Change Gender Gap in Medicine," *Baton Rouge Sunday Advocate* (8 September, 1991), sec. A, p. 18.

50. Schlesinger, *Health Care Social Work Practice,* 55,

312–313; Starr, *The Social Transformation of American Medicine,* 396.

51. Joseph A. Califano, Jr., Statement before the Joint Economic Committee of Congress, April 12, 1984.

52. Gregg Easterbrook, "The Revolution in Medicine," *Newsweek* (January 26, 1987): 50–52.

53. "Employers Taking Control of Health Marketplace," *MBGH Bulletin,* Midwest Business Group on Health (Number 6, 1987): 1–3; Friedman, "The Uninsured," 2494; Edwin Chen, "Companies Try Managing Employees' Health Care Costs," *Baton Rouge Sunday Advocate* (6 November 1991), sec. D, p. 6.

54. Arnold S. Relman, "The Future of Medical Practice," *Health Affairs 11* (1983): 9.

55. Relman, "The New Medical-Industrial Complex," *New England Journal of Medicine 303* (October 23, 1980): 963; Relman, "The Future of Medical Practice," 11.

56. *Statistical Abstracts: 1991,* 106; "Health Care Delivery to Undergo Further Changes," *Standard and Poor's Industry Surveys,* Vol. 1, October, 1991 (New York: Standard and Poor's Corporation, 1991), 32–33.

57. Starr, *The Social Transformation of American Medicine,* 436–439; Howard W. French, "Walk-In Doctors' Offices: Treatment for People Who Don't Want to Wait," *New York Times* (11 February, 1990), p. 25.

58. David Burda, "Hospitals' Pricing Puzzle," *Modern Healthcare* (February 19, 1988): 32; Conrad and Kern, *Sociology of Health and Illness,* 244.

59. Castro, "Condition: Critical," 38.

60. Easterbrook, "The Revolution in Medicine," 73.

61. Quoted in Starr, *The Social Transformation of American Medicine,* 436.

62. Linda B. Miller, "For-Profit Hospitals: What About the Poor?" *Washington Post National Weekly Edition* (11 February, 1985): 28; David Stoez, "Corporate Health Care and Social Welfare," *Health and Social Work 11* (Summer 1986): 170; Friedman, "The Uninsured," 2494.

63. Stephen M. Davidson, "Medicaid," in *Social Work and Health Care Policy,* 57–68.

64. *Health, United States, 1990,* 2; James S. Todd, Steven V. Seekins, John H. Krichbaum, and Lynn K. Harvey, "Health Access America—Strengthening the U.S. Health Care System," *Journal of the American Medical Association 265* (May 15, 1991): 2503.

65. Martha Shirk, "State's Rural Poor Lack Prenatal Care," *St. Louis Post Dispatch* (22 March 1987), 1, 11A.

66. Mary O'Neil Mundinger, "Health Service Funding Cuts and the Declining Health of the Poor," *New England Journal of Medicine 313* (June 4, 1985): 44–47.

67. American Hospital Association, *The Cost of Compassion* (undated pamphlet).

68. Julie S. Bach, ed., *Biomedical Ethics: Opposing Viewpoints* (St. Paul, MN: Greenhaven Press, 1987); Elisabeth Rosenthal, "As More Tiny Infants Live, Choices and Burden Grow," *New York Times* (29 September 1991), p. 1; Edwin M. Reingold, "Oregon's Value Judgement," *Time* (November 25, 1991): 37.

69. Blendon and Edwards, "Caring for the Uninsured," 2563.

70. Todd, "Health Access America," 2503–2506; Castor, "Condition: Critical," 36; Robert Pear, "President's Plans for Health Care Outlined to A.M.A.," *New York Times* (9 January 1992), 1.

71. Morganthau, "Health Care: Cutting Through the Gobbledygook," 25; Sherry Jacobsen, "Canadians Happy with Health Care," *USA Today* (11 February, 1991), sec. B, p. 3; Max Gates, "Study Says Costlier U.S. Hospital Care No Better than Canadian Care," *Kalamazoo (Michigan) Gazette* (11 May, 1990), sec. B, p. 6.

72. Stuart M. Butler, "Coming to Terms on Health Care," *New York Times* (28 January 1990), sec. F, p. 13.

73. David Mechanic, *Medical Sociology,* 2nd ed. (New York: Free Press, 1978), 335; Bates, *Health Systems and Public Scrutiny,* 54–55.

74. J. David Colfax, "Some Notes on Local Level Political Activism," *Sociological Focus 4* (Winter, 1970–71): 73; Vincente Navarro, "The Influence of Social Class Structure on the American Health Sector," 233–241; John Ehrenreich and Barbara Ehrenreich, *The American Health Empire: Power, Profits, and Politics* (Health Advisory Center, 1970); Bates, *Health Systems and Public Scrutiny,* 122–123.

75. Schnall and Kern, "Hypertension in American Society, 97–122.

76. Ehrenreich and Ehrenreich, *The American Health Empire,* 176–190.

77. Sandra Taylor-Owen, "The History of the Profession of Social Work: A Second Look" (Doctoral Dissertation, Brandeis University, 1986); Regina Kulip and Sister M. Adrian Davis, "Nurses and Social Workers: Rivals in the Provision of Social Services?" *Health and Social Work 12* (Spring 1987): 101–112. Taylor-Owen argues that social workers' historical roots lie in the work of nineteenth century nurses.

78. Schlesinger, *Health Care Social Work,* p. 256.

79. Salie Rossen, "Hospital Social Work," *Encyclopedia of Social Work,* vol. 1, 818–819.

80. Peter Hookey, "Social Work in Primary Health Care Settings," *Social Work in Health Care,* 211–223.

81. Peter Bracht, "Public Health Social Work: A Community Focus," *Social Work in Health Care,* 245–248.

82. National Association of Social Workers, "NASW Standards for Social Work in Health Care Settings" (Washington, D.C.: NASW, 1981), 1; NASW, Report of the Social Workers Task Force on AIDS, September, 1987.

C·H·A·P·T·E·R
thirteen

The Workplace

onsider the following situations which the authors have encountered during their years in social work practice.

Although hard to believe, the Brindel family had been an open child welfare case for nineteen years. The case involved a little of everything—neglect, abuse, exploitation, and alcoholism. When the case was transferred to the author, the Viet Nam conflict was at its height and good jobs were easy to come by in the Dallas-Ft. Worth area because of the booming defense industry. The Brindels availed themselves of the opportunity and both got, for the first time in their lives, good jobs. Mr. Brindel was hired as a janitor in an aircraft plant and Mrs. Brindel was hired as a tool room clerk in an electronics factory. Both were earning about two times the minimum wage, plus nearly unlimited overtime at a much greater wage. During the six months the author had contact with the Brindels, he saw virtually no sign of the pathological family described so vividly in the case record. In fact, their lifestyle and behavior appeared to be typical of any stable blue-collar family. Several years later the author visited his former office and asked the child welfare program director how the Brindels were doing. She said that Mr. and Mrs. Brindel had been laid off after America's involvement in Viet Nam ended and they had returned to their old ways.

Mary Ann Douglas, an attractive thirty-six-year-old widow, was coming to the community mental health center for help dealing with a number of problems she was experiencing following her husband's death. Her husband, Clifford Douglas, had left for work one morning and had never returned home. After a two-day search, he was found in his car on a deserted country road, dead from a self-inflicted gun shot wound. As the story unfolded it was discovered that Cliff, a hot shot electrical engineer with a masters degree from MIT, had been laid off six months before his death. Not wanting to upset his family, he had not told them of his layoff, thinking he would quickly get a new job and then would tell them. As it turned out the electronics industry was depressed and there were simply no jobs for people as specialized and as highly paid as Cliff. As weeks stretched into months, he became more and more depressed as he left home each morning dressed for a day in the office but heading for the mall to just hang out. When his unemployment benefits ran out and his savings began to dwindle, he selected what he saw as the best way out of the situation. In a note he left for Mary Ann, he explained that he had enough insurance to take care of her and the children, and he apologized to her, not for deceiving her or for taking his own life, but for being unemployed. He wrote, "You should not have to live out your life married to a bum."

Jim Patten was one of the most highly motivated members of the alcoholics treatment group at the mental health center. The social worker in charge of the group related the following to one of the authors. "You know, it's really funny. Jim has been a drunk for the past twelve years. During that time his drinking has resulted in the breakup of his marriage, his estrangement from his children, two arrests for driving while intoxicated, and an untold number of injuries and general health problems. But he never was really motivated to change his behavior until his boss fired him. He told Jim to come back in six months and if he could demonstrate that he had his drinking under control he would give him his job back. All that other stuff didn't really make an impact on Jim, but after a few weeks without his job he came in here more fired up to lick his problem than any client I can remember."

The preceding examples are only three from literally dozens we could think of that illustrate the immense importance of work to the welfare of individuals. With the possible exception of family, work is with little doubt the most important sphere of most individuals' existence. It has been noted in a number of places that each individual defines *self* in terms of what he or she does in work. In this chapter we will look at work as a central component of social welfare. We will discuss how work has changed in recent history and the effects this has had on families and individuals, and we will examine changes that are currently emerging. We will describe how the work and nonwork spheres of a person's life interact and how problems in one area often result in problems in the other. Our major focus throughout this chapter will be on work as a central concern of all areas of social work practice. However, we will devote a good deal of attention to an emerging, or more accurately we should say reemerging, area of social work specialization, occupational social work.

DEFINITION AND STATISTICAL DESCRIPTION

Work as a social welfare problem is more vague and hard to define than the other problems we deal with in this book. Yet there can be no doubt that it is immensely important. Work is closely related to, and in fact it undergirds, all social welfare problems. The relation of work to poverty is obvious, as is its relation to housing; if you don't have a job, you will have little money and with little money you won't have a decent place to live. A major school of thought relates crime to the lack of legitimate means of earning a living; the workplace and job opportunities were the first targets of those combating racism and sexism; an increase in unemployment guarantees an increase in intake at the child welfare office; and dissatisfaction with work is a major dynamic in problems dealt with at mental health centers. We will define work by first arguing that it is of central importance to individual adjustment, and therefore those concerned with social welfare of individuals must understand the importance of work to this welfare. We will then look at work as a central component of American culture. Finally, we will describe, conceptually and statistically, specific work-related problems which nearly all social workers encounter in their day-to-day practice with clients: unemployment, problems of the interaction of work with other spheres of workers' lives, and personal and interpersonal problems affecting work performance.

The Centrality of Work to Individual Adjustment

The relation of work to economic well-being is obvious. However, for some time psychologists and social workers have suggested that work serves a number of equally important, or even more important functions in individual growth and adjustment. The first person to develop this idea was Freud in his book *Civilization and its Discontents*. In this book Freud set out to explain how people achieve happiness. He developed the argument that two main factors were responsible for human well-being, *Eros* and *Anake,* which mean love and necessity. Freud argued that work, the primary component of *Anake*, attaches a person to reality and gives him or her a secure place in the human community. He summarized the psychological functions of work as, "The possibility it offers of displacing a large amount of libidinal components, whether narcissistic, aggressive or even erotic, on to professional work and on to the human relations connected with it lends it a value by no means second to what it enjoys as something indispensable to the preservation and justification of existence in society." Although

The work a person does is a central part of his or her self-image.

Freud believed that work performs an indispensable psychological function, he observed that people do not generally recognize this. "And yet, as a path to happiness, work is not highly prized by men. They do not strive after it as they do after other possibilities of satisfaction. The great majority of people only work under the stress of necessity, and this natural human aversion to work raises most difficult social problems."[1]

Psychologist Marie Jahoda studied the problems of the unemployed during the Great Depression and concluded that the problems of passivity, distress, and resignation she observed in the unemployed could be explained by looking at the manifest and latent functions of work. The manifest function of employment is income. The latent functions, which we are calling psychological, she identified as time structure, enlargement of social experience, participation in collective purposes, status and identity, and regular activity. All of these latent functions are necessary for a person to participate as a mature citizen in our society.[2]

Social worker Helen Harris Perlman has studied work as a central component of human growth and development. She argues that work "is potentially and often actually a potent force in the sustaining and stabilizing of the young adult's personality." She disagrees with Freud's belief that people have a natural aversion to work, arguing that people are naturally motivated to work and want to work. The functions which Perlman assigns to work are similar to those discussed by Jahoda: work provides a social identity ("I'm a police officer," or "My mom's a lawyer"); it maintains a linkage with other people; it is a socially recognized function; and it structures time and provides the conditions for the stabilization and ordering of daily living. Further, work provides a critical underpinning for other social roles—it binds people to their families and links them to the world outside.[3]

In this section we have purposely not differentiated between good jobs and bad jobs. Obviously, good jobs provide many psychological benefits in addition to those discussed earlier and bad jobs can do much psychological harm. That is not the point of this section. The point is that work, any work, is critical to the growth, development, and well-being of people. Work, in addition to providing for material wants and needs, anchors people to the social system, gives them an identity, and structures and regularizes their lives.

The Centrality of the Work Ethic in American Society

Sociologist Talcott Parsons has observed that if a distinctive focus of values can be found in this complicated culture, it is the strong positive appreciation for worldly, instrumental activism, in other words, work.[4] We value work not only for what it produces but also as an end to itself. As an illustration of this point, Perlman observes that around the turn of the century a number of wealthy young men left the United States and took up residence in Europe because in this country not working was neither understood nor socially tolerated.[5]

There are a number of historical factors which have combined to produce the strong work ethic we have in the United States. Among these are the fact that the United States began as a frontier nation with a labor shortage, leading to the attitude of, "He who will not work will not eat." Also important is the fact that the vast majority of people coming to the United States came from the working classes and therefore there was no aristocratic class to aggrandize leisure and place a stigma on work. However, probably the most important factor was identified over a century ago by the German scholar Max Weber, who labeled it the Protestant ethic. Weber argued that fundamental to the development of capitalism in the West, and particularly in the United States, was the Calvinistic belief in predestination. This belief asserts that people have been divinely selected for either salvation or damnation at birth and there is nothing they can do to alter their fate. Although a person's fate is sealed, so to speak, Calvinist philosophy posits that indications of this fate can be detected. Good deeds, hard work, and success at one's work were taken as signs that one was destined for salvation. Thus, according to Calvinist philosophy, secular activity such as work could have religious implications. Because hard work and success could be signs of one's fate, hard work and frugality came to have great value for the Puritans. They considered work to be a moral virtue and idleness to be a sin. Benjamin Franklin is famous for a number of memorable little sayings that capture the spirit of the Protestant ethic: "Time is money." "A penny saved is a penny earned." "After industry and frugality, nothing contributes more to the raising of a young man than punctuality." "He who sits idle . . . throws away money," and "Waste neither time nor money; an hour lost is money lost."[6] Although the influence of the Protestant ethic has declined during the twentieth century, it is still a major part of our national character.* We still believe that work is a moral virtue in and of itself and idleness is suspect. We may laugh about our new

---

*It is possible to argue that work is becoming an even more important value in American society. Less than a generation ago it was possible for a woman to gain identity and acceptance through her husband's career. This appears no longer to be the case. Women who stay home find themselves labeled as "just a housewife." There is evidence that an increasing number of women are seeking careers outside of the home even when they do not have to and really do not want to, in order to avoid the appearance of laziness and lack of ambition.

cultural hero being the "couch potato," but few people would seriously claim to be one.

The centrality of work in our culture has several implications for social welfare. The first is that people who are out of work are under great pressure to re-enter the labor market. Rarely will you find a person willing to admit that he or she is simply out of work. Usually the person will explain that he or she is trying to decide on the next career step to take or that he or she is evaluating options; the person might also give some other explanation that implies that he or she is still connected to the labor market and has the situation under control. The fact of being out of work with no immediate prospects is so stigmatizing in the context of the American work ethic that people will go to great lengths to avoid admitting that they are in this condition. The second implication is that work has become the major criterion through which the poor have been defined in our society. Social welfare benefits which are work-related, such as unemployment insurance or Social Security, are viewed as having much more legitimacy and less stigma than those which are not work-related, such as AFDC, or food stamps. We have long made an explicit or implicit distinction between the "worthy" and the "unworthy" poor. This distinction, in the case of the able-bodied person, is generally made in relation to the person's work history. If the person has a substantial record of work, that person is usually judged as being worthy and he or she is assumed to be experiencing a period of bad luck. If he or she has a sporadic work history or none at all, that person is usually judged to be lazy and therefore unworthy.[7] It is no accident that all recent attempts to reform the welfare system have come under the title of "workfare."

We should note that the work ethic is neither uniquely American nor is it modern. Wilensky and Lebeaux noted how the work ethic appeared to be as strong in the Soviet Union as in the U.S.[8] In fact, one of the Americans most admired by Joseph Stalin was Frederick Taylor, the developer of scientific management, an approach to management based on a radical conception of the work ethic. Daniel Bell notes that the early church fathers were perplexed and intrigued by the question of what Adam did before the fall. He says, "in the variety of speculations, none assumed he was idle. He devoted himself to gardening, 'the agreeable occupation of agriculture,' said St. Augustine."[9] However, in the United States work has come to take on an almost religious significance. Work is equated with virtue and idleness is equated with sin. Ozawa summarizes the situation when she says

> A nation . . . cannot be developed, let alone prosper, without a common belief in something. What, then, is it in the United States? If there is anything that has strongly linked the people of this country together, it may be the value attached to work. Apparently the United States does not wish to have a dominant religion, a dominant political ideology, or a powerful nationalism that might unite the people. Instead, one of the main foundation stones on which this nation has been built has been the common understanding that work by everyone is valued and will be fairly rewarded.[10]

Major Work-Related Problems of Significance to Social Welfare

In the two previous parts of this section we have attempted to make two major points. The first is that work, regardless of type, is central to individual growth and adjustment.

The second is that in our society we place immense, even moral, value on work. The major conclusion we draw from these two points is that an individual's relation to work is very important for his or her welfare, and consequently it is very important for social workers and allied professionals to have an understanding of work. Problems at work are likely to have a seriously disruptive effect on other spheres of a person's life, particularly family life. Let us now look at some major categories of work problems, namely unemployment; underemployment/lack of personal fulfillment from work; problems in the interaction of work with other spheres of life; and finally, personal/interpersonal problems affecting work performance.

Unemployment   Later in this section we will discuss the way the government defines unemployment. At this point we are not concerned with official definitions. For our purposes we define *unemployment* simply as the condition of a person who is out of work, and who would like to, or needs to be working. Given the importance of work to individuals as well as in the realm of values in our culture, unemployment is the most basic and most serious work-related problem. Consider the following quotes from interviews with unemployed people

> *Judy relates:* I . . . got what I considered to be the ideal job . . . from which I was fired after one month. That was crushing. There were weeks when I woke up completely filled with remorse that I was fired, going hopelessly over it and over it. [At my job] I had felt connected with the intellectual world and I felt like a human being with prospects. Over the past three months, since I lost that job, I've lost all my sense of self-worth. . . . These days I'm learning to live on very little money and to pass time at an incredibly slow rate. The hours weigh on me. I don't have to do anything—to keep things clean or to keep myself up. I haven't exercised. It's almost a mental problem at this point. I'm just depressed. In the morning I'm just crazy when I wake up. I jump out of bed and smoke cigarettes. I know I should relax, have a cup of tea and listen to the radio, but I can't. I try to sleep until noon, if possible, because then the mornings are out of the way and most of the day is gone. If necessary, I sleep in the afternoon. We watch a little bit of television and I have to worry about what to cook for dinner, then we go to bed early . . . I've taken note of the fact that I'm unhappy most of the time. Not terribly unhappy—I would say that I measure unhappiness in terms of nerve endings at this point, and if I'm calm, I consider myself happy. But I don't think that's a way to live. I would like to feel free . . . [but] I feel that I have to lie around until I get an idea about my next job application.

> *Ted recalls:* When you're not working, you somehow have this feeling that the world has made a decision that you're not as good as the people out there who are pulling in great salaries . . . Now, I have an all leather briefcase that cost about ninety dollars . . . It looks like a distinguished piece of luggage and makes me feel better. I didn't carry it around when I was working, but sometimes when I go to the unemployment office now, I use the briefcase . . . I carry the briefcase around with my resume and a few pencils and my date book—which is around 365 pages blank. It makes me feel like I am working towards something where I will be more productive instead of carrying myself like a schlump.[11]

As these quotes imply, unemployment as a social welfare problem has two dimensions. The first is the economic dimension. People in modern industrial societies such as ours live from paycheck to paycheck. Very few people own their homes outright and even fewer maintain gardens and animals sufficient to feed their families. We exchange our work for pay and our pay for the things we need to live. To make matters worse, if you will recall the discussion on wealth in Chapter 6, only a very small percentage of our population, about 10 percent, has any real assets to fall back upon during hard times. Therefore, when a person loses his or her job, if that person cannot find another one right away, a very severe financial problem almost immediately occurs. Most workers are eligible for unemployment insurance payments, but these only make up a portion of lost wages and eligibility only lasts for a short time, generally twenty-six weeks. There are two programs which can extend unemployment insurance programs beyond the twenty-six-week limit. The first is a permanent extended benefits program, enacted in 1970, which provides up to an additional thirteen weeks of benefits to workers in states with particularly high unemployment rates. Unfortunately, the required rate is so high that very few states have ever qualified for this program. A second emergency unemployment program was passed in the fall of 1991 which utilized a different means of determining the unemployment rate in states and made it easier for states to qualify to provide up to thirteen weeks of extended benefits to insured workers. The purpose of unemployment insurance is to tide a person over until he or she finds another job. If this does not happen, the person will have to go on welfare, if the eligibility requirements are met.

The second dimension is psychological. People who lose jobs, particularly those who do not rapidly find new employment, report severe psychological pressures. Harvey Brenner has statistically correlated a 1 percent increase in the aggregate unemployment rate sustained over a period of six years with 37,000 total deaths, 920 suicides, 650 homicides, 500 deaths from cirrhosis of the liver, 4,000 admissions to state mental hospitals, and 3,300 sentences to state prisons.[12] Research indicates that even when unemployment is clearly the result of factors over which the worker has no control, most people still tend to blame themselves. Psychologist Paula Raymond conducted a study of the adjustment of workers who were laid off from aircraft industries in Hartford, Connecticut, when the industry became depressed in the early 1970s. She found that the laid-off workers expressed the psychology of blaming the victim. The people in her sample were so convinced of their own blame for their situations that many refused to accept any services paid for out of public funds because they felt they did not deserve these.[13]

Let's now look at some statistics regarding unemployment. To understand these statistics we must first understand how the government, the source of most unemployment data, defines unemployment. The basic concepts the government uses are:

- People with jobs are *employed*.
- People who are jobless, looking for jobs, and available for work are *unemployed*.
- People who are neither employed nor unemployed are *not in the labor force*.

All people age sixteen and over and not in prison or a mental hospital are counted. To be counted as unemployed, a jobless person must have made a specific effort to obtain employment within the four weeks prior to being counted. It is important to understand that unemployment figures are not the same thing as the actual number of jobless people who need to or would like to be working. People who have given up looking because they are discouraged, and people who have applied everywhere they can think of and are at a loss for what else to do, are not counted as being in the labor force and so they are not counted as unemployed. This is strange, but true.[14]

TABLE 13-1			U.S. civilian unemployment rate						
	All			**White**			**Non-White**		
	Total	Men	Women	Total	Men	Women	Total	Men	Women
1951	3.3	2.8	4.4	3.5	3.4	3.8	5.9	5.8	6.1
1961	6.7	6.4	7.2	6.0	5.7	6.5	12.4	12.8	11.9
1971	5.9	5.3	6.9	5.4	4.9	6.3	9.9	9.1	10.9
1981	7.6	7.4	7.9	6.7	6.5	6.9	15.6	15.7	15.6
1991	6.7	7.0	6.3	6.0	6.4	5.5	12.4	12.9	11.9

Source: Adapted from data in *Monthly Labor Review 114* (December 1991): 76–91.

Recent official statistics on unemployment are presented in Table 13–1. The figures presented are for rates (percentages) because they make comparisons simpler than those with raw numbers do. To get some idea of the numerical size of the various groups, you need only to know that the size of the labor force in 1991 was about 125 million. Therefore, when we talk of an unemployment rate of 6.7 percent, we are referring to over 8 million people. There are two general facts you should get from inspecting this table. The first is that the rate of unemployment fluctuates quite a bit, but that over time it has increased. In the 1950s and 1960s an unemployment rate of 5 percent was high; we have not seen a rate below 5 percent in over twenty years. The second is that the unemployment rate is significantly greater for minorities than for whites, currently almost double.

At the beginning of this section we defined unemployment, for our purposes, as the condition of a person who is out of work, and who would like to, or needs to be working. This is a much larger number of people than is covered by the government figures in Table 13–1. How much larger is not known, but some estimates have been made. A survey conducted by the Office of Federal Statistical Policy and Standards in 1976 counted 911,000 people who were not working but were not counted as unemployed because they were not actively seeking employment, who said they would like to have a job if one were available. It named these people "discouraged workers." In 1981, the Bureau of Labor Statistics counted discouraged workers and reported that their numbers had increased to 1.1 million, of whom 65 percent were women, and 32 percent were members of minority groups. Based on this data *Dollars & Sense* magazine estimated that the actual unemployment rate (as we are defining it) may have been four points higher than the official government figures.[15]

Underemployment/Lack of Personal Fulfillment from Work   *Underemployment* is defined as a situation in which a person is employed, but at a level significantly below what would generally be perceived as appropriate for a person with his or her credentials. The classic example is a person with a Ph.D. who is working as a cab driver. Most colleges and universities have dozens of BA-level employees who are underemployed as secretaries or typists. People who are underemployed are generally in routine, menial, and low-skill jobs, but this is not always the case. One of the authors once had an office in a suite that was primarily occupied by welfare department medical claims examiners. These folks spent their days reviewing medical records and making judgments as to whether the applicants qualified for medical assistance. This was fairly high paying, complex, and technical work. However, several of the claims examiners were physicians whose careers had, for one reason or another, veered off course. Although they had what would be considered by most people to be desirable employment, they were in fact underemployed because the job of medical claims examiner holds few challenges and little interest for a person with an MD degree.

Underemployment can range from mild to severe with associated problems varying accordingly, as illustrated by the following case examples.

Bill Spiker, a thirty-one-year-old black male, came to the community mental health center for help dealing with vague feelings of depression, anxiety, and general life dissatisfaction. After several interviews it was determined that Bill felt he was trapped in a boring, dead-end job. A life-long high achiever, Bill had completed all requirements for a Ph.D. in English from a prestigious university. In the middle of writing his dissertation Bill's major professor had died, Bill got involved in the losing side of a departmental feud, and consequently he was never able to finish his degree. Bill had found a rather high paying job teaching English in a large community college, but he felt he was wasting his talents in a job that was way below his potential.

Once the problem was clarified, Bill and his social worker determined that he had to choose among three courses of action. The first was to return to school and finish his doctorate even though this would involve nearly starting over. The second was to look at career options outside of an academic setting. The final option was to accept the advantages of his job (good pay, low pressure, and being a "big fish in a small pond") and seek growth and development activities outside of work. After much thought and discussion, Bill decided to pursue the second option. Following a thorough job search, he found a job as assistant director of communications for a large technical manufacturing company. Today, three years later, Bill has been promoted to director and his company has sent him back to school in an executive MBA program. He feels his career, and consequently his life, has gotten back on track.

Sara and David Thorp came to the family guidance agency for help with what they felt was a rapidly deteriorating marriage. The presenting problem was that Sara was chronically irritable; she constantly criticized David, who retaliated by withdrawing from her; and their sexual relationship had become almost nonexistent. During the course of the counseling it was revealed that a major problem was the fact that Sara was seriously underemployed; she was bored and frustrated as a result; and she held David responsible for her situation. Sara had a BA degree in philosophy and, after her daughter had entered school, she had enrolled in divinity school and spent three years, full time, earning a masters degree in divinity and becoming an ordained minister. Following Sara's graduation David, a junior high school principal, accepted an offer to become assistant superintendent of a school system in a small midwestern city. After searching for a ministerial position for nearly a year, Sara finally had to accept a position as a data entry clerk for a bank so she could begin paying off her student loans. She was devastated by the turn her life had taken, saying, "I hate to even get up in the morning. It's bad enough that my job is dull and, as far as I'm concerned, totally meaningless, but what's worse is the attitude the bank has toward me. I'm not even a person. I'm just a machine that punches numbers into the computer all day. Our division manager even said one day that he couldn't wait until someone invented a machine to take our place. I think I'm going crazy, and I *know* I'm driving my family crazy."

After several months of counseling, Sara and David began to realize that they had fallen into a trap without really thinking about it. David had assumed that Sara would follow him wherever his career took him, and Sara had shared this assumption. She had passively followed him to what for her was a graveyard for her dreams and ambitions. However, her subservience had its price—she was so unhappy that she made the rest of her family miserable without ever coming to grips with the source of the problem. Once the dynamics of the problem were uncovered, Sara and David began to discuss how to deal with it. They decided that they would begin a joint job search and would not move anywhere that did not contain opportunities for them both. After nearly a year of searching they moved to a large southern city where David works for an educational consulting firm and Sara is the associate minister of a large church. In a Christmas card to their former social worker, David wrote, "I sometimes miss my job as assistant superintendent; it was really my ideal job and probably would have led to a superintendency some day. However, the happiness that Sara brings into our home after a day where she feels she has grown as a person and contributed something to the world more than compensates for my minor sacrifice."

Briar has observed that underemployment produces many of the same symptoms as does unemployment. In fact, it has been argued that the symptoms of underemployment may be even more severe than those of unemployment because, as is illustrated by the last example, workers feel trapped and angry and all the attendant spillover effects hurt their personal functioning and family life.[16]

As you can well imagine, underemployment is much more difficult to measure than unemployment. The Bureau of Labor Statistics recognizes underemployment as a serious problem, saying, "underemployment represents a waste of resources and, therefore, is a subject of continuing interest," however, "though easy to illustrate, [underemployment is] not so easily quantified." To get some idea of the size of this problem, we have to rely on surveys of worker satisfaction and of the relation of education to job complexity. Data from the University of Michigan's Survey Research Center provides some interesting clues as to the size and trend of the problem. The Center has undertaken a series of surveys of American working conditions which include items on the quality of work life. The most recent report, based on 1977 data, indicates that about one-third of all American workers report that their skills, training, and education are underutilized in their jobs. The researchers report that overall there was a "slight but significant" drop in job satisfaction between the 1973 and 1977 survey results.[17] Other surveys have had similar findings. Duncan and Hoffman found that 42 percent of employees felt overeducated for their jobs.[18] Rumberger conducted a complex analysis in which he classified jobs into varying categories of complexity, empirically determined the levels of skills necessary to perform the jobs, and classified the American labor pool by level of education and skill, and then he compared the job market with the labor market. He concluded that about 40 percent of all college-educated workers are overeducated for their jobs. Further, like the other researchers, Rumberger's data indicated that the number of people who are underemployed is increasing.[19]

Problems of Interaction of Work with Other Spheres of Life   As we discussed in Chapter 2, people occupy a number of statuses and they have a number of roles associated with their various statuses. Work and family involve what sociologists have called *master roles,* meaning that these are the primary roles which define and structure much of a person's life. It is not uncommon for there to be role conflict between these two master roles, and these conflicts account for many work-related problems.

There has always been conflict between work roles and family roles for poor people and for single-parent families because the role of full-time homemaker has never been possible for these groups. However, until fairly recently the pattern for the majority of American families was to have one member, nearly always the man, who filled the role of breadwinner, and one person, nearly always the woman, who filled the role of homemaker. Thus, there was little spillover of routine family duties and problems such as child care, care for elderly parents, care for the sick, housework, or meal planning from family life into work life, at least for middle-class people. This situation has rapidly changed and indications are that it will continue to change.

Business, industry, and government have become aware of the problems of two-worker families in recent years as these problems have led to higher absenteeism, lower productivity, and lower morale among employees. Every employer is familiar with what has come to be called the "three o'clock slump," when worker productivity declines drastically at the time children come home from school. At that time many parents become distracted from their work as they spend time on the phone looking for their children, checking up on what they are doing, helping them solve problems, or simply worrying and feeling guilty about the children being home alone. Because of these problems, employers have begun to call on social workers to help, as the following situation illustrates.

Bob Andrews, President of Data Systems Incorporated, was concerned by what he perceived as steadily declining morale at his company. A study conducted by the personnel division revealed that the problem was largely a result of the fact that the employees were pre-dominantly young professionals in high-pressure jobs who were either single parents or

The rapid increase in the number of mothers who work while their children are small has led to increasing conflicts between home and work.

else members of two-career families. The pressure of combining career and parenthood was proving to be very difficult for many of the employees and, consequently, morale and productivity were declining.

Bob and his personnel director contacted Employee Assistance Associates, a company run by three social workers who specialize in studying companies and developing employee assistance programs for them that are effective and efficient. After a thorough study it was recommended that Bob's company do two things. The first was to contract with a local day care provider to set up a center in a building which the company would remodel on a lot adjacent to the main office. This would allow parents with preschool children to be close to their kids, to have lunch with them, and to see school programs. The second thing was to implement a flex time system where people would be required to be in the office between 10 AM and 3 PM, but could fit the other four hours of work anywhere between 6 AM and 7 PM. Thus, a person with school-age children could let their spouse get the children up and to school in the morning and could, by coming to work at 6 AM, be home when they returned from school in the afternoon.

There are, of course, problems other than child care that cause difficulties for people at work. Caring for elderly parents, having a sick family member, struggling with legal problems, and any other time-consuming family responsibility will overtax a working person. However, child care and other parenting responsibilities are the major problem of the current generation of employees.

As may be inferred from the preceding discussion, the major statistical measures relevant to the topic of problems in the interaction of work with other spheres of life are those which describe the entry of women into the workforce either as single parents or as members of two-career couples. Let us now look at these statistics. First, from Tables 13–2 and 13–3 you will see that they confirm conventional logic which would

TABLE 13–2	Labor force participation rates of widowed, divorced, or separated men, 1947–1987					
	Age					
Year	**16–19**	**20–24**	**25–34**	**35–44**	**45–64**	**65 +**
1947	—	—	85.2	89.6	78.8	32.8
1952	—	78.2	81.1	88.2	79.0	27.3
1957	—	85.8	81.2	86.8	76.3	24.5
1962	—	70.7	80.8	85.0	77.4	16.7
1967	—	78.4	81.0	82.6	74.6	15.2
1972	—	88.4	91.4	90.8	73.6	16.9
1977	—	93.6	92.7	89.7	72.8	12.1
1982	69.7	92.9	91.7	92.4	73.5	13.9
1987	—	90.6	92.9	91.1	73.1	11.1

Source: Adapted from data in U.S. Department of Labor, Bureau of Labor Statistics, *Labor Force Statistics Derived from the Current Population Survey, 1948–87* (Washington, D.C.: U.S. Government Printing Office, August, 1988), 797.

	Age					
Year	16–19	20–24	25–34	35–44	45–64	65+
1947	—	—	63.8	67.6	45.4	7.6
1952	41.0	59.0	63.0	68.7	49.6	8.2
1957	35.5	53.1	62.1	69.4	56.0	12.3
1962	34.0	54.7	57.5	63.3	60.2	11.2
1967	41.1	60.9	62.4	68.9	60.2	9.6
1972	44.7	57.7	62.1	71.7	61.0	9.8
1977	50.0	62.8	75.7	72.5	57.5	8.6
1982	45.6	67.1	77.1	77.2	61.9	7.8
1987	—	67.2	77.1	83.0	61.9	7.6

TABLE 13–3 Labor force participation rates of widowed, divorced, or separated women, 1947–1987

Source: Adapted from data in U.S. Department of Labor, Bureau of Labor Statistics, *Labor Force Statistics Derived From the Current Population Survey, 1948–87* (Washington, D.C.: U.S. Government Printing Office, August, 1988), 797.

indicate that widowed, divorced, or separated people (thus likely to be single parents) have always had a high rate of labor force participation. However, even for this group the rates have increased in recent years, especially for women. The rate of labor force participation for women in the twenty-five to thirty-four-year-old group, the group most likely to have young children at home, has increased from 64 to 77 percent between 1947 and 1987, with the majority of the change occurring in the last fifteen years. Table 13–4 records the most significant area of change—married women with children entering the labor force in great numbers. In 1952, only 14 percent of women with children under age six worked; and by 1987, this had increased to 57 percent. In 1952, 31 percent of women with children six to seventeen years of age worked, and by 1987, this had increased to 71 percent. Now, add to this the percent of unemployment for 1987, which was 6.2 percent and you get 77.9 percent; then add a conservative estimate of "discouraged people" of 3 percent and you begin to see the magnitude of the social change with which we are dealing—the actual labor force of women with children under age six equals about 66 percent of this group, and the labor force of women with children from age six to seventeen equals about 80 percent.

The Children's Defense Fund recently made the following observations regarding the relation of parental employment to children for the immediate future:

- By 1990 about 45 percent of the labor force will be parents of children under eighteen (in two-thirds of these families, both parents will be employed).
- Single-parent families will increase to include about one in ten of these working parents.
- About 80 percent of female employees will become pregnant during their working years (there will be about 4 million babies born per year, almost as many as during the 1950s baby boom).

TABLE 13–4	Labor force and labor force participation rates of married women, spouse present, by presence and age of children, March 1952–1987				
Year	Total	With No Children under 18	With Children 6 to 17	With Children under 6
1952	9.2 (25%)	5.0 (31%)	2.5 (31%)	1.7 (14%)
1957	11.5 (30%)	5.8 (36%)	3.5 (37%)	2.2 (17%)
1962	13.5 (33%)	6.2 (36%)	4.4 (42%)	2.9 (21%)
1967	15.9 (37%)	7.2 (39%)	5.3 (45%)	3.5 (26%)
1972	19.3 (42%)	8.8 (43%)	6.7 (50%)	3.8 (30%)
1977	22.7 (47%)	10.4 (45%)	7.7 (56%)	4.5 (39%)
1982	25.8 (51%)	11.8 (46%)	8.3 (63%)	5.7 (49%)
1987	29.2 (56%)	13.2 (48%)	9.0 (71%)	7.0 (57%)

(Numbers in millions followed by participation rate in parentheses)

Source: Adapted from data in U.S. Department of Labor, Bureau of Labor Statistics, *Labor Force Statistics Derived From the Current Population Survey, 1948–87* (Washington, D.C.: U.S. Government Printing Office, August, 1988), 801.

- Fifty-seven percent of school-age children and 44 percent of preschool children had mothers in the labor force in 1982.
- Children from families with higher incomes were even more likely to have had working mothers; almost 60 percent of all children with family incomes over $25,000 and more than two-thirds of all black children with family incomes over $15,000 had working mothers.
- The proportion of children with working mothers increased 36 percent over the decade of the 1970s, from 38.8 percent in 1970 to 52.8 percent in 1980; continued increases in subsequent decades are forecast.[20]

The fact that most people are now trying to combine two master roles, that of worker and that of homemaker, is frequently resulting in role overload, where one role, or often both roles, is not adequately carried out. This is an even greater problem because there is evidence that the fact of women joining the workforce has not resulted in greater role symmetry in families; in other words, the wife assumes a major responsibility for bringing in income but the husband generally does not assume an equivalent share of the homemaking tasks. Studies have consistently found that employed wives continue to do most of the child care and housework, and that husbands' contributions to homemaking and parenting tasks increase little, if at all, when the wife goes to work. For example, Vanek calculated that employed wives worked an average of 71 hours per week on household and paid work, while their husbands averaged 62.5 hours per week. In families with young children the gap was even wider, with the wife working 80 hours per week and the husband working 65.[21] Thus, working mothers often suffer extreme role strain and role overload as they essentially attempt to occupy two full-time jobs.

Personal and Interpersonal Problems which Affect Work Performance   Just as work can adversely affect the performance of people in nonwork roles, problems in other areas of people's lives can affect their work performance. Although the range of personal problems which people can bring to their work setting is immense, there are a few major categories of problems which have caught the attention of managers and social workers. The first is a wide range of personal/emotional problems. These problems may be short-term crises—a man is going through a divorce or a woman is experiencing anxiety related to a transfer to a new city—or they may be of a longer term variety—a woman experiences frequent and intense anxiety attacks, a worker enters a deep depression, or a man thinks his co-workers are plotting against him. All of these problems are serious in their own right, but they become even more serious when they impinge on a person's work environment. They adversely affect a person's ability to do a job, they disrupt the workplace, and they can lead to a person losing his or her job, thus making an already serious problem even more serious.

The second major category of personal/interpersonal problems affecting work performance, and the one currently receiving the most attention, is chemical dependency. The most frequently abused drug is alcohol, but there are many problems with a number of others, including marijuana, cocaine, crack, and heroin. Also, prescription drugs, often legally obtained, constitute a problem of massive proportion. DiNitto states that chemical dependency manifests itself in the workplace in four ways: employees themselves may be chemically dependent; an employee may be affected by a significant other (spouse, child, parent, or other loved one) who is chemically dependent; an employee may be the adult child of a chemically dependent parent; and, finally, an employee may be selling or using drugs on the job.[22]

There have been a number of studies which have come up with widely disparate estimates of the incidence of personal/interpersonal problems affecting work performance, but all agree that the problem is large. Winch has estimated that 10 to 12 percent of the workforce has serious personal problems of some type.[23] In a study now considered to be a classic, Kornhouser found that of his sample of 407 autoworkers, approximately 40 percent had some symptoms of mental health problems.[24] Bertram Brown lists the following facts regarding the relation of mental health to work:

- Accidents, low productivity, and high personnel turnover are concrete industrial problems significantly related to mental health and mental illness.
- Emotional problems are responsible for approximately 20 to 30 percent of employee absenteeism.
- Personal factors cause 80 to 90 percent of industrial accidents.
- It is estimated that from 15 to 30 percent of the workforce are seriously handicapped by emotional problems . . . evidence shows that about a quarter of any large workforce is in serious need of help for some kind of psychological and social trouble.
- At least 65 and possibly as much as 80 percent of the people who are fired by industry are dropped from their jobs because of personal rather than technical factors.
- Although the exact dimensions are unknown, there are considerable data which suggest that drug abuse and addiction is emerging as a serious and major problem in many work settings.

- At least a $15 billion loss to the economy occurs annually as a result of alcoholism and alcohol abuse.[25]

DYNAMICS AND PERSPECTIVES

In other chapters we have dealt with dynamics and perspectives in separate sections. With regard to work-related problems, these topics are so heavily intertwined that such conceptual separation is not practical. Basically, from the conservative perspective, the dynamics of work-related social welfare problems are almost always rooted in something the individual has, or has not, done. This is a result of the conservative belief, discussed in Chapter 1, in individual autonomy and hence responsibility for one's own situation, combined with the conservative contempt for environmental explanations of individual problems. The liberal perspective is likely to view work-related problems as being rooted in the structure of work organizations, which liberals see as often being insensitive to the needs of employees. They believe that if work organizations were humanized, if management became sensitive to the needs of workers, many, if not most work-related problems would disappear. From the radical perspective, work-related problems are inherent in the very nature of capitalism. Capitalism, they argue, is fundamentally inhumane and is based on the exploitation of labor and so the problems are inherent to the system. There is, supposedly, a perverse logic to capitalism that demands that workers be reduced to cogs in a great machine, and to do this jobs are continually made more and more simple, more and more routine, and hence, more and more alienating. Let's now look at the categories of work-related problems in more detail.

Unemployment

The dynamics of unemployment are so complex, and understanding them requires such an extensive background in economics, that anything more than a cursory treatment is beyond our scope here. We can, however, provide a few basic concepts which will allow us to explain unemployment in a simplified manner. The concepts are the three types of unemployment, deindustrialization and plant closure, and the relation of unemployment to inflation. After a discussion of these concepts, we will look at perspectives on unemployment.

Three Types of Unemployment Economists differentiate among three types of unemployment: frictional, structural, and cyclical. *Frictional unemployment* is that which is considered normal, unavoidable, and in the opinion of some economists, desirable. Frictional unemployment is caused by normal processes in the labor market, such as people quitting jobs, or people being fired or laid off. These processes cause a number of people to be without jobs, not because the jobs are not available, and not because the unemployed lack qualifications, but because it normally takes a certain amount of time for an employee and an employer to find one another. Frictional unemployment is caused by (1) employers not being fully aware of available workers and their job qualifications and (2) available workers not being fully aware of the jobs available.

Thus, frictional unemployment is seen as being a result of imperfect information. There is not complete agreement on what the "normal" rate of frictional unemployment should be, but estimates range from 3 to 5 percent. Because it is a temporary condition for individuals, frictional unemployment is not considered a major problem. There are several well-established programs in place which deal with this type of unemployment, namely unemployment insurance to provide financial support while a worker is searching for a new job and state employment services to improve the dissemination of information to both employers and job seekers and thus make job searches shorter.

The second type of unemployment is *structural unemployment*. Structural unemployment is caused by conditions in the economy which cause jobs and workers to be mismatched. The skills (or human capital) possessed by potential employees and those required by available jobs are different. Thus, there are workers wanting jobs and employers needing workers, and they may well be aware of each other, but because the workers do not possess the necessary skills, the jobs go unfilled and the workers go unemployed. The United States has been experiencing a good deal of structural unemployment in recent years because of what has been termed the "post-industrial revolution." The major response to structural unemployment is the development of training programs that attempt to develop skills which will match workers to jobs.

Economists have known for a long time that our economy (as well as others) goes through cycles. For a period of time the economy will grow and then it will go into a decline. Periods of growth are known as *boom periods,* declines are known as *recessions,* and severe declines are called *depressions.* These down cycles account for the final type of unemployment, *cyclical unemployment.* Cyclical unemployment is caused by businesses laying off workers or not hiring new workers because of a reduction in demand for the goods and services they produce. Thus, cyclical unemployment is a result of a decline in the aggregate demand for labor. In contrast to the other two types of unemployment, where there are enough jobs but some are unfilled because of either imperfect information or inadequate skills, in cyclical unemployment the problem is that there are not enough jobs to go around. The only response to cyclical unemployment is macroeconomic policies designed to increase the general level of aggregate demand. Services to individuals will have absolutely no effect on cyclical unemployment because helping one person get a job merely will result in someone else not being employed.

Deindustrialization and Plant Closure   In recent years the United States has been hit with a special type of structural unemployment caused by plant closures related to what has come to be called *deindustrialization.* This is a phenomenon in which manufacturing plants are shutting down in old locations and reopening in new ones in another community or in another country. The reason for the relocation of plants is generally to take advantage of lower labor costs; laborers in Korea will work for a whole day for less than workers in Detroit earn for one hour. This problem is compounded by technological developments which have changed the production process in such a way that the manufacturing jobs which remain require fewer employees to perform; one person can now run a machine which replaces several former workers. The exact size of the problem has been the subject of widely varying estimates. Using a data set gathered by Dun and Bradstreet Corporation, Bluestone and Harrison conclude that between 1969 and 1976, "22.3 million jobs had disappeared as a result of plant closings and the interstate and overseas movement of business establishments. This was equivalent to nearly 39 percent of all the jobs that had existed in 1969." Using the same data set Birch concluded that only 1.5 percent of job losses in the Northeast and Midwest were caused by plant relocations. The actual extent of the problem probably lies somewhere between these two estimates. In spite of the fact that no one really knows the exact extent of the problem, most researchers agree that it is a serious problem which is extensive in numerous industries throughout the nation.[26]

Unemployment and Inflation   Unemployment and inflation are generally recognized as the two biggest economic woes. Unemployment is considered an evil for reasons we have already discussed. Inflation is considered bad because it causes a deterioration in the standard of living of people whose incomes do not rise along with inflation. It does not take too many years of 10 percent inflation to completely impoverish someone on a fixed income, such as a retiree living on a pension. Ironically, economic data indicates that there is a close relationship between unemployment and inflation. In an article written in 1958, British economist A. W. Phillips analyzed historical data and demonstrated that any time British unemployment was lower than 5.5 percent, inflation began to rise. The Phillips curve he developed from the data showed that the farther below 5.5 percent unemployment became, the greater the inflation rate became.[27]

There are several reasons that low unemployment leads to higher inflation. The first is the old economic idea of supply and demand. When unemployment is low, businesses must compete with one another for employees and the most obvious way of competing is to offer higher wages. These higher wages are then reflected in higher prices for goods and services which, taken together, add up to higher inflation. The second reason is what economists call the *accelerationist hypothesis*. This hypothesis asserts that when, because of low unemployment, workers receive wage increases, their real wages do not increase because each dollar is worth less due to inflation. This will cause workers to demand greater wage improvements, leading to greater inflation, once again decreasing real wages, and the process goes round and round. The final ingredient in the process is what economists call the *rational expectations hypothesis*. This hypothesis asserts that people will take information about economic variables into account when formulating their expectations. Thus, if there has been high inflation, workers will factor this in when negotiating wage agreements with employers. For example, if there has been an inflation rate of 7 percent, workers will consider an offer of a 6 percent salary improvement to actually represent a 1 percent cut in pay. To summarize the whole process, low unemployment causes employers to bid up the price of labor; this causes an increase in the cost of the goods and services produced, which causes real wages to decline. In response to the decline in real wages, workers demand higher pay increases. Finally, in response to past inflation, workers factor this into wage demands, which causes further inflation.

Perspectives on Unemployment   Conservatives, liberals, and radicals have sharp disagreements on what unemployment means and what should be done about it. Conservatives tend to favor approaches to the problem which emphasize the improvement of human capital in order to reduce structural unemployment. They feel that, in a sense, structural unemployment is nature's way of telling people that they are no longer contributing members of society and that they had better get on the bandwagon and learn some new skills. People need the threat of poverty to keep them productive. In a similar fashion, conservatives do not feel that deindustrialization is a major problem. They believe that it is a transitory phenomenon that reflects natural adjustments in both the economy and the labor force. Foreign inroads into domestic markets, like business cycles, come and go. Businesses can and do adjust to downturns, and displaced workers move on to new jobs in growing segments of the labor market. Eventually, they argue, the economy will adjust and employment opportunities will grow, provided that the government does not interfere and spoil the natural processes. Conservatives will point out the lower standard of living in former Eastern Bloc countries and argue that the major explanation is the fact that people were guaranteed a job, and therefore they had little motivation to learn new skills. They say that the governments in these countries interfered with the operation of the free market and kept industries alive which were not productive or profitable. This belief is logically derived from the conservative view of human nature (basically negative), of human behavior (autonomous and pleasure seeking/pain avoiding), and of the proper relation of the government to the economy (that which governs least governs best).

Based on their belief in the efficiency of the free market and their opposition to government involvement in the economy, conservatives believe in a natural rate of unemployment and argue that attempts to lower this rate by job creation are undesirable. Conservatives argue that government intervention to lower the unemployment below the "natural" rate is undesirable for two reasons. The first is their belief that if a job is needed it will be created by the free market; if a job has to be created by government, then it is, by definition, not needed. Gwartney and Stroup say, "Full employment is an empty concept if it means employment at unproductive jobs. The meaningful goal of full employment is *productive employment*—employment that will generate at the lowest possible cost goods and services desired by consumers."[28] The second reason is a belief in the Phillips curve discussed earlier. Friedman says, "the market rate [of unemployment] can be kept below the natural rate only by inflation. And . . . only by accelerating inflation."[29]

Based mainly on their belief in the possibility of improving society through planned intervention and their faith in government as the source of this intervention, liberals believe that unemployment can be reduced through job creation. While conservatives define a productive job as one which creates goods and services at the lowest cost to consumers, liberals have a different idea. They believe that there are many productive tasks which would benefit our society that are outside of the market system. Leff and Haft, for example, say, "the high U.S. unemployment rate is a matter of policy; it is not the 'natural' outcome of some regrettable but unavoidable limit to our economy. There is more than enough work to be done—building housing, rebuilding our decayed inner cities, roads, and bridges, preserving our landmarks, raising our literacy standard, caring for the neglected needs of senior citizens, delivering basic health care to all our communities, cleaning our water and our air, ridding the land of toxic wastes—the list could go on and on—to provide jobs for all who want them." If there is no such thing as a "natural" unemployment rate, why do conservatives argue against policies which would lower it? The reason, according to liberals such as Leff and Haft is "the fact that our economy is oriented toward profit rather than human well-being."[30] And what of the inflation-unemployment tradeoff that conservatives such as Friedman use as an argument against government job creation? To the extent that they would agree that this does exist, liberals would argue that unemployment is a far greater evil than inflation. Thus, it is worth raising the inflation rate to lower unemployment.

In a similar vein, liberals challenge the arguments that plant closures and deindustrialization are a result of natural market adjustments and that workers will eventually regain lost ground. They argue that plant closures are generally a result of unchecked corporate profiteering and that some form of government regulation is necessary. An often cited example is that of the decision of the General Electric Corporation to close its steam iron plant in Ontario, California, and relocate it in South America. The reason for the decision was that the plant in California was "only" turning a 14 percent profit and by relocating this could be increased to 16 percent. Liberal critics argue that the damage done to the United States economy and the damage done to the lives of individual workers far exceed any advantage which would result from a 2 percent increase in G.E.'s profits.[31] Liberals argue that the assumption by conservatives that workers displaced by plant closures will eventually find their way into the high technology work which is taking over the manufacturing process is erroneous. Looking at the old mill-based workers in the Northeast who lost their jobs when these industries relocated, Bluestone asks, "What happened to all the workers? Did these workers find their way into high technology?" Based on his research he says

> The answer was a resounding no. Between 1957 and 1975, 833,000 workers were employed in the old mill-based industries (apparel, textiles, shoes, rubber goods, and the like) sometime during the period. By 1975, 674,000 no longer worked in these industries, largely because the firms had closed down. Some of the companies relocated in the South; some went to Singapore, South Korea, or Brazil. What happened to the workers? Of the 674,000 no longer in these industries, fewer than 3 percent were able to make the transition to the new high-tech sector. Five times as many (16 percent) skidded downward into retail trade and low-wage service jobs like those at K-Mart or McDonald's. Many left the labor force altogether, unable to find suitable employment . . . In short, the high-tech revolution, despite its great promise, has held out little hope for the victims of deindustrialization.[32]

Although it at first seems rather strange, the radical perspective on unemployment has substantial areas of agreement with the conservative perspective. Like conservatives, radicals argue that a certain rate of unemployment is built into our economic system. Radicals also agree with conservatives that for our system to prosper, unrestricted capital mobility is necessary even though this results in higher unemployment rates and the erosion of our industrial base. Finally, with one major qualification, radicals agree that unemployment is natural and that there is little that can be done about it. The one major qualification is that these conditions apply *within the system as it is currently structured.* Conservatives accept the system and so conclude that a certain rate of unemployment is natural and necessary. Radicals reject the system and thus argue that the only thing for which unemployment is natural and necessary is to preserve and enlarge the power and wealth of the capitalist ruling class. They argue that to reduce, and perhaps even to eliminate unemployment, a new social and economic system is necessary, one which would put the security needs of average people above the perceived needs for wealth and power of a small, elite group. Radicals also challenge the work ethic upon which our society is built. They argue that technology has evolved to a point where there is not enough meaningful work to go around and so we now have more workers than we have work to be done. The proper societal response to this situation, radicals argue, is to stop stigmatizing people who are unemployed, to recognize that their unemployment is caused by no fault of their own, and to develop legitimate opportunities for individuals to develop identities not tied to work.

Underemployment/Lack of Personal Fulfillment from Work

Conservative and liberal perspectives and explanations about the dynamics of underemployment and the lack of fulfillment from work are not markedly different. They tend to explain the problem mainly as the result of two characteristics of the workplace that have been increasing throughout modern history—specialization and automation—and of one characteristic of workers—overeducation. *Specialization* refers to the process of individual workers being responsible for a narrower and narrower part of the production process. This is a result of the replacement of the craft system, where one worker produces a complete product, by the mass production system, where each worker completes only one specialized task out of a large number necessary to produce the complete product. A famous early example of this process was given by Adam Smith, who described a new method of producing pins:

> One man draws out the wire; another straights it, a third cuts it; a fourth points it; a fifth grinds it at the top for receiving the head; to make the head requires two or three distinct operations; to put it on is a peculiar business; to whiten the pin is another; it is even a trade by itself to put them into the paper; and the important business of making a pin is in this manner divided into about eighteen distinct operations, which in some manufactories are all performed by distinct hands.[33]

The result of specialization is that jobs require less skill, and they are less interesting and fulfilling. It has been estimated that 80 percent of all jobs in our society require few skills.[34] Also, when a person produces a complete product, even one so mundane as a card of pins, he or she feels a sense of pride and accomplishment. When a worker merely repeats one step over and over, stamping a part, grinding a part, entering a piece of data, or whatever, he or she feels no sense of accomplishment for producing a product and, therefore, gets little fulfillment from the job.

As a phenomenon leading to a decrease in fulfillment from work, *automation* is closely related to specialization. More and more jobs are being done partially, or wholly, by machines. The result is that once again workers are distanced from what they are producing, and they are denied the satisfaction which comes from directly producing a product. The work of producing pins which Smith described is probably now done by a few workers monitoring the control panels of machines which do all the actual work.

Overeducation creates a problem for worker satisfaction for two reasons. The first is the obvious reason that workers who have skill levels greater than those required by their jobs are going to be bored. The second, and perhaps more important, reason is that as level of education increases, workers' expectations increase. Fifty years ago most people entering a career expected little more from it than a reasonably secure and economically rewarding future. Evidence indicates that as educational level increases, the expectations people have of their jobs also increase. A longitudinal study by Dowling and O'Brien found that the length of education increased students' desire for skill-utilization, autonomy, and variety in their eventual jobs.[35] These increasing expectations are not restricted to income and security; people begin to expect work to provide fulfillment and meaning for life. O'Toole has observed, "one of the main problems [with worker satisfaction] is that work has not changed fast enough to keep up with the rapid and wide scale changes in worker attitudes, aspirations and values. A general increase in their educational and economic status has placed many American workers in a position where having an interesting job is now as important as having a job that pays well."[36]

The mainstream (that is to say, the liberal and conservative) solutions to the problems of underemployment and lack of satisfaction from work generally involve what is called *job enlargement*. Job enlargement refers to the concept of increasing the scope and/or depth of a job. *Scope* is the number and variety of tasks performed by the worker. For example, a small office may have three clerical workers, one acting as receptionist, one as production typist, and one as office manager. A manager who wanted to increase the scope of these jobs would divide the tasks up among the positions so the workers would each do a wider variety of things during the day. Job *depth* refers to the amount of planning and control responsibility a worker has. If the manager wanted to increase the job depth of the workers referred to earlier, she might allow the workers to schedule their own breaks, divide the work up among themselves, and decide on their own procedures for getting the work done. Studies of job enlargement have indicated that it is often successful in substantially improving worker satisfaction, but that it does not necessarily lead to greater productivity.[37]

While radicals would generally agree that specialization and automation are partially responsible for worker dissatisfaction, they argue that those areas are themselves symptoms of a larger problem. This problem is the capitalist system with its concern for profits over everything else. In order to increase profits, the argument goes, jobs have been specialized and automated regardless of the fact that the effects of these developments on workers have been known for years. Radicals argue that the result has been the development of alienation among workers. *Alienation* refers to the separation of workers from ownership of the means of production and from any control over the final product of their labor. Marx said

> In what does this alienation consist? First, that work is external to the worker, that it is not part of his nature, that consequently he does not fulfill himself in his work but denies himself, has a feeling of misery, not well-being, does not develop freely a physical and mental energy, but is physically exhausted and mentally debased . . . His work is not voluntary but imposed, forced labor. . . . Finally, the alienated character of work for the worker appears in the fact that it is not his work but work for someone else, that in work he does not belong to himself but to another person.[38]

Research has shown that alienation among workers leads to feelings of powerlessness (a feeling that one has little control over the direction of one's life), meaninglessness (the feeling that one does not understand the events occurring around one nor how one's personal contribution fits into these events), self-estrangement (the feeling that one engages in activities for purely utilitarian reasons and with ulterior motives rather than for the intrinsic enjoyment of these activities), and social isolation (the feeling of separation from individuals and groups around one).[39]

Radicals argue that job enlargement, while a potentially useful activity, is not in itself enough to counteract the effects of alienation. The reason is the research cited previously, which concludes that while job enlargement may increase satisfaction, it does not increase productivity. Because productivity is the major goal of capitalist society, and because job enlargement can be costly and inconvenient, it will not be employed to any great extent. Radicals argue that the only way to decrease alienation is to restructure our social and economic system in such a way that human needs take precedence over the desire for ever-increasing profits. Only when we have substituted humanistic goals for the goals of greed that we currently pursue will job enlargement really work.

Problems of Interaction of Work with Other Spheres of Life

At various points throughout this book we have used role theory as a framework to explain social welfare problems. We turn once again to this theory to explain the dynamics of the interaction of work with other spheres of life. Sociologist Talcott Parsons once observed that American families were characterized by role differentiation in which husbands performed instrumental roles, mainly working outside the home to economically support the family, and wives performed expressive roles, engaging in family- and friend-related activities inside the home. Parsons argued that this was a good arrangement because it prevented competition and increased cohesion. According to Parsons, women working outside the home would be bad for families because it would disrupt this role symmetry.[40] More recently, sociologists, notably Scanzoni, have argued that just the opposite is true. Scanzoni argues that the fact of wives working outside the home strengthens families because when wives fulfill instrumental duties, then husbands perform expressive activities; he feels that the mutual exchange of expressive activities is associated with marital happiness and satisfaction.[41] Whatever the effect on marital satisfaction, one thing is clear—the fact of women working outside the home leads to *role conflict*. In the great majority of American households there is no longer one person who devotes full time to the roles of homemaker, parent, and recreation planner, so some accommodation must be made between work and family roles.

Role conflict as described by sociologists refers to situations in which a person holds a position or positions where he or she is confronted with contradictory expectations such that compliance with one makes compliance with the others difficult or impossible. There are three major types of role conflict relevant to our discussion of the conflict of work with other spheres of a person's life. The first, and most relevant here, is *role overload*. This is the situation that occurs when an individual is confronted with a large number of expectations and he or she cannot satisfy them all within the available time. By far the most common type of role overload revolves around the issue of parenting. Any working parent is confronted several times a month with days where they are expected to be at work, but also feel they should be: at home with a sick child; at school to see their child in a play; taking the Cub Scouts to the museum; meeting with teachers to discuss problems with school work; or helping the child with his or her homework, bug collection, or science project. The list could go on and on. The point is, when both parents work, and especially if they have inflexible work schedules, there are not enough hours in the day to adequately fulfill the roles of worker and parent. Because most jobs allow very little flexibility, it is generally the parent role which suffers.

The second type of role conflict is *inter-sender role conflict*. This is the situation in which a person is subjected to conflicting expectations from two or more significant others. A man whose wife is pursuing a career will likely be expected by her to perform half of the expressive roles in the family, including child care, entertaining, and housework. However, the man's boss and co-workers may well have no understanding of this and may have little sympathy when he refuses to work late because it is his night to pick up the kids and to cook dinner.

The third type of conflict is *intra-sender role conflict*. This is the type of situation in which a person is receiving conflicting expectations from one significant other. In this era of rapidly changing expectations, women are particularly susceptible to intra-sender role conflict. As a society we now expect that women will pursue successful careers, but we have not relieved them of the expectation that they will also be old-style wives and mothers. Therefore, it is not at all uncommon for social workers in family counseling settings to find marital stress resulting from a husband who expects his wife to be both a successful worker who contributes to the family coffers, and a homemaker who prepares home-cooked meals every night, takes full responsibility for the kids, keeps the house spotless, and plans and executes beautiful dinner parties.

Role conflicts are, of course, not limited to married people in two-career families. The conflicts are even greater in single-parent families because in these situations the parent often gets absolutely no help with family roles. Also, these conflicts are not limited to conflict between work and parental roles. Work roles often conflict with other important roles such as the role of son or daughter, particularly when parents become elderly and/or experience failing health; or the role of citizen, when a person feels obligated to be heavily involved in community affairs.

Liberals believe that the solution, or at least the mitigation, of problems of the conflict between work and other spheres of a person's life will occur through the government and employers adopting more humanistic policies which allow more flexibility and provide more recognition and support for other roles in employees' lives. The number one recommendation of the 1980 White House Conference on Families was for family-oriented personnel policies including flex-time, more part-time work which pays fair wages and provides the same benefits as full-time jobs, job sharing, more generous and flexible leave and transfer policies, and more support for quality child care from both employers and the government.[42] A frequently mentioned idea is to give employees a choice of "cafeteria benefits." With this system employees receive certain "core" benefits, such as medical insurance and a pension plan, and then they have a choice of other benefits, up to a certain dollar value, from a list which would include things like profit sharing, child care, or home health care. Employees can then tailor their benefits to their individual situations and stage of life. For example, for a twenty-five-year-old parent, child care might be of far greater value than participation in a profit sharing plan. The employee might well reason that when the children enter school, there will still be over thirty working years to build up an investment portfolio.

Many conservatives also support the types of reforms discussed previously. Their support stems from their concern with a smoothly functioning economic system and their perception that the conflict between work roles and other roles is becoming a disruptive factor which must be dealt with (for example, concern about the "three o'clock slump" mentioned earlier). However, there is a group of conservatives who, based on their belief in tradition, their opposition to change, and their fear of government programs, oppose any programs which make it easier for women to choose a career rather than the traditional roles of wife and mother. Conservative opposition to programs in this area has focused on day care. A recent study by the very conservative and influential Heritage Foundation says

> The critical factor in judging day care is point of view. If you are looking at it from the point of view of economically and socially ambitious parents, day care is clearly a great convenience. But in the rush to simplify and cushion the lives of adults, it is easy to overlook the interests of the children involved. Indeed, I have been amazed as I've followed the day-care debate to see how infrequently it is approached with a child's-eye view. It is argued as a "women's issue," as an "employment issue," as a "productivity issue"; but scarcely anyone asks, "Is it good for children?" . . . The question is: can you substitute a paid relationship for the natural parent-child bond without seriously harming children and society? It appears the answer may be no.

The policy recommendations of the report are summarized as

> Rather than further subsidizing substitute parenting, with its many risks, we ought to endeavor to create options for the large number of Americans who would like to care for their own children when they are very young. There is much we can do in this area, from enacting tax credits for parents raising preschoolers to encouraging more home-based work to changing social attitudes about the contributions of stay-at-home parents.[43]

Conservative opinion on this subject is clearly based on the assumption that the majority of women who work are doing so for noneconomic reasons and thus staying home is a viable option. The data does not support this assumption. After reviewing available data on women's labor force participation, Spitze concludes

> almost all women work to support or to help support themselves or their families. Even if we maintain the traditional assumption that the income of a male breadwinner is taken into account first, a majority of employed women work due to economic need. Forty-three percent of all women over 18 are single, widowed, separated, or divorced and thus may be the sole support of themselves or children. An additional 13 percent have husbands who earn less than $10,000, the approximate poverty line for a family of four.[44]

HISTORICAL PERSPECTIVE

The work-related problems we have been discussing in this chapter—unemployment, underemployment, conflict between work and other spheres of life, and personal/interpersonal problems—are viewed by individuals as largely personal difficulties. For employers, however, they have always been viewed as problems of productivity and labor relations. When people are unemployed, this means something is wrong with the economy and the most work possible is not getting done; when workers are dissatisfied with their jobs, they do not work as diligently and as efficiently as possible; and when people are worrying about who is taking care of the kids, their minds will not be 100 percent on their work. In addition, alcoholism, drug addiction, and mental illness tremendously increase the cost of doing business. While business people may be as humanitarian as any other group, we begin our historical survey of social services related to work with the observation that charity has always been a secondary concern to business people promoting social services. The bottom line has always been the bottom line.

In this historical survey we will not attempt to look at the history of each of the problem areas we have been discussing. That task would be beyond the scope of this chapter. Rather, we will be looking at the development of social services to deal with these problem areas. This history can be divided into two cycles of growth and decline, from approximately 1875 to the 1930s, and from 1940 until the early 1960s, and one period of growth which began in the mid-1960s and is still going on.

The First Cycle—from 1875 to the 1930s[45] In the late nineteenth century, businessmen were faced with a number of labor problems. The increasing size of businesses prevented personal contact between labor and management. An increasing proportion of the labor force was made up of women and immigrants, groups whom management did not understand. Startling rates of labor turnover, malingering, sabotage, and, most ominous, the tendency toward labor organization indicated labor's discontent. All of these tendencies were viewed by a worried management as being threats to the paternalistic, autocratic style that had been their norm.

In the late 1800s, in an effort to deal with these problems, businessmen initiated policies and programs that were known at the time as the *welfare movement* and that are currently referred to as *welfare capitalism*. Although it was rationalized as humanitarianism, the welfare movement had two additional, and probably more important, goals. One was the creation of a new, improved, loyal working man who kept in line with management values and ideals; that is, he was one who would drink little, play wholesomely, work hard, and be thrifty, efficient, and diligent. The second goal was to create a labor force so contented that it would have no desire to unionize but, rather, would trust management to look out for its best interests. The major goal of the welfare program at the Plymouth Cordage Company, for example, was stated by an official as, "When we get our men to say Plymouth Cordage in the way and with the feeling a man says 'Dartmouth' 'Harvard' or 'Yale' we will get results."[46]

The welfare movement took the form of a number of services offered by management to labor for the purpose of mitigating various management-defined problems of life in industrial society. The acculturation of immigrants and young people was felt to be a pressing problem. For this purpose, American businesses ran a large variety of schools and training programs. Another set of problems revolved around the basic necessities of food and shelter. To meet these needs, businessmen set up nonprofit lunchrooms and company stores, and they built literally hundreds of thousands of company houses and apartments. Because the mills and factories were dangerous, and work-related injuries often resulted in lawsuits, many companies began programs to aid employees in case of sickness or accident. Clinics were established and staffed by company doctors, and a visiting nurse was often provided to visit convalescing employees in their homes.*

---

*The services of the visiting nurse provide insight into the dual humanitarian/social control aspect of the welfare movement. Responding to a survey, an executive of the Walworth Manufacturing Co. said, in regard to the duties of the visiting nurse, "When a man is away from his job a nurse will be down within a day or two, not more than two, to determine the cause. If there is a reason for his being out, she will help him and if there is not, he will have to change his habits if he is to remain in our employ." (Manufacturers Research Association, "Dispensary Survey" [1927] Manufacturers Research Association Papers, Baker Library, Harvard University, Boston, MA.)

Employers were concerned that their workers, particularly women, would fall under the evil influence of the saloon or dance hall, so they provided various "wholesome" recreational programs such as garden clubs, baseball teams, libraries, and company resorts. Finally, some companies distributed material aid to employees, former employees, or their families who had fallen on hard times.[47]

Following its beginning in the late 1800s, the welfare movement experienced a rapid and steady growth. A Bureau of Labor Statistics survey reported that by 1926, 80 percent of the 1,500 largest companies in the United States had at least one type of welfare program and about half had comprehensive programs.[48] These programs required staff. This need, combined with the trend toward functional specialization, gave rise to the profession of the social or welfare secretary, the forerunner of the occupational social worker. Statistics regarding the number of welfare secretaries are scanty at best, but what figures are available indicate that the specialization grew steadily into the 1920s. The first welfare secretary appears to have been Mrs. Aggie Dunn, hired in 1875 by the H.J. Heinz Company in Pittsburgh to look after the needs of the young women working in its plant. Dunn was probably the only welfare secretary in the United States until 1900 when the specialization began to grow; Nathan reports eight to ten secretaries employed in 1902 and Cranston reports twenty-seven in 1906.[49] A 1919 Bureau of Labor Statistics survey of 431 of the largest companies in the United States found that 141 employed at least one full-time secretary and 154 contracted with outside agencies for social work services.[50] By 1920, more graduates of the New York School of Social Work were taking jobs in industry than in any other setting.[51]

Although many types of employee benefit programs flourished in the 1920s and there is evidence that businessmen were pleased with the results of these programs, the occupation of welfare secretary was losing support. Very few references to welfare secretaries are found in the literature of the 1920s, and those that are available are generally critical. There appear to be a number of reasons for this decline. A major source of opposition to the welfare secretary was the laborers themselves, who considered the job paternalistic. There is little doubt that this complaint was justified, even though contemporary accounts decried paternalism and denied that welfare secretaries were guilty of this behavior. The following quote is fairly typical of descriptions of the welfare secretary and illustrates the paternalistic (or maternalistic) attitude with which the work was approached.

> The social secretary in a department store is practically a house mother to a great big family, and there is ample need for all the mothering she can spare. The great majority of immigrants are very illiterate; their children after a few years schooling seek work, perhaps in a department store. Not having the guidance of a mother capable of instructing them intelligently, they are drawn to the social secretary, who, by her thorough knowledge of what they need, advises them intelligently and helpfully.[52]

As might be expected, workers did not react favorably to being patronized and thus they often opposed welfare programs and welfare secretaries. Because businessmen hired welfare secretaries to decrease tension between management and labor, the fact that the position sometimes had the opposite effect was very discouraging.

Another source of opposition to the welfare secretary was labor leaders, who considered welfare secretaries (and, in fact, all management-sponsored welfare programs) to be anti-union. They believed that the purpose of the welfare secretary was to defuse employee unrest without bringing about any fundamental change in the relationship between capital and labor. Bloomfield, for example, reported, "The ideal of the welfare supervisor [union leaders] claim is docile, obedient, and machine like women workers. The good welfare worker is the most dangerous because she destroys the independence of the workers and turns them from unionism. Her responsibility to the employer makes her a more efficient kind of slavedriver."[53]

When the Great Depression began in 1929, unemployment rapidly grew and businesses either closed or struggled for survival. Welfare programs became a luxury and were dropped from most companies. Several factors contributed to the decline of welfare programs and of welfare secretaries, the forerunners of occupational social workers. First, many of the functions of the welfare secretaries were taken over by the new profession of personnel management. Second, because business was so bad, most companies simply could not afford welfare programs. Third, because unemployment was so high, businesses could hire all the people they needed and if they did not work out, they could fire them. Thus, from the businessman's point of view, there was no reason to spend money on people and programs to help workers resolve problems. Finally, most businessmen did not deny that welfare programs were anti-union. Accordingly, as unions gained a foothold in various industries, and as legislation was passed during the Depression to make the formation of unions easier, one of the main motivations for employing a welfare secretary was lost.

The Second Cycle—from 1940 to the 1960s At the same time that social services for employees were declining during the 1930s, the seeds for their reemergence were being sown in what came to be called the *human relations school of management*. This school of management had its beginning in some of the most interesting and widely publicized research ever conducted—the Hawthorne Experiments. This research, beginning in the late 1920s, was conducted by a team from the Harvard Business School at the Western Electric Hawthorne plant, a facility which assembled telephones. The original purpose of the study was to ascertain the effects of different variables, such as amount of light, on productivity. The research was eventually to look at almost every possible physical variable, including humidity, temperature, number and length of breaks, amount of sleep, and nutrition. The researchers found that when they began the study, productivity increased and, as long as the study continued, almost nothing would cause it to decrease. In fact, they once reduced illumination to see what effect this would have. It was not until the illumination became about the level of moonlight that production declined. The conclusion of this research was that the attention being paid to the workers by the researchers was the variable affecting productivity and, therefore, traditional theories of management which stressed the physical organization of work needed to be replaced by a theory recognizing the complex social nature of workers. As one of the researchers, Fritz Roethlisberger, wrote, "Workers are not isolated, unrelated individuals; they are social animals and should be treated as such . . . . Our technological development in the past hundred years has been tremendous. Our methods of handling people are still archaic. If this civilization is to survive, we must obtain a new understanding of human motivation and behavior in business organizations—an understanding which can be simply but effectively practiced."[54] The human relations approach, which stresses that the psychological and social well-being of workers is the most important variable determining productivity, came to be the dominant theory of management. This approach paved the way for the reintroduction of social services into the workplace during the 1940s and again in the 1960s.

After the decline of social services during the years of the Depression, they were rapidly reintroduced when the United States entered the Second World War in 1941. There were several reasons for the reintroduction of services at this time. The two main reasons were related to the departure of a large proportion of the labor force into military service. This caused a labor shortage, and thus it was no longer practical for employers to simply fire employees who were having difficulties; the provision of a service which could lead to salvaging an employee once again became cost-effective. The second reason was that the new employees were different from those they replaced. These workers were more likely to be unexperienced, female, older, and members of minorities; and they often needed supports the departing labor force had been able to do without. Recognizing these problems, the federal government made funds available to support social services to the workforce, especially in the rapidly expanding aircraft industry. Unions also began to provide services to their members to help them deal with the many problems and stresses the war was placing on workers. In 1941 the CIO (Congress of Industrial Organizations) formed its National Community Service Committee, which trained union counselors who worked in a number of plants during the war.[55] Social worker Bertha Reynolds worked with labor and management to establish a social service program for the members of the National Maritime Union and their families. Also during the war the different branches of the military service for the first time employed professionally trained social workers, as commissioned officers, to deal with the many problems that military persons encounter in relation to their work.[56]

When the Second World War ended in 1945, occupational social services went into another decline. With the return of the military personnel it once again became possible for employers to easily hire replacements for workers experiencing difficulties. Also, the traditional labor force returned and women returned to the home. This meant that once again employers did not have to worry about issues such as who was minding the children; once again, problem workers could simply be fired.

There was one exception to the decline of occupational social service programs after World War II, and this was the development during the 1940s and 1950s of occupational alcoholism programs. Evidence had been steadily accumulating about the tremendous cost to business of alcohol abuse, and the spread of Alcoholics Anonymous led to a view that alcoholism could, with help, be conquered. By the late 1950s a number of large companies had established occupational alcoholism programs (OAP), generally located in their medical divisions. Among these were DuPont, Eastman Kodak, Consolidated Edison, Bell Telephone, and North American Aviation.[57] The majority of these programs did not actually provide any treatment for alcoholic employees; rather, they focused on identifying employees who were having work problems related to alcohol and getting them into treatment and self-help groups, notably Alcoholics Anonymous.[58]

The Third Cycle—from the Mid-1960s to the Present   Two things occurred, beginning in the mid-1960s, which have lead to the reemergence of occupational social service programs. The first, which we discussed in a previous section, is the change in the composition of the labor force. Once again women entered the labor force in large numbers, leading to a need for family supports that are not necessary when only one member of a family works and the other is available for support roles. Business people have become increasingly aware that this trend is permanent and that the problems related to it negatively affect productivity and competitiveness. They therefore are beginning to take an interest in services to help with these problems.

The second thing that has happened is that as a part of the larger movement toward increasing recognition of the civil rights of various groups, legislation has been passed that requires that services be provided to groups defined as having special needs. Among the more important work-related legislation enacted during the past twenty years are the Hughes Act, Vocational Rehabilitation Act, Occupational Safety and Health Act, Employee Retirement Income Security Act, Age Discrimination in Employment Act, and Title VII of the Civil Rights Act. All of these have affected the relationship of employers and employees by emphasizing the need to address the problems facing workers.[59]

In the 1960s, for the first time since the decline of the welfare secretary before the Great Depression, the social work profession began to exhibit an interest in practice in work settings. Social workers, such as Leo Miller at the Polaroid Corporation, entered the business world and demonstrated the effectiveness of social services to employees; research and demonstration programs on the effectiveness of employee assistance were conducted, such as that developed by Weiner, Akabas, and Sommer with the Amalgamated Clothing Workers of America in New York; research and training centers were opened, such as the Center for Social Policy and Practice in the Workplace at the Columbia University School of Social Work and the World of Work Program at the Hunter College School of Social Work; and national conferences on the role of social work in the world of work were held and proceedings were published, such as *Labor and Industrial Settings: Sites for Social Work Practice; Proceedings of a National Conference June 7–9, 1978*. The interest of organized social work in practice in work settings has continued to grow. In the past few years a number of schools of social work have developed field placements and specializations in what is now called *occupational social work*. It is to roles in this increasingly important practice specialization that we now turn.

SOCIAL WORK ROLES

Occupational social work specialists find employment in both business and union settings. In businesses they are most frequently located either in the medical department or in the personnel office. However, they are also found in training units, affirmative action offices, corporate social responsibility departments, and human resources divisions. Common job titles used to describe the functional positions of occupational social workers in business settings are employee counselor, affirmative action officer, community relations consultant, substance abuse service coordinator, employee resources manager, corporate relocation officer, human resources policy advisor, career planning and development counselor, training consultant, charitable allocations analyst, urban affairs advisor, coordinator of corporate health and wellness programs, employee

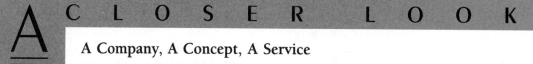

A Company, A Concept, A Service

When Rick Hellan, MSW, and his partner, Carl Tisone, founded Personal Performance Consultants, Inc. (PPC) in 1975, little did they realize that their concept of employer-based counseling services would contribute to a revolution in the way the average consumer receives—and perceives—counseling services.

Today, PPC, based in St. Louis, has become the world's largest privately held provider of Employee Assistance Programs (EAPs). The company recently embarked on a joint venture with Willis Faber plc, a British insurance firm, to provide EAPs to employers throughout the United Kingdom. PPC has been named to *INC.* magazine's list of the 500 fastest growing companies in the U.S. for the last two years in a row. And the firm's managed care systems—counseling programs which incorporate mental health and substance abuse treatment cost-containment features—are recognized as being on the leading edge of the EAP industry.

PPC's employee assistance programs range in size and design, but most include a professionally staffed, short-term counseling element as well as a closely monitored referral system. The recent focus in programs for large employers has been on cost containment and quality control, and PPC has responded with custom-designed, "managed care" systems.

Hellan explained that within a comprehensive managed care system, the EAP is the point-of-entry vehicle for employees seeking assistance with emotional, mental health, and substance abuse problems. But that gatekeeping function is not the program's only focus; the EAP then acts as the employee's advocate throughout the course of care, and is responsible for assuring that the employee is referred for the highest-quality, most appropriate care for his or her problem. This employee advocacy orientation is an important part of PPC's approach to managed care systems.

What does PPC see down the line for EAPs? "An even heavier shift towards managed care," Hellan said. "As employers see the cost- and quality-control evidence coming from other programs, they're going to want to integrate their EAPs into their employee benefits management systems too. It is clear that social work can make a major contribution to helping our country gain control of rising health care costs, while ensuring quality care."

Expanding EAPs and managed care systems are having an impact on the way social workers practice in clinical settings. Heightened levels of accountability for outcome, together with the need to precisely define social worker intervention, are resulting in higher expectations from the consumer for quality care. Hellan also pointed out that for counselors in private practice, the continuing growth of managed care systems will make EAPs a major and growing referral source.

Source: Margie Newman, "A Company, A Concept, A Service," *Links,* Alumni Association Newsletter, George Warren Brown School of Social Work, Washington University in St. Louis, MO (Fall 1988), 1.

---

assistance officer, and outplacement specialist.[60] A few social workers have gone beyond working for businesses and have set up businesses of their own to provide consultation to managers regarding employee benefit programs.

In union settings, social workers generally work in union counseling programs, which are often called personal or membership service units. Common titles for social workers in unions and union-sponsored programs are personal service worker, education program director, occupational safety and health officer, health and security plan manager, membership services coordinator, career training and upgrading adviser, preretirement services worker, day care consultant, legislative analyst, benefit plan administrator, community services coordinator, alcoholism program supervisor, and director of retiree services.[61]

A number of occupational social work specialists have found employment in the nonprofit sector of the economy. An increasing number of colleges and state and local governmental agencies are setting up comprehensive employee assistance programs which provide a wide range of services, including career development, health and fitness training, help with alcohol and drug dependence, and mental health and family counseling. The employee assistance program at the university of one of the authors even offers small garden plots and the help of a horticulturist so employees can have gardens even if they live in apartments. Social workers in these settings usually have titles such as employee assistance administrator or counselor.

A final employment setting for occupational social workers is the military. All three branches of the military employ graduate-level social workers, with the title of social worker, as commissioned officers. These people are assigned to the medical service corps and they provide clinical mental health and substance abuse services to members of the military and their families. In addition, the military employs a number of civilian social workers on a contract basis to work in mental health and family assistance programs. Bachelor-level social workers also work in the military, with titles such as social work assistant and mental health technician.

What do social workers do in this wide range of settings? The answer is that the things they do cover as wide a scope as the settings, ranging from administration of programs, to clinical treatment, to advocacy; they even include social action roles such as specialist in corporate social responsibility. Akabas and Kurzman have listed the following items which may be found in the job descriptions of social workers in occupational settings:

- Counseling and other activities with troubled employees or [union] members in jeopardy of losing their job to assist them with their personal problems and to help them achieve and maintain a high level of performance.
- Advising on the use of community services to meet the needs of clients and establishing linkages with such programs.
- Training front-line personnel (union representatives, foremen, line supervisors) to enable them to determine when changes in an employee's job performance warrant referral to a social service unit and carrying out an appropriate approach to the employee that will result in a referral.
- Developing and overseeing the operations of a union or management information system which will record information on services and provide data for analyzing the unit's program.
- Conceiving a plan for the future direction of the program that is based on the identification of unmet needs and current demographic trends.
- Offering consultation to labor management decisionmakers concerning the development of a human resource policy.
- Helping to initiate welfare, community health, recreational, or educational programs for active and retired employees or [union] members.

- Assisting in the administration of the benefit and health care structure and helping plan for new initiatives.
- Advising on corporate giving or labor coalition building and on organizational positions in relation to pending social welfare legislation.[62]

C O N C L U S I O N

As we have proceeded with this chapter, our focus has progressively narrowed until at the end we have been discussing occupational social work as a social work specialization. By way of conclusion we wish to return to a broader focus and to reemphasize a point we made several times in the earlier sections of the chapter. This point is that work is a central component of the well-being of nearly everyone. The security, identity, and future of people are intimately tied to their work situations. There are interpenetrations of work with almost every sphere of a person's life. If a person's work is not going well, it will tend to adversely affect his or her family and personal life. On the other hand, if a person is having difficulty with his or her personal life, it will most likely adversely affect his or her work performance. Therefore, concern with work is not the exclusive domain of those social workers who choose this as an area of specialization. All social workers, whether they are public welfare workers, clinical social workers, child welfare workers, or whatever, need to be concerned with and sensitive to work problems if they are to be effective in helping their clients.

E N D N O T E S

1. Sigmund Freud, *Civilization and its Discontents* (New York: W.W. Norton, 1961), 27.
2. Marie Jahoda, *Employment and Unemployment: A Social Psychological Analysis* (Cambridge, England: Cambridge University Press, 1982), 22–27.
3. Helen Harris Perlman, *Persona: Social Role and Personality* (Chicago, IL: The University of Chicago Press, 1968), 59–86.
4. Talcott Parsons, *The Social System* (New York: The Free Press, 1959), 180–200.
5. Perlman, *Persona*, 64.
6. Thomas J. Sullivan, Kenrick S. Thompson, Richard D. Wright, George R. Cross, and Dale R. Spady. *Social Problems: Divergent Perspectives* (New York: John Wiley & Sons, 1980), 300.
7. John E. Tropman, *American Values and Social Welfare; Cultural Contradictions in the Welfare State* (Englewood Cliffs, NJ: Prentice Hall, 1989), 4.
8. Harold Wilensky and Charles Lebeaux, *Industrial Society and Social Welfare* (New York: Russell Sage Foundation, 1958), 46–47.
9. Daniel Bell, *Work and its Discontents: The Cult of Efficiency in America* (Boston, MA: Beacon Press, 1956), 54.
10. Martha Ozawa, "Work and Social Policy," in *Work, Workers, and Work Organizations: A View from Social Work,* Sheila H. Akabas and Paul A. Kurzman, eds. (Englewood Cliffs, NJ: Prentice-Hall, 1982), 34–35.
11. Walli F. Leff and Marilyn G. Haft, *Time Without Work* (Boston, MA: South End Press, 1983), 117–126.
12. Barry Bluestone, "Deindustrialization and Unemployment in America," in *Deindustrialization and Plant Closure,* Paul D. Staudohar and Holly E. Brown, eds. (Lexington, MA: D.C. Heath, 1987), 6–7.
13. Maya Pines, "Recession is Linked to Far-Reaching Psychological Harm," *New York Times,* April 6, 1982, C-1.
14. U.S. Department of Labor, Bureau of Labor Statistics, *How the Government Measures Unemployment* (Washington, D.C.: U.S. Government Printing Office, 1987), 1–5.
15. Office of Federal Statistical Policy and the Bureau of the Census, *Social Indicators* (Washington, D.C.: U.S. Government Printing Office, 1977), 383; "Eight

Percent, or Maybe Twelve," *Dollars & Sense* (January 1982): 14–15.

16. Katherine Hooper Briar, *Social Work and the Unemployed* (Silver Spring, MD: National Association of Social Workers, 1988), 12.

17. Graham L. Staines and Robert P. Quinn, "American Workers Evaluate the Quality of Their Jobs," *Monthly Labor Review 102* (January 1979): 3–12.

18. Greg Duncan and Saul Hoffman, "The Economic Value of Surplus Education," in *5000 American Families,* Vol. 6, Greg Duncan and James Morgan, eds. (Ann Arbor, MI: Institute for Social Research, 1978), 223–246.

19. Russell W. Rumberger, *Overeducation in the U.S. Labor Market* (New York: Praeger, 1981), 67–98.

20. Jacquelyn McCroskey, "Employer-Supported Child Care," in *Social Work in the Workplace,* Gary M. Gould and Michael L. Smith, eds. (New York: Springer, 1988), 173.

21. Joanne Miller and Howard H. Garrison, "Sex Roles: The Division of Labor at Home and in the Workplace," *Annual Review of Sociology 8* (1982): 237–262; J. Vanek, "Household Work, Wage, and Sexual Equality," in *Women and Household Labor,* Sarah Fenstermaker Berk, ed. (Beverly Hills, CA: Sage, 1980).

22. Dianna M. DiNitto, "Drunk, Drugged, and on the Job," in Gould and Smith, *Social Work in the Workplace,* 75–95.

23. Cited in Judy Winkelpleck and Michael Lane Smith, "Identifying and Referring Troubled Employees to Counseling," in Gould and Smith, *Social Work in the Workplace,* 45.

24. Arthur Kornhauser, *Mental Health of the Industrial Worker* (New York: Wiley, 1965).

25. Bertram Brown, "Foreward," in *Mental Health Care in the World of Work,* Hyman J. Wiener, Shiela H. Akabas, and John J. Sommer, eds. (New York: Association Press, 1973), 11.

26. Barry Bluestone, "Deindustrialization and Unemployment in America," H. Craig Leroy, "The Free-Market Approach," and "Introduction," in *Deindustrialization and Plant Closure,* Paul D. Staudohar and Holly E. Brown, eds. (Lexington, MA: Lexington Books, 1987), 4, 17, xviii–xix.

27. A. W. Phillips, "The Relation between Unemployment and the Rate of Change of Money Wage Rates in the United Kingdom, 1861–1957," *Economica,* New Series, 25 (November 1958): 283–299.

28. James D. Gwartney and Richard Stroup, *Macroeconomics: Private and Public Choice,* 3rd ed. (New York: Academic Press, 1982), 136.

29. Milton Friedman, "The Role of Monetary Policy," *American Economic Review 58* (March 1968): 10.

30. Leff and Haft, *Time Without Work,* 16–17.

31. Gilda Haas, *Plant Closures: Myths, Realities and Responses* (Boston: South End Press, 1985).

32. Barry Bluestone, "Deindustrialization and Unemployment in America," 6.

33. Adam Smith, *The Wealth of Nations* (New York: The Modern Library, 1936), 4–5. (Originally published in 1776.)

34. Briggitte Berger, "The Coming Age of People Work," *Change 9* (May 1976): 24–30.

35. Cited in Gordon E. O'Brien, *Psychology of Work and Unemployment* (Chichester, Australia: John Wiley and Sons, 1986), 27.

36. James O'Toole, ed., *Work in America,* Report of a Special Task Force to the Secretary of Health, Education, and Welfare (Cambridge, MA: MIT Press 1973), xv–xvi.

37. Christopher Orpen, "The Effects of Job Enrichment on Employee Satisfaction, Motivation, Involvement, and Performance: A Field Experiment," *Human Relations 32* (1979): 189–217.

38. Karl Marx, *Selected Writings in Sociology and Social Philosophy,* translated by T.B. Bottomore (New York: McGraw-Hill, 1964), 85–86.

39. Melvin Seeman, "Empirical Alienation Studies: An Overview," in *Theories of Alienation,* R. Felix Geyer and David R. Schweitzer, eds. (Leiden, Netherlands: Martinus Nijhoff, 1976), 265–305.

40. Talcott Parsons, "The Stability of the American Family System," in *Family, Socialization and Interaction Process,* Talcott Parsons and Robert F. Bales, eds. (New York: Free Press, 1955), 3–9.

41. John Scanzoni, *Opportunity and the Family* (New York: Free Press, 1970).

42. White House Conference on Families, *Listening to America's Families* (Washington, D.C.: U.S. Government Printing Office, 1980).

43. Karl Zinsmeister, "Hard Truths about Day Care," *Readers Digest* (October 1988): 91–93.

44. Glenna Spitze, "The Data on Women's Labor Force Participation," in *Women Working; Theory and Facts in Perspective,* Ann Helton Stromberg and Shirley Harkness, eds. (Mountain View, CA: Mayfield Publishing Company, 1988), 45.

45. Much of this section appeared as part of Philip R. Popple, "Social Work Practice in Business and Industry, 1875–1930," *Social Service Review 55* (June 1981): 257–269. © 1981 by The University of Chi-

cago. Reprinted with permission of the University of Chicago.

46. Mr. Marshall's report, February 29, 1922, Plymouth Cordage Co. (Plymouth Cordage Co. Files, Baker Library, Harvard University, Boston, MA).

47. Stuart D. Brandes, *American Welfare Capitalism: 1880–1940* (Chicago, IL: University of Chicago Press, 1970).

48. U.S. Bureau of Labor Statistics, *Health and Recreation Activities in Industrial Establishments, 1926,* Bulletin No. 458 (Washington, D.C.: U.S. Government Printing Office, 1928), 86.

49. Maud Nathan, "The Social Secretary," *World's Work 4* (May 1902): 2100; Mary R. Cranston, "The Social Secretary: An Opportunity for Employer and Employee to Understand Each Other," *Craftsman 10* (July 1906): 489.

50. U.S. Bureau of Labor Statistics, *Welfare Work for Employees* (Washington, D.C.: U.S. Government Printing Office, 1919), 119.

51. New York School of Social Work, "News Notes," *Alumni Magazine* (July 1921): 10–11.

52. William Tolman, *Social Engineering* (New York: McGraw-Hill, 1909), 51.

53. Daniel Bloomfield, *Labor Maintenance: A Practical Handbook of Employees' Service Work* (New York: Ronald Press, 1920), 16.

54. Fritz J. Roethlisberger, *Management and Morale* (Cambridge, MA: Harvard University Press, 1941), 26.

55. Irl Carter, "Social Work in Industry: A History and a Viewpoint," *Social Thought 1* (Winter 1977): 7–17.

56. Michael Lane Smith, "Social Work in the Workplace: An Overview," in *Social Work in the Workplace; Practice and Principles,* Gary M. Gould and Michael L. Smith, eds. (New York: Springer, 1988), 7.

57. Harrison M. Trice and Mona Schonbrunn, "A History of Job Based Alcoholism Programs," in *Employee Assistance Programs: A Basic Text,* Fred Dickman, B. Robert Challenger, William G. Emener, and William S. Hutchison, Jr., eds. (Springfield, IL: Charles C Thomas, 1988), 9–47.

58. Bradley Googins and Joline Godfrey, *Occupational Social Work* (Englewood Cliffs, NJ: Prentice-Hall, 1987), 23.

59. Michael Lane Smith, "Social Work in the Workplace: An Overview," 7.

60. Paul A. Kurzman, "Industrial Social Work (Occupational Social Work)," in National Association of Social Workers, *Encyclopedia of Social Work,* 18th ed. Vol. 1 (Silver Spring, MD: NASW, 1987), 900.

61. Kurzman, "Industrial Social Work," 900.

62. Paul Kurzman, "Industrial Social Work," 900–901; originally in Sheila H. Akabas and Paul Kurzman, "The Industrial Specialist: What's So Special?" in Akabas and Kurzman, *Work, Workers, and Work Organizations: A View From Social Work.* ©1982, pp. 201–202. Reprinted by permission of Prentice-Hall, Inc., Englewood Cliffs, NJ.

C·H·A·P·T·E·R

fourteen

Housing and Homelessness

Hank Beal stares morosely at the door to the Columbus, Ohio, Homeless Families Shelter. It's 2:00 PM and the shelter won't open until 5:00. In the meanwhile, his two daughters, Sonya and Susan, play in the school yard across the street—the closest they've been to a school in four weeks. A month ago Mr. Beal, divorced from his wife, moved up to Columbus from Nashville, Tennessee, where he'd been laid off from his construction job. The family came to Columbus with a job lined up and temporary arrangements to live with a cousin and her family. But the job fell through at the last minute and after two weeks the cousin's landlord ordered the extra family out of her small apartment. Mr. Beal's savings covered only one week's stay in a motel. After a discouraging five days of sleeping in the family car, Mr. Beal has reluctantly decided to move with his children to a crowded shelter for the homeless. He continues to look for work, but finds it difficult to shake a sense of disorientation and powerlessness.

Kate is an intelligent and independent young woman with a good job. She is also a wheelchair user. Her life is full of too many curbs and stairways and too few ramps and elevators. In order to cook for herself, she had to have her apartment kitchen redesigned with lower counters and appliances. With members of the local Center for Independent Living and other advocacy groups, she had to picket the city transportation department in order to get buses with lifts, so that she could take a bus to and from work, shopping, and recreation like other people.

Errol is an intelligent and independent young man who does not have a good job. He'd like to find one. Growing up in public housing wasn't easy. His mother's salary barely covered rent and food. The hallways, playgrounds, and streets provided daily opportunities to become a victim of crime (or to become a criminal). There was never enough heat in the winter and the elevator rarely worked. Against great odds, he graduated from high school. But his large, big-city neighborhood has very few jobs to offer. He must travel two hours by bus and subway to find any employment opportunities. Some of his friends said he was a fool to stay in school when he could make much better money selling "crack" for the local drug runners. He's beginning to think they were right.

Ella has maintained a keen mind and vigorous body throughout her seventy years of life. She has no trouble cooking for herself or maintaining the inside of the large, old house in which she raised her family, but the exterior repairs are a problem. Most of her old neighbors have moved away. Young families cannot afford to buy houses in the neighborhood because of high mortgage rates. Other old houses around her have been divided into apartments and their absentee landlords are allowing them to run down. She can no longer drive because of her poor eyesight. There is no public transportation in her area, but the grocery store, the shopping mall, the doctor's office, the library, the Cinema Six, and most of her friends are beyond walking distance. She doesn't need a nursing home, and the "retirement village" apartment complex is on the edge of town where she would be even more isolated than she is now.

Mary Ann is a single parent with two small children. Apartments near the center of the city where she works as a secretary are either too expensive (costing over 30

This chapter was co-authored by Robert D. Leighninger, Jr. and Leslie Leighninger.

percent of her salary) or run down and dangerous, so she lives half an hour away and commutes by car. There is no day care center near her office or her apartment. She takes her children to her cousin, who is also half an hour away, but in a different direction. The three-way commute leaves little time or energy for cooking, but convenience foods and fast foods are a strain on the budget. She finds herself short-tempered with the children and hits them when they misbehave. Guilt, anger, and frustration are daily companions.

Bill and Jennifer live in a distant suburb. Bill is a young executive who often must work late. Jen, an occupational therapist, has chosen to stay at home with their three children. She spends a good part of her day chauffeuring them to schools, lessons, soccer practices, choir rehearsals, and other events in their active lives. She would like to work part-time, but cannot find a position close enough to home. She likes her house and garden; its only problem is its distance from everything else. She has no contact with her former colleagues, and some days pass without a single adult conversation. Bill comes home late, sometimes after the children have gone to bed. He regularly must miss school plays and soccer games. He envies Jen's regular involvement with the children; she envies his opportunities to grow and be rewarded in his chosen profession. Sometimes the envy becomes resentment, and quarrels start over insignificant things.

DEFINITIONS OF THE PROBLEM

Homelessness is a nightmare for increasing numbers of Americans. It is the most recent and dramatic sign of the difficulties we are having in providing shelter, a basic human need, to all citizens. Unfortunately, it is not the only problem with the way Americans are housed. Even more unfortunately, social workers have paid little attention to these problems.

Housing, like the weather, is something we tend to take for granted. It's there, like it or not; there's not much we can do about it. Social workers usually confront only the most dramatic housing problems: babies bitten by rats or old people dying of heatstroke because they are afraid to open their windows. They rarely consider how the availability of decent housing and the way it is designed and distributed can cause problems or make existing problems (jobs, health, or education) worse.

Housing conditions can spawn contagious diseases (a fact that brought about the first government intervention in housing), traumatic injuries (children falling out of windows that have loose screens), and death (whole buildings burned because of faulty wiring, gas leaks, or overloaded space heaters). Housing conditions can encourage crime (insecure entrances, dark hallways, or lack of windows to allow observation of public areas). They can also adversely affect a child's psychosocial development (by lack of stimulation or its opposite—chaos, lack of privacy, or lack of basic security). Housing can strain family and marital relationships to the breaking point (too many people in too few rooms, or too much of the family income needed to cover rent or mortgage payments).

There is a further problem of housing that is even more subtle. Americans tend to think of home as a place to get away from the world: a haven, or a castle ("be it ever so humble"). Perhaps this is why we so often ignore the fact that our homes may lack important links with the rest of the world. Housing isolates and segregates people as often as it unites them. It separates them from family members and friends who can help them and from services they need to sustain life. Although some aspects of housing involve problems of dependence, most of them involve interdependence.

Thus, housing becomes a social welfare problem (1) when there is not enough of it; (2) when it is too expensive for people to afford; and (3) when its design, location, or quality cause problems for those who live in it. The problem is complicated by the fact that housing can be seen both as a basic right to which all are entitled and as a commodity that is bought like other things in the marketplace. As we will see, these two perspectives are frequently in conflict and lead to different solutions to housing problems.

Housing is not like the weather. We can understand the complex forces that have produced it and we can change it. Let us begin with a look at the variety of actors involved in the field of housing.

Builders

Home building is a labor-intensive industry. Traditionally, most home builders have been relatively small, local businesses because it is expensive to transport materials long distances. Building is a seasonal occupation in most parts of the country. It is also very sensitive to changes in the economy; if interest rates go up or wages go down, fewer people can buy homes.

Since World War II, more large home-building companies have entered the market. They are able to cut their costs by building many identical houses on large tracts of cheap suburban land. They have achieved further economies by prefabrication and by using their own raw materials and transportation. Their size is also an advantage in persuading local municipalities to provide the necessary services for these tracts and in lobbying all levels of government for favorable tax and subsidy policies. Their main representative is the National Association of Home Builders. This group, like the organizations representing bankers, realtors, and insurance companies, makes major financial contributions to political campaigns and is highly influential in local, state, and federal policymaking.[1]

Developers

Developers coordinate the acquisition of land and they arrange for it to be used in new ways. They recruit investors, arrange for bank loans, plan the use of the land they acquire, and hire builders to execute the plans. Often they re-sell what is built to still other investors. Part of their plans may involve houses, apartment buildings, and condominiums, but a variety of other constructions are likely to be involved, including office buildings, shopping centers, parking lots, and industrial parks. Sometimes these developments are carefully planned to accommodate the varied interests of the people who will use these new facilities as well as the impact the developments will have on existing neighborhoods around them. Will nearby neighborhoods be disrupted by noise and traffic? Will there be enough parking? Will water supplies be adequate? What has to be torn down to make room for the development? Will people and businesses be displaced? Sometimes these considerations are inadequately planned for or ignored.

Some cities and states have laws and ordinances to regulate what builders and developers can do. Some do not. Zoning, which specifies certain uses for certain areas, is a very common method of regulation. Zoning can forbid commercial activities in some residential areas, it can require a minimum number of parking spaces for new businesses or apartments, and it can discourage the cutting up of single-family houses into apartments. Some cities, like Houston, have no zoning.

Developers, like large builders (who are sometimes also developers themselves) have considerable political clout because of their ability to provide jobs and to make large profits for their investors. They use this power to insure the cooperation of local governments in the provision of rezoning, services, and often tax breaks.

Bankers

Most people cannot afford to pay the entire cost of a house at the time of purchase, so they must borrow money in order to become homeowners. Banks lend the money and earn interest on their investments. A special type of bank, the savings and loan, came into existence to meet this need. Banks are also important in the maintenance of houses because they provide loans for home repair and improvement.

Bankers, like builders, are interested in housing as a commodity, as something to be exchanged. They profit from the exchange. Homeowners may share that perspective because they too will profit if the market value of the house appreciates. But they are also concerned that the house be safe and comfortable, and that it otherwise meet their shelter needs. This "use value" is different from, and sometimes at odds with, the "exchange value" of the house.

If the homeowner cannot continue to make the mortgage payments, the bank will become the owner of the home. This fact requires banks to make judgments about both the abilities of a borrower to make the payments and the quality and resale value of the house. In making these judgments, bankers may be influenced by biases against African Americans, women, old houses, ultra-modern houses, or inner city neighborhoods. It is often difficult to separate these general biases from judgments about the worth of an individual buyer or house. Such biases are often felt to be based on sound business practice. However, if bankers systematically refuse to lend to buyers of a certain group or a certain neighborhood, for whatever reason, this has important consequences; it usually guarantees the decline of the neighborhoods affected. A refusal to loan money to certain geographic areas is known as *red-lining* and is now prohibited by federal law.

Bankers also carry considerable weight in local politics because of their control of business and home loans. They are represented at the national level by the American Bankers Association, the Mortgage Bankers Association, and other organizations.

Insurance Companies

A house is a major investment for individuals and banks, and it must be protected from destruction by fire, flood, or storms. Insurance companies provide that protection for a fee. The fees are set based on their judgment of the risk and profit offered by a particular homeowner, house, or neighborhood. Like bankers, insurance executives can be influenced in their judgments by a variety of biases. They too can accelerate the decline of a neighborhood by refusing to insure buildings in it. This means buyers can't get mortgages, and it is another form of red-lining.

Government

Federal, state, and local governments have been heavily involved in housing for more than a century. This involvement has benefited a variety of parties, often private developers.

Governments usually provide the roads, sewers, and electrical and water connections to new housing tracts and businesses. Governments make this investment in the belief that the development will provide jobs for residents and because the new residents will increase the tax base. Of course, this will be offset by tax breaks that are sometimes granted to encourage developers. Recently, cities like Cleveland have begun to question whether the tax breaks demanded by developers are a good investment. They may actually outweigh any financial benefit to the city the development may bring.

In some areas, development is highly profitable, and it does not need to be encouraged. In these cases, the process is reversed and governments can get help or concessions from developers. In some cities, builders of luxury condominiums are required to either build or contribute to the building of low-income housing.

The federal government has a very prominent role in encouraging homebuilding and homeowning by providing low-cost, below market mortgage loans. By allowing the deduction of the interest on mortgage payments from income tax, it also provides a huge subsidy to homeowners. The size of the subsidy increases directly with the size of the mortgage, so the wealthy benefit much more than the middle-income owner.

Governments, especially the federal government, may also build subsidized dwelling units and attempt to prevent discrimination against minorities in the housing market. As we shall see, the federal government's involvement in many of these activities has declined dramatically in recent years.

City governments, like private organizations, often need to act in concert on the national level and to lobby the federal government. The National League of Cities, formed in 1924, acts as an advocate for its members in Washington and makes proposals on national urban policy.

Realtors

Most people who buy houses do so through real estate agents. These people connect buyers with sellers and they receive a commission, usually based on the sale price of the house, as payment for their service. Realtors and their agents can "steer" buyers by showing them only houses in certain neighborhoods. Steering can reinforce racial segregation (by showing black buyers only houses in black neighborhoods and vice-versa) and neighborhood decay (by not showing old houses in inner city neighborhoods). Racial steering is illegal by federal law, but proving its occurrence is difficult. As with bankers and insurance executives, it is often hard to know to what extent prejudice enters this process and to what extent it is driven by pure financial consideration. Because the agent's commission is based on the price of the house, showing expensive houses in expensive neighborhoods is in the realtor's interest.

Local boards of realtors are usually active in politics, particularly in zoning and school tax issues. They are represented in Washington by the National Association of Realtors, a powerful lobbying group representing over 800,000 members and 1,840 local boards.[2]

Landlords

Renting a home to others can be a service or a source of profit, or both. For a landlord who wants to maintain a house in good condition and benefit the neighborhood, renting can be risky. While the majority of renters take good care of their units, a lot of damage can be done in a very short amount of time by an irresponsible tenant. Landlords protect themselves by practices such as charging security deposits as well as the first and last month's rent at the time of occupancy. This can have the effect of making it impossible for a person with a low income and no savings to rent a home.

Landlords may also screen tenants carefully. This presents another opportunity for prejudice to enter the process. Landlords with only a few units cannot be prosecuted for discrimination.

Making a profit, or even breaking even, is not always easy for the responsible landlord. For those who do not care about the quality of the houses they own or the neighborhoods their houses are in, it is much easier to make a profit. Charging the highest rents the market will bear and neglecting repairs guarantees maximum profit. When the building has deteriorated to the point where no one will rent it or the city condemns it (something that can take quite a long time), it is abandoned. Abandonment can also occur when a landlord with limited resources cannot pay maintenance costs and taxes.

Homeowners and Renters

Homeowners and renters, as individuals, can have some effect on the quality of their housing. They can maintain and improve it or they can allow it to decay. But much of what happens to their housing is outside of their immediate control. Even homeowners who want very much to keep their houses in good repair may be prevented from doing so. Older people on fixed incomes may not be able to maintain large old houses without help. Families with low to middle incomes who must spend 40 to 50 percent of their salaries on mortgages may have nothing left over for repairs.

Homeowners with the resources to rehabilitate old houses have been an important force in recent housing changes. Middle- and upper-income buyers have returned to inner city neighborhoods in many cities because of the appeal of older houses, the convenience of central location, and the boredom of the suburbs. They have often been able to buy the large older houses for very little money and thus have been able to afford the extensive repairs often necessary. If they do some of the work themselves ("sweat equity"), the process of rehabilitation is less expensive. This process has both benefits and costs to the housing market, which will be discussed later.

Community Groups

Neighborhoods of all types and income levels can organize neighborhood associations to further their interests. One important purpose can be simple socializing: providing opportunities for people to get to know each other. But most neighborhood groups have a larger agenda: dealing with burglars or a "crack house," getting their share of community services like street lights or garbage pick-ups, maintaining the quality of the local school, combatting "red-lining," providing information, or planting flowers.

Because builders and developers are usually able to secure the cooperation of local governments, it is often neighborhood organizations that mobilize opposition to projects that may threaten resident interests: a shopping center that will triple traffic through the neighborhood, a fast-food restaurant that will increase litter, a factory that will level an entire neighborhood, or lights at Chicago's Wrigley Field. (They also may fight for less noble causes like opposing group homes for people with disabilities.) Community groups don't always win against the developers or city halls, but their efforts can result in modifications of a project and can encourage developers to plan more carefully on the next project.

Advocacy Organizations

There are a number of advocacy groups which promote community interests and housing concerns on the local, state, and national levels. In New York City, homeless families work through the group "Parents on the Move" to lobby local officials for permanent housing. The Chicago Coalition for the Homeless promotes state legislation to provide shelters. State welfare rights organizations, formed in the 1960s to address the problems faced by welfare recipients, have now moved into the housing arena. Increasingly, those interested in organizing the poor are using housing as a mobilizing issue.

On the national level, National People's Action speaks for the social and physical preservation of neighborhoods. The Community for Creative Non-Violence, a former antiwar group, was transformed by the late Mitch Snyder, a housing activist, into an organization which advocates for the homeless. The group has supported legislation such as the Affordable Housing Act, which is aimed at increasing the nation's stock of low income housing. The National Coalition for the Homeless is a federation of local advocacy groups. The National Union of the Homeless organizes homeless people to advocate for themselves, and it provides job training as well.

Research

An important role in the housing system, which is often overlooked, is that played by people who collect information about housing. This has been particularly important to individuals with an interest in housing reform. Housing surveys have provided the evidence which convinced politicians and policymakers that something had to be done. Until recently, the federal government collected information about the condition of the nation's housing stock in an Annual Housing Report. As part of its withdrawal from housing, the Reagan Administration decided to produce the report every two years.

A CLOSER LOOK

The Loss of Poletown

In Spring of 1980, the residents of the Detroit community known as Poletown learned that General Motors had delivered an ultimatum to the Detroit city government: give up 500 acres within the city so that GM could build an auto plant, or else lose two existing GM plants. With no input from the Poletown community, the city decided that the northern third of the area, about sixty square blocks, would be taken by eminent domain and given to GM as a plant site.

Poletown, first settled in the 1870s, was Detroit's original settlement area for Polish-Americans. It lies on the border between the city of Hamtramck, also a Polish area, and Detroit. In the early 1980s, Poletown was a stable working-class neighborhood of single-family homes, which were occupied not only by Poles but also by newer immigrants from Albania, the Philippines, Yugoslavia, and Yemen, as well as by African Americans. At the time of GM's demand, the community was actively involved in commercial revitalization and rehabilitation of senior citizen housing.

Once the plans to raze the area became known, Poletown residents and neighborhood organizations fought the city's decision in the courts and through demonstrations and picketing at GM headquarters. The city and GM argued that the new plant would bring needed jobs to the surrounding communities. The defenders of Poletown countered that little hard evidence was available about the number of new jobs. Hamtramck officials contended that the plant was necessary to keep their city from dying; because one-third of the plant site was on Hamtramck land, their city stood to gain one-third of the taxes paid by the new factory.

Poletown residents were unable to change the joint decision of business and government to build the new plant. In the end, some 3,500 residents were displaced. Fifteen hundred homes, sixteen churches, over one hundred forty businesses, two schools, and a hospital were demolished. While those owning homes and businesses were reimbursed for their losses, and residents received relocation allowances, a major part of an established community was destroyed.

Sources: Richard Hodas, "Neighborhood and Factory Could Coexist," and Corrine Gilb, "Detroit Must Move Forward," *Historic Preservation 33* (January/February, 1981): 47–49.

This practice was continued under George Bush. Producing data less often saves money, of course, but it also makes it more difficult to know what is happening to the quality of American housing and what effects the government's policies have had.

STATISTICAL PICTURE OF HOUSING

The most dramatic figures on housing in the last few years relate to the continuing phenomenon of homelessness in the United States. The problem has been noted in national and regional newspapers, weekly newsmagazines, and even such family magazines as *Better Homes and Gardens*. Estimates of the number of homeless persons in the nation vary widely, from 350,000 (a U.S. government figure) to 3 million (as assessed by the National Coalition for the Homeless). Exact figures are difficult to establish. People "without a fixed abode" are not always visible in our society. Two attempts at a more thorough count of the homeless illustrate these measurement problems. In 1987, the Urban Institute, a nonprofit policy organization, conducted the first national survey of the homeless. The study focused on homeless persons who used shelters and other services in 20 large cities of the U.S. The Institute extrapolated from its findings to reach a figure of 229,000 "service-using homeless" in cities over 100,000. In a further projection to the entire country, the study estimated that some 600,000 people were homeless during the month of the survey. Since these figures constitute projections based on a particular segment of the homeless, the Institute suggested caution in their use.[3]

The Census Bureau attempted its first national survey of the homeless in 1990; its results (230,000 homeless counted in a single night's study) have been criticized as reflecting only a portion of the total. The Census Bureau relied on counts of people in shelters and on the streets on a cold March night. Advocates and some local officials have argued that not all shelters were included and that many homeless individuals slept in their cars or hid elsewhere while the census was taking place. Even if all shelters had been surveyed, only one segment of the homeless would have been reached. By focusing primarily on shelter occupancy as an indicator of homelessness, one can even suggest, as did a recent writer in *Newsweek,* that the total number of homeless in the United States is diminishing.[4]

There are, of course, political overtones to estimating the extent of homelessness in the United States. Groups which are committed to helping the homeless might be inclined to overestimate their number. On the other hand, an administration trying to curtail social programs might not want to expose the dimensions of the housing problem. Yet most observers agree that the number of homeless people rose steadily in the 1980s and continues to constitute a problem in the 1990s.

Traditionally, the "typical" person without a home has been presumed to be a single male, often with drug or alcohol problems. More recently, the popular image of the homeless has broadened to include mentally ill persons discharged from state hospitals and "bag ladies" ("strange" older women roaming the streets of large cities, carrying all their belongings in large shopping bags). However, the actual characteristics of today's homeless population differ from this popular picture. It is true that a sizeable portion—from one-fifth to one-third—have suffered mental illness at some point in their lives (although one can argue that lack of housing in itself contributes to mental difficulties). About a quarter of the homeless may be substance abusers. Yet despite the picture of the homeless as a single, older, addicted to alcohol or drugs, and often mentally ill, 30 to 40 percent of America's homeless are families with dependent children. This group is, in fact, the fastest growing segment of the homeless population. Many of these are minority families, and 80 percent are single families headed by women. As many as half a million children may now lack a stable roof over their heads.[5]

Of those urban homeless who use shelters and meal services, most are male. (Most cities still lack adequate shelters for families.) Over half are African American or other minorities, and about half are between the ages of 31 and 50. The majority have been without a job for a long time. However, it is estimated that among the total number of homeless, about one in four have jobs. Another large proportion were employed in the recent past.[6]

Not all homeless people, then, are the long-term destitute. Many have their health and family supports; some even have jobs. What most lack is affordable housing, that is, housing that fits within their incomes. As real incomes have stagnated or dropped in the 1980s and 1990s, housing costs have risen. The widening gap between salary levels and housing costs has been particularly devastating for those at the lower end of the income scale. Many of these are renters. In 1970, the national median percentage of income paid for rent was 20 percent. By 1987, the median percentage had risen to 29 percent. Low-income families who rented were paying, on average, 66 percent of their income on housing. Not just people in the very lowest income bracket have suffered, however. A recent study found that in 1987, 42 percent of all renters were "shelter poor"—that is, they paid so much on housing that they did not have enough money left over for basic necessities.[7]

As rents increase, financial loss caused by sudden illness or unemployment can push individuals and families "over the edge" and out into the streets. In the Washington, D.C. area, one young family of four began its slide toward homelessness when the father broke his leg playing football with friends and lost his job driving a van for a printing company. His wife, who had missed some time at work because their car was in the shop, came down with the flu and was fired from her position as a mailroom supervisor at a local company. With no savings to help pay the rent on their $385 a month apartment, they were evicted. After a year of doubling up with friends and staying in cheap motels, the couple and their two children ended up in a family shelter. Both have since found part-time minimum wage jobs, but their combined salaries won't cover the costs of another apartment.[8]

The problem of homelessness has been made worse by the loss of low-income housing units over the last ten years. One type of housing, "single room only" residential hotels, or SROs, has typically served low-income single people in large cities. In the late 1970s, such hotels began to be torn down to make way for more lucrative upper-class housing or commercial development. Chicago, for example, lost nearly two-thirds of its SRO units between 1977 and 1987. At the same time, conversion to condominiums, abandonment, demolition, arson, and other factors have contributed to the loss of low-income dwelling units in general, including apartments for families. As many as half a million low-income units have disappeared annually in recent years. In New York City, there were over 60 percent fewer apartments renting for under $200 a month and 56 percent fewer renting for under $300 a month in 1987 than in 1981. Yet in 1987, the poorest two-fifths of the city's population could not afford to pay more than $250 a month.[9] (See Figure 14–1 on page 480.)

Little of this lost affordable housing is being replaced. In 1987, apartments renting for less than $350 accounted for only 5 percent of all new privately financed apartment construction. Public programs have failed to fill the gap. In past decades, the federal government countered low-income housing shortfalls through federal housing programs. Under presidents Ford and Carter, for example, 500,000 low-cost housing units were built. Under Reagan, the figure dropped to 17,000. In 1988, less than 10,000 units were under construction. Some cities are actually tearing down public housing, particularly high rise buildings that have been reduced by poor planning and lack of maintenance to delapidated structures plagued by crime. Even without reductions, public housing cannot meet the present need. In Washington D.C., 12,000 people were on the public housing waiting list in 1987. Officials projected a waiting period of seven years. In 1989, approximately 900,000 families were on waiting lists for the 1.4 million occupied units of public housing in the U.S.[10]

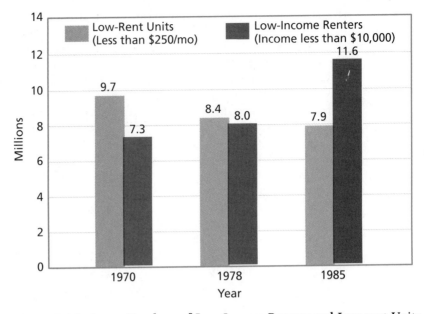

FIGURE 14–1   Numbers of Low-Income Renters and Low-rent Units
in the United States, 1970, 1978, and 1985

Source: Julee H. Kryder-Coe, Lester M. Salamon, and Janice M. Molner, *Homeless Children and Youth: A New American Dilemma* (New Brunswick, N.J.: Transaction Publishers, 1991), 187. © 1991 Transaction.

For families who suffer a loss of income, then, there is little low-income housing on which to fall back. And for low- to middle-income families in general, higher rents mean that other family expenditures must be skimped on and both parents must work. Families that cannot meet these rents may join the ranks of the homeless.

Rising homelessness, however, is only one factor in a complex and rapidly shifting housing picture. Homeownership, a basic feature of American society, is also undergoing change. While an impressive two-thirds of all Americans own their own homes, this figure has been dropping slightly each year since 1980. In that year, 65.6 percent of U.S. housing units were occupied by their owners. By 1989, the rate had fallen to 63.9 percent. Ownership rates among young Americans have dropped the most. For those aged 30 to 34, home ownership rates fell from 61.1 percent in 1980 to 52.6 percent in 1988. Rates of home ownership among 25- to 29-year-old household heads dropped from 43.3 percent to 36.2 percent in the same time period. (See Figure 14–2.) Because incomes have generally not risen as fast as housing costs, homeowners must spend greater and greater percentages of their salaries on home costs. First time home buyers, those who are hit the worst, now spend more than 31 percent of their incomes on mortgage payments alone, compared with 26 percent in the previous decade. Many younger families cannot even enter the housing market.[11] (See Figure 14–3 on page 482.)

Part of the problem has been the great increase in both mortgage interest rates and home prices. Older homes continue to appreciate and new home costs have risen far faster than inflation and salaries. In 1983, the average sales price of a new one-

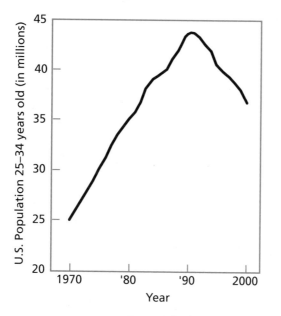

FIGURE 14–2   **Potential First-Time Home Buyers**

Source: Newsweek (January 25, 1989), Blumrich.

family home was $89,800. In 1990, the average new home cost $149,800; in some cities it is well over $200,000. In addition, despite the need for housing, new housing starts have fluctuated. In 1990, they dropped to their lowest point in eight years.[12]

Affordability and availability of housing are of course major facets of the housing picture for both renters and homeowners. Another, sometimes less tangible factor, is quality. Some elements of quality can be measured. A lack of plumbing, for example, now characterizes only 3 percent of American housing. But if other defects such as no kitchens, insufficient heating, and inadequate electrical systems are added, some 9 percent of American housing is still physically deficient. Rural areas fare the worst, and contain one-third of the nation's substandard units.[13] Other elements of quality—housing style, adaptability to special needs, such as those of the elderly or people with disabilities, accessibility of transportation, neighborhood atmosphere, caliber of local schools—are harder to measure, yet equally important.

One factor in housing quality, overcrowding, is an increasing problem. Because of housing shortages and expense, more and more families are doubling up. Over 3 million families now share housing, over twice the number in 1980. While it has been assumed that this phenomenon applies primarily to low-income families crowding into small apartments, crowding is also becoming a way of life in many suburbs. The serious lack of affordable housing in Long Island, New York, for example, has led to often illegal conversions of single-family homes to several family dwellings. Overcrowding not only puts a strain on the individuals and communities involved, but also constitutes a potential source of homelessness. Evictions for illegal doubling, or simply the difficulty of living in small, shared quarters for any length of time, have often precipitated a

Statistical Picture of Housing

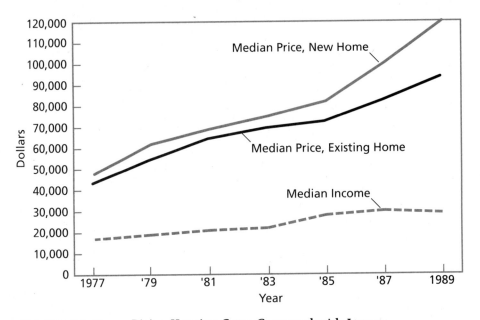

FIGURE 14–3 **Rising Housing Costs Compared with Income**

Sources: Adapted from *Better Homes and Gardens* (February, 1988), p. 40; *The New York Times* 26 March, 1989, Sec. E, p. 4; (Copyright © 1988/89 The New York Times Company. Reprinted by permission.); and U.S. Bureau of the Census, *Statistical Abstract of the United States: 1991* (Washington, D.C.: 111th Edition, 1991), 450.

family's move to a shelter for the homeless. In 1989, about 30 percent of families entering shelters in Philadelphia, and 71 percent doing so in New York City were previously doubled up.[14]

Certain populations have particular needs and problems related to housing quality. The elderly, for example, generally live on their own, and three-fourths remain in their own homes. Yet these homes tend to be located in the older, deteriorating parts of cities. In addition, older people often lack the resources to maintain home upkeep, and this can result in substandard housing conditions. Both the elderly and those with disabilities may require housing with special features, such as ramps and other adaptations. These are often not available. In addition, both groups face problems of affordability because many are on small, fixed incomes. About 33 percent of the elderly, for example, pay more than 30 percent of their income on housing.[15]

Minority status frequently affects housing accessibility, affordability, and quality. Despite the outlawing of discrimination in housing under the 1964 Civil Rights Act, residential segregation continues to be a major roadblock to the provision of adequate housing to all Americans. Housing experts measure neighborhood segregation and integration by what is called an "index of dissimilarity," or segregation index. The index looks at how closely the racial and ethnic makeup of a neighborhood matches that of the whole metropolitan area. For example, if 25 percent of the people in a given urban area are African American, and every neighborhood in the area is also 25 percent African American, the index for segregation would be 0, reflecting complete integration. If none of the area's neighborhoods had a mixture of African Americans and whites, the index would be 100, reflecting absolute segregation. Using this index, it has been found that the average level of segregation of African Americans and whites by block in the nation's twelve largest cities with a population of 100,000 or more was 81 percent in 1980. This figure constitutes only a 7 percentage point decline since 1950. A study of over 200 U.S. cities using 1990 census figures showed Detroit with the highest segregation index for African Americans and other minorities (83), followed by Cleveland (82), Gary/Hammond (79), and Buffalo (78). Lesser, but still serious levels of segregation exist for Hispanic Americans and Native Americans. The same study described the segregation index for Hispanic Americans, for example, as 63 in Los Angeles, 68 in New York City, and 65 in Chicago. Because segregation narrows the range of housing choices, African Americans and other minorities often pay more than whites for housing of comparable quality. In 1987, the median percentage of income spent on housing by African American and Hispanic American renters was 32 percent, while the median for all tenants was 29 percent. Moreover, homes occupied by African Americans have a much smaller value than those owned by whites. The median value of a home owned by an African American individual in 1989 was about $24,000 less than the median value of all homes in that year. In addition, African Americans and Hispanic Americans face discrimination both in renting homes and apartments and in obtaining home mortgages.[16] (See Figure 14–4.)

Minority status also has a strong impact on housing quality. Housing conditions for Native Americans and Hispanic Americans are among the worst in the country. Almost one-fourth of all Native American and Hispanic American households live in substandard housing. A number of studies also show discrepancies in quality between

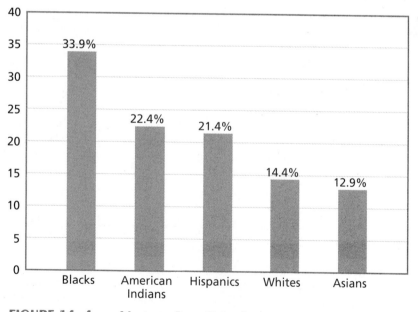

FIGURE 14–4   **Mortgage Loan Rejections**

Source: David Skidmore, "Regulators Cite Mortgage Discrimination," *Baton Rouge Morning Advocate* (22 October 1991), Sec. C., p. 1. Reprinted with permission of AP/Wide World Photos.

living conditions of whites and blacks. In 1980, almost 40 percent of all black owner-occupied units were 30 or more years old, compared to 35 percent for whites. Close to 16 percent of units rented by blacks lacked complete plumbing, but only 3.4 percent of those rented by whites did so. While housing conditions for African Americans have improved since 1980, the 1989 *American Housing Survey* still found that 18 percent of housing units occupied by African Americans had moderate to severe physical problems, compared to only 8 percent of total occupied housing units. Women of all races share similar problems. They pay large amounts of their incomes on housing, and stand a 20 percent chance of being inadequately housed.[17]

Given these broad scale problems in housing in America, what has been the level of government commitment to dealing with issues of accessibility, affordability, and quality? While never a major priority of the federal government, involvement in housing programs has diminished precipitously in recent years. As part of the Reagan administration's campaign to cut government expenditures, particularly in the area of social welfare, federal spending on housing dropped from $25 billion in 1981 to $8 billion in 1987. The Department of Housing and Urban Development had a budget equal to 7.4 percent of the total federal budget in 1978. In 1988, this figure had fallen to less than 1 percent. While federal spending on housing has increased somewhat under President Bush, the number of low-income households receiving federal housing assistance is still well under the figures for the late 1970s.[18]

Currently about 4 and a half million American families receive federal housing subsidies in some form (excluding mortgage interest rate deductions on income tax, a "hidden subsidy" which we will discuss later). These subsidies reach only about one in three low-income families. One of the most visible types of subsidies is public housing. Public housing projects house about 3.5 million people. Altogether, these units constitute less than 1.5 percent of the country's housing stock. State and local governments have attempted to fill some of the gap left by federal budget cuts, often in partnership with private corporations. Yet financing for these programs each year is counted in the millions, rather than in the billions the federal government used to spend on low-income housing.[19]

It is clear that we face a number of issues regarding housing. The most immediately pressing are housing shortages and the effects of residential segregation. However, ongoing issues of housing quality are also of concern. What lies behind these problems and issues? Why is affordable housing in such short supply? What factors affect the type and quality of housing available to Americans today? The following section examines these questions.

DYNAMICS OF HOUSING

Lack of Affordable Housing

The preceding statistics already tell much of the story behind the rise of homelessness in the United States. It is clear that homelessness has become a widespread phenomenon, affecting families as well as individuals, working- and middle-class people as well as low-income individuals, "normal" people as well as those with mental illness or addictions. This makes it apparent that the basic cause of homelessness is not the fault of the homeless, but a lack of affordable housing. This was the conclusion of a government committee in 1984:

> "The scarcity of low-income housing appears to be the main cause of homelessness," [reported] the House intergovernmental relations and human resources subcommittee after conducting extensive hearings on the homeless . . . "Poor people simply cannot afford the majority of available housing in the United States."[20]

Why this scarcity of affordable housing in a basically affluent society? Housing analysts Kim Hopper and Jill Hamberg argue that certain conditions gathered momentum in the 1970s and then erupted as the economy worsened and the housing market tightened in the early 1980s. The resulting rise in homelessness grew out of the coming together of a number of factors, especially the rise in housing costs and decline in incomes.[21]

Lower income levels and increases in housing costs are part of the overall economic picture of the 1970s through the 1990s. These years have witnessed the transformation from an industrial to a high-technology and service economy in the United States. In the 1970s, 38 million jobs in basic industry were lost. For many workers, this has meant a shift to newly created service jobs at lower wages, or part-time work. Recessions in 1979 and 1982 led to higher levels of unemployment. All these events increased people's vulnerability to homelessness, which began to spread in the early 1980s. Economic recovery in 1983 failed to counteract the phenomenon. (See Figure 14–5.) In part, this was because high levels of unemployment remained for certain population groups, such as African American males, and in certain areas of the country, such as the northeast "Rustbelt." In addition, the recovery aided some segments of the economy while bypassing others, particularly the poor. And while salaries have increased in the

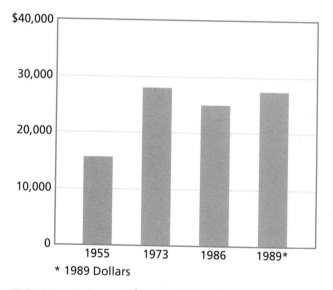

FIGURE 14–5   **Changes in Earnings 1955–1986**

*1989 Dollars

Source: Adapted from *The Washington Post Weekly Edition* (June 13–19, 1988), 7; U.S. Bureau of the Census, *Statistical Abstract of the United States, 1991* (Washington, D.C.: 111th Edition, 1991), 417.

Dynamics of Housing

last ten years, their real dollar value has fallen since the 1970s. Finally, the return of recession in the early 1990s has meant renewed problems with unemployment.[22]

In addition, government-funded income assistance levels have either decreased or stagnated, leaving recipients with less income available for housing. General assistance, social security, and SSI payments have not kept up with cost of living increases. There have been cuts in AFDC benefits as well as a general decline in the real dollar worth of AFDC payments. AFDC benefits are meant to cover housing as well as other expenditures, yet rarely do the grants enable families to pay for housing without using benefits intended to pay for food, clothing, and other necessities. In 35 states, the amount of the entire AFDC grant for a family of three is less than the fair market rent (a measure established by HUD) for a low-cost, two-bedroom apartment. Even where the state AFDC program includes specific shelter allowance, the money provided generally falls far short of prevailing rents. In New York City in 1987, for example, a family of four might have received a $280 housing allowance for apartments whose rents amounted to $400 or more.[23]

The rise of new populations needing shelter has added to the housing problem. Deinstitutionalization of people with mental illness and developmental disability in the 1970s increased the number of those seeking affordable places to live. Many of these individuals had no families or homes to which they could return. In addition, today's more stringent commitment policies mean that far fewer mentally ill people are admitted to mental institutions. With a lack of community facilities, the result for some is a life on the street. New immigration also affects the housing picture. Recent immigrants from Mexico, Central America, and East Asia often have difficulty finding shelter they can afford.

What we have just described is a growing number of people with limited resources available for housing. What brings this situation to crisis proportions is the lack of inexpensive housing in America today. Part of the problem is rising costs. Many of the materials used in housing construction are manufactured by large corporations with few incentives for cost control. Increases in interest rates, and rising costs of land and fuel also drive up house prices and rentals. Some people, especially builders, contend that local governments add to the scarcity and resulting high cost of land through tougher zoning laws and antigrowth policies. Others blame speculators, or individuals who buy and hold undeveloped land until they can sell it for inflated prices.[24]

At the same time that prices rise, much of the existing low-income housing disappears each year. In some cases, higher safety standards and stricter enforcement of building codes have meant the closing down of apartment buildings and other dwellings. In others, the decay of inner city neighborhoods has led to vandalism, arson, and abandonment. Neglect by landlords has contributed to this decay. Sometimes housing is demolished because of high maintenance costs or commercial development. In the 1960s and 1970s, urban renewal decimated much inner city housing stock; only part of this was replaced. Finally, developers and builders tend to construct or remodel dwellings into the type of housing that is most profitable—that is, housing for white, middle- and upper-income small family consumers. This intensifies the shortage of housing for larger families, minorities, and those with low incomes.

Another factor decreasing the supply of affordable housing is *gentrification,* or the displacement of low-income tenants by higher income individuals who buy and renovate older homes in run-down areas. Sometimes, as we noted earlier, these are people

Gentrification can bring new life to old neighborhoods, but often at the cost of increasing housing shortages.

who plan to live in the homes. But renovation is also carried out by developers, who re-sell the property at greatly increased prices. In a Chicago neighborhood full of poor immigrants, for example, a developer changed a dilapidated, 1892 three-story Victorian structure into a luxury home with a master bedroom suite and a walk-in wine cellar. She also converted two deteriorated graystone buildings containing thirty six single-room rentals into twelve luxury apartments. Each building will be sold for about $1,000,000.[25]

Reactions to gentrification are mixed. Some low-income residents, particularly the elderly, welcome what they see as a chance to revive a once-beautiful and viable, now run-down neighborhood. Individual renovators, who move into the homes they restore, are generally motivated by a love of old buildings and a desire to save structures with genuine historic significance. Renovation contributes to the economic revitalization of inner city neighborhoods because the new residents can support more stores, restaurants, and services. At the same time, however, low-income families are often forced out of the area by rising rents and home costs.

Beneath all these causes of the shortage of affordable housing exists an underlying dynamic: the tendency in the United States to view housing as a commodity rather than as a basic right. Although federal housing legislation since the 1940s has declared shelter to be a right of all citizens, the tendency, particularly in recent years, has been to think about housing in terms of its ability to produce a profit. When builders build to sell and each owner trades for profit in the marketplace, housing prices will tend to rise. One might argue that the laws of supply and demand would hold down prices; that is, that once there is an abundant supply of housing, sellers will no longer be able to attract high prices. However, high prices often exist even when housing supplies are adequate. The reasons behind this are complex and not entirely understood. Some analysts contend that the situation occurs because the housing market, particularly the rental market, is not truly competitive. The ownership of rental housing is often concentrated in a relatively small number of hands. These owners have the possibility of market control; they can raise rents without much competition from others. In addition, consumers of rental housing may not have a lot of choice in their decisions. Discrimination against minorities, families with children, or the poor can limit the possibilities of where they can rent. (However, discrimination against families was largely eliminated in 1989 when new federal rules prohibited "adult-only" housing except for strictly defined older adult complexes.) Finally, just as in the area of health care, consumers are to some extent a captive audience—housing is not something they can easily cut back on or go without.[26]

Profits, and concurrent high costs in housing, can also be bolstered by government intervention. As critics of current housing policy have noted, when housing policy is made in Washington, the process reflects the "interaction of the Administration and Congress on the one hand, and the various nationally organized interest groups on the other." Business interests are well represented and very influential in this process. The result is housing policies which operate, at least in part, to enhance "the profitability of the housing sector and of the business community as a whole."[27] Many of these policies are part of the federal tax structure. One example is the depreciation allowance, which is a tax break for owners of income producing property, allowing them to subtract a certain amount for depreciation from that income.

Residential Segregation

Minority status is also an important dynamic affecting housing price, availability, and quality. Discrimination against minorities, as we shall see, has been a significant factor in the history of housing in the United States. Its most obvious manifestation appears to be racial and ethnic residential segregation. There has been an ongoing debate among researchers, however, about the degree to which segregation is caused by socioeconomic factors, rather than by outright discrimination against minority groups. Some studies contend that factors such as income level or occupation explain much of the segregation existing in American communities. Other research contradicts this finding, presenting evidence that income differentials, for example, account for only a small amount of the segregated housing pattern. A solution to the debate seems to be emerging in recent reviews of the research, which conclude that while socioeconomic factors are important in the degree of segregation of ethnic groups, such as Hispanic Americans, these same factors are far less important in explaining the experience of African Americans. One study, for example, demonstrates that "whether measured in terms of education, income, or occupation, Spanish-white segregation declines unambiguously with increasing socioeconomic status."[28] Yet a review of the economic research on the causes of segregation of African Americans concludes that differences

> in black and white incomes account for only a small portion of segregation; a greater share of segregation seems to be accounted for by whites being willing to pay significantly more to live in all white neighborhoods than blacks are to penetrate them and by overt discrimination against blacks when they do try to enter white neighborhoods.[29]

Once Hispanic Americans and other ethnic groups rise in income, they are much more likely to be accepted into mainstream white society than are African Americans; in other words, skin color matters.

People trapped in segregated housing, particularly in the inner city, are likely to face overcrowding and poor housing quality. They may even pay more for this housing,

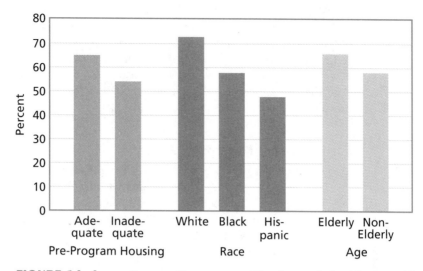

FIGURE 14–6   **Success Rates among Voucher and Certificate Holders**

Source: Mary Austin Turner and Veronica M. Reed, *Housing America* (Washington, D.C.: The Urban Institute, 1990), 8.

partly because they are a captive market. The federal government has done little in recent years to deal with housing discrimination and its effects. As the U.S. Justice Department has retreated from active civil rights enforcement, the amount of fair housing legal cases has declined. Also, one solution to the problem of the shortage of affordable housing—housing vouchers—flies in the face of existing segregation. Vouchers are government grants which low-income families can use on the open market to obtain better housing. African Americans with such vouchers may find it difficult to get landlords in white areas to accept them. A recent government study indicated that minority families looking for private housing for which they could use a voucher had a success rate of only 57 percent, compared to a nearly 75 percent success rate for white families.[30] Racial and other kinds of discrimination thus continue to add to our current housing problems. (See Figure 14–6.)

HISTORY OF HOUSING

One approach to the history of housing in America is to describe it as a reflection of social values. Writers like architectural historian Gwendolyn Wright view housing as embodying many images and attitudes in our society: ideas about gender roles, images of the ideal family, attitudes toward immigrants and African Americans, views about the role of government and the market, and beliefs about the nature of democracy. Housing can also be seen as an instrument of social control, that is, as a mechanism for maintaining a docile workforce, keeping women "in their place," or a race "in its place."[31] In addition, one can think about housing in terms of its relationship to other factors in the environment, such as health and employment. Social reformers dealing with problems in these and other areas have sometimes focused on changes in housing as the key to broader reform. Their story is an important piece in housing history. As we shall see, there is a certain degree of overlap between social reform and social control. Both proceed from the belief that if you structure housing, you can influence other aspects of people's lives as well. All of these themes will be interwoven as we trace the development of housing in the United States from colonial times to the present.

Early Housing Patterns in America

Ideas about religion, family, and the social order influenced housing in colonial America. The Puritans, for example, felt that buildings should reflect how God wanted them to live. They believed this included an orderly community with close, interacting families (partly so that family members could keep an eye on each other to stave off the influence of the Devil). Accordingly, they built fairly plain, wooden houses with one or two downstairs rooms in which all the family's daily living activities—cooking, eating, sewing, repairing tools, and reading Scripture—were conducted. No one was allowed to live alone, because all individuals were perceived to exist only in a social context. Homeless people, such as widows and orphans, were sheltered by other families.[32]

After the American Revolution, housing and community planning projected an image of equality in society. Plain, uniform, row houses in cities housed both craftsmen and wealthier merchants and professionals. These homogeneous buildings, along with simple rural homes and workers' cottages built by employers in milltowns, reflected the idea of the state as a collective of individual, more-or-less equal households.[33]

However, the ideal of equality expressed through housing was rarely realized. Increasingly, economic and social segregation became the norm. The pattern of uniform row houses remained in many cities, but middle-class row houses became more elaborate. By the 1820s, different classes and ethnic groups lived in different parts of the city. African Americans and the very poor were often shunted to the less desirable outskirts of an urban area.[34]

More and more housing, particularly workers' housing, was built on speculation, that is, by entrepreneurs who bought land and built houses to sell or rent rather than to live in themselves. With the rise of capitalism and the growth of cities in the early to mid-1800s, housing had become a commodity to be bought and sold for money. Housing thus reflected the growing value placed on a market economy. Only the more well-off could afford to buy their own housing, in part because mortgage financing as we know it today did not exist. By 1815, more than half the homes in America's larger cities were rented, generally by skilled craftsmen and unskilled laborers.[35]

While housing built on speculation was not necessarily of poor quality, various forces, including the profit motive, contributed to deficiencies in workers' dwellings. In the early 1800s, investors began acquiring larger and larger tracts, forcing up land prices and housing costs. As the United States industrialized, more and more people moved to the cities, leading to overcrowded housing conditions. The typical urban row house was only fifteen to twenty feet across. The backyard might allow room for a garden, some chickens, a pig, and a privy. In workers' areas, this space soon had to be shared with other families, as investors built additional houses in the back. Sometimes owners did this also, to house extended family in dwellings the tax collector might not see. Basements were rented out to the very poor. With the financial crises of the 1830s, houses built for one family were often subdivided. The standard of living for the worker declined, while that of the middle classes rose. Ironically, however, poor sanitation, noise, and lack of police protection plagued almost all neighborhoods in the early nineteenth century city. Residents had to put up with mud, open sewers, piles of horse manure, and the lack of municipal garbage collection.[36]

Housing conditions were also difficult for other groups in other localities. In the South, slaveholders used negative views about black culture, such as the idea that blacks were not bothered by pain and dirt, to justify the inferior quality of slave housing. Slave families usually lived in single-room dwellings with stark and poorly ventilated interiors. Housing was often used as a method of control by the plantation owner, with larger cabins for the overseers and favored slaves, and much poorer dwellings for the rest. Slaves resisted such oppression when they could. Black carpenters patterned slave homes after African dwellings where possible, using traditional construction techniques, but hiding them from slaveowners. To deal with overcrowding in the small cabins, slave families hung quilts or built partitions to provide a measure of privacy. Generally, however, home was not a haven for the black slave family.[37]

Beginning in the late 1700s, economic recessions increased poverty; this led to the formation of groups of wanderers, who traveled from place to place looking for work. As the earlier practice of sheltering widows and orphans in people's homes declined, they too joined the ranks of the homeless. At first, communities tried to deal with the problem through "settlement laws" imported from England. These laws forced vagrants to return to their original communities. When such laws failed, workhouses were built. By the mid-1800s, many of the people in jails and workhouses were skilled workmen whose numbers fluctuated with the availability of jobs.[38]

Housing Trends through the 1920s

Although they were not new, several housing patterns became prominent in nineteenth century and early twentieth century America. These included the city slum, the middle- and working-class suburb, and the company town.

The urban slum developed in the mid-1800s as poor immigrants from Ireland joined other impoverished groups crowded in cities like New York and Boston. Speculators responded to increased housing needs by constructing tenements, or multistory buildings built especially to house the poor. A typical design was the "railroad flat," which was a long and narrow, flimsily constructed building that might house twelve or more families. Only those rooms facing the street or the narrow back alley received direct light. Often a single backyard privy served all residents.[39]

These conditions prompted reformers to action. Physicians, charity workers, and concerned citizens saw slums as breeding grounds of poverty and disease. The Association for Improving the Conditions of the Poor (AICP) was a New York City-based charity organization founded in 1843. While AICP members believed that poverty stemmed in part from moral defects within individuals, they also saw crowded slums as contributing to laziness, crime, drunkenness, and sexual promiscuity. Like other reformers, AICP members also feared the effects the slum would have on the rest of the city. Epidemics and social unrest could spread beyond its borders. The AICP's solution to the problem was the "model tenement," which was a more spacious and sanitary building constructed by a socially minded private investor who was willing to limit profits. Other groups, like the New York Citizens' Association founded in 1864, promoted the resettlement of the poor to working-class cottages outside the city.[40]

Neither the model tenement nor resettlement proposals met with much success. An AICP-sponsored tenement delivered only a tiny financial return, and the building deteriorated quickly. Resettlement plans were hindered by the lack of good transportation systems to connect workers with jobs in the city. In the meantime, reformers did achieve the beginnings of government regulation of health and housing conditions. In New York in the late 1860s, lobbying on the part of reform groups led to the establishment of a Metropolitan Board of Health and the enactment of a local tenement house law (the first in the country). The law set fairly low standards, such as one privy for every twenty persons, and it was not well enforced. However, it served a symbolic value in accepting the community's right to limit the freedom of the tenement builder and the landlord.[41]

Legislation and model tenements, fears of epidemics and social unrest, and the desire to reform and help poor individuals through improving their dwellings continued to characterize attempts at urban housing reform through the turn of the century. (See Figure 14–7.) The growth of the slum proceeded dramatically as the "New Immigration" from Italy, Poland, Russia, and the Balkan countries flooded into New York, Chicago, Cleveland, and other metropolises in the 1880s and 1890s. Most of these immigrants were poor, unskilled laborers or subsistence farmers. Lacking the knowledge and

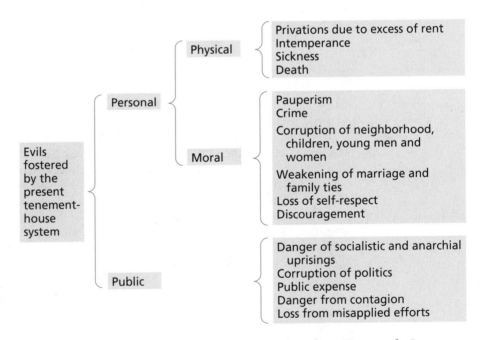

FIGURE 14–7 **"Evils of the Tenement" as Seen by a Nineteenth-Century Reformer**

Source: Marcus T. Reynolds, *The Housing of the Poor in American Cities* (College Park, MD: McGrath, 1893), 30.

resources to survive in rural areas, they remained in the cities, joining former countrymen in slum neighborhoods. Immigrant families often worked in their own homes, sewing garments and rolling cigars at piece-work wages. This added to the congestion of their living situations. In New York, 70 percent of the population lived in multiple-family dwellings by 1893. Four-fifths of these buildings were tenements, and almost all were privately owned and operated for profit.[42] (See Table 14–1.)

During this period, Jane Addams and others in the social settlement movement joined in the campaign to improve poor living conditions. Shocked by the crowding and filth in the slums around them, workers spoke of "garbage-strewn streets," "pale, dirty, undersized children," and sights such as the room on a hot summer day "crowded with scantily-clothed, dull-faced men and women sewing upon heavy woolen coats and trousers."[43]

In response to these experiences, settlement residents attacked the housing problem. One settlement worker surveyed housing conditions in Jersey City in 1902. As she gathered information, landlords threatened her and sometimes drove her away. However, when her results were published, the governor of the state was so impressed that he appointed a special tenement house commission to look into the problem. Other settlements also used studies to publicize deficient housing in order to gain public sympathy and an official response. Hull House, for example, prepared detailed maps and surveys of the tenements in its neighborhood. Through the efforts of settlements and other reform groups, Chicago got a tenement house ordinance in 1902.[44]

TABLE 14–1	Crowding in American dwellings in the 1890s	
Percentage of Population Hiring* Dwellings Having More Than 10 Occupants		**More than 20**
United States	13.59	—
New York	83.50	66.70
Chicago	49.18	16.63
Philadelphia	12.79	3.41
Brooklyn	56.65	25.70
St. Louis	36.26	10.14
Boston	47.80	13.93
Baltimore	14.14	2.55
Cincinnati	51.52	21.92
Buffalo	30.02	—
Newark	40.01	10.25
Jersey City	49.41	23.53
Providence	37.76	7.49

*"Hiring" means renting.

Source: Marcus T. Reynolds, *The Housing of the Poor in American Cities* (College Park, MD: McGrath, 1893), 18.

Many housing reformers at the turn of the century believed that laws defining minimum construction and sanitation standards would do much to solve the problem of the slum. A major accomplishment was the New York Tenement Law of 1901. This law, written by housing expert Lawrence Veiller, established strict standards dealing with fireproofing, ventilation, and overcrowding. The legislation was an improvement over the earlier New York housing code, in that standards were higher and more carefully enforced.[45]

Housing codes and legislation improved the situation to some degree, but they did not eliminate the bulk of slum housing. An alternative approach, the building of model tenements and other private housing schemes, continued through the early 1900s. In New York, reporter Jacob Riis was a major publicizer of the model tenement idea. Riis exposed the realities of life in the slum in gripping photographs and in books like *How the Other Half Lives,* which included chapters on "Cheap Lodging Houses," "The Down Town Back Alleys," and "Stale-Beer Dives." Riis was convinced that model tenements, built through private enterprise, were an important tool for dealing with the problems of the slum. He believed that many of these problems were caused by the shiftlessness and ignorance of the tenants themselves. The model tenement, then, with its improved living conditions and careful rules, could serve as a mechanism for improving the character of the people who lived there.[46]

Like the earlier AICP model tenements, these also failed. Two hundred were built in New York City between 1855 and 1905, a drop in the bucket compared to the 50,000 buildings put up by speculators in the same period. Moreover, the model housing proved to be a poor investment, rarely making even the 5 percent profit to which philanthropists were willing to limit themselves. This inability to build low-income housing that was even moderately profitable suggested the need to go outside the private market to find ways to house working people and the poor. Yet the reformers gave no consideration to the possibility of government-financed shelter. Along with most Americans, they saw public ownership as ideologically out of step with American values.[47]

While working families were at least housed, no matter how inadequately, wandering transient workers, now called "tramps," found little cheap housing as they moved from mine to harvest to factory—wherever a mobile labor force was needed. Economic downturns increased their numbers. At first they slept in almshouses and lodgings maintained by the police. But reformers, concerned about the "idle, dangerous tramp," promoted "anti-tramping" laws that outlawed vagrancy and replaced police lodgings with imprisonment. When this harsh measure proved ineffective, reformers helped to create public lodging houses with regulations and trained staff. The municipal lodging house and the rescue mission became the predominant forms of shelter for vagrants by the turn of the century. Neither was an adequate solution to the problem. Rescue missions required attendance at religious services and the lodging houses soon became squalid residential warehouses.[48]

While the urban poor lived in slums or public lodging houses, other trends developed for the more affluent. These included apartment living for the well-to-do in cities and a move to the idyllic home in the suburbs for the middle class. Migration out of the cities intensified in the 1870s. The suburbs began to be seen as an avenue of escape from the health hazards, social unrest, and vice of urban areas (a phenomenon which continues today). Development of public transportation, such as the street car, made it possible to commute to work and shopping in the city. The growth of building-and-loan associations enabled middle-class and more well-off working-class families to borrow money for mortgages.[49]

The suburban home was fast becoming the symbol of personal expression and middle-class status. It also represented the importance of the nuclear family, and particularly of that family pattern in which the father dealt with the demanding world of work and the mother provided a nurturing, private haven in the home. This "cult of domesticity," as historians now call it, stressed the importance of women providing a strong moral and educational influence within their families. The suburban home, protected from the evil influence of the city, seemed the perfect setting in which to do this.[50]

The company town represented another, less congenial counterpart to city living, this time aimed at the working class. Beginning with the early nineteenth-century textile mill industry in New England and the South, manufacturers built factories and rental housing for workers in areas away from the congested and supposedly corrupting cities. The houses, while small, were meant to accommodate six to ten people. Families generally took in boarders to help pay the rent. Despite the cramped conditions, inadequate sanitation facilities, and poor ventilation of these houses, factory owners felt the regular rows of identical cottages presented an organized system which would inculcate middle-class values in the minds of employees and their families. They also built dormitories for young working-class women; in these dormitories the lives of residents were strictly regulated.[51]

The planned industrial communities of the early 1900s were expanded versions of the earlier mill towns. Factory owners hoped that the provision of housing and other amenities would keep workers content, make them more efficient, and prevent the rise of unions. Some industrialists built large communities for their employees, complete with churches, schools, libraries, and social facilities. They hired welfare secretaries (an early version of the industrial social worker) to act as moral police, recreational planners, and counselors for their tenants. Some company towns were reasonably democratic. Others, like that erected by George Pullman of the Pullman railway car company, were autocratically run. These fit a popular slogan among manufacturers: "A Housed Labor Supply is a Controlled Labor Supply."[52]

The idea of planned communities, which was pioneered in company towns, was utilized in a different way for the middle class in the early 1900s. Planned residential areas, particularly in the suburbs, were seen as ideal environments for providing small-town virtues and urban amenities. Developers, municipal zoning boards, and homeowners' associations joined in the movement. Both the appearance of the houses and the social class of the homeowners were carefully regulated. To ensure homogeneity, "restrictive covenants" were developed in the 1920s. These prevented the sale of property in particular areas to Asians, Jews, or African Americans.[53]

Restrictive covenants were upheld by the courts. A more violent way of enforcing segregation existed in working-class and poorer neighborhoods in the big cities. In Chicago, for example, blacks moving in from the South were relegated to a congested "black belt" in the city's south side. When they attempted to escape deterioration and crowding by moving into white neighborhoods, they met with furious opposition. Whites, particularly those in close-knit ethnic neighborhoods, countered the mobility of blacks by bombing their homes and attacking them in the streets. Violent race riots

Pullman

George Pullman's company made railroad sleeping cars. In 1880 he began construction on a new factory south of Chicago which would include a complete town for his workers. He may have been inspired by a visit to Saltaire, a town near Bradford, England, that was built by woolen manufacturer Titus Salt. Salt believed that his workers would be more productive if they had good working conditions and decent housing. Pullman seems to have been more influenced by the Railroad Strike of 1877. He thought that by moving his workers out of the city, he would be "removing them from the feeling of discontent and desire for change which so generally characterize the American Workman."

Pullman's town looked very impressive to visitors. They saw a broad town square surrounded by substantial buildings. A hotel with seventy rooms welcomed them. A church of shining green stone promised spiritual rectitude. A three-level shopping arcade (a prototype of our suburban malls) included a theater, library, and offices. There was a Market Square with indoor and outdoor stands. And, of course, there was housing for almost 12,000 people.

Like George Cadbury, another English industrialist who built a planned community, Pullman did not allow bars or the sale of alcohol in his town. There was a bar in the hotel for visitors and company executives, but the price of drinks assured that even a worker who was bold enough to enter could not afford to stay. Cadbury felt that if he provided his workers with good houses and ample gardens, they would stay at home and not need the diversion of the local pub. Pullman's plan was much less generous with gardens.

The houses nearest the square were attractive and well-equipped, but a few blocks away there were tenements with one water faucet for every five families. Further out were 14 feet × 20 feet wooden structures called "cottages" by the company and "dens" by everyone else. There were no streets, sidewalks, gas or sewer connections; and the communal water faucets were outside.

Salt and Cadbury hoped their planned communities would uplift the physical and moral lives of their workers and enhance their productivity. Pullman expected more immediate benefits: the town was to make a 6 percent profit. Rents on an average house were $15.00 to $17.50 per month; water, gas, fire protection, and garbage removal were additional. This was all subtracted from the worker's paycheck. The average daily wage was $1.84. One worker reported coming home with a check for eight cents after two weeks' work.

All community space, even the church, had to return a profit. For two years after it was built no congregation could afford to rent the church. There was a charge to use the library. The school, named after Pullman, was regarded as excellent, but the taxes supporting it were higher than any of the fourteen surrounding school districts.

In response to the financial panic of 1893, Pullman laid off thousands of workers and cut wages by 25 to 50 percent. He did not, however, adjust rents or fees. The company continued to pay 8 percent to stockholders and enjoyed a profit of $25 million. The famous Pullman Strike of 1894 followed.

Sources: William Adelman, *Touring Pullman: A Study in Company Paternalism,* 2nd ed. (Chicago, IL: Illinois Labor History Society, 1977); Stanley Buder, *Pullman: An Experiment in Industrial Order and Community Planning, 1880–1930* (New York: Oxford University Press, 1967); Walter Stranz, *George Cadbury, 1839–1922,* (Aylesbury, England: Shire Publication 1973); Bill Risebero, *Modern Architecture and Design: An Alternative History,* (Cambridge, MA: MIT Press, 1983), 134–138.

in 1919 were a culmination of whites' efforts to show black Chicagoans that their only safety lay in remaining in the ghetto—the counterpart to the turn-of-the-century immigrant slum.[54]

The Development of Modern Housing Policy

The 1930s saw the continuation of racial segregation and other housing problems, along with unprecedented housing shortages brought on by the Depression. The era witnessed a major change in responses to shelter issues: the entry of the federal government into the housing arena. New federal policies and programs affected housing not only for poor and working-class families but also for the middle class. By the end of the 1930s, and especially after World War II, government agencies oversaw the financing and construction of a sizeable portion of American housing. Directly or indirectly, federal policies sought to boost employment, stabilize the nuclear family, and maintain existing patterns of economic and racial segregation.[55]

Mass unemployment, coupled with paralysis in the construction industry, created tremendous housing shortages during the 1930s. In 1933, only twenty-one apartment units were built in all of Chicago. About one-third of the city's families had incomes that were too low to obtain decent housing on the private market.[56] Homeless people drifted across the country in search of jobs. Often their only source of shelter was "Hoovervilles," or depressing shanty towns named after President Herbert Hoover, whose government refused to aid the homeless. When Franklin D. Roosevelt came to office, housing joined unemployment and aid to business on the national agenda.

Public, or federally sponsored housing was not a completely new idea. Many European countries had been constructing such housing for some time.[57] The U.S. government built homes for defense workers during World War I, although it sold them off immediately after the war ended. In the 1920s, various groups, including social workers, clergy, and labor leaders, advocated the development of public housing in the United States. But it took the crisis of the Depression to overcome American reluctance to turn to the federal government rather than to the private market to meet social welfare needs. Even then, the Roosevelt Administration proceeded cautiously, in part because of continued opposition from the powerful private real estate lobby. Housing programs developed during the Depression were as much an attempt to boost employment in the construction industry as they were a way to provide needed shelter.

One of the earliest New Deal public housing efforts was the slum clearance and low-rent housing construction carried out by the Public Works Administration (PWA). A major function of this activity was to provide jobs for laid-off construction workers. Generally, individuals who were displaced by the destruction of the slums could not afford the new housing, which went largely to moderate-income families. Half of the new housing was allocated to African Americans. However, the PWA officially accepted the prevailing custom of segregation; no African American families were admitted into PWA projects in all-white neighborhoods.[58]

The 1934 Housing Act brought relief to moderate and middle-income families by making it more possible for them to buy their own homes. It thus shored up the private housing industry. The act established long-term, low-down-payment, and low-interest mortgages through a new Federal Housing Administration (FHA). The FHA mortgage program allowed many white families to become homeowners for the first time. It also allowed them to take advantage of the federal tax deduction for mortgage interest, an aid to homeowners in existence since income taxes began in 1913. Still, the program did not reach the lowest income groups. The program was also of little help to African American families, because the FHA refused to underwrite mortgages in the central cities, where segregation patterns forced most African Americans to live.[59]

When a series of court decisions held that the PWA could not continue its acquisition of slum properties for clearing, public housing proponents pushed for a more permanent program. The Housing Act of 1937 established public housing on an ongoing basis. In order to meet charges by private builders and others that the act was socialistic, its supporters had to focus the legislation on the housing needs of the poor, rather than the general public. They thus avoided competition with the middle- and upper-class private housing market. The act granted discretion to local communities by loaning them the money to build housing projects based on federal guidelines. Local housing authorities, created by special legislation in each state, were responsible for constructing and operating the projects. Because the local governments were given a role in choosing housing sites, the location of the housing usually followed prevailing patterns of economic and racial segregation.[60]

Tenants were carefully screened in the early years of public housing. In part to win acceptance of the program, local housing authorities chose two-parent families who had been investigated by social workers for employment and social stability and checked for police records. The authorities wished to convey an image of public housing tenants as being well-motivated, upwardly mobile low-income families. They often rejected applications from the very poor. Most of the projects were purposely stark, with standard units and rules designed to regulate occupants' lives.[61]

By 1939, 21,000 dwelling units had been built. Then World War II diverted resources from public housing. Most of the federal housing constructed in the early 1940s was targeted for war industry workers. Controversies arose when some housing authorities attempted to accommodate black war workers or veterans in previously all-white areas. In Chicago, a slum inhabited by Italian families had been cleared before the war for a large housing project. When the war began, the federal government converted the project from one housing the local poor to one accommodating migrant war workers, who were primarily black. The resentment felt by some of the dispossessed Italian families turned to hatred and led to an incident in which gunshots were fired into an apartment occupied by blacks. (This is a good example of the way in which prejudice can stem in part from competition over scarce resources such as housing.) Three years later, Chicago had its first large-scale integration battles, when the Chicago Housing Authority brought black veterans into prefabricated units in white areas. Community pressure and mob violence caused black residents to leave many of these projects.[62]

The end of the war brought a second housing shortage. Returning veterans sought homes for their families. Large numbers of Southern blacks migrated to Northern cities both during and after the war. Public housing continued to grow. Much of it was built in the deteriorated central cities, partly because working- and middle-class communities put pressure on local officials not to locate projects in their areas. A good deal of this opposition was motivated by racial and class prejudice.

To house more tenants on expensive inner city land, planners turned to the high-rise project. Elizabeth Wood, head of the Chicago Housing Authority, saw an additional advantage to groups of fifteen- and twenty-story public housing buildings. In order to create new neighborhoods, Wood felt, planning "must be bold and comprehensive. If it is not . . . , the result will be a series of small projects, islands in a wilderness of slums."[63]

Typical of this "bold planning" was Grace Abbott Homes, ten square blocks of housing, including seven 15-story buildings, which opened in 1955. But higher density and the decreasing size of individual apartments made public housing an increasingly unpleasant and impersonal place in which to live. Parents had little chance of watching over children playing fifteen stories below. People lost touch with their neighbors and the communal life of the street. Police officers found high-rise buildings more difficult to patrol.[64]

Even the increase in large projects, however, did not fill the need for affordable housing for the poor. Housing shortages persisted for middle-income families as well. The Housing Act of 1949 was designed in part to deal with these persistent shortages. The bill had conflicting purposes: to increase housing for middle- and low-income families and to meet the demands of merchants, bankers, and builders for larger profits and the revitalization of commercial areas in the central city. While the act was most helpful to middle-class families and business interests, it also included some measures aiding the poor.

In the 1949 Act, the national government officially recognized the importance of providing "a decent home and a suitable living environment for every American family." It expanded the FHA mortgage program. This, coupled with VA mortgages established earlier by the Veterans Administration, helped to fuel the massive move of white middle-class families to suburban tract developments in the 1950s. The act also increased low-income housing by authorizing additional public housing units. However, the act's most important change in housing policy was its promotion of the widespread use of a new tool for dealing with slum neighborhoods: urban renewal.[65]

While at first glance, the new approach seemed a humanitarian response to the poor living conditions of low-income groups, urban renewal as established in the 1949 Act served the needs of business interests. Downtown merchants and real estate entrepreneurs in many cities had begun to worry about the effects of suburbanization and the deterioration of the central city on their businesses. Following examples set in Washington, D.C., and Chicago, the act responded to their concerns by authorizing over $1 billion to purchase downtown land and sell it at a discount to private developers for slum clearance. Because the act included only general provisions for rehousing the people dislocated by the tearing down of their homes, developers were relatively free to build what they wished on the sites. This could include luxury housing. Slum clearance became "poor and minority clearance," enlarging old ghettos. It also increased integration battles as minority families attempted to find decent housing in white areas. Some realtors preyed on the fears of white homeowners by practicing "block-busting." Convincing white residents that blacks were about to move into their neighborhoods, realtors would buy homes from panicked citizens at considerably less than market value and sell these houses to black families at considerably higher prices. Black families displaced by urban renewal also moved into the public housing units now being vacated

The dynamiting of Pruitt-Igoe, 1972. Bad policy, not bad architecture,
rendered this St. Louis housing project unlivable.

by veterans and many of the original, predominantly white residents. These families
were moving on as their incomes rose.[66]

This mixture of public housing for the poor, mortgage insurance for the middle-
class, and urban renewal designed primarily to help real estate and business interests
remained in place through the 1960s. During the War on Poverty, attacks on the
deterioration and impersonalization of high-rise public housing led to restrictions
against new buildings over three stories tall (the Housing Act of 1968) and greater
endorsement of "scattered site" housing, or small units located in various neighborhoods
of a city. The banning of discrimination in housing in the 1964 Civil Rights Act was
of some help toward housing integration, although by the 1960s public housing had
become almost totally black in many large cities. The federal government attempted
to revitalize older areas without simply clearing them by providing loans for the
rehabilitation of older buildings and authorizing demonstration projects for upgrading
inner city neighborhoods under the Demonstration Cities and Metropolitan Development Act. These projects involved local community residents and leaders. Finally,
the Johnson Administration experimented with public/private partnerships in the provision of housing. Section 236 of the 1968 Housing Act established federal subsidies
to private lenders and developers for the construction of multi-family low- and moderate-income units.[67]

These programs achieved a certain degree of success. For example, about half a
million new and rehabilitated subsidized housing units were created each year in 1971
and 1972. However, in 1973, a newly reelected President Nixon established a mora-
torium on federal housing and community development assistance and called for
reevaluation of housing and urban programs. A number of factors supported this move:
a growing backlash against the federal antipoverty programs of the 1960s; a preoccupation of developers and thrift institutions with suburban housing, using largely

The Destruction of Pruitt-Igoe

The Wendell Oliver Pruitt Homes and the William L. Igoe Apartments, thirty-three high-rise buildings built by the St. Louis Housing Authority, were occupied in 1954. They were designed by a famous architect, Minoru Yamasaki, and were considered models of modern public housing. By 1972 the buildings were notorious centers of crime, vandalism, and destruction. Few apartments were occupied; the empty ones were looted of pipes and plumbing fixtures. Residents were attacked in the halls and on the grounds. Nonresidents refused to enter the area. The elevators were broken and used as bathrooms. The Housing Authority declared the buildings unfit for habitation and dynamited them. What went wrong with this "model" project?

Some critics believe that the style of Modern architecture, with its simple geometric forms and plain surfaces, is sterile and monotonous, and stigmatizing and alienating to residents. Others believe that high-rise living is inappropriate for most people, particularly families with small children. This does not seem to be a problem for high-income apartment dwellers, however.

Specific problems with the Pruitt-Igoe design must be considered. These included lack of security at the building entrances, and no private or semiprivate spaces outside the buildings to offer defense and surveillance by the residents. The open spaces outside the building became the turf of roving gangs.

Site planning was completely absent. The relationship of the dwelling spaces to other aspects of life was not considered. There was no day care center, no school, no health facility, no recreation center in the project and no shopping or services nearby.

The architect attempted to provide "vertical neighborhoods" within the buildings. Every third floor had a screened gallery which combined laundry and storage facilities with a play area for small children. Families could gather here and keep an eye on their children. In practice, however, these vertical neighborhoods never developed. They were overcrowded from the beginning. Two-thirds of the apartments had one or two bedrooms, while the average resident had four or more children. In public areas paint was considered a "luxury", and lighting was minimal. The middle-income families originally in residence soon moved out and the Housing Authority began concentrating welfare-dependent, multiproblem families in the project. This, of course, meant a decline in rent revenue and the Housing Authority tried to save money by performing minimal maintenance.

The elevators were not maintained. Because of overcrowding, the elevators broke down frequently. They were unpleasant to use even when they were repaired. To save money, they were designed to stop only on the gallery floors, so two-thirds of the residents had to walk up or down a floor. Also eliminated from the design were first-floor bathrooms.

So, what went wrong? The design had some weaknesses from the beginning, but more important were the cost-cutting measures imposed by the Housing Authority: the skip-stop elevator, no first-floor bathrooms, and no paint in the public areas. Garden apartments, which might have provided defensible space on the first floor and prevented the grounds from becoming "no man's land," were cut out of the design. Landscaping was also cut out.

Overcrowding, concentrating the poorest and neediest families in one place, and then withdrawing maintenance were the fatal blows. No buildings, however well designed, can be expected to stand up to those conditions. The dynamite that destroyed Pruitt-Igoe was social as well as chemical.

Sources: "Slum Surgery in St. Louis," *Architectural Forum* (April 1951): 129–136; Jane Holtz Kay, "Architecture," *The Nation* (September 24, 1973): 284–286; George McCue, "$57,000,000 Later," *Architectural Forum* (May 1973): 42–45; William Moore, Jr., *The Vertical Ghetto* (New York: Random House, 1969); Lee Rainwater, *Behind Ghetto Walls* (Chicago, IL: Aldine, 1970); Katherine G. Bristol, "The Pruitt-Igoe Myth," *The Journal of Architectural Education 44,* 3 (May, 1991), 163–171.

private mortgage insurance; and a continued concern about deterioration and crime in public housing. (One reason public housing deteriorated was that federal support was limited to building construction. Maintenance expenditures had to be covered by rents. As the buildings aged, rents did not provide enough revenues for upkeep and repairs.)[68]

Following the reassessment period, the Nixon Administration turned to two different approaches to low-income housing: increasing the use of public housing for the elderly, and developing subsidies to nonprofit and private developers and to tenants. The creation of public housing for the elderly actually began in the late 1950s, but the change from federally sponsored family housing to housing for low-income older Americans accelerated in the 1970s. Neighborhoods reluctant to accept projects for poor minority families were much more likely to approve of housing for the elderly, "the only remaining reservoir of poor people who are also white, orderly, and middle-class in behavior." Because Congress provided higher levels of funding for these units, public housing for older citizens often resembled conventional apartment buildings. By the end of the 1970s, the elderly constituted one-third of all public housing residents.[69]

Housing subsidies were another move away from the often negative image of the government-built shelter. These subsidies, which were developed first under President Johnson, rely on the private housing market. They use federal funds to stimulate the private sector to produce moderate and low-income housing. These supports work in two ways: (1) they provide a subsidy to the housing unit itself, such as government support of the mortgage interest rate so that it is a below-market interest rate for the buyer, or (2) they provide assistance directly to the tenant, subsidizing that person's rent. Both types of subsidies were provided under Section 8 of the 1974 Housing Act, which became the main housing assistance program for those with low income. In the tenant subsidy portion of Section 8, the government pays the difference between the actual rent of the unit and 30 percent (originally 25 percent) of the household's income. Renters can live anywhere as long as the unit meets certain standards and it is being rented for a certain maximum allowable amount. Housing developers have also been aided under the act. First, government-subsidized Section 8 units helped to bail out financially insecure projects. Owners could count on the rents from assisted tenants. Second, the Section 8 program also included direct subsidies to owners, including help with low-cost financing. Some analysts contend that the Section 8 program has helped developers far more than it has helped individual renters.[70]

The 1970s brought a shift away from direct federal involvement in housing. The Section 8 subsidies put money directly into the hands of tenants and private developers. The 1974 Act also replaced the Demonstration Cities program of the 1960s with Community Block Development Grants. These are locally controlled grants which do not have to be used specifically for housing and which are funded at lower levels than earlier programs.

In the 1980s, the Reagan Administration called for the transfer of the federal government's domestic commitments to state and local governments and the private market wherever possible. In the housing arena, this meant drastic cuts in federal funding. Relatively little new public housing was created. The Department of Housing and Urban Development slashed operating subsidies for existing public housing and encouraged localities to sell off their older units. In 1981, Section 8 rules were changed so that renters could not qualify unless their rent was 30 percent (not 25 percent) of

TABLE 14–2	HUD funding, 1978–1989 (in billions of dollars)	
Fiscal Year	Budget Authority	Budget Outlays
1978	$38.0	$ 7.6
1979	31.1	9.2
1980	35.7	12.6
1981	33.4	14.0
1982	20.1	14.5
1983	16.0	15.3
1984	17.9	16.5
1985	31.7[1]	28.7[1]
1986	15.9	14.1
1987	14.7	15.5
1988	15.4	18.9
1989[1]	13.6	19.7
1990	23.7	22.8 (est.)

Note: This includes items other than low-income housing.

[1]Reflects a one-time purchase of $14.3 billion of outstanding notes for public housing as directed by Congress.

Source: "Plan to Revamp Housing Policy Faces Same Old Problem: Funds," *Congressional Quarterly 46* (April 2, 1988), 892–895; U.S. Bureau of the Census, *Statistical Abstracts of the United States, 1991* (Washington, D.C.: 111th Edition, 1991), 321; Jill Zuckman, "Space Scores Win in Spending Test," *Congressional Quarterly* (11/3/90): 3744.

their income. By 1987, Section 8 subsidies to builders had almost disappeared. Instead of expanding the allowances to individuals, Reagan promoted the use of housing vouchers. Unlike Section 8 allowances, vouchers do not have to be used solely for rent. The housing chosen does not have to meet the same standards required in the Section 8 program. To date, a relatively small number of vouchers has been issued. Thus, even where federal subsidies are being used to stimulate the private market, their production has been limited. This reluctance to engage in federal housing assistance was succinctly summed up by a HUD official in 1985: "We're basically backing out of the business of housing, period."[71] (See Table 14–2.)

CURRENT ISSUES AND TRENDS

Homelessness

The rise in homelessness and lack of affordable housing for Americans of varying incomes represent serious issues. Decreasing federal housing assistance under the Reagan Administration contributed to these problems. In recent years, the Bush Administration has taken steps to renew federal involvement in housing policy. In the meantime, attempts to shelter the homeless and provide low-income housing have occurred largely at the local level.

Communities have developed several ways of coping with the problem of homelessness. One has been to return to the use of the Single Room Occupancy hotel. This use had declined in recent years, as SRO buildings were torn down to make way for luxury housing and commercial development. Lately, however, housing advocates have successfully opposed the destruction of these low-rent facilities for single people. In some areas, new or rehabilitated SROs have been established. In downtown Kalamazoo, Michigan, for example, a deteriorated SRO hotel has been refurbished to serve as a home for elderly persons, individuals released from the nearby state mental institution, and other people with low incomes who prefer to live in the center of the city, often because they lack transportation. The hotel has a social services staff which offers counseling, help in locating jobs, referrals to public welfare, and other assistance.

Another, more problematic response to lack of housing is the "welfare hotel." Used especially in New York City, these are large hotels housing families on public assistance who cannot find apartments at the rent allowed them in their welfare budgets. The AFDC program, which is based on a combination of federal, state, and city funds, covers the cost of accommodating entire families in small hotel rooms with minimal cooking and other housekeeping facilities. By the late 1980s, New York had over 60 welfare hotels, the largest one sheltering over 440 families. The average length of stay was at least six months in 1989. In some cases, families remained in hotel housing for several years. Despite a pledge by then Mayor Ed Koch that the city would stop using welfare hotels by 1990, Koch's successor, David Dinkins, found it impossible to fulfill that pledge, as well as to meet his own campaign promise to remove people from barracks-like shelters in one year and to house them in more permanent situations.[72]

Jobs might provide the means for getting off welfare and out of the hotel, yet generally the salaries to be earned are simply too small to cover apartment rental in New York. In fact, one-fifth of the adults living in welfare hotels are already employed. People are thus trapped for long periods of time, and the pathway out of the welfare hotel is often limited to doubling up with other families in private housing (and risking eviction) or moving out of the area. New York City officials and advocates for the homeless now fear that homelessness has become embedded in the city's life for the forseeable future.[73]

What is life like in a welfare hotel? Imagine that you and your family live in two hotel rooms. You have no refrigerator (only some welfare hotels supply these); you have only a hot plate on which to cook; and you must wash dishes in the bathroom tub or sink. Because cooking facilities are primitive, your meals are cooked and eaten one item at a time. There is no table large enough for the family, so you eat on newspapers spread on the bed or the floor. You are given a "restaurant allowance" to eat some of your meals out of the hotel, but this consists of about 70 cents per person per meal. In addition, unlike the hotels you are used to, this one has roaches, dirty halls and stairwells, and maintenance staff who can enter your room without invitation or warning. These conditions are typical of most New York City welfare hotels.

The cost of placing families in welfare hotels is extremely high. The rent for a family of four is about $2,400 a month, $29,000 a year. In a number of instances, hotel owners receive large profits from providing welfare housing. New York's Holland Hotel, eventually shut down by the city for numerous housing and management violations, made profits of $3 to $4 million a year for the corporation that owned it. The high cost of welfare hotels has prompted many critics to suggest that it would be far more economical to raise the public welfare housing allowance, so that families could live in less expensive rental housing. However, this solution requires increasing the overall AFDC benefit, something which the state legislature has not been willing to do.[74]

For many localities, the major response to homelessness is the shelter—temporary, free, communal living quarters for people without housing. At first, communities provided shelters for single men and women. One of the largest and most famous is Federal City Shelter in Washington, D.C. This 1,700-bed facility, run by the city, was set up in 1984 after a fifty-one day hunger strike by housing activist Mitch Snyder. More recently, with the rising number of homeless families, cities have begun to build shelters for parents and children. Sponsors for both types of shelter vary, and include municipal and county governments, churches, and charitable groups.

Shelters often offer only the very basics for survival—a temporary roof for the night (they are generally not open during the day) and possibly a soup kitchen. There is usually little privacy or space to store belongings. A shelter for men near the Bowery in New York, for example, sleeps about 250 men on cots that are two inches apart. Each night, the door is locked to keep additional applicants out. One observer, visiting the shelter in winter, commented, "You could actually see marks on the door where men had clawed at it to get in after hours."[75] Many shelters, because they are crowded and understaffed, have become settings for theft and violence. Homeless people sometimes prefer the streets to this more frightening and dangerous alternative.

Of course, not all shelters are this unpleasant. A number of New York's churches and synagogues, supported in part by city and state finances, maintain small shelters that are well staffed by volunteers. These settings offer a friendly atmosphere and encouragement to residents. However, one way these shelters survive is by careful screening of clients and strict rules against drugs and alcohol. This has the effect of increasing the concentration of the most troubled and uncooperative people at the large municipal shelters.[76]

Family shelters also vary in quality. Some put up large numbers of families in barracks-style arrangements without privacy or special care for children. Stays are limited to two or three weeks. Others, like the Salvation Army shelter in Los Angeles, allow a longer stay and offer better living conditions as well as a variety of services. These include child care and help with job-seeking and apartment-hunting. To give families an even better chance to get back on their feet, some organizations run more permanent shelters. New York's Henry Street Settlement has developed the Urban Family Center, which is considered a model family shelter program. Using a building provided by the New York City Housing Authority, the center houses families for six months in conventional apartments. Social workers and other staff are available on a 24-hour basis. The center's many services include educational programs for children and adults and short-term counseling to help families with specific problems.[77]

Transitional housing such as the Urban Family Center is the middle level of a three-tier solution to homelessness recommended by advocates for the homeless. The first level is temporary crisis shelters and the third level is permanent housing. Local governments and private groups have already put a fair amount of funding into crisis and transitional housing. Advocates achieved a goal of increased federal assistance to the homeless in 1987, when president Reagan reluctantly signed the McKinney Homeless Assistance Act. The Act provides $1 billion annually for emergency shelters, some long-term housing for the homeless, and various services. A typical program funded through the Act is Project Hope in Louisville, Kentucky, which provides remedial schooling and vocational training to adult residents of shelters. Yet even as shelters and services have proliferated, so have the numbers of people who are homeless. It is also more and more apparent that shelters can become institutionalized and dead-end answers to the problem—permanent fixtures which allow us to forget about trying to prevent homelessness in the first place. As a result, many advocates have begun to question the wisdom of concentrating on temporary and crisis housing and are turning instead to the basic problem of the lack of permanent and affordable housing.[78]

There are new reasons to be alarmed about the housing deficit. The tax reforms of 1986 cut out many of the incentives to private business for building rental housing. This means that the loss of rental units, including low-income units, will continue. In addition, the 20-year contracts for Section 8 housing are now expiring. This means that many subsidized low- to moderate-rent apartments will be converted by their owners to higher rent housing.

What can be done to provide more housing at a reasonable cost? The Reagan approach of relying on vouchers has had little effect. This leaves two other ways of dealing with the housing problem: (1) preserve existing units and keep rents and mortgages low, and (2) provide new housing. Today both solutions are being tackled through innovative combinations of public and private action on the local and state level, and new initiatives at the federal level.

To preserve existing housing, cities have passed laws halting the demolition of buildings. Communities have developed house-sharing schemes in which elderly people in large homes are matched with younger people who move in as tenants. Some areas are using zoning changes to allow homeowners to add on separate apartment units for rental to relatives or others. Rehabilitation of older homes and apartments can be an important activity, as long as rents in the remodeled units are kept low. Where they are not, gentrification occurs. In opposition to this trend, the Neighborhood Reinvestment Corporation, a national nonprofit housing organization, has established Neighborhood Housing Service programs in 137 cities to rehabilitate housing specifically for low-income tenants. The Chicago Neighborhood Housing Service, for example, has used $50 million to provide over 10,000 rehabilitated units.[79]

Financing and construction of new moderate and low-income housing is now being carried out by nonprofit organizations, unions, and state and local governments. Often, these sponsors work cooperatively with each other and with banks and private, for-profit developers. Federal monies, through Community Development Block Grants and other sources, may constitute part of their funding. For example, states like New York and Massachusetts now have special housing trust funds, which can be used to finance private, nonprofit housing. The Greater Miami Neighborhoods organization has raised over $1.5 million from local governments and businesses to create several hundred low-income dwelling units. Montgomery County, Maryland provides zoning density bonuses to private developers. To receive the bonus, builders set aside one-eighth of the units in new residential developments for moderate-income families. Habitat for Humanity, a nonprofit organization made famous by one of its volunteers, former President Jimmy Carter, brings prospective homeowners and volunteers together to build homes which are then sold at cost. In Boston, a local bricklayers union has started a nonprofit corporation to build affordable housing. A number of firms are now offering home-loan assistance to their employees. Finally, community banks, committed to revitalizing their local communities through investment, can do much to improve housing. Chicago's South Shore Bank, for example, makes millions of dollars of loans to low- and moderate-income residents for mortgages and building rehabilitation. It has also set up affiliates which use state and federal funds and private foundation grants to remodel units in the community's most deteriorated housing. Along with its affiliates, the bank has helped to rehabilitate one out of every six multifamily housing units in the South Shore neighborhood.[80]

One of the largest cooperative ventures is the rise of Community Development Corporations (CDCs). These nonprofit organizations, which have evolved from church and community groups, help low-income neighborhoods with both jobs and housing. CDCs are funded by local businesses and major foundations, such as the Ford Foundation. They build housing for the elderly and the poor and they help to revive local businesses to create jobs. One CDC director explains, "We're really nonprofit entrepreneurs. We combine the public purpose of government with the flexibility . . . of the private sector, and we're directly accountable to the community."[81]

The inventiveness of these solutions, and their ability to bring together government, nonprofit, and business spheres, is impressive. Yet policy analysts and others have pointed out that regional and local efforts cannot in themselves solve our housing difficulties. They have called for the return of the federal government to the housing arena on a comprehensive scale. To the National Housing Task Force—a group of people from banking, business, and community service organizations established by congressional initiative to study housing—the answer lies in greatly increased federal funding for state and local initiatives, including partnerships with the private sector. To housing analysts like Chester Hartman, federal involvement means following the example of many European countries and developing a substantial network of government-funded "social housing," perhaps through collaboration with nonprofit housing corporations and community organizations.[82]

Another possibility for change lies in the existing tax system, which gives large tax deductions to homeowners based on home mortgage interest payments. As can be seen in Figure 14–8 on page 508, these deductions produce a federal expenditure many times greater than direct housing subsidies. Homeowner deductions are a form of federal housing assistance which benefits the rich far more than the poor. Many low- and middle-income homeowners, for example, do not itemize their deductions and thus they do not receive the tax break. In a novel proposal, a National League of Cities report suggests redressing the balance by limiting the amount of deduction a homeowner may take, and using the revenues gained to fund housing programs for low-income individuals and families.[83]

Comprehensive changes like these would be costly for the government, although suggestions to move more housing out of the profit sector would lower the nation's total expenditures for housing. The Bush Administration has embarked on a more modest program of change. In 1990, the president signed the National Affordable Housing Act, which includes initiatives favored by conservatives as well as approaches appealing to a broader spectrum of those concerned about housing problems. A major objective of the Act is "to forge a nationwide partnership of public and private insti-

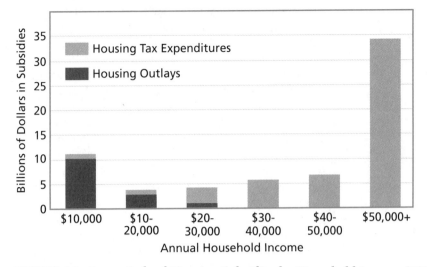

FIGURE 14–8   **Federal Housing Subsidies by Household Income (1988)**

Source: Mary Austin Turner and Veronica M. Reed, *Housing America* (Washington, D.C.: The Urban Institute, 1990), 28.

tutions to ensure that every U.S. resident has access to decent shelter or assistance in avoiding homelessness." The Act includes the optimistically titled HOPE program (Homeownership and Opportunity for People Everywhere), developed by Bush Administration officials. This is a program to assist public housing residents to manage housing projects and eventually to buy their own housing units within these projects. In addition, the Act provides for new public housing development, bringing the government into financing the construction of low-income housing. The legislation also broadens the Community Development Block Grant system to include funding for housing development at the local level. Other provisions of the Act include increases in rent subsidies for low-income tenants as well as efforts to maintain the stock of low-income housing. One effort to accomplish the latter is to provide incentives to Section 8 housing owners to keep their housing in the Section 8 program; another is to allow those owners who wish to do so to sell their Section 8 units to others who will maintain them as low-income housing.[84]

Some housing advocates have praised the new legislation. "It's a great step forward," reports the president of the National Low Income Housing Coalition. "It's far less than is needed, but it's also a major reversal of 10 years of neglect and retreat." Others have been less optimistic. The Twentieth Century Fund Task Force on Affordable Housing views the Act as providing relatively modest steps toward dealing with our national housing problems. An editorial in the *New York Times* finds the HOPE program "big on hype," and concludes that the Act fails to set out a national housing policy for low-income households who receive no public housing assistance. The Act does bring the potential for substantial increases in federal funding for housing; the extent to which this potential is realized and effects felt remains to be seen.[85]

Gender and Household Stereotypes

There is one problem of housing that is present even where there seem to be no problems at all. Imagine a "dream" house: ample space, appliance-filled kitchen, safe neighborhood, huge lawn, and affordable mortgage. What else could one need? Well, one needs to ask where the house is located. Where is it in relation to work, shopping, schools, doctors, or libraries? If it is placed in a typical American suburb, the answer is that all of those things are some distance away. (So, add a two-car garage to our dream list.) If the house is in an older city neighborhood, many of the facilities may be within walking distance, with the exception of the workplace. Chances are that the factories and offices where we work are not close by. We may be just as happy that they are not. Who needs smoke, noise, and parking lots? As long as we fit the traditional family pattern for which these houses and neighborhoods were built, we can deal with the problem of isolation in the traditional way: Dad can commute to work and enjoy the quiet of the home at night. Mom can take care of the house and the kids.

The traditional pattern (traditional only since 1950) has a price. Dad is cut off from most of domestic life and Mom has little else. Many have found this a reasonable bargain. But many of both genders have felt trapped, because they found that the house and its location did not allow much variation from the traditional pattern. The traps inherent in the suburban dream were among the many contributors to the women's movement of the 1970s.[86]

Now, those who fit the traditional pattern are a minority. Both women and men, willingly or unwillingly, no longer conform to the stereotypes. Women want to work outside the home. Many women must work whether they want to or not; either they have become the sole source of support for their families or they have found that two incomes are necessary to pay the bills. Some men want a bigger part in domestic life. (Some like domesticity, but not the work that goes with it: employed wives still do more than half of the housework.) Many households are headed by single parents, often women, but not always. Some households contain several families. The traditional house doesn't fit this wide variety of needs very well.

For a single parent, the daily routine is very complex. The distances between home, work, day care, schools, and shopping become major obstacles. Each in itself may be minor, but all must be added together. If work is more than half an hour away, as it can easily be in any large city, and if the other deliveries and pick-ups that must be accomplished are not on a direct route from home to work, then a lot of time, money, and energy can be consumed in transportation.

The home and its location are built according to gender stereotypes, and they serve as a daily reminder to both men and women that they are not following the expected pattern. Both men and women may have left the pattern by choice, but it is hard not to feel guilty or resentful under the stress this kind of living pattern creates.

The dream house in the suburbs has become so much a part of our national mythology in the last forty years that it is hard to imagine any other way of arranging the relationships of house and workplace. Are there other ways? Imagine a group of houses and apartments overlooking a shipyard where cargo ships are built. Those living in the houses and working at the shipyard are mostly single parents. Not only is work close by but also so are the school and the attached day care center. From one window in the Center, children can watch on the days when one of "Mommy's ships" is being launched. The Center also includes a large kitchen. When the parents pick up their children at the end of the day, they can also take home a hot meal that has been cooked and packaged for them.

This community existed, briefly, not in fantasy but in Vanport City, Oregon, and during the Second World War. It was created by the Federal Public Housing Authority Kaiser Steel Corporation for its shipyard workers. Most of the women workers were replaced in the shipyard, some willingly and some not so willingly, when men returned from the Armed Services. The community where work and home were integrated with a minimum of stress was dismantled and most of the occupants went off to create the "traditional" pattern of gender separation.[87]

What can social workers do? Rebuilding cities is not usually within their power. They can, however, begin by recognizing the stress that is placed on marriages and families by their living arrangements. They can appreciate and support the struggles of men and women against the gender stereotypes that their housing imposes. They can look for and support ways to relieve stress, including neighborhood day care cooperatives; programs initiated in the workplace, such as company day care centers, flex-time, and job sharing; and respite care arrangements for families with invalid grandparents or children with disabilities or other special needs.

Social workers can support planning efforts to make cities and neighborhoods more flexible and responsive to human needs, particularly ways that will allow a better integration of work and home life. This includes issues most social workers consider irrelevant to their practice, such as zoning or transportation. Zoning regulates the separation of work and residence, the possibility of subdividing a single-family house to create an apartment for an elder relative (a "granny flat"), or the different sizes and forms of family groups allowed to share the same neighborhood. For example, 20 percent of those seeking housing now are single-parent families.[88] Given the scarcity of affordable apartments, it may be more practical and economical for two or more single-parent families to share a large house. But if the neighborhood is zoned for single-family occupancy, this would not be permitted. More flexible zoning may create more livable cities. Social workers can also strive to save the decaying public transportation systems that for some people are the only means of getting around in our spread-out cities. Social workers are supposed to be specialists in working with people in their situational contexts. Housing arrangements present a broader and more complex situation than most others.

Housing for People with Special Needs

We all have individual preferences in home design and decoration, but most of us could adapt quickly to almost any type of house, even a tepee or an igloo. For others, adaptation is more difficult. It can help enormously if their special needs are considered in the design and location of the house. People who have low vision or total blindness, people who use wheelchairs, older people with medical problems, and people with mental illnesses or developmental disabilities all face barriers to independence in the built environment. Their communities can ignore these barriers and keep them imprisoned and dependent, or they can remove the barriers and facilitate free access for them to all aspects of community life. Not only is this access a necessary part of "normal" life but it can also improve physical and mental health.[89]

People who use wheelchairs need ramps and elevators to allow them to move about independently. Imagine the frustration of being in a department store or office building and confronting a bathroom door that is too narrow to get your chair through. Federal legislation requiring access to public facilities and cities which have purchased buses with lifts have made it easier for wheelchair users to lead a normal life, but many barriers remain even in areas that we assume are accessible. Spend a day in a wheelchair on your campus and discover for yourself the many places you cannot go.

When a wheelchair user returns home, another set of obstacles is encountered. Stoves, sinks, and counters are too high to use sitting down. The freezing compartment in the average refrigerator is completely out of reach. Obviously, preparation and clean-up for even a simple meal requires gymnastics in this kind of environment. There may be no community-wide solution to this problem, but planning for special needs can be practical in some situations. A student housing complex on the campus of George-town University includes an apartment with scaled-down counters and reachable appliances and sinks. The University knew from experience that it regularly enrolled students who could use such an apartment.

Many features that are essential to people with special needs could also be enjoyed by the rest of us. Wider doors and hallways make it easier to move furniture in and out. Adjustable shelves and clothes rods in closets expand options for everyone. Room to turn around in a bathroom should not be a luxury. Builders could accommodate a broader range of the population with small changes in construction standards and little added cost. As our population ages, more of us will appreciate homes designed with freedom and mobility in mind. We may not need grab bars in the bathroom now, but if the walls were properly reinforced when the house was built, we could easily add them later. Social workers can help communicate the value of these "universal design" principles.[90]

The location of a home in relation to other parts of the community is, as we have seen, as important as its interior accommodations. The separation of home from work, shopping, entertainment, and health services is a problem even for those in the prime of health and with access to an automobile. For those whose mobility is impaired, the possibility of a normal life is severely limited. Nursing homes provide an integration of living space, health services, and communal meals, but they usually do this in a manner that is impersonal, inflexible, and institutional. Recently, "retirement villages" have been designed to maximize the privacy and independence of residents while providing cooking, cleaning, and health services when needed. Such design is usually associated with only the more expensive facilities. Does it need to be? Convenience stores can be built into the ground level of apartment buildings. Day care centers and communal kitchens are a feature of some European apartments for single parents. Gradually, the same idea may be extended to all of us.

Just as some people need to have the outside world brought closer to home, others need a home in the outside world. People with developmental disabilities, who have been segregated in public institutions or carefully protected by their families, are now living in group homes and finding employment. They are learning to find their way around their neighborhoods, to take public transportation, and to gain access to the full range of community activities. Many now earn real salaries outside of sheltered workshops. With their new incomes, they shop, go to movies, and eat in restaurants. They need a safe, nurturing community environment. Similarly, an effort is being made to bring people with serious emotional problems out of the institution and into the community, and to support them once they are out, not just dump them. Social workers are heavily involved in these efforts. The design, adaptation, and location of homes and apartments for these re-emerging populations require special attention to make integration successful.

Group homes cause little disruption in residential communities, but there is usually initial resistance to them. The NIMBY phenomenon ("Not In My Backyard"), where people recognize the necessity of certain facilities but prefer to have them located somewhere else, is common. Some social service agencies counteract this with careful community preparation. Others avoid the hassle and concentrate their efforts in neighborhoods that are less likely or less able to protest. Such ghettoization defeats the purpose of normalization.

Social workers need to be aware of the special housing needs of some people. They need to be sensitive to the frustration and anger that a restrictive environment can create, as well as to the growth and health that participation in the community can foster. Not all needs can be satisfied and not all barriers are removable. This is true for any of us. But barriers and restrictions should not be taken for granted. Individual adaptations, group supports, and environmental changes can be made.

The Retreat from Public Life

The second half of the twentieth century has presented Americans with greater opportunities for privacy. It is easier to get away, and stay away, from others than it used to be. Television, newspapers, stereo tape decks, video cassette recorders, large refrigerators, and frozen food greatly reduce the need to go out. When we do go out, we need not share our trips with other people on buses, streetcars, or trains; we go in private cars. Our trips are speeded by highways that avoid the neighborhoods of others, so we have little idea of how other people live in our cities. The people in our own neighborhoods are all pretty much like us: same income level, same race, even the same age.

Technology allows us to stay at home. Our recent history has reduced our desire to go out. The civil rights, antiwar, environmental protection, and women's movements brought many people into public life. Their struggles brought solid accomplishments, but they also brought disillusionment and exhaustion. Most public problems resisted permanent solution. Corruption and deceit remained common. Many people lost confidence in our public institutions. A retreat from public life might have been expected. But some people have begun to worry that by becoming more private, we are losing some skills and attitudes which are necessary to keep American society working properly.[91]

We have a long tradition of regarding our houses as havens from the world. This has increased as more people have fled the problems of the cities for the seeming refuge of the suburbs. Not only do public problems seem too complex to solve but also much public space seems unsafe to inhabit. Urban renewal, with its concentration on office buildings and parking lots, has helped to make downtown areas places to fear. When the offices close, large areas become deserted; anyone working late or traveling through is an easy target for muggers. One response to this is cities composed of segregated, homogeneous neighborhoods where one does not have to interact with others very often and where people of other races or income levels are rarely seen at all (except on television).[92]

Diplomats are people specially trained by our government and sent to other nations to maintain peaceful political relationships and to encourage productive economic trade and cultural enrichment. But in our own cities and neighborhoods, we are all diplomats who must encounter people we don't know, people who may be different from us. We must interact peacefully and productively with them. This, too, takes special skills. Our national history has included considerable intolerance and conflict, but our cities have consistently offered examples of fruitful diversity. As we turn inward and focus exclusively on family life, enjoy the privacy that technology now allows us, and avoid the public life that threatens or depresses us, will we lose the minimal appreciation of differences and the tolerance of disagreements that are necessary to operate a nation of diverse groups? Will we lose the skills of civility that make our local and national life possible? Will we ultimately lose the intellectual stimulation that produces scientific and artistic creativity? Or can we reestablish the right balance of security and adventure: a safe home within a nurturing but diverse community?

What can social workers do about this? First, as citizens and as professionals, they can take advantage of all the opportunities available to them to participate in public life. Any neighborhood, community, or city event or organization that brings people together from different classes, races, ages, or religions is a possible antidote to isolation. These are simple, preliminary measures. The long-term revitalization of public life will require structural changes. Some of these involve housing.

Social workers connected with city planning operations can encourage policies that create and preserve a balance of private, semiprivate (communal), and public spaces. Community spirit and neighborliness are the keys to security. Life can be returned to sterile downtown areas with mixed-use developments. Public housing projects, where personal safety is often threatened, can be redesigned. Low-rise buildings with windows on the street, front porches, and front yards (even tiny, token spaces) can help define areas that are not open to just anyone, but are at least partially under the control of the residents. Such spaces also encourage residents to take the responsibility to maintain them.[93]

Social work has a long tradition of sensitivity to the needs of communities and neighborhoods. In the spirit of the settlement house movement, social workers can still be found in community centers throughout the country. A new style of community organizer, one with management skills as well as advocacy, group work, and counseling abilities, is finding work in such centers.

Social workers, whether in community centers or private agencies, often help people in difficulty to develop social support networks. The problem may be a disability or illness, the loss of work, a frail parent, or a rebellious teen. Relatives, neighbors, or strangers who have the same problem can be brought together to offer support. In order to do successful networking, social workers must understand the environmental conditions that inhibit people from coming together.

At all levels of social work practice—individual, agency, neighborhood, community, city, state, and national—there are things that can be done to help create and maintain private, communal, and public spaces where people can live with a fruitful combination of security with stimulation, and privacy with community. The retreat from public life represents a conviction that the larger problems of our society—crime, poverty, and discrimination—cannot be solved. People believe our political institutions, either local or national, have failed us, and the only reasonable response is to seek refuge behind the walls of our own tiny castles. Counteracting this woeful conclusion will take vigorous action at all levels of government and at all levels of group activity. Although the size of this problem may be discouraging, we must remember that it can be attacked on many levels. All of us can play a part, whatever our individual skills and interests.

PERSPECTIVES

The Conservative Perspective

The conservative point of view maintains that housing can best be provided by market forces. Consumers exercise choices; these choices guide producers of housing in deciding what to build. The major cause of homelessness, many conservatives argue, is not the lack of affordable housing. Most homeless people are deviants or members of an entrenched underclass, and they lack the motivation or ability to better their lives.[94] If some consumers are without the necessary resources to enter the marketplace, the government should give them vouchers which will allow them to purchase the housing of their choice (within the limits of the voucher). They should not be forced to accept public housing, which stigmatizes them as poor and deprives them of the dignity that other consumers are given in the market. Public housing, like other welfare programs, encourages dependency. These programs should be phased out and residents should be encouraged to move toward self-sufficiency.[95]

One way of encouraging public housing residents to enter the private market as owners is to divert part of their rental payments to a savings account. The savings can be used to make a down payment on a house once enough money has accumulated.

Public housing is unfair competition for private builders. Existing public housing should be sold to private buyers. The deterioration of housing is often caused by tenants' ignorance of maintenance or their lack of responsibility.[96]

The flight to the suburbs after World War II was an expression of consumer choice. It is an essential part of the American Dream to want to own a house with land around it. Everyone who wants to can own good quality housing by saving money, investing in a modest home, and "trading-up" as market and personal resources allow. As middle-income homeowners move up to better housing, those with lower incomes will move up behind them. Everyone benefits eventually.

The Liberal Perspective

Liberals feel the market is a necessary device for providing everyone with housing, but it needs regulation and stimulation. It usually cannot provide the poorest members of society with adequate housing and it does not always respond to those with special needs. Therefore, government must intervene to offer subsidies, tax incentives, and regulations to encourage private developers to provide for all consumers and to curtail unfair or destructive practices. Low-interest home loans and Section 8 programs will aid the disadvantaged, and laws against red-lining and restrictive covenants will discourage discrimination.[97]

As a last resort, the government must build new housing to replace the loss of low-income options in the market. This housing should, wherever possible, be scattered throughout the city and it should be designed to avoid stigmatizing its residents. As a short-term response to the current rise in homelessness, the government should also provide emergency shelters and encourage private sponsors to do likewise.

The flight to the suburbs was a popular choice of consumers, but liberals point out that it could not have happened without considerable aid from the government. Low-cost loans through the Veterans Administration and the Federal Housing Administration, mortgage tax credits, municipal water and sewage services, and arterial highways which allowed easy commuting to the suburbs were necessary before consumers could exercise this choice.

Finally, liberals argue that job opportunities and a responsive public transportation system are a necessary part of any effort to insure adequate housing for all.

The Radical Perspective

Radicals believe the market is not the appropriate model for housing provision. They assert that housing is a right, not a commodity. Decent housing should be guaranteed to all. The market encourages speculation, which drives up prices and makes profits from other people's misery.[98]

The shape of cities is determined by the interests of those with wealth and power. The "flight" to suburbia happened because large developers found it easier and cheaper to build outside cities. They mobilized their political influence to persuade government to provide the necessary loans, highways, and other services. The consumers had little choice, because these same speculators had decided to disinvest in cities and to allow them to decay.[99]

Similarly, the deterioration of inner city neighborhoods was aided by red-lining by banks and insurance companies. When the urban decay had proceeded past the point where profits could be extracted from slum properties, the federal program of "urban renewal" was created. This allowed developers to remove low-income and African American residents from inner city areas so that they could, with tax breaks and other incentives, build again in the decayed areas. Similar tax breaks were made available when middle-income professionals decided to move into older city neighborhoods. These government programs, supported by liberals as well as conservatives, have compounded the current housing crisis.

Housing is made available to the poor only in periods when the poor pose some threat. In the nineteenth century, communicable diseases spread across class lines, so governments were empowered to clear slums. After World War I, when the British government feared that returning veterans might follow the example of the Russian Revolution, a massive housing program was begun (and discontinued once a depression took away that threat).[100] The urban riots of the 1960s in the United States brought brief concern for the housing of African Americans. With public housing available, wages can be kept low, but the promise of eventual homeownership helps workers accept their position.

Change comes when oppressed groups organize. Tenants in public housing can take over management of their projects and seek collective solutions to problems of crime, maintenance, rehabilitation, and service delivery. The homeless can take over abandoned buildings and demand the materials to repair them. They can protest the destruction of low-income housing and lobby for the creation of alternatives. To provide adequate housing for all Americans, the federal government can develop a comprehensive "social housing" program. This would guarantee housing for all citizens through a major system of nonprofit housing produced and operated by local, state, and federal governments.[101]

SOCIAL WORK ROLES

Our earlier discussion of housing issues suggested a number of roles social workers can and do play in the housing arena. At the very least, social workers can be sensitive to the impact of particular kinds of housing (or the lack of it) on their clients' lives. They can help people cope with difficult housing situations or change them. Social workers can also choose to work directly within a housing setting, such as a public housing program. Finally, they can become specialists who work specifically on housing policy, often advocating for change.

Social workers who engage in counseling, case management, or other types of direct service to clients witness a variety of kinds of housing problems. A single parent reports living in deteriorated and crowded conditions; an elderly client fears living alone; or a person with visual impairment is told he cannot have a guide dog in the apartment he wishes to rent. In these cases, the social worker can make referrals and act as an advocate. The single parent might be referred to a federal assistance program or to a community group which helps people find decent and affordable housing. The elderly client might be introduced to a home-sharing program or aided in the development of a supportive social network. The visually impaired man might be given information about his rights as a person with a disability, and he and the social worker could plan how he might best assert those rights with potential landlords.

Some social workers are employed within housing settings. A traditional role is screening applicants for public housing. In the 1960s, this role was broadened to include provision of social services. The community service division within a public housing project might coordinate programs provided by outside agencies (day care centers, for example), offer some services on its own, such as counseling, and organize tenant groups. In some instances, social workers have been employed as managers of public housing. In Chicago, for example, social workers from the Uptown Branch of Hull House manage scattered site public housing units for the Chicago Housing Authority. In addition to acting as landlords, they help integrate building residents into neighborhood life, they develop tenant councils, and they work with these councils on areas such as tenant selection and building improvements. Such a job involves management skills, community organizing tactics, and an ability to counsel residents with difficult life problems. Hull House has found social workers to be excellent candidates for such positions.[102]

Social workers also help staff temporary and long-term shelters. There they might serve as managers, provide referral and counseling services, or simply act as good listeners. A social work student assigned to a daytime "drop-in center" for street people found that much of his time was spent talking with people and offering support and encouragement.

Such activities, particularly in shelter settings, may strike people as putting band-aids on serious problems. For this reason, social workers have been drawn into the arenas of housing provision and the development of housing policy. Some social workers do such work as one portion of their jobs. For example, community center and neighborhood organization workers may be involved in housing rehabilitation programs in their areas. In other cases, social workers take on full-time roles as advocates in low-income housing coalitions, researchers and policy analysts in social welfare "think-tanks" such as the Urban Institute, lobbyists for housing groups, or members of political staffs.

C O N C L U S I O N

All of the roles described here are demanding but exciting ones for social workers. The state of America's housing has become a crucial issue in the 1990s. Except for the early 1900s and the Depression years, social workers have managed to relegate housing to a minor niche within their broad concern for people's well-being. Current housing issues demand that affordable and appropriate shelter be returned to the social work agenda.

E N D N O T E S

1. Chester Hartman, ed., *America's Housing Crisis* (Boston: Routledge and Kegan Paul, 1983), 12–13.
2. Hartman, *America's Housing Crisis,* 12–13.
3. Jonathan Kozol, *Rachel and Her Children* (New York: Crown Publishers, 1988), 9–10; Martha R. Burt and Barbara E. Cohen, *America's Homeless: Numbers, Characteristics, and Programs That Serve Them* (Washington, D.C.: The Urban Institute Press, 1989), 19–32.
4. Barbara Vobejde, "Census Spotted Nearly 230,000 Homeless People," *The Washington Post* (13 April 1991), Sec. A, 3; Jay Mathews, "Rethinking Homeless Myths," *Newsweek* (April 6, 1992), 29.
5. James D. Wright, "The Mentally Ill Homeless: What is Myth and What is Fact?" *Social Problems 35* (April 1988): 182–191; Kozol, *Rachel and Her Children,* 3–5; The National Alliance to End Homelessness, *What You Can Do to Help the Homeless* (New York: Simon and Schuster, 1991), 11–12; Julee H. Kryder-Coe, Lester M. Salamon, and Janice M. Molnar, *Homeless Children and Youth: A New American Di-*

lemma (New Brunswick, NJ: Transaction Publishers, 1991), 19–20.
6. Burt, *America's Homeless,* 36.
7. Kim Hopper and Jill Hamberg, *The Making of America's Homeless: From Skid Row to New Poor* (New York: Community Service Society of New York, 1984), 30–31; "Housing the Poor," *Public Welfare* 47 (Winter 1989): 5–12; National Housing Task Force, *A Decent Place to Live* (National Housing Task Force, March, 1988), 6–7; U.S. Bureau of the Census, *Statistical Abstract of the United States: 1991* (Washington, D.C.: 111th Edition, 1991), 728; Ann Mariano, "Housing Costs Outpace Income by Wide Margin," *The Washington Post* (11 August 1990), Sec. E, 1.
8. Ruth Marcus, "The New Homeless Crowd Shelters," *The Washington Post* (18 February 1985), 20.
9. Steve Kerch, "Norman Hotel Commitment Sets Pace for Low-Rent Rehabs," *Chicago Tribune* (16 August 1987), Sec. 16, 1; Jonathan Kozol, "No Stereotype Can Capture Broad Diveristy of Victims," *Detroit*

Free Press (14 February 1988), Sec. B, 4; Kryder-Coe, *Homeless Children and Youth,* 234.

10. U.S. Bureau of the Census, Current Housing Reports, H130-87, Q 4, *Market Absorption of Apartments* (Washington, D.C.: U.S. Department of Commerce, March, 1988), p. 2; Tom Hundley, "Homeless are Victims of Nation's Indifference," *Detroit Free Press* (14 February 1988), Sec. B, 4; *Statistical Abstract: 1991,* 732; Kozol, *Rachel and Her Children,* 8, 34; Bill Turque, "When Tenants Take Charge," *Newsweek* (November 27, 1989), 44.

11. William E. Schmidt, "Home Buying is an Official Cause Again," *New York Times* (26 March 1989), Sec. E, 4; U.S. Bureau of the Census, *American Housing Survey for the United States in 1989* (Washington, D.C.: U.S. Department of Commerce, 1991), 1; John Gallagher, "A Nation of Renters? Early Ownership Rate Falls," *Detroit Free Press* (9 July 1989), Sec. K, 1.

12. U.S. Bureau of the Census, Current Construction Reports, Series C25, "New One-Family Houses Sold," (Washington, D.C.: U.S. Department of Commerce, August, 1991), 6; U.S. Bureau of the Census, Current Construction Reports, Series C20, "Housing Starts" (Washington, D.C.: U.S. Department of Commerce, July, 1991), 3.

13. National Housing Task Force, *A Decent Place to Live,* 7; Cushing N. Dolbeare, *Federal Housing Assistance: Who Needs It? Who Gets It?* (Washington, D.C.: National League of Cities, 1985), 6; *American Housing Survey,* 4; Linda Dravitz and Art Collings, "Rural Housing Policy in America: Problems and Solutions," in *Critical Perspectives on Housing,* Rachel G. Bratt, Chester Hartman, and Ann Meyerson, eds. (Philadelphia: Temple University Press, 1986), 325. "Substandard housing" is measured in this instance by overcrowding and lack of complete plumbing.

14. Kozol, *Rachel and Her Children,* 11; Iver Peterson, "Subdividing the Single-Family House, *New York Times* (24 July 1988), 7; Kryder-Coe, *Homeless Children and Youth,* 17.

15. *Statistical Abstract: 1991,* 728; The National Alliance to End Homelessness, *What You Can Do to Help the Homeless,* 11.

16. Joe T. Darden, "Accessibility to Housing: Differential Residential Segregation for Blacks, Hispanics, American Indians, and Asians," in *Race, Ethnicity, and Minority Housing in the United States,* Jamshid A. Momeni, ed. (New York: Greenwood Press, 1986), 109–126; Patricia Edmunds, "By the Numbers, Tracking Segregation in 219 Metro Areas,"

USA Today (11 November 1991), Sec. 3A; Michael Quint, "Racial Gap Found on Mortgages." *New York Times* (22 October 1991), Sec. C, 4; *Statistical Abstract,* 728; *American Housing Survey,* 79, 239.

17. Jamshid A. Momeni, "The Housing Conditions of Black Female-headed Households: A Comparative Analysis," in Momeni, *Race, Ethnicity, and Minority Housing,* 90, 99–107; Bratt, *Critical Perspectives on Housing,* xvii-xviii; *American Housing Survey,* 40, 193.

18. Tom Morganthau with Bob Cohen and Monroe Anderson, "The Housing Crunch," *Newsweek* (January 4, 1988), 18–20; Michael A. Stegman, *More Housing, More Fairly: Report of the Twentieth Century Fund Task Force on Affordable Housing* (New York: The Twentieth Century Fund Press, 1991), 25–28.

19. Tom Morganthau, "The Housing Crunch," 18; Rachel Bratt, "Public Housing: The Controversy and Contribution," in Bratt, *Critical Perspectives on Housing,* 342; National Housing Task Force, *A Decent Place to Live,* 26–27.

20. Quoted in Greer, "The Homeless," 56.

21. Hopper and Hamberg, *The Making of America's Homeless,* 4.

22. Greer, "The Homeless," 57–58.

23. Kryder-Coe, *Homeless Children and Youth,* 21, 251–253; Kozol, *Rachel and Her Children,* 57.

24. Emily Paradise Achtenberg and Peter Marcuse, "Towards the Decommodification of Housing: A Political Analysis and a Progressive Program," in Hartman, *America's Housing Crisis,* 208; Alan S. Oser, "Scarcity and High Cost," *New York Times,* Real Estate Report (November 9, 1988), 20.

25. Elizabeth Hopp-Peters, " 'Dumps' Become Arguments in Favor of Gentrification," *Chicago Tribune* (August 16, 1987), Sec. 16, 1C and 2F.

26. Richard P. Applebaum and John I. Gilderbloom, "Supply-side Economics and Rents: Are Rental Housing Markets Truly Competitive?" in Bratt, *Critical Perspectives on Housing,* 167–172.

27. Chester Hartman, "A Radical Perspective on Housing Reform," in Hartman, *America's Housing Crisis,* 11–12; Achtenberg and Marcuse, "Towards the Decommodification of Housing," in Hartman, *America's Housing Crisis,* 208.

28. Darden, "Accessibility to Housing," in Momeni, *Race, Ethnicity, and Minority Housing,* 109–111.

29. Peter Mieszkowski and Richard Syron, "Economic Explanation for Housing Segregation," *New England Economic Review* (November/December 1979): 33–39.

30. Chester Hartman, "Housing Policies Under the Reagan Administration," in Bratt, *Critical Perspectives on Housing,* 376; Henry B. Gonzales, "Is Public Housing the Answer?" *Public Welfare 47* (Winter 1989): 38.
31. Gwendolyn Wright, *Building the Dream* (New York: Pantheon Books, 1981), 4, 46–47, 66.
32. Wright, *Building the Dream,* 3–17.
33. Wright, *Building the Dream,* 21–26.
34. Wright, *Building the Dream,* 26–39.
35. Michael S. Stone, "Housing and the Economic Crisis: An Analysis and Emergency Program," in Hartman, *America's Housing Crisis,* 118–119; Wright, *Building the Dream,* 26.
36. Stone, "Housing and the Economic Crisis," 118–119; Wright, *Building the Dream,* 34–40.
37. Wright, *Building the Dream,* 41–50.
38. Charles Hoch, "A Brief History of the Homeless Problem in the United States," in *The Homeless in Contemporary Society,* Richard D. Bingham, Roy E. Green, and Sammis B. White, eds. (Beverly Hills, CA: Sage, 1987), 17–18.
39. Roy Lubove, *The Progressives and the Slums: Tenement House Reform in New York City, 1890–1917* (Pittsburgh, PA: University of Pittsburgh Press, 1962), 1–3; Wright, *Building the Dream,* 118.
40. Lubove, *The Progressives and the Slums,* 4–11.
41. Lubove, *The Progressives and the Slums,* 11–23.
42. Wright, *Building the Dream,* 123.
43. Allen F. Davis, *Spearheads for Reform: The Social Settlements and the Progressive Movement, 1890–1914* (New York: Oxford Press, 1967), 65.
44. Davis, *Spearheads for Reform,* 66–67.
45. Wright, *Building the Dream,* 128–129.
46. Devereux Bowly, Jr., *The Poorhouse: Subsidized Housing In Chicago, 1895–1976* (Carbondale, IL: Southern Illinois University Press, 1978), 1–6; Jacob Riis, *How the Other Half Lives* (New York: Hill and Wang, 1957, [1890]), 203–226.
47. Wright, *Building the Dream,* 123; Peter Kivisto, "A Historical Review of Changes in Public Housing Policies and Their Impacts on Minorities," in Momeni, *Race, Ethnicity, and Minority Housing,* 3.
48. Hoch, "A Brief History of the Homeless Problem," in Bingham et al., *The Homeless in Contemporary Society,* 20–22.
49. Wright, *Building the Dream,* 96–102.
50. Dolores Hayden, *Redesigning the American Dream* (New York: W. W. Norton, 1984), 22–23; Wright, *Building the Dream,* 96–113.
51. Wright, *Building the Dream,* 58–60.
52. Wright, *Building the Dream,* 177–184.
53. Wright, *Building the Dream,* 193–212.
54. Thomas Lee Philpott, *The Slum and the Ghetto: Neighborhood Deterioriation and Middle-Class Reform, Chicago, 1880–1930* (New York: Oxford University Press, 1978), 162–180.
55. Wright, *Building the Dream,* 217–219.
56. Bowly, *The Poorhouse,* 17.
57. Catherine Bauer, *Modern Housing* (New York: Arno Press, 1974 [1934]).
58. Kivisto, "A Historical Review of Changes in Public Housing Policies" in Momeni, *Race, Ethnicity, and Minority Housing,* 3.
59. R. Allen Hays, *The Federal Government and Urban Housing* (Albany, NY: State University of New York Press, 1985), 81–84; Arnold R. Hirsch, *Making the Second Ghetto* (Cambridge, England: Cambridge University Press, 1983) 10.
60. Kivisto, "A Historical Review of Changes in Public Housing Policies" in Momeni, *Race, Ethnicity, and Minority Housing,* 3–4.
61. Bowly, *The Poorhouse,* 33; Wright, *Building the Dream,* 229–232.
62. Hirsch, *Making the Second Ghetto,* 45–56; Bowly, *The Poorhouse,* 45–53.
63. Quoted in Wright, *Building the Dream,* 235.
64. Bowly, *The Poorhouse,* 91–93.
65. Wright, *Building the Dream,* 246; George Sternlieb and David Listokin, "A Review of National Housing Policy," in *Housing America's Poor,* Peter D. Salins, ed. (Chapel Hill, NC: University of North Carolina Press, 1987), 21–22.
66. Sternlieb and Listokin, "A Review of National Housing Policy" in Salins, *Housing America's Poor,* 21–22, 26; Wright, *Building the Dream,* 232–234; William R. Barnes, "A Battle for Washington: Ideology, Racism, and Self-Interest in the Controversy over Public Housing, 1943–1946" *Records of the Columbia Historical Society of Washington D.C.* (1980) Vol. 50, 452–483; Ira S. Lowry, "Where Should the Poor Live?" in Salins, *Housing America's Poor,* 96–97.
67. Sternlieb and Listokin "A Review of National Housing Policy" in Salins, *Housing America's Poor,* 23–24; Hays, *Federal Government and Urban Housing,* 104; Bowly, *The Poorhouse,* 184–191.
68. Sternlieb and Listokin "A Review of National Housing Policy" in Salins, *Housing America's Poor,* 30–31; Wright, *Building the Dream,* 237–239, 260–261.

69. Wright, *Building the Dream*, 237–239; Elizabeth D. Huttman, *Introduction to Social Policy* (New York: McGraw-Hill, 1981), 292.

70. Huttman, *Introduction to Social Policy*, 298; Sternlieb and Listokin "A Review of National Housing Policy" in Salins, *Housing America's Poor*, 30–31; John I. Gilderbloom and Richard P. Appelbaum, *Rethinking Rental Housing* (Philadelphia; PA: Temple University Press, 1988), 75–76.

71. Hartman, "Housing Policies Under the Reagan Administration" in Bratt, *Critical Perspectives on Housing*, 363–376.

72. Kozol, *Rachel and Her Children*, 16–17; Clare Collins, "Limits Placed on State Rental Help," *New York Times* (8 August 1990), Sec. C, 4; Alan Finder, "New York Lags in Effort to Move Families from Hotels," *New York Times* (19 February 1990), Sec. B, 1; Todd S. Purdum," Dinkins' Aides Will Delay on Homeless Bill," *New York Times* (24 February 1990), Sec. I, 27.

73. Alan Finder, "Homelessness in New York: Years of Plans, No Solution," *New York Times* (30 December 1990), Sec. I, 1.

74. *Struggling to Survive in a Welfare Hotel* (Community Service Society of New York, 1984), 3–4, 12, 20–22, 25; Kozol, *Rachel's Children*, 18; Josh Barbanel, "New York Seeking to Buy Welfare Hotel," *New York Times* (19 March 1988), Sec. B, 2.

75. Greer, "The Homeless," 58; Collins, "Limits Placed on State Rental Help."

76. Josh Barbanel, "Alternatives to Despair: Shelters Hearten America's Homeless," *New York Times* (13 March 1988), Sec. A, 1, 35.

77. Hank Whittemore, "We Can't Pay the Rent," *Parade* (January 10, 1988), 6; *Alternatives to the Welfare Hotel* (Community Service Society of New York, 1987), 13, 22–23.

78. Robert Pear, "President Signs $1 Billion Bill to Aid Homeless, *New York Times* (24 July 1987), Sec. A, 1; Peter K. Kilborn, "In Small Steps, Program Puts Homeless into Jobs," *New York Times* (28 January 1990), 1.

79. National Housing Task Force, *A Decent Place to Live*, 25, 29; James Wheaton, Neighborhood Housing Services, Statement at Field Hearing, Subcommittee on Housing and Community Development of Committee on Banking, Finance, and Urban Affairs, House of Representatives, 101st Congress, 1st Session, Chicago, IL, August 21, 1989.

80. National Housing Task Force, *A Decent Place to Live*, 24–31; Paul Goldberger, "High Marks for Low-Cost Housing in Boston, *New York Times* (6 November 1988), Sec. H, 33; Mary Sit, "Fringe Benefits: Some Companies are Helping Employees with Housing," *Boston Globe* (20 July 1991), 37; Annual Report, 1986, South Shore Bank and Affiliates.

81. Margaret Daly, "Sharing the American Dream," *Better Homes and Gardens* (May, 1988), 32; Avis C. Vidal and Bob Komines, "Community Development Corporations: A National Perspective, *National Civic Review 78* (May–June, 1989): 168–186.

82. National Housing Task Force, *A Decent Place to Live*, 18–20; Chester Hartman and Michael E. Stone, "A Socialist Housing Alternative for the United States," in Bratt, *Critical Perspectives on Housing*, 480–490.

83. Cushing N. Dolbeare, *Federal Housing Assistance: Who Needs It? Who Gets It?"* (Washington, D.C.: National League of Cities, 1985).

84. Jill Zuckman, "Housing Authorizations," *Congressional Quarterly* (December 8, 1990), 4091–4104.

85. Jill Zuckman, "Conferees' Authorization Bill Marks Turnabout in Policy," *Congressional Quarterly* (October 20, 1990), 3514–3516; Stegman, *More Housing, More Fairly*, 6, 13–15; "More Hype than HOPE," *New York Times* (18 February 1990), IV, 1.

86. Betty Friedan, *The Feminine Mystique* (New York: W.W. Norton, 1963).

87. Dolores Hayden, *Redesigning the American Dream*, 3–4.

88. Karen A. Franck and Sherry Ahrentzen, eds., *New Households, New Housing* (New York: Van Nostrand, 1989), ix.

89. Elizabeth Huttman, *Housing and Social Services for the Elderly* (New York: Praeger, 1977); Raymond Lifchez and Barbara Winslow, *Design for Independent Living; The Environment and Physically Disabled People* (New York: Watson-Guptill, 1979); Sandra C. Howell, *Designing for Aging; Patterns of Use* (Cambridge: MIT Press, 1980); Anne M. Donnellen, et al., "A Time-Limited Intensive Intervention Program Model to Support Community Placement for Persons with Severe Behavior Problems," *Journal of the Association for Persons with Severe Handicaps 10* (1985), 123–131.

90. Ronald Mace, "Design for Special Needs," in *Housing: Symbol, Structure, Site*, Lisa Taylor, ed. (New York: Rizzoli, 1990), 50–51.

91. Richard Sennett, *The Fall of Public Man* (New York: Alfred Knopf, 1977); David Popenoe, *Private Pleasure, Public Plight: American Metropolitan Community Life in Comparative Perspective* (New Brunswick, NJ:

Transaction, 1985); Lyn Lofland, "Private Life-styles, Changing Neighborhoods, and Public Life: A Problem in Organized Complexity," Paper presented at the International Research Conference on Housing, Policy, and Urban Innovation (Amsterdam, 1988).

92. Wright, *Building the Dream;* Hayden, *Redesigning the American Dream;* Robert C. Wood, *Suburbia: Its People and Their Politics* (Boston: Houghton Mifflin, 1958); Oscar Newman, *Defensible Space* (New York: Macmillan, 1972).

93. Oscar Newman, *Community of Interest* (Garden City, NY: Doubleday, 1981).

94. Myron Magnet, "The Homeless," *Fortune* (November 23, 1987), 170–190.

95. *The Report of the President's Commission on Housing* (Washington, D.C., 1982), xvii–xviii; Peter Salins, "America's Permanent Housing Problem" in Salins, *Housing America's Poor,* 1–13.

96. Salins, "America's Permanent Housing Problem," in Salins, *Housing America's Poor,* 5.

97. National Housing Task Force, *A Decent Place to Live,* 12–17.

98. Hartman, "A Radical Perspective on Housing Reform," in Hartman, *America's Housing Crisis,* 1–25; Achtenberg and Marcuse, "Towards the Decommodification of Housing," in Hartman, *America's Housing Crisis,* 202–230.

99. Barry Checkoway, "Large Builders, Federal Housing Programs, and Postwar Suburbanization," in Bratt, *Critical Perspectives,* 119–138.

100. Mark Swenarton, *Homes Fit for Heroes* (London: Heinemann, 1981).

101. Gilderbloom and Appelbaum, *Rethinking Rental Housing,* 181–204.

102. Interview with Dennis Marino and Sue Brady, Hull House, Uptown Branch, Chicago, (June 18, 1988).

C · H · A · P · T · E · R

fifteen

Aging

Seventy-year-old Hattie Brown lived alone in a run-down house in the central city. Determined to be independent, she refused to move in with relatives, even though her house lacked heat and the roof leaked badly. On a particularly chilly winter day, a neighbor found Mrs. Brown lying sick and cold on her kitchen floor. Mrs. Brown refused her neighbor's offer to take her to a hospital and turned away the police officer and social worker who later came to help. Convinced after talking with the older woman that she fully understood both her predicament and her alternatives, the social worker and police officer felt their hands were tied—they could not legally remove Mrs. Brown by force. Hattie Brown died in her home two days later.

Diane Lenski, a social worker in a nursing home, has called an informal meeting of all nursing home social service workers in her area. "The reason for this meeting," she tells them, "is to try to do something about the way the hospitals keep 'dumping' patients on us. I know my institution can't handle all the severely ill people that keep getting referred—and the hospital staff doesn't even tell us the real extent of their problems." Others at the meeting agree. New federal policies regulating the length of stay of Medicare patients seem to be resulting in discharges of sicker patients who aren't able to return to their homes. "Why can't this field get its act together?" one worker exclaims. "It seems like all these programs and policies for the aged are contradicting each other." The meeting ends with a plan to set up a conference with the hospital social workers in order to try to negotiate a solution.

Horace Randolph is an 82-year-old African American resident of a small midwestern city. A widower whose health has been declining over the last ten years, he is just getting by on his Social Security payments (low because he held poorly paying jobs all his life) and federal Supplemental Security Income benefits. Recently, Mr. Randolph has become confused and disoriented. His two sons and their wives have done their best to care for him in his home, but they feel that now he probably needs to be in a nursing home. They worry about the fact that the predominantly white nursing homes in the area don't seem to welcome African American residents.

Sarah Levin, who is 86, recently suffered a stroke which left her with some speech problems and a weakness in her left arm. She was transferred from the hospital to a rehabilitation center near her home in Brooklyn. There she receives daily physical and speech therapy. Her 81-year-old "baby sister" drops in regularly to see her, along with her daughter and three grandchildren. Her older brother, Max, brings her the Sunday New York Times each weekend "so we can do the crossword puzzle together." Sarah is making remarkable progress, she has recovered her famous sense of humor, and she plans to return to her apartment in a few weeks.

"My talk went really well," Jolene French tells her social work instructor. "I told the older people at the congregate meal site about my idea for a telephone-check-in-network and a lot of them want to sign up. Now I have to finish recruiting the volunteers who will call them each day to see how they are doing. For this rural area, it's going to be a great way to keep people in touch."

Today, one in eight Americans is age 65 or over. These older individuals have diverse needs and interests. Although they are often perceived as being a homogeneous category of people, older Americans in fact vary broadly in income level, health status, degree of educational attainment, ethnic and racial background, and level of independence. While certain problems—chronic disease, low income, and loss of important life roles and abilities—plague a number of the elderly, these are by no means the rule for everyone over 65. Yet because problems of ill health, reduced income, and dependency have frequently been linked to increasing age, a variety of policies and programs have been developed to address them. Unfortunately, as noted earlier by the nursing home social worker, such programs and policies frequently lack coordination and consistency. In addition, social workers and other helping professionals are sometimes reluctant to work with the elderly, even though the field presents many challenges and rewards. This chapter tells you more about the field and tries to dispel common myths about aging. It examines age-related social welfare programs in the United States and analyzes the images of aging upon which they are based. In doing so, it looks at both the historic and contemporary position of the elderly in America.

DEFINITIONS OF AGING

What exactly is the nature of old age, and when does it occur? Philosophers, physicians, and physical and social scientists have debated these questions over the years. Is old age, as some people fear, an incurable disease, the inevitable decline of one's physical and intellectual powers? Or, to put it more positively, is it simply a stage of growth and development, associated with wisdom and reflection? Does it begin at age 50, 65, or later? The answers to these questions have varied over time and across cultures. The Social Security Act of 1935 selected 65 as the age at which benefits begin, but this was an arbitrary choice based on economic and policy considerations, rather than on medical or scientific judgments. The policy makers could have chosen 62, 66, or some other dividing line between middle and old age.

Thus, the definition of aging and the notion of when it begins are by no means universally agreed upon. Some social scientists have even argued that the category of "old age" is a relatively useless concept. Perhaps it makes no more sense than speaking of all people aged 20 to 45 as belonging to one group. Bernice Neugarten emphasizes the great diversity among elderly people. She suggests that chronological age can be a less powerful influence in people's lives than their socioeconomic status, sex, race, ethnic background, or the area of the country in which they live. For example, a newly widowed woman, age 60, who has never worked outside the home and is living solely on Social Security in a small, isolated community, has a very different life experience from a 65-year-old married man who continues to be involved in a part-time law practice in a large city. Because of such diversity among the elderly, age-related policies, based on general conceptions about old age, may not relate accurately to people's needs.[1] The older woman in our example might most need income assistance and social supports. The lawyer's concerns might be recreational opportunities and investment planning.

Despite awareness of divergence among the elderly, many researchers and planners still rely on chronological age as a meaningful category. In an attempt to make the concept of old age more precise, some researchers draw a distinction between the "young-old" and the "old-old." The first group covers individuals aged 65 to 74. Most people in this age range lead active, reasonably independent lives and they are only moderately restricted, if at all, by physical or mental disabilities. The second group includes all people over the age of 75. These are the individuals more likely to be "frail elderly," those with incapacitating chronic diseases or serious deficiencies in mental functioning. Members of the two groups often have quite different needs in terms of social, health, and other services. Programs and services should be developed with this distinction in mind.[2]

The concept of aging can be discussed not only on an individual level but also on a social level. "The Graying of America" has become a popular way of referring to the effects of having an increasing proportion of elderly people in our society. As this proportion grows, certain issues rise to national prominence. These include the capacity of Social Security to continue to provide for all qualified beneficiaries; the problem of poverty among specific groups of elderly, especially women and minorities; rapidly rising health care costs; and the need for adequate housing for older people. "The Graying of America" suggests increases in these problems and it also often implies a growing conservatism, as older citizens become more numerous among the nation's voters.

Those who study the biological, psychological, and social aspects of aging are known as specialists in the multidisciplinary field of *gerontology.* A subfield within gerontology is *geriatrics,* which focuses on the medical treatment and prevention of diseases among older people.

America has more elderly people today than ever before. There are currently more than 31 million individuals aged 65 and over in the United States, representing about

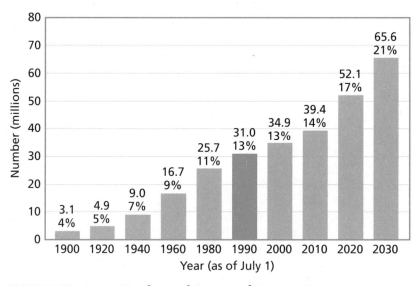

FIGURE 15–1   **Number and Percent of Persons 65+: 1900 to 2030**

Note: Increments in years on horizontal scale are uneven.

Source: Adapted from American Association of Retired Persons, *A Profile of Older Americans: 1990* (Washington, D.C.: AARP, 1990); © 1990 American Association of Retired Persons. Reprinted with permission. U.S. Congress, Senate, Special Committee on Aging, *Developments on Aging: 1987,* Vol. 1, 100 Congress, 2nd Session, 1987, 2.

12.5 percent of the total population. This proportion has changed radically between the Colonial period and the present. In 1776, only one out of every 50 people was 65 or over; in 1900, it was one in 25, and by 1987, it was one in 8. There are now more older Americans than there are teenagers.[3] (See Figure 15–1 and Table 15–1.)

Growth in the absolute number of elderly is caused by factors such as the influx of immigrants up to World War I, decreases in infant mortality rates since the turn of the century, control of infectious diseases, and improvements in environmental and social conditions. (See Figure 15–2 on page 528.) Changes in the proportion of older people in the United States stem largely from decreases in birth rates, although recent dramatic increases in survival rates among the old have also played a part.

This increase in the number and proportion of elderly will continue on into the twenty-first century, particularly with the aging of the "baby boom" generation of the 1940s and 1950s. Demographers predict that by the year 2030, every fifth American will be at least 65. The number of elderly people in 1990 will more than double in forty years.

At present older Americans tend to be concentrated in certain areas of the country. Over half of all the elderly live in nine states: California, New York, Florida, Pennsylvania, Texas, Illinois, Ohio, Michigan, and New Jersey. The migration of older people to the sunbelt states is a frequently noted phenomenon. So far, however, the size of that trend has been exaggerated. The state of Florida is one exception; 18 percent of its residents are 65 and over. A number of cities in the state have elderly populations that comprise over 20 percent of the total. In general, though, most elderly live near where they grew up.[4] (Figure 15–3 on page 529 shows the geographic distribution of those over 65.)

The proportion of "young-old" (65–74) and "old-old" (75 and over) within the category of elderly has undergone interesting shifts. The most rapid growth is occuring within the oldest group. In 1950, under a third of all elderly were aged 75 and over. In 1989, the figure had grown to 41 percent, with the largest growth among women over 75. By the year 2000, almost half of the elderly population will be 75 or more. The group aged 85 and over has seen the greatest increase of all. Improved medical care and environmental conditions appear to be helping to increase the remaining life expectancy for persons who reach the age of 65. A woman who celebrated her 65th

TABLE 15–1   **Selected age groups of total U.S. population: 1960–1989**

Percent Distribution

Age:	Under 5	5–13	14–17	18–24	65–74	75+	65+	Median Age
1960	11.3	18.2	6.2	8.9	6.1	3.1	9.2	29.4
1970	8.4	17.9	7.8	12.1	6.1	3.7	9.8	27.9
1980	7.2	13.7	7.1	13.3	6.9	4.4	11.3	30.0
1989	7.5	12.8	5.4	10.7	7.3	5.1	12.5	32.6

Source: Adapted from U.S. Bureau of the Census, Current Population Reports, Series P-25, Nos. 519, 917, and 1000; U.S. Bureau of the Census, *Statistical Abstract of the United States: 1991* (Washington, D.C.: 111th Ed.), 13.

Age as of July 1, 1987

| 65 and over | 55 to 64 | 45 to 54 | 35 to 44 | 25 to 34 | 18 to 24 | 14 to 17 | 5 to 13 | Under 5 |

Influenza Epidemic

Stock Market Crash

Beginning of Baby Boom

Legalized Abortion Begins

Oral Contraceptives

World War II Ends

World War I Ends

U.S. Entry into World War II

Year of Birth (July 1 – June 30)

FIGURE 15–2   Number of Births, by Year, 1910 to 1987, and Relationship to 1987 Age Groups

Source: U.S. Bureau of the Census, Current Population Reports, Series P-25, No. 1022, *United States Population Estimates, by Age, Sex, and Race: 1980 to 1987* (Washington, D.C.: U.S. Government Printing Office, 1988), 2.

birthday in 1989, for example, could expect to live almost another nineteen years; a man age 65 could expect about fifteen more years.[5]

This expanded number of elderly is a better educated group than ever before. In 1965, about a quarter of those 65 and over had completed high school. Twenty-five years later, over 50 percent were high school graduates. There has also been a steady, if less dramatic increase in the proportion of elderly who have attended college. By 1990, over a tenth were college graduates.[6]

The figures we have discussed so far, while useful, fail to convey the heterogeneous nature of that group labeled "the elderly." As we noted earlier, there is much diversity among older Americans. A number of these differences relate to race and sex. Women, for example, far outnumber men among older Americans. By 1989, there were three women aged 65 and over to every two men of that age. For those 85 and over, the ratio had grown to about five to two. Life expectancies of men and women are correspondingly different. For those born in 1989, the life expectancy for women was 78, and for men it was almost 72.[7] (See Table 15–2 on page 530.)

One of the most dramatic variations among men and women relates to marital status. Overall, 63 percent of persons 65 to 74 are married and living with their spouse; for those 75 and over, the figure is 40 percent. Yet while 74 percent of all older men are married and living with their spouse, only 40 percent of older women fit this category. Some 14 percent of older men are widowed, compared to half of all women over 65. These differences can be explained not only by greater longevity among women, but also by the greater tendency of widowed or divorced men to remarry and to choose

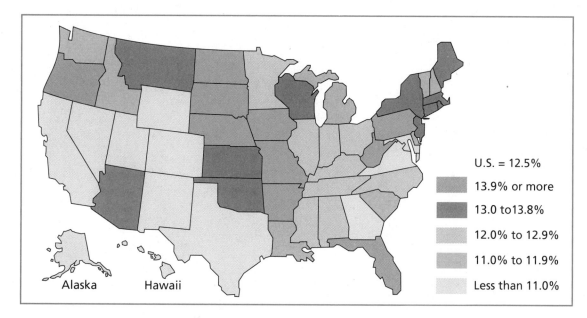

U.S. = 12.5%

13.9% or more

13.0 to13.8%

12.0% to 12.9%

11.0% to 11.9%

Less than 11.0%

FIGURE 15–3   **Persons 65+ as Percentage of Total Population: 1989**

Source: American Association of Retired Persons, *A Profile of Older Americans: 1990* (Washington, D.C.: AARP, 1990). © 1990 American Association of Retired Persons. Reprinted with permission.

younger spouses. Partly because of the high rate of widowhood, two-fifths of all women over 65 live alone.[8]

Race is another element differentiating the elderly. African Americans do not live as long as whites, on average, and a higher proportion have lost a spouse. While 12 percent of the total population is African American, they constitute only 8 percent of those 65 and over. In 1989, an African American man's life expectancy was more than 6 years less than that of his white counterpart. African American women over 75 are the most likely of all groups to have lost a spouse. On the other hand, the percentage of African American elderly is growing at a greater rate than that of white elderly. The greatest increase, however, is among the "other races" population, or Native Americans, Alaskan Natives, Asian Americans, and Pacific Islanders.[9]

Educational attainment can also be affected by sex, race, and ethnicity. In all educational categories except completion of eight years of elementary school and four years of college, elderly women surpass elderly men. (See Table 15–3.) In 1988, the median number of years of school completed by older persons was 12.2 for whites, 8.4 for African Americans, and 7.5 for Hispanic Americans.[10]

Living Arrangements

The vast majority of older Americans live alone or in a household, rather than in an institution or a group setting. At any one time, only about 5 percent are residents of a nursing home. As noted, far more women live alone than men. Few elderly people live with their children. However, despite the widespread belief that many elderly are abandoned by their offspring, a large number report frequent contact. According to a

TABLE 15-2   Expectation of life at birth: 1920–1989

	Total			White			Black		
	Total	Male	Female	Total	Male	Female	Total	Male	Female
1920	54.1	53.6	54.6	54.9	54.4	55.6	na	na	na
1930	59.7	58.1	61.6	61.4	59.7	63.5	na	na	na
1940	62.9	60.8	65.2	64.2	62.1	66.6	na	na	na
1950	68.2	65.6	71.1	69.1	66.5	72.2	na	na	na
1960	69.7	66.6	73.1	70.6	67.4	74.1	na	na	na
1970	70.8	67.1	74.7	71.7	68.0	75.6	64.1	60.0	68.3
1980	73.7	70.0	77.4	74.4	70.7	78.1	68.1	63.8	72.5
1989	75.2	71.8	78.5	75.9	72.6	79.1	69.7	65.2	74.0

Source: U.S. Bureau of the Census, *Statistical Abstract of the United States: 1988* (Washington, D.C.: 108th. Ed. 1988) 106; National Center for Health Statistics, *Health, United States, 1990,* DHHS Pub. No. (PHS) 91-1232, Public Health Service (Washington, D.C.: U.S. Government Printing Office, 1990), 67.

1984 survey, four out of five older persons who lived alone and had children were in personal or telephone contact with a child at least once a week. Twenty-three percent saw a child daily. Fifty percent said that at least one child could get to them in a matter of minutes in case of emergency. (See Table 15–4.) Other studies have noted that the children of African American and Hispanic American elderly are even more likely than those of white parents to visit and give support.[11]

About three-fourths of all elderly own their own homes. Because these tend to be older homes, often in inner city neighborhoods or poor rural areas, housing conditions may be less than adequate. Insufficient weatherproofing, exposed electrical wiring, and

TABLE 15-3   Education of persons 65 years old and over, by sex: 1960–1988

Years of School Completed	Male					Female				
	1960	1970	1980	1985	1988	1960	1970	1980	1985	1988
8 years or less	72.5	61.5	45.3	37.2	31.7	66.4	56.1	41.6	34.1	29.7
1–3 years of high school	10.4	12.6	15.5	15.7	15.6	12.8	13.9	16.7	17.0	15.8
4 years of high school	7.8	12.5	21.4	26.4	29.4	11.6	18.1	25.8	30.7	35.5
1–3 years of college	4.9	5.6	7.5	9.1	9.8	6.1	6.7	8.6	10.3	10.5
4 years or more of college	4.3	7.9	10.3	11.5	13.5	3.2	5.2	7.4	8.0	8.5

Source: U.S. Bureau of the Census, *Statistical Abstract of the United States: 1988* (Washington, D.C.: 108th. Ed., 1988), 35; *Statistical Abstract: 1991,* 111th Ed., 1991, 37.

TABLE 15–4   **Persons 65 years old and over with children who do not live in the same household—contacts, 1984***

Frequency of Contact	Total	65–74 Years Old	75 Years Old and Over	75–84 Years Old	85 Years Old and Over
			Age Group		
Total (1,000)	17,526	11,284	6,243	5,234	1,009
			Percent Distribution		
Total	100.0	100.0	100.0	100.0	100.0
Frequency of seeing or talking with child:					
Daily	41.4	39.8	44.3	42.6	53.2
2 or more times per week	21.3	22.6	19.1	19.2	18.5
Weekly	20.2	20.1	20.3	21.5	14.2
2 or more times per month	6.6	6.8	6.2	6.3	5.9
Monthly	5.0	5.2	4.6	5.0	2.9
Less than monthly[1]	5.5	5.6	5.4	5.5	5.3
Frequency of seeing child:					
Daily	22.6	21.5	24.6	23.7	29.5
2 or more times per week	17.7	17.7	17.7	17.1	20.9
Weekly	21.3	21.5	21.0	21.0	21.3
2 or more times per month	8.0	8.5	7.1	7.3	6.1
Monthly	7.9	7.6	8.5	8.9	6.5
Less than monthly[1]	22.4	23.2	21.0	22.1	15.8
Frequency of talking with child:					
Daily	33.5	32.6	35.2	33.8	42.5
2 or more times per week	20.9	22.1	18.7	18.9	17.7
Weekly	21.9	21.8	22.2	23.4	15.7
2 or more times per month	7.8	8.0	7.4	7.5	6.7
Monthly	6.8	7.3	5.9	6.5	2.9
Less than monthly[1]	9.1	8.2	10.5	9.8	14.4
Time for child to get to parent:					
Within 10 minutes	25.6	24.6	27.2	26.8	29.6
10–29 minutes	28.6	28.5	28.6	27.8	32.9
30–59 minutes	11.6	11.8	11.3	10.9	13.3
1–2 hours	13.2	13.7	12.2	13.0	8.6
3–23 hours	13.8	14.0	13.4	14.2	9.3
More than a day[1]	7.3	7.3	7.1	7.3	6.3

*(Covers persons 65 years old and over who were living in communities outside of nursing homes or other institutions)

[1]Includes unknown and other responses, not shown separately.

Source: Statistical Abstract of the United States: 1989 (Washington, D.C.: 109th Edition, 1989), 37.

worn-out furnaces are frequent problems. Renters, especially minority elderly and those living in rural areas, are particularly likely to have poor housing.[12]

Income

The elderly, like other age groups, have a range of income levels. Contrary to popular opinion, advanced age does not necessarily mean a life of straitened circumstances and careful budgeting. One quarter of the elderly still have money enough for luxuries after covering the expenses of a comfortable level of living. On the other hand, the median family income of persons 65 and over was $23,179 in 1989, or less than half that of those in the 45–54 age range. The elderly are more likely than any other age group to be among the "near poor," with resources just above the poverty line. The drop in the number of older people actually living below the poverty line is a bright spot in this income picture. In contrast to the situation of other age groups, poverty among the elderly has decreased dramatically since the early 1960s, when one-third of older Americans were poor. Yet a stubborn level remains, with about 11.4 percent of older people still living below the poverty line. Women, minorities, and persons over 85 are disproportionately represented in this group. Older women account for three-fourths of the poor elderly. One out of every ten elderly whites was poor in 1989, compared to about one-third of elderly African Americans and one-fifth of Hispanic Americans over 65. Some 65 percent of Native American elderly have incomes below the poverty level. African American women living alone have the lowest incomes of all.[13] (See Figures 15–4 and 15–5.)

Most elderly rely on Social Security benefits and assets as major sources of income. Since the turn of the century, fewer and fewer Americans have continued to work after

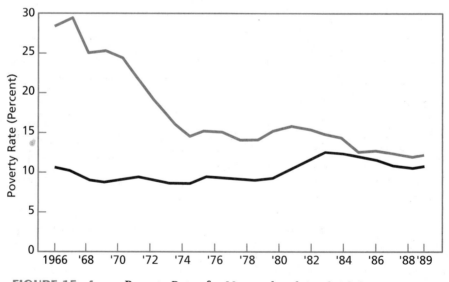

FIGURE 15–4   **Poverty Rates for Nonaged and Aged Adults, 1966–1989**

Source: U.S. Congress, Senate, Special Committee on Aging, *Developments in Aging: 1986,* Vol. 3, 100 Congress, 1st session, 1986, 42.

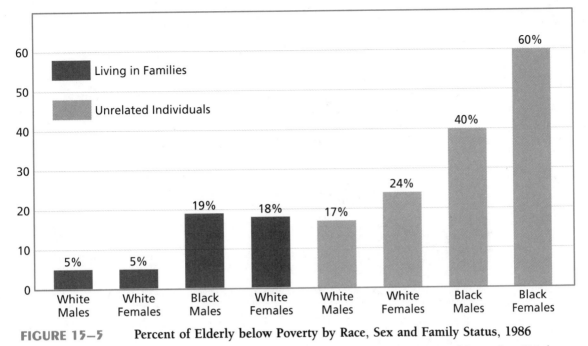

FIGURE 15–5   Percent of Elderly below Poverty by Race, Sex and Family Status, 1986

Source: U.S. Bureau of the Census, Current Population Reports, Series P-60, No. 161, *Money Income and Poverty Status United States: 1987* (Washington, D.C.: U.S. Government Printing Office, 1988), 28–31.

65. In 1900, 60 percent of older men were employed. Now, about 12 percent of all those over 65 are wage earners. The development of Social Security has much to do with this change. On average, Social Security payments account for almost 40 percent of the income of older Americans. The average monthly Social Security benefit for a retired worker was $629 in 1991, for a male worker and his wife, $1,067. Assets, such as savings and personal property, provide another 25 percent of average income. However, about a third of the elderly have no asset income at all. A number of older persons need additional government help beyond Social Security pension benefits. Some 7 percent of older Americans receive Supplemental Security Income, or federally administered public assistance payments to people who are below a set income level. Minorities and women are particularly likely to need such assistance.[14] (See Figure 15–6 on page 534.)

Older people generally have less cash income than the rest of the population. On the other hand, a number of non-cash factors favor the elderly, including paid-up mortgages, smaller family size, and favorable tax treatment. In addition, older Americans qualify for a number of in-kind benefits from the government. Some, like Medicare, are available to almost all elderly; others, like Medicaid, are income-based. Ninety-six percent of older Americans are covered by Medicare, and about 8 percent are also insured by Medicaid. However, since these government programs do not cover all medical costs, and also because these costs are rising, households headed by an elderly person spend an average 12.5 percent of after-tax income on health care. This compares to an average 5 percent spent by all households.[15]

Definitions of Aging   **533**

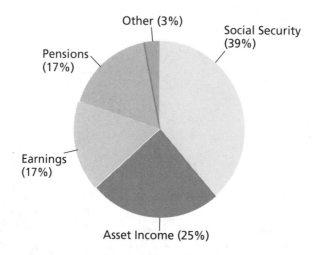

Other (3%)

Social Security (39%)

Pensions (17%)

Earnings (17%)

Asset Income (25%)

FIGURE 15–6   Shares of Income by Source, Couples and Unmarried Persons Aged 65 and Older, 1988

Source: American Association of Retired Persons, *A Profile of Older Americans, 1990,* 10. © 1990 American Association of Retired Persons. Reprinted with permission.

Health

According to one survey, a quarter of the elderly see poor or failing health as a major problem of old people today. Yet the health status of the elderly is varied, and the picture is not as negative as many may think. Although most older individuals have at least one chronic disease, such as arthritis, interview surveys find over two-thirds of the non-institutionalized elderly describing their health as good to excellent. About 62 percent of non-institutionalized older persons report no limitations in their daily activities. Only about 10 percent of all those over 65 are severely disabled. It is true, however, that the older the person, the greater the probability of encountering disease or impairment. About 40 percent of those aged 75 and over, for example, have health constraints on their normal activities. Men are more likely to encounter illness and limitations than women. Non-white and low-income elderly are also more susceptible to disease and disability. These groups account for a disproportionate number of the elderly with severe disability.[16]

Government Expenditures for the Elderly

Those who worry about "the Graying of America" often have rising public expenses in mind. Since 1960, the share of the federal budget spent on programs serving the aging has almost doubled. Currently, over a quarter of the federal budget goes for programs for the elderly, with the major cost being the contributory social insurance system. Individual states contribute their share, accounting for half the money spent on Medicaid, for example.

The cost of old age and survivors benefits under Social Security rose from $31.8 billion in 1970 to $118 billion in 1980, and to almost $250 billion in 1990. Currently, over a quarter of the federal budget goes for programs for the elderly, with all but 5 percent of that amount being spent on Social Security. But the more serious increase has been in Medicare and Medicaid payments, with Medicare now accounting for about a tenth of all federal spending. As we noted in Chapter 12, rising health costs are a major problem for our economy.[17]

Summary

As we survey the statistics related to aging, no single picture emerges. True, older Americans are more likely to have moderate to low incomes and to have one or more chronic diseases. These characteristics, along with some restrictions in activities, are more typical in the old-old group than among those between 65 and 74. Moreover, income level, health status, and living arrangements among the elderly are influenced not only by age but also to a great degree by previous income level, race, and sex.

DYNAMICS: CAUSES AND EFFECTS OF AGING

It is possible to construct several pictures of the causes and effects of aging. Each relates to our theme of dependency. One version might be the following: Aging is an incurable disease. Upon reaching old age, the individual steadily deteriorates physically, intellectually, and emotionally. He or she encounters illness and disability, loses mental capacity, becomes more conservative and ill-tempered, loses interest in sex, comes to depend more and more on others, and gradually becomes isolated from the larger society.

A different picture would depict aging this way: Aging is a natural phenomenon of uncertain causes. The older person faces some physical and intellectual deterioration, but this generally proceeds at a modest rate and does not affect daily functioning in a major way. He or she remains involved in political and community activities, not necessarily changing attitudes, but becoming more interested in issues related to the needs and priorities of older people. Social interaction and sexual interest generally do not decline and most individuals continue to lead independent and satisfying lives.

Neither picture, of course, portrays the "truth" about aging for all people. The first is more heavily laden with myths and stereotypes about the elderly than the second. In order to sort through the many myths and facts about aging, it is helpful to review existing theories about its nature and causes. Because gerontology is a relatively new study, however, such theories are still tentative.

Biological Theories

Why do people age? Is aging inevitable? These questions are still difficult to answer. At present, most scientists believe that aging is an inevitable phenomenon for human organisms. Aging is not a disease, but instead represents natural losses of function. Examples of such losses include decline in short-term memory, reduced exercise capacity, and deficiencies in the body's immune system.

The ultimate sources of aging are still poorly understood. Aging probably stems from the fact that the ability of normal somatic cells (any cell other than a germ cell) to replicate and function is limited. After a certain period of time, these cells no longer reproduce. Specialists in geriatrics have posited a number of explanations as to why this occurs. Many look to genetic bases of aging, hypothesizing for example that a purposeful sequence of events is programmed into human genes. These events lead to age changes. Another theory suggests that cells accumulate defective proteins in the course of aging; still another holds that "control systems" such as the endocrine system are responsible for eventual loss of cell function. Research on these and other biological theories of aging is still in a beginning phase.[18]

While biological gerontologists have not yet uncovered the ultimate cause or causes of aging, they are learning more and more about the physiological effects of aging. Current understanding about these effects tends to challenge earlier views of the large and irreversible declines experienced by the elderly. True, sensory input (taste, touch, smell, hearing, and vision) decreases with age. Age brings a decline in the pumping function of the heart, and the respiratory system does not work as well. Older people also show a diminishing ability to respond to stress and to return to a pre-stress level in a reasonable length of time. For example, an older person takes longer to adjust to changes in temperature. Also, while age itself is not a disease, it has the effect of making people more vulnerable to illness. Cardiovascular disease and cancer have their greatest incidence among the elderly.

However, individuals experience these effects of aging differently and at varying points in their lives. And despite the various changes brought by age, the majority of older people have more than enough skills and capacities to meet the demands of contemporary lifestyles.[19]

One important element in these lifestyles is sexuality. The myth that older people lose sexual interest and ability is largely unfounded. While sexual activity does tend to decrease with age, much of this is due to lack of partners and the inhibiting effect of societal expectations and assumptions. Our society has difficulty accepting the fact that older people may be as interested in sex as anyone else. In actuality, capacity for sexual activity and enjoyment changes relatively little as people age.

Common images of aging also link advancing years with loss of intellectual ability. Yet recent studies indicate that brain capacity does not decline greatly with age. These studies do show a slowing of brain waves and reaction time among the elderly. However, in tasks that do not demand a rapid response, there is little difference in intellectual ability between younger and older subjects. In fact, researchers now feel that an individual's intelligence peaks at quite a late age, perhaps in the mid-fifties.[20]

Those age-related losses in physiological and intellectual capacity which do occur are not necessarily irreversible. For example, exercise can counter declines in cardiac and respiratory functioning. Through biofeedback techniques, older people can increase their brain wave activity. Additional sensory stimulation may also counter intellectual decline.

Physiological aspects of aging, then, are real, but not necessarily fixed. In addition, biological aspects of aging tell only one part of the story. Contrary to the phrase "biology is destiny," both social and social psychological dimensions need to be added to our understanding of the aging process.

Social Psychological Theories of Aging

Social psychologists stress that personality and behavior are shaped by socialization experiences and assigned social roles. Adult personality change stems from the varying demands society places on individuals as they grow older. Roles shift also, as the individual moves from parent to grandparent, married person to widow or widower, employed person to retiree. New roles demand new responses, beliefs, and different ways of behaving. Some researchers argue that the elderly pick up few new roles that compensate for the major life activities that are lost. Retirement, widowhood, and other changes can lead to loneliness and the loss of meaningful functions in life.[21]

Psychologist Erik Erikson sees life development as a series of tasks to be mastered. The task for the middle-aged person is to achieve "generativity" rather than stagnation, that is, to produce something of value for future generations. Erikson describes the work of the final stage as achievement of integrity. Ideally, the older person comes to accept his or her life as having been meaningful and worthwhile. Failure to do so can lead to despair.[22]

Other theorists offer similar descriptions of adult development as a series of different periods or phases. Most of these models characterize the later years as a time of heightened introspection and increasing awareness of personal mortality.

If one adds the idea of role loss to this picture, it is possible to think of the elderly as gradually withdrawing from daily activities and social interaction. This act of withdrawal has in fact been described as a successful adaptation to aging. Writing in 1961, Elaine Cumming and William Henry advanced the *disengagement theory* of aging. They posited that such isolation and turning inward were helpful for the elderly, allowing them to approach death, the final separation, with acceptance and a sense of peace. Because the elderly face the loss of loved ones, resources, and traditional roles, disengagement becomes a healthy, mutual process between the individual and society. There is a certain reality to this concept. Losses *do* occur, and some older individuals do withdraw from social contacts and future planning. In one survey of older people, almost half said they had not made plans for things they would be doing "a month or a year from now."[23]

On the other hand, the majority of older people report active family ties, close friends, and good relations with their neighbors. This finding is more in line with a different perspective on successful aging, known as *activity theory*. The idea that keeping active keeps one young has been around for a long time. More formally stated in the early 1960s, activity theory stresses that aside from changes in biology and health, older people are the same as middle-aged people. They have the same psychological and social needs and will gain greatest satisfaction from staying active and resisting isolation. It is through continued activity that older individuals maintain their skills and their sense of social value.[24]

Evidence exists to support both theories. A number of studies suggest that age brings increased introversion and attention to the inner self. It may also bring greater conformity, cautiousness, and passivity. Yet these findings may in fact be due not to age changes, but to generational differences in values, experiences, and socioeconomic status (a point we will return to shortly). As evidence of continued activity on the part of the elderly, one might note that about 75 percent of those aged 60 to 69 belong to a church or synagogue. The elderly and near-elderly (ages 55–64) are the most likely age groups to vote. In the 1988 presidential election, for example, 69 percent of those 65 and over voted, as opposed to 48 percent of those aged 25 to 34. Three-quarters of the elderly read a daily newspaper regularly. In a survey on life satisfaction, almost 70 percent of the older individuals questioned reported "the things I do are as interesting to me as they ever were."[25]

Social psychological theories of aging offer different perspectives on the issues of dependence and interdependency. Discussions of role change among the elderly some-times stress the significance of the "dependent person" role. Disengagement theory pictures a passive individual who is no longer interdependent with others. Activity theory emphasizes the independence of most elderly, as well as their ability to help others. Reality is more complex. As gerontologist Nancy Hooyman notes, there is

> growing recognition that the role of "dependent person" is not inevitable with age. Rather, the life course is characterized by varying periods of greater or lesser dependency in social relationships, with most people being emotionally dependent on others regardless of age.

In addition, many older people are in turn *depended upon* by others. A recent report on the interdependence of generations reminds us of the many ways in which older Americans help families and others, including child care, financial and emotional support, and community service.[26]

This review of social psychological theories suggests that rather than a single pattern of optimum aging, what we see is "a diversity of patterns of aging based on combinations of personality type, role activity, and life satisfaction."[27] In addition, social factors affect these differential responses to aging.

Sociological Theories of Aging

Major social influences on aging include a person's sex, ethnicity, socioeconomic status, occupation, and birth cohort. These and other factors color each individual's encounter with old age. A white, college-educated, 80-year-old retired business executive who lives with his wife in a Florida condominium will experience a different aging process from that of an elderly, widowed Hispanic woman with a sixth-grade education, who has worked all her life as a farm laborer, and now lives with her youngest daughter. The two will probably vary in terms of lifestyle, attitudes toward aging, support systems, and health status.

As we noted in our earlier section on statistics, men and women over 65 differ along the dimensions of income, health and longevity, marital situation, and living arrangements. Older men face more acute health problems and a shorter life expectancy than women. Many married women will spend the last twenty years of their life without a spouse. Relatively few will move in with their children. Sociologists like Helena Lopata have pointed out that widowhood represents a serious problem in middle-class America. A husband's death "removes the major segment in the social role of wife and reduces the social circles of mother, friend, housewife [and] neighbor." It can lead to ongoing loneliness and depression.[28]

Race and ethnicity are other potent determinants of a person's experience with aging. Up until the 1960s, most gerontologists focused exclusively on white subjects.

Now that picture is changing, with researchers investigating the effects of race, national origin, and culture on individual and population aging. The existence of income differences between white, African American, and Hispanic American elderly is one obvious finding. A more subtle difference is the way in which education's effects on income are muted by race. For example, among those with some college education, three times as many African American aged as white are likely to be poor. Minority and ethnic status also affect: (1) housing arrangements (minority aged generally have the least adequate housing); (2) health status (older Hispanic American males, for example, have unusually high levels of stress and health and mental health dysfunction); and (3) familial patterns and social roles (in contrast to the predominant pattern in the United States, many Native American families assign to the older generation meaningful roles as transmitters of traditional culture, values, and religion). Support systems also differ, with foreign-born and minority elderly often relying more on churches, extended family, and community ties than native-born Americans.[29]

Previous and present income level carry obvious implications for one's experience with aging. Middle- and upper-class individuals are much more likely to enter retirement with assets and private pension funds, along with their Social Security benefits. In addition, income often interacts with occupational status to affect aging. For example, men from lower socioeconomic classes leave school earlier and begin working earlier, generally in blue collar or service jobs. These men may retire sooner and thus see themselves as being old at younger ages than do middle-class men.

A particularly useful construct within the sociological perspective on aging is the idea that individuals' attitudes and behaviors are greatly influenced by the particular age cohort into which they were born. The term *cohort* is used to describe those born within a specific unit of time, generally a five or ten year interval. Each cohort undergoes certain similar sociocultural experiences and possesses a broad historical heritage. That is, despite differences of sex and ethnicity, all Americans born between 1915 and 1920 share the common experience of being young adults during the period of World War II. Cohorts differ from one another in terms of general educational levels achieved, commitment to political activism, and other factors. Many stereotypes about the elderly are in fact applicable only to specific cohorts. For example, the observation that people become more conservative as they age may reflect the fact that recent cohorts of elderly grew up in conservative times and reflect this in their voting patterns. Social reform and activist stances may be very different among the elderly of the early 2000s, who were young adults in the politically active 1960s. Education levels also change from cohort to cohort. The elderly of the 1990s are a much better educated group than those of the 1970s.[30]

A final variation of the sociological approach is to think about aging within the broad context of the organization of work in our society. In other words, the elderly can be viewed in terms of their productivity level in a modern industrialized economy. Historians and social scientists have observed that since the late 1800s, older Americans have been helped or pushed out of the workforce. The notion of mandatory retirement has been based on assumptions that older workers lack the up-to-date skills, strength, and appropriate attitudes necessary for their jobs. (It also reflects the concern that the job market needs to be opened up to younger people.) We will assess the validity of these assumptions later in this chapter. The important point here is that the social role of retiree or nonworker can carry with it a stigma of "uselessness" which affects the self-perceptions of older people and can be used to justify their segregation from mainstream society.

HISTORY OF AGING IN AMERICA

The history of old age in America chronicles a variety of attitudes toward aging. Interestingly, despite popular belief, there has probably never been a truly "golden epoch" for the elderly in America. Instead, Americans have persistently demonstrated ambiguous, conflicting feelings about old age, with specific differences in the ways we have described the elderly over time.

There are two major themes in this history of aging. The first, described by historian Andrew Achenbaum and others, pertains to the change from a generally positive conception of old age before the Civil War to a largely negative picture from the 1870s on. The second theme relates to ways of dealing with dependency among older people. While there has always been a mixture of public and private responses to this problem, over time the federal government has taken on more and more responsibility for meeting the needs of the elderly. This section will explore changing attitudes toward the elderly as well as the development of age-related policies and programs.

During the colonial period, older individuals were generally looked upon with respect. Early Americans saw a definite role for the elderly, believing their wisdom to be an important asset in a new, developing nation. While their proportion in the population was relatively small, older Americans seemed to show, through their survival, that the American environment promoted a long and vigorous life. Many older people still worked and carried out useful family functions. Men remained active in farming, government, and other activities. Women were often in their sixties before the last child of a large family left home.[31]

Not all elderly, of course, were held in high esteem. Those who had had power and wealth as younger people were most likely to be respected and revered in old age. Poorer individuals were less likely to be admired. Americans also recognized that old age could bring pain and suffering. They saw chronic illness as an inevitable problem of aging and they realized that economic problems increased with age.[32]

In the colonial period and in the early 1800s, a variety of measures were developed in a piecemeal way to supplement the role of families in caring for the poor and dependent elderly. These included the poorhouse and outdoor relief. However, care by one's own family members constituted the most common type of help.

Despite recognition of the problems of old age, the elderly continued to be viewed in a generally positive light during the early 1800s. However, attitudes began to shift by the mid-1800s, and by World War I, many Americans had come to equate old age with ugliness, disease, and uselessness. The reasons for this change have intrigued historians. The simple answer would be to attribute the new attitudes to changes in the economy because of a large increase in the elderly population. One might argue, for example, that a newly industrializing nation had little room for workers with outdated ideas and lessened physical capabilities and that there were now many more frail elderly in need of help. However, the proportion of older people in the United States did not greatly increase until the late 1800s. The biggest jumps in the elderly population occurred after World War I. Also, the majority of elderly continued to work; in 1890, for example, almost three-quarters of men over 65 were still employed. However, older workers did tend to be found in the more traditional trades, such as farming and mining. In addition, the elderly were moving into cities at a greater rate in the later 1800s, and by doing so they often lost supportive ties with both family and community.[33]

The dramatic shifts in attitudes, however, seem to have come more from broader cultural and intellectual changes in American society than from occupational trends or differences in the elderly population itself. Achenbaum argues that negative ideas about the aging stemmed in part from the new philosophy of Social Darwinism, which stressed survival of the fittest, and in part from a growing stress on the importance of science and efficiency in American life. The expansion of medical knowledge was a crucial factor in the change. Earlier, the elderly had been seen as possessing the secrets of long life. Now, modern scientific medical knowledge could teach those secrets. In addition, physicians began to change their ideas about old age, stressing the degeneration and weakening of cells and organs as people grew older. The notion that old age was in itself a disease grew in popularity.[34]

While physicians appeared to be increasing their knowledge about the aging process, they were not yet successful in making the aged more healthy. Historian Carole Haber argues that it was the experts themselves—doctors, social scientists, and professional charity workers—who despaired of improvement in the lives of the elderly and focused instead on their social, physical, and economic problems. Social scientists in the late 1800s, for example, spoke of aging as "a unique and particularly perilous stage of existence."[35]

While the new ideas were not at first based on significant changes in the situation of the aged, reality began to catch up with these concepts after 1890. By then, larger numbers of poor elderly could be found in big cities, where they were perceived as a growing welfare problem. In addition, businessmen enamored of the modern concept of efficiency had begun to view the elderly as outmoded and unproductive workers. The late 1800s brought the first retirement programs, through which businesses could pension off older workers. While these might be viewed as humanitarian measures and as a final payment for service to the company, they gave employers greater control over the workforce and reinforced the idea that the elderly were incapable of useful work. (See Figure 15–7 on page 542.)

At the same time, the number of elderly people in institutions grew. This happened in part because of changes in family life, such as fewer adult children to care for older parents, and in part because of diminished resources among the elderly, less of whom now worked or owned farms. While the percentage of older people in poorhouses remained fairly small, their presence had become much more visible. This was because by the early 1900s most other groups had been siphoned off to specialized institutions—the mental asylum, the training school for the mentally retarded, or the reformatory. By 1910, poorhouses had been transformed into old age homes. In that year, 45 percent of all native-born residents and 70 percent of all foreign-born in poorhouses were age 60 or over.[36]

By the 1920s, the aged as a group had come to be characterized as a "social problem." Their numbers had increased almost 60 percent since 1870. The proportion of old-old in the group had begun to grow. Only 60 percent of older men now worked,

FIGURE 15–7

Source: W. Andrew Achenbaum and Peggy Ann Kusnerz, *Images of Old Age in America* (Ann Arbor, MI: Institute of Gerontology, 1978), 33. Reprinted with permission of the author.

compared to 73 percent in 1890. The decline in agriculture deprived the elderly of one traditional source of employment.[37]

Researchers began to focus on physical and intellectual problems and undesirable character traits in the elderly. One writer saw old age as "simply a mass of bad habits." Reformers and philanthropists concentrated on work with younger people, who seemed more capable of change. Writing as late as 1939, a social worker noted, "Perhaps we may regard old age as a 'twilight' where the light is too dim to allow for useful service."[38]

Despite these negative views, many older people continued to live useful lives with adequate financial resources. However, the economic crash of the thirties served to bring the problems of poorer elderly to a head. While countless Americans were adversely affected by the Great Depression, the elderly were particularly at risk. Many lost their jobs, their savings, and other assets following the 1929 market collapse. It was not, therefore, surprising that a system of old age insurance—Social Security—served as the cornerstone of Franklin D. Roosevelt's New Deal social welfare programs.

The idea of pension systems was not entirely new in the 1930s. Private businesses had been establishing pension programs on a small scale since the latter part of the nineteenth century, although by 1925 only 280 programs existed nationwide. In addition, the federal government began providing compulsory old age and disability insurance to civil servants in the 1920s. More important, public pensions for United States war veterans had been established after the Civil War. At first these applied only to financially needy veterans and to those with disabilities. By 1912, however, veterans pensions became strictly age-related. In other words, any veteran over 62 could qualify.[39]

Nevertheless, the idea of a national system of old age benefits did not catch on in the early 1900s. Although England, Germany, and other European countries established pension plans during this period, American beliefs in individual responsibility and private responses to need continued to hold sway. Even the developing labor movement did not at first back old age benefits, with workers preferring to trust the union's ability to improve wages and provide security rather than the government's paternalistic measures.[40]

A number of forces interacted to bring about change in this situation in the 1930s. First of all, as we discussed in Chapter 8, a social insurance movement had been growing quietly through the early years of the century. The idea of social insurance was seen as an alternative to direct charity. Generally, it meant following the same principles used in life insurance or property insurance, in which people pay a certain fee and contract with a company or organization to reimburse them in the case of loss. Social insurance was first conceived as government-sponsored insurance for urban industrial workers, who could be insured against sickness, accident, or unemployment. After World War I, the social insurance movement broadened to cover the idea of old age pensions. Abraham Epstein, an economist who spent much of his career promoting the old age pension idea, founded the American Association for Old Age Security in 1927. This group and other organizations lobbied for old age pension legislation in the 1920s and early 1930s. A number of state and municipal retirement systems emerged during this period.[41]

The Townsend Movement was another factor in the move toward Social Security. Dr. Frances Townsend, a retired physician in California, proposed a program to end the Depression by providing everyone over 60 with a pension of $200 a month. The program was to be funded through public taxation. Recipients would have to spend their $200 within the month, thus bolstering the economy. This rather simple idea found a good deal of popularity, with "Townsend Clubs" spreading among older Americans in 1934. Soon, Townsend claimed 5 million supporters. Similar proposals were made by other groups. In promoting these ideas, the elderly were beginning to demonstrate their power as a political lobbying group.[42]

The various pension plans evoked controversy. Radical observers saw pensions, particularly private ones, as measures to control workers—to weed out older, supposedly unproductive employees and to ensure a labor force of younger workers compelled to remain with a particular employer for the sake of retirement benefits. Conservatives, on the other hand, accepted the necessity of some type of social welfare help for the elderly, but wanted this carried out under voluntary, rather than governmental auspices. They felt that public old age pensions would sap people's self-respect. If public relief was necessary for dependent elderly, it should be provided through a means test which would deter individuals from "irresponsible" use of public monies. Finally, liberals saw social insurance as one way to bring about reform through a better distribution of wealth in the United States. They hoped that social insurance programs would replace the old punitive relief approach and establish welfare benefits as a right for both the elderly and other categories of people. Many social workers joined in this view. Some were active in the drafting of Roosevelt's Social Security legislation.[43]

The Social Security Act of 1935 constituted a compromise between different proposals and different political points of view. It offered some federal aid for means-tested public assistance for the elderly (as well as for two other groups: dependent children and the blind). Through this program, the federal government matched funds spent by the states for needy elderly, who could be considered among the "deserving" poor. The Social Security Act also established a social insurance system for individuals aged 65 and over, regardless of financial need. The system was funded through a payroll tax levied on both employers and employees. The notion that workers "paid into" their old age pension fund fit well with the American stress on individualism and hard work, and made the act more palatable to both politicians and the public. Unlike European systems, in which social insurance was paid for through general tax revenues, the Social Security program would be financed largely through the private sector. As President Roosevelt put it:

> We put the payroll contributions there so as to give the contributors a legal, moral and political right to collect their pensions . . . . With those taxes in there, no damn politician can ever scrap my social security program.[44]

The program made moderate attempts at redistribution of income. That is, benefits were weighted to provide proportionately higher returns to lower income workers.

The Social Security system soon expanded. In 1939, an important amendment added Survivors Insurance, which provided benefits to the widow and other surviving dependents of a worker who died prematurely. The initial act had not insured everyone; domestic and agricultural workers, for example, had been excluded. When payments began in 1940, only one-fifth of all workers qualified. Gradually most groups of employees were included, so that at the present time almost all retired Americans receive Social Security benefits. Also, by 1939, Congress had decided to tie old age benefits not to lifetime contributions, but to average earnings over a shorter period of work. Finally, the Social Security Administration broadened its coverage of disabled workers in the 1940s and 1950s, so that people with disabilities qualified for more benefits than they had actually put into the system.

This expansion of coverage signaled a shift in the makeup and philosophy of Social Security. It had become a more complex system, taking need into account as well as contributions. Financing principles had also changed. Initially, the government "was to be a piggy bank, storing contributions and paying them back with interest at age sixty-five."[45] People would be contributing money to a fund set aside for their own retirement benefits. Now, current workers were paying benefits for those already retired. As we will see, this shifting forward of obligations to future workers would eventually lead to predictions of crisis in the system.[46]

Social Security was the first national institutional structure set up to assist older Americans. It helped bring about a major change in the source of financial support for the elderly, a shift from dependence on family aid and wages to reliance on social insurance benefits and private pensions. In the following decades, national interest in the aging continued. A number of organizations and programs evolved to meet the needs of older citizens. These developments attested to the growing numbers and political power of the elderly.

Scientific study of the problems and needs of the older population was not new to the 1940s and 1950s. The founding of the New York Geriatrics Society in 1915 reflected attention given to the medical aspects of aging in the early years of this century. Social and behavioral scientists had also been studying the nature and effects of aging. However, because of the increase in the number of elderly and the visibility given to them by the development of Social Security, research on aging expanded greatly after 1940. In 1946 the National Institute of Health in Washington established a Gerontological Research Unit, which set the stage for the creation of the National Institute for Aging in 1974. The Institute conducts and sponsors research on aging in the biomedical and social sciences. The Gerontological Society of America, founded in 1945, promoted interdisciplinary discussion in the field. The first National Conference on Aging was held in 1950; this was followed by three White House Conferences on Aging between 1961 and 1981. These developments led to joint activity by scientists and policy makers in the areas of research and legislation.[47]

The federal government was gradually becoming a clearinghouse for information and research on old age. In addition, attention to the problems of the elderly led to the creation of special committees on aging in the House and Senate. Crucial legislation emerged in the 1960s and 1970s. Programs for the elderly, such as Medicare and Medicaid (1965), were an important contribution of Lyndon Johnson's Great Society. Extensions of the Social Security Act increased the economic security of older Americans. Of particular significance was the establishment of automatic adjustments of monthly benefits for inflation (Cost of Living Adjustments, or COLAs) in 1972. Also in the 1970s, Congress enacted the Supplementary Security Income program (SSI), in which the federal government took over the old age assistance programs for needy elderly persons that had previously been run by the states. Housing and low-income energy assistance constituted two other areas of legislation. Finally, the Older Americans Act of 1965 demonstrated the commitment of the Great Society to a broad array of social, nutritional, mental health, and other needs of the elderly.

The Older Americans Act established what has been dubbed the "aging network," a partnership of federal, state, and local public and private agencies offering a range of programs and services for older Americans. The Act and its subsequent amendments "changed the federal government's focus from income maintenance to coordination and funding of a comprehensive service system for the elderly." This coordination is carried out through a three-level administrative structure, with a national Administration on Aging, state units on aging, and local area agencies on aging (AAA). The types of programs planned and sponsored by these units have focused on nutrition, recreation, transportation, employment, housing, and information.[48]

By the 1970s, then, the federal government had made enormous strides in legislating to meet a broad array of needs of an aging population. The proportion of the federal budget related to programs for the elderly rose to approximately 25 percent. A major reason for this expansion lay in the growth of lobbying efforts by a larger, more articulate, and better organized population of older Americans. The so-called "Gray Lobby" developed out of a number of citizen and professional organizations for older individuals. One of the largest and most powerful organizations is the American Association of Retired Persons (AARP), which grew out of a retired teachers' organization founded in 1947. By 1975, AARP had a membership of 9 million people, making it the largest voluntary association in the world. The organization's goals included political

After retiring from a key executive post with the United Presbyterian Church, Maggie Kuhn became a national leader promoting the rights of the elderly.

involvement as well as provision of various benefits to members, including insurance and discounts on pharmaceutical products. The National Association of Retired Federal Employees (1921) and the National Council of Senior Citizens, a union-related association which developed in the 1960s, are two other important grass-roots organizations. In 1950, public and private health, recreation, community action, and social work agencies dealing with the elderly formed the National Council on the Aging to serve as a central resource for planning, information, and consultation relative to the needs of the elderly. The most colorful of all these organizations is the Gray Panthers, established in 1972 by social activist Maggie Kuhn. The Gray Panthers took a more radical stance than other groups in the Gray Lobby, striving for the liberation of older persons from the "paternalism and oppression with which society keeps us powerless."[49]

A number of factors have thus contributed to the distinct "presence" of the elderly and their concerns in current national policy considerations. From a small proportion of the population in the Colonial period, older Americans have become a significant percentage of all citizens. A group whose weaknesses had been stressed in the 1800s, the elderly now belong to well-organized lobbying groups which have helped win important social legislation. However, the position of the elderly in modern society still contains a number of ambiguities and problems.

CURRENT ISSUES AND TRENDS

Social Welfare Expenditures for Older Americans

One of the most publicized issues regarding the elderly in recent years has been the so-called "Social Security Crisis." This, in turn, is linked to concerns about rising public expenditures for older people and the impact of a growing elderly population on the size of the social welfare budget.

Fears about the solvency of Social Security arose first in 1977 and again in 1980. In both cases, the mandatory cost-of-living adjustment, higher unemployment rates, and slow wage growth caused a decline in the program's trust funds. Until recently, Social Security trust funds had maintained a reserve equal to a full year of benefit payments (a cushion against severe problems in the national economy). By 1980, reserves had declined to less than three months' benefit payments. Congress "rescued" the program several times by raising Social Security taxes for workers, reducing the growth of benefits, and borrowing money from Medicare trust fund reserves. A more long-term solution was achieved under the Social Security Amendments of 1983. This complex set of changes included higher Social Security payroll taxes, a gradual rise in the retirement age, and taxation of benefits received by taxpayers with incomes over certain limits. Although conservative politicians and others continue to warn Americans of the inevitable demise of the system, Social Security fund trustees predict that the funds will remain solvent for the next seventy years.[50]

One factor which continues to make people nervous about the long-term solvency of the system is the rising number of elderly in the United States. As the proportion of working people to retirees decreases, the *dependency ratio* changes. Although that term applies to the relationship between the working population and all dependent members of society, including children, what is generally stressed is the ratio between workers and the elderly. In 1910, there were ten working people per older person. In 1980, there were five or six. This ratio will continue to decline into the next century. Theoretically, this means that fewer and fewer workers will be responsible for the support of more and more elderly.[51]

However, the picture may not be as grim as it seems. A number of those older individuals will have private pensions and other assets. Many may work longer. Economic growth and increased real wages can also offset effects of a changing dependency ratio. In addition, if the United States were willing to alter the nature of Social Security financing and to adopt the general tax revenue approach of European countries, the nation would be better able to support its elderly. Finally, as Crystal notes, "Today's benefit levels could be sustained even in the worst coming years if we were willing to pay . . . at the level currently imposed in a number of European countries."[52] The United States has the money to support its elderly, but the country would have to alter its spending priorities.

Evaluation of spending priorities would necessitate discussion of the degree to which the government should assume responsibility for the well-being of older people in our society. Such responsibility can be costly. In a comparative study of social welfare expenditures among affluent countries, Harold Wilensky found that the level of total government welfare spending (not just programs specifically for the elderly) is affected more by the proportion of aged in the population than by any other variable.[53] In other words, a high number of older people leads to growth in the social welfare system. Rising expenditures in this system, particularly related to Social Security and health care for the elderly, rekindle debates over the proper mix between private and governmental commitments.

Some argue that support for the elderly should be lodged more firmly in the private sector of our economy. A number of conservatives have contended that growth in Social Security benefits undercuts the public's reliance on the market, increases individuals' dependency on the government, and reduces incentives for personal savings that "provide a major source of essential investment capital for economic growth."[54] During the Reagan Administration, one proposed solution was a national system of private pensions that would supplement or completely replace Social Security. However, public acceptance of Social Security has so far prevented moves in this direction. Currently, about one-half of private-sector employees are covered by a pension plan. A smaller percentage will actually receive benefits upon retirement. Critics of a broad private pension system have argued that because such pensions would most likely be tied to workers' actual wage levels, this kind of arrangement would not do anything to redistribute income. In addition, large, private pension schemes might benefit business more than workers, giving corporations large amounts of capital funds to invest for their own purposes.[55]

Health care is an area in which private sponsorship of services for the elderly figures prominently. For-profit nursing homes constitute a major factor in this care. Private homes for the elderly first developed in the 1800s, as an alternative to the almshouse for middle-class clients. Later, they were seen as appropriate institutions for a broad range of elderly people. Their growth was spurred in the 1930s when the old age assistance portion of Social Security prohibited benefits to elderly residents of public institutions. Those living in private "rest homes," however, could qualify. Since the 1960s, Medicaid funding has further promoted nursing home growth. Heavy reliance on institutional care for the elderly is in part a result of the government's failure to put much of its resources into alternative kinds of services. It also reflects the increase in frail elderly needing long-term care.

Presently, about 80 percent of the country's nursing homes are run for profit. A number of these are part of large corporate chains. (See Table 15–5.) Ironically, of course, while these nursing homes are privately owned and managed, much of their funding comes through public assistance, chiefly Medicaid payments. Thus, although we tend to think of private and public sponsorship of services for the elderly as two separate phenomena, a more accurate picture is that of interdependence of the market and the governmental sectors.

While the source of funding may not distinguish private and public sector approaches to health care for the elderly, the difference between private market, private non-profit, and governmental perspectives does emerge in debates over regulation versus competition. Those favoring for-profit systems of care argue, for example, that competition between nursing home care providers results in better, more cost-efficient services. Critics point to abuses and deficiencies in care and complain about profiteering in the system. The solution, they say, is tighter state and federal regulation of homes along with strict enforcement of these standards.[56] One example of such regulation is the recent development of federal rules discouraging the use of physical or chemical restraints on elderly nursing home residents. Such rules are important for nursing homes no matter what their sponsorship. In 1990, for example, about 41 percent of all nursing home residents were put in some type of restraint.[57]

A serious problem affecting both private and public programs is the pattern of governmental spending cut-backs established by the Reagan administration and continued under President Bush. While Social Security remains basically intact, Medicare and Medicaid beneficiaries now pay a greater portion of their medical expenses than they used to. Federal funding for other programs used by the elderly, including food stamps and low-income energy assistance, has also been curtailed. These cut-backs

| TABLE 15–5 | Leading investor-owned nursing home systems (Ranked by number of beds—1990) | | | |

System	Number of Beds		Number of Units	
	1989	1990	1989	1990
1. Beverly Enterprises	96,268	91,414	885	849
2. Hillhaven Corp.	45,177	45,052	363	364
3. ARA Living Centers	26,180	24,738	240	230
4. Manor Care	21,637	23,051	160	167
5. United Health	16,018	16,475	141	148
6. Health Care & Retirement Corp.	16,799	16,397	132	132
7. National HealthCorp	8,684	9,666	72	78
8. National Heritage	19,960	9,147	181	84
9. Meritcare	5,923	6,132	58	61
10. Meridian Healthcare	5,100	5,500	35	36
11. GranCare*	. . .	5,453	. . .	38
12. Britthaven	4,265	5,356	42	53
13. Horizon Health Corp.	5,093	4,977	49	44
14. Brian Center Management	4,162	4,965	32	41
15. Geriatrics & Medical Centers	4,703	4,470	23	23

*GranCare reflects the merger of HostMasters and American Medical Services effective December 1990.

Source: Modern Health Care as reported in Standard & Poor's Industry Surveys, Vol. 1, October, 1991, p. H34.

reflect the philosophy that solutions to the problems of the elderly should come not from the institution of national policies and programs, but rather from state and local government efforts and from initiatives of the private sector and the family. However, the shifting of responsibility to states and localities has come at a time when their budgets are seriously restricted.[58] At the same time, family care for the elderly has become increasingly difficult as more and more women, the traditional caregivers, enter the labor force. It remains to be seen, as we move through the 1990s, whether the federal government will renew its commitment to major support for older Americans.

Community Services: Problems of Coordination and Adequacy

The first half of this century witnessed major strides in the development of income maintenance for older Americans. More recently, social welfare programs for the elderly have broadened to include a wide array of community-based health and social services. Such services are provided by many types of public and private organizations: hospitals, hospices, county departments of social service, churches, private social service agencies,

Nursing homes are appropriate institutions for a portion of the older population. Yet their spread may also reflect the failure of our society to devote resources to alternate types of services.

legal aid bureaus, visiting nurse associations, and home health care agencies. Ideally, the programs of these organizations help the elderly, including those with chronic disability, remain in their communities. However, these services can be fragmented. Without some type of centralized planning, gaps in particular kinds of care can exist.

Since the 1960s, the federal government has played an increasingly greater role in the financing and coordinating of community services. Through the Older Americans Act of 1965, planning and program development became major emphases in federal aging policy. The Older Americans Act (OAA) established an Administration of Aging at the national level. It also created State Units on Aging in each state. These units are responsible for planning and advocacy on behalf of the elderly on a state-wide basis. State Units on Aging designate local Area Agencies on Aging (AAAs). These funnel federal funds to "direct service providers," or those agencies, such as social agencies or legal aid bureaus, actually responsible for delivering federally mandated services. The AAAs also carry out area-wide planning for social services for the elderly. This planning includes, but is not limited to, the programs of organizations funded through the OAA. The Area Agencies monitor and evaluate policies and programs affecting the aged, they assess needs for services, they evaluate the services provided, and they coordinate federal programs serving the elderly. (See Figure 15–8.)

Funding for the OAA program is mandated in four areas: access services, including information and referral, transportation, and case coordination; in-home services, such as personal care, home health programs, homemaker chore assistance, and home-delivered meals; community services, including congregate meals, senior centers, and adult day care; and legal services. All services are provided free of charge, although donations are encouraged.

Currently, the bulk of OAA funding goes to nutrition programs. The major food programs are congregate meals (meals served to senior citizens in group settings such as churches or community centers) and "meals on wheels" (nutritionally balanced noon meals delivered to homebound elderly in their residences). These are vital resources for many elderly, who have nutritional deficiencies because of lack of income, difficulty

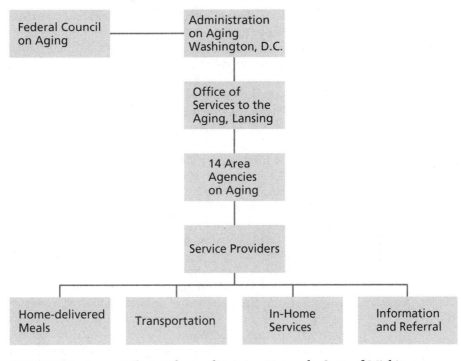

FIGURE 15–8   Who's Who in the Aging Network: State of Michigan

buying and preparing food, and disinterest in cooking or eating full meals when living alone. The home-delivered meals service is a particularly important source of support for the frail elderly.

Senior centers, another area of OAA funding, are multipurpose facilities which offer health, social, and educational services to older adults. One such center in Jacksonville, Florida, offers a dining room, auditorium, classrooms, a ceramics studio, library, and miniature golf course. Typical services of such a center include congregate meals, a telephone reassurance network, information and referral regarding other programs aiding the elderly, employment and volunteer opportunities, and recreational activities.[59] While senior centers fill important socialization and other needs, they are underutilized by minority and frail elderly, and are used by under 20 percent of older Americans over all.

The AAAs coordinate, sponsor, and plan other services as well. These include adult day care centers, which provide day time programming for ambulatory elderly with physical or mental difficulties; home health care, in which nurses and health aides provide nursing care, rehabilitation therapy, medication, and other assistance; and homemaker chore services, to help individuals with personal care and housekeeping. In addition, AAAs can carry out a variety of innovative coordination activities, many, but not all of which are related to services funded by the OAA. An AAA in Michigan, for example, recently took part in the following projects. It brought together staff members of local senior centers to discuss common issues and to compare notes on programming. It arranged meetings between legal aid bureau representatives and service providers, so that human service workers would be sensitized to the legal aspects of problems faced by their older clients. It carried out gerontology training for home care aides and individuals providing low-income housing for the elderly. It trained a group of older people in advocacy techniques. Finally, it sponsored a project aimed at building closer ties between nursing homes and local communities.

While AAAs and the OAA mark an important step in building an organized network of services for the elderly, the endeavor has encountered several difficulties. First, federal appropriations for the Administration on Aging and its programs have been modest. Largely because of funding problems, services have often been understaffed and otherwise inadequate. Some adult day care centers, for example, serve chiefly as recreational "holding programs," offering little or no counseling or rehabilitation for emotionally and/or physically impaired older adults. Local AAAs often face problems in coordinating agencies and programs. They must deal with fragmented community services. The area of home health care, for example, is "cluttered with a melange of small and changing suppliers, both public and private."[60] Finally, the coordination goal is undercut by serious gaps in services. The United States has developed few alternatives for older people discharged from mental institutions, other than nursing and boarding homes. Although home health programs have been an important breakthrough, we do not yet have an effective system of services for the frail elderly. Nevertheless, AAAs are making a significant contribution to supports for the elderly in general. This is seen particularly in their recent focus on in-home services to improve the quality of life for older Americans and to decrease the need for institutionalization.

Any discussion of community services for the elderly would be incomplete without recognition of the importance of the informal support network offered by families, friends, and neighbors. Such informal caregiving is actually the dominant type of long-term assistance to the frail elderly. Women family members—wives and daughters—are most likely to be the caregivers for elderly relatives. Family support for the elderly takes many forms. In one case, a spouse might provide companionship, financial security, and physical care. In another, a child might run errands, give gifts, and provide transportation. Generally such caregiving is not one-sided, but part of a mutual exchange between family members. Recently, planners and policymakers have sought ways in which government and the formal service system might enhance this informal aid. In some localities, AAAs have developed programs such as respite care and in-home services to support the efforts of families and friends in assisting older people.[61]

Ageism and Advocacy

The Administration on Aging's emphasis on in-home services results in part from continued pressure on elected officials and policy makers by organized groups of older citizens. These groups have banded together to promote better health, economic, and living conditions for the elderly and to counter *ageism,* that special brand of discrimination against those 65 and over. They have focused both on extending and reforming existing services and on changing public attitudes.

The stated goals of many programs for the aged are to maintain the independence and dignity of older people and to enhance their quality of life. Yet general attitudes toward the elderly can undermine these goals, both within services themselves and within the larger society. For example, older individuals may be patronized, treated as dependent, or directly exploited in institutions and programs. Nursing home abuses range from the condescending "Let's all do crafts, dears" of the well-meaning activities director to the over-medication which creates lethargic and depressed patients. Boarding home staff may hold back residents' public assistance allowances or fail to heat their rooms properly. Physicians may not give full attention to the ailments of older clients, stating, "Oh well, you have to expect this because you're growing old." Social workers and nurses may care *for* elders rather than help them make their own decisions.

On the broader social level, older Americans encounter subtle media put-downs as they watch programs and commercials focusing on the joys and attractiveness of youth. They also face the more overt problems of job discrimination and the denial of their legal rights. An older person might be declared legally incompetent without adequate definition of that term or careful examination of his or her particular case. While the use of court-appointed legal guardians was designed to be a protection for the frail elderly, a recent investigation found a dangerously overburdened system "where judges routinely place senior citizens under guardianship with little or no evidence and then frequently lose track of the wards and their money."[62]

More and more, older people are turning to advocacy groups for the resolution of these problems. The American Association of Retired Persons (AARP), the largest of these organizations, now numbers about 33 million members. Its magazine, *Modern Maturity,* has the third largest circulation of any periodical in the United States. AARP has significant grass-roots lobbying strength, which it uses to promote better health care, the preservation of Social Security benefits, and older workers' rights. Its lobbying efforts include state legislative committees, which have brought about such changes as agreements allowing generic drug substitutions in every state in the country.[63]

While AARP uses mainstream political activities to promote the views of its constituents, the Gray Panthers organization employs more of an activist approach. A smaller, more loosely structured advocacy group, the Panthers have taken to the streets with picket signs and banners to promote their concerns. Through their 120 local chapters or networks, they have brought class action suits on behalf of nursing home patients to ensure protection of their rights, they have monitored the treatment of the institutionalized elderly, and they have testified before Congress on numerous issues involving older Americans. While groups like the AARP focus primarily on obtaining services for older people, the Gray Panthers emphasize the need for basic social change.[64]

The activities of the "Gray Lobby," along with advocacy by professionals, have brought about a number of changes in society's behavior toward and treatment of older people. Recent amendments to the 1967 Age Discrimination in Employment Act have eliminated age-based mandatory retirement in almost all job settings. A Resident Rights Statement for intermediate care nursing home facilities has been incorporated into federal regulations for such facilities. A 1981 amendment to the OAA mandates a nursing home ombudsman system in every state. Grounds for declaring older people legally incompetent to carry out their own affairs have been tightened in a number of states. States have developed "Adult Protective Services," similar to those for children, in an attempt to prevent physical and emotional abuse of the elderly. Finally, older citizens have won impressive victories in maintaining the basic integrity of the Social Security system. The fight against more subtle forms of ageism is of course more difficult, but with the increased number and spending power of older citizens, even traditional media fascination with the young has begun to give way to television programs like NBC's "Golden Girls" and new magazines that tap the older market.

PERSPECTIVES

Public policies related to the needs and status of the elderly reflect a variety of political perspectives. Such perspectives differ along at least two major dimensions: (1) which facet of society should be responsible for meeting the needs and ensuring the rights of the elderly, and (2) what the role of the elderly themselves should be in shaping programs and policies affecting them.

The Conservative Perspective

Conservative approaches to policies and programs for the elderly stress the responsibility of the individual, family, and community in meeting social, health, and economic needs. While conservatives accept the necessity for a minimum level of governmental social welfare provisions for older Americans, they look to the voluntary sector and to private initiatives as being the major solutions to the problems of old age. Thus, the Reagan Administration spoke of Social Security as part of the basic safety net for older Americans, but at the same time promoted growth in private pensions and privately operated nursing homes, boarding homes, home health programs, and other forms of care. The conservative approach to services for the elderly has stressed decentralization, or the planning and provision of services on the state and local levels wherever possible. Finally, family care of elderly relatives receives a good deal of emphasis from conservative policy makers, in part because it highlights the nuclear family in meeting social needs, and in part because it reinforces the image of women as traditional caregivers in their immediate and extended families.

Belief in the primacy of family life, decentralization of programs, and fiscal responsibility underlie conservative approaches to policies for older Americans. Conservatives argue that private and local government initiatives will prove more cost-effective than the provision of services by a complex national government bureaucracy. They also contend that decentralization will bring the realm of decision making closer to the people who will be affected. Finally, they see individual, family, and community responsibility as part of an important self-help tradition in America.

The Liberal Perspective

While liberals, too, believe in the importance of community and family, they are wary of the wholesale decentralization of programs and planning activities to the state and local level. They feel that only the federal government has adequate resources to meet the income maintenance, health, and other needs of older Americans. They argue that states and localities may follow discriminatory practices which are less likely to occur when policy is decided nationally. They are not necessarily opposed to private sponsorship of programs, but are concerned that profit making and lack of accountability will interfere with fair and adequate provision of services. Finally, they believe that families often lack sufficient resources to care for their elderly members.

These beliefs lead liberals to promote the maintenance and expansion of broad national social welfare programs: Social Security, Medicare, and Medicaid, and the social service system created by the Older Americans Act. Liberals see such services as basic rights of all citizens. Liberals also stress the need for governmental regulation of private programs, such as nursing homes and home health care. They think the federal government should provide more direct help to families and communities as they support elderly individuals. Such help could consist of more adult day care facilities, information and referral services, and greater provision of in-home services to elderly individuals. Lobbying by organized groups of elderly is seen as a legitimate way to have an impact on existing policies and programs.

The Radical Perspective

Radicals offer a critical analysis of present systems of aid for the elderly. A common version of this critique focuses on the need of the capitalist system to control the nation's work force. Both Social Security and private pensions provide a way for employers to remove "less-productive" older workers and to keep nonworking groups from dissatisfaction and possible revolt. Sociologists like John Williamson and activists like Maggie Kuhn note the use of stereotypes about the aged in this process. Labels like "less-productive" and "old fashioned" support a system which separates older individuals from the labor force.[65] Radicals also point out that America's welfare measures do little to redistribute income or to counter the control of large corporations over our lives. They are critical of the growth of the "senior industry," which includes huge nursing home chains and profitable communal living facilities for the affluent elderly.

Radical agendas for change vary. However, most support a broad extension of social welfare measures for all Americans, including the aged, particularly those provisions which help to redistribute income. In addition, radicals call for the empowerment of the elderly. They would support such measures as workers' and retirees' control over their pension systems, for example. Thus, while conservatives, liberals, and radicals all envision a role for the elderly in ensuring their own welfare, radicals are the most likely to seek the involvement of older people in all decisions affecting their lives.

SOCIAL WORK ROLES

Rita Yepez is a social worker at a large city hospital. Much of her work consists of discharge planning for elderly patients. Today she visits with Anna Reilly, an eighty-four-year-old widow who was hospitalized with a broken arm and a mild concussion. Mrs. Reilly had fallen down her cellar stairs while carrying a large basket of laundry. Rita has already consulted with the physical therapist and Mrs. Reilly's physician, so she has a good idea of Mrs. Reilly's needs and capabilities once she is discharged. Together, she and Mrs. Reilly discuss the older woman's plan to return to her own home. For the next few weeks, Mrs. Reilly's daughter will look in on her every day on her way home from work. Because Mrs. Reilly has a low income, Rita has been able to arrange through the Department of Social Services for the permanent assignment of a homemaker aide to spend one day a week doing household chores, such as laundry, for Mrs. Reilly. Today they talk about Mrs. Reilly's other needs and interests. By the end of the session, they agree that Rita will also contact John Hartman, a social worker at the Senior Center in Mrs. Reilly's neighborhood. He will arrange for delivery of a hot meal to Mrs. Reilly's home every noon. Mrs. Reilly tells Rita that she gets lonely now that several of her close friends have died, so the social worker encourages her to look into the other services offered by the center once she is able to get up and about.

Rita's approach to this case covers many of the roles carried out by social workers with elderly clients. As a hospital social worker, one of her major functions is discharge planning. This involves assessing the client's need, often in consultation with other hospital staff, involving relatives as well as the client in the discharge plan, locating appropriate resources, carrying out referrals, helping the client to use these resources, and encouraging independence. If Mrs. Reilly were unable to attend to personal needs or required further medical care, Rita would have thought about which part of what is called the "continuum of care system" would be most appropriate for her client. Her choices would include a skilled nursing home facility for a frail elderly person needing 24-hour nursing care, an intermediate care facility for an ambulatory client requiring primarily health supervision, a boarding home or home of a relative, or home health services.[66]

The same roles of assessment, consultation, work with families, decision making with the client, and referral can be carried out in a variety of settings. Social workers dealing with the elderly are found in nursing homes, senior centers, adult day care centers, hospice programs, and information and referral services. In these and other jobs, social workers can also function as advocates for elderly clients, counselors, case managers, and developers of community networks or support systems for the elderly. Such community networks may be made up of friends, neighbors, members of the same church or synagogue, and volunteers.

Some social workers serve in protective services units for the elderly, which are usually housed in departments of social services. In this position, they intervene in cases where clients appear to be abused, exploited, neglected, or unable to function independently. Sometimes this intervention leads to referral of the older person for guardianship. In this case, the court appoints a guardian for an individual whom it determines to be mentally incompetent.

Finally, social workers can act as administrators, planners, policy makers, and advocates in Area Agencies on Aging, health and social service organizations, lobbying groups, and legislative offices. There, as in the direct service roles described earlier, one of the social worker's major functions is to mediate between the client and the service system, and between the elderly person and the larger environment. As you can see from the preceding description, social work with elderly offers a wide and interesting variety of settings and tasks.

CONCLUSION

Today's elderly are a diverse group—some rich, some poor; some healthy, some frail; and some living in the community and others residing in institutions. The present system of social, economic, and health services for older Americans reflects this complexity. Both the idea of a continuum of services and the model of a coordinated array of pro-

grams relate well to the existence of a range of needs and interests within the elderly population. The challenge in social services for the elderly is to ensure adequacy, comprehensiveness, and coordination of services and benefits, as well as a meaningful role for older citizens in the decisions affecting their lives.

ENDNOTES

1. Bernice L. Neugarten, "Policy for the 1980s: Age or Need Entitlement?" in *Age or Need? Public Policies for Older People,* Bernice L. Neugarten, ed. (Beverly Hills, CA: Sage, 1982), 19–22.

2. Elizabeth D. Huttman, *Social Services for the Elderly* (New York: Free Press, 1985), 4; Neugarten, *Age or Need?,* 22–23.

3. Frank L. Schick, ed., *Statistical Handbook on Aging Americans* (Phoenix: Oryx Press, 1986), xx, 1.

4. American Association of Retired Persons, *A Profile of Older Americans: 1990,* pamphlet (Washington, D.C.: American Association of Retired Persons, 1990), 5–8.

5. U.S. Congress, Senate, Special Committee on Aging, *Developments in Aging: 1986,* Vol. 3, 100 Congress, 1st Session, 1986, 1, 23; U.S. Bureau of the Census, *Statistical Abstract of the United States: 1991* (Washington, D.C.: 111th Ed., 1991), 13, 37.

6. Schick, *Statistical Handbook,* p. 60; *Statistical Abstract: 1991,* 37.

7. U.S. Congress, Senate, Special Committee on Aging, *Developments in Aging: 1987,* Vol. 1, 100 Congress, 2nd Session, 1987, 3; *Statistical Abstract: 1991,* 37.

8. *Statistical Abstract: 1991,* 37.

9. National Center for Health Statistics, *Health, United States, 1990,* DHHS Pub. No. (PHS) 91-1232, Public Health Service (Washington, D.C.: U.S. Government Printing Office, 1990), 67.

10. American Association of Retired Persons, *A Profile of Older Americans,* 12.

11. U.S. Congress, Senate, Special Committee on Aging, *Developments in Aging: 1987,* Vol. 3, *The Long-Term Care Challenge,* 100 Congress, 2nd Session, 1987, 18–19; Wilbur H. Watson, "Family Care, Economics, and Health" and Charles M. Barresi and Geeta Menon, "Diversity in Black Family Caregiving," in *Black Aged: Understanding Diversity and Service Needs,* Zev Harel, Edward A. McKinney, and Michael Williams, eds. (Newbury Park, CA: Sage, 1990), 50–54; 221–235.

12. Nancy Hooyman and H. Asuman Kiyak, *Social Gerontology: A Multidisciplinary Perspective* (Boston: Allyn and Bacon, 1988), 353–355; American Association of Retired Persons, *A Profile of Older Americans,* 11.

13. American Association of Retired Persons, *A Profile of Older Americans,* 9–10; Paul Stuart and Eloise Rathbone-McCuan, "Indian Elderly in the United States," in *North American Elders: Canadian and U.S. Comparison,* Eloise Rathbone-McCuan and Betty Havens, eds. (Westport, CT: Greenwood Press, 1988), 242.

14. *Statistical Abstract: 1991,* 37; Robert Pear, "Social Security Benefits to Go Up 3.7%," *New York Times* (18 October 1991), sec. A, p. 10.

15. Robert Pear, "Medicare Prognosis: Unwieldy Growth Fueled by More Fees and Beneficiaries," *New York Times* (10 March 1991), 4; *Statistical Abstract: 1991,* 100; *Health, United States, 1990,* 209.

16. Lou Harris and Associates, *Aging in the Eighties: America in Transition* (Washington, D.C.: National Council on Aging, 1981), 22; *Health, U.S., 1990,* 121.

17. *Statistical Abstract: 1991,* 316; Pear, "Medicare Prognosis," 4.

18. Leonard Hayflick, "Biological Aging Theories," in *The Encyclopedia of Aging,* George L. Maddox, ed.

(N.Y.: Springer Publishing Co., 1987), 64–68; Paul Denny, "The Biological Basis of Aging," in *Aging: Scientific Perspectives and Social Issues,* Diana S. Woodruff and James E. Birren, eds. (Monterey, CA: Brooks/Cole, 1983), 226–241.

19. Ruth B. Weg, "Changing Physiology of Aging," in Woodruff, *Aging,* 248–251.

20. K. Warner Schaie, "Age Changes in Adult Intelligence," in Woodruff, *Aging,* 138–145.

21. Huttman, *Social Services for the Elderly,* 10–12.

22. Erik Erikson, *Childhood and Society* (New York: W.W. Norton, 1963), 266–269.

23. Elaine Cumming and William Henry, *Growing Old— The Process of Disengagement* (New York: Basic Books, 1961); Robert C. Atchley, "Disengagement," *The Encyclopedia of Aging,* 186–187; Harris, *Aging in the Eighties,* 26.

24. Neugarten, "Older People: A Profile," in Neugarten, *Age or Need?,* 41–42; Robert C. Atchley, "Activity Theory," *The Encyclopedia of Aging,* 5; David Mechanic, *From Advocacy to Allocation: The Evolving American Health Care System* (New York: Free Press, 1986), 169.

25. Margaret Neiswender Reedy, "Personality and Aging," in Woodruff, *Aging,* 120–121; Schick, *Statistical Handbook,* 77, 82; U.S. Congress, Senate, *Developments in Aging: 1897,* Vol. 1, 10–11; Harris, *Aging in the Eighties,* 26.

26. Hooyman and Kiyak, *Social Gerontology,* 66; Eric Kingson, Barbara A. Hirshorn, and John M. Cornman, *The Ties That Bind: The Interdependence of Generations,* A Report from the Gerontological Society of America (Washington, D.C.: Seven Locks Press, 1986), 9–12.

27. Bernice L. Neugarten, "Kansas City Studies of Adult Life," *Encyclopedia of Aging,* 372–373.

28. Helena Z. Lopata, *Widowhood in an American City* (Cambridge, MA: Schenkman, 1973), 89–92.

29. Watson, "Family Care, Economics, and Health," 50–68; Barresi and Menon, "Diversity in Black Family Caregiving," 221–235; Ramon Valle, "The Demography of Mexican-American Aging," in *Aging in Minority Groups,* R. L. McNeely and John N. Colen, eds. (Beverly Hills, CA: Sage, 1983), 68–69; Stuart and Rathbone-McCuan, "Indian Elderly in the United States," 251.

30. Martha Riley, et al, *Aging from Birth to Death* (Boulder, CO: Westview Press, 1982), II: 11–24.

31. W. Andrew Achenbaum, *Old Age in the New Land* (Baltimore: The Johns Hopkins Press, 1978), 10–25; Carole Haber, *Beyond Sixty-Five: The Dilemma of Old Age in America's Past* (Cambridge, England: Cambridge University Press, 1983), 10.

32. Haber, *Beyond Sixty-Five,* 16–18.

33. Achenbaum, *Old Age in the New Land,* 39–40, 57–75; Haber, *Beyond Sixty-Five,* 30–31.

34. Achenbaum, *Old Age in the New Land,* 40–47.

35. Haber, *Beyond Sixty-Five,* 28–29.

36. Michael B. Katz, *In the Shadow of the Poorhouse: A Social History of Welfare in America* (New York: Basic Books, 1986), 86–93; Achenbaum, *Old Age in the New Land,* 80.

37. Achenbaum, *Old Age in the New Land,* 74, 95–102.

38. Achenbaum, *Old Age in the New Land,* 110–112; James R. Reinardy, "Social Casework with the Elderly between World Wars I and II," *Social Service Review* 61 (1987): 502.

39. Achenbaum, *Old Age in the New Land,* 82–84.

40. James Leiby, *A History of Social Welfare and Social Work in the United States* (New York: Columbia University Press, 1978), 199–200; Roy Lubove, *The Struggle for Social Security: 1900–1935* (Pittsburgh: University of Pittsburgh Press, 1968), 129–130.

41. Lubove, *Struggle for Social Security,* 113–143.

42. Leiby, *A History of Social Welfare and Social Work,* 230–232, 250–252; Achenbaum, *Old Age in the New Land,* 129.

43. Lubove, *Struggle for Social Security,* 116–118; Leiby, *A History of Social Welfare and Social Work,* 234.

44. Charles McKinley and Robert W. Frase, *Launching Social Security* (Madison, WI: University of Wisconsin Press, 1970), 17.

45. James T. Patterson, *America's Struggle Against Poverty: 1900–1980* (Cambridge, MA: Harvard University Press, 1981), 93.

46. Stephen Crystal, *America's Old Age Crisis* (New York: Basic Books, 1982), 108–110.

47. W. Andrew Achenbaum, *Shades of Gray: Old Age, American Values, and Federal Policies Since 1920* (Boston: Little, Brown and Company, 1983), 118–121.

48. Sharon Y. Moriwaki and Frances S. Kobata, "Ethnic Minority Aging," in Woodruff, *Aging,* 65; Huttman, *Social Services for the Elderly,* 49–58.

49. Henry J. Pratt, *The Gray Lobby* (Chicago: University of Chicago Press, 1976), 87–94; Achenbaum, *Shades of Gray,* 69–70; Dieter Hessel, ed., *Maggie Kuhn on Aging* (Philadelphia: Westminster Press, 1977), 9.

50. Willard C. Richan, *Beyond Altruism* (New York: The Haworth Press, 1988), 80–81; U.S. Congress, Senate, *Developments in Aging: 1987,* Vol. 1, 18–21, 12.

51. Deming, "Demography of the Aged," in Woodruff, *Aging,* 32–35.

52. Crystal, *America's Old Age Crisis,* 111.

53. Harold Wilensky, *The Welfare State and Equality* (Berkeley, CA: University of California Press, 1975), 22–28.

54. Carroll L. Estes, Robert J. Newcomer, and Associates, *Fiscal Austerity and Aging* (Beverly Hills, CA: Sage, 1983), 27.

55. John B. Williamson, Judith A. Shindul, and Linda Evans, *Aging and Public Policy: Social Control or Social Justice?* (Springfield, IL: Charles C Thomas Publisher, 1985), 115–116.

56. Linda Horn and Elma Griesel, *Nursing Homes: A Citizens' Action Guide* (Boston: Beacon Press, 1977), 5–16.

57. Tamar Lewin, "Using Restraint," *St. Louis Post-Dispatch* (3 January 1990), Sec. C, p. 1.

58. Carroll L. Estes, "Austerity and Aging: 1980 and Beyond," in *Readings in the Political Economy of Aging,* Meredith Minkler and Carroll L. Estes, eds. (Farmingdale, NY: Baywood Publishing Co., 1984), 243–247.

59. Huttman, *Social Services for the Elderly,* 107.

60. Huttman, *Social Services for the Elderly,* 56.

61. Pamela Doty, "Family Care of the Elderly: The Role of Public Policy," *Milbank Quarterly 64* (1986): 34–75; Karen A. Conner, *Aging in America: Issues Facing an Aging Society* (Englewood Cliffs, NJ: Prentice-Hall, 1992), 112–127; William J. Sauer and Raymond T. Coward, *Social Support Networks and the Care of the Elderly* (New York: Springer Publishing Company, 1985).

62. "Guardians," *Kalamazoo Gazette* (20 September 1987), Sec. B, p 2.

63. Cyril F. Brickfield, "AARP," *Encyclopedia of Aging,* 31–32.

64. Hessel, *Maggie Kuhn,* 106–107; Horn and Griesel, *Nursing Homes,* 120–165; Pratt, *The Gray Lobby,* 52.

65. Williamson, *Aging and Public Policy,* 206–208; Hessel, *Maggie Kuhn,* 70.

66. Betsy Ledbetter Hancock, *Social Work with Older People* (Englewood Cliffs, NJ: Prentice-Hall, 1987), 136–152.

C·H·A·P·T·E·R

sixteen

Developing Your Own Perspective on Social Welfare

The following are samples of a conversation among three students after a social work class, following a heated debate about the causes of social problems and possible solutions:

Martha: "I just can't imagine why he thinks he wants to go into social work. He's so judgmental about clients—he thinks teens get pregnant because they can't be bothered to take precautions, or because they want to go on welfare and move out on their own. And did you catch what he was saying about the homeless? If they tried hard enough, they'd get jobs and work their way out of poverty. That's ridiculous! The system is screwed up. Teens need more birth control information in the schools. They need a world they can believe in. And they need real options in their lives. The homeless are that way because a minimum wage job can't decently support and house a family, and because the real estate investors want to make profits off of housing for the rich instead of building low-income housing. I don't know how it's going to be done, but the system's got to be changed. Power and wealth have got to be shared."

Deirdre: "I don't know—I think sometimes he makes some good points. My mother is a product of social work school in the 1960s. She's convinced that government programs are the answer. She gets all starry-eyed about the War on Poverty, and government services for people on welfare, Job Corps, Head Start, people being 'helped to reach their full potential' and all that stuff. I keep trying to tell her we're in a different world now. There isn't all that government money floating around. People are going to have to become more responsible for themselves. The social work jobs are going to be in private agencies, or even in businesses or places like that."

Richard: "I think I'd like your mother. Yeah, maybe those really big government programs aren't the only answer. But we're still going to need government help to make sure all people get a chance for a decent life. Self-help approaches and private organizations are important, but it's up to the feds to set some standards for income and housing and health care, and to regulate private charity and big business so everyone gets a fair chance. We're living in one world together— we're all responsible for each other."

What stand would you take? Could you defend your position? Do you know where the others are coming from? Could you respond to their arguments? Or would you choose not to join this conversation at all, because it is pointless to debate these things, and more important to get on with the job of helping people?

We hope that you would join in, in this and other situations in which people present different perspectives on social welfare and the problems it seeks to solve. One of the goals of this book has been to convey the idea that social welfare and the social work profession are not simply "rational" or neutral entities. Instead, they are shaped by a variety of political ideas, values, and religious beliefs, some of which conflict with one another. A second goal has been to strengthen your ability to analyze different perspectives, particularly political ones, and to develop your own informed point of view.

Most Americans feel that poverty is a bad thing and that the country ought to devote at least a minimum level of resources to the poor and dependent. Yet beyond this, our society has developed different perspectives on poverty and other social problems, and on the ways in which to deal with these problems. As we have discussed in this book, three different political viewpoints have affected America's approaches to social welfare. The conservative perspective is suspicious of change and emphasizes people's accountability for their own life situations. In speaking of crime, for example, conservatives worry about a breakdown in the existing social order. They see criminals as making a conscious choice when they break the law. Conservatives propose a limited role for government in the welfare arena and look to the market economy to handle most human needs. In the health field, for example, conservative thinkers approve of competition between private providers of medical services, arguing that this competition improves quality of care and keeps costs down.

The liberal viewpoint finds moderate change or reform useful, stresses the importance of the external environment in shaping people's lives, and sees a positive role for government both in providing social welfare services and in regulating the excesses of a market economy. Liberals believe in government regulation of private nursing homes and group homes for those with developmental disability. They have long supported federal programs for the disadvantaged, such as public housing, Aid to Dependent Children, Medicare, and Medicaid.

Radicals see individuals as being both shaped by and shapers of their environment. They promote more fundamental alteration in the system, calling for changes leading to an equitable distribution of power and resources. They see many social problems as being inherent in the very nature of capitalism. The market economy exploits labor, for-profit group homes prey on those with mental illness and other handicaps, and unscrupulous real estate agents and ghetto landlords have a vested interest in maintaining residential segregation.

Each of these viewpoints carries baggage. That is, each perspective leads to particular ways of dealing with dependency and fostering interdependency. While various solutions are justified in terms of cost-effectiveness, "numbers helped," or other concrete measures, justification is almost always based, as well, on the solution's fit with a particular political position. That is, a workfare-welfare program conforms to a conservative stress on the work ethic and market economy, while Medicare reflects a liberal belief in the responsibility of government to supplement the market economy in meeting human needs. No one perspective is correct, or leads to the perfect program.

As a citizen, then, you will encounter variations of these perspectives, in pure and overlapping forms, whenever you hear people talking about social welfare issues or whenever you are asked to support certain solutions to social problems. And of course, these viewpoints will affect your work in a social welfare agency. The board members or advisory committee of your agency, the legislators or the community chest officials responsible for funding, the citizens in your state or community who give or withhold support for the organization's work, your administrators and co-workers, and the clients served—all represent a variety of values and political views. Your ability to understand these views and their consequences will increase your effectiveness at communication, compromise, and change.

Finally, you are not a blank slate in this process. Perhaps the most important contribution this book can make is in helping you as you develop and articulate your own perspective on social welfare. While finding *the* correct position is an unrealistic goal, it is important to try to look at social problems and tentative solutions in a thoughtful and ethical way. As we discussed in the chapter on the profession of social work, this involves reflecting carefully on the implications of your perspective for clients, agency, and community. Thoughtful practice will make a difference.

Name Index

Abbott, Edith, 63, 64, 70, 143
Abbott, Grace, 63, 64, 138, 143, 407
Abramovitz, Mimi, 133
Achenbaum, W. Andrew, 540, 542
Addams, Jane, 61–62, 74, 100, 137–138, 139, 140, 143, 493
Adelman, William, 496
Adler, Mortimer J., 302
Adorno, T. W., 132
Akabas, Sheila, 463
Allen, Mary Lee, 278
Allen-Hagen, Barbara, 317
Anderson, Martin, 179, 180
Arnow, Harriet, 400
Askerooth, Gary, 28
Atherton, Charles, 35, 39
Augustus, John, 327
Axinn, June, 229

Bailey, Walter, 329
Banfield, Edward C., 201, 213
Barnett, Samuel A., 99–100
Bartlett, Harriet, 407
Basu, Asoke, 191, 193
Beatty, Barbara R., 60
Beccaria, Cesare, 324
Beck, Bernard, 25
Becker, Howard S., 322
Beeghley, Leonard, 180, 209, 212
Beers, Clifford, 362, 363, 365
Bell, Daniel, 438
Bell, Winifred, 28–29
Berliner, Howard S., 402
Betten, Neil, 100
Binet, Alfred, 196, 371
Birtwell, Charles, 273
Black, Bruce L., 381, 382
Blau, Joel, 39
Blau, Peter, 211

Blendon, Robert J., 422, 423
Block, N. J., 197
Bloomfield, Daniel, 461
Bluestone, Barry, 167, 168, 450, 453
Bogue, Donald, 205
Boll, Eleanor Stone, 268
Books, Lester, 67
Booth, Charles, 171, 172
Booth-Tucker, Frederick, 114
Bossard, James, 268
Brace, Charles Loring, 101, 269, 271, 272
Breckinridge, Sophonisba, 63, 64, 70, 143
Bremner, Robert B., 233
Briar, Katherine Hooper, 443
Bristol, Katherine, 501
Brooks, Mary Potter, 362
Brown, Bertram, 448
Brunvand, Jan Harold, 222
Buckner, Howard, 119
Buder, Stanley, 496
Buell, Bradley, 197
Burns, Eveline, 28
Burt, Sir Cyril, 196
Bush, George, 15, 88, 104, 145, 244–248
Butler, Stuart, 179, 215, 245

Cabst, Richard, 406
Cadbury, George, 496
Calkins, Clinch, 240
Cannon, Ida, 407
Carroll, Nancy K., 79
Carstens, C. C., 274
Carter, Genevieve, 288
Carter, Jimmy, 244, 506
Chalmers, Thomas, 98–99
Chambers, Clarke, 143
Cloward, Richard, 48, 321
Cohen, Albert, 321

Coit, Stanton, 100
Coll, Blanche D., 30, 71
Collier, Christopher, 288
Collier, James Lincoln, 288
Compton, Beulah R., 34, 40
Costin, Lela B., 64, 284, 285, 286
Craven, John, 163
Cressey, Donald, 329
Cullen, Frances T., 326
Cumming, Elaine, 537

Dahl, Robert, 11
Darwin, Charles, 234
De Francis, Vincent, 276
DeMause, Lloyd, 269
Dershowitz, Alan M., 324
Desai, Meghnad, 173
de Schweinitz, Karl, 224, 225
de Sismonde, J.C.L.S., 222
Devine, Edward, 63, 65
Dillingham, Steven, 318
Diner, Steven, 139
DiNitto, Dianna M., 448
Dinkins, David, 504
Disraeli, Benjamin, 232
Dix, Dorothea, 58, 74, 231, 361
Dobson, James, 281, 282
Dohrenwend, Bruce P., 354
Donahue, William A., 46–47
Douglas, James, 97
Downey, Thomas, 245
Dressel, Paula, 143
Duke, David, 145
Duncan, Greg J., 193, 443
Duncan, Otis D., 211
Dussich, J. P. J., 335
Dwight, Theodore, 325
Dworkin, Gerald, 197

565

Subject Index

Federal Housing Administration (FHA), 497,
    499–500, 515
Federal programs:
    antipoverty (see Antipoverty program de-
        velopment; New Deal; War on
        Poverty)
    community-based programs for mentally
        ill, 374
    cutbacks in 1990s, 73
    for disabled, 373–374
    for elderly, 545
        expenditures on, 534–535, 546–549
        health (see Medicare and Medicaid)
        Social Security (see Social Security)
    during Great Depression, 68–72
    growth of, 103
    health, 405, 408, 422, 425 (see also Medi-
        care and Medicaid)
    housing, 474, 479, 503
        discrimination in, 489 (see also
            Segregation)
        mortgage programs, 499–500
        research, 476–477
        subsidies, 484, 486
    social agencies of 1920s, 66
    victim assistance, 335
Fee-for-service basis, 413, 414
Female-headed households (see also Single-
        parent families)
    gender and household stereotypes, 509–
        510
    and poverty, 190, 193
Feminization of poverty, 190
Feudal system, 223
Fiscal policy, 14
Flex-time, 457
Food programs, elderly, 550–551
Food Stamp Act, 243
Food Stamp Program, 43, 243
    Jobs and Income Security Program, 244
    Reagan administration and, 244
Ford administration, housing programs, 479
Foster care, 276–278, 289
    class action lawsuits on behalf of children
        in, 279–281
    institution of by Children's Aid Society,
        272–273
    matching, 146–148
    permanency planning, 276–278
    social work roles, 289–290
Four-dimensional model of social work prac-
        tice, 79–80, 81
Freedmen's Bureau, 69,74, 138, 139
Frictional unemployment, 449–500
Functional inferiority, cultural deprivation
        theory, 202
Functionalist perspective (see also Conserva-
        tive perspective)
    conservative views as, 10–11
    on deviance, 345

Gender:
    and child maltreatment, 260
    and criminal behavior, 310
    elderly
        demographics of, 538
        and poverty, 533, 534
    and health, 397–398, 400
        life expectancy, 528, 529
        medical school admissions, 405

mental illness, 354
    and homelessness, 478
    and poverty, 193, 533, 534
    unemployment rates, 441
Gender inequality, 133–134
    social work leadership position, 143–144
    as structural component of poverty, 212
Gender stereotypes, 509–510
General assistance, 42, 484
General deterrence, 306
General systems theory, 392
Genetic factors:
    eugenics movement, 196, 371
    as explanation of poverty, 195–197
    in mental retardation, 371
    in schizophrenia, 348–349
Gentrification, 484–485
Geographical distribution of crime, 319
Geographic distribution:
    elderly, 527
    poverty, 161, 188, 189, 190
Gerontological Society of America, 545
Gerontologists, biological, 536
Ghettos, 212–214
Gini coefficient, 162, 164, 166, 181
G.L. v. Zumwalt, 280
Government, 34 (see also Federal programs)
    definitions of poverty, 175–178
    growth of services, 103
    and parent-child relationship, 285–287
    role of, views of conservatives, liberals, and
        radicals, 5–6, 12–17, 563
    state (see State governments)
Government job creation, 452
Graying of America, 526
Gray Lobby, 545, 546, 553
Gray Panthers, 546, 553
Great Awakening, 227
Great Depression, 165, 233
    antipoverty program development during,
        238–240
    elderly during, 542
    federal program development, 68–72
    housing during, 497–498
    private domination of social welfare, 237
    structural factors, 240
    unemployed during, 436
Great Society, 545
Gross National Income (GNI) of U.S., 160
Gross National Product (GNP), 233, 341,
        392
Group homes, 511–512
Group social work, 66
Guardians, of parolees, 326
Guardianship of elderly, 553

Habitat for Humanity, 506
Handicapped (see Developmental disability;
        Disability)
Hawthorne Experiments, 461
Head Start, 72
Health:
    definitions of, 391–392
    of elderly, 534, 535–536
    minority status and, 127
    poverty cycle, 210
    unemployment and, 440
    work and, 436–437, 438–439
Health care:
    current issues and trends, 413–422

corporate and entrepreneurial practice,
        416–417
    costs, 413–415
    ethical issues, 421
    inequities, 417–421
    reform of system, 421–422
    specialization, 415
    definition of health and illness, 391–392
    dynamics of health and illness, 398–402
    elderly, 548, 549
        expenditures on, 533
        government programs (see Medicare and
            Medicaid)
        home, 550, 552
    history of, 402–413
        health care in 1960s and 1970s, 407–
            413
        medical social work, 406–407
        rise of scientific medicine, 403–406
    in-kind services, 42
    and mental retardation, 358, 359
    perspectives, 422–425
    poverty line calculations, 179
    social work roles, 425–428
    statistics, 392–398
        causes of death, 397, 398, 399
        costs, 392–393
        mortality rates and life expectancy, 394–
            395, 396, 397, 398, 399
        self-assessment reports, 393–394
        socioeconomic factors, 396–398
    in workplace, welfare movement and,
        459–460
Health care crisis, 411–412
Health case workers, 553
Health insurance, 408, 418–419
    costs of, 413, 414–415
    Medicaid/Medicare (see Medicare and
        Medicaid)
    private, 408, 203
Health Maintenance Organizations, 412
Health planning agencies, 412
Health promotion programs, 415
Heart disease, 396–397, 399
Henry Street Settlement, 505
Heritage Foundation, 458
Highrise projects, 499, 500, 501
Hill-Burton program, 406
Hispanic Americans* (see Discrimination;
        Race and ethnicity)
    crime, 311, 315
    health, 395, 397, 398
    health insurance, 418
    housing, 482–483, 488–489
    medical school enrollment, 412
Historical development of social work, 56–
        73, 74
    Charity Organization Society, 58–61
    chronology, 74
    diversity and unification, 66–68
    Great Depression and federal program de-
        velopment, 68–72
    growth of profession, 63–66, 72–73
    ideological perspectives, 56–57
    social settlement, 61–63
    state charitable institutions, 58
Holistic health, 392, 401–402, 410
Home health care, 550, 552
Homelessness:
    advocacy organizations, 476

Intrarole conflict, parents, 257
Intra-sender role conflict, 457
Involuntary mental health services, 44
IQ (intelligence quotient) tests, 196–197, 356

Jewish agencies, 106–107
Jewish roots of social welfare, 95–96
Jim Crow laws, 139
Job Corps, 242
Job depth, 455
Job enlargement, 455
Job opportunities, 85–86
Jobs and Income Security Programs, 244
Job scope, 455
JOBS (Job Opportunities and Basic Skills), 245–247
Jobs Training Partnership Act (JTPA), 247
Johnson administration:
    elderly issues, 545
    housing policy, 502
    War on Poverty, 72, 74, 179, 242–244, 500
Judeo-Christian value system, 18–19
Just deserts theory, 305, 319
Justice model, 305, 332
Justice system (see also Corrections system)
    Jewish roots, 96
    juvenile (see Juvenile justice system)
Juvenile delinquency, 304–305, 327–328
    definition of, 305
    incidence of, 311
    rates of, 319
Juvenile justice system:
    diversion program, 332
    Juvenile Court, 327–328
    treatment programs outside criminal justice system, 334

Kinship, 33–34

Labeling theory:
    crime, 322
    developmental disability, 357
    mental illness, 344–345, 351, 353
Labor crisis of 14th century, 223–224
Labor movement:
    planned communities and, 495
    settlement movement and, 62, 63
Landlords, 475, 485–486
Law enforcement as social work, 336–337
League for Protection of Immigrants, 138
Legal definitions of crime, 302–305
Legal guardians, 553
Legal services, 179, 550
Legislation:
    developmentally disabled, 378
    elderly issues:
        community issues, 550
        Great Society, 545
        Social Security, 544, 545
    in England, 223, 224–225
    during Great Depression, 238–240
    Health Maintenance Organizations, 412
    health planning, 412
    historical developments, 74
    housing, 485
        Bush administration, 507
        New Deal, 497–498

nineteenth century, 492, 494
    after Second World War, 499–500
    immigrant protection in early 20th century, 138
lobby groups (see Interest groups)
Jim Crow law, 139
maternal and child health, 141
medical practitioners licensing, 403–404
mothers' and old age pensions, 237
public charity, 231
retarded citizen service, 372
settlement movement and, 62
welfare reform, 245–247
work-related, 463
Liaison, 44
Liberalism, 4
Liberal perspective, 563
    child welfare:
        causes of mistreatment, 283, 284
        on discipline of children, 281–282
        rights of children and parents, 286
    on discrimination and disadvantage, 135
    on criminal justice, 301–302
    elderly, 554–555
    on health care, 424
    on housing, 514–515
    on mental illness and developmental disability, 380
    on unemployment, 452–453
    social welfare, 46–47, 49
    social work as profession, 57
    work role conflicts, 457
    world view
        comparison of perspectives, 16
        on family, 10
        on government and economy, 6–7, 14, 16–17
        on human nature, 8, 16, 9
        on social system, 11, 12
        value system, 17–18, 19
Libertarian philosophy, 115
Licensing:
    medical practitioners, 403
    social workers, 86–87
Life expectancy, 394–395, 528, 529
Lifestyles:
    elderly, 536
    and health, 401
Liver disease, 397, 399
Living arrangements of elderly, 530–532
Lobby groups, 405 (see Interest groups)
Local government:
    housing programs, 474, 486, 506–507
    services for mentally ill, 374, 376
Lorenz curve, 162, 163, 164, 165, 166, 168
Low-Income Home Energy Assistance Program (LIHEAP), 43
Low-income housing, 479, 484, 486

Mainstreaming, 147, 378
Majority, 129
Mala in se, 304
Mala prohibita, 304
Malpractice insurance costs, 419
Managed care, 415
Management theories, 459–462
Mandatory employment and training programs, 44
Mandatory retirement, 539–540

Manpower Development and Training Act (MDTA), 247
Marginally employed (see Underemployed)
Marginal poor, 192
Marital status:
    of elderly, 538
    and employment, 444–447
Marriage:
    culture of poverty theory, 202
    poverty cycle, 211
Massachusetts General Hospital Social Service Department, 407
Mass society thesis, 46
Master roles, 444–447
Masters degrees, 68, 86, 105
Matching client worker, 144–148
Maternal and child health programs, 407
McKinney Homeless Assistance Act, 506
Mediator role, 80
Medical care (see Health care)
Medical-industrial complex, 416–417
Medical model, 283, 398–400
    of health and illness, 391–392
    of mental illness, 346
Medical profession, 419
    and elderly, 553
    medical chains, 416–417
    specialization in, 415
Medical social work, 406–407
Medicare and Medicaid, 42, 414, 424, 545
    elderly
        budget expenditures, 534, 535
        coverage, 533
        and nursing homes, 548
    establishment of, 408–409
    inadequacies of, 418, 419, 420
    Reagan administration and, 244
Medicare and Medicaid amendments to Social Security Act, 243
Mental health:
    employment and:
        role of work, 436–437, 438–439
        unemployment, 440
    historical development of social work, 58, 74
    social welfare programs, 43–44, 45
    and work performance, 448
Mental health facilities, 66
Mental health services, 43–44
Mental health social workers, 382
Mental hygiene movement, 362–365
Mental illness:
    and child abuse, 263
    current issues and trends, 372–379
    definitions of mental illness, 345–348
    dynamics of, 348–352
    historical perspective, 359–368
        asylums, 360–361
        colonial society, 359–360
        community mental health, 365–368
        drugs, 365, 367–368
        industrialization and, 361–362
        mental hygiene movement, 362–364
        women's role, 362, 363–365
    housing
        deinstitutionalization and, 478, 484
        special needs facilities, 510–512
    perspectives on, 379–387
    social work roles, 381–382
    statistics, 352–353
    and unemployment, 440

Mental retardation (*see* Developmental disability)
Methods, social work, 78–79
Milieu therapy, 365, 366, 371
Military, occupational social work, 465
Mill towns, 495
Minority group, as label, 129
Minority group status (*see* Discrimination; Race and ethnicity)
Mobilizer, social worker role, 80
Model tenements, 492–494
Morbidity and mortality rates, 396, 400, 440
Mortgage Bankers Association, 473
Mortgage insurance, 500
Mortgage loans:
    interest rates, 480
    programs after World War II, 499–500
    rejections, race and, 483
Mothers' pension law, 237
Multiculturalism, 146
Multidisciplinary practice, 88, 425–426
Multihospital systems, 416–417
Mutual support, 33

National Affordable Housing Act, 476, 507–508
National Association for the Advancement of Colored People (NAACP), 140
National Association of Home Builders, 472
National Association of Retired Federal Employees, 545–546
National Association of Schools of Social Service Administration, 70, 74
National Association of Social Workers (NASW), 72, 74
National Association of Social Workers (NASW) Code of Ethics, 76
National Center for Child Abuse and Neglect, 276
National Center for the Prevention and Treatment of Child Abuse and Neglect, 276
National Coalition for the Homeless, 476
National Committee for Mental Hygiene, 362
National Committee for Prevention of Child Abuse Study, 259–262
National Conference of Charities and Correction, 58, 61, 65, 74, 63
National Conference of Social Work, 66
National Council of Senior Citizens, 546
National health insurance, 408, 422
National health system, 425
National League of Cities, 474
National Low Income Housing Coalition, 508
National People's Action, 476
National Union of the Homeless, 476
National Urban League, 67
Native American health services, 43
Native Americans (*see also* Discrimination; Race and ethnicity)
    crime, 311, 315
    elderly, 530, 532, 539
    health, 391, 394
    housing, 483
Natural unemployment rate, 452
Neighborhood associations, 476
Neighborhood Housing Service programs, 506
Neighborhood Reinvestment Corporation, 506

Neighborhood Youth Corps, 242
Neoclassical control theory of crime, 318–319
New Deal, 69, 70 (*see also* Great Depression)
    public housing efforts, 497
    Social Security, 542
New immigrants (*see* Immigrants and immigration, new)
New left, 103
New penology, 326
Nixon administration:
    Health Maintenance Organizations, 412
    housing policy, 502
Noblesse oblige, 45–46
Non-denominational groups, populations funded or served by, 106–107
Nonmarket economic transfers, social welfare as, 28–29
Nonprofit hospitals, 416
Nonprofit sector:
    affordable housing ventures, 506–507
    housing corporations, 507
    social work specialists, 465
Normalization, developmentally disabled, 373
North American Association of Christians in Social Work, 104
Nuclear families, 36
Nurses, 405
    and social workers, 427
    visiting, 459n.
Nursing homes, 414, 511, 548, 549, 553
    discharge planning, 427
    mental health, 377
Nutrition, 43, 550–551

Occupational alcoholism programs, 462
Occupational Safety and Health Act, 463
Occupational social workers, 463–466
Office of Economic Opportunity, 242
Official poverty line, 175–178
Official poverty rate, 192
Old Age, Survivors, and Disability Insurance (OASDI), 41, 239
Old Age Assistance (OAA), 239
Old age pensions, 237
Older Americans Act (OAA), 545, 550, 551, 552
Old-old, 525, 527
Omnibus Budget Act in 1981, 374
Operation Head Start, 242
Organizational charts, practice settings, 83, 84
Outdoor relief, 230, 345
Outpatient programs, mental health, 367
Outreach worker, 80
Overcrowding, 481
    in nineteenth century, 493
    in segregated housing, 488–489
Overeducation, 454–455

Parens patriae, 285, 327
Parents:
    child abuse, factors in, 255–256
    rights of, 285
Parole, 44, 308, 325–326, 330–331
Parole officers, 328, 331
Part-time work, 457
Patient dumping, 417, 421
Patterns of crime, 309
Paupers, 231

Peabody House, 137
Penology (*see* Corrections system)
Pension laws, 237
Pension plans, 543
Permanency Planning, 276–278
Persistently poor, 192–193
Perspectives on social welfare issues (*see also* Conservative perspective; Liberal perspective; Radical perspective)
    political, 3–7
    world view of conservatives, liberal and radicals, 7–19
Personality development:
    traits of abusing parents, 263
    work and, 436–437, 438–439
Personality disorders, 263
Phillips curve, 451, 452
Physiological explanations of mental illness, 348–349
P.L. 96-272, 278, 279–280
Planning, community, 495, 510, 513
Plant closure, 450–451
Pluralism, 131
Police work as social work, 336–337
Political activity (*see* Interest groups)
Political perspectives, 3–7 (*see also* Conservative perspective; Liberal perspective; Radical perspective)
Politics, 34
Poorhouse, 229–230, 271
Population, 32
"Post-marital family," 248
Poverty, 159–170 (*see also* Antipoverty program development)
    and child abuse, 268
    definitions of, 170–175
        absolute, 170–173
        official poverty line in U.S., 175–178
        relative, 173–174
    and developmental disability, 358
    economic trends, 165–167
    elderly, 532–533, 534, 538, 539, 540
    explanations of, 194–215
        cultural, 199–209
        individual characteristics, 194–199
        structural, 209–215
        theories of early 19th century, 229
    and health, 400
    and health care inequities, 417–421
    and homelessness, 478–479
    and incidence of child mistreatment, 261
    and labeling, 323
    major issues and common terms, 159
    measurement and definition, 161–162, 178–182
    minority status and, 126
    perspectives on inequality, 167–170
    settlement movement and, 62–63
    statistical description of poverty population, 187–191
    types of, 191–194
    wealth and income distribution, 163–165
Poverty line:
    criteria, 175–178
    criticism of, 178–182
Power:
    alienation of work and, 455
    and labeling, 323, 345
    poverty cycle, 210
    and prejudice and discrimination, 133

Practice, social work (see Social work practice; Social work practice areas)
Practice settings, 81–85
Prejudice, defined, 130
Preventive approaches to health, 362, 401
Prison reform, 324–325, 328–329
Private agencies:
    antipoverty, 230–231
    child welfare, 290
    establishment of, 66
    racial discrimination by, 140
    social work practice settings, 82, 513 (see also Social work practice areas and settings)
Private corporations, housing initiatives, 486
Private health insurance, 408, 423
Private housing market, subsidies, 502
Private pensions and retirement programs, 15, 42
Private troubles and public issues, 37–38
Privatization of care of mentally ill and handicapped, 376–378, 380
Probation, 44, 307, 326–327, 331
Probation officers, 328
Production-distribution-consumption functions, 32
Professional organizations, social work, 72, 74, 104–105
Professional status of social work (see also Historical development of social work)
    education for, 86
    historical development, 56–72, 73
    methods, 78–79
    perspectives on practice, 88–89
    practice model, 79–81
    practice settings, 80–85
    professionalism, 54–56
    professional issues, 86–87
    roles, 80
    salaries and job opportunities, 85–86
    social welfare context, 87–88
    values and ethics, 72, 74–78
Programmatic welfare, 39, 40
Progressive Era, 232, 234–235
    juvenile court formation, 327–328
    scientific medicine in, 403
Project Hope, 506
Protective services, development of, 273–275
Protestant ethic, 437
Pruitt-Igoe, 500
Psychiatric nurses, 381
Psychiatric social work, 365
Psychiatrists, 383
Psychodrama, 367
Psychological control theory of crime, 316–317
Psychological explanations of mental illness, 350
Psychological health (see Mental health)
Psychological problems:
    abusing parents, traits of, 263
    and poverty, 197–198
Psychologists, 383
Psychopathic hospitals, 362
Psychotropic drugs, 348, 365, 366, 367
Public agencies:
    child welfare, 288–290
    practice settings, 82 (see also Social work practice areas and settings)
Public assistance programs, 41–42 (see also specific programs)

Public health approach, 401
Public hospitals, 417
Public housing, 43, 479, 486
    in Great Depression, 498
    New Deal, 497
    poverty line calculations, 179
    social work roles, 516
    urban renewal, 500
    War on Poverty projects, 500
    after World War II, 499–502
Public issues, 37–38
Public transportation, 515
Public Works Administration (PWA), 497, 498
Punishment approach to crime, 305–306

Qualified Clinical Social Worker, 87

Race and ethnicity, 130, 161 (see also Discrimination; Poverty)
    and child abuse, 261
    criminal behavior statistics, 311, 315
    elderly, 529–530
        and family financial support, 530
        and health, 534
        and income, 532–533
        sociological theories of aging, 538–539
    and health, 400
        of elderly, 534
        medical school admissions, 405, 411, 412
        mental illness, 354
        self-assessment, 393–394
        utilization of services, 418–419
    and health status, 396–397, 398
    and housing, 482–484
        restrictive covenants, 495
        segregation, 488–489
    and labeling, 323
    matching policies, 146, 147–148
    medical school admission, 411, 412
    and mental retardation, 359
    and poverty, 195
        cultural definitions, 205
        income, 161
        poverty populations, 188, 189
        structural components of poverty, 212
Racism, 129, 130
Radical criminology, 323
Radical perspective, 4, 5, 563
    on aging, 543, 555
    on criminal justice, 302
    on discrimination and disadvantage, 135–136
    on health care, 424–425
    on housing, 515–516
    on mental illness and developmental disability, 380–381
    on unemployment, 453–454
    on social welfare, 48, 49
    on social work as profession, 57
    on work, 457
    world view
        comparison of perspectives, 16
        on family, 10
        on government and economy, 6–7, 14–15
        on human nature, 8, 9, 16
        on individual behavior, 9
        on social system, 11, 12
        value systems, 17–18, 19

Rank and File movement, 69, 70, 74
Rate of poverty, 192–193, 194
Rational expectations hypothesis, 451
Rationalization, 207
Reagan administration:
    Annual Housing Report, 476
    antipoverty programs, 244–245
    elderly programs, cuts in, 548–549
    health-care policy, 413, 414
    and health planning agencies, 413
    housing policy, 502–503, 504, 506
    housing programs, 479, 486
    and services to mentally ill, 374
Real estate sector:
    elements of, 472–474
    and homelessness, 479
    and public housing, 497
Recessions, economic, 450, 491
Recreation and socialization services, 44
Redistributive welfare state, 39
Regional differences (see Geographic distribution)
Rehabilitation Act of 1973, 378
Rehabilitation of developmentally disabled, 369–370, 378
Rehabilitation of offenders, 334
    corrections system approaches, 306–308
    effectiveness of, 332–333
    juvenile justice system, 305, 312
    reality of, 328–329
    outside corrections system, 334
Rehabilitation of older homes, 506
Relative definitions of poverty, 173–174
Relative deprivation, 173
Relative poverty, 181–182
Religion, 34, 229
    and attitudes about poverty, 233
    and child maltreatment, 267
    and concepts of mental illness, 359
    conflicts with social work, 108–119
        conservative religion and social change, 111–115
        of interest, 111
        of values, 115–119
    current sectarian services, 105–109, 110
    roots of social welfare, 95–97
    roots of social work, 98–103
        Charity Organization Society movement, 98–99
        institution development, 100–101
        Settlement House movement, 99–100
    secularization, reversal of, 103–105
    and work ethic, 437, 438
Rental housing, 488
    costs of, 479
    minority status and, 483
    ownership of, 485–486
    tax reforms and, 506
Research, 86, 463
    housing system, 476–477
    Progressive Era, 234
Residential schools for developmentally disabled, 369
Residential segregation, 488–489
Residual conception of social welfare, 38
Residual poor, 192, 202
Respite care services, 378
Restitution, 305
Restrictive covenants, 495
Retirement programs, 539–540, 541

Retribution, 305
Reverse discrimination, 145
Rights:
    of children and parents, 284–285
    liberal perspective focus (see Liberal
        perspective)
Rights versus responsibilities, 45–47
Role:
    concept of, 31–32
    mental illness as, 351
Role blurring, 367
Role conflict, types of, 456–457
Role dependency, 40, 43–45 (see also
        Dependency)
Role expectation, 32
Role functioning in parent-child-community
        network, 254–259
Role overload, 456–457
Role performance, 32
Role rejection by parent, 256–257
Roles, social work, 80
Role theory, 32
Roosevelt administration, 497 (see also New
        Deal)
Runaways, 106–107, 108–109
Rural health care, 409, 419

Salaries, 85–86
Salvation Army shelter, 505
Scapegoating, 265
Scientific medicine, 403–406
Sectarian agencies, 105–109, 110
Section 8 programs, 502–503, 515
Secularization of social work, 101–103
Secularization of society, reversal of, 103–105
Segregation:
    housing, 482–483, 488–489
        New Deal projects, 497–498
        restrictive covenants, 495
    special needs people, 511
Segregation index, 482–483
Self-fulfilling prophecy, 322
Semi-profession, social work as, 55
Senior centers, 551
Sentencing, indeterminate, 325–326
Separate but equal principle, 146
Separatism, 132
Separatism versus integration, 146
Settlement houses:
    churches and, 99–100
    Hull House, 61, 62, 74, 64, 137–138,
        141, 516
    mother's clubs in, 141
Settlement laws, 491
Sex differences, demographic data (see
        Gender)
Sexism, 129
Sexual abuse of children, 260, 266
Sexual discrimination (see Gender inequality)
Sexuality:
    culture of poverty theory, 204
    in eighteenth century, 228
    elderly, 536
    homosexuality, 128, 129, 146, 347
Shelter (see Housing)
Sheltered workshop system, 378
"Shelter poor", 479
Shelters for homeless, 478, 505, 516–517
Sheppard-Towner Act, 141, 407
Sin concept, 116

Single-parent families, 248
    child abuse in, 265
    gender and household stereotypes, 509–
        510
    work-family role conflicts, 444, 445, 446,
        447, 457
Single Room Occupancy hotel, 504
Single room only residential hotels, 479
Situational adaptation theory, 205–206, 214
Slums, 491
    New Deal housing programs, 497
    urban renewal, 500
Smith College School of Social Work, 365
Smoking, 395, 397, 399, 402
Social adaptation:
    mental illness definitions, 347
    work and, 436, 437
Social attitudes, 5
Social buffer, 213
Social casework, 65
Social change, 33, 63
Social class:
    and child abuse, 260, 267
    elderly, 538, 539
    explanations of poverty, 211
    and health, 400–401
        mental illness, 353–354
        utilization of services, 418
    and intelligence, 196–197
    and mental retardation, 359
    planned communities, 495
Social construct, developmental disability as, 357
Social control, 33
Social control theory of crime, 317–318
Social Darwinism, 234
Social democracy, 46
Social Diagnosis, 61, 74
Social/environmental model of disease, 400
Social factors (see Socioeconomic factors)
Social housing, 507
Social institutions:
    essential functions, 32–33
    social welfare, 38
Social insurance, 236–237, 543 (see also So-
        cial Security)
Social integration, 33
Social isolation:
    alienation of work and, 455
    traits of abusing parents, 263
Social isolation hypothesis, 212–214
Socialization, 32
Social learning theory, 334
Social order, 33
Social psychological theories of aging, 537–
        538
Social role (see Role)
Social Security, 526, 532–533, 547
    advocacy groups and, 553
    English roots, 223
    establishments of, 542–544
    expenditures, 534
    housing costs, 484
    stigma, 438
Social Security Act, 238–239, 239, 241, 247,
        544
    child welfare provisions, 275–276
    American Medical Association and, 406
    Medicare and Medicaid amendments, 243
Social Security Amendments of 1967, 243
Social Security Amendments of 1983, 547

Social services:
    poverty line calculations, 179
    racial discrimination in, 140
Social settlement movement, 61–63
    and African Americans, 138–139
    and new immigrants, 137–138
Social-structural factors in social problems
        (see Liberal perspective)
Social structure, 31–34
Social system:
    behavioral norms, 344
    views of conservatives, liberals, and radi-
        cals, 10–12, 16
Social transformation (see Industrialization;
        Urbanization)
Social treatment, 37
Social victim theory, 322–323
Social welfare, 38–39 (see also Welfare
        system)
    classification of services, 40–45
    and crime, 311–312
    crime as problem of, 305–306
    definitions, 28–40
        descriptive, 28–30
        functional, 30–40
    expenditures for older Americans, 546–549
    housing costs, 484
    and new immigration, 136–138
    perspectives on, 3–7, 15, 45–49
    stigma and, 25–27
    work-related, 438
Social workers:
    client-worker matching, 147–148
    professional status (see Professional status
        of social work)
    roles of, 80
Social work method, 78–79
Social work practice, 73
    controlling entry, 87
    mental health and developmental disability,
        382
    model of, 79–81
    multidisciplinary team, 87–88
    perspectives on, 88
Social work practice areas and settings, 81–
        85
    aging, 555–556
    child welfare issues, 287–290
    crime and corrections issues, 333–337
    discrimination issues, 149–150
    health care issues, 425–428
    housing issues, 513, 515, 516–517
    mental health and developmental disability
        issues, 381–384
Societies for the Prevention of Cruelty to
        Children, 274, 276
Societies for the Prevention of Pauperism, 231
Socioeconomic factors:
    and child abuse, 268
    and developmental disability, 358
    and discrimination, 132, 135
    and health, 396–398
Socioeconomic status (see Social class)
Sociological theories:
    of aging, 538–540
    of mental illness, 350–351, 352
Special Intensive Parole Unit (SIPU), 331
Specialization, occupational, 454
Specialization in medical profession, 415
Special needs people, 510